Web Standards Programmer's Reference: HTML, CSS, JavaScript®, Perl, Python®, and PHP

Steven M. Schafer

Wiley Publishing, Inc.

Web Standards Programmer's Reference:
HTML, CSS, JavaScript®, Perl, Python®, and PHP

Published by
Wiley Publishing, Inc.
10475 Crosspoint Boulevard
Indianapolis, IN 46256
www.wiley.com

Copyright © 2005 by Wiley Publishing, Inc., Indianapolis, Indiana

Published simultaneously in Canada

ISBN-13: 978-0-7645-8820-4
ISBN-10: 0-7645-8820-6

Manufactured in the United States of America

10 9 8 7 6 5 4 3 2 1

1MA/SQ/QX/QV/IN

Library of Congress Cataloging-in-Publication Data:

Schafer, Steven M.
  Web standards programmer's reference : HTML, CSS, JavaScript, Perl, Python, and PHP / Steven M. Schafer.
    p. cm.
  Includes index.
  ISBN-13: 978-0-7645-8820-4 (paper/website)
  ISBN-10: 0-7645-8820-6 (paper/website)
  1. HTML (Document markup language) 2. Web site development. I. Title.
  QA76.76.H94S2525 2005
  006.7'4--dc22
                          2005012600

Credits

Senior Acquisitions Editor
Jim Minatel

Development Editor
Marcia Ellett

Technical Editors
Bill Patterson
David Schultz
Dilip Thomas

Production Editor
Gabrielle Nabi

Copy Editor
Publication Services

Editorial Manager
Mary Beth Wakefield

Vice President & Executive Group Publisher
Richard Swadley

Vice President and Publisher
Joseph B. Wikert

Project Coordinator
Kristie Rees

Graphics and Production Specialists
Kelly Emkow
April Farling
Carrie A. Foster
Lauren Goddard
Denny Hager
Jennifer Heleine
Julie Trippetti

Quality Control Technicians
Laura Albert
Leeann Harney
Jessica Kramer
Carl William Pierce

Proofreading and Indexing
TECHBOOKS Production Services

About the Author

Steve Schafer is a veteran of technology and publishing. He programs in several languages, works with a variety of technologies, and has been published in several technical publications and articles. He currently is the COO for Progeny, an open source-based service and support company. Steve can be reached by email at sschafer@synergy-tech.com.

Contents

Contents

Contents

Contents

Part Two: Cascading Style Sheets (CSS)

Contents

Contents

Contents

Contents

Contents

Contents

Contents

Contents

Contents

Introduction

The Web has matured quickly from a textual reference to a medium suitable for publishing just about any document imaginable, conveying any idea, containing any type of information. As the Web grows, it envelopes people of all types—research professionals, companies, and even individuals. People from all walks of life and with all levels of technical ability are expected to have a Web presence.

As a consequence, most technical people have been relied upon to know more about the technologies involved in publishing on the Web. Unfortunately, despite what most non-technical people think, technical people don't automatically understand all things Web-related. The evolving standards, increasing number of platforms that are Web capable, and number of technologies that can be employed in Web publishing conspire to create a morass of technologies that must be addressed.

That's where this book comes in.

This book does its best to cover the basics of all of the technologies central to Web publishing:

❑   **XHTML**—The latest Hypertext Markup Language standard, incorporating XML constructs in the language used to describe Web content.

❑   **CSS**—Cascading Style Sheets, a structured method for defining and applying formatting to Web documents.

❑   **JavaScript**—The premier, client-side scripting language providing scripting access to document content and base-level automation to Web documents.

❑   **CGI Scripting**—Server-side, common gateway interface scripts (via the Perl and Python languages) that bring even more power, capability, and interconnectivity to Web content.

❑   **PHP**—The revolutionary Hypertext Pre-Processing scripting language built from the ground up to deliver dynamic Web content.

This book is not designed to be a comprehensive beginner's tutorial for every standard in Web publishing. That would require six or seven books each this size or larger. In fact, if you've never done any Web publishing or other programming, this may not be the right book for you to start with. (See the next section, "Who Is This Book For?") However, if you don't need an exhaustive tutorial on each language and are looking for core usage examples and syntax for several popular Web standards, this book is the all-in-one reference for Web standards that programmers should turn to when needing to learn or reference information on the core publishing technologies.

Wiley and WROX have several additional books that should be considered as supplements to this book. Almost all of the technologies covered in this book have appropriate Beginning and Professional titles that cover the technology in more depth. Browse for the subjects that most interest you at http://www.wrox.com.

Who Is This Book For?

This book is in the WROX *Programmer's Reference* series, designed for programmers. However, this book expands the concept of "programmer" to include Web coders familiar with HTML. Essentially, there are two categories of readers that can benefit from this book:

❑ Programmers familiar with traditional programming languages who wish to learn more about Web technologies so they can expand their programming capabilities to deliver standards-compliant Web content

❑ Web designers familiar with HTML and related-technologies who wish to become familiar with scripting languages to expand their capabilities on the Web

The first third of this book covers XHTML and CSS, the backbone technologies for Web content. Programmers who want to learn about the current XHTML and CSS standards and how they are used to format and convey content should spend time working through the chapters in these parts.

The second third of the book covers scripting—client-side JavaScript, server-side CGI (Perl and Python), and PHP are covered. These parts of the book introduce the programming technologies prevalent on the Web. These programming languages (commonly known as scripting languages) can be used to help create and deploy more dynamic and powerful content via the Web. Anyone looking to learn how to use scripting to expand the capabilities of their online documents should read this part of the book.

The last third of the book contains reference Appendices useful for looking up the syntax and capabilities of the specific technologies.

See the section, "How This Book Is Organized" later in this Introduction for a full breakdown of the book's contents.

A Word about Standards

Standards are vastly more important than most people give them credit for. Fortunately, most programmers are familiar with learning and adhering to standards of many types. However, the Web has become a very forgiving platform, allowing Web developers to create and deploy documents that only loosely conform to the published standards. However, as the publishing platforms for Web content continue to expand and grow, the need for standards becomes more important to ensure content can be viewed on as many platforms as possible.

Personally, I've been coding for the Web for several years. However, only recently have I begun to adhere to the W3C specifications and produce standards-compliant HTML. The road to this point has been a bit painful, but also very rewarding and something I hope to communicate in every example within this book.

It's important to understand that you *can* code for the Web while ignoring the standards, but you *shouldn't*. Most browsers (especially the oft-used Microsoft Internet Explorer) will allow sloppy coding, actually correcting common code errors. However, this doesn't guarantee that your document will appear the way you intended. The auto-correcting behavior of some browsers can also make designers complacent in their non-conformance. I've often heard designers claim, "It looks fine in browser X," when trying to defend a non-standards-conforming document.

You should do the following:

❏ Code to the standards, not the browsers. Trust that most browsers will support the W3C standards and correctly render documents that are coded to said standards.

❏ Test your documents against the most popular browsers (Microsoft IE and Mozilla Firefox) or your target browser(s), if known.

This book does its best to cover only the published standards for XHTML and CSS, ignoring browser-specific extensions, transitional DTDs, quirks-modes, and anything else non-standard. There are a few areas where this approach is difficult to achieve:

❏ Some tags/attributes that have been deprecated have not had their features replaced with CSS. In those cases, the deprecated tags or attributes are covered, but discouraged.

❏ JavaScript is especially testy when required to be cross-platform (Internet Explorer and Mozilla). As such, the JavaScript chapters cover tricks to help your scripts exist peacefully on both platforms.

In the event that a desired effect can only be achieved by deprecated methods, the methods are covered but disclaimed as deprecated, and their use is not recommended.

The author recognizes that there are more user agent platforms than just Internet Explorer and Mozilla Firefox, such as Opera, for example. However, the author also recognizes that the most popular browsers are IE and Firefox themselves, or are based on the IE or Mozilla (Gecko) codebase. As such, this book highlights these two browsers—the few times we highlight any specific browser.

How This Book Is Organized

This book is broken up into distinct Parts, each Part covering a specific Web technology.

Part I—HyperText Markup Language (HTML)

The first part of this book concentrates on HTML, specifically the XHTML standard. The chapters in this part of the book start with the basics of HTML (Chapter 1) and progresses through coverage of how XHTML is used to format specific elements in a document (Chapters 2–10). The last chapter in this section discusses XML, its structure, schema(s), and role in XHTML (Chapter 11).

Part II—Cascading Style Sheets (CSS)

The second part of this book concentrates on CSS. It starts with a description of how CSS works and how selectors are defined to apply styles in a document (Chapters 12 and 13). Specific chapters cover specific formatting uses of CSS—text, margins, colors, and so on (Chapter 14–17). The last chapter in this section covers using CSS to arrange and position elements (Chapter 18)—a topic that is revisited in the next part's coverage of Dynamic HTML.

Part III—JavaScript and DHTML

This part of the book covers the JavaScript client-side scripting language. The first chapter covers the basics of the language, how and why it is used, and its basic syntax (Chapter 19). The next chapter dives into the guts of the language, covering its constructs, functions, objects, and more (Chapter 20). The next chapter covers the Document Object Model, a standard method of identifying document elements and working with their attributes and properties (Chapter 21). The concept of Dynamic HTML—the practice of creating dynamic content through the synergy of JavaScript and HTML—is covered in the next chapter (Chapter 22). The last chapter in this part shows you practical examples of JavaScript in use, including sample code and explanations thereof (Chapter 23).

Part IV—Common Gateway Interface (CGI)

This part of the book covers the technology involved in using CGI—using server-side scripting languages to deliver XHTML content. The first chapter of this section covers the basics of the technology, how and why it is used, and so forth (Chapter 24). The next two chapters cover the specific language conventions of the two most prominent CGI scripting languages, Perl and Python (Chapters 25–26). CGI can be accomplished with most any executable language, a concept that is demonstrated in the next chapter (Chapter 27). Practical examples using Perl and Python are shown in the last chapter in this part (Chapter 28).

Part V—PHP

This part of the book covers the relatively new, but exciting and powerful, Web scripting language PHP. The first chapter in this part covers the basics of the PHP language (Chapter 29), the second chapter covers the language in-depth (Chapter 30), and the third chapter covers practical examples of using PHP (Chapter 31).

Part VI—Appendixes

The reference appendixes of this book provide comprehensive referential material on the technologies covered in this book. These references are designed to be used with the chapters where the technology is covered. The chapters cover learning and using the technologies while the appendixes provide the comprehensive reference into the technologies as a whole.

Conventions Used in this Book

This book follows fairly standard technical book conventions, outlined in the next few sections.

Terminology

This book uses fairly unique terminology regarding the World Wide Web and content published thereon. Most references of this type refer to content on the Web in terms of *pages* or *sites*. However, the author maintains that the Web has grown into an actual publishing medium, allowing rich content to be easily developed and deployed, allowing for use of the term "document" in lieu of page or site. On today's Web, content can be as rich as any book, magazine, or other document-based medium.

> *In fact, with the abundance of multimedia options available, the Web often exceeds "document" publishing standards.*

To the same end, this book routinely refers to XHTML tags by their name, not their coding. For example, you will see descriptions of the *span element*, instead of <span>. Also, because all XHTML tags need to have open and closed pairs in XHTML, when we do refer to the tags by their codes we will only refer to the open tag (for example, <body> tags, instead of <body> and </body> tags).

This book also avoids using the familiar term *browser* when referring to the application rendering XHTML and other Web-related technologies into visual presentations. Instead, the book refers to such applications as *user agents*. This is due to the fact that a wide range of software and devices now render Web technologies into presentation formats. The scope of serviceable XHTML rendering tools isn't as narrow as it once was—reserved for a few applications known as browsers (Internet Explorer, Mozilla, Opera, and so on). This book assumes that the reader wants to provide content for as many platforms as possible, even those outside the familiar application (browser) setting.

Code Listings

There are several ways that code is conveyed in this book.

When code is represented in line, within normal text, it is presented in a special, monotype font such as: The Wiley Web site can be found at `http://www.wiley.com`.

Inline code is reserved for short examples, URLs, and other short pieces of text.

When longer listings are required, they appear in a listing format similar to the following:

```
<!DOCTYPE html PUBLIC "-//W3C//DTD XHTML 1.0 Strict//EN"
    "http://www.w3.org/TR/xhtml1/DTD/xhtml1-strict.dtd">
<html>
<head>
  <title>Document Title</title>
</head>
<body>
<p>Document body text goes here.</p>
</body>
</html>
```

If particular sections of the listing need to be specially referenced, they will appear with a gray background like the `<title>` section in the preceding listing.

Within code listings we often need to show that the listings contain placeholder information that may be different in actual use. For example, the following code shows that the `margin-top` property needs an argument indicating what the margin should be set to:

```
margin-top: margin-value;
```

In such cases, we will use italic keywords representing the variable information. In the preceding listing, `margin-value` is the placeholder for the value of the margin. In actual use, `margin-value` would be replaced by an actual value, such as the following:

```
margin-top: 25px;
```

Tips, Notes, and Cautions

Text that deserves special attention will appear offset in special box as shown in the following paragraph:

> *This paragraph contains important information that deserves the reader's attention. It is reserved for special notes outside the normal flow of the text, cautions that the reader should be aware of, and other information of special importance.*

Source Code

Code from this book can be found on the WROX Web site, namely http://www.wrox.com. You can use the search function to search for this book or use the topical listings to find it. Note that many books are similar in title and searching for the ISBN (0-7645-8820-6) instead of the title might yield quicker results.

What You Need to Work with Examples in This Book

This book is full of examples that you can use to help learn the technologies discussed. To replicate code from the book as well as build your own code, you will need the following:

❏   Access to a Web server, preferably Apache

❏   Shell/command prompt-level access on the system running the Web server

❏   A robust text-editing program, preferably one that does syntax highlighting. On Linux, vim and Emacs are good choices. Windows users should use TextPad (http://www.textpad.com/), Homesite (http://www.macromedia.com/software/homesite/) or other full-featured code editors.

❏   Installed copies of PHP, Perl, and Python. (Needed only for the appropriate chapters that cover those languages.)

❏   A computer running a recently released browser for testing your code—Mozilla Firefox or Microsoft Internet Explorer is recommended.

The Basics of HTML

Before you begin to code HTML pages for the Web, it is important to understand some of the technology, standards, and syntax behind the Web. This chapter introduces you to HTML and answers the following questions:

❑   What is the World Wide Web?

❑   How does the Web work?

❑   What is HTML?

❑   What is the basic syntax of HTML?

Subsequent chapters in this section delve into the specifics of HTML, covering various tags you can use to format your pages.

What Is the World Wide Web?

The Internet is a worldwide network of computers all attached in a global networking scheme. This scheme, known as TCP/IP, assigns and uses unique addresses to communicate between computers on the Internet.

The World Wide Web is a network of computers that, using the Internet, are able to exchange text, graphics, and even multimedia content using standard protocols. *Web servers* — special computers that are set up for the distinct purpose of delivering content — are placed on the Internet with specific content for others to access. *Web clients* — which are generally desktop computers but can also be dedicated terminals, mobile devices, and more — access the servers' content via a browser. The *browser* is a specialized application for displaying Web content.

For example, Google maintains many Web servers that connect to their database of content found on the Web. You use your home or office PC to connect to the servers via a browser such as Microsoft's Internet Explorer or Mozilla's Firefox (shown in Figure 1-1).

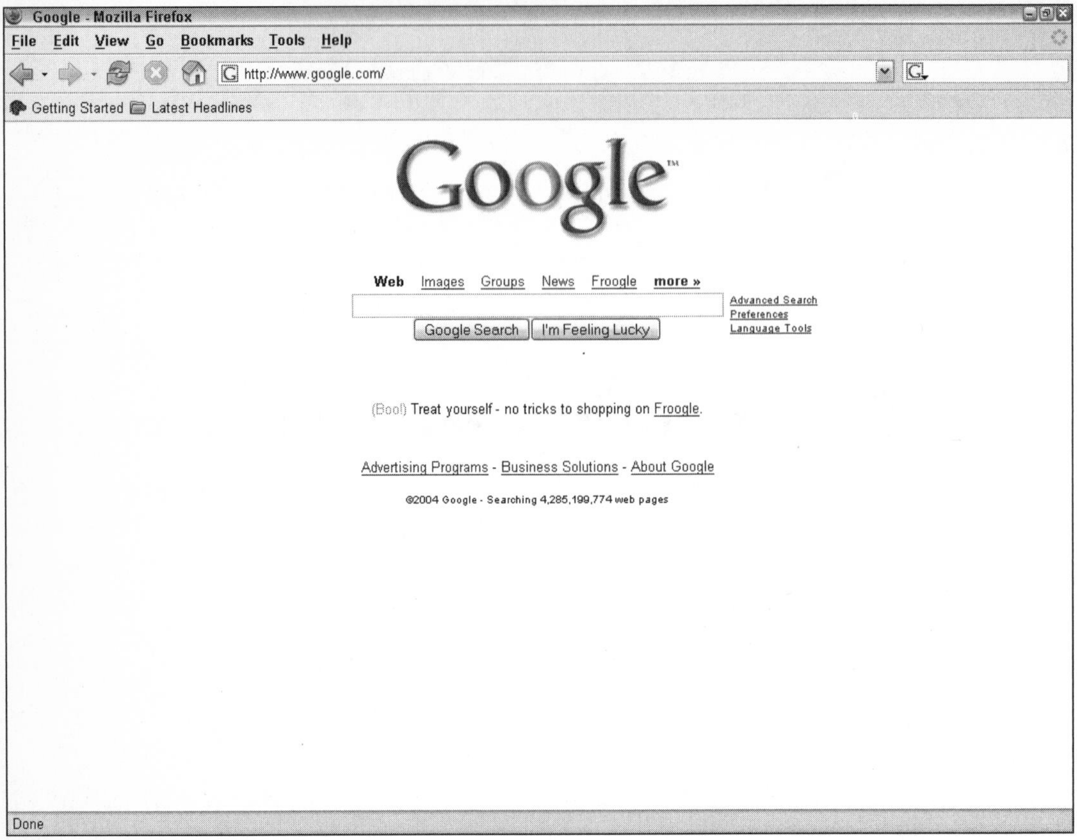

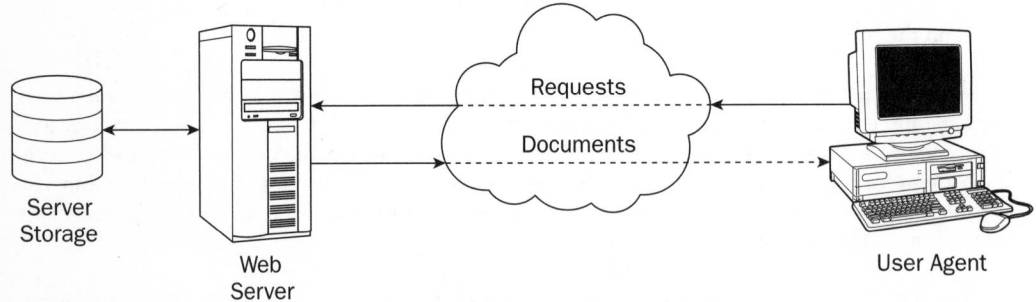

Figure 1-1

If you were to make a diagram of the relationships between all the technical components involved in requesting and delivering a document over the Web, it would resemble the diagram shown in Figure 1-2.

Requests

Documents

Server
Storage

Web
Server

User Agent

Figure 1-2

Creating a Web

The Web was created as a replacement for the aging Gopher protocol. Gopher allowed documents across the Internet to be linked to each other and searched. The inclusion of *hyperlinks*—embedded links to other documents on the Web—gives the resulting technology its name because it resembles a spider's web.

Figure 1-3 shows a graphic representation of a handful of sites on the Web. When a line is drawn between the sites that link to one another, the *web* becomes more obvious.

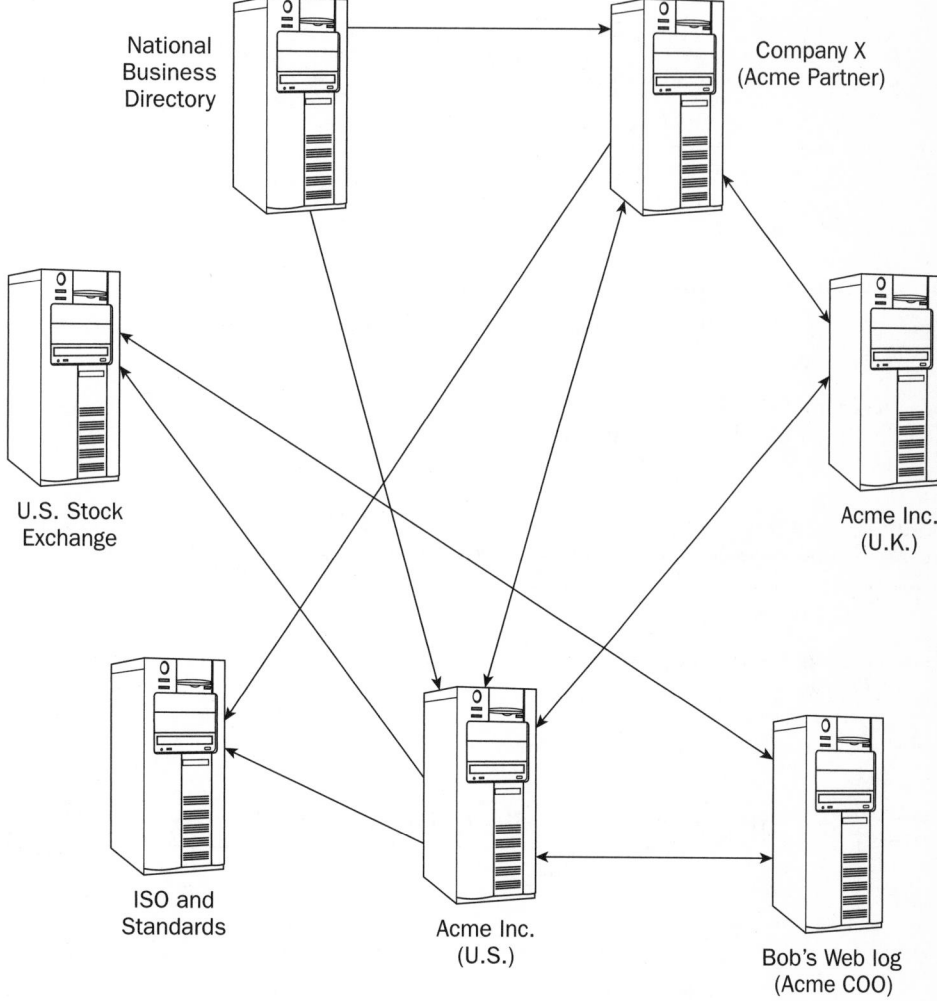

National Business Directory

Company X (Acme Partner)

U.S. Stock Exchange

Acme Inc. (U.K.)

ISO and Standards

Acme Inc. (U.S.)

Bob's Web log (Acme COO)

Figure 1-3

However, the Web doesn't operate as the diagram would have you believe. One Web site doesn't go to another for information; your browser requests the information directly from the server where the information can be found. For example, suppose you are on the Acme Inc US site in Figure 1-3 and click the link to Company X. The Acme Inc US server doesn't handle the request for the external page; your browser reads the address of the new page from the hyperlink and requests the information from the server that actually hosts that page (Company X in the example from Figure 1-3).

Hyperlinks contain several pieces of vital information that instruct the Web browser where to go for the content. The following information is provided:

❑   The protocol to use (generally HTTP)

❑   The server to request the document from

❑   The path on the server to the document

❑   The document's name (optional)

The information is assembled together in a URL. The information is presented in the following form:

❑   The protocol followed by a colon (for example, `http:`)

❑   The fully qualified domain name of the server, prefixed by two slashes (for example, `//www.google.com`)

❑   The path to the file being requested, beginning with a slash, with a slash between each directory in the path and a slash at the end (for example, `/options/`)

❑   The name of the file being requested (for example, `index.html`)

*Most Web servers are configured to deliver specific documents if the browser doesn't explicitly request a document. These specific documents differ between server applications and configurations but are generally documents such as **index.html** and **home.html**. For example, the following two URLs will return the same document (**index.html**):*

http://www.google.com/options/
http://www.google.com/options/index.html

Taken all together, a URL resembles that shown in Figure 1-4.

Figure 1-4

HTTP: The Protocol of the Web

As previously mentioned, the Web operates by sending data using specific protocols. The main protocol used for the Web is Hypertext Transfer Protocol (HTTP). HTTP defines how the computers on the Web, specifically the server and client, exchange data.

Although HTTP is the protocol of choice for the Web, most browsers support additional protocols such as the File Transfer Protocol (FTP).

Much like other protocols, an HTTP conversation consists of a handful of commands from the client and a stream of data from the server. Although discussing the whole HTTP protocol is beyond this book's scope, it is important to grasp the basics of how the protocol operates. By using a telnet client, you can "talk" to a Web server and try the protocol manually as shown in the following code (text typed by the user appears with a gray background):

```
telnet localhost 80
Trying 127.0.0.1...
Connected to localhost.
Escape character is '^]'.
GET /index.html HTTP/1.1
Accept: text/plain,text/html
Host: localhost
User-Agent: Telnet

HTTP/1.1 200 OK
Date: Sun, 17 Oct 2004 23:47:49 GMT
Server: Apache/1.3.26 (Unix) Debian GNU/Linux PHP/4.1.2
Last-Modified: Sat, 26 Oct 2002 09:12:14 GMT
ETag: "19b498-100e-3dba5c6e"
Accept-Ranges: bytes
Content-Length: 4110
Keep-Alive: timeout=15, max=100
Connection: Keep-Alive
Content-Type: text/html; charset=iso-8859-1

<!DOCTYPE HTML PUBLIC "-//W3C//DTD HTML 3.2//EN">
<HTML>
<HEAD>
    <META HTTP-EQUIV="Content-Type" CONTENT="text/html; charset=iso-8859-1">
    <META NAME="GENERATOR" CONTENT="Mozilla/4.05 [en] (X11; I; Linux 2.3.99-pre3
i686) [Netscape]">
    <META NAME="Author" CONTENT="johnie@debian.org (Johnie Ingram)">
    <META NAME="Description" CONTENT="The initial installation of Debian/GNU
Apache.">
    <TITLE>Welcome to Your New Home Page!</TITLE>
</HEAD>
<BODY TEXT="#000000" BGCOLOR="#FFFFFF" LINK="#0000EF" VLINK="#55188A"
ALINK="#FF0000">

<BR>

<H1>Welcome to Your New Home in Cyberspace!</H1>

<HR NOSHADE>
<BR>

<IMG ALIGN="right" ALT="" HEIGHT="247" WIDTH="278" SRC="icons/jhe061.gif">
```

```
<P>This is a placeholder page installed by the <A
HREF="http://www.debian.org/">Debian</A>
release of the <A HREF="http://www.apache.org/">Apache</A> web server package,
because no home page was installed on this host.
...
</BODY>
</HTML>
Connection closed by foreign host.
```

The telnet client is started with the name of the host to connect to and the port number (80):

```
telnet localhost 80
```

Once the client is connected, the server waits for a command. In this case, the client (our telnet session) sends a block of commands, including the following:

❑   The document to be retrieved and the protocol to return the document (GET and HTTP 1.1)

❑   The types of documents the client expects or can support (plain text or HTML text)

❑   The host the request is destined for (typically the fully qualified domain name of the server)

❑   The name of the user agent (browser) doing the requesting (Telnet)

```
GET /index.html HTTP/1.1
Accept: text/plain,text/html
Host: localhost
User-Agent: Telnet
```

Note that only the first three pieces of data are necessary; the user agent name is provided only as a courtesy to the Webmaster on the server as it gets recorded in the server logs accordingly.

This block of commands is known as the header and is required to be followed by a blank line, which indicates to the server that the client is done with the header. The server then responds with information of its own, including the following:

❑   A response to the command

```
HTTP/1.1 200 OK
```

❑   The current date (as known by the server)

```
Date: Sun, 17 Oct 2004 23:47:49 GMT
```

❑   The server identification string, which usually identifies the type and capabilities of the server but can be configured differently

```
Server: Apache/1.3.26 (Unix) Debian GNU/Linux PHP/4.1.2
```

❑   Information about the document being delivered (date modified, size, encoding, and so on)

```
Last-Modified: Sat, 26 Oct 2002 09:12:14 GMT
ETag: "19b498-100e-3dba5c6e"
Accept-Ranges: bytes
Content-Length: 4110
Keep-Alive: timeout=15, max=100
Connection: Keep-Alive
Content-Type: text/html; charset=iso-8859-1
```

❑   The content of the document itself (in this case, the default Debian/GNU Linux Apache welcome page)

```
<!DOCTYPE HTML PUBLIC "-//W3C//DTD HTML 3.2//EN">
<HTML>
<HEAD>
   <META HTTP-EQUIV="Content-Type" CONTENT="text/html; charset=iso-8859-1">
 . . .
```

A few seconds after the full document is delivered, the server closes the connection.

```
Connection closed by foreign host.
```

This dialog is HTTP at its simplest, but it does a good job of illustrating how the protocol works.

Hypertext Markup Language

Hypertext Markup Language (HTML) was devised as an easy means to format textual documents. HTTP is the method for delivering HTML documents, which the client browser then renders into an on-screen image. This section covers the development and evolution of HTML.

In the Beginning — HTML

HTML and HTTP were both invented by Tim Berners-Lee, who was then working as a computer and networking specialist at a Swiss research institute. He wanted to give the institute's researchers a simple markup language that would enable them to share their research papers via the Internet. Berners-Lee based HTML on Standard Generalized Markup Language (SGML), an international standard for marking up text for presentation on a variety of physical devices. The basic idea of SGML is that the document's *structure* should be separated from its *presentation.*

To date, HTML has gone through four major standards, including the latest, 4.01. In addition to HTML, Cascading Style Sheets (CSS) and Extensible Markup Language (XML) have also provided valuable contributions to the way of the Web.

Most of the standards used on the Web are developed and/or ratified by the World Wide Web Consortium (W3C). The resulting specifications can be found online at the W3C Web site, www.w3c.org.

HTML 1.0

HTML 1.0 was never specified by the W3C, as it predated the organization. The standard supported a few basic tags and graphics, although the latter needed to be in GIF format if used in-line or JPEG format if the image was out-of-line. You couldn't specify the font, background images, or colors, and there were no tables or forms. At the time, only one browser, Mosaic 1.0, was available to view Web documents. However, the standard became the stepping-stone to the modern Web.

HTML 2.0

The HTML 2.0 standard provided a wealth of improvement over the 1.0 version. Background colors and images were supported, as were tables and rudimentary forms. Between 1.0 and 2.0, a new browser was launched (Netscape), and several HTML features created to support features in the new browser became part of the 2.0 standard.

HTML 3.2

The HTML 3.2 standard significantly increased the capability of HTML and the Web. Many of the new features enabled Web designers to create feature-rich and elegant designs via new layout tags. Although the 3.2 specification introduced Cascading Style Sheets (CSS level 1), browsers were slow to adopt the new way of formatting. However, the standard did not include frames, but the feature was implemented in the various browsers anyway.

> There was an HTML 3.0 proposed standard, but it could not be ratified by the W3C in time. Hence, the next ratified standard was HTML 3.2.

HTML 4.0

HTML 4.0 did not introduce many new features, but it ushered in a new way of implementing Web design. Instead of using explicit formatting parameters in HTML tags, HTML 4.0 encouraged moving the formatting parameters to style sheets instead. HTML 3.2 had become burdensome to support with several dozen tags with several parameters each. The 4.0 standard emphasized the use of CSS, where formatting changes could be made within one document (the style sheet) instead of individually editing every page on a site.

XML 1.0

The Extensible Markup Language (XML) was created as a stepping-stone to bring Standard Generalized Markup Language (SGML) concepts to HTML. Although it was the precursor to HTML, SGML was not widely endorsed. As such, the W3C sought to create a usable subset of SGML targeted specifically toward the Web. The new standard was meant to have enough flexibility and power to provide traditional publishing applications on the Web. XML became part of the new XHTML standard.

CSS 1.0 and 2.0

As mentioned previously, Cascading Style Sheets were devised to move formatting methods used in Web documents into centralized, formal style sheets. A CSS document contains formatting specifics for various tags and is applied to applicable documents. This mechanism provides a formal means to separate the formatting from the content of a page.

When the formatting needs to change, the CSS document alone can be updated, and the changes are then reflected in all documents that use that style sheet. The "cascade" in the name refers to the feature that allows styles to be overridden by subsequent styles. For example, the HR department Web pages for Acme Inc. can use the company style sheet but also use styles specific for the individual department. The result is that all of the Acme Inc. Web pages look similar, but each department has a slightly unique look and feel.

Note: CSS is covered in depth in Part II of this book.

HTML 4.01

Heralded as the last of the HTML standards, 4.01 fixed errors inherent in the 4.0 specification and made the final leap to embracing CSS as the vehicle for document formatting (instead of using parameters in HTML tags).

XHTML 1.0

Extensible Hypertext Markup Language is the latest standard for Web documents. This standard infuses the HTML 4.01 standard with extensible language constructs courtesy of XML. It was designed to be used in XML-compliant environments yet be compatible with standard HTML 4.01 user agents. As of this writing, adoption of the XHTML standard for Web documents has been slow. Although most browsers natively support HTML 4.01, most do not support the extensibility features of XHTML 1.0.

HTML Concept and Syntax

The concept and use of HTML is straightforward. Individual tags — special text strings that are interpreted as formatting commands by the browser — are placed within a document to lend structure and format accordingly. Each tag has a beginning and an ending tag; everything between the tags is formatted according to the tag's parameters or related style sheet.

HTML Tags

Each tag begins with a left-pointing angle bracket (<) and ends with a right-pointing angle bracket (>). Between the brackets are keywords that indicate the type of tag. Beginning tags include any parameters necessary for the tag; ending tags contain only the keyword prefixed by a slash.

For example, if you want a word to be bold in a document, you would surround it with bold tags (<b> and </b>) similar to the following:

```
If I wanted this word to be <b>bold</b> I would use bold tags.
```

Many tags require children tags to operate. For example, the <table> tag itself only marks the position in the document where a table will appear; it does nothing to format the table into rows and columns. Several child tags — <tr> for rows, <td> for cells/columns, and so on — are used between the beginning and ending <table> tags accordingly:

```
<table border="0" >
<tr>
  <td>Cell 1</td>
  <td>Cell 2</td>
</tr>
```

```
<tr>
  <td>Cell 3</td>
  <td>Cell 4</td>
</tr>
</table>
```

Notice how the tags are closed in the opposite order they were opened. Although intuitive for structures like tables, it isn't always as intuitive. For example, consider the following fragment where the phrase "italic and bold" is formatted with italic and bold tags:

*This sentence uses ****italic and bold**** tags for emphasis.*

Although this example would generally not cause a problem when rendered via a user agent, there are many instances where overlapping tags can cause problems. Well-formed HTML always uses nested tags — tags are closed in the exact opposite order that they were opened.

Simple Rules for Formatting HTML Documents

As with most programming languages, formatting plays a big role in writing Web documents that not only display as intended but also are easily understood and maintained. These simple rules should always be followed when creating Web documents:

❑ **Use liberal white space.** Browsers ignore superfluous white space, so you can make use of it to create documents that are more easily read and maintained. Insert blank lines and follow standard coding rules for indentation whenever possible.

❑ **Use well-formed code.** This means following the XHTML standard to the letter — not taking shortcuts that some browsers allow. In particular, you should pay attention to the following:

   ❑ Always include a `<doctype>` tag (`<doctype>` and other document-level tags are discussed in Chapter 2.

   ❑ Elements (tags) must be nested, not overlapping.

   ❑ All nonempty elements need to be terminated. Most browsers allow for nonclosed elements, but to meet the XHTML standard you need to supply closing tags for each open one (for example, supply a closing paragraph tag [`</p>`] for every open one [`<p>`]).

   ❑ All tags need to be closed. Although the HTML standard allows tags such as `<hr>` without a closing tag — in fact, the `<hr>` tag has no closing mate — in XML all tags must be closed. In the case of tags like `<hr>`, you close the tag by putting a slash at the end of the tag: `<hr />`.

   ❑ All attribute values must be quoted. Again, most browsers allow nonquoted attributes, but the XHTML standard does not.

   ❑ All attributes must have values. Older HTML standards allowed for tags similar to the following:

```
<input type="checkbox" checked>
```

However, XHTML does not allow attributes without values (for example, `checked`). Instead, you must supply a value, such as the following:

```
<input type="checkbox" checked="checked">
```

❑ **Comment your code.** Using the comment tag pair (`<!--` and `-->`) should be as natural as commenting code in programming languages. Especially useful are comments at the end of large blocks, such as nested tables. It can help identify which part of the document you are editing:

```
</table>  <!-- End of floating page -->
```

Your First Web Page

As you will see in the other chapters within this section, many elements can make up a Web document, and you can use many HTML entities to format your documents. However, the following simple example uses only the basic, necessary tags to produce a page.

Example: A Simple Web Page

This example produces a simple HTML document with one line of text, using the bare minimum number of HTML tags.

Source

Type the following code into a document and save it, in plain text format, as `sample.html` on your local hard drive.

```
<!DOCTYPE HTML PUBLIC "-//W3C//DTD HTML 4.01//EN"
    "http://www.w3.org/TR/html4/strict.dtd">
<html>
<!-- sample.html - A simple, sample web document -->
<head>
  <title>A simple HTML document</title>
</head>
<body>
<p>This is sample text.</p>
</body>
</html>
```

Output

Now open the document in a Web browser. In most graphical operating environments, you can simply use a file manager to find the `sample.html` file and then double-click on it. Your default Web browser should open and load the file. If not, select Open (or Open File) from the File menu and find the `sample.html` file using the browser's interface.

Your screen should resemble that shown in Figure 1-5.

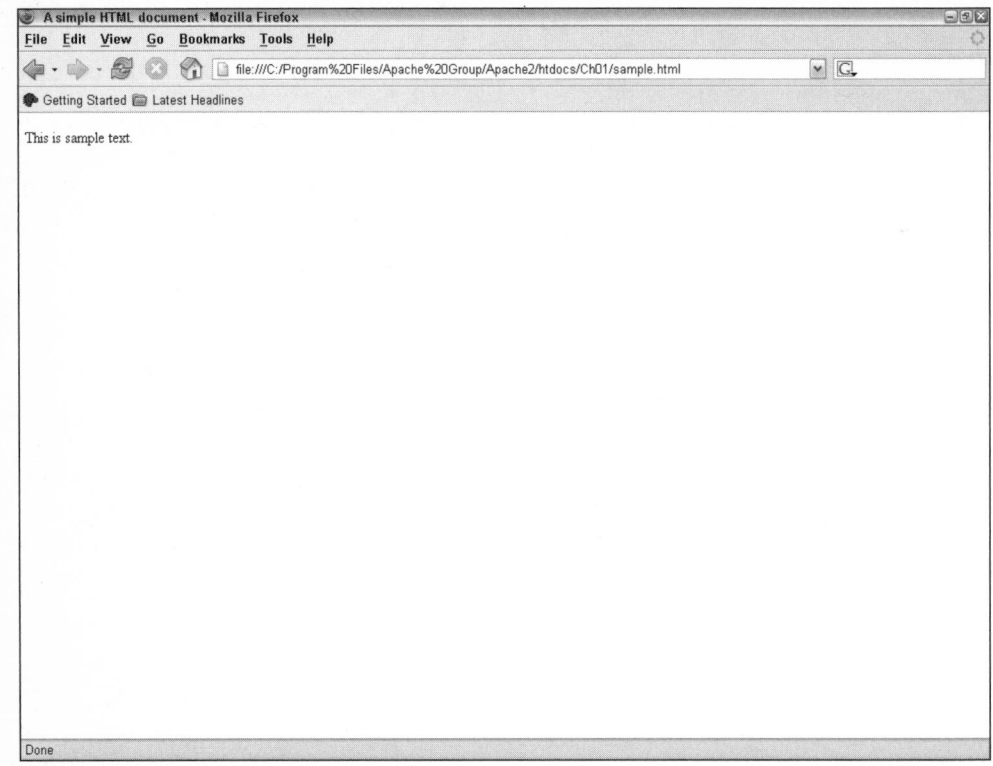

Figure 1-5

At this point, you may be asking yourself, "Why don't I need a Web server?" The reason is simple: The browser loads and interprets the HTML file from the local hard drive; it doesn't have to request the file from a server. However, the file uses only HTML, which is interpreted only by the client side. If you used any server-side technologies (Perl, PHP, and so on), you would have to load the sample file onto a Web server that had the appropriate capabilities to process the file before giving it to the client. More information on server-side technologies can be found in Parts V and VI of this book.

Summary

This chapter introduced you to the World Wide Web and the main technology behind it, HTML. You saw how the Web works, how clients and servers interact, and what makes up a hyperlink. You also learned how HTML evolved and where it is today. This basic background serves as a foundation for the rest of the chapters in this section, where you will learn more about specific HTML coding.

2

Document Tags

HTML documents are much like word processing documents — they contain information about the document itself, not just its contents. Understanding the layout of the document is as important as forming the document itself. This chapter delves into the details of document-level tags.

Understanding Document-Level Tags

Web documents are made up of several nested layers, and each layer is typically delimited by a particular HTML tag. Most Web veterans know that HTML documents start and end with <html> tags. However, those new to HTML or those who haven't kept up with the HTML standards might not realize that the document should start with a doctype tag and that the top layer doesn't have to be <html> (although it usually is).

The tags that make up the framework of a typical HTML document include the following:

- ❑ A document type tag
- ❑ The top-level tag, generally <html>
- ❑ A header section, delimited by <head> tags
- ❑ Title, style, and script information enclosed in the <head> section

The following sections detail the various tags and sections in a typical Web document.

> Web document is used in this book to refer to HTML documents due to the Web becoming closer to a true publishing platform.

Chapter 2

Document Type Tag

The DOCTYPE tag is one of the most overlooked tags in HTML. Strictly speaking, it isn't an HTML tag but a generic document identifier used to tell validation tools and clients what format and conventions the document content follows. A typical document type tag resembles the following:

```
<!DOCTYPE html PUBLIC "-//W3C//DTD XHTML Basic 1.0//EN"
    "http://www.w3.org/TR/xhtml-basic/xhtml-basic10.dtd">
```

This tag specifies the following information:

❏   The document's top tag level is HTML (html).

❏   The document adheres to the formal public identifier (FPI) "W3C XHTML Basic 1.0 English" standards (PUBLIC "-//W3C//DTD XHTML Basic 1.0//EN").

❏   The full DTD can be found at the URI http://www.w3.org/TR/xhtml-basic/xhtml-basic10.dtd.

The DTD specifies each valid element that can be contained in the document, including the attributes for the element and types of values each can contain. For example, the XHTML 1.0 Strict DTD contains the following section for the anchor tag (<a>):

```
<!--================== The Anchor Element ====================================-->

<!-- content is %Inline; except that anchors shouldn't be nested -->

<!ELEMENT a %a.content;>
<!ATTLIST a
  %attrs;
  %focus;
  charset     %Charset;       #IMPLIED
  type        %ContentType;   #IMPLIED
  name        NMTOKEN         #IMPLIED
  href        %URI;           #IMPLIED
  hreflang    %LanguageCode;  #IMPLIED
  rel         %LinkTypes;     #IMPLIED
  rev         %LinkTypes;     #IMPLIED
  shape       %Shape;         "rect"
  coords      %Coords;        #IMPLIED
  >
```

This section specifies the relationship the <a> tag has to the document (in-line) as well as the valid attributes (charset, type, name, and so on). The structure of the sections within the DTD also indicates where elements can appear in relationship to one another.

The XHTML Basic 1.0 DTD is a bit different because it applies to a modular standard — its sections refer to other modular DTD that contains the actual specification. For example, the DTD contains the following section on tables:

```
<!-- Tables Module ......................................... -->
<!ENTITY % xhtml-table.module "INCLUDE" >
<![%xhtml-table.module;[
<!ENTITY % xhtml-table.mod
     PUBLIC "-//W3C//ELEMENTS XHTML Basic Tables 1.0//EN"
            "xhtml-basic-table-1.mod" >
%xhtml-table.mod;]]>
```

*The **xhtml-basic-table-1.mod** document contains the specifications on table elements within XHTML.*

The DTD is important because without it validation tools and certain clients won't know how to validate or otherwise handle your document. You should get in the habit of always including a valid document type tag at the beginning of your documents.

You can find a list of valid, public DTDs on the W3C Web site at `http://www.w3.org/QA/2002/04/valid-dtd-list.html`.

*This book uses the XHTML 1.0 DTD (**http://www.w3.org/TR/xhtml1/DTD/xhtml1-strict.dtd**) unless otherwise indicated.*

HTML Tag

The HTML tag (`<html>`) is the tag that indicates the beginning and end of an XHTML document. Your documents should always begin with the opening HTML tag (`<html>`) and end with the closing HTML tag (`</html>`).

A variety of browsers (including Microsoft's Internet Explorer) correctly handle documents that are missing one, or both, of these tags. However, you should never count on your audience using a particular user agent or browser and should therefore strive to always write standards-compliant code.

Head Tag Section

The head section of a document provides extra information about the document as well as serving as a container for sections such as styles and global scripts. A document's head section begins with the opening head tag (`<head>`) and ends with the closing head tag (`</head>`). Added to the other two elements previously discussed in this chapter, your HTML document should always resemble the following structure:

```
<!DOCTYPE html PUBLIC "-//W3C//DTD XHTML 1.0 Strict//EN"
    "http://www.w3.org/TR/xhtml1/DTD/xhtml1-strict.dtd">
<html>
<head>
  <title>Title of Document Goes Here</title>
</head>
<body>
Body text of document goes here...
</body>
</html>
```

The `<title>` and `<body>` elements are discussed in the appropriately titled sections later in this chapter.

The following sections detail some of the various elements found in the head section.

Specifying the Document Title

The document title element supplies the title of the document to the user agent, who treats it appropriately: GUI-enabled agents usually display the title in their title bar, audible agents speak it aloud, and so on. As you would expect, the title appears in between opening and closing title tags (<title> and </title>).

For example, a document with the following title code would cause Mozilla's Firefox to display "A synopsis of last quarter's earnings" in its title bar:

```
<title>A synopsis of last quarter's earnings</title>
```

The document title is also routinely used as a label for the document when added to user favorites, as the descriptive text for the document in search engines, and so forth. Because of the limited space granted to document titles, it's important to keep the title to a reasonable length and on one line. However, given the wide range of places it can appear, to describe your document you should make the title as apropos to the document content as possible.

Meta Tags

Meta tags enable Web authors to embed extra information in their documents. Meta tags are used to provide information to search engines, control browser caching of documents, and much more. Most of a document's meta information is generated by the Web server that delivers the document. However, by using <meta> tags, you can supply different or additional information about the document.

A typical meta tag follows this syntax:

```
<meta name="name_of_data" content="data_content" />
```

For example, a meta tag that provides a description of a document's content would resemble the following:

```
<meta name="description" content="A site where programmers can vent" />
```

The full breadth of meta tag uses is outside the scope of this book because, since meta tags are simple data containers, any entity, program, or user agent can accept unique meta tags if required. For example, a user agent may require the author's name on every page. For pages displayed with that user agent, you could use the following tag:

```
<meta name="author" content="Steve Schafer" />
```

The following sections detail some of the more popular meta tag uses.

Over the last few years, meta tag use and support has been declining. As a result, you should never depend on meta tags to drive any functionality of your documents.

Providing Search Engine Information

A meta tag can be used to provide more information about a document so that when a search engine indexes the page it can include the extended information. A sample of providing a description was shown in the previous section; you can also provide keywords and ask that search engine robots (programs that automatically search and categorize Web documents) not index or follow links in a particular document.

```
<meta name="keywords" content="open, source, PHP, programming, code" />
```

The preceding tag provides keywords (to those agents requesting them) for the document. Some search engines use these keywords to categorize the document for searching.

```
<meta name="robots" content="noindex, nofollow" />
```

The preceding tag tells conforming robots not to index the current document or follow any links from it. Note that not all robots follow such directions.

Setting the Default Path

When defining links and other elements requiring paths and URIs, it is important to be as exact as possible with your references. For example, when defining the path to an image for use with an image tag (`<img>`), you should consider using an *absolute path*. An absolute path provides all the information necessary to find the content regardless of the scope of the current document. For example, the following is an absolute path because it includes the server address and the full path to the image:

```
http://www.example.com/products/images/imscr.jpg
```

Relative paths provide information relative to the location of the current document. For example, if the same image was referenced in a document contained in the `products` directory, you could use a relative path such as the following:

```
images/imscr.jpg
```

When the user agent receives that path, it typically appends the path to the content onto the path of the current document (`http://www.example.com/products/`). This creates the absolute path to the content being referenced.

However, both approaches have their drawbacks:

❑   When you move a document, for example, to the `legacy_products` directory, internal absolute paths will be broken — they will still refer to resources in the `products` directory.

❑   Some servers do not handle relative links properly, resulting in broken links due to the server or user agent incorrectly building the absolute path. This is mostly due to configuration issues but is something to consider if you don't have control over the server configuration.

One method to help ensure that all your links continue to function is to provide the correct context to all parties (server and user agent) via the base tag (`<base>`). For example, the following tag indicates that the document exists in the `products` directory and all relative links should be applied against that path:

```
<base http="http://www.example.com/products/" />
```

Thereafter, if you have to move the documents in a particular path, you can simply change the base tag at the top of each:

```
<base http="http://www.example.com/legacy_products/" />
```

The rest of the links in the document (if relative) will be correctly handled.

Directing User Agent Caching

You can control the caching behavior of some user agents with appropriate meta tags. For example, you can direct the user agent not to cache the current document with one of the following tags:

```
<meta name="Cache Control" content="no-cache"
<meta http-equiv="pragma" content="no-cache">
```

The first tag (Cache Control) is generally understood by modern browsers. The second should be used for browsers that are only HTTP 1.0 compliant, as they do not recognize Cache Control. (When in doubt as to the user agents accessing your content, include both.)

Furthermore, you can control how long the document stays in the cache:

```
<meta name="Cache Control" content="max-age=86400"
```

*The value of **max-age** is given in seconds from the user agent receiving the document. In the preceding example, the user agent is instructed to cache the document for one day (86,400 seconds), at which point the cached copy should expire.*

As previously stated, it is up to the user agent as to whether it will abide by such requests; you should never design documents that rely on behavior specified in meta tags.

Creating Automatic Refreshes and Redirects

You can direct the user agent to automatically reload the current document or another document after a specified amount of time has passed. The syntax of the corresponding meta tag is as follows:

```
<meta http-equiv="refresh" content="seconds_to_wait; url=path_to_document">
```

For example, the following tag will reload the document specified after 5 seconds:

```
<meta http-equiv="refresh" content="5;
    URL=http://www.example.com/new_products/index.html">
```

Typical uses of such tags include the following:

❑ **Notifying users of a moved page.** I'm sure you have seen at least one page resembling the following:

```
This page has moved. You will be redirected in 5 seconds.
```

Such pages use the meta tag to direct the user to the appropriate location after the specified time. Note that the redirection is done by the user agent, not the server.

❏ **Refreshing content that changes.** A document that tracks stock prices or inventory quantities should be refreshed automatically so that the data is reasonably accurate. In this case, the document specified in the tag should be the current document, causing the document to simply reload, refreshing its contents. Note that this use generally requires a no-cache directive as well, helping prevent the user agent from simply loading the same copy from cache.

Overriding Server Meta Information

As previously mentioned, most of the meta data sent to user agents is sent from the server delivering the Web document. However, if you use the HTTP-EQUIV parameter in the <meta> tag, you can replace HTTP header information. For example, the following <meta> tag defines the content type of the document as HTML with the Latin character set (ISO-8859-1):

```
<meta http-equiv="Content-Type" content="text/html; charset=ISO-8859-1" />
```

For a comprehensive list of HTTP 1.1 headers, including cache and other directives, see the HTTP 1.1 definition on the W3C Web site: **http://www.w3.org/Protocols/rfc2616/rfc2616.html**.

Style Section

The head section is also the area where you should declare any general and local styles for the document. All style definitions should be contained within style tags accordingly:

```
<head>
  <title>ACME Products Corporate Web Site</title>
  <style type="text/css">
    ...style definitions go here ...
  </style>
...
</head>
```

Note that the opening style tag includes a type definition so that the user agent knows what to expect — textual information in CSS format.

Styles are covered in depth within Part II of this book.

You can also refer to an external document containing style definitions (commonly referred to as a style sheet) using the <link> tag. For example, the following code refers the user agent to an external style sheet named site.css:

```
<link rel="stylesheet" type="text/css" href="site.css" />
```

*The **<link>** tag can also be used to provide information on documents that are related to the current document — an index, the next or previous document in a series, and so on. For more information on attributes and values necessary to specify such information, see Appendix A.*

Script Section

You should also place any global scripts inside the head section of the document. For example, if you use JavaScript for certain features, your head would include a section similar to the following:

```
<script type="text/javascript">
  ...script code goes here...
</script>
```

As with other non-HTML content containers, the opening `<script>` tag includes identifiers of the content contained in the section (in this case, textual JavaScript code).

Scripting is covered in Part III of this book.

The `<script>` tag can also be used to refer to an external document containing the script code by adding the `src` (source) attribute:

```
<script type="text/javascript" src="myscripts.js" />
```

The preceding code would direct the user agent to find the code for the scripts in the file `myscripts.js`.

Note that you can (and usually should) include an absolute or relative path to the external script file.

Body Section

The body section of the document is where the visible content appears. This content is typically a series of block tags containing in-line content — similar to paragraphs containing words and sentences.

The body section is delimited by opening and closing <body> tags and appears after the <head> section but within the <html> tags. For example, the following code shows the typical structure for a Web document:

```
<!DOCTYPE html PUBLIC "-//W3C//DTD XHTML 1.0 Strict//EN"
   "http://www.w3.org/TR/xhtml1/DTD/xhtml1-strict.dtd">
<html>
<head>
  <title>...document title goes here...</title>
  <style type="text/css">
    ...style definitions go here ...
  </style>
  <script type="text/javascript">
    ...script code goes here...
  </script>
</head>
<body>
...document body goes here...
</body>
</html>
```

Prior to HTML 4.01 the <body> tag played host to a wealth of document format information, including the following:

❏ Background color

❏ Background image

❏ The color of text

❏ The color of links in the document

However, those attributes have been deprecated, and the appropriate CSS styles are now used instead.

Styles are covered in depth within Part II of this book.

The <body> tag does retain all of its event attributes — onload, onunload, onclick, and so on. These events can be used to trigger scripts upon the appropriate action. For example, the following <body> tag will cause the current document to close when the user clicks anywhere in the document:

```
<body onclick= "self.close()">
```

Events and scripts are covered in depth in Part III of this book. Dynamic HTML, which makes good use of events and scripting, is covered in Chapters 24 and 25.

Summary

This chapter discussed the various document-level tags and how they are used to set up the basic format of HTML documents. You learned that a <doctype> tag should be mandatory for all Web documents and how the other document tags relate to one another. As you progress through the rest of the chapters in this section, you will learn about content-level tags and how to construct and format the actual document contents.

3

Paragraphs and Lines

In Chapter 2, you learned how to correctly set up an HTML document. Now that you have the basic framework for a document, you can get to work on filling it with content. The first elements that you need to learn are block tags, which define blocks of content within the body of a document. This chapter teaches you about the top-level block elements—paragraphs, line breaks, and divisions—as well as some of the additional block elements.

Paragraphs — The Basic Block Element

Like most documents, Web documents are broken up into discrete blocks. The main textual blocks are delimited by paragraph tags (<p>). Paragraph tags surround each paragraph in the document.

Using Paragraph Tags

For example, consider the following paragraphs from Homer's *Iliad*:

"Thus did he speak, and they did even as he had said. Those who were about Ajax and King Idomeneus, the followers moreover of Teucer, Meriones, and Meges peer of Mars called all their best men about them and sustained the fight against Hector and the Trojans, but the main body fell back upon the ships of the Achaeans.

"The Trojans pressed forward in a dense body, with Hector striding on at their head. Before him went Phoebus Apollo shrouded in cloud about his shoulders. He bore aloft the terrible aegis with its shaggy fringe, which Vulcan the smith had given Jove to strike terror into the hearts of men. With this in his hand he led on the Trojans."

Note how the lines within the paragraph are spaced using single line spacing, with double-spacing between the paragraphs.

Source

To display the paragraphs similarly in a Web document, you would simply place each paragraph within paragraph tags:

```
<p>Thus did he speak, and they did even as he had said. Those who were about
Ajax and King Idomeneus, the followers moreover of Teucer, Meriones, and Meges
peer of Mars called all their best men about them and sustained the fight
against Hector and the Trojans, but the main body fell back upon the ships of
the Achaeans.</p>
<p>The Trojans pressed forward in a dense body, with Hector striding on at their
head. Before him went Phoebus Apollo shrouded in cloud about his shoulders. He
bore aloft the terrible aegis with its shaggy fringe, which Vulcan the smith had
given Jove to strike terror into the hearts of men. With this in his hand he led
on the Trojans.</p>
```

Output

In a browser, the code generates the document shown in Figure 3-1.

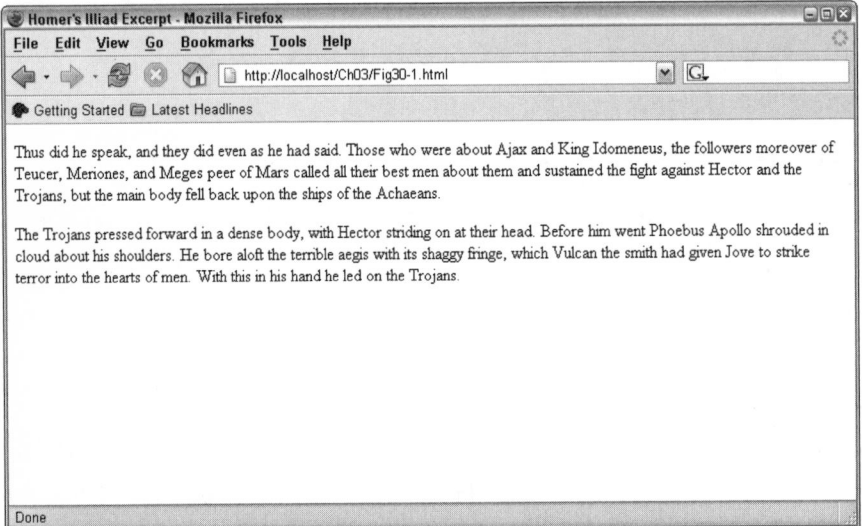

Figure 3-1

Despite the name of the tag implying text (paragraph), the `<p>` tag can be used to enclose any distinct piece of a document. In fact, the `<p>` tag is the block tag most used within documents.

*Each element within the body of an HTML document (anything between the **<body>** tags) must be enclosed within block tags.*

For example, a document body with two tables would resemble the following code:

```
<body>
<p>
  <table>
    ...body of table one...
  </table>
</p>
<p>
  <table>
    ...body of table two...
  </table>
</p>
</body>
```

Early Web developers used **<p>** *tags only to create space. For example, two paragraphs would be coded similarly to the following:*

```
...paragraph one...
<p>
...paragraph two...
```

No closing tags (**</p>** *) were used and therefore no elements were enclosed within block tags. This practice will still render basic text properly in most browsers but is not standards compliant and impacts some of the features of cascading style sheets.*

Manual Line Breaks

Occasionally, you need to break a text line prematurely (that is, before the paragraph break). In such cases, use the line break tag (<br />).

Use of Line Break Tags

For an example of how line breaks are used, consider these lines from William Shakespeare's play *Hamlet*:

```
Fran.
I think I hear them.--Stand, ho! Who is there?

[Enter Horatio and Marcellus.]

Hor.
Friends to this ground.

Mar.
And liegemen to the Dane.

Fran.
Give you good-night.
```

```
Mar.
O, farewell, honest soldier;

Who hath reliev'd you?
```

This text has the distinct format of a play script where each paragraph is formatted like the following example:

```
Actor

Dialog
```

For example, dialog for Fran would resemble the following:

```
Fran.

Give you good-night.
```

Source

To format text such as in the preceding example, you make each actor-dialog pair a separate paragraph with a line break between the two:

```
<p>Fran.<br />
I think I hear them.--Stand, ho! Who is there?</p>
<p>[Enter Horatio and Marcellus.]</p>
<p>Hor.<br />
Friends to this ground.</p>
<p>Mar.<br />
And liegemen to the Dane.</p>
<p>Fran.<br />
Give you good-night.</p>
<p>Mar.<br />

O, farewell, honest soldier;<br />Who hath reliev'd you?</p>
```

*Notice the following two things about the preceding code: (1) The code uses white space to help break up the document; this will have no effect on how the browser renders the text. (2) The **
** tag, because it has no closing tag, includes the slash (**
**) so that it closes itself and is XHTML compliant.*

Output

When rendered by a Web browser, the preceding code results in the display shown in Figure 3-2.

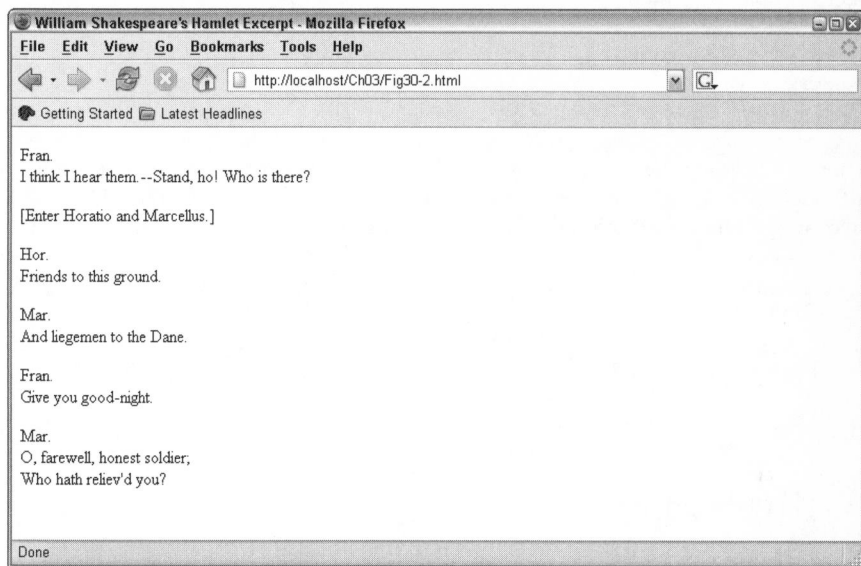

Figure 3-2

*Unlike the **<p>** tag, you can use multiple **
** tags to create vertical white space in documents. However, the use of CSS is still preferred for spacing issues; see the information in Part II of this book, especially Chapters 15 and 16.*

Headings

Standard HTML tags allow for six levels of headings, <h1> through <h6>. The higher the heading number, the smaller the heading. Figure 3-3 shows a simple page with all six headers and a line of standard text.

The user agent's settings affect the size of the different headings.

The code to generate the document shown in Figure 3-3 appears here:

```
<!DOCTYPE html PUBLIC "-//W3C//DTD XHTML 1.0 Strict//EN"
   "http://www.w3.org/TR/xhtml1/DTD/xhtml1-strict.dtd">
<html>
<head>
  <title>Sample Headings</title>
</head>
<body>
<p>
```

```
<h1>Heading One</h1>
<h2>Heading Two</h2>
<h3>Heading Three</h3>
<h4>Heading Four</h4>
<h5>Heading Five</h5>
<h6>Heading Six</h6>
A line of normal text.</p>
</body>
</html>
```

Notice how the headings have implicit line breaks and how the entire document is set inside paragraph tags. Although there are no attributes that you can use to modify the format and behavior of heading tags, you can change their appearance and behavior with styles (which are discussed in Part II of this book).

As a general rule, you should not include any other tags within a heading.

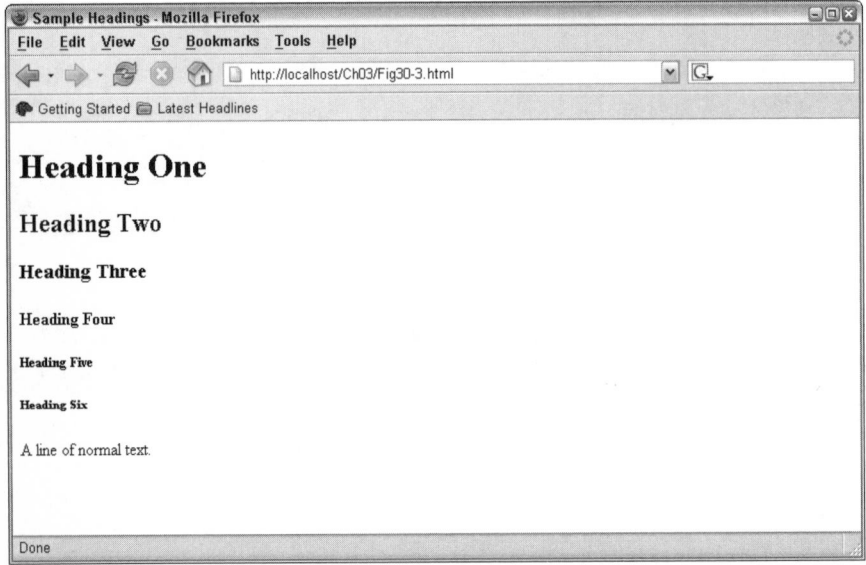

Figure 3-3

Horizontal Rules

Horizontal rules appear as lines across the user agent screen, and they are generally used to separate information visually. A typical <hr/> is shown in Figure 3-4.

The tag to generate a horizontal rule is <hr />. Like any other nonpaired tag, the <hr /> tag should include a slash so that it operates as an open and close tag.

Previous versions of HTML included various attributes that could be used to modify the width, thickness, and look of the line. These attributes have been deprecated in favor of applicable styles.

You will learn more about styles in Part II of this book. Figure 3-5 shows a few sample rules using different styles.

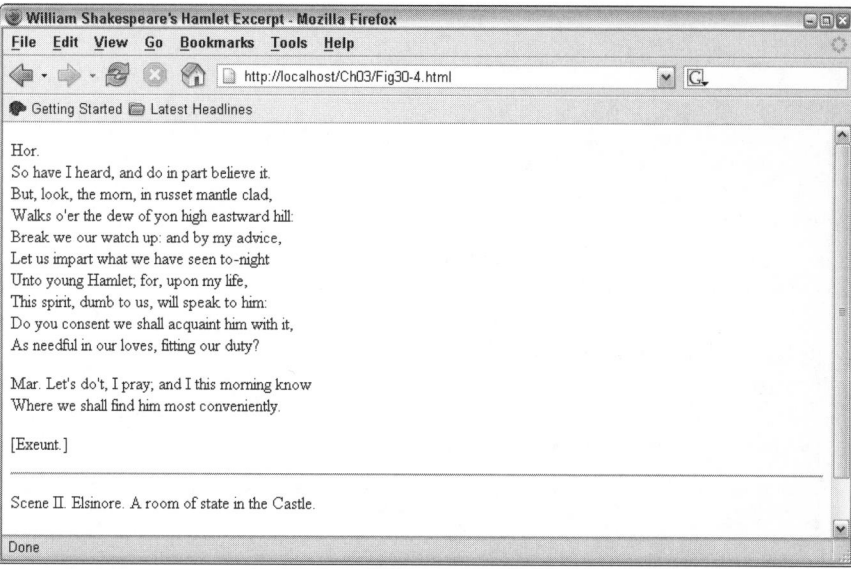

Figure 3-4

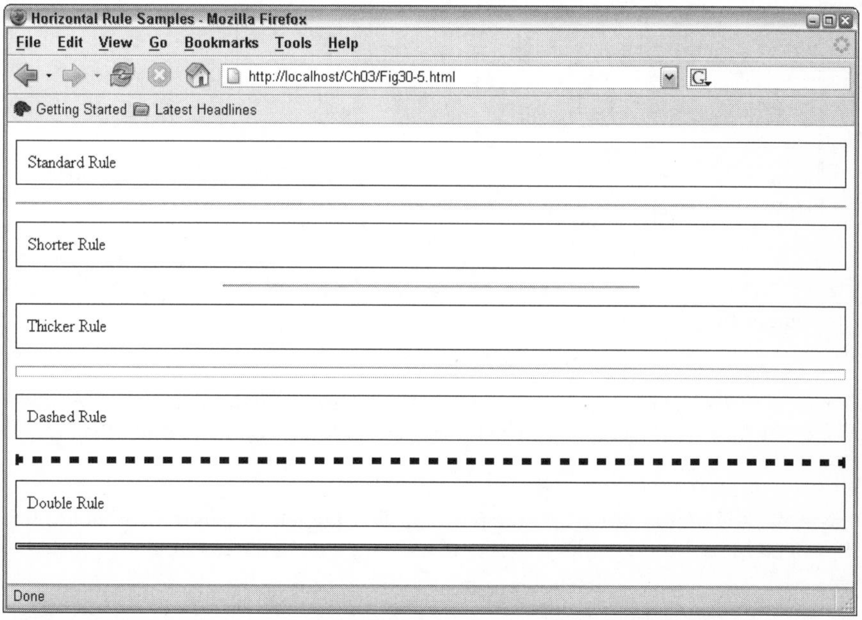

Figure 3-5

Preformatted Text

Occasionally you will need to present content that has already been formatted — tabbed or spaced data, for example — that you do not want the user agent to reformat. For example, suppose you had the following output from a SQL query:

```
+---------------+-------------------+
| name          | value             |
+---------------+-------------------+
| newsupdate    | 1069455632        |
| releaseupdate | Tue, 1/28, 8:18pm |
| status        | 0                 |
| feedupdate    | 1069456261        |
+---------------+-------------------+
```

If you allow a user agent to reformat this text, it will end up looking something like what is shown in Figure 3-6, which is nothing like what was intended.

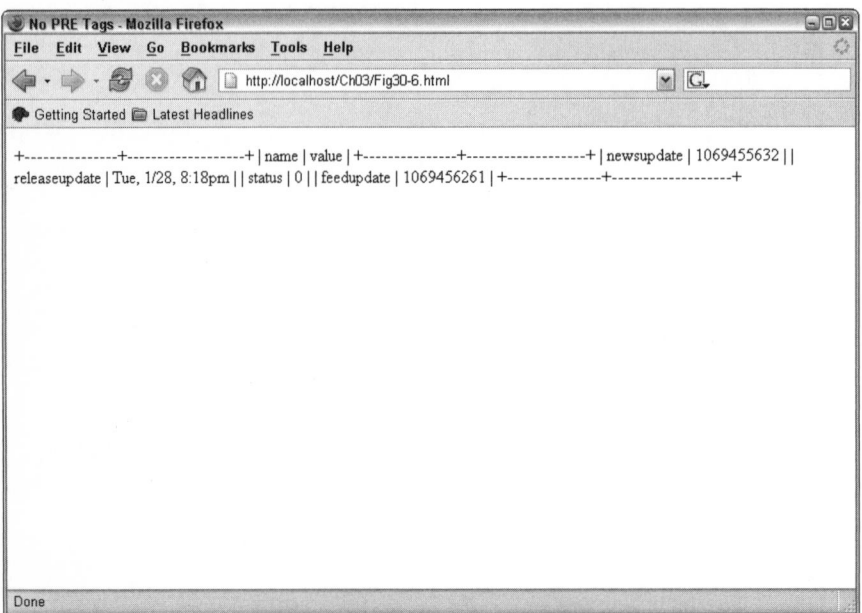

Figure 3-6

Keep in mind that all white space (spaces, line breaks, and so on) will usually be condensed by the user agent into one single space. Use the **<pre>** *tag as required to have the user agent interpret and render white space verbatim.*

In such cases, use the preformatted text tag (<pre>). This tag tells the user agent not to reformat the text within the <pre> block but to render it verbatim as it appears in the document.

If you use a `<pre>` block with the example text (as shown in the following code), the user agent will render it correctly, as shown in Figure 3-7.

```
<pre>
+---------------+-------------------+
| name          | value             |
+---------------+-------------------+
| newsupdate    | 1069455632        |
| releaseupdate | Tue, 1/28, 8:18pm |
| status        | 0                 |
| feedupdate    | 1069456261        |
+---------------+-------------------+
</pre>
```

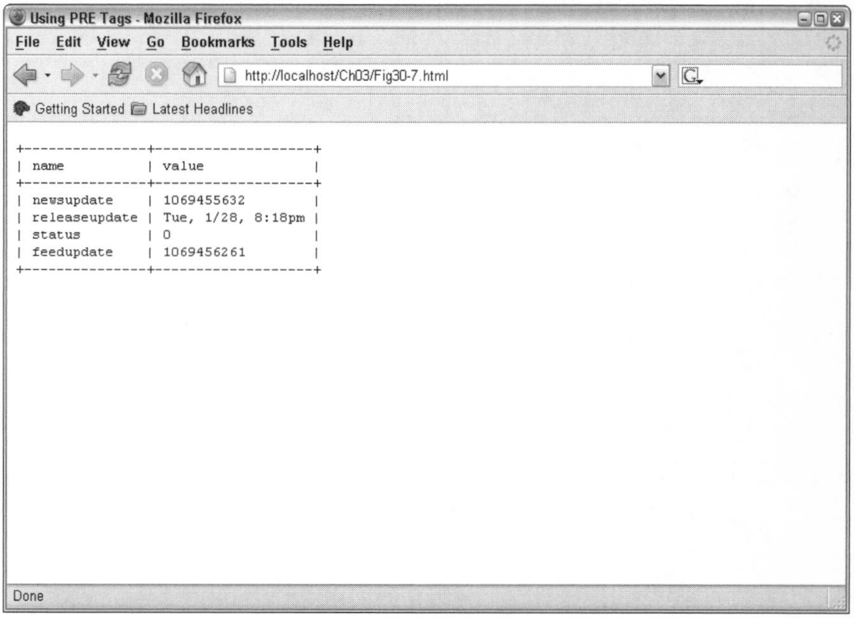

Figure 3-7

Block Divisions

You may sometimes want to format a large block of text in a similar fashion but in a way that is different from other block(s) in the same document. For example, you might want to set apart a quote so that it appears in a different style than the text around it.

You could change the format of the paragraphs manually or you could set them off in their own block using the division tag (`<div>`).

Using the <div> Tag

The use of the <div> tag is straightforward. Simply place the tags around sections of text you want to treat as a special division.

Source

The following shows a few paragraphs of text, surrounding a quote that should be set off in a different format.

```
<p>Despite recent setbacks, Acme Inc still intends on releasing its super-
duper gaming console on Tuesday. Company CEO Morgan Webb had this to say:</p>

<div class="quote"><p>&#147;Although the company has seen better times, we
are confident that the release of the new system will prove our continued
strength in the market. I'm sure that our customers--who have waited
patiently for the X22-B12--will not be disappointed.</p>
<p>The release of multiple games and the launch of our online servers will
further increase our lead over the competition. At the next industry event we
will also be launching a new controller interface that will leave gamers
breathless.&#148;</p></div>


<p>Although Acme has not released a single product in over four years, the
new X22-B12 console holds the promise of revolutionizing gameplay--that is,
if it arrives on time and garners enough support from the masses.</p>
```

The styles for the document, inserted into the document <head> section, include the format for the quote class of <div>:

```
<style type="text/css">
  div.quote { padding-right: 4em; padding-left: 4em;
             font-style: italic; }

</style>
```

Output

The resulting output, once rendered in a user agent, is shown in Figure 3-8. Note how the quote is indented from the right and left margins and is in italic type, as defined by the style.

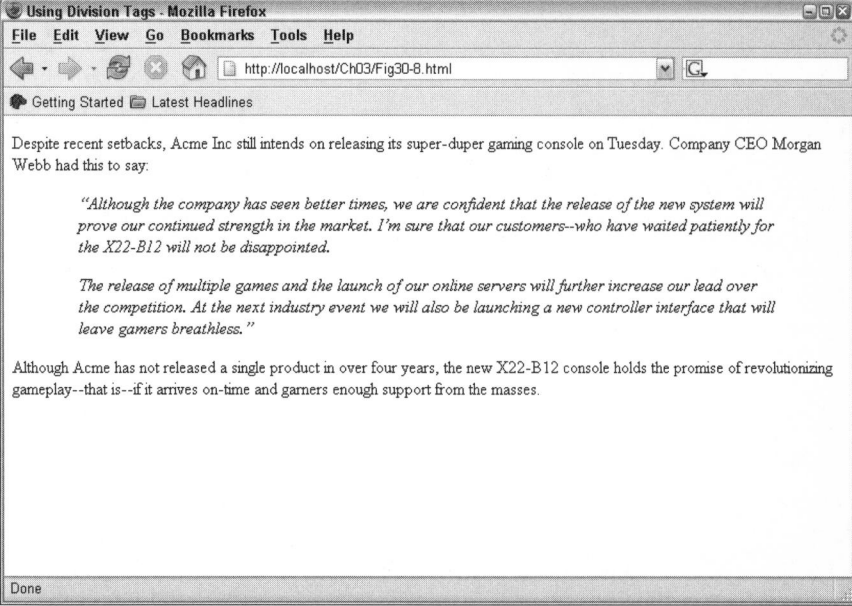

Figure 3-8

Summary

This chapter introduced you to the basic block tags and how best to use them within your content. The coverage in this chapter was pretty basic, formatting-wise. You saw how the block tags can be used to separate text but not to format it. That is because most of the formatting attributes have been deprecated in favor of styles, which are covered in Part II of this book. Chapter 4 introduces the list tags, and subsequent chapters introduce other elements of HTML.

Lists

XHTML supports many different block text elements due to its roots as a text document description and formatting language. One of the more often used blocks is lists, of which XHTML supports three different varieties:

❑ **Ordered lists** — Lists whose elements must appear in a certain order. Such lists usually have their items prefixed with a number or letter.

❑ **Unordered lists** — Lists whose elements can appear in any order, usually referred to as bulleted or laundry-style lists. Such lists usually have their items prefixed with a bullet or other graphic symbol.

❑ **Definition lists** — Lists that contain two pieces of information — a term and a definition of said term — for each list element.

This chapter covers all three lists, their syntax, and various options that can be used to customize their appearance.

This chapter introduces several Cascading Style Sheet concepts. For more information about Cascading Style Sheets, see Part II of this book.

Understanding Lists

Both ordered and unordered lists share a similar syntax in XHTML, as shown in the following pseudocode example:

```
<list_tag>
  <item_tag>List item</item_tag>
  <item_tag>List item</item_tag>
  <item_tag>List item</item_tag>
</list_tag>
```

Definition lists are different in syntax due to their unique structure — that is, two items for each list element. See the section on definition lists later in this chapter for more information.

Each list is encapsulated in opening and closing list tags, and each list element in turn is encapsulated in opening and closing list item tags.

Ordered lists have their list items prefixed by incrementing numbers or letters indicating the order of the items. Unordered lists have their list items prefixed by a bullet or other symbol, indicating that their order does not matter.

The following is an example of an ordered list:

1. Choose `Open` from the `File` menu.
2. Use the `File Open` dialog to navigate to the file you want to open.
3. Double-click the file or click the file and then click the `Open` button.

The following is an example of an unordered list:

- Banana
- Chocolate
- Strawberry

Definition lists have two pieces of information per list item, usually a term and a definition, as shown in the following example:

- Mozilla
- Developed by the Mozilla Project, an open source browser for multiple platforms

Ordered and unordered lists have many options that can be used to customize their appearance.

- Ordered lists can have their items preceded by the following:
  - Arabic numbers
  - Roman numerals (upper- or lowercase)
  - Letters (upper- or lowercase)
  - Numerous other language-specific numbers/letters
- Unordered lists can have their items preceded by the following:
  - Several styles of bullets (filled circle, open circle, square, and so on)
  - Images

More information on the individual list types is provided in the following sections.

Ordered (Numbered) Lists

Ordered lists have a simple format, but many options can be used to customize their appearance in a document. Each ordered list is encapsulated in ordered list tags (<ol>), and each item within the list is encapsulated in list item tags (<li>), as shown in this example:

```
<ol>
  <li>List item 1</li>
  <li>List item 2</li>
  <li>List item 3</li>
</ol>
```

The default numbering method uses Arabic numbers. When rendered in a user agent, this basic list resembles that shown in Figure 4-1.

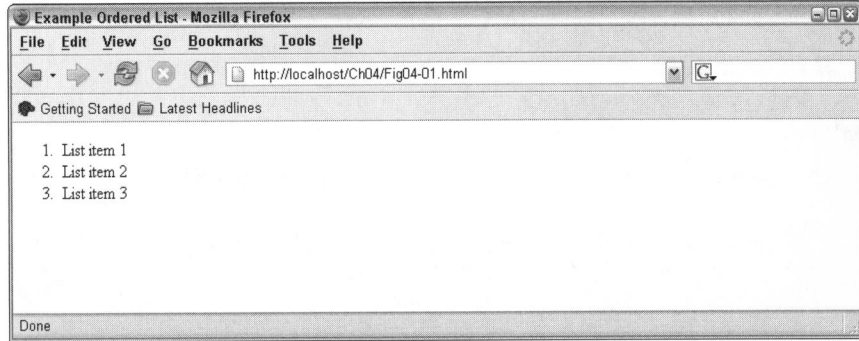

Figure 4-1

Previous versions of HTML did not require the closing item tag (</li>). However, as you should know by now, XHTML requires each tag to have a closing mate. Therefore, it is important always to close your list items with an appropriate tag.

Changing the Number Style

To change the numbering method for the list, you would use the list-style-type property to define the style you want for the numbers.

Example: Using Letters for an Ordered List

This example shows how to use the list-style-type property to change an ordered list's ordinal to uppercase letters.

Source

The source code for the list would resemble the following code. Note the use of the style attribute in the <ol> tag.

```
<!DOCTYPE html PUBLIC "-//W3C//DTD XHTML 1.0 Strict//EN"
    "http://www.w3.org/TR/xhtml1/DTD/xhtml1-strict.dtd"><html>
<head>
  <title>Example Ordered List - Letters</title>
</head>
<body>
<p>
<ol style="list-style-type: upper-alpha">
  <li>In Internet Explorer, open the Web page that displays
the graphic you wish to use as wallpaper for your
desktop.</li>
  <li>Right-click on the image to open the context menu.</li>
  <li>Choose Set as Background to save the image and use it
as your desktop wallpaper.</li>
</ol>
</p>
</body>

</html>
```

Output

When rendered in a user agent, the list appears as shown in Figure 4-2.

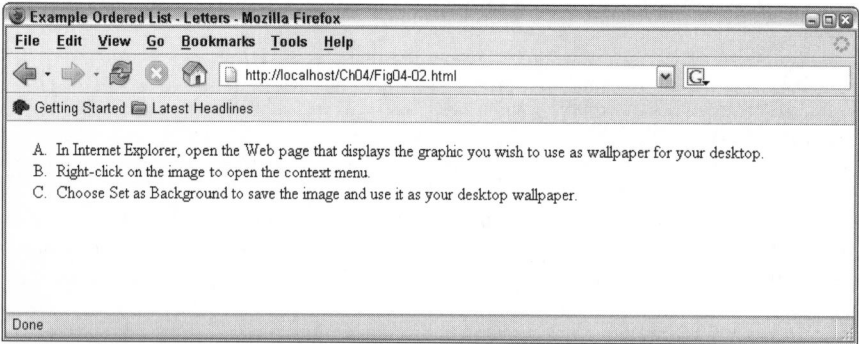

Figure 4-2

The `list-style-type` property supports the following values in CSS2:

- ❑ `decimal`

- ❑ `decimal-leading-zero`

- ❑ `lower-roman`

- ❑ `upper-roman`

- ❑ `lower-greek`

- ❑ `lower-alpha`

- ❑ lower-latin
- ❑ upper-alpha
- ❑ upper-latin
- ❑ hebrew
- ❑ armenian
- ❑ georgian
- ❑ cjk-ideographic
- ❑ hiragana
- ❑ katakana
- ❑ hiragana-iroha
- ❑ katakana-iroha
- ❑ none

The values are self-explanatory. For example, the decimal-leading-zero will produce numbers with leading zeros ("01" instead of "1"). Keep in mind that the default style is decimal on most user agents, but if you want to ensure that the list displays as decimal on all agents, you should explicitly set it to such using the list-style property.

> *Some of the **list-style-type** values are font dependent (that is, they are supported only on certain fonts). If you are using a type such as **hiragana** with a Latin-based font, you will not get the results you intend.*

Changing the Position of the Ordinal

Ordered lists also support the list-style-position property, which controls where the ordinal appears in relation to the list item. The list-style-position property supports three values: inherit, inside, and outside.

The inherit value causes the list to adopt the list style of its parent(s). The inside value moves the ordinal inside the paragraph of the item, for a more compact list. The outside value (the default) places the ordinal outside the list item. A sample of inside and outside items is shown in Figure 4-3, which uses the following list code:

```
<!DOCTYPE html PUBLIC "-//W3C//DTD XHTML 1.0 Strict//EN"
   "http://www.w3.org/TR/xhtml1/DTD/xhtml1-strict.dtd"><html>
<head>
  <title>Example Ordered List - Positioning</title>
</head>
<body>
<p>Outside positioning
<ol style="list-style-position: outside">
  <li>Lorem ipsum dolor sit amet, consectetur adipisicing elit, sed do eiusmod
tempor incididunt ut labore et dolore magna aliqua. Ut enim ad minim veniam, quis
nostrud exercitation ullamco laboris nisi ut aliquip ex ea commodo consequat. Duis
```

```
aute irure dolor in reprehenderit in voluptate velit esse cillum dolore eu fugiat
nulla pariatur. Excepteur sint occaecat cupidatat non proident, sunt in culpa qui
officia deserunt mollit anim id est laborum.</li>
  <li>Lorem ipsum dolor sit amet, consectetur adipisicing elit, sed do eiusmod
tempor incididunt ut labore et dolore magna aliqua. Ut enim ad minim veniam, quis
nostrud exercitation ullamco laboris nisi ut aliquip ex ea commodo consequat. Duis
aute irure dolor in reprehenderit in voluptate velit esse cillum dolore eu fugiat
nulla pariatur. Excepteur sint occaecat cupidatat non proident, sunt in culpa qui
officia deserunt mollit anim id est laborum.</li>
  <li>Lorem ipsum dolor sit amet, consectetur adipisicing elit, sed do eiusmod
tempor incididunt ut labore et dolore magna aliqua. Ut enim ad minim veniam, quis
nostrud exercitation ullamco laboris nisi ut aliquip ex ea commodo consequat. Duis
aute irure dolor in reprehenderit in voluptate velit esse cillum dolore eu fugiat
nulla pariatur. Excepteur sint occaecat cupidatat non proident, sunt in culpa qui
officia deserunt mollit anim id est laborum.</li>
</ol></p>
<p>Inside positioning
<ol style="list-style-position: inside">
  <li>Lorem ipsum dolor sit amet, consectetur adipisicing elit, sed do eiusmod
tempor incididunt ut labore et dolore magna aliqua. Ut enim ad minim veniam, quis
nostrud exercitation ullamco laboris nisi ut aliquip ex ea commodo consequat. Duis
aute irure dolor in reprehenderit in voluptate velit esse cillum dolore eu fugiat
nulla pariatur. Excepteur sint occaecat cupidatat non proident, sunt in culpa qui
officia deserunt mollit anim id est laborum.</li>
  <li>Lorem ipsum dolor sit amet, consectetur adipisicing elit, sed do eiusmod
tempor incididunt ut labore et dolore magna aliqua. Ut enim ad minim veniam, quis
nostrud exercitation ullamco laboris nisi ut aliquip ex ea commodo consequat. Duis
aute irure dolor in reprehenderit in voluptate velit esse cillum dolore eu fugiat
nulla pariatur. Excepteur sint occaecat cupidatat non proident, sunt in culpa qui
officia deserunt mollit anim id est laborum.</li>
  <li>Lorem ipsum dolor sit amet, consectetur adipisicing elit, sed do eiusmod
tempor incididunt ut labore et dolore magna aliqua. Ut enim ad minim veniam, quis
nostrud exercitation ullamco laboris nisi ut aliquip ex ea commodo consequat. Duis
aute irure dolor in reprehenderit in voluptate velit esse cillum dolore eu fugiat
nulla pariatur. Excepteur sint occaecat cupidatat non proident, sunt in culpa qui
officia deserunt mollit anim id est laborum.</li>
</ol></p>
</body>
</html>
```

*The various list properties can all be defined within one property, **list-style**. The **list-style** property has the following syntax:*

```
list-style: <list-style-type> <list-style-image> <list-style-position>
```

*You can use this one property to specify one, two, or all three **list-style** properties in one style declaration.*

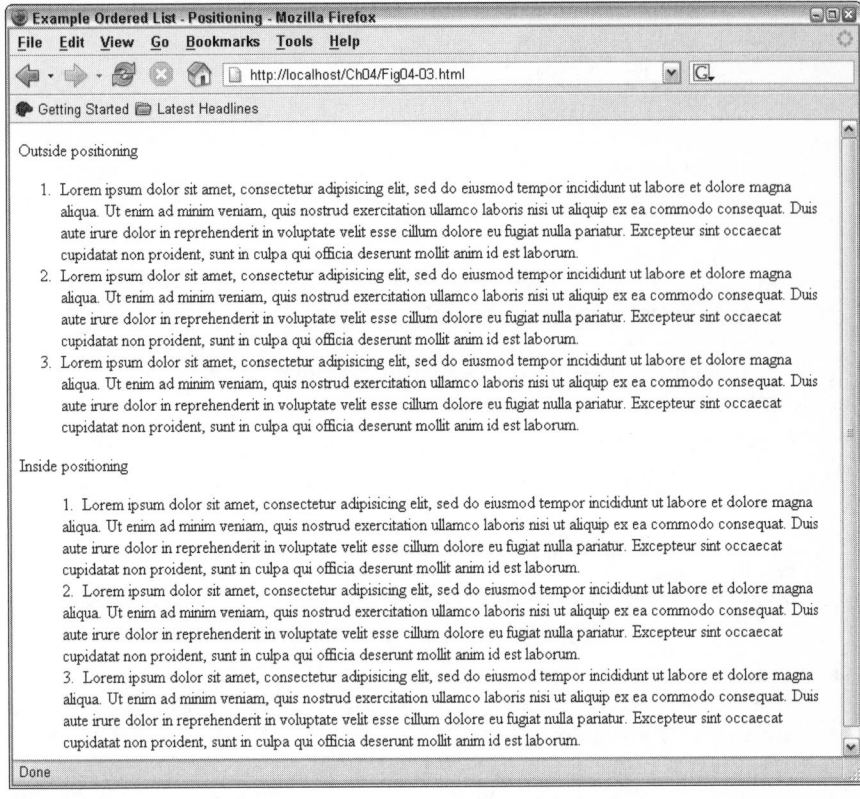

Figure 4-3

Changing the Starting Number of Ordered Lists

Previous versions of HTML allowed the use of the `start` attribute in the ordered list tag to control what number or letter the list would begin with. For example, the following code would have started a list with the decimal number 10:

```
<ol start="10" style="list-style: decimal;">
```

However, the start attribute of the `<ol>` tag has been deprecated. To date, no replacement CSS style has been defined. Although you can use the `start` attribute, your document will no longer be XHTML compliant.

To implement flexible numbering, use the new CSS2 automatic counters and numbering feature. This feature uses the `content` property along with the new `counter-increment` and `counter-reset` properties to provide a flexible yet powerful automatic counter function.

The following style code will define a counter and cause any <ol> list to begin with 10:

```
<style type="text/css">
ol { counter-reset: list 9; }
li { list-style-type: none; }
li:before {
    content: counter(list,decimal) ". ";
    counter-increment: list; }
</style>
```

This code introduces quite a few CSS2 concepts — pseudoelements, counters, and related properties and methods. However, it isn't as complex as it might first appear:

❑ The ol definition sets the counter (list) to be reset to 9 every time an <ol> tag is used in the document.

❑ The li definition sets the list-style-type to none — the counter will display our number. If the type was left alone or set to decimal, there would be an additional number displayed with each item.

❑ The li:before definition accomplishes two distinct purposes:

  ❑ It causes the counter to be displayed before the item (using the begin pseudoelement and the content property) along with a period and a space.

  ❑ It also increments the counter. Note that the counter increment happens first, before the item is displayed. That is why the counter is initialized to one lower than the starting number desired (9 instead of 10).

Using the preceding styles along with the following list code in a document results in a list with items numbered 10–15:

```
<ol>
  <li>Item 10</li>
  <li>Item 11</li>
  <li>Item 12</li>
  <li>Item 13</li>
  <li>Item 14</li>
  <li>Item 15</li>
</ol>
```

Unfortunately, at the time of this writing, only the Opera browser fully supports counters. However, the other user agents should adopt this feature in the future.

Unordered (Bulleted) Lists

Unordered lists are generally used to present lists whose order does not matter. For example, when listing the flavors of milkshakes available, you might use a list similar to the following:

❑ Chocolate

❑ Vanilla

❑ Strawberry

❑ Mocha

This same list can be implemented in HTML documents using the unordered list tag (<ul>), as shown in the following HTML code:

```
<ul>
  <li>Chocolate</li>
  <li>Vanilla</li>
  <li>Strawberry</li>
  <li>Mocha</li>
</ul>
```

Note that the use of the unordered list tag is very similar to the use of the ordered list tag—only the output is different, as shown in Figure 4-4.

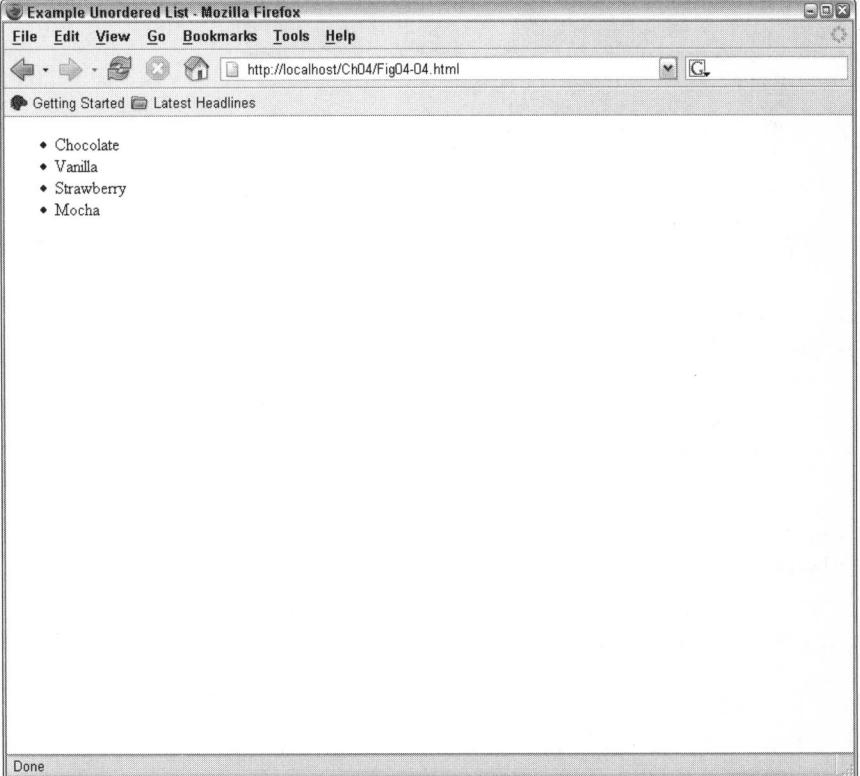

Figure 4-4

Changing the List Item Marker

As you can with ordered lists, you can change the marker used to prefix each unordered list item. To do so, use the `list-style-type` property with one of the following values:

- ❏ disc
- ❏ circle
- ❏ square
- ❏ none

You can also use the `list-style-image` property to specify a graphic image for use as the list item marker.

Changing the List Item Marker Example

This example shows how to change the list item marker, specifying one of the preset markers or a specific graphic image.

Source

The following code uses several different types of list markers:

```
<!DOCTYPE html PUBLIC "-//W3C//DTD XHTML 1.0 Strict//EN"
    "http://www.w3.org/TR/xhtml1/DTD/xhtml1-strict.dtd"><html>
<head>
  <title>Example Unordered List Markers</title>
  <style type="text/css">
    ul.normal { }
    ul.circle { list-style-type: circle; }
    ul.image  { list-style-image: url("shake.jpg"); }
    ul.none   { list-style-type: none; }
  </style>
</head>
<body>
<p>
<ul class="normal">
  <li>Chocolate</li>
  <li>Vanilla</li>
  <li>Strawberry</li>
  <li>Mocha</li>
</ul>
<ul class="circle">
  <li>Chocolate</li>
  <li>Vanilla</li>
  <li>Strawberry</li>
  <li>Mocha</li>
</ul>
<ul class="image">
  <li>Chocolate</li>
  <li>Vanilla</li>
  <li>Strawberry</li>
  <li>Mocha</li>
</ul>
<ul class="none">
  <li>Chocolate</li>
  <li>Vanilla</li>
  <li>Strawberry</li>
```

```
        <li>Mocha</li>
    </ul>
    </p>
    </body>

    </html>
```

Note that to use an image for a marker, the image must conform to the following:

❑ Accessible to the document via HTTP (be on the same Web server or deliverable from another Web server)

❑ In a suitable format for the Web (jpg, gif, or png)

❑ Sized appropriately for use as a bullet

If the image used in the **list-style-image** *property is not found, most user agents will substitute the default marker.*

Output

The code results in a document that resembles that shown in Figure 4-5.

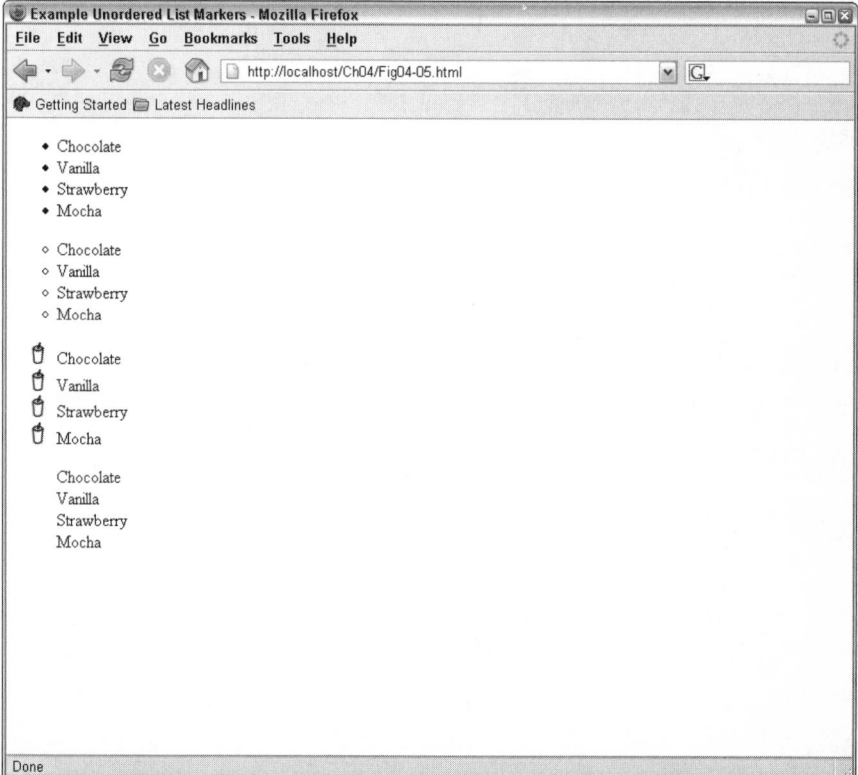

Figure 4-5

As you can see from Figure 4-5, all user agents do not use a standard round bullet for the default **<ul>**
*item marker. In this case, Mozilla Firefox uses a solid diamond for the standard bullet. If you want to
ensure that your document is always displayed using a particular marker in its unordered lists, you
should explicitly define it.*

Changing the Position of the Ordinal

Unordered lists support the list-style-position property, controlling where the marker appears in
relation to the list item. The list-style-position property supports three values: inherit, inside,
and outside. The effect is similar to that of ordered lists, as demonstrated in the ordered list section earlier in this chapter.

Definition Lists

Definition lists seem more complex than the other two lists due to their having two elements per list item.
However, the sparse number of options available for definition lists makes them easy to implement.

The definition list itself is encapsulated within definition list tags (<dl>). The list items consist of a definition term (<dt>) and definition (<dd>), each delimited by its own tag pair.

For example, the following code results in the document shown in Figure 4-6:

```
<!DOCTYPE html PUBLIC "-//W3C//DTD XHTML 1.0 Strict//EN"
   "http://www.w3.org/TR/xhtml1/DTD/xhtml1-strict.dtd"><html>
<head>
  <title>Example Definition List</title>
</head>
<body>
<p>
<dl>
  <dt>Internet Explorer</dt>
  <dd>Developed by Microsoft, an integral piece of Windows
      products.</dd>
  <dt>Mozilla</dt>
  <dd>Developed by the Mozilla Project, an open source
      browser for multiple platforms.</dd>
  <dt>Netscape</dt>
  <dd>Developed by Netscape Communications Corporation, one
      of the first graphical browsers.</dd>
  <dt>Safari</dt>
  <dd>Developed by Apple Computer, Inc, for Apple's OSX
      operating system.</dd>
  <dt>Firefox</dt>
  <dd>A "next generation" open source browser developed by Mozilla
      and available on multiple platforms.</dd>
</dl>
</p>
</body>
</html>
```

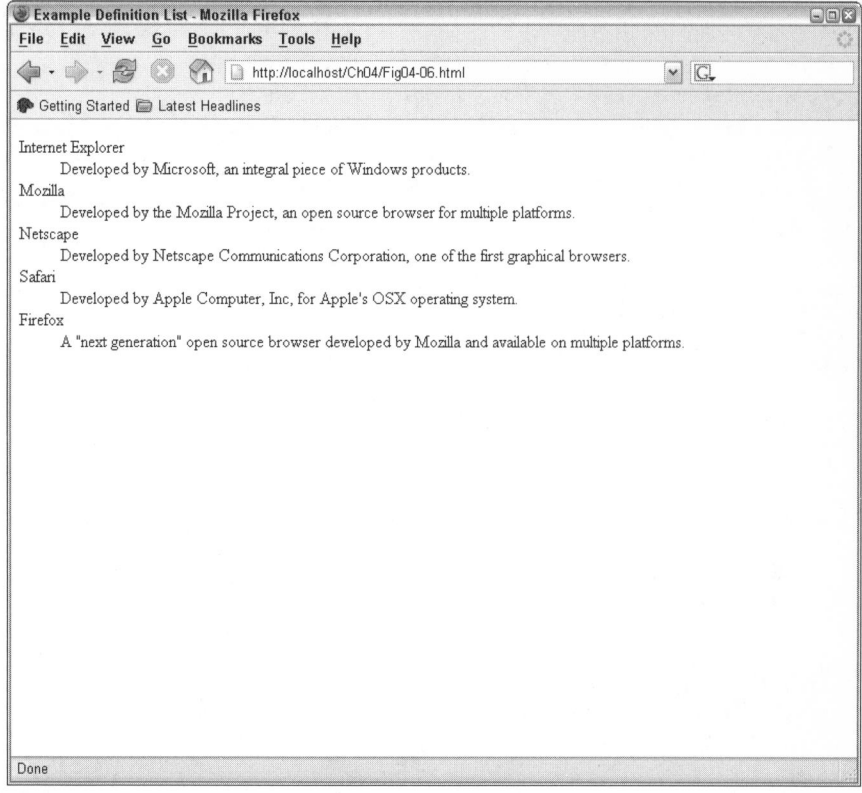

Figure 4-6

Nesting Lists

You can nest lists of the same or different types as necessary. For example, you can generate a list similar to the following, incorporating an ordered list within an unordered one:

- Call the number below.
- Send us a letter, being sure to include the following:
    1. Your full name
    2. Your order number
    3. Your contact information
    4. A detailed description of the problem
- Use the Web form to send us an e-mail.

This combination of lists can be constructed using the following code and results in the display shown in Figure 4-7:

```
<!DOCTYPE html PUBLIC "-//W3C//DTD XHTML 1.0 Strict//EN"
    "http://www.w3.org/TR/xhtml1/DTD/xhtml1-strict.dtd"><html>
<head>
  <title>Example Nested Lists</title>
</head>
<body>
<p>
<ul>
  <li>Call the number below</li>
  <li>Send us a letter, being sure to include:</li>
  <ol>
    <li>Your full name</li>
    <li>Your order number</li>
    <li>Your contact information</li>
    <li>A detailed description of the problem</li>
  </ol>
  <li>Use the Web form to send us an email</li>
</ul>
</p>
</body>
</html>
```

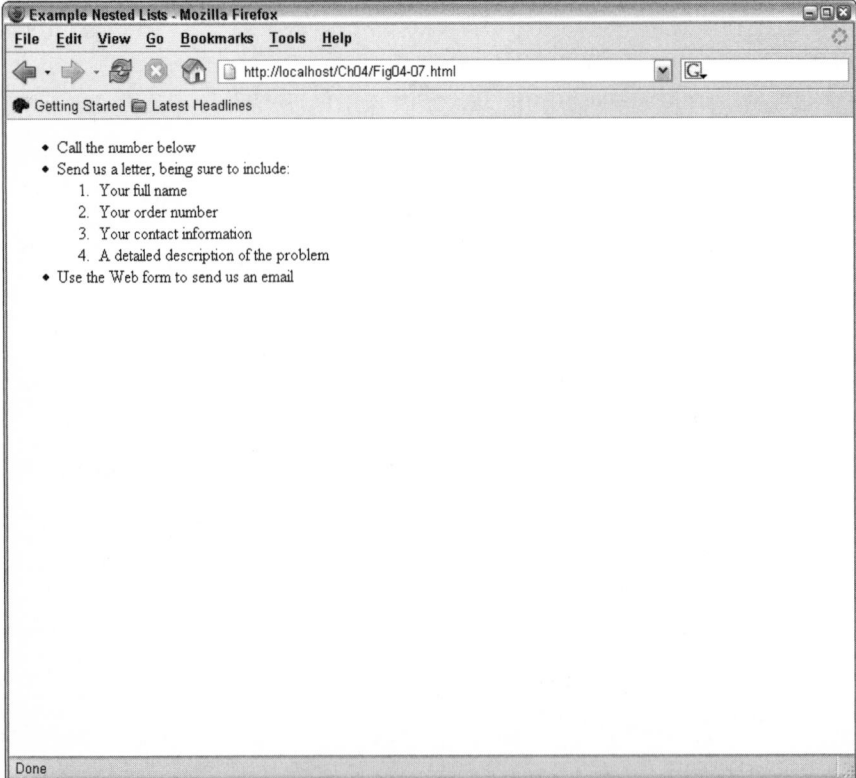

Figure 4-7

Summary

As you learned in this chapter, XHTML lists are flexible text constructs that can be used for a variety of purposes. Using the many optional formatting options, you can construct a list, or nested series of lists, for just about any purpose. The new counters feature of CSS can also be used to extend even more functionality and flexibility to your lists.

5

Images

Previously a haven of text-only mediums, the Internet became mainstream due to graphic content on the Web. Today capabilities exist to deliver much more than static graphics — multimedia of every variety can be found on Web pages. This chapter covers the inclusion of basic graphic format — static images — in Web documents.

Including other multimedia formats in Web documents is covered in Chapter 10.

Image Formats

Although static images can seem unexciting in today's world of Web-delivered content, the Web would be a very boring place without their use. As you will see in the following sections, there are plenty of options and formats to consider when using images in your Web documents.

Web Formats

The Web supports three main formats of graphics — GIF, JPEG, and PNG. The following sections detail the capabilities and suggested uses for each type of graphic.

GIF

The Graphics Interchange Format (GIF) was created in the late 1980s. It was originally used by the CompuServe online service to deliver graphic content to their subscribers. The GIF format uses LWZ compression to help keep the file size small. Version 89a of the GIF format added the ability to encapsulate several images within one file, giving the format animation functionality.

The GIF format has the following characteristics:

- ❏ Supports up to 8-bit color (256 colors)
- ❏ Supports transparency
- ❏ Is stored in a compressed, lossless format
- ❏ Can be interlaced and used for rudimentary animations

As you can see, GIF is a versatile format. The main drawback to the GIF format is the limit of 256 colors, which can limit what the format can display.

Patent problems plagued the GIF format's adoption in the late 1990s. Unisys, the patent holder of LWZ compression, chose to terminate their royalty-free licenses and charge royalties for use of the format. This practice spurred the development of alternative formats for platforms like the Web, resulting in new and/or more robust JPEG and PNG format support.

JPEG

The Joint Photographic Experts Group (JPEG) graphic file format is actually two standards: one specifies how an image is translated into a series of bytes, and the second (JPEG File Interchange Format [JFIF]) specifies how the data is encapsulated into a file format. JPEG files are stored using one of several lossy compression methods — to keep images at a reasonable size, the compression scheme sacrifices being able to accurately reconstruct all data present in the original image.

The JPEG format has the following characteristics:

❑   Supports 24-bit color (64,000 colors)

❑   Does not support transparency

❑   Is stored using a lossy compression format; the smaller the file, the lower the quality of the image (although the compression level can be configured when an image is created in an image editing program)

❑   Can be stored in a "progressive" format

The JPEG format is not as versatile as the GIF format, but its support of 24-bit color and compression make it a good format for quality images across a bandwidth-constrained medium.

PNG

The Portable Network Graphics (PNG) format was developed during the GIF patent confusion. PNG was created specifically for delivery over online services such as the Web and specifically to solve some of the problems with the GIF format. PNG uses a nonpatented lossless compression scheme to keep file sizes smaller while maintaining image quality.

The PNG format has the following characteristics:

❑   Supports 24-bit color (64,000 colors)

❑   Supports transparency

❑   Is stored using a lossless compression scheme

❑   Can be stored and displayed in interlaced format

PNG is a relatively new format, and as such, support for the format and its various features is still some-what spotty. For example, as of this writing, Microsoft's Internet Explorer supports only the single-color transparency option of the PNG format. However, this format promises to be a large step in the evolution of online graphics.

In 2004 an animation standard was proposed for the PNG format. As of this writing, the standard has not made it into the mainstream and is not in use on the Web.

Transparency

Transparent graphics can be displayed with one or more of their colors transparent, causing what is under the image to be shown instead of the image data. The effect is as if the specified colors were turned to clear glass. For example, consider the two images in Figure 5-1.

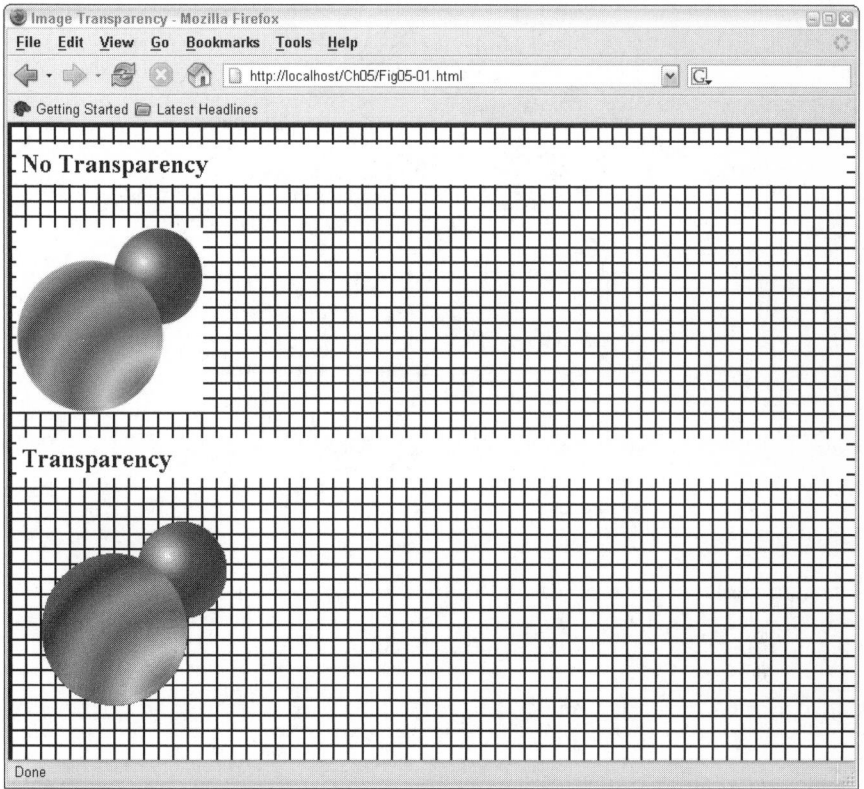

Figure 5-1

The first image was not saved with transparency information — its white background clearly outlines the image. The second image contains transparency information — the white background is transparent, allowing the grid to show through areas of the image that are completely white.

As previously mentioned in the "Web Formats" section of this chapter, both GIF and PNG formats support transparency, though many user agents do not fully support PNG's transparency feature set.

Interlaced and Progressive Storage and Display

In the days before broadband went mainstream, large images took far too long to transfer across modem lines. An interlaced encoding scheme was created to help solve this problem. An image was stored so that when it was displayed it would display alternating scan lines, revealing the picture a bit at a time; as the image loaded, it would also display the full length of the image. Images that are not interlaced display each scan line in turn, and the user must wait for the full image to load to see the bottom of the image.

Figure 5-2 shows how an interlaced graphic and a noninterlaced graphic load in a user agent.

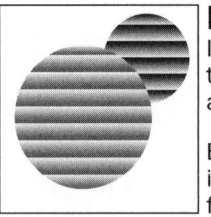
Interlaced
Image is revealed
top-to-bottom,
alternating scan lines.

Bottom of image
is revealed in piecemeal
fashion while image loads.

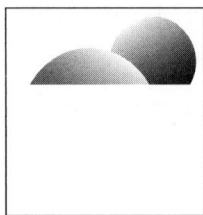
Non-Interlaced
Image is revealed
top-to-bottom, one
scan line at a time.

Bottom of image
cannot be seen until
entire image is loaded.

Figure 5-2

The effect of an interlaced image is similar to horizontal blinds being opened. Pieces of the image, top to bottom, are revealed at the same time, allowing the user to get the general idea of what the image contains without having to wait for the entire image to load.

The JPG image format supports a similar feature. An interlaced JPG image is saved in *progressive* format but displays similarly to that of an interlaced GIF image.

> *Interlaced and progressive images are not used very often, due to the proliferation of broadband throughout the Web's intended audience (consumers). Most images load fast enough that the advantages provided by interlacing or progressive display are negligible. However, you should avoid going overboard with images to keep your documents' load times to a minimum.*

Animation

The GIF format supports displaying, encapsulating several images within one image file. The images can then be displayed one after another, resulting in a rudimentary animation technique. The technique is similar to that of an animator's flipbook: basic sketches are drawn on the pages of the book, and when the book's pages are rapidly flipped, the images seem to animate.

> *Keep in mind that an animated GIF file contains one image for each frame of animation. As such, they are significantly larger than static images.*

Animated GIFs have several options that can be used to aid in the animation:

❑ Each image within the file can be displayed with its own delay value so the animation can be slowed or sped up as necessary.

❑ Each image can replace the previous image in a variety of ways — by overwriting it with transparency, a palette color, and so on.

❑ The animation can be set to play a limited number of times or set to repeat indefinitely.

Example: GIF Animation Example

This example animates a clock's hour hand.

Source

You need to assemble all the images in your animation. For this example, you will take a clock face and move the hour hand through a 12-hour cycle, saving each image as shown in Figure 5-3 (images viewed in Jasc Software's Media Center application).

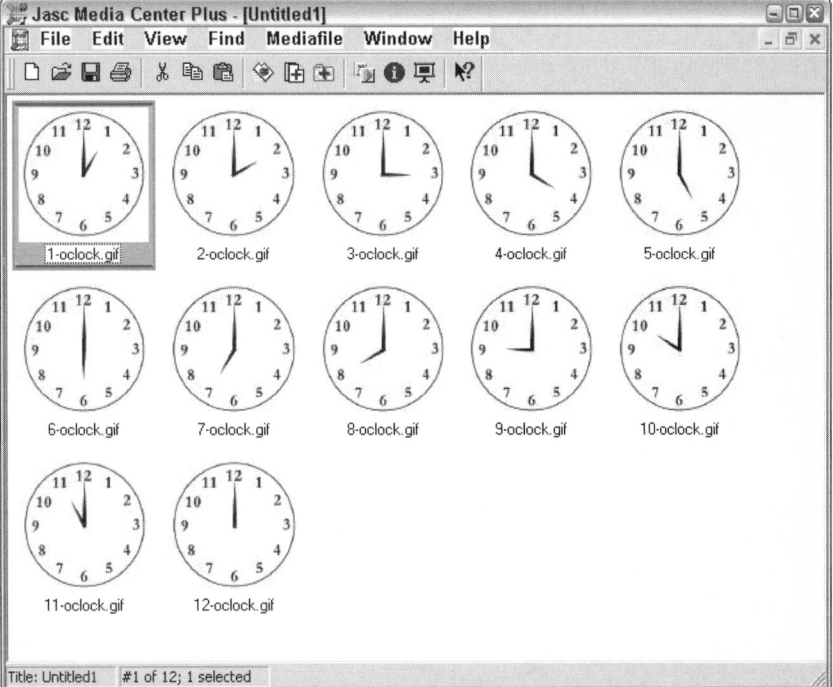

Figure 5-3

Assembling the Animation

Using an animation tool (such as JASC Software's Animation Shop, shown in Figure 5-4), you assemble the individual images into an animated GIF file, specifying the options for each frame and the entire animation.

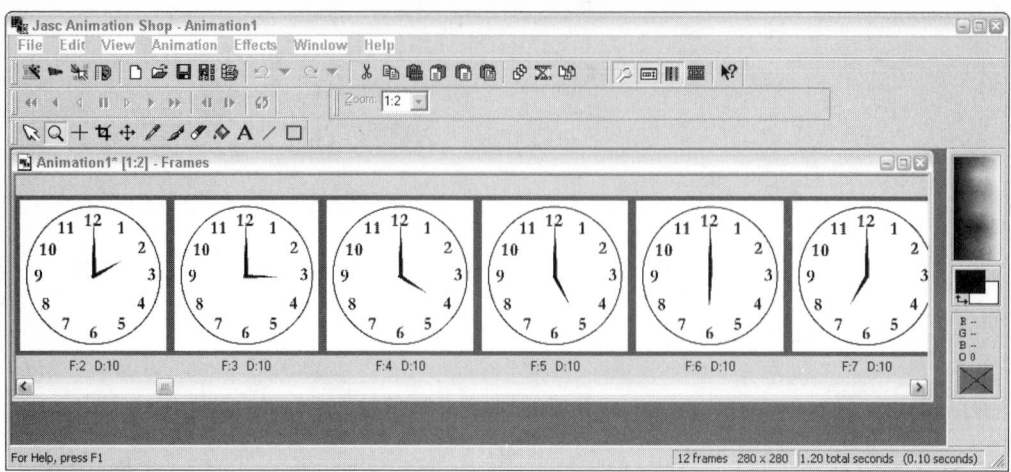

Figure 5-4

Output

When placed in a Web document, the finished image animates the clock by showing each image/frame in order (see Figure 5-5).

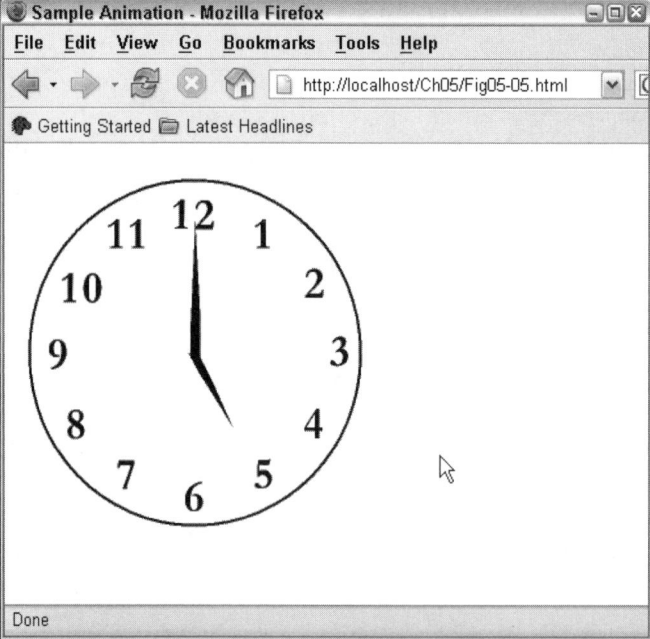

Figure 5-5

Animated GIFs do not interpolate motion between the individual frames. As such, extreme changes between frame images will appear very jerky and sudden. When creating the images for animation frames, try to keep your motions slow and spanning several frames.

There are several graphic editing programs that support animated GIFs. This example shows JASC Software's Animation Shop, available as part of their Paint Shop Pro product (www.jascsoftware.com).

Creating Images

Many graphic editing packages and applications are available to create images for your Web documents. This section lists a few of the more popular solutions.

Commercial Applications

Several commercial editing applications can be purchased to create and edit graphic images:

❑ **Adobe Photoshop** — Known for its high-end feature set, Adobe Photoshop is the extreme top end of graphic editing products. Its numerous features, large number of add-ons, and huge install base are among its benefits; its large price tag is among its deficits.

❑ **Adobe Illustrator** — Another Adobe product, Illustrator, is known for its vector editing abilities. Its native editing of Postscript-compatible files is one of its benefits, though it also is fairly expensive and doesn't handle raster graphic formats as well.

❑ **JASC Software Paint Shop Pro** — Paint Shop Pro has been a contender for second place in the graphic editor championships. However, its latest versions all but put it in the same class as Adobe's products. Its ability to handle both vector and raster graphics and its compatibility with many Photoshop add-ons mean that Paint Shop Pro can handle almost any task.

❑ **Macromedia Freehand and Fireworks** — Although known mainly for its Flash and Director products, Macromedia has its own suite of graphic editing programs as well. Of those products, Freehand and Fireworks are of particular note. Freehand is similar to Adobe's Illustrator product, excelling in editing vector graphics. Fireworks, by comparison, edits raster graphics and has a host of animation features as well.

Several of the commercial packages are available in suite form. For example, the Macromedia suite bundles Dreamweaver, Fireworks, Flash, and Freehand in one package (for less than the individual applications bought separately). If you need more than one capability (vector editing, raster editing, animation, and so on), look for one of the suites instead of individual applications.

Open Source Applications

A few open source graphical editors are also available. These applications tend to be free for use but support varies from community-driven to nonexistent.

The most full-featured and supported open source application is the GNU Image Manipulation Program (GIMP). Rivaling Photoshop in features and capabilities, GIMP is a great solution for the cash conscious — its price (free) belies its wide range of features and Photoshop compatibility. Visit www.gimp.org for more information.

Operating System Built-In Applications

Most operating systems come with rudimentary graphic editing programs. Windows, for example, includes the Windows Picture Viewer (which can only resize and rotate) and Paint (which can edit raster graphics). If your needs are meager, you can get by using these applications.

Using Premade Images

Several sources for premade images may also suit your needs. You can find several commercial image packages at your favorite software store and several image repositories online.

One important issue when dealing with other people's content is rights. It's important to be aware of what rights are granted for the images' use. For example, some image products and sites do not allow their images to be used for commercial purposes. You can use them for internal company use or for things like greeting cards or party invitations. However, you might not be able to use the images for a commercial Web site.

> *Before using an image for online and/or commercial use, read the license info that accompanies the graphic (if from a retail package) or query the author for license information. When in doubt, don't use the image.*

In addition, although it may be tempting to use images you find elsewhere on the Web, you should remember that someone else holds the rights on almost every image, rights that don't automatically translate to anyone who downloads and reuses them.

Inserting Images into Web Documents

The image tag (`<img>`) is used to insert images into XHTML documents. The tag has the following minimal syntax:

```
<img src="url_to_image" alt="text_for_non_graphical_agents" />
```

The two parameters, `src` and `alt`, define where to find the image and text to display if the user agent can't display the image (or is set not to display images at all). These two parameters comprise the minimal set of parameters for any image tag.

> *As with other tags that lack a closing mate, you should end the **<img>** tag with a slash to be XHTML compliant.*

For example, the following tag will insert an image, `cat.jpg`, into the document with the alternate text "A picture of a cat":

```
<img src="cat.jpg" alt="A picture of a cat" />
```

In this case, because the `src` does not contain a server and full path, the image is assumed to be in the same directory, on the same server, as the XHTML document. The following tag gives the full URL to the image, which could conceivably be on a different server than the document:

```
<img src="http://www.example.com/animal_images/cat.jpg" alt="A picture of a cat" />
```

Note that it is a good practice to store images separately from documents. Most Web authors use a directory such as **images** *to store all images for their documents.*

The user agent will attempt to display the image in-line (that is, alongside elements around it). For example, consider the following code snippet:

```
<p>Lorem ipsum dolor sit amet, consectetur adipisicing elit, sed do eiusmod tempor
incididunt ut labore et dolore magna aliqua. Ut enim ad minim veniam, quis nostrud
exercitation ullamco laboris nisi ut aliquip ex ea commodo consequat. <img
src="book.jpg" alt="A book" /> Duis aute irure dolor in reprehenderit in
voluptate velit esse cillum dolore eu fugiat nulla pariatur. Excepteur sint
occaecat cupidatat non proident, sunt in culpa qui officia deserunt mollit anim id
est laborum.</p>
```

When displayed in a user agent, the code results in the document being rendered similarly to that shown in Figure 5-6.

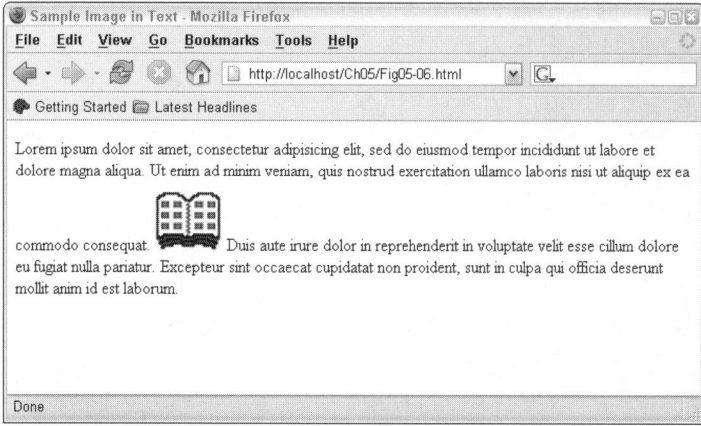

Figure 5-6

As you can see, the image doesn't quite fit where placed. However, the user agent dutifully renders it where the tag appears. A better choice would be to place the image at the beginning or end of the text, as in the following code (whose results are shown in Figure 5-7):

```
<p><img src="book.jpg" alt="A book" /> Lorem ipsum dolor sit amet, consectetur
adipisicing elit, sed do eiusmod tempor incididunt ut labore et dolore magna
aliqua. Ut enim ad minim veniam, quis nostrud exercitation ullamco laboris nisi ut
aliquip ex ea commodo consequat. Duis aute irure dolor in reprehenderit in
voluptate velit esse cillum dolore eu fugiat nulla pariatur. Excepteur sint
occaecat cupidatat non proident, sunt in culpa qui officia deserunt mollit anim id
est laborum.</p>
```

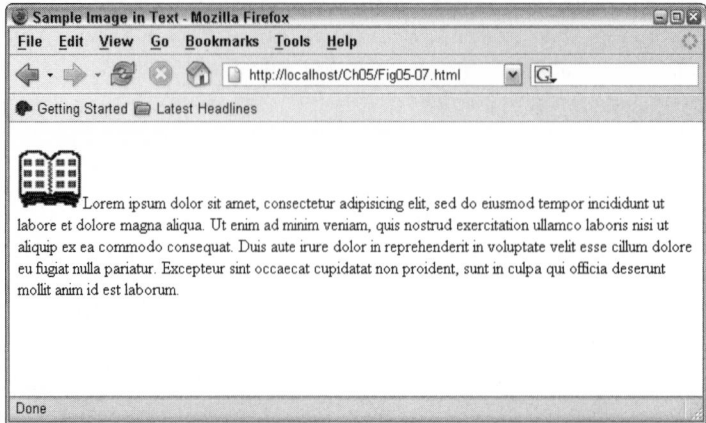

Figure 5-7

The `<img>` tag has several attributes to help control how user agents will display an image; those attributes are covered in the next section. You can also use several CSS style attributes to control how an image is formatted in relation to other elements. Part II of this book covers CSS in detail.

Image Attributes

The `<img>` tag supports several attributes that can be used to help adjust how an image is rendered in a user agent. The basic XHTML attributes are described in the following sections.

*Earlier versions of HTML supported additional attributes such as **align**, **border**, **hspace**, and **vspace** to help position the image. However, those attributes have been deprecated; to adjust the factors controlled by those attributes, you must now use their CSS equivalents.*

Specifying Text for Nongraphical Browsers

As previously mentioned in this chapter, the `alt` attribute is used to provide text for nongraphical browsers. This text is generally displayed in place of the graphic in text-only browsers or in browsers that have images disabled. Alt-text is also used by nonvisual browsers — for example, audio browsers will speak the value of the `alt` attribute as it renders the page. Lastly, some user agents will use the `alt` tag's value as a tooltip or other textual hint, as shown in Figure 5-8.

Because of the utility of the attribute, you should endeavor to always include the `alt` tag with a descriptive value.

*Resist the urge to embed extra information in an **alt** attribute value. Doing so will obscure the information from browsers that display the image and otherwise don't use the alt-text. Additionally, it will not give alternative user agents (nongraphical) the information they need to understand the purpose of the graphic that they cannot see.*

*If you have a lot of information to convey, consider using the **longdesc** (long description) attribute as well as the **alt** attribute. The **longdesc** attribute specifies a URL to a document that is to be used as the long description for the figure. Note that it is up to the user agent to decide how to enable access to the long description, if at all.*

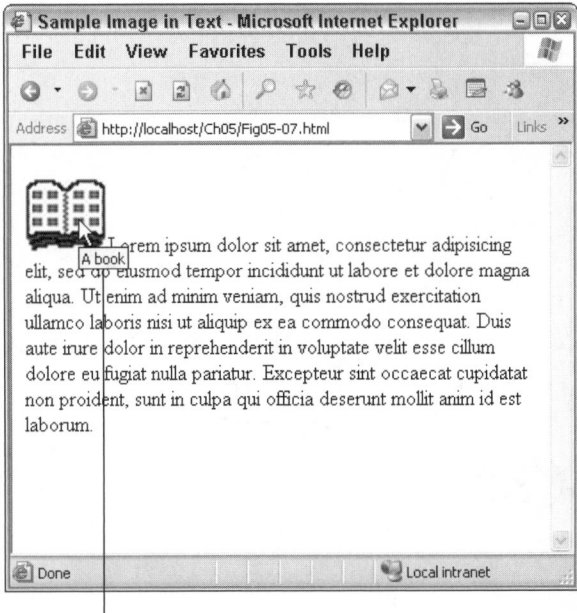

Tooltip showing the `alt` text

Figure 5-8

Image Size

Two attributes exist to control the physical image size. The attributes are suitably named `width` and `height`. Both attributes support pixel and percentage values. You can use a pixel value to specify an exact size that the image should be rendered at in the user agent. A percentage value will size the image according to the size of the user agent's window.

Note that changing the image's display size, via tag attributes, does not alter the amount of data transmitted to the user, only the size at which it displays.

For example, if you wanted a square image to be rendered to 100 pixels square, you could use the following tag:

```
<img alt="A 100 pixel square" src="square.jpg" width="100" height="100" />
```

Note that you can use only one of the size attributes if you want; the user agent will use the image's proportion to determine the other dimension's correct value. However, the value in specifying both dimensions is that the user agent can reserve the space for the image—rendering the rest of the page as it waits for the image data.

Contrary to what you might think, using percentage values for width and height scales the image according to the user agent's window. For example, consider the following tag, shown in two differently sized browser windows in Figure 5-9:

```
<img alt="A 200 pixel square" src="200pxSquare.jpg" width="200" height="200" />
<img alt="A 200 pixel square" src="200pxSquare.jpg" width="25%" />
```

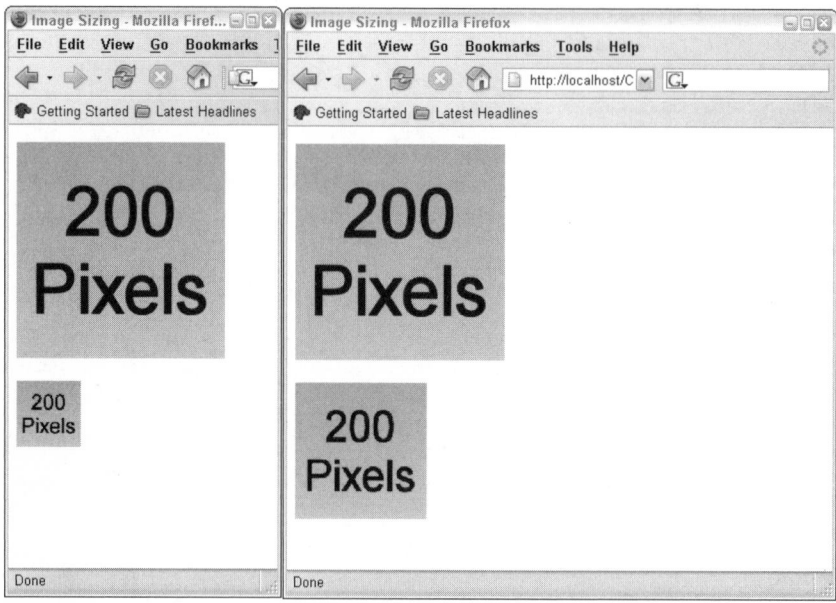

Figure 5-9

As you can see, instead of resizing the image to 50 pixels square (25% of 200), the image is sized to 25% of the browser's width.

*Be careful to preserve an image's aspect ratio when specifying both dimensions in an **alt** tag. Specifying dimensions that do not adhere to the same aspect ratio as the original image will cause the image to appear distorted in the user agent much like a funhouse mirror distorts reflections.*

Image Alignment and Borders

Previous versions of HTML contained an `align` attribute for the `<img>` tag to aid in aligning the image to other elements around it. This attribute has been deprecated in favor of CSS alignment styles. Previous HTML versions also contained a `border` attribute to control the border shown around an image.

The images shown in the figures of this chapter are vertically aligned to the baseline of neighboring text. Although some user agents use this default alignment, not all user agents can be relied on to exhibit this default behavior; if you need an image aligned in a certain manner, it is best to explicitly code the alignment.

The CSS styles for positioning are covered in Chapter 19. The CSS styles for controlling margins and borders are covered in Chapter 16.

Image Maps

Image maps provide a method to map areas of images to actions. For example, a company Web site might want to provide a map of the United States that allows customers to click on a state to find a local office or store.

There are two types of image maps: client-side and server-side. Client-side image maps rely on the user agent to process the image, the area where the user clicks, and the expected action. Server-side image maps rely on the user agent only to tell the server where the user clicked; an agent on the Web server does all the processing.

Between the two methods, client-side image maps are preferred. The user agent is able to offer immediate feedback to the user (like being over a clickable area). Most user agents support client-side image maps. Server-side agents can also bog down a server if the map draws consistent traffic, hides many details necessary to provide immediate feedback to the user, and might not be compatible with some user agents.

*If you want images to be clickable and take the user to one particular destination, you don't have to use an image map. Instead, embed the **<img>** tags in appropriate anchor tags (**<a>**) similarly to the following:*

```
<a href="catpage.html"><img alt="Go to the cat page"
src="cat.jpg"></a>
```

Specifying an Image Map

A client-side image map's data (clickable regions) is specified within the contents of a <map> tag and linked to an appropriate <img> tag with the usemap attribute. For example, to specify a map for an image, travel.jpg, you could use this code:

```
<img alt="Travel reservations" src="travel.jpg"
  usemap="#map1">
<map name="map1">
...
</map>
```

*Note that all **src** attributes should usually include a full relative or absolute path to the resource.*

Inside the <map> tag pair, you specify the various clickable regions of the image, as covered in the next section.

Chapter 5

Specifying Clickable Regions

To create an image map, a list of polygonal regions must be defined on an image and referenced in the HTML document. Three different types of polygons are supported: rectangle, circle, and free-form polygon.

❑ rect — Defines a rectangular area by specifying the coordinates of the upper-left and lower-right corners of the rectangle

❑ circle — Defines a circular area by specifying the coordinates of the center of the circle and the circle's radius

❑ poly — Defines a free-form polygon area by specifying the coordinates of each point of the polygon

All coordinates of the image map are relative to the top-left corner of the image (referenced as 0, 0) and are measured in pixels. For example, suppose you wanted to create an image map for a travel site with an icon of a car, plane, and hotel. When users click on one of the icons, they are taken to the reservation page for auto rentals, airfare, or hotel reservations, respectively. Such an image would resemble the image shown in Figure 5-10.

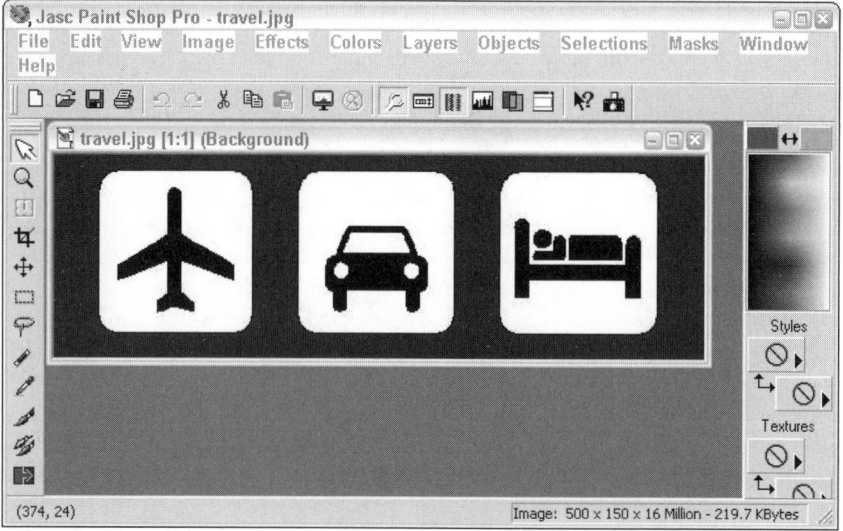

Figure 5-10

The regions that will be used for the map are within the three icon squares (the white squares around the icons). The regions are all rectangular, are uniform in size (121 pixels square), and have the following upper-left coordinates:

❑ car — 35 x, 11 y

❑ plane — 190 x, 11 y

❑ hotel — 345 x, 11 y

Knowing the upper-left corner coordinates and the size of each rectangle, you can easily figure out the coordinates of the bottom-right corner of each rectangle by adding the width (121) and height (121) to the upper-left coordinates.

Several tools are available to help create image map coordinates. Use your favorite search engine to find software dedicated to mapping regions, or examine your graphics program to see if it can create regions for you. Paint Shop Pro is an excellent Windows-based image editor that has image mapping tools built in.

Specifying Regions Using Anchor Tags

You can use anchor tags to specify regions with `shape` and `coords` attributes. For example, to specify the three regions previously outlined, you could use the following code:

```
<map name="map1">
<a href="plane.html" shape="rect" coords="35,11,156,132">
Plane Reservations</a>
<a href="car.html" shape="rect" coords="190,11,311,132">
Rental Cars</a>
<a href="hotel.html" shape="rect" coords="345,11,466,132">
Hotel Reservations</a>
</map>
```

The link text (between the anchor tags) helps the user determine what the clickable area leads to, as shown by the Internet Explorer tooltip in Figure 5-11.

Specifying Regions Using Area Tags

Another way to define regions is by using `<area>` tags instead of anchor tags:

```
<map name="map1">
<area href="plane.html"
  shape="rect" coords="35,11,156,132"
  alt="Plane Reservations">
<area href="car.html"
  shape="rect" coords="190,11,311,132"
  alt="Rental Cars">
<area href="hotel.html"
  shape="rect" coords="345,11,466,132"
  alt="Hotel Reservations">
</map>
```

Using the `alt` attribute helps the user determine what the clickable area leads to, as shown by the Internet Explorer tooltip in Figure 5-11.

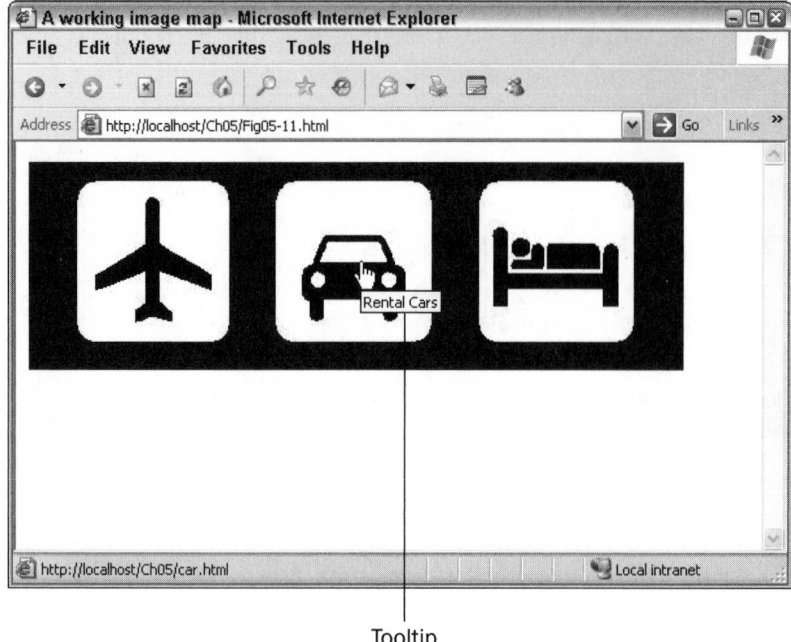

Tooltip

Figure 5-11

Putting It All Together

A document with a working image map (as outlined in this section) would resemble the following code:

```
<!DOCTYPE html PUBLIC "-//W3C//DTD XHTML 1.0 Strict//EN"
    "http://www.w3.org/TR/xhtml1/DTD/xhtml1-strict.dtd">
<html>
<head>
  <title>A working image map</title>
</head>
<body>
<img alt="Travel Plans" src="travel.jpg" usemap="#map1">
<map name="map1">
  <area href="plane.html"
    shape="rect" coords="35,11,156,132"
    alt="Plane Reservations">
  <area href="car.html"
    shape="rect" coords="190,11,311,132"
    alt="Rental Cars">
  <area href="hotel.html"
    shape="rect" coords="345,11,466,132"
    alt="Hotel Reservations">
</map>
</body>
</html>
```

The image map example in this chapter is somewhat simplistic. Image maps can be used for more complex purposes, such as letting customers click on a U.S. map as mentioned earlier in this chapter or allowing users to click on various buildings on a map or parts on an exploded diagram of a machine for more information on the building or part clicked.

Summary

This chapter introduced you to the <img> tag and the various graphic formats it supports. You also learned about image qualities such as transparency, interlacing, and animation, which can be used to make your image use more inventive and visually appealing. As you can see, adding graphics to a Web document is straightforward, but using them to increase the value and usability of your documents can be more challenging. Use this chapter as a basis for including images, but supplement it with information from Part II of this book for how to effectively position images within your documents.

6

Links

Links are what turn plain documents into Web-enabled content. Each document on the Web can contain one or more links to other documents — allowing users to easily access information related to the current document or entirely different information. As you will see in this chapter, you can also include information within links to describe the actual relationship between the document doing the linking and the document being linked to.

Understanding URLs

A Uniform Resource Locator (URL) is the unique address of a resource (usually a document) on the Web. This addressing scheme allows user agents and other Internet-enabled programs to find documents and ask for their contents.

URLs are made up of several different parts, all working together to provide a unique address for Internet content. Figure 6-1 shows an example of a typical URL and its various parts.

The various pieces of the URL are described as follows:

❑ The protocol section is a protocol abbreviation followed by a colon. For example, the standard HTTP protocol is designated as `http:`. Another popular protocol supported by many user agents is File Transfer Protocol (FTP), designated in URLs as `ftp:`.

❑ The server name is prefixed with two slashes and typically includes a fully qualified domain name, as in `//www.example.com`. The `www` is the server name, and `example.com` is the domain. Note that it is a misnomer that Web servers need to be named `www`; although `www` (World Wide Web) is a common convention, the server name can be any valid name. For example, the fully qualified name of the U.S.-based server for the Internet Movie Database is `us.imdb.com`. Note that an IP address can be specified instead of a server name.

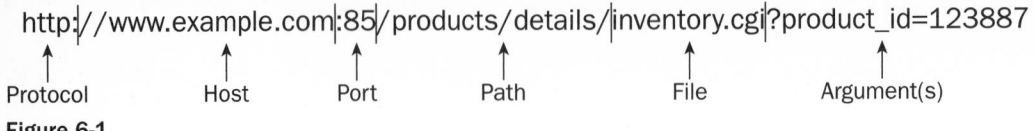

Figure 6-1

The URL can also include a username and password before the server name (description follows). This is especially true for FTP URLs. The username and password should appear after the protocol, separated by a colon (:) and ending with an ampersand (@). When used in this form, the URL would resemble the following:

```
http://username:password@www.example.com/...
```

❏ If necessary, the server name is followed by a port number — a colon separates the name and port. For example, some Web servers run their HTTP services on a port other than port 80. In those cases, the URL needs to include the alternate port number. In the example shown in Figure 6-1, the port number is 85.

The standard port for HTTP is port 80. For FTP the standard port is 25. Most user agents know the default ports and will use the default if no port is specified.

❏ After the server name (and optional port number) is the path on the server where the document or file can be found. In this case, the path to the document is /products/details/, that is, the details subdirectory of the products directory, which is off the root of the server. Note that the path of the URL doesn't directly correspond to the path on the file system of the server — the Web server software is configured to remap file system directories into URLs.

❏ The next piece of the URL puzzle is the actual document or filename. In this example, the name is inventory.cgi and the server looks for that file in the directory specified to return to the requesting user agent.

❏ After the filename, the URL can contain optional arguments for the server to pass to the file. If the file is an executable (CGI or other script), the arguments can be used for a variety of purposes. The argument list is separated from the filename by a question mark; the arguments appear in name/value pairs (separated by equal signs), the pairs separated by ampersands (&). For example, suppose you need to pass inventory.cgi the following name/value pairs:

  ❏ product_id = 123887

  ❏ description = long

  ❏ lang = EN

That list of arguments would appear as follows:

```
?product_id=123887&description=long&lang=EN
```

Strictly speaking, the arguments are not a part of the URL — the URL itself contains only information about where to find a resource. Arguments are covered here for the sake of completeness. See Part IV of this book for more on URL arguments and programs to interpret them.

Absolute versus Relative Paths

Two styles of paths can be used in URLs: absolute and relative. Absolute paths contain all the relevant information to find the resource indicated by the URL. Relative paths contain information relative to the current document. For example, suppose that the user agent had loaded a document from the following URL:

```
http://www.example.com/products/gizmo.html
```

Suppose the document has a link to another document, `doodad.html`, which resides on the same server, in the same directory. Both of the following URLs can be used to reference the other document:

```
http://www.example.com/products/doodad.html
doodad.html
./doodad.html
http:doodad.html
```

The first URL uses an absolute path to the document — everything from the protocol, server name, and path to the document are specified. The other three URLs are relative — they contain only enough information for the document to be found relative to the location of the current document.

If you don't specify the protocol in a URL, the user agent will attempt to use its default protocol to request the document.

Note that relative paths can be used only with documents on the same Web server because documents on other servers require substantially more information to guide the user agent to them. Relative paths are best used on sections of Web sites where the documents in the section never change relationships to one another. In most cases, absolute paths should be used in URLs.

Using the Anchor Tag

The anchor tag (`<a>`) is used to provide links within Web documents to other documents or resources on the Internet. The anchor tag has a simple format:

```
<a href="url_to_resource">textual_description_of_link</a>
```

The anchor tag can appear by itself or around other HTML elements. For example, a link to product information could appear in a document as follows:

```
<p>More information on product XYZ can be found <a
href="http://www.example.com/productXYZ/info.html">here</a>.</p>
```

In this case, the paragraph would appear as shown in Figure 6-2, with the word `here` being the link to the other document.

According to the XHTML standard, anchor links need to be placed within block elements (headings, paragraphs, and so on).

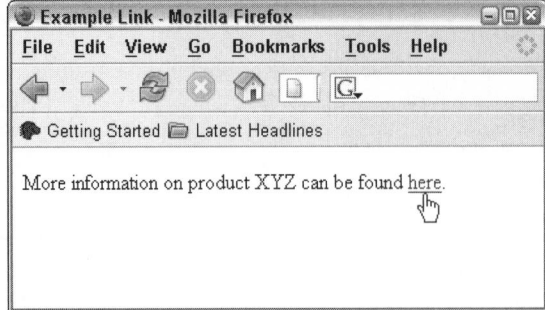

Figure 6-2

As previously mentioned, URLs can refer to other resources besides HTML documents. You can refer to other resources to be delivered via other protocols by specifying the correct protocol and server in the anchor tag. For example, the following tag would refer to a ZIP compressed file delivered via the FTP protocol:

```
<a href="ftp://ftp.example.com/somefile.zip">ZIP version of the file</a>
```

You can also use an anchor tag to spawn helper applications on the user's computer. For example, this anchor would open the default e-mail application on the user's computer to send an e-mail message to sschafer@example.com:

```
<a href="mailto:sschafer@example.com">Email me</a>
```

You can also embed other elements within the anchor to use as links. For example, you can include an image in the anchor so that the user can click on the image to activate the link:

```
<a href="http://www.example.com"><img src="companylogo.gif"
alt="Company Logo" /></a>
```

There are many other ways to link documents, including using image maps (covered in Chapter 5) and using event attributes in other elements (covered in Chapters 20 and 21).

Attributes of the Anchor Tag

The anchor tag supports several different attributes. This section details the various attributes you can use with the anchor tag.

Link Titles

The `title` attribute can be used to give more information about the document being linked to. It takes one argument, a string of characters, to title the link. For example, the following anchor tag uses a title attribute:

```
<a href="http://www.example.com/about.html" title="About Company XYZ">About</a>
```

The use of the title is left up to the user agent. Some agents, such as Mozilla Firefox, use the title as a tooltip, as shown in Figure 6-3.

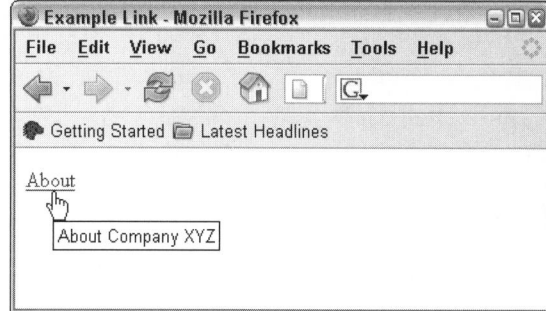

Figure 6-3

Keyboard Shortcuts and Tab Orders

In the modern world of computers, it is easy to make assumptions about users, their hardware, and capabilities. Several years ago, no one would have dreamt of delivering rich, multimedia content over the Web. Today, however, it is easy to assume that everyone is using the latest browser, on a high-end computer, across a broadband connection.

However, that isn't always the case. In fact, some users who visit your site may not even have a mouse to aid in browsing. The reason could be a physical handicap, a text-only browser, or just a fondness for using the keyboard. It is important to accommodate these users by adding additional methods to access links on your page.

The anchor tag includes two attributes to aid non-mouse users, keyboard shortcuts, and tab ordering.

Keyboard shortcuts define a single key that can be used to access the link. The `accesskey` attribute takes one letter as its value. For example, the following link defines "C" as the access key:

```
<a href="http://www.example.com/contents.html" accesskey="C">Table of
<b>C</b>ontents</a>
```

Note that different user agents and different operating systems treat shortcut keys differently. For example, Windows users on Internet Explorer need to hold the Alt key while they press the access key. Note also that different browsers handle the actual access of the link differently; some browsers will activate the link as soon as the access key is pressed, while others only select the link, requiring another key to be pressed to actually activate the link (usually Enter).

As with most graphical operating systems, the Tab key can be used to move through elements of the interface, including links. Typically, the tab order of links corresponds to the order in which the links appear in the document. The `tabindex` attribute can be used to define an alternate order in which the links in a document should be accessed. The `tabindex` attribute uses a number to define the position the link should occupy in the tab order. For example, the following three links have the tab order reversed — pressing the tab key several times will select the last link, then the second, and finally the first:

```
<a href="http://www.example.com/first.html" tabindex="3">First link</a>
<a href="http://www.example.com/first.html" tabindex="2">Second link</a>
<a href="http://www.example.com/first.html" tabindex="1">Third link</a>
```

As with most interface elements in XHTML, the browser defines how `tabindex` is implemented and how tabbed elements are accessed.

Link Colors

To differentiate text used for links from other text in the document, user agents use different text colors. Different colors are used to show different modes of links:

❑   **Link** — The standard link in the document that is not active and has not been visited (see other modes).

❑   **Active** — The target of the link is active in another browser window.

❑   **Visited** — The target of the link has been previously visited (typically, this means the target can be found in the browser's cache).

❑   **Hover** — The mouse pointer is over the link.

The various links are colored differently so that the user can tell the status of each link on your page. The standard colors of each link status are as follows:

❑   **Link** — Blue, underlined text

❑   **Active** — Red, underlined text

❑   **Visited** — Purple, underlined text

❑   **Hover** — No change in the appearance of the link (remains blue, red, or purple)

As with other presentation attributes in HTML, the user agent plays a significant role in setting link colors and text decorations. Most user agents follow the color scheme outlined in this section, but there are those that don't conform to this scheme.

To change the color of links, you use CSS. For example, to choose another color (and possibly display property) for visited links, you could use something similar to the following:

```
<head>
  <style type="text/css">
    a:visited  { color: yellow;  font-weight: bold; }
  </style>
</head>
```

This changes the visited links in the document to yellow, bold text. The `link`, `active`, and `hover` style properties can be used to change the other link modes.

More information on using CSS can be found in Part II of this book.

Document Relationships

There are a host of other attributes that you can add to your anchor tags to describe the form of the target being linked to, the relationship between the current document and the target, and more.

The following table lists these descriptive attributes and their possible values.

Link Target Details

Attribute	Meaning	Value(s)
charset	The character encoding of the target	char_encoding for example, "ISO 8859-1"
hreflang	The base language of the target	language_code for example, "en-US"
rel	The relationship between the current document and the target	alternate designates stylesheet start next prev contents index glossary copyright chapter section subsection appendix help bookmark
rev	The relationship between the target and the current document	alternate designates stylesheet start next prev contents index glossary copyright chapter section subsection appendix help bookmark
type	The MIME type of the target	Any valid MIME type

An example of how the relationship attributes (rel, rev) can be used is shown in the following code snippet:

```
<!DOCTYPE html PUBLIC "-//W3C//DTD XHTML 1.0 Strict//EN"
    "http://www.w3.org/TR/xhtml1/DTD/xhtml1-strict.dtd">
<html>
<head>
<title>Chapter 10</title>
</head>
<body>
<p><a href="contents.html" rel="chapter" rev="contents">Table
of Contents</a></p>
<p><a href="chapter9.html" rel="next" rev="prev">Chapter
9</a></p>
<p><a href="chapter11.html" rel="prev" rev="next">Chapter
11</a></p>
 .  .  .
```

The anchor tags define the relationships between the chapters (next, previous) and the table of contents (chapter, contents).

The Link Tag

The link tag (<link>) can be used to provide additional information on a document's relationship to other documents, whether the document links to those other documents or not. The link tag supports the same attributes as the anchor tag but uses slightly different syntax:

❑   The link tag must appear in the <head> section of the document.

❑   The link tag does not encapsulate any text.

❑   The link tag does not have a matching close tag.

For example, the following code could be used in chapter10.html to define that document's relationship to chapter9.html and chapter11.html:

```
<head>
  <title>Chapter 10</title>
  <link href="chapter9.html" rel="next" rev="prev" />
  <link href="chapter11.html" rel="prev" rev="next" />
</head>
```

Link tags do not result in any text being rendered by the user agents but can be used to provide other information, such as to provide alternate content for search engines. For example, the following link references a French version of the current document (chapter10.html):

```
<link lang="fr" rel="alternate" hreflang="fr"
      href="http://www.example.com/chapter10-fr.html" />
```

Other relationship attribute values (`start`, `contents`, and so on) can likewise be used to provide relevant information on document relationships to search engines.

Summary

This chapter reviewed the anchor tag (`<a>`), how it is used to provide links to other documents, and how additional information can be provided to illustrate the relationship between linked documents. You also learned how to provide alternative navigational methods through the use of the `tabindex` and `accesskey` attributes. As you learn the rest of the XHTML tags and elements, you will see how to effectively weave links into your documents' structure.

7

Text

Although most Web documents are chock-full of graphics and multimedia, text still plays a very important part in communicating on the Web. Previous versions of HTML (prior to 4.01) included several tags for direct text formatting. Many of those tags have been deprecated in favor of CSS, but many still exist and can be used and still be in XHTML compliance.

Methods of Formatting Text

Previous chapters have shown you how to format different block elements. You have seen many tags that can be used to format large chunks of a document. As you can imagine, there are several additional tags and methods to format text. However, the road through text formatting options is complex; many of the text formatting methods used in previous versions of HTML have been deprecated. Still, many other legacy methods still survive in XHTML. The following sections detail some of the more popular methods of formatting text.

The Font Tag

The font tag (`<font>`) used to be the predominant way to control text within documents. However, with HTML 4.01 (and hence, XHTML) the `<font>` tag was deprecated and should not be used. To aid in understanding legacy document coding, the format of the `<font>` tag is as follows:

```
<font face="font_name" size="relative_size"
color="font_color">...text...</font>
```

The font size is given relative to the default document font size. The default size is typically controlled via the `<basefont>` tag (also deprecated). The `<basefont>` tag supports the same arguments as the `<font>` tag, but it has no closing mate.

Default font types and sizes are left up to the user agent. No standard correlation exists between the size used in a ***<font>*** *tag and the actual font size used by the user agent.*

To be XHTML compliant, you should use CSS methods for font control.

Inline Text Attributes

Several tags still exist in the XHTML standard for emphasizing text. These tags are shown in the following table.

Tag	Use
`<cite>`	Citation
`<code>`	Computer code text
`<dfn>`	Definition term
`<em>`	Emphasized text
`<kbd>`	Keyboard text
`<samp>`	Sample computer code text
`<strong>`	Strongly emphasized text
`<var>`	Variable(s)

Examples of these tags in action are shown in Figure 7-1.

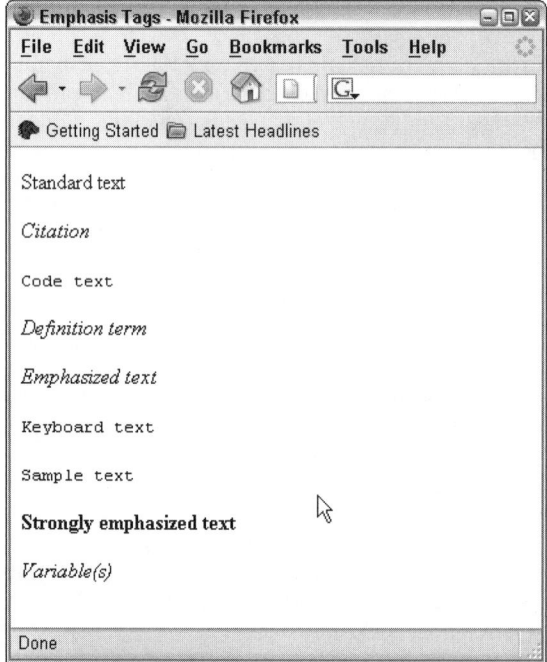

Figure 7-1

The adoption and support of these tags is very haphazard across the various user agents. As such, these tags are best avoided. Use of CSS instead of these tags is strongly encouraged.

Tags for italic and bold text are still part of the current XHTML specification and are covered in their own section later in this chapter.

CSS Text Control

CSS is the preferred method of text control in all versions of HTML, 4.01 and above (including XHTML). Some of the more popular CSS text control properties are listed in the following table.

CSS Property	Values	Use
color	color	Change the color of text
font	font-style font-variant font-weight font-size	Shortcut property for setting font style, variant, weight, and size
font-family	family-name	Set the font family (face)
font-size	font-size	Set the font size
font-stretch	normal | wider | narrower | ultra-condensed | extra-condensed |condensed | semi-condensed |semi-expanded | expanded |extra-expanded | ultra-expanded	Expand or compress the letter spacing
font-style	normal | italic | oblique	Set font to italic
font-variant	normal | small-caps	Set small-caps
font-weight	normal | bold | bolder | lighter	Set font to bold
text-decoration	none | underline | overline | line-through | blink	Set under/overlining
text-transform	none | capitalize | uppercase | lowercase	Transform font capitalization

Control of text via CSS involves creating style definitions in style sections within your document, in an externally linked style sheet, or within individual tags. For example, both of the paragraphs in the following code will be rendered in all caps, the first via a definition in a <style> section and the second from style code directly in the paragraph tag:

```
<!DOCTYPE html PUBLIC "-//W3C//DTD XHTML 1.0 Strict//EN"
    "http://www.w3.org/TR/xhtml1/DTD/xhtml1-strict.dtd">
<html>
<head>
  <style type="text/css">
    p.caps { text-transform: capitalize; }
  </style>
</head>
<body>
<p class="caps"> Lorem ipsum dolor sit amet, consectetur adipisicing elit,
sed do eiusmod tempor incididunt ut labore et dolore magna aliqua. Ut enim
ad minim veniam, quis nostrud exercitation ullamco laboris nisi ut aliquip
ex ea commodo consequat.</p>

<p style=" text-transform: capitalize;"> Lorem ipsum dolor sit amet, consectetur
adipisicing elit, sed do eiusmod tempor incididunt ut labore et dolore magna
aliqua. Ut enim ad minim veniam, quis nostrud exercitation ullamco laboris nisi
ut aliquip ex ea commodo consequat.</p>
</body>
</html>
```

Smaller sections of text can use the span tag (<span>) to incorporate text changes in-line. For example, to specify that a handful of words should be rendered in red, you would use a span tag similar to the following:

```
<p> Lorem ipsum dolor sit amet, consectetur adipisicing elit, sed do eiusmod
tempor incididunt <span style="color: red">ut labore et dolore magna aliqua</span>.
Ut enim ad minim veniam, quis nostrud exercitation ullamco laboris nisi ut aliquip
ex ea commodo consequat.</p>
```

*More information on the **<span>** tag appears in a separate section later in this chapter. More information on CSS can be found in Part II of this book.*

Special In-Line Text Elements

Usually, you can leave the formatting of text lines up to the user agent, allowing it to flow text freely according to the width of its window. However, at times you will want to prevent the user agent from breaking lines across certain phrases. There are also times when you may want to allow a user agent to hyphenate long words to help preserve formatting.

Nonbreaking Spaces

Just as you will want to break some text into discrete chunks, other times you will want to keep text together. For example, you wouldn't want words separated in dates (December 25, 2004), awkward phrases that include letters and numbers (24 hours), or in some company names (International Business Machine Corporation).

Suppose you were to use the phrase "12 Angry Men." You would not want a user agent to split the "12" and "Angry" across two lines as shown in the following:

```
A good example of this argument appears in the movie 12
Angry Men.
```

Whenever you don't want the user agent to break text, you should use a nonbreaking space entity ( ) instead of a normal space. For example, when coding the "12 Angry Men" paragraph, you could use something similar to the following:

```
<p>A good example of this argument appears in the movie
<i>12 Angry Men</i>.</p>
```

As discussed in previous chapters, user agents tend to collapse white space. This is typically a desirable effect—allowing you to be more liberal with white space when formatting your documents. However, sometimes you need to explicitly include spaces in your documents. The nonbreaking space entity can also be used to space-fill text. For example, to indent a line of text by three spaces, you could use code similar to the following:

```
   Indented by three spaces
```

However, space-fill formatting techniques should be avoided—the use of CSS instead is highly recommended.

> *The nonbreaking space code, ** **, is known as an entity in HTML-speak. There are entities for many characters that can't be typed on a conventional keyboard. Many of the supported entities are listed in Appendix A.*

Soft Hyphens

Soft hyphens can be used to indicate where a user agent can hyphenate a word, if necessary. For example, consider the following code and its resulting output shown in Figure 7-2:

```
<p style="text-align: justify;">The morbid fear of the number
13, or triskaidekaphobia, has plagued some important historic
figures like Mark Twain and Napoleon.</p>
```

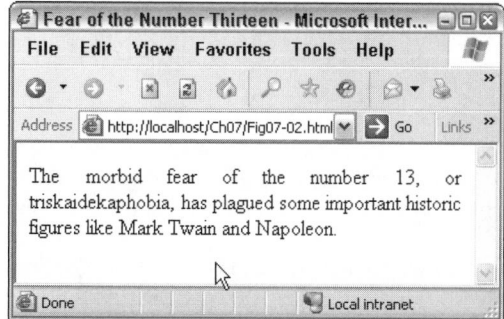

Figure 7-2

To tell the user agent where a word can be hyphenated, you insert a soft-hyphen entity (`&shy;`). Using the preceding example, you can hyphenate the word "triskaidekaphobia" with soft hyphens, as follows:

```
<p style="text-align: justify;">The morbid fear of the number
13, or tris&shy;kai&shy;deka&shy;pho&shy;bia, has plagued
some important historic figures like Mark Twain and
Napoleon.</p>
```

The resulting output, shown in Figure 7-3, shows how the optional hyphens are used to achieve better justification results.

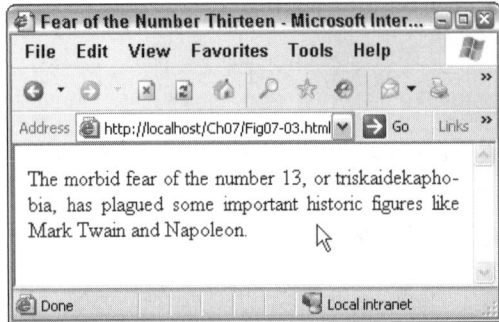

Figure 7-3

Note that not all user agents support soft hyphens.

Bold and Italic

Two tags are used to designate text as bold (`<b>`) and italic (`<i>`). As with other XHTML tags, both tags have opening and closing elements and are used to surround the text you want to modify. For example, consider the following code and the results rendered in a user agent as shown in Figure 7-4:

```
<p>This is normal text.</p>
<p><b>This is bold text.</b></p>
<p><i>This is italic text.</i></p>
```

Previous versions of HTML contained an underline attribute. However, the underline tag has been deprecated. Underlining should be accomplished using CSS.

Not every font has a bold and/or italic variant. Whenever possible, the user agent will substitute a similar font when bold or italic is asked for but not available. However, not all user agents are font savvy. In short, your mileage with these tags may vary depending on the user agent being used.

For the same reasons mentioned elsewhere, it is advisable to use CSS instead of hard-coded bold and italic tags.

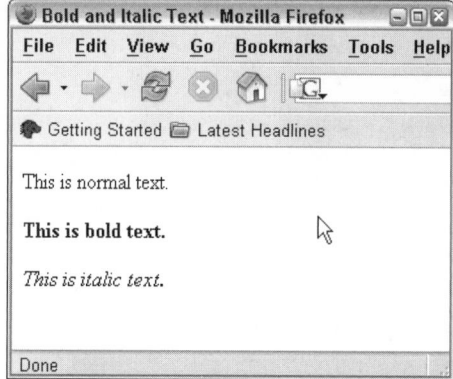

Figure 7-4

Monospaced Text

Another text formatting tag that has survived deprecation in XHTML is the teletype (`<tt>`), or monospaced, tag. This tag tells the user agent that text should be rendered in a monospaced font. You can use this tag to format reserved words in documentation, code listings, and so on. The following code shows an example of the teletype tag in use:

```
<p>Consider using the <tt>date()</tt> function for this purpose.</p>
```

This tag is named for the teletype terminals used with the first computers, which were capable of printing only in a monospaced font.

Again, the use of styles is preferred over individual in-line tags. If you need text rendered in a monospaced font, consider using styles instead of the `<tt>` tag.

Superscript, Subscript, Big, and Small Text

The superscript (`<sup>`) and subscript (`<sub>`) tags can be used to specify superscript and subscript text. For example, consider the following code and the results shown in Figure 7-5:

```
<p>This is normal text.</p>
<p>This is the 16<sup>th</sup> day of the month. (superscripted "th")</p>
<p>Water tanks are clearly marked as H<sub>2</sub>O. (subscripted "2")</p>
```

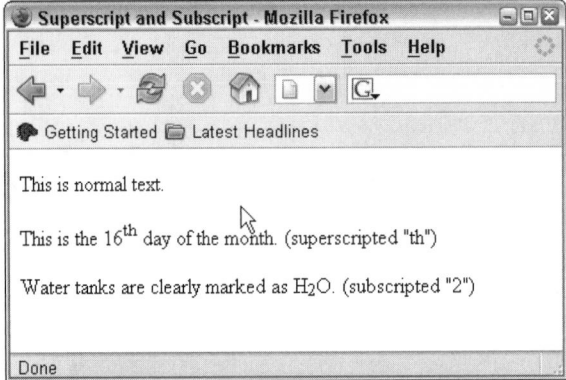

Figure 7-5

The big (`<big>`) and (`<small>`) tags are used as you would expect: to delimit text you want rendered bigger or smaller than the default text. For example, consider the following example code and the result shown in Figure 7-6:

```
<p>This is default text.</p>
<p>This word is <big>bigger</big> than the default text.</p>
<p>This word is <small>smaller</small> than the default text.</p>
```

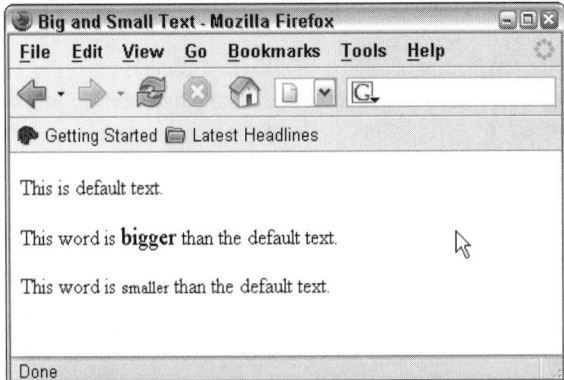

Figure 7-6

Insertions and Deletions

To strengthen the printed-material capabilities of Web documents, the insert (`<ins>`) and delete (`<del>`) tags have been added to HTML. Both tags are used for redlining documents—that is, a visually marked-up document showing suggested changes.

The following paragraph has been marked up with text to be inserted (underlined) and deleted (strikethrough). The output of this code is shown in Figure 7-7.

```
<p>Peter <del>are</del><ins>is</ins> correct, the proposal
from Acme is lacking a few <del>minor </del>details.</p>
```

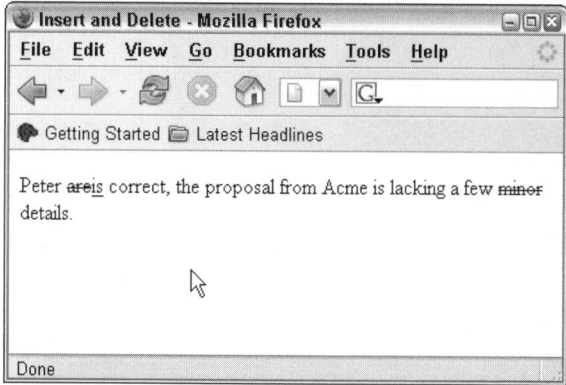

Figure 7-7

Abbreviations

The abbreviation tag (<abbr>) can be used to mark a word as an abbreviation and to give users the expansion of the acronym. For example, consider the following code:

```
<abbr title="Hypertext Markup Language">HTML</abbr>
```

It is up to the user agent as to how the title attribute's value will be shown, if at all. Some user agents will display the value when the mouse is over the acronym.

Grouping In-Line Elements

When using CSS for text formatting, you need a method to combine several text-formatting attributes into one delimiting tag. If you are coding block elements, you can use the division (<div>) tag to delimit the block, but with smaller chunks (in-line elements) you should use the span tag (<span>).

The <span> tag is used like any other in-line tag (<b>, <i>, <tt>, and so on), surrounding the text/ elements that it should affect. You use the style or class attribute to define what style should be applied. For example, both of the paragraphs in the following code sample would cause the word "red" to be rendered in red, bold text:

```
<head>
  <style type="text/css">
    .boldredtext { color: red; font-weight: bold; }
  </style>
</head>
<body>
<!-- Paragraph 1, using direct style coding -->
<p>We should paint the document <span style="color: red; font-weight: bold;">
red</span>.</p>

<!-- Paragraph 2, using a style class -->
<p>We should paint the document <span class="boldredtext">
red</span>.</p>
</body>
```

Of the two methods, the use of the `class` attribute is preferred over the `style` attribute because `class` attribute avoids directly (and individually) coding the text. Instead, it references a separate style definition that can be repurposed for other text or changed globally, as required.

Summary

As Web publishing evolves, so do the tools to adequately provide publishing capabilities to Web documents. As you have seen, most of the document-formatting capabilities — including textual formatting — have been relegated to CSS instead of direct coding via HTML tags. However, there are still quite a few formatting tags that can be used to format text in your Web documents. This chapter introduced those remaining tags that are still XHTML compliant. However, you should always strive to encode text formatting in CSS instead of directly coding text using tags.

Tables

Tables were created in HTML as a means to display tabular data — typically scientific or academic data. However, as the Web became more of a traditional publishing medium, tables evolved from only supporting plain textual data to being a flexible platform for arranging all sorts of elements to accomplish all sorts of layouts.

Today, XHTML tables can be used to display tabular data, align elements in a form, or even provide entire document layout structures. This chapter introduces you to tables and their various uses and formats.

Parts of a Table

A table in XHTML can be made up of the following parts:

- Header row(s)
- Column groupings
- Body row(s)
- Header cells
- Body cells
- Rows
- Columns
- Footer row(s)
- Caption

Figure 8-1 shows an example of a table with its various parts labeled.

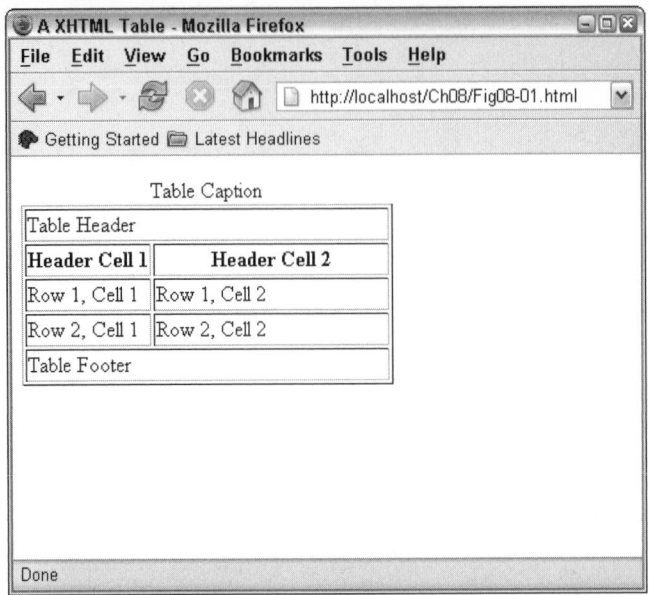

Figure 8-1

The table in Figure 8-1 was rendered from the following code:

```
<!DOCTYPE html PUBLIC "-//W3C//DTD XHTML 1.0 Strict//EN"
    "http://www.w3.org/TR/xhtml1/DTD/xhtml1-strict.dtd"><html>
<html>
<head>
  <title>A XHTML Table</title>
</head>
<body>
  <p>
  <!--  Table definition -->
  <table border="1">
    <!-- Column grouping -->
    <colgroup>
      <col width="35%">
      <col width="65%">
    </colgroup>
    <!-- Table caption -->
    <caption>Table Caption</caption>
    <!-- Table header -->
    <thead>
      <tr><td colspan="2">Table Header</td></tr>
    </thead>
    <!-- Table footer -->
    <tfoot>
      <tr><td colspan="2">Table Footer</td></tr>
    </tfoot>
```

```
    <!-- Table body -->
    <tbody>
      <tr><th>Header Cell 1</th><th>Header Cell 2</th></tr>
      <tr><td>Row 1, Cell 1</td><td>Row 1, Cell 2</td></tr>
      <tr><td>Row 2, Cell 1</td><td>Row 2, Cell 2</td></tr>
    </tbody>
  </table>
  </p>
</body>
</html>
```

Not all of the parts contained in this example are mandatory. It is possible to create a table using only the table tag (<table>) and row (<tr>) and cell/column (<td>) tags. For example, the following table is completely valid:

```
<table>
  <tr><td>Row 1, Cell 1</td><td>Row 1, Cell 2</td></tr>
  <tr><td>Row 2, Cell 1</td><td>Row 2, Cell 2</td></tr>
</table>
```

However, as you will see in the rest of this chapter, the breadth and depth of table tags and options allow you to encapsulate a lot of information within XHTML tables.

It is possible to nest tables within one another. In fact, a particularly popular XHTML technique is to use tables for sophisticated page layout (covered later in this chapter) — doing so depends on nested tables.

> *It's important to note that most user agents build tables in memory before displaying them. This can cause a delay in displaying a large table.*

Formatting Tables

Tables are one of the most versatile elements in XHTML. You can use them to simply align other elements or as layout control for a full document. Along with functionality usually comes complexity, and tables are no exception — you can use many options and attributes to format tables. The following sections detail the various formatting options available.

Table Width and Alignment

Typically, a table will expand to accommodate the data stored within its cells. For example, consider the two tables in the following code, whose output is shown in Figure 8-2:

```
<p>
  Short Text Table<br />
  <table border="1">
      <tr><td>Short Text 1</td><td>Short Text 2</td></tr>
  </table>
</p>
```

```
<p>
  Longer Text Table<br />
  <table border="1">
      <tr><td>Much Longer Text 1</td><td>Much Longer Text 2</td></tr>
  </table>
</p>
```

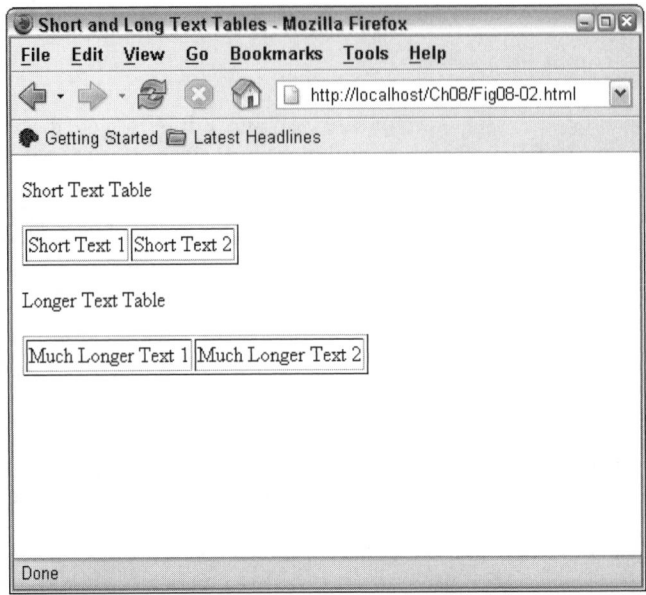

Figure 8-2

Once a table expands to the limits of the user agent's window, the content of its cells will wrap within their respective cells.

Note that both tables are left-aligned in the user agent window.

However, there are times when you want to explicitly define a table's width and possibly its alignment.

Controlling Table Width

Using the width attribute in the `<table>` tag, you can set a table's size by specifying the table width in pixels or as a percentage of the containing object. For example, consider the following table whose width is set to 50 percent.

```
<p>
  50% Table Width<br />
  <table border="1" width="50%">
    <tr>
      <td>Cell 1</td><td>Cell 2</td>
      <td>Cell 3</td><td>Cell 4</td>
    </tr>
  </table>
</p>
```

The containing object is a nonconstrained paragraph that spans the width of the user agent. The result is that the table will occupy 50 percent of the user agent's window width, as shown in Figure 8-3.

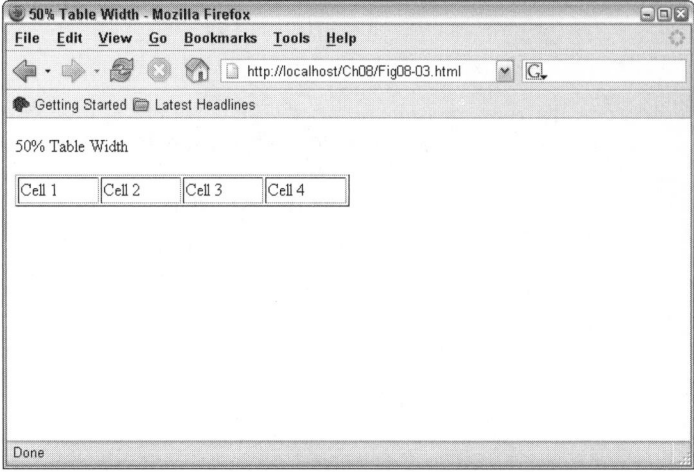

Figure 8-3

To specify an exact width of a table, use pixel width specifications instead. For example, if you need a table to be 500 pixels wide, you could use a table definition similar to the following:

```
<table width="500px">
```

If the specified table width exceeds the user agent's window width, it is up to the user agent to handle the overflow, via resizing the table, wrapping it, or providing scroll bars as shown in Figure 8-4.

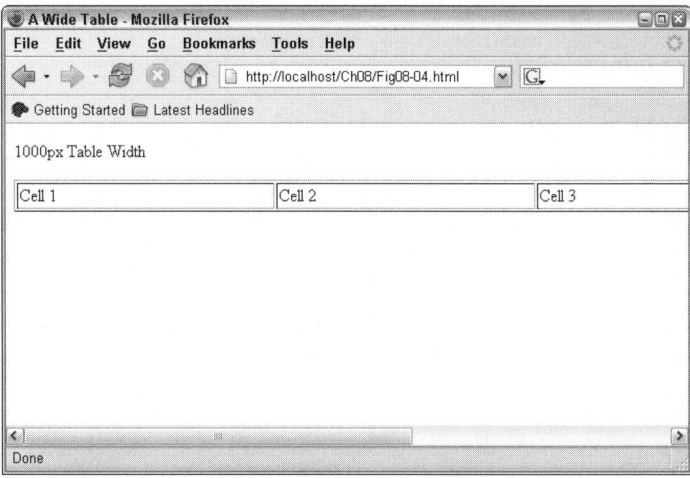

Figure 8-4

Besides specifying the width of the table as a whole, you can also specify the width of each column within the table, using width attributes in **`<th>`** *and* **`<td>`** *tags or specifying width within* **`<col>`** *or* **`<colgroup>`** *tags. These techniques are covered in the "Cells" and "Grouping Columns" sections later in this chapter.*

Aligning a Table Horizontally

The <table> tag supports an `align` attribute to control how the table is aligned horizontally in its containing block. The `align` attribute supports three values: `left` (default), `right`, and `center`.

For example, if you wanted a table to be centered in the user agent's window, you could use code similar to the following (whose result is shown in Figure 8-5):

```
<p>Centered Table</p>
<p>
  <table border="1" align="center">
    <tr>
      <td>Cell 1</td><td>Cell 2</td>
      <td>Cell 3</td><td>Cell 4</td>
    </tr>
  </table>
</p>
```

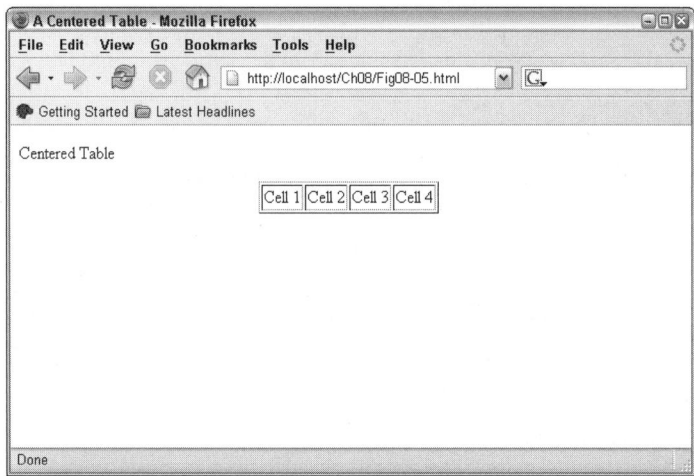

Figure 8-5

Note that the `align` attribute has no visible effect on a table that occupies the full width of its container object.

Cell Spacing and Padding

There are two attributes to table cell spacing: padding and spacing. *Padding* refers to the distance between a cell's contents and its border. *Spacing* refers to the distance between cells (that is, the distance between a cell's border and neighboring elements' boundaries).

Figure 8-6 shows a graphical representation of cell padding and spacing.

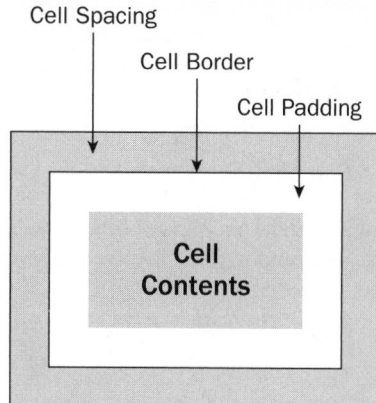

Figure 8-6

Cell padding is controlled with the `<table>` tag's `cellpadding` attribute and can be specified in pixels or percentages. When specified by percentage, the browser uses half of the specified percentage for each side of the cell. The percentage is of the available space for the dimension (size of the cell), vertical or horizontal.

Cell spacing is controlled with the `cellspacing` attribute. Like `cellpadding`, the `cellspacing` attribute can be specified in pixels or percentages. Figure 8-7 shows a table whose `cellspacing` attribute has been set to 20 percent using the following `<table>` tag:

```
<table border="1" width="100%" cellspacing="20%">
```

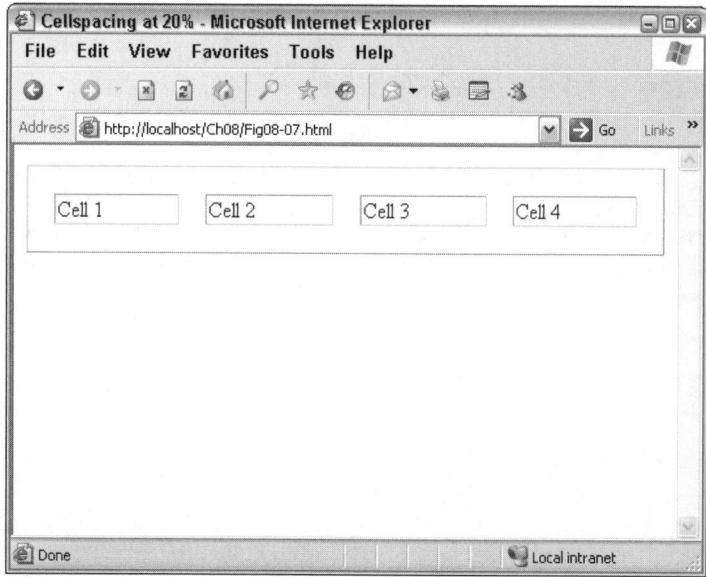

Figure 8-7

Borders and Rules

The border around tables and between cells can be configured in many ways. The following sections cover the various ways you can configure table borders and rules.

CSS offers several additional formatting options for tables and their elements. CSS is covered in Part II of this book.

Table Borders

The `<table>` tag's `border` attribute can be used to control the width of the border surrounding the table. For example, consider the following three tables and the resulting output shown in Figure 8-8:

```
<p>
   No Borders<br />
   <table border="0">
       <tr><td>Cell 1</td><td>Cell 2</td></tr>
       <tr><td>Cell 3</td><td>Cell 4</td></tr>
   </table>
</p>
<p>
   Border = 1<br />
   <table border="1">
       <tr><td>Cell 1</td><td>Cell 2</td></tr>
       <tr><td>Cell 3</td><td>Cell 4</td></tr>
   </table>
</p>
<p>
   Border = 5<br />
   <table border="5">
       <tr><td>Cell 1</td><td>Cell 2</td></tr>
       <tr><td>Cell 3</td><td>Cell 4</td></tr>
   </table>
</p>
```

The `border` attribute's value specifies the width of the border in pixels. The default border width is 0, or no border.

Borders can be an effective troubleshooting tool when dealing with table problems in XHTML. If you are having trouble determining what is causing a problem in a table, try turning on the borders to better visualize the individual rows and columns. If you are using nested tables, turn on the borders of individual tables (possibly using different border values for different tables) until you narrow down the scope of the problem.

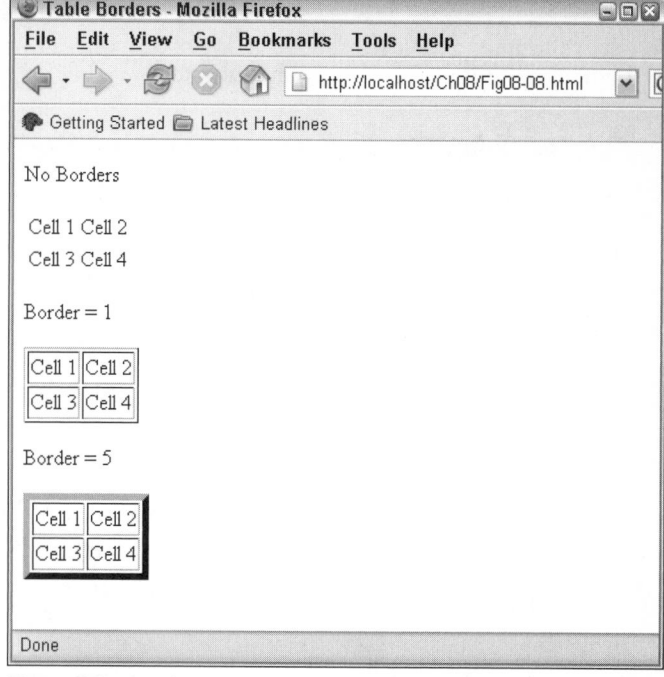

Figure 8-8

To specify which outside borders are displayed, use the `frame` attribute with the `<table>` tag. The `frame` attribute supports the values displayed in the following table:

Value	Definition
void	Display no borders.
above	Display a border on the top of the table only.
below	Display a border on the bottom of the table only.
hsides	Display borders on the horizontal sides (top and bottom) only.
lhs or rhs	Display only the left side or the right side border.
vsides	Display borders on the vertical sides (right and left) only.
box or border	Display borders on all sides of the table (the default when the border attribute is set without specifying frame).

Not all user agents use the same defaults for table borders. If you want a table rendered a particular way, use care to explicitly define each border option.

Table Rules

The `<table>` tag's `rules` attribute controls which rules (borders between cells) are displayed within a table. The `rules` attribute supports the values shown in the following table:

Value	Definition
none	Display no rules.
groups	Display rules between row groups and column groups only.
rows	Display rules between rows only.
cols	Display rules between columns only.
all	Rules will appear between all rows and columns.

For example, the following table code will cause the table to render with rules between columns only, as shown in Figure 8-9:

```
<table cellpadding="5px" rules="cols">
    <tr><td>Cell 1</td><td>Cell 2</td></tr>
    <tr><td>Cell 3</td><td>Cell 4</td></tr>
</table>
```

Figure 8-9

Note that the width of rules is governed by the setting of the `cellspacing` attribute. For example, setting `cellspacing` to a value of `3px` will result in rules 3 pixels wide.

Rows

Rows are the horizontal elements of the table grid and are delimited with table row tags (`<tr>`). For example, a table with five rows would use the following pseudocode:

```
<table>
   <tr>   row 1   </tr>
   <tr>   row 2   </tr>
   <tr>   row 3   </tr>
   <tr>   row 4   </tr>
   <tr>   row 5   </tr>
</table>
```

The rows are divided into columns (individual cells within the row) via table data (`<td>`) or table heading (`<th>`) tags, which are covered in the next section.

The `<tr>` tag supports the options shown in the following table:

Attribute	Definition
align	Set to `right`, `left`, `center`, `justify`, or `char` (character), this attribute controls the horizontal alignment of data in the row. Note that if you use `char` alignment, you should also specify the alignment character with the `char` attribute described below.
char	Specifies the alignment character to use with character (`char`) alignment.
charoff	Specifies the offset from the alignment character to align the data on. Can be specified in pixels or as a percentage.
valign	Set to `top`, `middle`, `bottom`, or `baseline`, this attribute controls the vertical alignment of data in the row. Baseline vertical alignment aligns the baseline of the text across the cells in the row.

Bottom vertical alignment aligns the row to the bottom of neighboring elements. Setting the vertical alignment to **baseline** *will cause the row to be aligned to the baseline of neighboring text (the line text rests upon when written on ruled paper).*

You can use the `align` value of `char` to align columns on a particular character—a decimal (.) if you want to align numbers, for example. If you set alignment to `char`, you will also need to specify the alignment character using the `char` attribute. For example, to align a cell's data on a decimal point, you would use something similar to the following:

```
<td align="char" char=".">145.99</td>
```

You can also use the charoff value for alignment to set the alignment to be offset from a particular character. When using charoff alignment, you also need to use the char attribute to specify the character to offset from.

Note that using alignment attributes in a table row tag will cause all cells in that row to be formatted accordingly. If you want to format individual cells in the row differently, use attributes in the appropriate table data or table header tags instead.

Cells

The *cells* of a table are the elements that actually hold data. The cell definitions also define the column in which they reside. Table cells are delimited by table data tags (<td>), as shown in the following example:

```
<table>
  <tr>  <!-- Row 1 -->
    <td>Column 1</td><td>Column 2</td><td>Column 3</td>
  </tr>
  <tr>  <!-- Row 2 -->
    <td>Column 1</td><td>Column 2</td><td>Column 3</td>
  </tr>
</table>
```

Formatting your tables with ample white space (line breaks and indents) will help you accurately format and understand your tables. There are just as many ways to format a table in XHTML as there are Web programmers—find a style that suits your tastes and stick to it.

This code defines a table with two rows and three columns, due to the three sets of <td> tags within each row (<tr>).

You can also use table header tags (<th>) to define cells that are to be used as headers for the columns. Expanding on the previous example, the following adds column headers:

```
<table>
  <tr>  <!-- Header Row -->
    <th>Header 1</th><th>Header 2</th><th>Header 3</th>
  </tr>
  <tr>  <!-- Body Row 1 -->
    <td>Column 1</td><td>Column 2</td><td>Column 3</td>
  </tr>
  <tr>  <!-- Body Row 2 -->
    <td>Column 1</td><td>Column 2</td><td>Column 3</td>
  </tr>
</table>
```

Most user agents render the table header cells (those delimited by <th> tags) in a different font, usually bold. This allows an easy method to format headings without using additional character formatting tags. However, as with all formatting defaults, each user agent is free to define its own default formatting for table headers. If you want your headers to appear with specific textual formatting, you should take care to explicitly code them as such.

*Some user agents will not properly render an empty cell (for example, **<td></td>**). When you find yourself needing an empty cell, get in the habit of placing a nonbreaking space entity (** **) in the cell (for example, **<td> </td>**) to help ensure that the user agent will render your table correctly.*

Although cells represent the smallest element in a table, they have the most attributes for their tags. Supported attributes include those shown in the following table:

Attribute	Definition
abbr	An abbreviated form of the cell's contents. User agents can use the abbreviation where appropriate (using a voice synthesizer to speak a short form of the contents, displaying on a small device, and so on). As such, the value of the abbr attribute should be as short and concise as possible.
align	The horizontal alignment of the cell's contents — left, center, right, justify, or char (character).
axis	Used to define a conceptual category for the cell, which can be used to place the cell's contents into dimensional space. How the categories are used (if at all) is up to the individual user agent.
char	The character used to align the cell's contents if the alignment is set to char.
charoff	The offset from the alignment character to use when aligning the cell's contents by character.
colspan	How many columns the cell should span (the default is 1). See the "Spanning Columns and Rows" section of this chapter for more information.
headers	A space-separated list of header cell id attributes that correspond with the cells used as headers for the current cell. User agents use this information at their discretion — a verbal agent might read the contents of all header cells before the current cell's contents.
rowspan	How many rows the cell should span (the default is 1). See the "Spanning Columns and Rows" section of this chapter for more information.
scope	The scope of the current cell's contents when used as a header — row, col (column), rowgroup, or colgroup (column group). If set, the cell's contents are treated as a header for the corresponding element(s).
valign	The vertical alignment of the cell's contents — top, middle, bottom, or baseline.

*Previous versions of HTML also supported a **nowrap** attribute for cell tags. In HTML version 4.01 (and hence, XHTML) that attribute was deprecated in favor of CSS formatting.*

Captions

Captions allow you to annotate your tables, detailing the contents or its meaning for the reader. The caption section of an XHTML table is encapsulated in caption tags (`<caption>`) within the table tags (`<table>`). For example, consider the following table and the resulting output shown in Figure 8-10:

```
<!DOCTYPE html PUBLIC "-//W3C//DTD XHTML 1.0 Strict//EN"
    "http://www.w3.org/TR/xhtml1/DTD/xhtml1-strict.dtd">
<html>
<head>
  <title>Table with a Caption</title>
</head>
<body>
<p>
<table border="1" width="25%">
  <caption>The Nobel Gases occupy the last
column of the Periodic Chart of the Elements</caption>
  <tbody>
    <tr><th>Element</th><th>Symbol</th></tr>
    <tr><td>Helium</td><td>He</td></tr>
    <tr><td>Neon</td><td>Ne</td></tr>
    <tr><td>Argon</td><td>Ar</td></tr>
    <tr><td>Krypton</td><td>Kr</td></tr>
    <tr><td>Xenon</td><td>Xe</td></tr>
    <tr><td>Radon</td><td>Rn</td></tr>
  </tbody>
</table>
</p>
</body>
</html>
```

Note that the caption must come immediately after the `<table>` tag so that the user agent will know to reserve space for it. Also, the caption generally appears centered above the table, but different user agents may display it differently.

You can use styles to format the caption. For more information on styles, see Part II of this book.

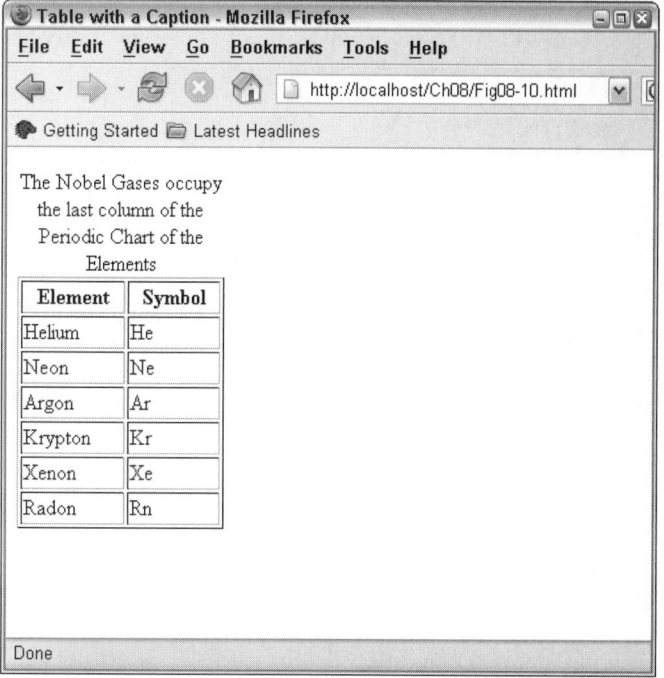

Figure 8-10

Header, Footer, and Body Sections

There are three section tags that can (and should) be used to delimit sections of your table: the header (`<thead>`), footer (`<tfoot>`), and body (`<tbody>`) tags. There are several advantages to using the section tags within your table, including the following:

❑ Each section can be easily styled differently.

❑ The user agent allows the user to scroll the body separately from the headers and footers.

❑ The various sections can be easily identified for later modification.

Each section supports the same tags delimiting columns and rows — table rows (<tr>), table headings (<th>), and table data (<td>). For example, a table heading section might resemble the following:

```
<thead>
  <tr>
    <th>Cust #</th>
    <th>Customer Name</th>
    <th>Last Order Date</th>
  </tr>
</thead>
```

Note that, in this case, <th> tags are used to ensure that the cells are formatted as headings. However, you could just as easily use <td> tags if you wanted.

A sample use of these tags is shown in the following code, and the result is displayed in a user agent within Figure 8-11:

*Notice the use of the **rules="groups"** attribute in the **<table>** tag. This causes the rules to be inserted between the sections (row groups) only (see Figure 8-11).*

```
<!DOCTYPE html PUBLIC "-//W3C//DTD XHTML 1.0 Strict//EN"
    "http://www.w3.org/TR/xhtml1/DTD/xhtml1-strict.dtd">
<html>
<head>
  <title>Page Estimates</title>
</head>
<table border="1" cellpadding="3" cellspacing="2"
    rules="groups">
<caption>Page estimates for the first four chapters.</caption>
<thead align="center">
  <tr>
    <th>Chapter</th><th>Pages</th><th>Figures</th>
      <th>Illustrations</th>
  </tr>
</thead>
<tfoot align="center">
  <tr>
    <td>Totals</td><td>51</td><td>13</td><td>6</td>
  </tr>
</tfoot>
<tbody align="center">
  <tr>
    <td>1</td><td>10</td><td>0</td><td>2</td>
  </tr>
  <tr>
    <td>2</td><td>12</td><td>4</td><td>1</td>
  </tr>
  <tr>
    <td>3</td><td>9</td><td>2</td><td>0</td>
  </tr>
```

```
    <tr>
      <td>4</td><td>20</td><td>7</td><td>3</td>
    </tr>
  </tbody>
  </table>
  </body>
  </html>
```

Although counterintuitive, the <tfoot> section should be placed *before* the <tbody> section in the table code. This allows the user agent to anticipate the footer section when rendering the table.

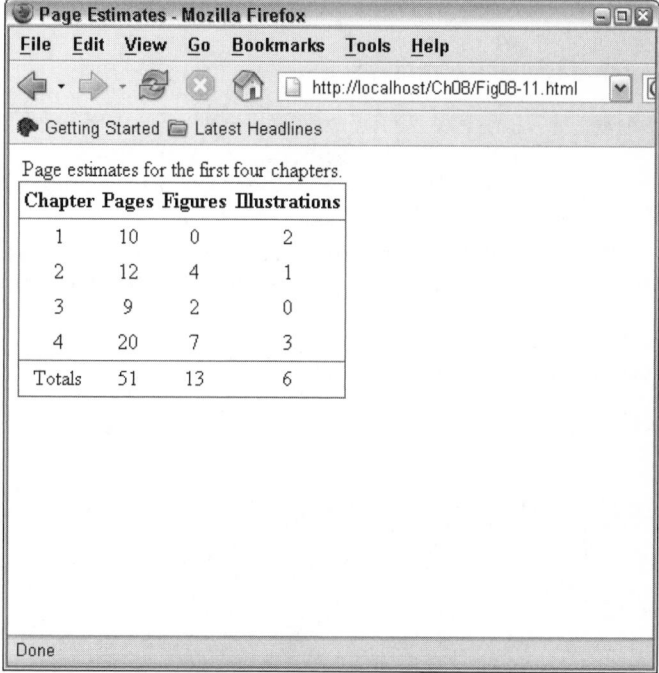

Figure 8-11

Backgrounds

Previous versions of HTML supported a bgcolor attribute in table, row, header, and cell tags. The attribute was used to define a color for the element it was included with. However, in HTML 4.01 that attribute was deprecated. To specify background colors in table elements, you must now use CSS.

For example, the following style definition defines a CSS class for a table with a red background:

```
table.redbg { background-color: red; }
```

Using CSS, you can also use graphic images as backgrounds for tables:

```
table.graphic { background-image: url("marble.jpg"); }
```

Many user agents do not currently support color or image backgrounds in tables.

More information on CSS and backgrounds can be found in Chapter 16.

Spanning Columns and Rows

You can use the `colspan` and `rowspan` attributes to span cells across multiple columns and rows, respectively. The following two sections outline the use of both attributes.

Spanning Columns

Using the `colspan` attribute in table header (`<th>`) and table data (`<td>`) tags, you can span a cell over two or more columns. For example, consider the following table and the result in a user agent, shown in Figure 8-12:

```
<table border="1" cellpadding="5">
<caption>Respondent Summary by Answer</caption>
<tr align="center">
  <!-- Spanning group headers -->
  <th> </th>
  <th colspan="2" width="150">Aggressive</th>
  <th colspan="2" width="150">Passive</th>
  <th colspan="2" width="150">Passive/Aggressive</th>
</tr>
<tr align="center">
  <!-- Individual column headers -->
  <th>Respondent</th><th>A</th><th>B</th>
  <th>C</th><th>D</th><th>E</th><th>F</th>
</tr>
<!-- Table data -->
<tr>
  <td>Mike</td>
  <td>0</td><td>3</td><td>4</td><td>0</td><td>5</td><td>2</td>
</tr>
  <td>Terri</td>
  <td>0</td><td>0</td><td>4</td><td>6</td><td>2</td><td>2</td>
</tr>
```

```
   <td>Amy</td>
   <td>7</td><td>7</td><td>0</td><td>0</td><td>0</td><td>0</td>
</tr>
   <td>Ted</td>
   <td>2</td><td>2</td><td>4</td><td>2</td><td>2</td><td>2</td>
</tr>
   <td>Thomas</td>
   <td>7</td><td>3</td><td>4</td><td>0</td><td>0</td><td>0</td>
</tr>
   <td>Corinna</td>
   <td>0</td><td>0</td><td>4</td><td>10</td><td>0</td><td>0</td>
</table>
```

The colspan attributes were added to table header tags so the result is formatted as a header. The row where the colspan attributes are used has fewer columns (by necessity, one fewer for each column spanned).

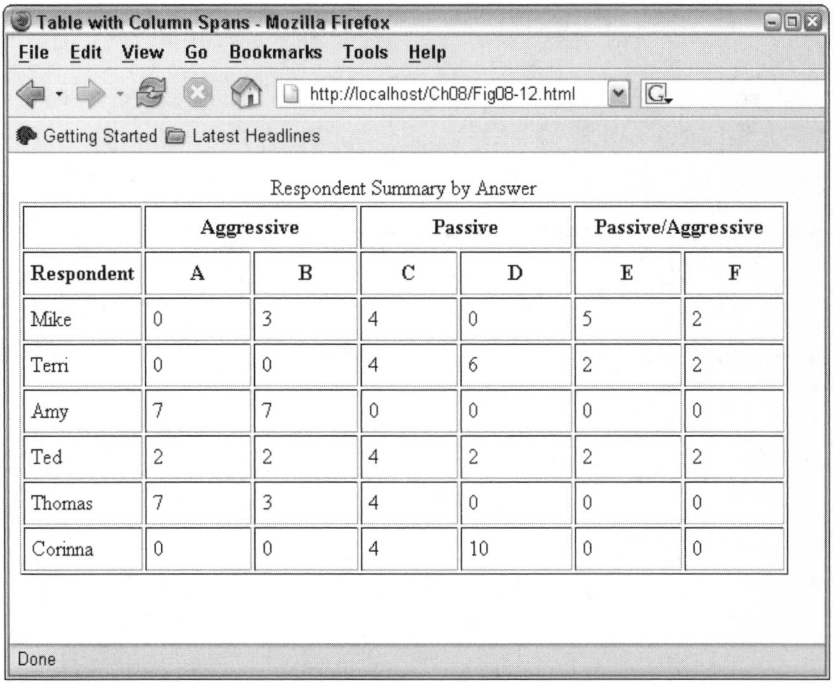

	Aggressive		Passive		Passive/Aggressive	
Respondent	A	B	C	D	E	F
Mike	0	3	4	0	5	2
Terri	0	0	4	6	2	2
Amy	7	7	0	0	0	0
Ted	2	2	4	2	2	2
Thomas	7	3	4	0	0	0
Corinna	0	0	4	10	0	0

Figure 8-12

Spanning Rows

You can use the rowspan attribute in table data (<td>) and table header (<th>) tags to span a cell across several rows. For example, consider the following table and the results shown in Figure 8-13:

```
<table border="1" cellpadding="5">
<caption>Respondent Summary to Questions 1-4</caption>
<tr align="center">
  <th>Category</th>
  <th>Age</th><th>#1</th><th>#2</th><th>#3</th><th>#4</th>
</tr>
<tr>
  <td rowspan="3">Male<br>Respondents</td>
  <!-- Above cell spans 3 rows -->
  <td>23</td><td>A</td><td>C</td><td>F</td><td>B</td>
</tr>
<tr>
  <!-- First cell is the span cell -->
  <td>29</td><td>B</td><td>F</td><td>A</td><td>A</td>
</tr>
<tr>
  <!-- First cell is the span cell -->
  <td>25</td><td>C</td><td>C</td><td>C</td><td>C</td>
</tr>
<!-- End of first span -->
<tr>
  <td rowspan="3">Female<br>Respondents</td>
  <!-- Above cell spans 3 rows -->
  <td>28</td><td>F</td><td>E</td><td>B</td><td>B</td>
</tr>
<tr>
  <!-- First cell is the span cell -->
  <td>21</td><td>B</td><td>B</td><td>B</td><td>A</td>
</tr>
<tr>
  <!-- First cell is the span cell -->
  <td>23</td><td>F</td><td>F</td><td>C</td><td>C</td>
</tr>
<!-- End of second span -->
</table>
```

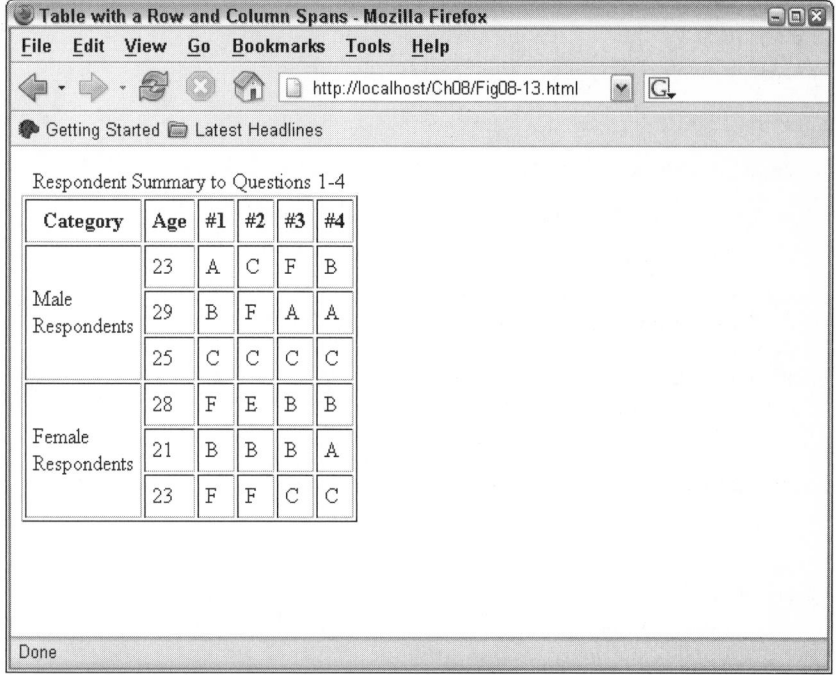

Figure 8-13

Grouping Columns

HTML 4.01 added a few extra tags to make defining and formatting groups of columns easier. The two tags, <colgroup> and <col>, are used together to define and optionally format column groups and individual columns.

The <colgroup> tag is used to define and optionally format groups of columns. The tag supports the same formatting attributes as the <tr> and <td>/<th> tags (align, valign, width, and so on). Any columns defined by the <colgroup> will inherit the formatting contained in the <colgroup> tag's attributes and styles.

The <colgroup> tag's span attribute indicates how many columns are in the group. For example, the following code defines the first three columns in a group and sets their alignment to center:

```
<table>
<colgroup span="3" align="center">
</colgroup>
...
```

Additional `<colgroup>` tags create additional column groups. You must use additional column groups if the columns you are grouping are not contiguous or do not start with the first column. For example, the following HTML table code creates three column groups:

❑ Columns 1 and 2, formatted with centered alignment

❑ Columns 3–5, formatted with decimal alignment

❑ Columns 6–10, formatted with right alignment and bold text

```
<table>
<colgroup span="2" align="center">
<!-- This group contains columns 1 & 2 -->
</colgroup>
<colgroup span="3" align="char" char=".">
<!-- This group contains columns 3 - 5 -->
</colgroup>
<colgroup span="5" align="right" style="font-weight: bold;" >
<!-- This group contains columns 6 - 10 -->
</colgroup>
. . .
```

Column groups that do not have explicit formatting attributes defined in their respective `<colgroup>` tags inherit the standard formatting for the columns of the table. However, the group is still defined as a group and will respond accordingly to table attributes that affect groups (`rules="groups"`, and so on).

What if you don't want all the columns within the group formatted identically? For example, in a group of three columns, suppose you wanted the center column (column number 2 in the group) to have its text formatted as bold text? To define specific formatting for the columns in the group, you use the `<col>` tag. To format a group using the preceding example (middle column bold), you could use code similar to the following:

```
<table>
<colgroup span="3">
<!-- This group contains columns 1 & 3 -->
<col></col>
<col style="font-weight: bold;"></col>
<col></col>
</colgroup>
. . .
```

The `<col>` tag follows similar rules to that of the `<colgroup>` tag:

❑ Empty tags (those without explicit formatting) are simply placeholders.

❑ You must define columns in order, and in a contiguous group, using blank `<col>` tags where necessary.

❑ Missing or empty `<col>` tags result in the corresponding columns inheriting the standard formatting for columns in the table.

In standard HTML the `<col>` tag has no closing tag. However, in XHTML the tag must be appropriately closed.

*Using the **`<colgroup>`** or **`<col>`** tags does not eliminate or change the necessity of **`<td>`** tags (which actually form the columns). You must still take care in placing the rest of the tags within the table to ensure proper formatting of your tables.*

Using Tables for Page Layout

One relatively new use for tables is using them for intricate page layout — aligning text and graphics. This method is quite popular because it is both easy and versatile. Other methods, such as CSS, are more exact but harder to code and aren't as well supported by user agents.

For example, take a look at Figure 8-14.

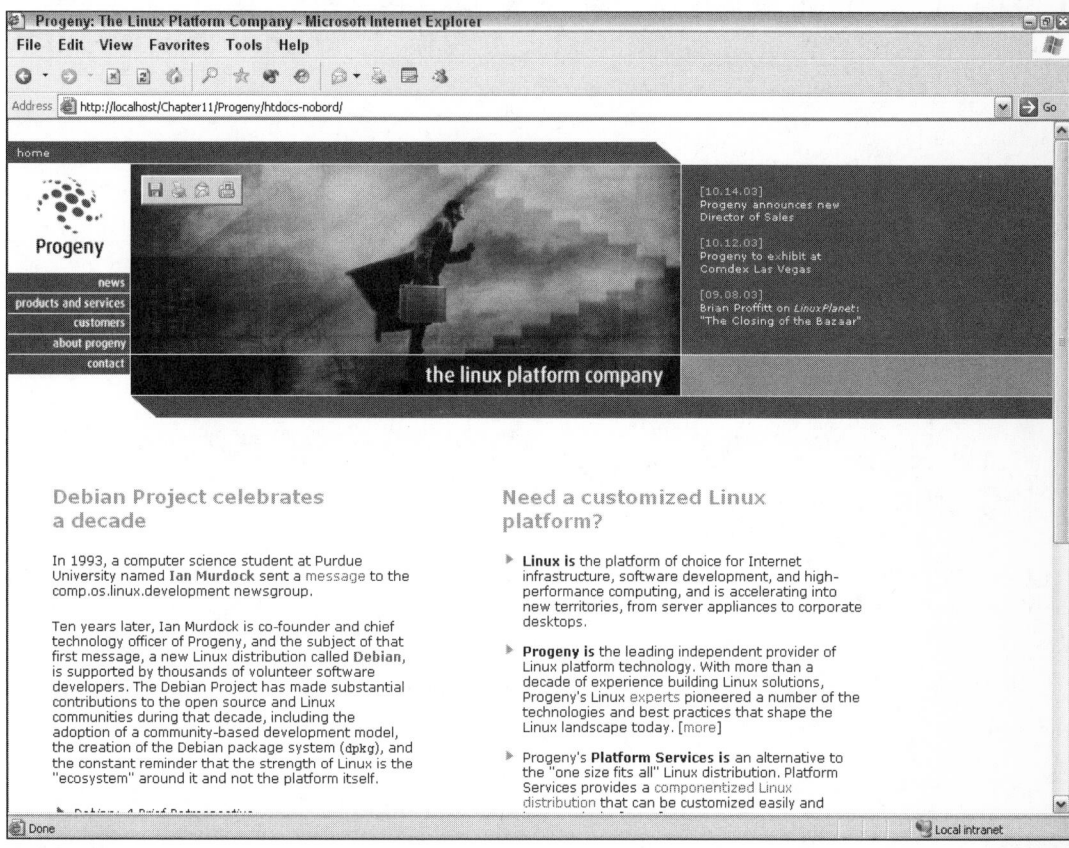

Figure 8-14

At first glance you wouldn't think that many tables were involved in this document's creation. However, if you enable borders on all the tables, their use and multitude becomes quite apparent, as shown in Figure 8-15.

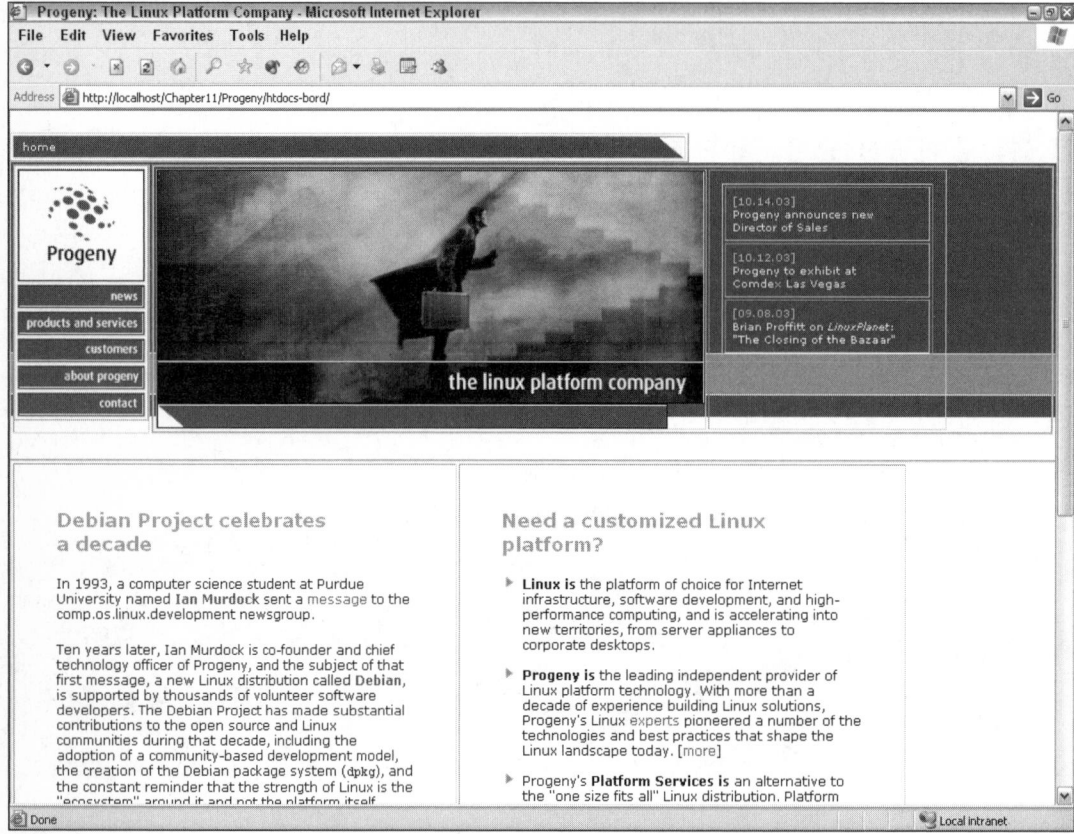

Figure 8-15

This section covers some of the more popular uses of tables for page layout purposes. However, the possibilities for using tables are endless; feel free to experiment with different layouts or with combining layouts.

> *Most table layout schemes use nested tables to accomplish their formatting. Remember that tables can be nested only within cells of other tables (between* **<th>** *or* **<td>** *tags).*

Floating Page

The floating page layout (as shown in Figure 8-16) is quite popular and used for documents of all kinds, from corporate sites to personal online diaries.

Figure 8-16

The effect is fairly easy to create using a few nested tables, as shown in the following code, the output of which is shown in Figure 8-17.

```
<!DOCTYPE html PUBLIC "-//W3C//DTD XHTML 1.0 Strict//EN"
    "http://www.w3.org/TR/xhtml1/DTD/xhtml1-strict.dtd">
<html>
<head>
  <title>Floating Table Format</title>
  <style type="text/css">
```

```
      <!-- Sets "desktop" color (behind page) -->
      body { background-color: #B0C4DE; }
    </style>
</head>
<body>
<p>
<!-- /Body container -->
  <!-- (background = border, padding = border width
       margin = centered table) -->
<table border="0" cellpadding="4px" cellspacing="0"
    style="background-color: black;
    margin: 0 auto;">
  <tr>
   <td>

     <!-- Floating page -->
       <!-- (padding = page margin) -->
     <table border="0" cellpadding="5px" cellspacing="0"
       width="732px" height="900px"
       style="background-color: #FFFFFF;">
      <tr align="left" valign="top">
        <td>

          <!-- Page content -->
          <p>Content goes here.<p>
          <!-- Page content -->

        </td>
      </tr>
     </table>
     <!-- /Floating page -->

   </td>
  </tr>
</table>
<!-- /Body container -->
</p>
</body>
</html>
```

The comments in the code delimit the individual tables and content areas. It is a good practice to follow standard code formatting (indentation, liberal white space, and so on) and to include sufficient comments to easily keep track of all your tables, how they are formatted, and what they accomplish.

For more of a drop-shadow effect, set two adjacent borders to a nonzero value, as shown in the following code:

```
<!-- Floating page -->
  <!-- (padding = page margin) -->
<table border="0" cellpadding="5px" cellspacing="0"
  width="732px" height="900px"
  style="background-color: #FFFFFF;
  border-right: 4px solid black;
  border-bottom: 4px solid black;">
```

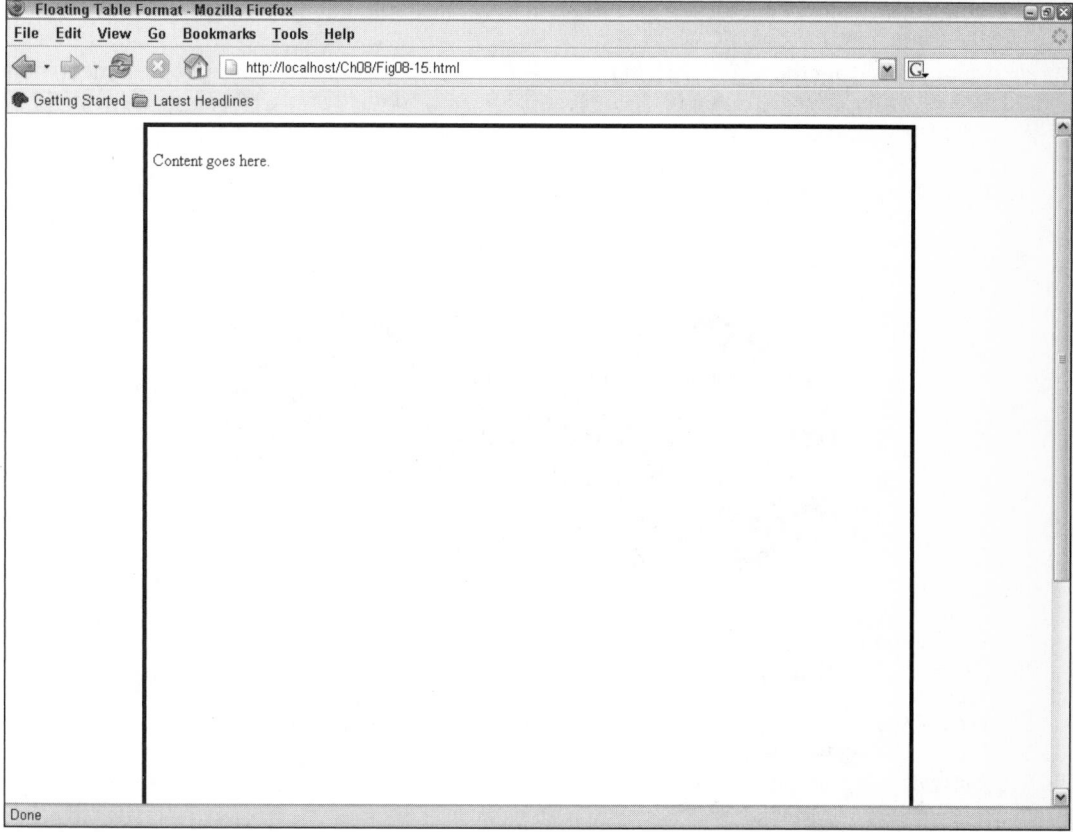

Figure 8-17

This will increase the width of the right and bottom borders, giving the page a more realistic, drop-shadow effect.

*Note that not all browsers correctly support attaching a **background-color** CSS style to the **body** tag.*

Odd Graphic and Text Combinations

As you have probably noticed, most HTML elements are rectangular, making it tough to combine irregularly shaped images with text. However, by breaking up the image(s) into rectangles and placing the chunks into table cells, you can combine images and text in almost any way you desire.

For example, consider the logo shown in Figure 8-18, which is typical of current Web document mastheads using a nonrectangular graphic. A sidebar containing nonvital information appears under the planet on the logo, while the main body of the document appears under the logo text.

Figure 8-18

Using a graphic editor like Paint Shop Pro, you can break the image into three parts, as shown in Figure 8-19.

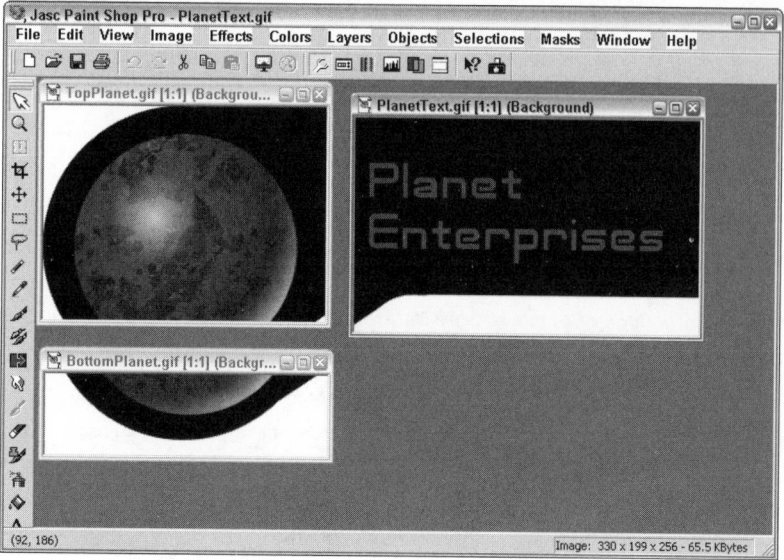

Figure 8-19

Those parts can then be placed into a table; the top of the planet and the text are placed in the first row, and the bottom of the planet and the main body of the document in the second row, as shown in the following code, which renders similarly to Figure 8-20.

```
<table border="0" cellpadding="0" cellspacing="0">
  <colgroup>
    <col valign="top" style="padding-left: 10px;"></col>
    <col valign="top" style="padding-right: 10px;"></col>
  </colgroup>
  <tbody>
  <tr>
    <td><img src="TopPlanet.gif" alt="TopPlanet Image"></td>
    <td><img src="PlanetText.gif" alt="Planet Enterprises"></td>
  </tr>
  <tr>
    <td><img src="BottomPlanet.gif" alt="BottomPlanet Image"><br/>

    <!-- Sidebar Content Here -->
    <p>Sidebar Content</p>

    </td>
    <td align="top">
```

117

```
        <!-- Main Page Content Starts Here -->
        <p>Main Page Content</p>

      </td>
    </tr>
    </tbody>
  </table>
```

The appropriate content replaces the placeholders, creating a seamless page design like that shown in Figure 8-19.

Many graphic editing programs have a Slice feature that can help break apart an image, and some applications will even build the appropriate HTML for you. The Slice feature in Paint Shop Pro (accessed via `File` ➪ `Export` ➪ `Image SLicer`) *is shown in Figure 8-20.*

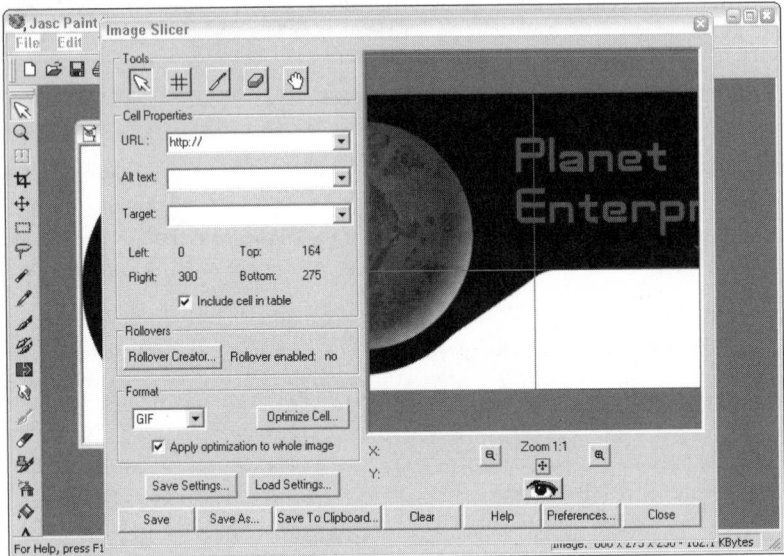

Figure 8-20

Note that white space in your code can create inadvertent problems when embedding graphics in table cells. Be careful not to leave any white space between table data tags (`<td>`) and the image tags (`<img>`). For example, the following code will result in a small margin between the image and the edge of the table cell due to the line breaks and spaces used to indent the `<img>` tag:

```
<td>
  <img src="logo_top.jpg" alt="top piece of logo">
</td>
```

Navigational Blocks

Tables can also be used to provide more simple layouts for navigational panes. For example, you can provide a navigational pane on top of a document or at either margin. Figure 8-21 shows an example of a navigational pane at the top of a document. Figure 8-22 shows an example of a navigational pane on the left margin of the document.

Figure 8-21

The table borders in both examples (Figures 8-21 and 8-22) have been turned on to show the layout of the tables involved. Although most layout designs use no borders, it may be advantageous to turn some borders on to help delimit certain sections of your documents.

The top navigation pane (Figure 8-21) provides an area where a menu can be placed. The left-margin pane (Figure 8-22) provides individual cells for individual menu items; you can use this approach to uniquely position the individual menu items.

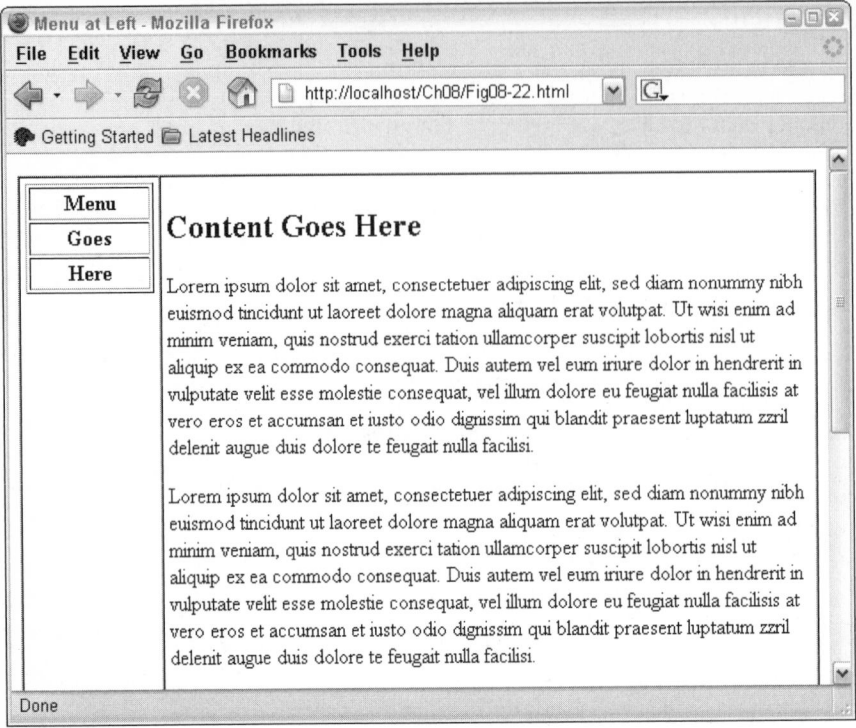

Figure 8-22

Multiple Columns

Tables can also be used to provide a newspaper-like format for your documents. This layout is quite simple, relying on two (or more) parallel columns, as shown in Figure 8-23.

Figure 8-23

A Word About Frames

Previous versions of HTML supported a flexible, multipane scheme called *frames*. Frames enable a user agent window to be divided into defined areas, each capable of displaying different content that can be set to scroll independently from one another.

XHTML allows a special document type definition (DTD) for frame support, the Extensible HTML version 1.0 Frameset DTD, available at `http://www.w3.org/TR/xhtml1/DTD/xhtml1-frameset.dtd`.

There is no frameset DTD for XHTML 1.1.

Although once very popular with Web designers, frames have become an outdated construct and should not be used for the following reasons:

❑ Frames are hard to code (requiring a special frameset document in addition to content documents) and are reasonably hard to manage.

❑ Frame support in user agents cannot be relied on as the Web moves to more resource-constrained platforms (mostly in the mobile arena).

❑ Frames are going the route of deprecation and aren't XHTML 1.1 compliant.

Summary

This chapter introduced you to one of the most powerful and flexible XHTML elements, the table. You learned about the various pieces that make up the table whole, as well as how to format each. You also learned about the evolution of the table and how some of the table-formatting attributes have migrated — much like other elements' formatting attributes — into CSS. In addition, you learned how to stretch the boundaries of tables to provide layout structures for text and even entire documents.

9

Forms

The Web was built as a one-way communication medium—designed to deliver content to a user but not gather data from the user. However, the usefulness of a *World Wide* Web soon drove constructs to enable users to send information as well as receive it. Enter the form, which allows graphical user controls to be placed in Web documents, allowing users to use methods they are familiar with to send data to interact with databases, submit orders to retailers, and more. This chapter details the ins and outs of XHTML forms and their controls.

Understanding Forms

HTML forms allow users to interact with Web documents by providing GUI controls for data entry. The HTML side of forms simply collects the data. A separate handler, usually a script of some sort, is used to do something useful with the data. A typical interaction with an HTML form resembles that shown in Figure 9-1.

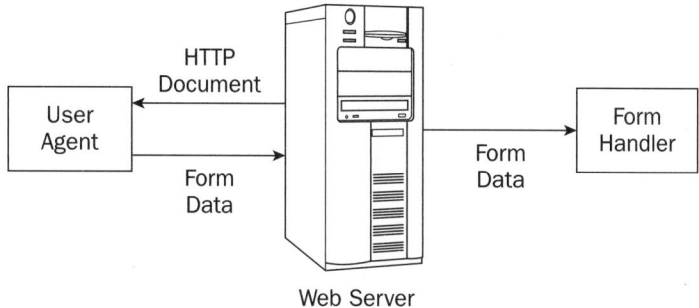

Figure 9-1

The steps in the flow are as follows:

1. The Web server sends the HTML document (containing the form) to the user agent.

2. The user uses the form's GUI controls to enter data and submits the completed form.

3. The form is submitted to a specified server (typically the same server that delivered the form document) to be passed to a handler.

4. The server passes the data stream to a specified handler, which uses the data in a prescribed method.

A sample form, using the various form fields, is shown in the following code and rendered in a user agent in Figure 9-2.

```
<!DOCTYPE html PUBLIC "-//W3C//DTD XHTML 1.0 Strict//EN"
    "http://www.w3.org/TR/xhtml1/DTD/xhtml1-strict.dtd">
<html>
<head>
  <title>A Simple Form</title>
</head>
<body>
<p>
<form action="formdata.cgi" method="post">
  <table cellspacing="20">
  <tr><td>

    <!-- Text boxes -->
    <p><label for="fname">First Name: </label>
      <input type="text" name="fname" id="fname" size="20"><br>
    <label for="lname">Last Name: </label>
      <input type="text" name="lname" id="lname" size="20">
    </p>

    <!-- Text area -->
    <p><label for="address">Address:</label><br>
      <textarea name="address" id="address"
        cols=20 rows=4></textarea>
    </p>

    <!-- Password -->
    <p><label for="password">Password: </label>
      <input type="password" name="password" id="password"
        size="20" />
    </p>

    </td>
    <td>

    <!-- Select list -->
    <p><label for="products">What product(s) are you<br>
    interested in? </label><br>
    <select name="prod[]" id="products" multiple="multiple"
      size="4" />
      <option id="MB">Motherboards</option>
      <option id="CPU">Processors</option>
      <option id="Case">Cases</option>
      <option id="Power">Power Supplies</option>
      <option id="Mem">Memory</option>
      <option id="HD">Hard Drives</option>
```

```
      <option id="Periph">Peripherals</option>
    </select>
    </p>

    <!-- Check boxes -->
    <fieldset>
      <legend>Contact me via: </legend>
      <p><input type="checkbox" name="email" id="email" checked="checked" />
        <label for="email">Email</label><br />
      <input type="checkbox" name="postal" id="postal" />
        <label for="postal">Postal Mail</label></p>
    </fieldset>

    </td>
    </tr>
    <tr>
    <td>

    <!-- Radio buttons -->
    <p>How soon will you be buying hardware?</p>
    <fieldset>
    <legend>I plan to buy:</legend>
    <p><input type="radio" name="buy" value="ASAP" id="buyASAP" />
      <label for="buyASAP">ASAP</label><br>
    <input type="radio" name="buy" value="10" id="buy10" />
      <label for="buy10">Within 10 business days</label><br />
    <input type="radio" name="buy" value="30" id="buy30" />
      <label for="buy30">Within the month</label><br />
    <input type="radio" name="buy" value="Never" id="buyNever" />
      <label for="buyNever">Never!</label></p>
    </fieldset>
    </td>

    <td>
    <!-- Submit and Reset buttons -->
    <p>
    <input type="submit" name="submit" id="submit" value="Submit"/>
       
    <input type="reset" name="reset" id="reset" />
    </p>

    <!-- Button -->
    <p>
    <input type="button" name="leave" id="leave" value="Leave site!" />
    </p>

    <!-- Image -->
    <input type="image" name="coupon" id="coupon" src="coupon.jpg" />

    <!-- Hidden field -->
    <input type="hidden" name="referredby" id="referredby" value="Google" />

</td>
</tr>
</table>
```

```
</form>
</p>
</body>
</html>
```

Text Legend and Fieldset Check Boxes

Text Area Password Select List Submit and Reset Buttons

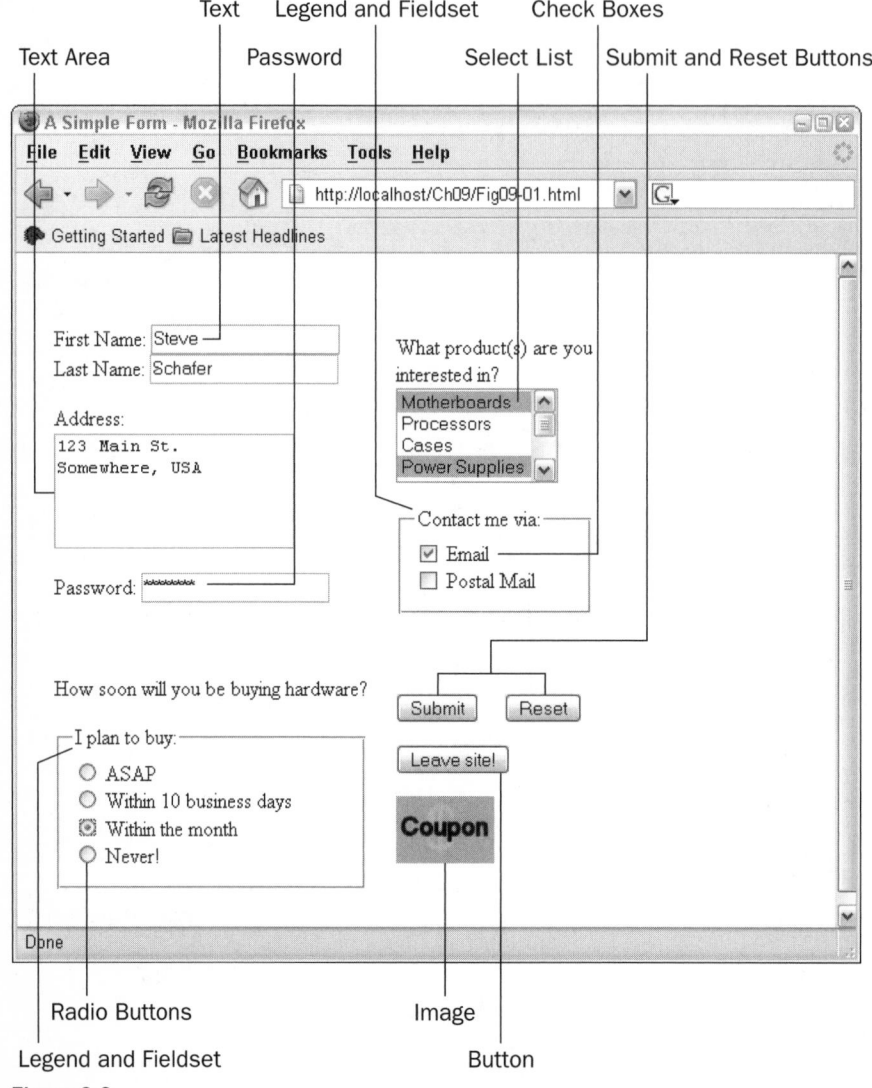

Radio Buttons Image

Legend and Fieldset Button

Figure 9-2

The various fields and options are covered in appropriate sections later in this chapter.

Form Handling

As previously mentioned, a separate form handler is necessary to do something useful with the data. Form handlers are generally script files designed to interact with e-mail, databases, or some other system. For example, a Perl program might be used to query a database based on user input and then pass the results back to the user via a separate document.

A simple PHP form handler that logs form data to a file might resemble the following:

```php
<?php

// Open LOG file
$log = fopen("formdata.log","a");

// For each value pair, output value to LOG
$firstvalue=TRUE;
foreach ($_POST as $key => $value) {
  if (!$firstvalue) { fwrite($log,", "); }

  // If value is array (multiple select list)
  //   output array to LOG (elements sep by - )
  if (is_array($value)) {
    $firstelement=TRUE;
    fwrite($log,"\"");
    foreach ($value as $element) {
      if (!$firstelement) {
        fwrite($log,"-");
        $firstelement=FALSE;
      }
      fwrite($log,$element);
    }
  } else {
    // Not array, output simple value
    fwrite($log,"\"$value\"");
    $firstvalue=FALSE;
  }
}

// Line feed and close LOG
fwrite($log,"\n");
fclose($log);

?>
```

Note that this form handler is very basic — it doesn't do any error checking, convert encoded values, or provide any feedback to the user. It simply takes the fields data passed to it and puts it in a comma-separated value (CSV) log file.

Common form handlers are created in Perl, Python, PHP, or other server-side programming languages.

More information on scripting languages that can be used for form handling can be found in Parts IV and V of this book.

Security is an issue that should be considered when creating form handlers. One of the earliest, most popular form handlers, `formmail.cgi`, was found to have a vulnerability that allowed anyone to send data to the script and have it e-mail the data to whomever the sender wanted. This functionality was an instant hit with e-mail spammers, who still use unsecured `formmail` scripts to send anonymous spam.

If you want a generic form handler to simply store or e-mail the data, you can choose from a few routes.

Several sites on the Internet have generic form handlers available. For example, CGI Resource Index, at `http://cgi.resourceindex.com/`, has several dozen scripts that you can download and use for your form handling.

Several services are also available that allow you to process your form data through their server and scripts. You may need such a service if you cannot run scripts on your server or want a generic, no-hassle solution. A partial list of script services is also available at the CGI Resource Index, `http://cgi.resourceindex.com/`. From the main page, select Remotely Hosted and browse for a service that meets your needs.

Passing Form Data

There are two methods that can be used to send the form data via HTTP, GET, and POST. Each method passes the form data back to the specified form handler in name/value pairs (name of the variable/form field and its value). Only the method for passing the data varies.

The HTTP GET protocol transfers data by attaching it to the URL text passed to the form handler. You have probably noticed URLs that resemble the following:

```
http://www.example.com/forms.cgi?id=45677&character=Taarna
```

The data appears after the question mark and is in name/value pairs. For example, the variable named `id` has the value of `45677`, and the variable `character` has the value of `Taarna`. In most cases, the variable name corresponds to field names from the form, but how they translate to values within the form handler is up to the handler itself.

Because the data is passed as plain text in the URL, it is easy to implement—you can pass data by simply adding the appropriate coding to the URL used to call the data handler. However, GET is also inherently insecure. You should never use GET to send confidential data to a handler, because the data is clearly visible in most user agents and can be easily sniffed by hackers.

The HTTP POST method passes data by encoding it in the HTTP protocol stream. As such, it is not normally visible to a user and is a more secure method to pass data, but it can be harder to implement. Thankfully, most Web technologies make passing data via POST trivial.

Note that GET data is also limited in size due to being encapsulated in the URL.

The Form Tag

You insert a form into your document by placing form fields within form (`<form>`) tags. The entire form or any of the tags within can be formatted like any other element in your document and can be placed within any element capable of holding other elements (paragraphs, tables, and so on).

The `<form>` tag has the following minimum format:

```
<form action="url_to_send_data" method="get|post">
```

The `action` attribute provides a URL to a suitable form handler that will process the form data accordingly. The `method` attribute specifies how the form data should be passed to the handler, via GET or POST.

The `<form>` tag has several additional attributes, shown in the following table:

Attribute	Values
accept	A comma-separated list of content types that the handler's server will accept
accept-charset	A comma-separated list of character sets the form data may be in
enctype	The content type the form data is in
id	The ID of the form (used instead of `name`)
name	The name of the form (deprecated, use the `id` attribute instead)
target	Where to open the handler URL (deprecated)

Although you may not need these attributes in all forms, they can be very useful. The `accept`, `accept-charset`, and `enctype` attributes are invaluable for processing nontextual and international data. The `id` attribute is used to uniquely identify a form in your document. This is essential for scripting, especially if you use more than one form in the same document.

The Input Tag

Many form fields share the same tag, namely the input (`<input>`) tag. This tag uses a `type` attribute to tell the user agent what type of field it signifies. The `input` tag is used for the following types of fields:

- ❏ button
- ❏ checkbox
- ❏ file
- ❏ hidden
- ❏ image
- ❏ password

❑   radio

❑   reset

❑   submit

❑   text

For example, the following two tags define a text field and a submit button:

```
<input type="text" name="username" id="username" size="30" />
<input type="submit" name="submit" id="submit" value="Submit" />
```

More information on the various fields supported by the input tag appears in appropriate sections later in this chapter.

The name and id Attributes

There are two attributes used in most form fields that serve similar purposes: name and id. However, their uses are extremely different.

HTML requires that all fields contain name attributes for their data to be submitted with the form. Any field that does not have a name attribute will not be included in the form data submission. Furthermore, HTML uses the name attribute to identify the value — as a sort of variable name, if you will. Therefore, it is important that you include name attributes in *all* your form fields. It is also suggested that the name values be succinct and machine-readable — that is, devoid of spaces and nonalphanumeric characters.

Some applications (some scripts and the <label> tag) require that fields also contain an id attribute. For example, user agents use the <label> tags' for attribute to match other fields' id attribute, resulting in a label-field match. JavaScript and other scripting languages can use the id attribute to directly access form fields.

To be on the safe side, it's usually best to include both attributes in all form fields.

Text Input Boxes

The text input field is one of the most used fields in HTML forms. This field allows for the input of one line of text — generally used for names, addresses, search terms, and so on.

The text input field tag has the following format:

```
<input type="text" name="name_of_field" id="id_of_field" value="initial_value"
  size="size_of_field" maxlength="max_characters_allowed" />
```

Although all the attributes previously listed are not required, they represent the minimum attributes that you should always use with text input fields. The following sample text box is displayed 30 characters long, accepts a maximum of 40 characters, and has no initial value:

```
<p>Name: <input type="text" name="username" id="username" value=""
  size="30" maxlength="40" /></p>
```

The following code example defines a text box that is displayed as a box 40 characters long, only accepts 40 characters, and has an initial value of "email@example.com" (supplied via the value attribute):

```
<p>Email: <input type="text" name="email" id="email"
value="email@example.com" size="40" maxlength="40" /></p>
```

Password Input Boxes

The password input box is similar to the text box, but it visually obscures data entered into the box by displaying asterisks or bullets instead of the actual characters entered into the field. The following example displays a password field that accepts 20 characters.

```
<p>Password: <input type="password" name="password" id="password" value=""
  size="20" maxlength="20" /></p>
```

Note that the password field only visibly obscures the data to help stop casual snoops from seeing what a user inputs into a field. It does not encode or in any way obscure the information at the data level. As such, be careful how you use this field.

Radio Buttons

The radio input field defines one in a series of radio buttons. When one is selected, the others in the group are deselected, making the buttons mutually exclusive from each other.

The radio button field has the following format:

```
<input type="radio" name="name_of_group" id="id_of_group" [checked="checked"]
  value="value_if_selected" />
```

The value attribute defines what value is returned to the handler if the button is selected. This attribute should be unique between buttons in the same group. Note that all radio buttons within a group share the same name attribute value, which defines them as a group.

The following code defines a group of radio buttons that allows a user to select their gender:

```
<p>Gender:
<input type="radio" name="gender" id="male" value="male"> Male
<input type="radio" name="gender" id="female" value="female"> Female</p>
```

If you want a radio button selected by default, use the `checked` attribute within the appropriate button's tag. Remember that XML and its variants do not allow attributes without values. Although HTML will allow the `checked` attribute to be used with or without a value, you should specify the `checked` attribute as `checked="checked"` instead of just `checked` to remain XHTML compliant.

Fieldsets are handy elements to use with radio buttons. More information on fieldsets appears in a separate section later in this chapter.

Checkboxes

The checkbox field has the following format:

```
<input type="checkbox" name="name_of_field" id="id_of_field" [checked="checked"]
  value="value_if_selected" />
```

Checkboxes are very similar in definition to radio buttons; however, unlike radio buttons, multiple checkboxes can be selected from the same group. The following example displays a checkbox allowing the user to select whether they should receive solicitous e-mails:

```
<p><input type="checkbox" name="spam_me" checked="checked"
value="spam_me" /> Add me to your email list</p>
```

You can use the `checked` attribute to preselect checkboxes in your forms. Also, just like radio buttons, the `value` attribute is used as the `value` of the checkbox if it is selected. If no value is given, selected checkboxes are typically given the value of "on" by the user agent.

List Boxes

List boxes are used to allow a user to pick one or more textual items from a list. The list can be presented in its entirety, with each element visible, or as a drop-down list where users must scroll to their choices.

List boxes are delimited using select (`<select>`) tags, with their options delimited using option (`<option>`) tags. Optionally, you can use the option group (`<optgroup>`) tag to group related options within the list.

The `<select>` tag provides the container for the list and has the following format:

```
<select name="name_of_field" id="id_of_field" size="number_of_items_to_show"
  [multiple="multiple"]>
```

The `size` attribute determines how many items will initially be displayed by the control. If the number of items in the list exceeds the number of lines to display, the user agent will provide scroll bars so that the user can navigate to the additional items in the list. If the `size` attribute is set to 1, the list will become a drop-down list; clicking the list will expand it to show multiple items with a scroll bar.

The select tag does not include an attribute to control the width of the control. The select box is automatically sized according to the longest element (`<option>`) it contains. If you wish a select list to be wider, a common practice is to include a placeholder option of the appropriate length, similar to the following:

```
<option value="null">-------- Please make a selection --------</option>
```

However, including such an option places an additional burden on the form handling; you must ensure that this option is not selected if the field is not optional.

The `<option>` tag delimits the items to be contained in the list. Each item is given its own `<option>` tag pair. The option tag has the optional attributes shown in the following table:

Attribute	Values
label	A shorter label for the item that the user agent can use
selected	Indicates that the item should be initially selected
value	The value that should be sent to the handler if the item is selected; if omitted, the text of the item is sent

The `label` attribute is useful for fields where you need to provide human-readable text (including spaces, punctuation, and so on) in the field for the user's benefit but wish to return a more succinct value to the form handler.

An example of an `<option>` list follows:

```
<option value="sun">Sunday</option>
<option value="mon">Monday</option>
<option value="tue">Tuesday</option>
<option value="wed" selected="selected">Wednesday</option>
<option value="thr">Thursday</option>
<option value="fri">Friday</option>
<option value="sat">Saturday</option>
```

Occasionally, you will want to group options of a list together for clarity. For this, you can use option group (`<optgroup>`) tags to delimit the groups of options. For example, the following code defines two groups for the preceding list of options, weekend and weekday:

```
<optgroup label="Weekend">
  <option>Sunday</option>
  <option>Saturday</option>
</optgroup>
<optgroup label="Weekday">
  <option>Monday</option>
  <option>Tuesday</option>
  <option>Wednesday</option>
  <option>Thursday</option>
  <option>Friday</option>
</optgroup>
```

It is up to the user agent as to how to display the option groups. A popular method of displaying the groups is to display the group label above the options to which they apply, as shown in Figure 9-3.

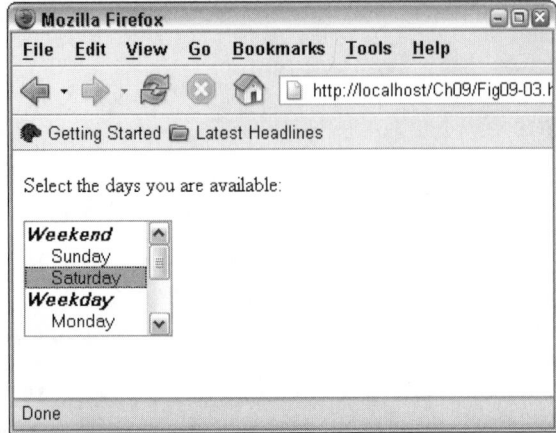

Figure 9-3

Combining the various list tags to create a list would look similar to the following code:

```
<p>Select the days you are available: </p>
<p>
<select name="DaysAvail" size="5" multiple="multiple">
  <optgroup label="Weekend">
    <option>Sunday</option>
    <option>Saturday</option>
  </optgroup>
  <optgroup label="Weekday"
    <option>Monday</option>
    <option>Tuesday</option>
    <option>Wednesday</option>
    <option>Thursday</option>
    <option>Friday</option>
  </optgroup>
</select>
</p>
```

Large Text Areas

The text area tag (`<textarea>`) is used for larger pieces of text — this tag can accept up to 1024 characters and uses a multiline text box for input.

The `<textarea>` tag has the following format:

```
<textarea name="name_of_field" cols="number_of_columns"
rows="number_of_rows">default_value_of_field</textarea>
```

The `cols` and `rows` attributes define the size of the text box in the user agent. If the content of the box exceeds its dimensions, the user agent will provide a vertical scroll bar to scroll the content appropriately. Note that the text area tag is one of the few form tags that has a formal closing tag. If the field should have a default value, it is placed between the tags. The tags should be adjacent to one another if the field is to be blank.

It is important to carefully watch the formatting of your code around a text area tag. For example, if you want the field to be initially blank, you *cannot* place the open and close tags on separate lines in the code:

```
<textarea>
</textarea>
```

This would result in the field containing a newline character — it would not be blank.

The text entered into the `<textarea>` field wraps within the width of the box, but the text is sent as one long string to the handler. However, where the user enters line breaks, those breaks are also sent to the handler, embedded in the string.

*Previous versions of HTML supported a **wrap** attribute for the **<textarea>** tag. This attribute was used to control how text wrapped in the text box as well as how it was sent to the handler. However, user agent support for this attribute was inconsistent — you could not rely on an agent to follow the intent of the attribute. The attribute has been deprecated and should not be used.*

Hidden Fields

You can place additional, nonvisible data in your forms using hidden fields. The hidden field has the following format:

```
<input type="hidden" name="name_of_field" value="value_of_field" />
```

Other than not being visibly displayed, hidden fields are much like any other field. Hidden fields are used mostly for tracking data and the state of a process. For example, in a multipage form, a `userid` field can be hidden in the form to ensure that subsequent forms, when submitted, are tied to the same user data. For instance, the following code could be used to track a user by a unique number:

```
<input type="hidden" name="userid" value="4384572332" />
```

Keep in mind that while hidden fields do not display in the user agent interface, they are still visible in the code of the document. Hidden fields should never be used for sensitive data.

Buttons

You can add custom text buttons on your forms using the button field. The button field has the following format:

```
<input type="button" name="name_of_field" value="text_for_button" />
```

This tag results in a simple button being displayed on the form using the style of the current GUI. The following code results in the button shown in Figure 9-4:

```
<input type="button" name="BuyNow" id="buynow" value="Buy Now!" />
```

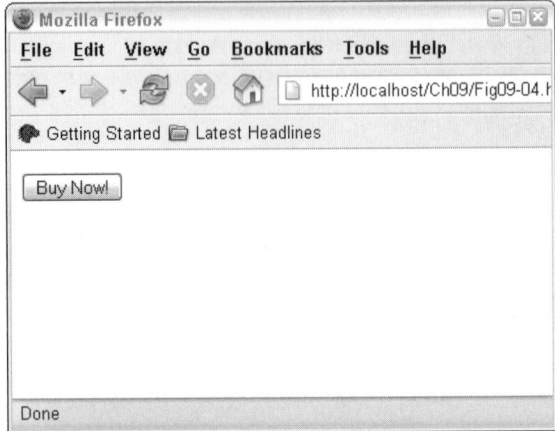

Figure 9-4

Buttons by themselves are relatively useless on a form. To have the button actually perform an action, you need to link it to a script via the `onclick` or other event attribute. For example, the following code results in a button that, when clicked, executes the JavaScript function `buynow()`:

```
<input type="button" name="buynow" id="buynow" value="Buy Now!"
  onclick="JavaScript:buynow()" />
```

More information on JavaScript and events can be found in Part III of this book.

Images

You can include additional graphic images in your form to help convey a message. The image field displays a graphic image much like the image tag (`<img>`) and has the following format:

```
<input type="image" name="name_of_field" src="url_to_image_file" />
```

However, much like the button field, the image field is useless without being tied to an event handler. The following example causes the image `buynow.jpg` to be displayed on a form. When the image is clicked, the JavaScript function `buynow()` is executed:

```
<input type="image" name="buynow" src="buynow.jpg" onclick="JavaScript:buynow()" />
```

Images by themselves are not intuitive user interface mechanisms. The image field exists to help encapsulate graphics into the form element within the document object model. If you use images for user interface purposes, be sure to include enough hints as to their purpose using nongraphical (text, and so on) means.

File Fields

File fields allow files to be attached to form data and sent along with the data to the handler. File fields have the following syntax:

```
<input type="file" name="name_of_field" size="display_size_of_field" />
```

The file field renders as a text box with a button that enables the user to browse for a file using their platform's file browser. Alternately, the user can manually type the full path and name of the file in the text box. Figure 9-5 shows an example of a file field.

Figure 9-5

However, to use this control in your forms, you must do the following:

❑   Specify your form encoding as `multipart`, which allows the file to be attached to the rest of the data.

❑   Use the POST, not the GET, method of form delivery. File information cannot be encapsulated using the GET method.

In other words, when using a file field, your `<form>` tag should resemble the following:

```
<form action="form_handler" method="post" enctype="form/multipart">
```

Submit and Reset Buttons

Submit and reset buttons provide control mechanisms for users to submit the data entered to a handler and reset the form to its default state, respectively. These buttons have similar formats:

```
<input type="submit" name="submit" id="submit" [value="text_for_button"] />
```

and

```
<input type="reset" name="reset" id="reset" [value="text_for_button"] />
```

The value attribute for both tags is optional; if this attribute is omitted, the buttons will display default text (usually "Submit" and "Reset," but the text is ultimately determined by the user agent).

The submit button, when clicked, causes the form to be submitted to the handler specified in the `<form>` tag's `action` attribute. You can also use the `onclick` event attribute to call a script to preprocess the form data prior to submission.

The reset button, when clicked, causes the form to be reloaded and its fields reset to their default values. You can also use the `onclick` event attribute to change the button's behavior, calling a script instead of reloading the form. However, the user will expect the reset button to ultimately reset the form; if you tie a script to the button using the `onclick` event, you should ensure that the script also resets the form.

Field Labels

The label tag (`<label>`) is used to define text labels for fields. This tag has the following format:

```
<label for="id_of_related_tag">text_label</label>
```

For example, the following code defines a label for a text box:

```
<p><label for="FirstName">First Name: </label>
<input type="text" name="FirstName" id="FirstName" value=""
size="30" maxlength="40"></p>
```

The label field's `for` attribute should match the `id` of the field for which it is intended. The main purpose of the label tag is accessibility—most users will be able to ascertain the purpose of fields in your forms by sight. However, if the user agent does not have a visual component, or if the user is visually impaired, the visual layout of the form cannot be relied on to match labels and fields. Note that if the user agent supports it, the user can also click on the field label to select the appropriate field.

The `<label>` tag's `for` attribute ensures that the user agent can adequately match labels with fields for the user, if necessary.

*Notice the use of both the **id** and **name** attributes in the text input field tag. HTML requires a field to have a name tag for its data to be submitted. However, the label tag requires an **id** value in its matching input field.*

Fieldsets and Legends

Sometimes it is advantageous to visually group certain controls on your form. This is a standard practice for graphical user agents, as in the Mozilla Firebird Options dialog shown in Figure 9-6.

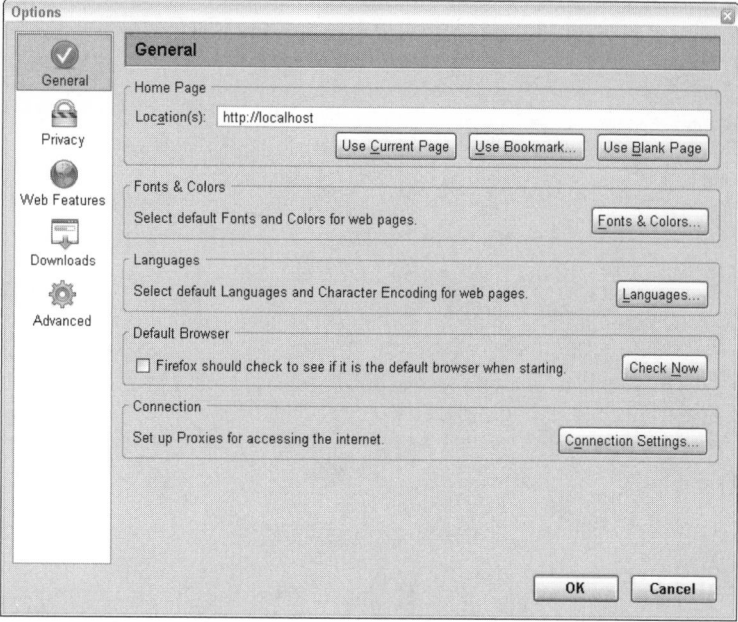

Figure 9-6

The fieldset tag (`<fieldset>`) is used as a container for form elements and results in a thin border being displayed around the contained elements. For example, the following code results in the output shown in Figure 9-7.

```
<fieldset>
<p>Gender: <br>
<input type="radio" name="gender" id="male" value="male"> Male <br>
<input type="radio" name="gender" id="female" value="female"> Female</p>
</fieldset>
```

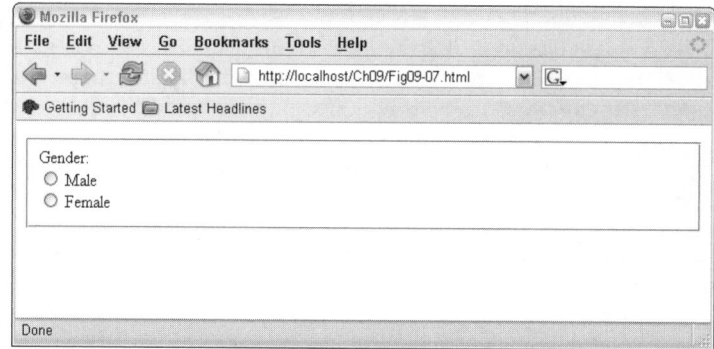

Figure 9-7

The legend tag (`<legend>`) allows the surrounding fieldset box to be captioned. For example, the following code adds a "Gender" caption to the previous example. The output of this change is shown in Figure 9-8.

```
<fieldset>
<p><legend>Gender </legend>
<input type="radio" name="gender" id="male" value="male"> Male <br>
<input type="radio" name="gender" id="female" value="female"> Female</p>
</fieldset>
```

Figure 9-8

Tab Order and Keyboard Shortcuts

Two additional attributes, `tabindex` and `accesskey`, should be used with your form fields to increase their accessibility.

The `tabindex` attribute defines what order the fields are selected in when the user presses the Tab key. This attribute takes a numeric argument that specifies the field's order on the form. The fields are then accessed in their numeric, `tabindex` order—`tabindex` 1, then 2, and so forth.

The `accesskey` attribute defines a key that the user can press to directly access the field. This attribute takes a single letter as an argument; that letter becomes the key the user can press to directly access the field. Keys specified in `accesskey` attributes typically require an additional key to be pressed with the specified key. For example, user agents running on Microsoft Windows typically require the `Alt` key to be pressed along with the letter specified by `accesskey`. Other platforms require similar keys; such keys typically follow the GUI interface conventions of the platform.

The following example defines a text box that can be accessed by pressing Alt+F (on Windows platforms) and is third in the tab order:

```
<p><label for="FirstName"><span class="und">F</span>irst Name: </label>
<input type="text" id="FirstName" name="FirstName" value=""
tabindex="3" accesskey="F" size="30" maxlength="40"></p>
```

Note the use of the **<span>** *tag to delimit the corresponding letter ("F") in the field's label. Deprecation of the underline element caused a slight problem when using* **accesskey** *attributes. It is customary to underline shortcut keys in GUI interfaces so that the user knows what key is mapped to what field/function. However, with the deprecation of the underline element, you must use CSS (hence the span tag) to appropriately code the letter corresponding to the access key.*

The **<span>** *tag is covered in Chapter 7, while CSS is covered in Part II of this book.*

Preventing Changes to Fields

There are two ways to display information in form fields without allowing a user to change the data: by setting the field to read only or by disabling the field.

You can add the `readonly` attribute to text fields to keep the user from being able to edit the data contained therein. This method has the advantage of displaying the data in field form while prohibiting the user from being able to modify it.

The `disabled` attribute causes the corresponding field to appear as disabled (usually graying out the control, consistent with the user agent's platform method of showing disabled controls) so the user cannot use the control.

The following code shows examples of both a read-only and a disabled control. The output of this code is shown in Figure 9-9.

```
<!DOCTYPE html PUBLIC "-//W3C//DTD XHTML 1.0 Strict//EN"
   "http://www.w3.org/TR/xhtml1/DTD/xhtml1-strict.dtd">
<html>
<head>
  <title>Read Only and Disabled Fields</title>
</head>
<body>
  <p>
<form action="formhandler.php" method="post">
<table cellspacing="10" width="600">
  <tr>
    <td width="25%">
    <p>Customer Code (readonly):</p>
    </td><td>
    <input type="text" size="12" value="X234GG"
      name="code" id="code" readonly="readonly">
    </td>
  </tr>
  <tr>
    <td>
    <p>Discount (disabled):</p>
    </td><td>
    <input type="text" size="10" value=""
      name="discount" id="discount" disabled="disabled">
    </td>
  </tr>
```

```
  </table>
  </form>
  </p>
  </body>
  </html>
```

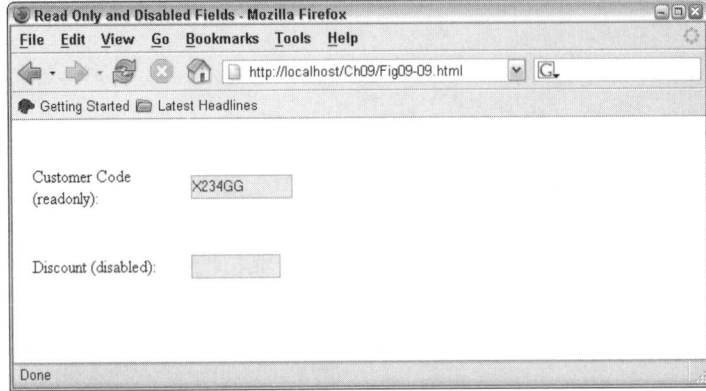

Figure 9-9

Although the two attributes make the fields look similar on-screen, the `readonly` field can be selected but not edited. The `disabled` field cannot be selected at all. You should also note the field's read-only or disabled status in text—whether in the field label or additional text near the field. This courtesy is for non-GUI users or users of agents that do not plainly indicate the field's status.

Summary

This chapter detailed XHTML forms, showing you how to define a form and populate it with appropriate controls for gathering data from users. You learned the basics of form handling and how to create documents to effectively gather and submit data. Parts IV and V of this book cover scripting and give examples of how to create script handlers for various purposes.

Objects and Plugins

The Web isn't just for text anymore. Today's user agents support many different types of data — from sound files to rich multimedia presentations. Including such content in your Web documents is not only welcome but also expected.

Many helpful applications — known as plugins — help extend a user agent's capability. The most popular plugin, Macromedia's Flash Player, allows for complex animation and even full navigation through non-HTML content delivered via the user agent.

This chapter introduces you to the world of non-HTML content, plugins, and how to use them in your documents.

Understanding Plugins

Plugins are small applications that extend the capabilities of user agents by running on the client machine and handling data delivered via HTTP supplied by the user agent. A typical plugin works with a user agent as shown in the diagram in Figure 10-1.

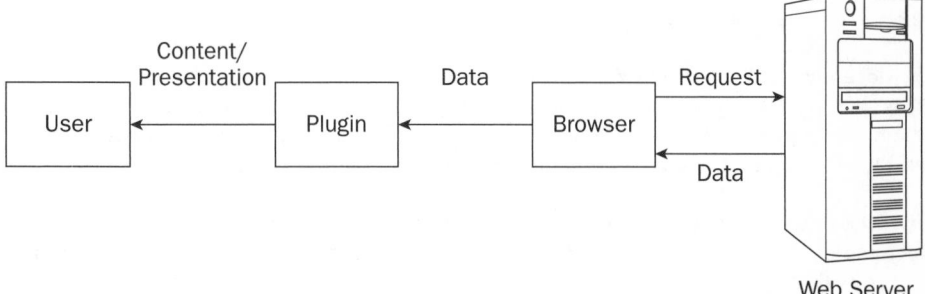

Figure 10-1

The user agent requests the content as normal but receives a file it doesn't know how to deal with. However, it has a plugin registered for the file it receives. The browser launches the plugin and passes the file to the plugin for processing. The plugin presents the data to the user in an environment native to the data while remaining in the browser environment.

Note that plugins are specialized applications requiring the end user to install and maintain them on their system(s). Although plugins (especially Flash and the like) are common on the Web, you should use caution in deciding to use plugin-enabled content in your pages, as it does have an impact on the end user.

The first plugins enabled the Netscape browser to deliver content other than text and basic graphics. The earliest plugins included programs from Macromedia for its Shockwave product and from Adobe for its Acrobat (PDF) product. These programs enabled users to view Shockwave graphic presentations and Adobe PDF files.

Today, plugins are available for almost all types of data. The old standbys are still available (Adobe Acrobat Reader, Macromedia Flash/Shockwave, and so on), but a host of new plugins exists to allow files to be transferred via HTTP and viewed by the end user.

There are other means for user agents to handle nonnative files. For example, Windows users can rely on file associations. If a received file is a registered file type, Windows will automatically spawn the correct application to handle it. However, note that the file is then being handled outside of the user agent, requiring another full application with all the associated overhead.

The Old Way — The Embed Tag

Early versions of HTML used the embed tag (<embed>) to represent non-HTML data within HTML documents. The <embed> tag has the following syntax:

```
<embed src="file_to_embed" name="name_of_embedded_object" width="width_in_pixels"
    height="height_in_pixels" hidden="true|false">
```

For example, the following could be used to embed a MIDI file (jinglebells.mid) in a Web document:

```
<embed src="jinglebells.mid" name="jinglebells">
```

When the document is displayed in Windows Microsoft Internet Explorer, a small media player control appears, as shown in Figure 10-2, and the MIDI file begins to play. Note that the hidden attribute could be used to hide the player from the user and the space the player occupies can be modified with the width and height attributes (but using values that are too small will hide some of the control).

Note, however, that many other platforms will not handle the embedded file as shown in Figure 10-2 — Windows handles it deftly because of the built-in media player control available to applications. Other user agents on other platforms will require a separate plugin to utilize the content. For example, Mozilla Firefox will display a prompt, as shown in Figure 10-3, and will attempt to install Apple's QuickTime player if the user chooses Install Missing Plugins.

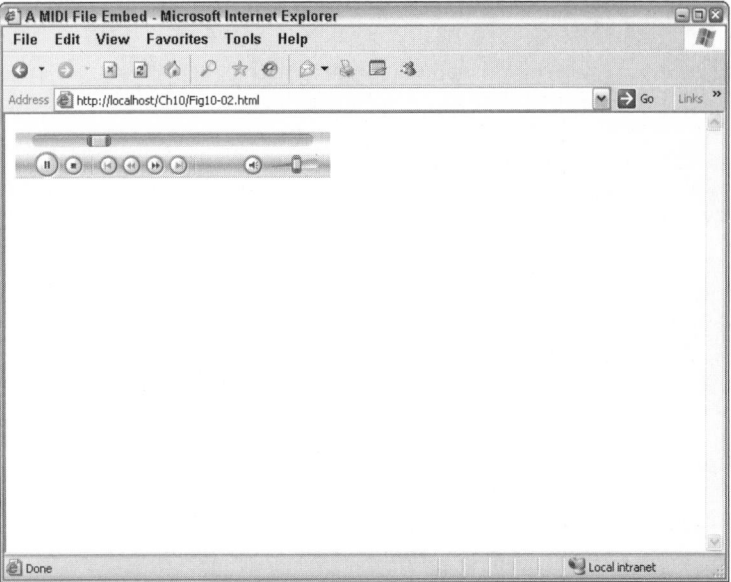

Figure 10-2

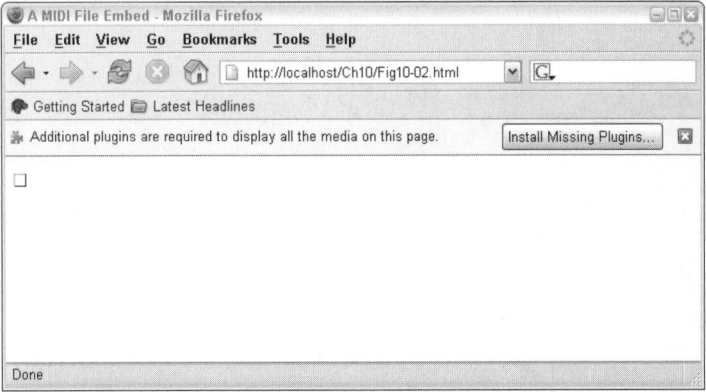

Figure 10-3

Another seldom-used tag for embedding non-HTML content in HTML documents was the **<applet>** *tag. This tag was used mainly to call on a small application (applet) to do something useful with or in addition to the document's contents.*

Later versions of HTML deprecated the <embed> tag, replacing it with the <object> tag, which was designed to be more flexible.

The Object Tag

The object tag (`<object>`) was introduced to replace both the `<embed>` and `<applet>` tag means of embedding objects (non-HTML content) within HTML documents. The `<object>` tag has the following syntax:

```
<object classid="class_id" id="object_id" codebase="base_for_object_code_URI"
    codetype="MIME_type_of_object" width="width_of_object"
    height="height_of_object" >
Alternate_text_for_object
    ...parameters...
</object>
```

The object tag encapsulates alternate text that is used if the object cannot be handled by the destination user agent and parameters defined by parameter tags (`<param>`).

*The **<param>** tag is covered in the next section.*

The object tag's attributes are listed in the following table:

Attribute	Value(s)	Use
archive	URL(s)	URLs to archives related to the object
classid	class_id	A URL to the implementation for the object
codebase	URL	A URL to the location of the code to utilize the object
codetype	MIME type	The MIME type of the object
data	URL	A URL to the object's data
declare	true|false	Determines if the object should only be declared but not initialized (true), or initialized and displayed after loaded (false)
height	pixels|percentage	The displayed height of the object
name	unique_name	A unique name for the object (used in scripting)
standby	text	Defines text to display while the object loads
type	MIME type	The MIME type of the data specified by the data attribute
usemap	URL	Specifies the location of a client-side image map to use with the object
width	pixels|percentage	The displayed width of the object

*The object tag can be used in the **<head>** or **<body>** section of a document. If used in the **<body>**, the object appears where placed in the document and uses the format of its containing block. If it is placed in the head, its positioning is determined by other criteria — options in the **<object>** block, styles dictating object placement, and so on.*

The `classid` and `codebase` attributes are essential — they tell the user agent what plugin should be used to display the content. The `classid` attribute corresponds to the internal identifier of the plugin. For example, on Windows platforms this value is stored in the Windows Registry along with the location of the plugin. The `codebase` attribute points to the Flash player (plugin) that can be downloaded if the plugin isn't already available on the platform.

The rest of the attributes are important to help tailor the appearance of the object (`width`, `height`, `declare`) or to provide the user agent more information about the object's data.

Note that the `<object>` tag can be formatted like any other block tag using CSS.

Parameters

Most objects require parameters to customize their appearance and operation. The `<param>` tag is used within the `<object>` tag to provide the appropriate parameters. The `<param>` tag has the following syntax:

```
<param name="name_of_param" value="value_of_param" type="MIME_type_of_param"
  valuetype="data|ref|object" />
```

*The **<param>** tag has no closing mate. To be XHTML compliant, the tag should end with the slash.*

The `name` and `value` attributes are necessary; they are the two attributes that provide the actual *parameter* for the object. The other attributes are necessary in certain circumstances to help define the type and scope of the parameter.

Multiple parameters can be added to an object by using multiple parameter tags.

Object Examples

More data/media formats are delivered via the Web than can be readily counted. Each of the non-HTML-based formats has its own plugin, format for the `<object>` tag, and parameters. The best way to determine the correct format of the `<object>` tag is to consult the owner of the data format or applicable plugin (Macromedia for Flash content, Apple Computer Inc. for QuickTime, and so on).

Many GUI-based HTML editors include features to help embed non-HTML content in Web documents. For example, Macromedia's Dreamweaver provides several features to embed and control various objects within your documents.

The following two examples show how to embed commonly used data types: a MIDI file and a Flash file.

Example: Adding a MIDI Sound File to a Web Document

Although not as popular as it once was, background music on Web documents is still common. This example shows how to use the `<object>` tag to place a MIDI file (and appropriate media controls) in a Web document.

Source

```
<!DOCTYPE html PUBLIC "-//W3C//DTD XHTML 1.0 Strict//EN"
    "http://www.w3.org/TR/xhtml1/DTD/xhtml1-strict.dtd">
<html>
<head>
  <title>A MIDI Object</title>
</head>
<body>
<p>
<object classid="clsid:22D6F312-B0F6-11D0-94AB-0080C74C7E95" id='jinglebells'
  height="45" width="300" />
  Jingle Bells!
  <param name="autostart" value="true" />
  <param name="filename" value="jinglebells.mid" />
</object>
</p>
</body>
</html>
```

This example will work only on Windows, with Microsoft Internet Explorer or a browser with an appropriate plugin allowing access to the Windows Media Player controls.

Output

The code results in a media player panel being displayed in the document at the <object> tag's location, as shown in Figure 10-4. The MIDI file begins to play as soon as the document is loaded.

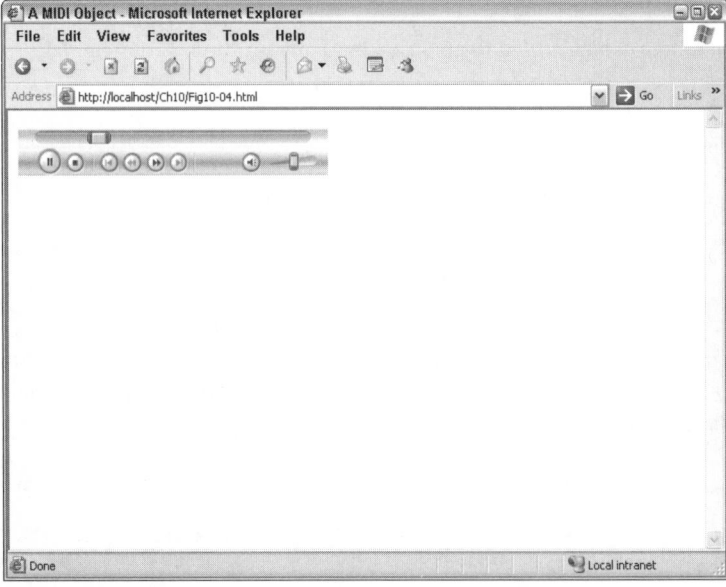

Figure 10-4

Example: Adding Shockwave Flash to a Web Document

Flash content is perhaps the most dominant multimedia content on the Web. This example shows how to use the `<object>` tag to place a Flash animation in a document.

Source

```
<!DOCTYPE html PUBLIC "-//W3C//DTD XHTML 1.0 Strict//EN"
    "http://www.w3.org/TR/xhtml1/DTD/xhtml1-strict.dtd">
<html>
<head>
  <title>A Flash Object</title>
</head>
<body>
<p>
<object classid="clsid:D27CDB6E-AE6D-11cf-96B8-444553540000"
codebase="http://download.macromedia.com/pub/shockwave/cabs/flash/swflash.cab#ve
rsi
on=6,0,40,0" width="150" height="150">
  Radar Screen
  <param name="movie" value="radar.swf" />
  <param name="quality" value="high" />
  <param name="loop" value="1" />
  <param name="play" value="1" />
</object>
</p>
</body>
</html>
```

Output

The preceding document displays as shown in Figure 10-5, with the Flash movie in the place of the `<object>` tag.

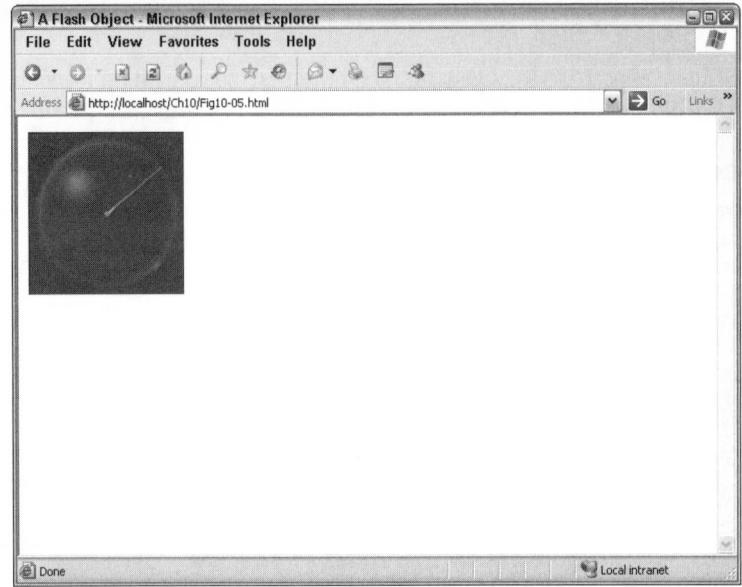

Figure 10-5

Support for Older, Netscape Browsers

Older, Netscape-based browsers do not support the `<object>` tag. If you need to include support for these browsers, you have only one choice — use the `<embed>` tag. However, you shouldn't use only the `<embed>` tag; some newer browsers do not support it. Using both tags is also problematic; some user agents support both tags, resulting in the object data being embedded twice in the document.

The answer is to include an appropriate `<embed>` tag within the `<object>` tag. Newer browsers will ignore the `<embed>` tag because it doesn't belong within the `<object>` tag, while older browsers will ignore the `<object>` and `<param>` tags but will process the `<embed>` tag.

For example, to use `<embed>` with the earlier Flash example, you would use code similar to the following:

```
<object classid="clsid:D27CDB6E-AE6D-11cf-96B8-444553540000"
codebase="http://download.macromedia.com/pub/shockwave/cabs/flash/swflash.cab#versi
on=6,0,40,0" width="150" height="150">
  Radar Screen
  <param name="movie" value="radar.swf" />
  <param name="quality" value="high" />
  <param name="loop" value="1" />
  <param name="play" value="1" />
  <EMBED src="radar.swf" quality="high" width="150" height="150"
    type="application/x-shockwave-flash"
    pluginspage="http://www.macromedia.com/go/getflashplayer" />
</object>
```

Placing the `<embed>` tag within the `<object>` tag will cause newer user agents to ignore it; they will perceive it as an invalid part of the `<object>` block due to its context. Older user agents (that don't support `<object>`) will ignore the `<object>` tags but will recognize and use the embed block. Note that if you place the embed section outside of the object block, the older user agents will still handle it properly, but the newer user agents will understand both tags individually, displaying the object twice.

Use of the **`<embed>`** *tag will cause your code to be non–XHTML compliant.*

Summary

This chapter introduced you to non-HTML content and how you can embed it in your documents. You learned how plugins operate, how to tell the user agent that it needs a plugin, as well as how to pass parameters to the plugin to help control the content.

Unfortunately, multimedia is one of the areas where the user agent market has fragmented. Microsoft builds a lot of functionality into Internet Explorer through the native Windows platform, while other user agents rely on plugins to handle non-HTML content. Properly coding for all cases becomes a chore not easily accomplished. The best advice is to stick to popular formats (such as Flash) or ensure that a plugin exists (and is accessible via your code) for most platforms.

11

XML

The Extensible Markup Language (XML) is a popular scheme for representing data. Although created as a more portable version of SGML, XML lives mostly on the application side of the computer world. XML is used to store preferences and data from applications, provide unified data structure for transferring data, encapsulate syndicated feeds from Web sites, and more. The XML standards are being adopted by other data formats such as HTML (creating XHTML).

This chapter presents a primer on XML, including its format, methods, and tools.

> *Full coverage of XML is outside the scope of this book—full coverage of XML can occupy an entire book of its own. In the case of the Web, XML is a bystander technology, useful to know but not entirely critical for publishing on the Web. However, because XHTML is XML compliant, coverage is mandatory. If you desire more information about XML, you would do well to pick up a book dedicated to the subject, such as WROX Beginning XML, 3rd Edition, WROX XSLT 2.0 Programmer's Reference, 3rd Edition, or Wiley's XML Weekend Crash Course or XML Programming Bible.*

XML Basics

The Extensible Markup Language (XML) was created to bring the advantages of the bloated Standard Generalized Markup Language (SGML) standard to smaller platforms such as Web browsers. XML retains the flexibility of its older sibling but has been redesigned for the Web with the ability to be easily transmitted via the Internet's architecture and displayed with less overhead.

The XML design strategy attempted to address the following points:

❑   Form should follow function. In other words, the language should be flexible enough to encapsulate many types of data. Instead of shoehorning multiple forms of data into one structure, the structure should be able to change to adequately fit the data.

❑   Documents should be easily understood by their content alone. The markup should be constructed in such a way that there is no doubt about the content it frames. XML documents are often referred to as self-describing because of this attribute.

- ❏ Format should be separated from presentation. The markup language should represent the difference in pieces of data only and should make no attempt to describe how the data will be presented. For example, elements should be marked with tags such as <emphasis> instead of <b> (bold), leaving the presentation of the data (which should be emphasized, but not necessarily bold) to the platform using the data.

- ❏ The language should be simple and easily parsed, with intrinsic error checking.

These attributes are evident in the goals stated in the W3C's Recommendation for XML 1.0 (found at http://www.w3.org/TR/1998/REC-xml-19980210):

1. XML shall be straightforwardly usable over the Internet.

2. XML shall support a wide variety of applications.

3. XML shall be compatible with SGML.

4. It shall be easy to write programs that process XML documents.

5. The number of optional features in XML is to be kept to the absolute minimum, ideally zero.

6. XML documents should be human-legible and reasonably clear.

7. The XML design should be prepared quickly.

8. The design of XML shall be formal and concise.

9. XML documents shall be easy to create.

10. Terseness in XML markup is of minimal importance.

As-is, XML is ill-suited for the World Wide Web. Because XML document elements can be author-defined, user agents cannot possibly interpret and display all XML documents in the way the author would have intended. However, standardized XML structures are excellent for storing application data. For example, consider the following applications of XML:

- ❏ The popular RSS syndication format defines particular element tags in XML format to encapsulate syndicated news and blog feeds. This enables many applications to easily disseminate the information contained within the feed.

- ❏ Several online statistic sites (computer game stats, and so on) store their information in XML because it can be easily parsed and understood by a variety of applications.

- ❏ Many applications store their preferences in XML-formatted files. This format proves to be easily parsed, changed, and rewritten, as necessary.

- ❏ Many word processing and other document-based applications (spreadsheets, and so on) store their documents in XML format.

- ❏ Many B2B applications use XML to share and transfer data between each other.

Note that while XML provides an ideal data structure, it should be used only for smaller, sequential collections of data. Data collections that require random access or have thousands of records would benefit from an actual database format instead of XML.

XHTML was designed to bring HTML into XML compliance (each element being properly closed, and so on), not the other way around (add extensibility to HTML). In short, XHTML adheres to XML standards, but it is not itself an extensible markup language.

XML Syntax

XML follows guidelines we have already set forth for XHTML:

❑   Element and attribute names are case sensitive.

❑   All elements must be properly closed.

❑   Elements must be properly nested, not overlapping.

❑   All attributes must have values.

❑   All attribute values must be quoted.

Within documents, the structure is similar to that of HTML, where element tags are used to encapsulate content that may itself contain tag-delimited content.

The following sections outline the particular syntax of the various XML document elements.

XML Declaration and DOCTYPE

Each XML document should begin with an XML declaration similar to the following:

```
<?xml version="1.0" encoding="UTF-8"?>
```

The declaration is `<?xml?>`, with `version` and `encoding` attributes. The `version` attribute specifies the version of XML the document uses, and the `encoding` attribute specifies the character encoding used within the document's content.

As with other markup languages, XML supports document type definitions (DTDs), which specify the rules used for the elements within documents using the DTD. Applications can then use the DTD to check the document's syntax. An XML document's DTD declaration resembles that of an XHTML document, specifying a SYSTEM or PUBLIC definition. For example, the following DTD is used for OpenOffice documents:

```
<!DOCTYPE office:document-content PUBLIC
   "-//OpenOffice.org//DTD OfficeDocument 1.0//EN" "office.dtd">
```

The following is an example of an XHTML document's DTD definition:

```
<!DOCTYPE html PUBLIC "-//W3C//DTD XHTML 1.0 Strict//EN"
   "http://www.w3.org/TR/xhtml1/DTD/xhtml1-strict.dtd">
```

Elements

XML elements resemble XHTML elements. However, due to the nature of XML (extensible), elements are generally not of the HTML variety. For example, consider the following snippet from an RSS feed, presented in XML format:

```xml
<?xml version="1.0" ?>
<rss version="2.0">
  <channel>
    <title>Liftoff News</title>
    <link>http://liftoff.msfc.nasa.gov/</link>
    <description>Liftoff to Space Exploration.</description>
    <language>en-us</language>
    <pubDate>Tue, 10 Jun 2003 04:00:00 GMT</pubDate>
    <item>
      <title>Star City</title>
      <link>http://liftoff.msfc.nasa.gov/news/2003/news-starcity.asp</link>
      <description>How do Americans get ready to work with Russians aboard the
 International Space Station? They take a crash course in culture, language and
protocol at Russia's <a href="http://howe.iki.rssi.ru/GCTC/gctc_e.htm">Star
City</a>.</description>
      <pubDate>Tue, 03 Jun 2003 09:39:21 GMT</pubDate>
    </item>
    <item>
      <description>Sky watchers in Europe, Asia, and parts of Alaska and Canada
will experience a <a
href="http://science.nasa.gov/headlines/y2003/30may_solareclipse.htm">partial
eclipse of the Sun</a> on Saturday, May 31st.</description>
      <pubDate>Fri, 30 May 2003 11:06:42 GMT</pubDate>
    </item>
  </channel>
</rss>
```

In this case, the following elements are used. `<channel>`, the container for the channel (that is, the feed itself), has the following subcontainers:

❑   `<title>` — the title of the channel or feed

❑   `<link>` — the link to the feed on the Web

❑   `<description>` — the description of the feed

❑   `<language>` — the language of the feed's content

❑   `<pubDate>` — the publication date for this feed

The feed then encapsulates each news item within an `<item>` element, which has the following subelements:

❑   `<title>` — the title of the item

❑   `<link>` — a link to the item on the Web

❑   `<description>` — a short description of the item

❑   `<pubDate>` — the publication date of the item

Note that several elements have multiple contexts. For example, the `<channel>` and `<item>` elements both provide context for `<title>` elements; the placement of each `<title>` element (usually its parent) determines what element the `<title>` refers to.

Attributes

XML elements support attributes much like XHTML. Again, the difference is that the attributes can be defined in accordance with the document's purpose. For example, consider the following code snippet:

```
<employee sex="female">
  <lastName>Moore</lastName>
  <firstName>Terri</firstName>
  <hireDate>2003-02-20</hireDate>
</employee>
<employee sex="male">
  <lastName>Robinson</lastName>
  <firstName>Branden</firstName>
  <hireDate>2000-04-30</hireDate>
</employee>
```

In this example, the sex of the employee is coded as an attribute of the `<employee>` tag.

In most cases, the use of attributes instead of elements is arbitrary. For example, the preceding example could have been coded with sex as a child element instead of as an attribute:

```
<employee>
  <sex>female</sex>
  <lastName>Moore</lastName>
  <firstName>Terri</firstName>
  <hireDate>2003-02-20</hireDate>
</employee>
<employee>
  <sex>male</sex>
  <lastName>Robinson</lastName>
  <firstName>Branden</firstName>
  <hireDate>2000-04-30</hireDate>
</employee>
```

The mitigating factor in deciding how to code data is whether the content is ever to be used as data, instead of just a modifier. If an application will use the content as data, it's best to code it within an element where it is more easily parsed as such.

Comments

XML supports the same comment tag as HTML:

```
<!-- comment_text -->
```

You can embed comments anywhere inside an XML document as long as the standard XML conventions and corresponding DTD rules are not violated by doing so.

Nonparsed Data

On occasion, you will need to define content that should not be parsed (interpreted by the application reading the data). Such data is defined as character data or CDATA. Nonparsed data is formatted within a CDATA element, which has the following syntax:

```
<!CDATA [non_parsed_data]]>
```

CDATA elements are generally used to improve the legibility of documents by placing reserved characters within a CDATA element instead of using cryptic entities. For example, both of the following paragraph elements result in identical data, but the first is more legible due to the CDATA elements:

```
<p>The &lt;table&gt; element should be used instead of the &lt;pre&gt; element
whenever possible.</p>

<p>The <!CDATA [<table>]]> element should be used instead of the <!CDATA [<pre>]]>
Element whenever possible.</p>
```

Entities

XML also allows for user-defined entities. Entities are content mapped to mnemonics; the mnemonics can then be used as shorthand for the content within the rest of the document. Entities are defined using the following syntax:

```
<!ENTITY entity_name "entity_value">
```

Entities are defined within a document's DTD. For example, the following document prologue defines "Acme, Inc." as the entity company:

```
<?xml version="1.0"?>
<!DOCTYPE report SYSTEM "/xml/dtds/reports.dtd" [
  <!ENTITY company "Acme, Inc.">
]>
```

Elsewhere in the document, the entity (referenced by &entityname;) can be used to insert the company name:

```
<report>
  <title>TPS Report</title>
  <date>2005-01-25</date>
  <summary>The latest run of the regression test have yielded perfect results. The
job for &company; can now determinately be completed and final code
delivered.</summary>
  ...
```

Entities can also be declared as external resources. Such external resources are generally larger than a few words or a phrase, like complete documents. A system entity, used for declaring external resources, is defined using the following syntax:

```
<!ENTITY entity_name SYSTEM "URL">
```

For example, the following code defines a `chapter01` entity that references a local document named `chapter01.xml`:

```
<!ENTITY chapter01 SYSTEM "chapter01.xml">
```

The `chapter01` entity can then be used to insert the contents of `chapter01.xml` in the current document.

Namespaces

The concept of namespaces is relatively new to XML; they allow you to group elements together by their purpose using a unique name. Such groupings can serve a variety of purposes, but they are commonly used to distinguish elements from one another.

For example, an element named `<table>` can refer to a data construct or a physical object (such as a dining room table):

```
<!-- Data construct -->
<table>
  <tr><th>Date</th><th>Customer</th><th>Amount</th></tr>
  <tr><td>2005-01-25</td><td>Acme, Inc</td><td>125.61</td></tr>
...
</table>

<!-- Home furnishing -->
<table>
  <type>Dining</type>
  <width>4</width>
  <length>8</width>
  <color>Cherry</color>
</table>
```

If both elements are used in the same document, there will be a conflict because the two refer to two totally different things. This is a perfect place to specify namespaces.

Namespace designations are added as prefixes to element names. For example, you could use a furniture namespace to identify the table elements that refer to furnishings:

```
<furniture:table>
  <type>Dining</type>
  <width>4</width>
  <length>8</width>
  <color>Cherry</color>
</furniture:table>
```

Style Sheets

XML also offers support for style sheets. Style sheets are linked to XML documents using the `xml-stylesheet` tag, which has the following syntax:

```
<?xml-stylesheet type="mime_type" href="url_to_stylesheet"?>
```

For example, to link a CSS style sheet to a document, you could use a tag similar to the following:

```
<?xml-stylesheet type="text/css" href="mystyles.css"?>
```

Using XML

Actual use of an XML document requires that the document be transformed into a usable format. There are many means and formats to translate XML — the limits are governed only by your imagination and tools at hand.

Viewing XML documents doesn't require special tools. Many of the modern user agents can view XML documents and even add capabilities such as tag highlighting and the ability to collapse portions of the document, as shown in Figure 11-1, where Internet Explorer is displaying an RSS document.

Collapsed elements

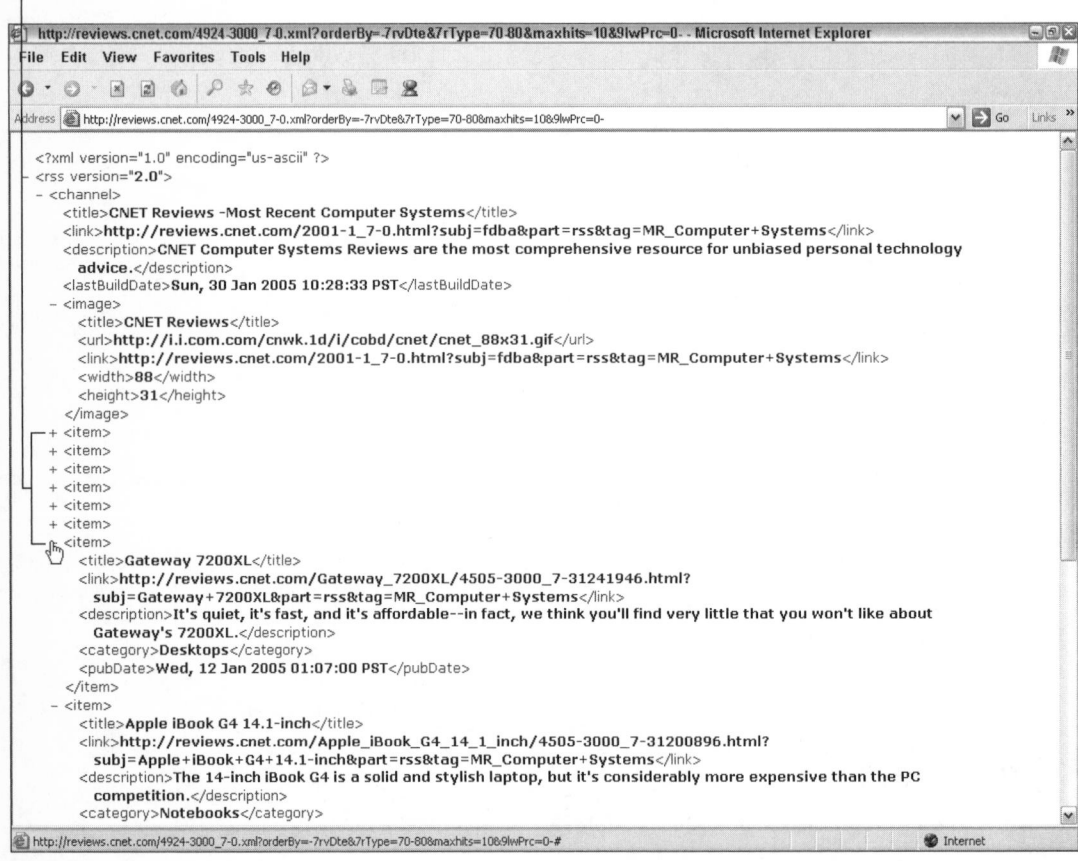

Figure 11-1

Extensible Stylesheet Language Transformations (XSLT)

The Extensible Stylesheet Language transforms XML documents into formatted documents and can also rearrange document contents to generate new document elements. XSLT takes two items as its input, the XML document (sometimes referred to as the *source tree*) and a style sheet to determine the transformation. The output document (sometimes referred to as the *result tree*) is in the desired format ready for output to the desired device.

There are many tools that can help you manage XML documents and perform XSLT, including many open source solutions (search for "XSLT" on `sourceforge.org`).

XML Editing

You have many choices for editing XML files. Because XML is a text-only format, you can use any text editor (emac, vi, notepad, and so on) to create and edit XML documents. However, dedicated XML editors make the editing job easier by adding syntax highlighting, syntax checking, validation, auto-code completion, and more.

- ❑ Many open source XML editors are available (search "XML editor" on `sourceforge.net`).

- ❑ Lennart Staflin has developed a major mode for Emacs called PSGML (`http://www.lysator.liu.se/projects/about_psgml.html`).

- ❑ XMetal — formerly owned by Corel, now owned by Blast Radius — is a well-known, capable (albeit commercial and expensive) XML editor (`http://www.xmetal.com`).

- ❑ XMLSpy, by Altova, is another capable XML editor in the same price range as XMetal, though the personal edition is free (`http://www.altova.com`).

- ❑ <oXygen/>, by SyncRO Soft Ltd., is a lower-cost, multiplatform XML editor and XSLT debugger (`http://www.oxygenxml.com`).

XML Parsing

You may choose to use XML to store various types of data, or you may have the need to access other people's data that is stored in XML.

Many XML parsing applications are available, including many open source applications (search for "XML parsing" on `sourceforge.org`). In addition, there are XML parsing modules for most programming languages:

- ❑ James Clark's XML parser, expat, is well-known as the standard for XML parsing (`http://expat.sourceforge.net` and `http://www.jclark.com/xml/expat.html`).

- ❑ Many XML modules are available for Perl via CPAN (`http://www.cpan.org`).

- ❑ Several XML tools are available for Python, including the many found at the Python Web site (`http://pyxml.sourceforge.net/topics`).

❏   PHP has a handful of XML functions built in as extensions to support expat (`http://www.php .net/manual/en/ref.xml.php`).

❏   The PHP Extension and Application Repository has several additional extensions for XML maintenance and manipulation (`http://pear.php.net`).

Summary

This chapter covered the basics of XML, its format, structure, and use. The basics of creating and maintaining an XML document and tools for working with XML data were all covered. You should now have a basic understanding of the standard and how it is affecting other data schemes and Web technologies.

CSS Basics

In the grand scheme that is the World Wide Web, Cascading Style Sheets (CSS) are a relatively new invention. The Web was founded on HTML and plain text documents. Over the last few years, the Web has become a household mainstay and has matured into a viable publishing platform thanks in no small part to CSS.

CSS enables Web authors and programmers to finely tune elements for publishing both online and across several different types of media, including print format. This chapter serves as the introduction to CSS. Subsequent chapters in this section will show you how to use styles with specific elements.

The Purpose of Styles

Styles are an electronic publishing invention for dynamically coding text and other document elements with formatting. For example, a style called "Heading" would be attached to every heading in the document. The style definition would contain information on how headings should be formatted. In this book, for example, headings (such as "The Purpose of Styles," above) use a larger, bold font.

The advantage of styles is that you can change the definition once and the change affects every element using that style. Coding each element individually, by contrast, would require that each element be recoded when you wanted them all to change. Thus, styles provide an easy means to update document formatting and maintain consistency across a site.

Also, coding individual elements is best done while the document is being created. This means that the document must be formatted by the author — not always the best choice. Instead, the elements can be tagged with appropriate styles (such as `heading`) while the document is created, and the final formatting can be left up to another individual who defines the styles.

Styles can be grouped into purpose-driven style sheets. *Style sheets* are just that, groups of styles relating to a common purpose. Style sheets allow for multiple styles to be attached to a document all at once. It also allows for all the style formatting in a document to be changed at once. This allows documents to be quickly formatted for different purposes — one style sheet can be used for online documents, another for brochures, and so on.

Styles and HTML

For a tangible example using XHTML, consider the following code:

```
<p><b><u>Heading One</u></b></p>
<p>Lorem ipsum dolor sit amet, consectetur adipisicing elit, sed do eiusmod tempor
incididunt ut labore et dolore magna aliqua. Ut enim ad minim veniam, quis nostrud
exercitation ullamco laboris nisi ut aliquip ex ea commodo consequat.</p>
<p><b><u>Heading Two</u></b></p>
<p>Lorem ipsum dolor sit amet, consectetur adipisicing elit, sed do eiusmod tempor
incididunt ut labore et dolore magna aliqua. Ut enim ad minim veniam, quis nostrud
exercitation ullamco laboris nisi ut aliquip ex ea commodo consequat.</p>
<p><b><u>Heading Three</u></b></p>
<p>Lorem ipsum dolor sit amet, consectetur adipisicing elit, sed do eiusmod tempor
incididunt ut labore et dolore magna aliqua. Ut enim ad minim veniam, quis nostrud
exercitation ullamco laboris nisi ut aliquip ex ea commodo consequat.</p>
```

For the purpose of this example, ignore the fact that most of the text formatting tags (underline, center, and so on) have been deprecated.

Note that all three headings are coded bold and underlined. Now suppose that you wanted the headings to be larger and italic. Each heading would have to be recoded similar to the following:

```
<p><font size="+2"><i>Heading One</i></font></p>
```

Although using a decent editor with global search and replace makes this change pretty easy, consider managing an entire site, with several documents — if not tens or hundreds — each with several headings. Each document makes the change exponentially harder.

Now, let's look at how styles would change the example. Using styles, the example could be coded similarly to the following:

```
<p class="heading">Heading One</p>
<p>Lorem ipsum dolor sit amet, consectetur adipisicing elit, sed do eiusmod tempor
incididunt ut labore et dolore magna aliqua. Ut enim ad minim veniam, quis nostrud
exercitation ullamco laboris nisi ut aliquip ex ea commodo consequat.</p>
<p class="heading">Heading Two</p>
<p>Lorem ipsum dolor sit amet, consectetur adipisicing elit, sed do eiusmod tempor
incididunt ut labore et dolore magna aliqua. Ut enim ad minim veniam, quis nostrud
exercitation ullamco laboris nisi ut aliquip ex ea commodo consequat.</p>
<p class="heading">Heading Three</p>
<p>Lorem ipsum dolor sit amet, consectetur adipisicing elit, sed do eiusmod tempor
incididunt ut labore et dolore magna aliqua. Ut enim ad minim veniam, quis nostrud
exercitation ullamco laboris nisi ut aliquip ex ea commodo consequat.</p>
```

There are several ways to apply styles to document elements. Various ways to define and use styles are covered in Chapter 13.

The style is defined in the head section of the document, similar to the following:

```
<head>
  <style type="text/css">
    p.heading { font-weight: bold; text-decoration: underline; }
  </style>
</head>
```

This definition defines a `heading` class that formats text as bold and underlined.

Style definitions are covered in Chapter 13. Style properties are covered in appropriate chapters ("Text," and so on) later in this part of the book.

To change all the headings in the document to a larger, italic font, the *one* definition can be recoded:

```
<head>
  <style type="text/css">
    p.heading { font-size: larger; font-style: italic; }
  </style>
</head>
```

CSS Levels 1, 2, and 3

There are three levels of CSS — two levels are actual specifications while the third level is in recommendation status. The main differences between the three levels are as follows:

❑　CSS1 defines basic style functionality, with limited font and limited positioning support.

❑　CSS2 adds aural properties, paged media, and better font and positioning support. Many other properties have been refined as well.

❑　CSS3 adds presentation-style properties, allowing you to effectively build presentations from Web documents (similar to Microsoft PowerPoint presentations).

You don't have to specify the level of CSS you are using. However, you should be conscientious about what user agents will be accessing your site. Most modern browsers support CSS, but the level of support varies dramatically between user agents. It's always best to test your implementation on target user agents before widely deploying your documents.

When using styles, it is important to keep in mind that not all style properties are well supported by all user agents. This book attempts to point out major inconsistencies and differences in the most popular user agents, but the playing field is always changing. One invaluable reference for style compatibility is Brian Wilson's excellent resources at **http://www.blooberry.com/indexdot/index.html**.

Defining Styles

Styles can be defined in several different ways and attached to a document. The most popular method for defining styles is to add a style block to the head of a document:

```
<head>
  <style type="text/css">
    Style definitions
  </style>
</head>
```

Using this method, all style definitions are placed within a style element, delimited by `<style>` tags. The opening style tag has the following syntax:

```
<style type="MIME_type" media="destination_media">
```

In most cases, the MIME type is "text/css." The `media` attribute is typically not used unless the destination media is nontextual. The `media` attribute supports the following values:

- ❏   all
- ❏   aural
- ❏   braille
- ❏   embossed
- ❏   handheld
- ❏   print
- ❏   projection
- ❏   screen
- ❏   tty
- ❏   tv

Note that multiple definitions, each defining a style for a different medium, can appear in the same document. This powerful feature allows you to easily define styles for a variety of document usage and deployment.

Alternately, the style sheet can be contained in a separate document and linked to documents using the link (`<link>`) tag:

```
<head>
  <link rel="stylesheet" type="text/css" href="mystyles.css" />
</head>
```

The style sheet document, `mystyles.css`, contains the necessary styles:

```
p.heading { font-size: larger; font-style: italic; }
```

Then, when the style definitions in the external style sheet change, *all* documents that link to the external sheet reflect the change. This presents an easy way to modify a document's format — whether to affect new formatting for visual sake or for a specific purpose.

Attaching external style sheets via the link tag should be your preferred method of applying styles to a document, as it provides the most scalable use of styles — you have to change only *one* external style sheet to affect many documents.

You can add comments to your style section or style sheet by delimiting the comment with /* and */. For example, the following is a style comment:

/* Define a heading style with a border */

Cascading Styles

So where does the "cascading" in Cascading Style Sheets come from? It comes from the fact that styles can stack, or override, each other. For example, suppose that an internal corporate Web site's appearance varies depending on the department that owns the various documents. It is important that all the documents follow the corporate look and feel, but the Human Resources department might use people-shaped bullets or other small changes unique to that department. The HR department doesn't need a separate, complete style sheet for its documents. The department needs only a sheet containing the differences from the corporate sheet. For example, consider the following two style sheet fragments:

corporate.css

```
body {
   font-family:verdana, palatino,  georgia,  arial, sans-serif;
   font-size:10pt;
}

p {
   font-family:verdana, palatino,  georgia,  arial, sans-serif;
   font-size:10pt;
}

p.quote {
   font-family:verdana, palatino,  georgia,  arial, sans-serif;
   font-size:10pt;
   border: solid thin black;
   background: #5A637B;
   padding: .75em;
}

h1, h2, h3 {
   margin: 0px;
   padding: 0px;
}

ul {
   list-style-image: url("images/corp-bullet.png")
}
...
```

humanresources.css

```
ul {
    list-style-image: url("images/hr-bullet.png")
}
```

The `humanresources.css` sheet contains only the style definitions that differ from the `corporate.css` sheet, in this case, only a definition for `ul` elements (using the different bullet). The two sheets are linked to the HR documents using the following `<link>` tags:

```
<head>
    <link rel="stylesheet" type="text/css" href="corporate.css" />
    <link rel="stylesheet" type="text/css" href="humanresources.css" />
</head>
```

When a user agent encounters multiple styles that could be applied to the same element, it uses CSS rules of precedence, covered later in this section.

Likewise, other departments would have their own style sheets, and their documents would link to the corporate and individual department sheets. As another example, the engineering department might use their own style sheet and declare it in the head of their documents:

```
<head>
    <link rel="stylesheet" type="text/css" href="corporate.css" />
    <link rel="stylesheet" type="text/css" href="engineering.css" />
</head>
```

Furthermore, individual XHTML elements can contain styles themselves:

```
<ul style="list-style-image: url("images/small-bullet.png");" >
```

The styles embedded in elements take precedence over all previously declared styles.

CSS refers to the location of declarations as follows:

❑   **Author** origin — The author of a document includes styles in a `<style>` section or linked sheets (via `<link>`).

❑   **User** origin — The user (viewer of document) specifies a style sheet.

❑   **User Agent** origin — The user agent specifies default style sheet (when no other exists).

Styles that are critical to the document's presentation should be coded as important by placing the text **!important** *at the end of the declaration. For example, the following style is marked as important:*

```
<ul style="list-style-image: url("images/small-bullet.png"); !important" >
```

Such styles are treated differently from normal styles when the correct style to use is determined from the cascade.

The CSS standard uses the following rules to determine which style to use when multiple styles exist for an element:

1. Find all style declarations from all origins that apply to the element.

2. For normal declarations, author style sheets override user style sheets, which override the default style sheet. For !important style declarations, user style sheets override author style sheets, which override the default style sheet.

3. More specific declarations take precedence over less specific declarations.

4. Styles specified last have precedence over otherwise equal styles.

Summary

This chapter taught you the basics of CSS—how styles are attached to a document, how they are best used, what the different levels of CSS are, and how the *cascade* in Cascading Style Sheets works. You learned the various ways to embed and define styles and more about the separation between content and formatting that CSS can provide. Chapter 13 delves into the ins and outs of style definitions. Subsequent chapters in this part of the book will show you how styles are best used with various elements.

13

Style Definitions

By this point in the book, you should recognize the power, consistency, and versatility that styles can bring to your documents. You have seen how styles can make format changes easier and how they adhere to the content versus formatting separation. Now it's time to learn how to create styles — the syntax and methods used to define styles for your documents.

The Style Definition Format

CSS style definitions all follow this format:

```
selector_expression  {
  element_property: property_value(s);
  element_property: property_value(s);
  ...
}
```

The selector_expression is an expression that can be used to match specific elements in the document. Its simplest form is an element's name, such as h1 to match all <h1> elements. At its most complex, you can match individual subelements of particular elements or elements that have particular relationships to other elements.

Selectors are covered in depth within the next section of this chapter.

The element_property specifies which properties of the element the definition will affect. For example, to change the color of an element, the color property is used. Note that some properties affect only one aspect of an element, while others combine several properties into one declaration. For example, the border property can be used to define the width, style, and color of an element's border; each of the properties (width, style, color) has its own property declarations, as well (border-width, border-style, and border-color).

Individual properties are covered within chapters relating to the type of element they affect. For example, the font properties are covered in the next chapter, "Text."

The `property_values(s)` specify how the property should affect the element to which it applies. For example, to specify an element's color as red, you would use the value `red` as the property value for the color property.

More information on property values can be found in the "Property Values" section later in this chapter.

Now let's look at the elements of a style declaration in a real example. The following style definition can be used to change all the heading-one (`<h1>`) elements in a document to have red text:

```
h1  {
   color: red;
}
```

The actual formatting of the style declarations can vary. The syntax is as follows:

```
declaration { property:value; property:value; property:value;... }
```

The declaration should be separated from the left brace (which begins the property/value section) by white space, and each property/value pair should end in a semicolon. The property/value pair section ends in a right brace. Extra white space can appear between all elements, and the amount of white space (whether spaces, new lines, or tabs) doesn't matter. For example, both of the following definitions produce identical results, but they are formatted quite differently:

```
h1 { color: red; border: thin dotted black; font-family: helvetica, sans-serif;
text-align: right; }

h1 {
   font-family: helvetica, sans-serif;
   border: thin dotted black;
   text-align: right;
   color: red;

}
```

Property Values

Throughout this chapter, you will see how to apply values to properties using CSS. First, it is important to talk a bit about the values themselves. Property values can be expressed in several different metrics according to the individual property and the desired result.

CSS supports the following metrics for property values:

❑ CSS keywords and other properties, such as thin, thick, transparent, ridge, and so forth

❑ Real-world measures

    ❑ Inches (in)

    ❑ Centimeters (cm)

    ❑ Millimeters (mm)

❏   Points (pt) — The points used by CSS2 are equal to 1/72 of an inch

❏   Picas (pc) — 1 pica is equal to 12 points

❏   Screen measures in pixels (px)

❏   Relational to font size (font size (em) or x-height size (ex))

❏   Percentages (%)

❏   Color codes (`#rrggbb` or `rgb(r,g,b)`)

❏   Angles

❏   Degrees (deg)

❏   Grads (grad)

❏   Radians (rad)

❏   Time values (seconds (s) and milliseconds (ms)) — Used with aural style sheets

❏   Frequencies (hertz (Hz) and kilohertz (kHz)) — Used with aural style sheets

❏   Textual strings

Which metric is used depends on the value you are setting and your desired effect. For example, it doesn't make sense to use real-world measures (inches, centimeters, and so on) unless the user agent is calibrated to use such measures or your document is meant to be printed. The em unit can be quite powerful, allowing a value that changes as the element sizes change. However, using the em unit can have unpredictable results. The em metric is best used when you need a relational, not absolute, value.

In the case of relational property values (percentages, em, and so on), the value is calculated on the element's parent values.

Understanding Selectors

Selectors are essentially patterns that enable a user agent to identify what elements get what styles. For example, the following style in effect says, "If it is a paragraph tag, give it this style":

```
p { text-indent: 2em; }
```

*The selector is the first element before the brace, in this case, **p** (which matches the **<p>** tag).*

This section shows you how to construct selectors of different types to best match styles to your elements within your documents.

Matching Elements by Name

The easiest selector to understand is the plain element selector, as in the following example:

```
h1 { color: red; }
```

Using the actual element name (h1) as the selector causes all occurrences of those tags to be formatted with the property/values section of the definition (color: red). You can also specify multiple selectors by listing them all in the selector area, separated by commas. For example, this definition will affect all levels of heading tags in the document:

```
h1, h2, h3, 4h, h5, h6 { color: red; }
```

Matching Using the Universal Selector

The universal selector can be used to match any element in the document. The universal selector is an asterisk (*). As an extreme example, you can use the universal selector to match *every* tag in a document:

```
* { color: red; }
```

Every tag will have the color: red property/value applied to it. Of course, you would rarely want a definition to apply to all elements of a document — you can also use the universal selector to match other elements of the selector. The following selector matches any <ol> tag that is a descendant of a <td> tag, which is a descendant of a <tr> tag:

```
tr td ol  { color: red; }
```

More information on child/descendant selectors can be found in the "Matching Child, Descendant, and Adjacent Sibling Elements" section later in this chapter.

However, this selector rule is very strict, requiring all three elements. If you also wanted to include descendant <ol> elements of <td> elements, you would need to specify a separate selector or use the universal selector to match all elements between <tr> and <ol>, as in the following example:

```
tr * ol  { color: red; }
```

In essence, the universal selector is a wildcard, used to represent any one or more elements. For example, the selector immediately preceding would also match <ol> elements embedded within a paragraph element within a cell, within a row (tr td p ol). You can use the universal selector with any of the selector forms discussed in this chapter.

Matching Elements by Class

You can also use selectors to define element classes, which can be adopted by any element. Suppose that you had two areas on your page with different backgrounds, one light and one dark. You would want to use dark-colored text within the light background area and light-colored text within the dark background area. You could then define light_area and dark_area classes to ensure that the appropriate text styles were applied within the areas.

To specify a class to match with a selector, you append a period and the class name to the selector. For example, this style will match any paragraph tag with a class of dark_area:

```
p.dark_area  { color: white; }
```

For example, suppose that this paragraph was in the area of the document with the dark background:

```
<p class="dark_area">Lorem ipsum dolor sit amet, consectetuer
adipiscing elit, sed diam nonummy nibh euismod tincidunt ut
laoreet dolore magna aliquam erat volutpat. Ut wisi enim ad
minim veniam, quis nostrud exerci tation ullamcorper suscipit
lobortis nisl ut aliquip ex ea commodo consequat.</p>
```

The specification of the dark_area class with the paragraph tag will cause the paragraph's text to be rendered in white.

The universal selector can be used to match multiple elements with a given class. For example, the following style definition will apply to *all* elements that specify the dark_area class:

```
*.dark_area   { color: white; }
```

You can also omit the universal selector, specifying only the class itself (beginning with a period):

```
.dark_area   { color: white; }
```

You could also take the example one step further, specifying the background and foreground in the same style:

```
.dark_area   { color: white;
               background-color: blue; }
```

Matching Elements by Identifier

You can also match element identifiers (the id attribute). To match identifiers, you use the pound sign (#) in the selector as a prefix for the id. For example, the following style will match any tag that has an id attribute of comment:

```
#comment { background-color: green; }
...
<p id="comment">This paragraph is a comment.</p>
```

Matching Elements by Specific Attributes

You can use a selector to match any attribute in elements, not just class and id. To do so, you specify the attribute and the value(s) you want to match at the end of the selector, offset in square brackets. This form of the selector has the following format:

```
element[attribute="value"]
```

For example, if you want to match any table with a border attribute set to 3, you could use this selector:

```
table[border="3"]
```

You can also match elements that contain the attribute no matter what the value of the attribute by omitting the equal sign and attribute value. To match any table with a `border` attribute, you could use this selector:

```
table[border]
```

*Combine two or more selector formats for even more specificity. For example, the following selector will match table elements with a **class** value of **datalist** and a **border** value of **3**:*

```
table.datalist[border="3"]
```

You can also specify multiple attributes for more specificity. Each attribute is specified in its own bracketed expression. For example, if you wanted to match tables with a `border` value of 3 and a `width` value of 100%, you could use this selector:

```
table[border="3"][width="100%"]
```

You can also match single values within a space- or hyphen-separated list value. To match a value in a space-separated list, use tilde equal (~=) instead of the usual equal sign (=). To match a value in a hyphen-separated list, you use bar equal (|=) instead of the usual equal sign (=). For example, the following selector would match any attribute that has "us" in a space-separated value of the language attribute:

```
[language~="us"]
```

Matching Child, Descendant, and Adjacent Sibling Elements

The most powerful selector methods match elements by their relationships with other elements. For example, you can specify a selector style that matches italic elements only when appearing within a heading, or list items only within ordered lists.

Understanding Document Hierarchy

The elements in an XHTML document are related hierarchically to the other elements in the document. The hierarchy follows the same nomenclature as family trees — ancestors, parents, children, descendants, and siblings. For example, consider the following code and Figure 13-1, which shows a document and its hierarchy.

```
<html>
<body>
<div class="div1">
  <h1>Heading 1</h1>
  <table>
    <tr><td>Cell 1</td><td>Cell 2</td></tr>
    <tr><td>Cell 3</td><td>Cell 4</td></tr>
  </table>
  <p>Lorem ipsum dolor sit amet, consectetuer adipiscing
  elit, sed diam nonummy nibh euismod tincidunt ut laoreet
  dolore magna aliquam erat volutpat. Ut wisi enim ad minim
```

```
    veniam, quis nostrud exerci tation ullamcorper suscipit
    lobortis nisl ut aliquip ex ea commodo consequat.</p>
</div>
<div class="div2">
    <h1>Heading 2</h1>
    <p>Lorem ipsum dolor sit amet, consectetuer adipiscing
    elit, sed diam nonummy nibh euismod tincidunt ut laoreet
    dolore magna aliquam erat volutpat. Ut wisi enim ad minim
    veniam, quis nostrud exerci tation ullamcorper suscipit
    lobortis nisl ut aliquip ex ea commodo consequat.</p>
    <ol>An ordered list
      <li>First element
      <li>Second element
      <li>Third element
    </ol>
</div>
</body>
</html>
```

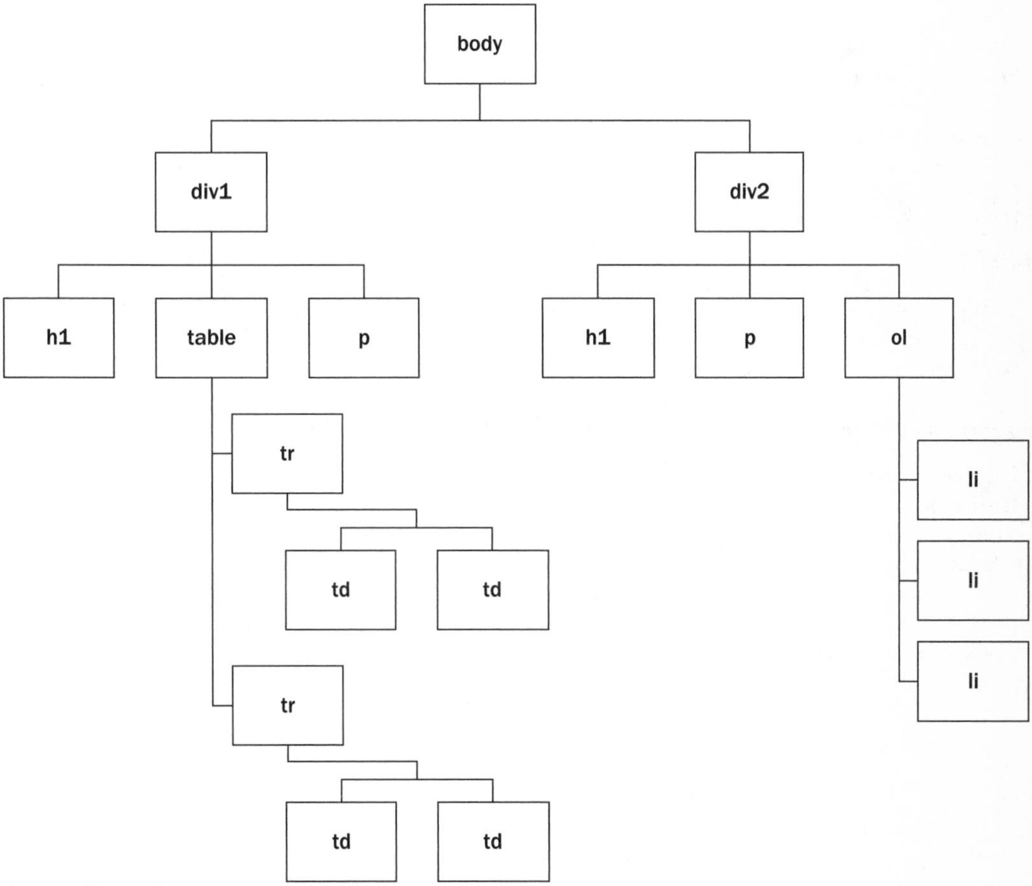

Figure 13-1

Ancestors and Descendants

Ancestors and descendants are elements that are linked by lineage, no matter the distance. For example, in Figure 13-1 the list elements under `div2` are descendants of the body element, and the body element is their ancestor, even though multiple elements separate the two.

Parents and Children

Parents and children are elements that are directly connected in lineage. For example, in Figure 13-1 the table rows (`<tr>`) under `div1` are children of the table element, which is their parent.

Siblings

Siblings are children that share the same, direct parent. In Figure 13-1, the list elements under `div2` are siblings of each other. The header, paragraph, and table elements are also siblings because they share the same, direct parent (`div1`).

Selecting by Hierarchy

You can use several selector mechanisms to match elements by their hierarchy in the document.

To specify ancestor and descendant relationships, you list all involved elements separated by spaces. For example, the following selector matches the list elements in Figure 13-1 (`li` elements within a `div` with a class of `div2`):

```
div.div2 li
```

To specify parent and child relationships, list all involved elements separated by a right angle bracket (>). For example, the following selector matches the table element in Figure 13-1 (a table element that is a direct descendant of a `div` with a class of `div1`):

```
div.div1 > table
```

To specify sibling relationships, list all involved elements separated by plus signs (+). For example, the following selector matches the paragraph element under `div1` in Figure 13-1 (a paragraph that has a sibling relationship with a table):

```
table + p
```

You can mix and match the hierarchy selector mechanisms for even more specificity. For example, the following selector will match only table and paragraph elements that are children of the `div` with a class value of `div1`:

```
div.div1 > table + p
```

Understanding Style Inheritance

Inheritance is the act of picking up property values from one's ancestors. In CSS, all *foreground* properties (properties that are used in displaying visible elements, font color, and so on) are inherited by descendant elements. The following definition would result in all elements being rendered in green, because every element in the document descends from the body tag:

```
body { color: green; }
```

Note that this inheritance rule is valid only for foreground properties. Background properties (background color, image, and so on) are not automatically inherited by descendant elements.

You can override inheritance by defining a style for an element with a different value for the otherwise inherited property. For example, the following definitions result in all elements, *except* for paragraphs with a `nogreen` class, being rendered in green:

```
body { color: green; }
p.nogreen { color: red; }
```

Instead of green, the `nogreen` paragraph elements are rendered in red.

Attributes that are not in conflict are cumulatively inherited by descendant elements. For example, the following rules result in paragraphs with an `emphasis` class being rendered in bold, green text:

```
body { color: green; }
p.emphasis { font-weight: bold; }
```

Using Pseudoclasses

You can use a handful of pseudoclasses to match attributes of elements in your document. Pseudoclasses are identifiers that are understood by user agents and apply to elements of certain types without the elements having to be explicitly styled. Such classes are typically dynamic and tracked by other means than the actual `class` attribute.

For example, there are pseudoclasses used to modify visited and unvisited anchors in the document (explained in the next section). Using the pseudoclasses, you don't have to specify classes in individual anchor tags — the user agent determines which anchors are in which class (visited or not) and applies the style(s) appropriately.

The following sections discuss the pseudoclasses available.

Anchor Styles

A handful of pseudoclasses can be used with anchor elements (<a>). The anchor pseudoclasses begin with a colon and are listed in the following table.

Pseudoclass	Matches
:link	Unvisited links
:visited	Visited links
:active	Active links
:hover	The link that the browser pointer is hovering over
:focus	The link that currently has the user interface focus

For example, the following definition will cause all unvisited links in the document to be rendered in blue, visited links in red, and when hovered over, green:

```
: link  { color: blue; }
:visited { color: red; }
:hover {color: green; }
```

The order of the definitions is important; because the link membership in the classes is dynamic, :hover must be the last definition. If the order of :visited and :hover were reversed, visited links would not turn green when hovered over because the :visited color attribute would override the :hover color attribute. Ordering is also important when using the :focus pseudoclass—it should be placed last in the definitions.

Pseudoclass selectors can also be combined with other selector methods. For example, if you wanted all nonvisited anchor tags with a class attribute of important to be rendered in a bold font, you could use the following code:

```
/* Add explicit "important" class to non-visited pseudo class */
:link.important { font-weight: bold; }
...
<!-- The following link is important! -->
<a href="http://something.example.com/important.html"
  class="important">An important message</a>
```

The :first-child Pseudoclass

The :first-child pseudoclass is used to assign style definitions to the first-child element of a specific element. You can use this pseudoclass to add more space or otherwise change the formatting of a first-child element. For example, if you need to indent the first paragraph inside specific <div> elements, you could use the following definition:

```
div > p:first-child { text-indent: 25px; }
```

This code results in only the first paragraph of all div elements being indented by 25px.

The :lang Pseudoclass

The :lang pseudoclass is used to change elements according to the language being used for the document. For example, the French language uses angle brackets (< and >) to offset quotes, while the English language uses quote marks (" and "). If you need to address this difference in a document (seen by both French and English native readers), you could use a definition similar to the following:

```
/* Two levels of quotes for two languages */
.quote:lang(en) { quotes: '"' '"' "'" "'"; }
.quote:lang(fr) { quotes: "«" "»" "<" ">"; }

/* Add quotes (before and after) to quote class */
.quote:before { content: open-quote; }
.quote:after  { content: close-quote; }
```

The pseudoelements ***:before*** *and* ***:after*** *are covered in the "Pseudoelements" section later in this chapter.*

The :lang selectors apply to all elements with a quote class within the document. The second two definitions in the preceding example add quote characters to any quote classed element.

Pseudoelements

Pseudoelements are another virtual construct to help apply styles dynamically to elements within a document. For example, the :first-line pseudoelement applies a style to the first line of an element dynamically — that is, as the first changes size (longer or shorter), the user agent adjusts the style coverage accordingly.

:first-line

The :first-line pseudoelement specifies a different set of property values for the first line of elements. This is a powerful feature; as the browser window changes widths, the "first line" of an element can grow or shrink accordingly, and the style is applied appropriately. This is illustrated in the following code and in Figure 13-2, which shows two browser windows of different widths:

```
<!DOCTYPE html PUBLIC "-//W3C//DTD XHTML 1.0 Strict//EN"
    "http://www.w3.org/TR/xhtml1/DTD/xhtml1-strict.dtd">
<html>
<head>
  <title>First-line formatting</title>
  <style type="text/css">
    p:first-line { text-decoration: underline; }
    p.noline:first-line { text-decoration: none; }
  </style>
</head>
<body>
<h1>IN CONGRESS, July 4, 1776.</h1>
<p class="noline">The unanimous Declaration of the thirteen
United States of America,</p>
```

```
<p>When in the Course of human events, it becomes necessary
for one people to dissolve the political bands which have
connected them with another, and to assume among the powers
of the earth, the separate and equal station to which
the Laws of Nature and of Nature's God entitle them, a decent
respect to the opinions of mankind requires that they should
declare the causes which impel them to the separation.</p>

</body>
</html>
```

*The preceding code example manages element formatting by exception. Most paragraphs in the document should have their first line underlined. A universal selector is used to select all paragraph tags. A different style, using a class selector (**noline**), is defined to select elements that have a class of **noline**. Using this method, you only have to add class attributes to the exceptions (the minority) instead of the rule (the majority).*

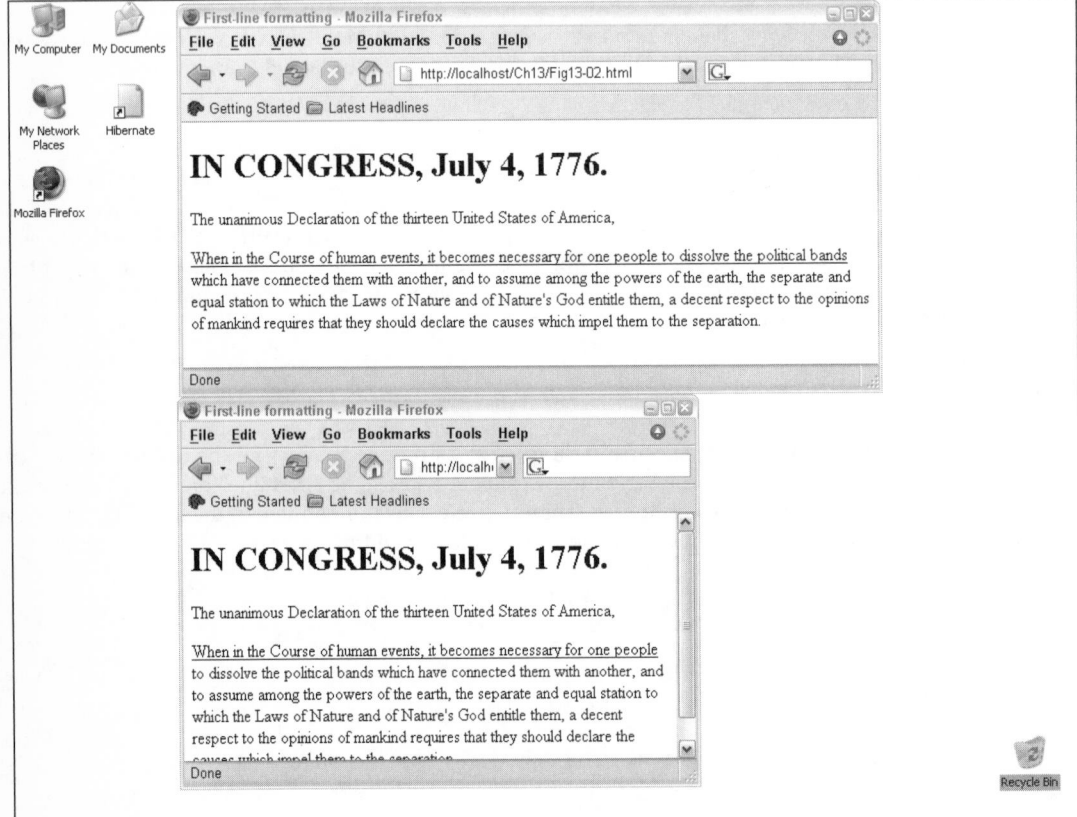

Figure 13-2

The :first-line pseudoelement has a limited range of properties it can affect. Only properties in the following groups can be applied using :first-line:

- ❑ Font properties
- ❑ Color properties
- ❑ Background properties
- ❑ word-spacing
- ❑ letter-spacing
- ❑ text-decoration
- ❑ vertical-align
- ❑ text-transform
- ❑ line-height
- ❑ text-shadow
- ❑ clear

:first-letter

The :first-letter pseudoelement is used to affect the properties of the first letter of an element. This selector can be used to achieve typographic effects such as drop caps, as illustrated in the following code and Figure 13-3:

```
<!DOCTYPE html PUBLIC "-//W3C//DTD XHTML 1.0 Strict//EN"
    "http://www.w3.org/TR/xhtml1/DTD/xhtml1-strict.dtd">
<html>
<head>
  <title>Drop cap formatting</title>
  <style type="text/css">
    p.dropcap:first-letter { font-size: 3em;
       font-weight: bold; float: left;
       border: solid 1px black; padding: .1em;
       margin: .2em .2em 0 0; }
  </style>
</head>
<body>
<h1>IN CONGRESS, July 4, 1776.</h1>
<p>The unanimous Declaration of the
thirteen united States of America,</p>
<p class="dropcap">When in the Course of human events,
it becomes necessary for one people to dissolve the political
bands which have connected them with another, and to assume
among the powers of the earth, the separate and equal station
to which the Laws of Nature and of Nature's God entitle them,
a decent respect to the opinions of mankind requires that
they should declare the causes which impel them to the
separation.</p>
</body>
</html>
```

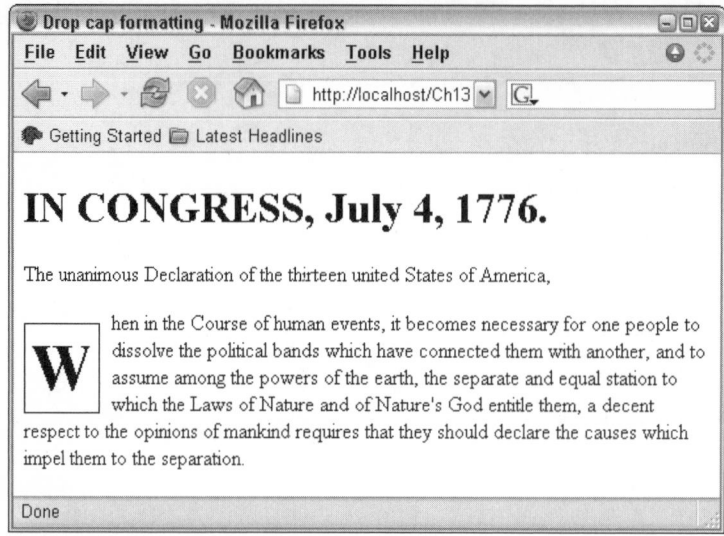

Figure 13-3

:before and :after

The `:before` and `:after` pseudoelements are used to add additional text to specific elements. These pseudoelements were used in the section "The `:lang` Pseudoclass" to add quote marks to the beginning and ending of elements with a `quote` class:

```
.quote:before { content: '"'; }
.quote:after  { content: '"'; }
```

Notice the use of the `content` property. This property assigns the actual value to content-generating selectors. In this case, quote marks are assigned as the content to add before and after elements with a `quote` class. The following code and Figure 13-4 illustrate how a supporting user agent (Opera, in this case) generates content from the `:before` and `:after` pseudoelements:

```
<!DOCTYPE html PUBLIC "-//W3C//DTD XHTML 1.0 Strict//EN"
    "http://www.w3.org/TR/xhtml1/DTD/xhtml1-strict.dtd">
<html>
<head>
  <title>Auto-quote marks</title>
  <style type="text/css">
  .quote:before { content: '"'; }
  .quote:after  { content: '"'; }
  </style>
</head>
<body>
<p class="quote">When in the Course of human events, it becomes necessary for
one people to dissolve the political bands which have connected them with another,
and to assume among the powers of the earth, the separate and equal station to
which the Laws of Nature and of Nature's God entitle them, a decent respect to the
```

```
opinions of mankind requires that they should declare the causes which impel them
to the separation.</p>
</body>
</html>
```

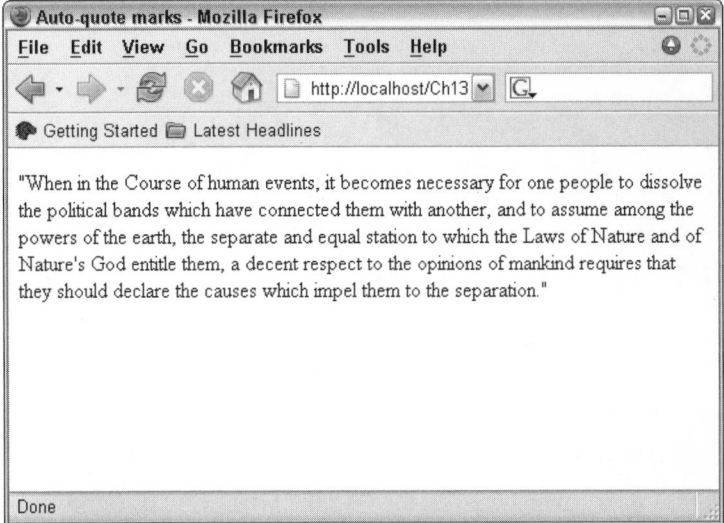

Figure 13-4

Generated content breaks the division of content and presentation. However, adding presentation content is sometimes necessary to enhance the content being presented. Besides adding elements such as quote marks, you can also create counters for custom numbered lists and other more powerful features.

Additional content-generating methods are covered in Chapter 14.

Shorthand Expressions

CSS supports many properties for formatting control over elements. For example, the following properties all apply to borders:

❑ border

❑ border-collapse

❑ border-spacing

❑ border-top

❑ border-right

❑ border-bottom

❑ border-left

❑ border-color

- ❑ border-top-color
- ❑ border-right-color
- ❑ border-bottom-color
- ❑ border-left-color
- ❑ border-style
- ❑ border-top-style
- ❑ border-right-style
- ❑ border-bottom-style
- ❑ border-left-style
- ❑ border-width
- ❑ border-top-width
- ❑ border-right-width
- ❑ border-bottom-width
- ❑ border-left-width

Several of these properties can be used to set multiple properties within the same definition. For example, to set an element's border, you could use code similar to the following:

```
p.bordered {
   border-top-width: 1px;
   border-top-style: solid;
   border-top-color: black;

   border-right-width: 2px;
   border-right-style: dashed;
   border-right-color: red;

   border-bottom-width: 1px;
   border-bottom-style: solid;
   border-bottom-color: black;

   border-left-width: 2px;
   border-left-style: dashed;
   border-left-color: red;
}
```

Alternately, you could use the shorthand property border-*side* to shorten this definition considerably:

```
p.bordered {
   border-top: 1px solid black;
   border-right: 2px dashed red;
   border-bottom: 1px solid black;
   border-left: 2px dashed red;
}
```

This definition could be further simplified by use of the `border` property, which sets all sides of an element to the same values:

```
p.bordered {
  border: 1px solid black;
  border-right: 2px dashed red;
  border-left: 2px dashed red;
}
```

This code first sets all sides to the same values and then sets the exceptions (right and left borders).

As with all things code, avoid being overly ingenious when defining your styles. Doing so will dramatically decrease the legibility of your code.

Summary

This chapter taught you the basics of defining styles — from formatting and using the various selector methods to formatting property declarations and setting their values. You also learned about special pseudoclasses and elements that can make your definitions more dynamic. The next series of chapters in this part delve into specific style use — for text, borders, tables, and more.

14

Text

Although the Web is rife with multimedia of all types, plain text is still the main medium used to convey messages across the Internet. As with other elements, CSS provides many properties for controlling how your text is rendered in your document, including alignment, letter and word spacing, white-space control, and even the font itself. This chapter covers how to use CSS to format text in your documents.

Aligning Text

Multiple properties in CSS can be used to align text, both horizontally and vertically. This section covers the various properties used to align text to other elements around it.

Horizontal Alignment

The `text-align` property can be used to align text horizontally using four different values/styles: left (default), right, center, and full. Consider the following code and the results shown in Figure 14-1:

```
<!DOCTYPE html PUBLIC "-//W3C//DTD XHTML 1.0 Strict//EN"
    "http://www.w3.org/TR/xhtml1/DTD/xhtml1-strict.dtd">
<html>
<head>
  <style type="text/css">
    p { border: thin solid black; padding: 10px; }
    p.left { text-align: left; }
    p.right { text-align: right; }
    p.center { text-align: center; }
    p.full { text-align: justify; }
  </style>
</head>
<body>
<h2>Left Aligned (default)</h2>
<p class="left">Lorem ipsum dolor sit amet, consectetuer adipiscing elit,
sed diam nonummy nibh euismod tincidunt ut laoreet dolore magna aliquam erat
volutpat. Ut wisi enim ad minim veniam, quis nostrud exerci tation ullamcorper
```

```
suscipit lobortis nisl ut aliquip ex ea commodo consequat.</p>
<h2>Right Aligned</h2>
<p class="right">Lorem ipsum dolor sit amet, consectetuer adipiscing elit,
sed diam nonummy nibh euismod tincidunt ut laoreet dolore magna aliquam erat
volutpat. Ut wisi enim ad minim veniam, quis nostrud exerci tation ullamcorper
suscipit lobortis nisl ut aliquip ex ea commodo consequat.</p>
<h2>Center Aligned</h2>
<p class="center">Lorem ipsum dolor sit amet, consectetuer adipiscing elit,
sed diam nonummy nibh euismod tincidunt ut laoreet dolore magna aliquam erat
volutpat. Ut wisi enim ad minim veniam, quis nostrud exerci tation ullamcorper
suscipit lobortis nisl ut aliquip ex ea commodo consequat.</p>
<h2>Fully Aligned</h2>
<p class="full">Lorem ipsum dolor sit amet, consectetuer adipiscing elit,
sed diam nonummy nibh euismod tincidunt ut laoreet dolore magna aliquam erat
volutpat. Ut wisi enim ad minim veniam, quis nostrud exerci tation ullamcorper
suscipit lobortis nisl ut aliquip ex ea commodo consequat.</p>
</body>
</html>
```

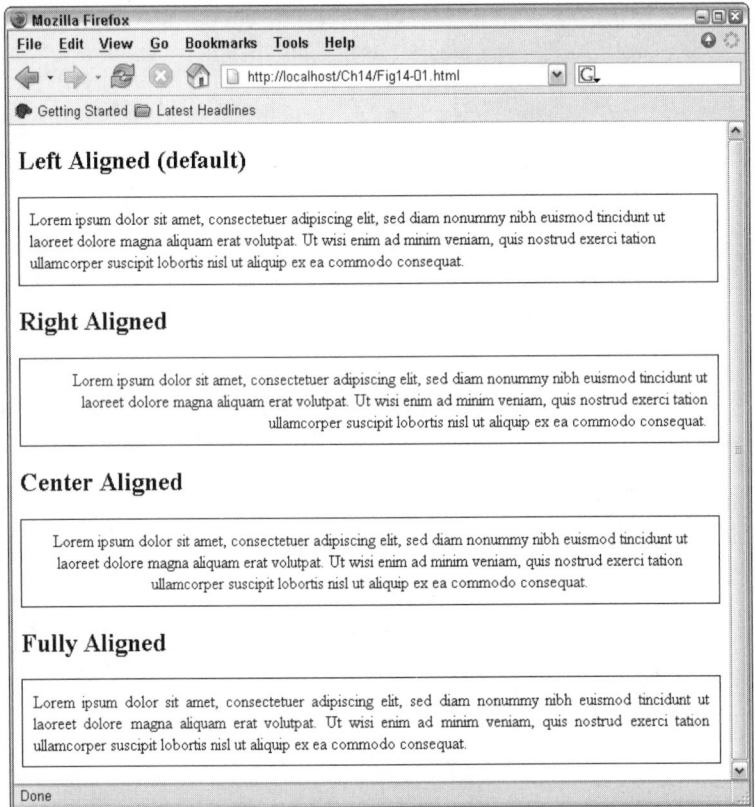

Figure 14-1

Note that justification is specified by how the text aligns to a specific margin. For example, left-aligned text aligns against the left margin while right-aligned text aligns to the right margin. Any side of the text not justified remains ragged.

You can also use the `text-align` property to align columns of text on a specific character, for example, monetary amounts aligned to a decimal point. The following code causes the numbers in the Amount Due column to align on their decimal points:

```
<!DOCTYPE html PUBLIC "-//W3C//DTD XHTML 1.0 Strict//EN"
    "http://www.w3.org/TR/xhtml1/DTD/xhtml1-strict.dtd">
<html>
<head>
  <title>Decimal Justification</title>
  <style type="text/css">
    td.dec { text-align: "."; }
  </style>
</head>
<body>
<p>
  <table border="1">
  <tr>
    <th>Customer</th>
    <th>Amount Due</th>
  </tr>
  <tr>
    <td>Acme Industries</td>
    <td class="dec">$50.95</td>
  </tr>
  <tr>
    <td>RHI LLC</td>
    <td class="dec">$2084.56</td>
  </tr>
  <tr>
    <td>EMrUs</td>
    <td class="dec">$0.55</td>
  </tr>
  </table>
</p>
</body>
</html>
```

*This use of **text-align** (character alignment) is not well supported in today's browsers. As such, you should avoid depending on it.*

Vertical Alignment

The `vertical-align` property can be used to align text on the vertical axis. The `vertical-align` property supports the values shown in the following table.

Value	Effect
baseline	The default vertical alignment; this value aligns the text's baseline to other objects around it.
bottom	Causes the bottom of the element's bounding box to be aligned with the bottom of the element's parent bounding box.
length	Causes the element to ascend (positive value) or descend (negative value) by the value specified.
middle	Causes the text to be aligned using the middle of the text and the midline of objects around it.
percentage	Causes the element to ascend (positive value) or descend (negative value) by the percentage specified. (The percentage is computed from the line height of the element.)
sub	Causes the text to descend to the level appropriate for subscripted text, based on its parent's font size and line height. (Has no effect on the actual size of the text, only the position of the element.)
super	Causes the text to ascend to the level appropriate for superscripted text, based on its parent's font size and line height. (Has no effect on the actual size of the text, only the position of the element.)
text-bottom	Causes the bottom of the element's bounding box to be aligned with the bottom of the element's parent text.
text-top	Causes the top of the element's bounding box to be aligned with the top of the element's parent text.
top	Causes the top of the element's bounding box to be aligned with the top of the element's parent bounding box.

The following code and Figure 14-2 illustrate the effect of each `vertical-align` value:

```
<!DOCTYPE html PUBLIC "-//W3C//DTD XHTML 1.0 Strict//EN"
    "http://www.w3.org/TR/xhtml1/DTD/xhtml1-strict.dtd">
<html>
<head>
  <title>Vertical Text Alignment</title>
  <style type="text/css">
    .baseline { vertical-align: baseline; }
    .sub { vertical-align: sub; }
    .super { vertical-align: super; }
    .top { vertical-align: top; }
    .text-top { vertical-align: text-top; }
    .middle { vertical-align: middle; }
    .bottom { vertical-align: bottom; }
    .text-bottom { vertical-align: text-bottom; }
    .length { vertical-align: .5em; }
    .percentage { vertical-align: -50%; }
```

```
      /* All elements get a border */
      body *  { border: 1px solid black; }
      /* Reduce the spans' font by 50% */
      p * { font-size: 50%; }
  </style>
</head>
<body>
  <p>Baseline: Parent
    <span class="baseline">aligned text</span> text</p>
  <p>Sub: Parent
    <span class="sub">aligned text</span> text</p>
  <p>Super: Parent
    <span class="super">aligned text</span> text</p>
  <p>Top: Parent
    <span class="top">aligned text</span> text</p>
  <p>Text-top Parent
    <span class="text-top">aligned text</span> text</p>
  <p>Middle: Parent
    <span class="middle">aligned text</span> text</p>
  <p>Bottom: Parent
    <span class="bottom">aligned text</span> text</p>
  <p>Text-bottom: Parent
    <span class="text-bottom">aligned text</span> text</p>
  <p>Length: Parent
    <span class="length">aligned text</span> text</p>
  <p>Percentage: Parent
    <span class="percentage">aligned text</span> text</p>
</body>
</html>
```

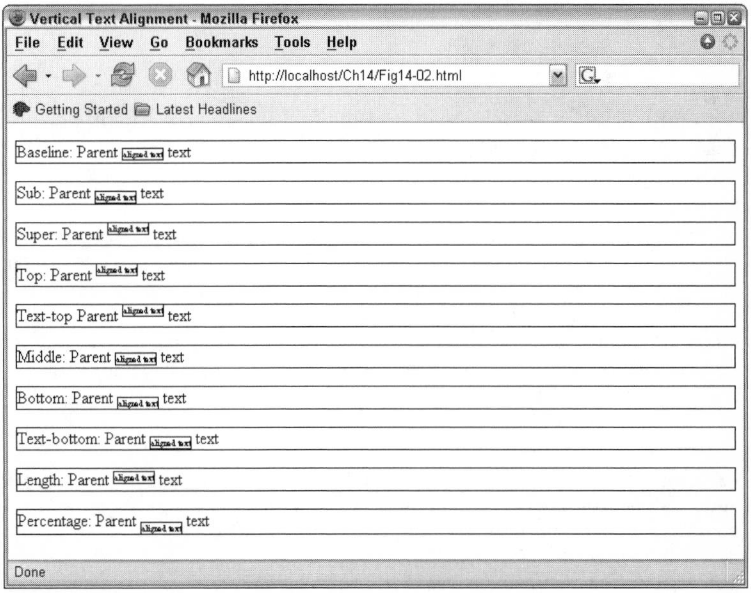

Figure 14-2

Text isn't the only type of element that you can affect with the `vertical-align` property. For example, note the document displayed in Figure 14-3; the sphere image has its `vertical-align` property set to `middle`. Note how the image and the text are aligned on their vertical midpoints.

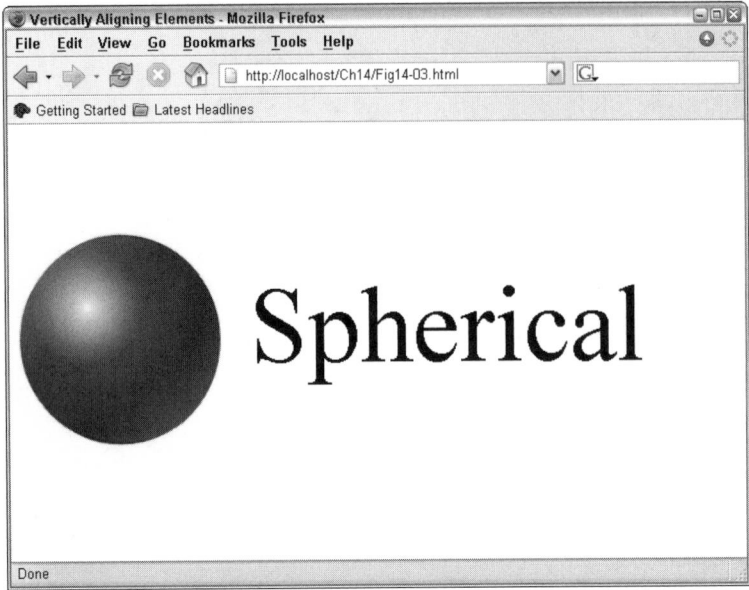

Figure 14-3

Indenting Text

The `text-indent` property can be used to indent the first line of an element. For example, to indent the first line of a paragraph by 5 percent of its overall width, you could use code similar to the following (whose results are shown in Figure 14-4):

```
<p style="text-indent: 5%;">Lorem ipsum dolor sit amet, consectetuer adipiscing
elit, sed diam nonummy nibh euismod tincidunt ut laoreet dolore magna aliquam erat
volutpat. Ut wisi enim ad minim veniam, quis nostrud exerci tation ullamcorper
suscipit lobortis nisl ut aliquip ex ea commodo consequat. Duis autem vel eum
iriure dolor in hendrerit in vulputate velit esse molestie consequat, vel illum
dolore eu feugiat nulla facilisis at vero eros et accumsan et iusto odio dignissim
qui blandit praesent luptatum zzril delenit augue duis dolore te feugait nulla
acilisi.</p>
```

*The **text-indent** property indents only the first line of the element to which it is applied. If you want to indent the entire element, use the margin property instead. The margin property is discussed in Chapter 15.*

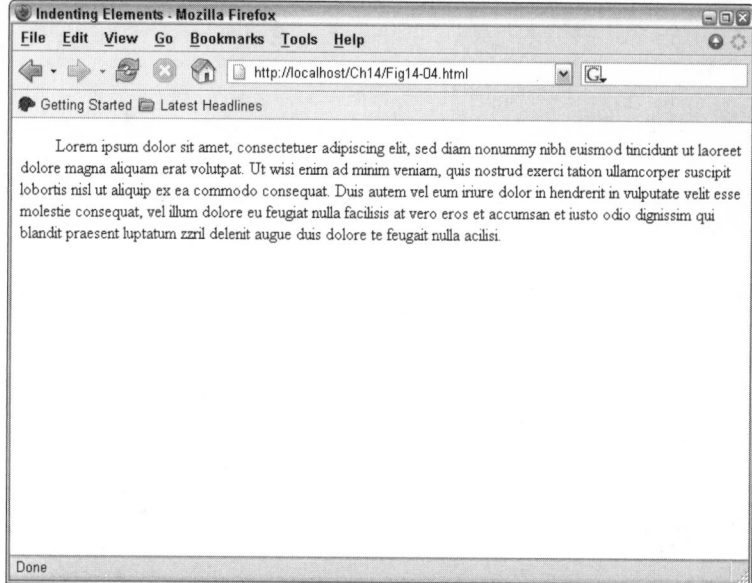

Figure 14-4

You can use any of the valid property value metrics in defining the value of the indentation. Note that the user agent's window size can play a significant role in the size of the actual indent if you use values computed from the containing block (percentages, em, and so on).

Possible metrics for CSS properties were covered in the "Property Values" section of Chapter 12.

Controlling White Space

Typically, you won't concern yourself over how white space is rendered in documents. However, there are times when you will need finer control over how a user agent pads elements or converts white space.

Floating Objects

Allowing elements to float in your documents can make them seem more dynamic. Floating elements *float* against a margin, allowing other elements to flow around them. For example, consider the following code and the results shown in Figure 14-5:

```
<p><b>Floating Image</b><br />
<img src="smsphere.jpg" alt="small sphere" style="float: left;"> Lorem ipsum
dolor sit amet, consectetuer adipiscing elit, sed diam nonummy nibh euismod
tincidunt ut laoreet dolore magna aliquam erat volutpat. Ut wisi enim ad minim
veniam, quis nostrud exerci tation ullamcorper suscipit lobortis nisl ut aliquip ex
ea commodo consequat. Duis autem vel eum iriure dolor in hendrerit in vulputate
velit esse molestie consequat, vel illum dolore eu feugiat nulla facilisis at vero
eros et accumsan et iusto odio dignissim qui blandit praesent luptatum zzril
delenit augue duis dolore te feugait nulla facilisi.</p>
```

```
<p><b>Non-Floating Image</b><br />
<img src="smsphere.jpg" alt="small sphere" style="float: none;"> Lorem ipsum
dolor sit amet, consectetuer adipiscing elit, sed diam nonummy nibh euismod
tincidunt ut laoreet dolore magna aliquam erat volutpat. Ut wisi enim ad minim
veniam, quis nostrud exerci tation ullamcorper suscipit lobortis nisl ut aliquip ex
ea commodo consequat. Duis autem vel eum iriure dolor in hendrerit in vulputate
velit esse molestie consequat, vel illum dolore eu feugiat nulla facilisis at vero
eros et accumsan et iusto odio dignissim qui blandit praesent luptatum zzril
delenit augue duis dolore te feugait nulla facilisi.</p>
<p>
```

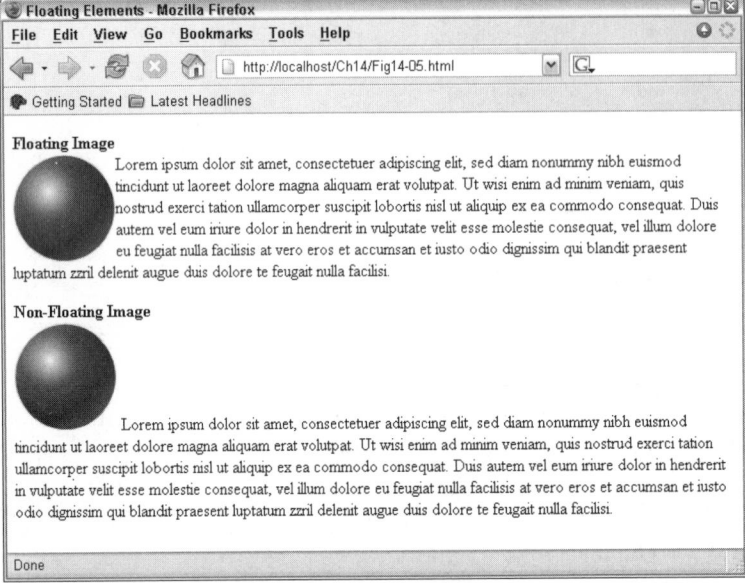

Figure 14-5

Floating images ignore the normal flow of the document, sticking to the margin closest to their location and allowing items to flow around them. You can set an element's float property to right, left, or none.

However, there are times when you might not want an element to flow around a floating element. For example, headings look odd when floated away from their home margin, as shown in Figure 14-6.

When you don't want an element to flow around floating elements, you should set its clear property. The clear property has four possible values: none (default), right, left, or both. This property makes sure that the specified side (or sides, if set to both) is clear of floated elements before the element is placed. For example, adding this style to the example shown in Figure 14-6 ensures that both sides of all headings are clear and results in the appearance shown in Figure 14-7 (the heading isn't placed until the left margin is clear):

```
h1, h2, h3, h4, h5, h6 { clear: both; }
```

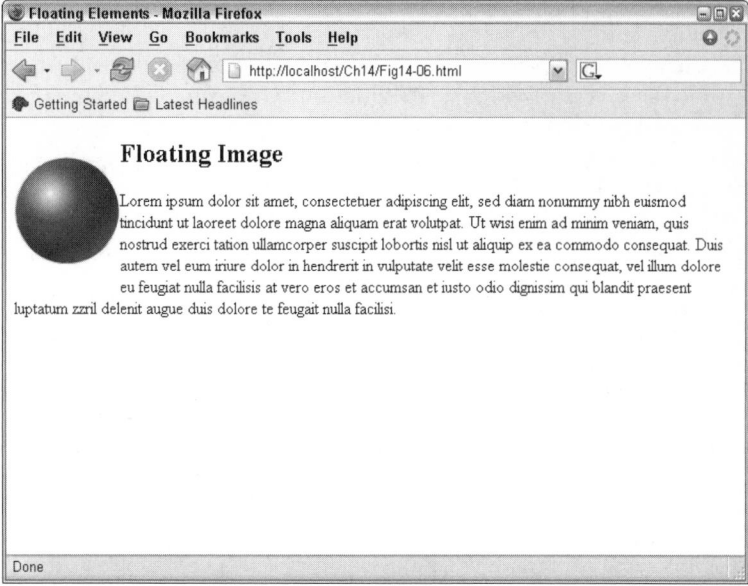

Figure 14-6

Figure 14-7

The white-space Property

You might occasionally want to preserve particular white space in a document. You have seen how the preformatted (<pre>) tag can be used to do this, but sometimes you might prefer to format the text with another tag instead and still preserve the white space.

The white-space property supports the following values:

❑ normal

❑ nowrap

❑ pre

The default value, none, allows the user agent to compress white space normally. Using the pre value causes the text to be formatted as preformatted text, preserving all the white space in the element. The nowrap value results in the element not wrapping at the border of the user agent's screen — the text continues on the current line until the next line break. Most user agents will add horizontal scroll bars to allow the user to scroll such content.

For example, the following paragraph will be rendered as is, with all its superfluous white space intact, but otherwise will inherit the formatting of the paragraph element (<p>):

```
<p style="white-space: pre;">Lorem        ipsum

dolor sit amet,
            consectetuer      adipiscing
elit, sed diam nonummy                   nibh euismod tincidunt
ut laoreet dolore          magna aliquam
erat volutpat.</p>
```

Letter and Word Spacing

The letter-spacing and word-spacing properties can be used to control an element's letter spacing and word spacing, respectively. Both properties take absolute or relative values — positive values add space; negative values remove space.

For example, consider the following code and output shown in Figure 14-8, which illustrates three different letter-spacing values:

```
<!DOCTYPE html PUBLIC "-//W3C//DTD XHTML 1.0 Strict//EN"
    "http://www.w3.org/TR/xhtml1/DTD/xhtml1-strict.dtd">
<html>
<head>
  <title>Letter Spacing</title>
  <style type="text/css">
    .normal { letter-spacing: normal; }
    .tight  { letter-spacing: -.2em; }
    .loose  { letter-spacing:  .2em; }
  </style>
</head>
<body>
```

```
   <h3>Normal</h3>
   <p class="normal">Lorem ipsum dolor sit amet, consectetuer
   adipiscing elit, sed diam nonummy nibh euismod tincidunt
   ut laoreet dolore magna aliquam erat volutpat. Ut wisi
   enim ad minim veniam, quis nostrud exerci tation
   ullamcorper suscipit obortis nisl ut aliquip ex ea commodo
   consequat.</p>
   <h3>Tight</h3>
   <p class="tight">Lorem ipsum dolor sit amet, consectetuer
   adipiscing elit, sed diam nonummy nibh euismod tincidunt
   ut laoreet dolore magna aliquam erat volutpat. Ut wisi
   enim ad minim veniam, quis nostrud exerci tation
   ullamcorper suscipit obortis nisl ut aliquip ex ea commodo
   consequat.</p>
   <h3>Loose</h3>
   <p class="loose">Lorem ipsum dolor sit amet, consectetuer
   adipiscing elit, sed diam nonummy nibh euismod tincidunt
   ut laoreet dolore magna aliquam erat volutpat. Ut wisi
   enim ad minim veniam, quis nostrud exerci tation
   ullamcorper suscipit obortis nisl ut aliquip ex ea commodo
   consequat.</p>
</body>
</html>
```

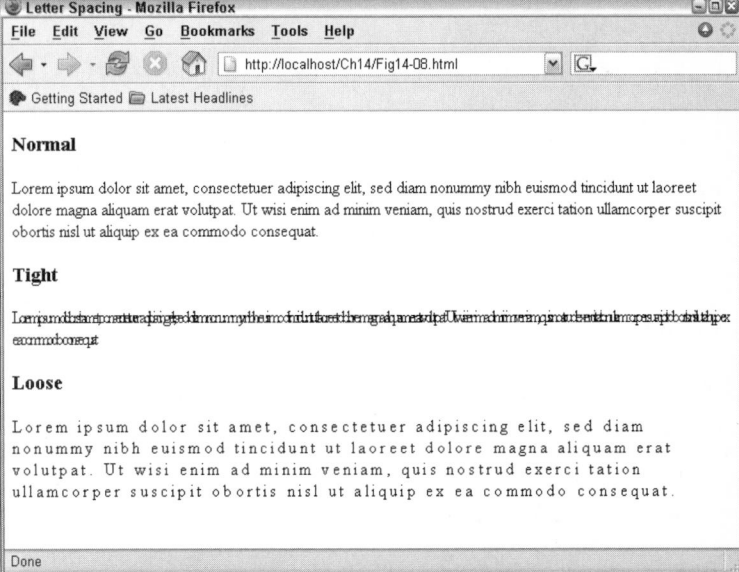

Figure 14-8

Note that the user agent can govern how much letter spacing is allowed to change. Also, changing the spacing by too drastic a value (as in the `tight` paragraph in Figure 14-8) can have unpredictable results.

The `word-spacing` property behaves exactly like the `letter-spacing` property, except that it controls spacing between words.

Capitalization

The `text-transform` property can be used to force particular capitalization on elements. This property has four possible values:

- ❑ none (default)
- ❑ capitalize
- ❑ uppercase
- ❑ lowercase

Setting the appropriate value will force the user agent to render the text (if possible) using that setting. For example, you may want all your headings in title case (as in this book, where most words begin with a capital letter). To do so, you could use a style similar to the following:

```
h1, h2, h3, h4, h5, h6  { text-transform: capitalize; }
```

This won't quite have the desired effect, as conjunctions (and, or, and so on) and other words not commonly capitalized in initial-caps schemes will still be capitalized.

Text Decorations

You can add additional text effects with the `text-decoration` and `text-shadow` properties.

The `text-decoration` property has five possible values:

- ❑ none (default)
- ❑ underline
- ❑ overline
- ❑ line-through
- ❑ blink

This property's use is straightforward, as shown in this style code example:

```
<p style="text-decoration: none;">No Decoration</p>
<p style="text-decoration: underline;">Underlined</p>
<p style="text-decoration: overline;">Overlined</p>
<p style="text-decoration: line-through;">Line Through</p>
<p style="text-decoration: blink;">Blink</p>
```

However, the use of this property isn't recommended. Blinking text has never had a welcome place on the Web, underlined text can be confused with links, and the delete tag (`<del>`) should be used to generate strikethrough text.

The advice to use a specific tag (namely, `<del>`) for formatting seems contrary to what we preach about styles — that is, use styles instead of dedicated tags. However, in this case, the recommendation is made because of the meaning of the tag, namely deletion, instead of its ornamentation function (strikethrough). The same way you would use `<emphasis>` instead of `<b>` when you wanted text to be emphasized (but not necessarily bold), you would use `<del>` to indicate that text is to be deleted, not just decorated in strikethrough. The advantage in this case is that the user agent could be configured not even to show text contained in `<del>` tags.

The `text-shadow` property, used to provide a drop shadow on affected text, is more complex than most properties discussed in this chapter, having the following syntax:

```
text-shadow: "[color] horizontal-distance vertical-distance [blur]"
```

At its most basic, the `text-shadow` property takes two distance arguments: one vertical, the other horizontal. Positive values will place the shadow down and to the right, negative values will place the shadow up and to the left. The `color` value sets the color for the shadow, and the `blur` value specifies the area of effect. You can also use multiple definitions to spawn multiple shadows of the same element. When using multiple definitions, you should separate them with a comma.

For example, consider the following code, which defines a shadow above and to the right (2em, -2em) of the heading and another lighter shadow directly underneath the text:

```
<h1 style="text-shadow: #666666 2em -2em, #AAAAAA 0em 0em 1.5em;">A Drop
Shadow Heading</h1>
```

Most user agents do not support the `text-shadow` property. If you desire this effect, you would be better off creating it in graphic image form.

Formatting Lists

Chapter 4 of this book covered XHTML lists, both of the ordered (or numbered) and unordered (or bulleted) variety. You learned how to embed list items (`<li>`) in both list types to construct lists. Using CSS, you can be much more creative with your lists, as this section will quickly demonstrate.

Any Element Can Be a List Item

CSS lists don't need to use the standard list item (`<li>`) tags. CSS supports the `list-item` value of the display property, which, in effect, makes any element a list item. The `<li>` tag is a list item by default.

*There is a **list-style** shortcut property that you can use to set list properties with one value assignment. You can use the **list-style** property to define the other list properties, as follows:*

```
list-style: <list-style-type> <list-style-position> <list-style-image>
```

To create a new list item, you can define a class as a list item:

```
.item { display: list-item; }
```

Then you can use that class to declare elements as list items:

```
<p class="item">This is now a list item, not just a normal paragraph.</p>
```

As you read through the rest of this section, keep in mind that the list properties can apply to any element defined as a `list-item`.

> *Both bullets and numbers that precede list items are known as markers. Markers have additional value with CSS, as shown in the "Generated Content" section later in this chapter.*

The list-style-type Property

The `list-style-type` property sets the type of the list and, therefore, what marker(s) are used with each item (bullet, number, Roman numeral, and so on).

The `list-style-type` property can have the following values:

- ❏ armenian
- ❏ circle
- ❏ cjk-ideographic
- ❏ decimal
- ❏ decimal-leading-zero
- ❏ disc
- ❏ georgian
- ❏ hebrew
- ❏ hiragana
- ❏ hiragana-iroha
- ❏ katakana
- ❏ katakana-iroha
- ❏ lower-alpha
- ❏ lower-greek
- ❏ lower-latin
- ❏ lower-roman
- ❏ none (default)
- ❏ square
- ❏ upper-alpha
- ❏ upper-latin
- ❏ upper-roman

Setting the style provides a list with appropriate item identifiers. For example, consider this code and the output shown immediately after:

HTML Code:

```
<ol style="list-style-type:lower-roman;">
  A Roman Numeral List
  <li>Step 1
  <li>Step 2
  <li>Step 3
</ol>
```

Output:

```
A Roman Numeral List
   i.   Step 1
  ii.   Step 2
 iii.   Step 3
```

You can also use the `none` value of `list-style-type` to suppress bullets or numbers for individual items. However, this does not change the number of those items; the numbers are just not displayed. For example, consider the following revised code and output:

HTML Code:

```
<ol style="list-style-type:lower-roman;">
  A Roman Numeral List
  <li>Step 1
  <li style="list-style-type:none;">Step 2
  <li>Step 3
</ol>
```

Output:

```
A Roman Numeral List
   i.   Step 1
        Step 2
 iii.   Step 3
```

Note that the third item is still number 3 (Roman iii), despite the fact that the number for item 2 is suppressed.

Positioning of Markers

The `list-style-position` property sets the position of the marker in relation to the list item. The valid values for this property are `inside` or `outside`. The `outside` value is the more typical list style; the marker is offset from the list item, and the entire text of the item is indented. The `inside` value sets the list to a more compact style; the marker is indented with the first line of the item. Figure 14-9 shows an example of both list marker positions:

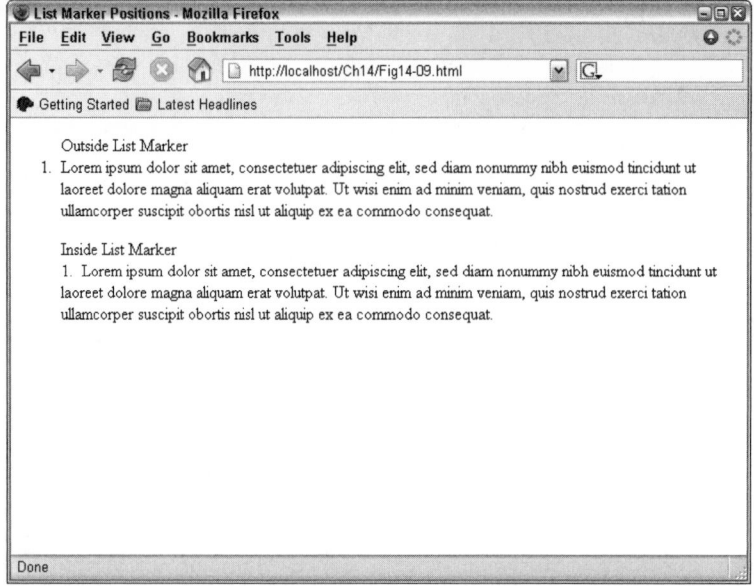

Figure 14-9

*To set the marker position for an entire list, use the **list-style-position** property in the list element (**<ol>** or **<ul>**) instead of in the list item element.*

Images as List Markers

Images can also be used as list markers by using the list-style-image property. The image to use is specified with the url construct. For example, the following code references sphere.jpg and cone.jpg as images to use in the list.

```
<ol>
    <li style="list-style-image: url(sphere.jpg)">
    Lorem ipsum dolor sit amet, consectetuer
    adipiscing elit, sed diam nonummy nibh euismod tincidunt
    ut laoreet dolore magna aliquam erat volutpat.
    <li style="list-style-image: url(cone.jpg)">
    Lorem ipsum dolor sit amet, consectetuer
    adipiscing elit, sed diam nonummy nibh euismod tincidunt
    ut laoreet dolore magna aliquam erat volutpat.
</ol>
```

Note that you can use any URL-accessible image with the list-style-image property. Remember to use images sized appropriately for your lists.

Autogenerating Text

One of the strengths of CSS is its ability to generate additional text, not just format existing text. You saw how the `:before` and `:after` pseudoelements could be used to add text in Chapter 13. This section expands on the autogenerated text mechanisms.

Many user agents do not support generated content.

Define and Display Quotation Marks

The autogeneration features of CSS can be used to both define and display quotation marks. First, you need to define appropriate quote marks, and then you can add them to elements.

The `quotes` property takes a list of arguments in string format to use for the open and close quotes at multiple levels. This property has the following form:

```
quotes: <open_first_level> <close_first_level>
<open_second_level> <close_second_level> ... ;
```

The standard definition for most English uses (double quotes on first level, single quotes on second level) is as follows:

```
quotes: '"' '"' "'" "'";
```

The opposite quote type is used to encapsulate each quote character (single quote enclosing double and vice versa).

Once you define the quotes, you can use them along with the `:before` and `:after` pseudoelements, as in the following example:

```
blockquote:before { content: open-quote; }
blockquote:after  { content: close-quote; }
```

*The **open-quote** and **close-quote** words are mnemonics for the values set in the **quotes** property. The **content** property also accepts string values, so you can use almost anything for its value.*

Automatic Numbering

The `content` property can also be used to automatically generate numbers, which, in turn, can be used to automatically number elements. The advantage to using automatic counters over standard list numbering comes in the form of flexibility, enabling you to start at an arbitrary number, combine numbers (for example, 1.1), and so on.

As with all generated content, most user agents do not support counters.

Chapter 14

The counter Object

A special `counter` object is used to hold the actual counter value. This object's value can be incremented and reset by other style operations. The `counter` object has the following syntax when used with the `content` property:

```
content: counter(counter_name);
```

This places the current value of the counter specified in the `content` object. For example, the following style definition will cause the user agent to display "Chapter" and the current value of the counter named `chapter_num` at the beginning of each `<h1>` element:

```
h1:before { content: "Chapter " counter(chapter_num) "  "; }
```

Of course, it's of no use to always assign the same number to the element. The `counter-increment` and `counter-reset` objects are used to change the value of the counter.

Changing a Counter's Value

The `counter-increment` property is used to increment a counter. It has the following syntax:

```
counter-increment: counter_name [increment_value];
```

If the increment value is not specified, the counter is incremented by 1. You can increment several counters with the same statement by specifying the additional counters after the first, separated by spaces. For example, to increment the chapter and section counters each by 2, you could use the following:

```
counter-increment: chapter 2 section 2;
```

You can also specify negative numbers to decrement the counter(s). To decrement the `chapter` counter by 1, you could use the following:

```
counter-increment: chapter -1;
```

The other method for changing a counter's value is to use the `counter-reset` property. This property resets the counter to 0 or a number expressly specified with the property. The `counter-reset` property has the following format:

```
counter-reset: counter_name [value];
```

For example, to reset the `chapter` counter to 1, you could use this definition:

```
counter-reset: chapter 1;
```

You can reset multiple counters with the same property by specifying all the counters on the same line, separated by spaces.

If a counter is used and incremented or reset in the same context (in the same definition), the counter is first incremented or reset before being used. For example, the following code will not use the value of the chapter counter before the heading; it will increment the counter and use the incremented value despite the fact that the `content` property comes before the `counter-increment` property:

```
h1:before {content: "Chapter " counter(chapter) ": ";
          counter-increment: chapter; }
```

Autonumbering Examples

Using counters, you can easily implement autonumbering schemes for many things. This section shows two examples—one for chapters and sections, the other for lists.

Example: Chapter and Section Numbers

To implement this autonumbering, use `<h1>` elements for chapter titles and `<h2>` elements for sections. You will use two counters: `chapter` and `section`, respectively.

First, set up your chapter heading definition, as follows:

```
h1:before {content: "Chapter " counter(chapter) ": ";
          counter-increment: chapter;
          counter-reset: section; }
```

This definition will display "Chapter *chapter_num:*" before the text in each `<h1>` element. The `chapter` counter is incremented and the `section` counter is reset for each `<h1>` element.

The next step is to set up the section numbering, which is similar to the chapter numbering:

```
h2:before {content: "Section " counter(chapter) "."
          counter(section) ": ";
          counter-increment: section;
```

Now the styles are complete.

Source

```
<!DOCTYPE html PUBLIC "-//W3C//DTD XHTML 1.0 Strict//EN"
   "http://www.w3.org/TR/xhtml1/DTD/xhtml1-strict.dtd">
<html>
<head>
  <title>Chapter Auto-Numbering</title>
  <style type="text/css">
    h1:before {content: "Chapter " counter(chapter) ": ";
              counter-increment: chapter;
              counter-reset: section; }
    h2:before {content: "Section " counter(chapter) "."
              counter(section) ": ";
              counter-increment: section; }
  </style>
</head>
<body>
```

```
    <h1>First Chapter</h1>
      <h2>Section Name</h2>
      <h2>Section Name</h2>
    <h1>Second Chapter</h1>
      <h2>Section Name</h2>
    <h1>Third Chapter</h1>
  </body>
</html>
```

Output

The code results in the output shown in Figure 14-10.

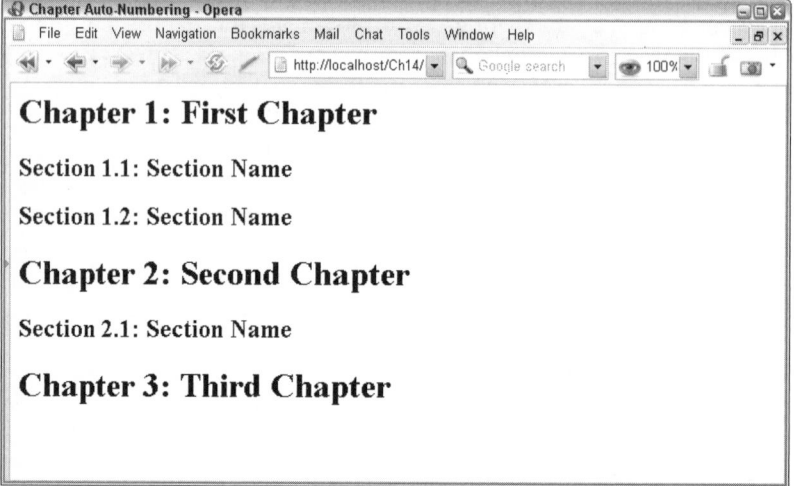

Figure 14-10

In this example, starting both counters at 0 is ideal. However, if you needed to start the counters at another value, the resets should be attached to a higher tag in the document hierarchy (such as **<body>**):

```
body:before {counter-reset: chapter 12 section 10;}
```

Example: Custom List Numbering

You can use a similar construct for custom list numbering.

Source

For example, consider the following code, which starts numbering the list at 30:

```
<!DOCTYPE html PUBLIC "-//W3C//DTD XHTML 1.0 Strict//EN"
    "http://www.w3.org/TR/xhtml1/DTD/xhtml1-strict.dtd">
<html>
```

```
<head>
  <title>List Auto-Number</title>
  <style type="text/css">
    li:before {content: counter(list) ": ";
               counter-increment: list; }
  </style>
</head>
<body>
  <ol style="counter-reset: list 29;
       list-style-type:none;">
    <li>First item
    <li>Second item
    <li>Third item
  </ol>
</body>
</html>
```

Output

The output of the preceding code appears in Figure 14-11.

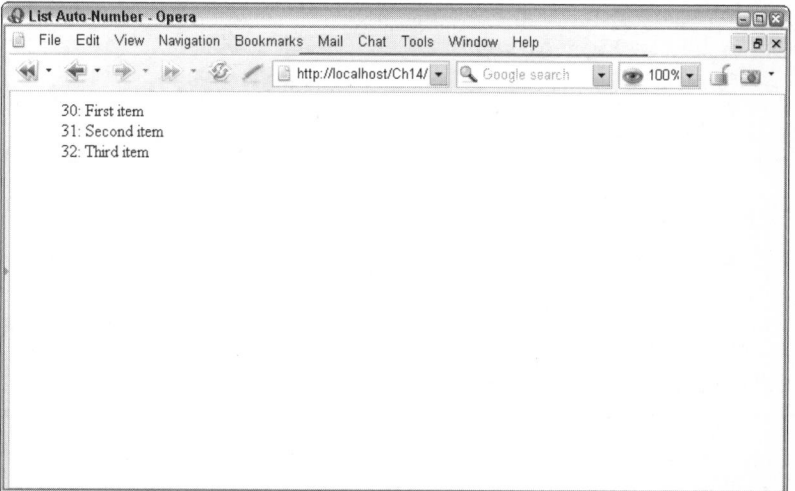

Figure 14-11

You can use multiple instances of a counter in your documents, and each instance can operate independently. The key is each counter's scope: A counter's scope is within the element that initialized the counter with the first reset. In the list example, it is the **<ol>** *tag. If you nested another* **<ol>** *tag within the first, the nested list could have its own instance of the* **list** *counter.*

Fonts

Fonts are stylized collections of letters and symbols. Different fonts can be used to convey different information; specialized fonts can be used to provide special characters or symbols. Although fonts can be quite different from each other, they share the same basic characteristics, as shown in Figure 14-12.

Figure 14-12

Fonts are mapped according to a system similar to ruled paper. The line that the characters or symbols sit on is called the baseline. The distance between the baseline and the top of the highest characters (usually capital letters and lowercase letters such as *l*, *f*, or *t*) is known as the ascension. The distance between the baseline and the lowest point of characters that dip below it (such as *p*, *g*, or *q*) is known as the *descension*.

> *Vertical font measurements, such as line spacing or leading, are typically measured between the baselines of text, at least as far as CSS is concerned.*

Just as CSS offers many properties to control lines and paragraphs, it also offers many properties to control the font(s) of the text in your documents.

Font Selection

CSS supports five different font family types. These general types can be used to apprise a user agent of the type of font face it should use. Those five families are as follows:

- ❑ **Serif**—Serif fonts have little ornamentation on each glyph (character—includes letters, numbers, and symbols). Typically, serif fonts are used in body text; the finishing strokes, flared or tapering ends, or serifed endings, make the lines of characters flow and tend to be easier on the eyes.

- ❑ **Sans serif**—These fonts are fairly plain, having little or no ornamentation on their glyphs. Sans serif fonts are typically used for headings or other large areas of emphasis.

- ❑ **Cursive**—Cursive fonts are quite ornate, approximating cursive writing. Such fonts should be used only in extreme cases where emphasis is on ornamentation rather than legibility.

- ❑ **Fantasy**—Fantasy fonts, much like cursive fonts, emphasize ornamentation over legibility. Fantasy fonts come in many styles but still retain the basic shape of letters. Like cursive fonts, fantasy fonts are generally used for logos and other ornamentation purposes where legibility is secondary.

❑ **Monospace** — Monospace fonts come in serif and sans serif varieties but all share the same attribute: all characters in the font have the same width. The effect is much like characters on a text-based terminal or typewriter. Such fonts are generally used in code listings and other listings approximating terminal output.

The `font-family` property defines the font or fonts that should be used for elements in the document. This property has the following format:

```
font-family: [[ <family-name> | <generic-family> ],]
  [<family-name> | <generic-family>] ;
```

For example, to select a sans serif font, you might use a definition similar to the following:

```
font-family: Verdana, Arial, Helvetica, Sans-Serif;
```

Note that this definition uses three family names (`Verdana`, `Arial`, `Helvetica`) and a generic family name (`Sans-Serif`) for versatility. The definition instructs the user agent that the sans serif font Verdana should be used. If it is unavailable, the Arial font (popular on Windows-based platforms) should be used. If neither of those fonts is available, the Helvetica font should be used (popular on Macintosh-based platforms and other PostScript systems). If none of the previously specified fonts are available, the user agent should use its default sans serif font.

The preceding font-family definition is a good, universal sans serif font specification that can be used for any platform. Likewise, the following definition can be used for a universal serif font specification:

```
font-family:  Palatino, "Times New Roman", "Times Roman", Serif;
```

Note that the `font-family` definition doesn't control the font variant (bold, italic, and so on) but the font that should be used as the basis for fonts in the element where the `font-family` definition is placed. Individual font variant tags and elements (`<b>`, `<i>`, and so on) determine the variant of the font used when such elements are encountered by the browser. If the base font cannot be used, one of the variants (if any) of the definition is used in its stead.

Style definitions to set up a document in traditional serif font body text with sans serif font headings would resemble the following:

```
body { font-family:  Palatino, "Times New Roman", "Times Roman", Serif; }
h1, h2, h3, h4, h5, h6 {
  font-family: Verdana, Arial, Helvetica, Sans-Serif;
  font-weight: bold; }
```

Font Sizing

Two properties can be used to control font sizing: `font-size` and `font-size-adjust`. Both properties can adjust a font absolutely or relative to the current font size. Possible value metrics are shown in the following table:

Metric	Description
Absolute size keywords	Keywords corresponding to user agent absolute font sizes. These keywords include xx-small, x-small, small, medium, large, x-large, and xx-large.
Relative size keywords	Keywords corresponding to user agent relative font sizes. These keywords include larger and smaller.
Length absolute	An absolute value corresponding to a font size. Negative values are not supported, but supported values include point sizes (for example, 12pt) and optionally (though not as exact) other size values such as pixels (for example, 10px).
Percentage relative	A percentage corresponding to a percentage of the current font. These values can be expressed in actual percentages (for example, 150%) or other relative metrics such as ems (for example, 1.5em).

Font Styling

Four properties can be used to affect font styling: font-style, font-variant, font-weight, and font-stretch. The syntax of each is shown in the following listing:

```
font-style: normal | italic | oblique;

font-variant: normal | small-caps;

font-weight: normal | bold | bolder | lighter | 100 | 200 |
   300 | 400 | 500 | 600 | 700 | 800 | 900;

font-stretch: normal | wider | narrower | ultra-condensed |
   extra-condensed | condensed | semi-condensed | semi-expanded |
   expanded | extra-expanded | ultra-expanded;
```

The font-style property is used to control the italic style of the text, while the font-weight property is used to control the bold style of the text. The other two properties control other display attributes of the font; font-variant controls whether the font is displayed in small caps, and font-stretch does exactly what its name implies.

The various values for the font-weight property can be broken down as follows:

❑ 100-900 — The darkness of the font, where 100 is the lightest and 900 the darkest. Various numbers correspond to other values as described below.

❑ lighter — Specifies the next lightest setting for a font unless the font weight is already near the weight value corresponding to 100, in which case, it stays at 100.

❑ normal — The normal darkness for the current font (corresponds to weight 400).

❑ bold — The darkness corresponding to the bold variety of the font (corresponds to weight 700).

❑ bolder — Specifies the next darkest setting for a font unless the font weight is already near the weight value corresponding to 900, in which case, it stays at 900.

The `font-style` and `font-weight` properties can be used to control a font's bold and italic properties without coding document text directly with italic (`<i>`) and bold (`<b>`) elements. For example, you might define a bold variety of a style using definitions similar to the following:

```
p { font-family:  Palatino, "Times New Roman", "Times Roman", Serif; }
p.bold { font-weight: bold; }
```

The `bold` class of the paragraph element inherits the base font from its parent, the paragraph element. The `font-weight` property in the `bold` class of the paragraph element simply makes such styled elements render as a bold variety of the base font.

Line Spacing

The `line-height` property controls the line height of text. The line height is the distance between the baselines of two vertically stacked lines of text. This value is also known as leading.

Refer back to Figure 14-12 for reference on the baseline of a font.

This property has the following syntax:

```
line-height: normal | <number> | <length> | <percentage>
```

This property sets the size of the surrounding box of the element for which it is applied. The normal value sets the line height to the default size for the current font. Specifying a number (for example, 2) causes the current line height to be multiplied by the number specified. Absolute lengths (for example, 1.2em) cause the line height to be set to that absolute value. A percentage value is handled like a number value; the percentage is applied to the value of the current font.

For example, the following two definitions both set a class up to double-space text:

```
p.doublespace { line-height: 2; }
p.doublespace { line-height: 200%; }
```

Font Embedding

There are two technologies for providing fonts embedded into your documents. Embedding fonts allows your readers to download the specific font to their local machine so that your documents use the exact font you designate. Unfortunately, as with most progressive Web technologies, the market is split into two distinct factions:

❑ OpenType is a standard developed by Microsoft and Adobe Systems. OpenType fonts, thanks to the creators of the standard, share similar traits to PostScript and TrueType fonts used in other publishing applications. Currently, only Internet Explorer supports OpenType.

❑ TrueDoc is a standard developed by Bitstream, a popular font manufacturer. Currently, only Netscape-based browsers natively support TrueDoc fonts; however, Bitstream does make an ActiveX control for support on Internet Explorer.

Even though a font is available for low cost or even for free, it doesn't mean you can reuse it, especially in a commercial application. When acquiring fonts for use on the Web, you need to ensure that you will have the appropriate rights for the use you intend.

To embed OpenType fonts in your document, you use an `@font-face` definition in the style section of your document. The `@font-face` definition has the following syntax:

```
@font-face { font-definition }
```

The `font-definition` contains various information on the font, including stylistic information and the path to the font file. This information is contained in typical style `property: value` form, similar to the following:

```
@font-face {
   font-family: Dax;
   font-weight: bold;
   src: url('http://www.example.com/fontdir/Dax.pfr');
}
```

To embed TrueDoc fonts in your document, you use the link (`<link>`) tag in a format similar to the following:

```
<link rel="fontdef" src="http://www.example.com/fontdir/Amelia.pfr">
```

To use TrueDoc fonts in Internet Explorer, you also have to include the TrueDoc ActiveX control using code similar to the following:

```
<script language="JavaScript" src="http://www.truedoc.com/activex/tdserver.js">
</script>
```

Several fonts are available for use on the TrueDoc Web site. Visit **www.truedoc.com** *for more information.*

Embedding fonts is not recommended for several reasons, including the following:

- ❑ The two standards make implementing embedded fonts difficult.
- ❑ Embedded fonts increase the download time of your document and increase the overall load on the user agent (many of which won't support the downloadable font).
- ❑ Embedded fonts decrease the flexibility of your documents, limiting how user agents can adjust the display of text.

Instead, it is recommended that you stick to CSS definitions for specifying font attributes. If you know your audience and their platform and you need your document to look *exactly* as you intend, investigate embedded fonts.

Summary

This chapter introduced you to the various CSS properties and definitions used to control text in your documents. You learned how to align text, control the spacing, and specify the font used. You also learned about two different font technologies that enable you to embed specific fonts in your documents.

15

Padding, Margins, and Borders

All elements in an XHTML document can be formatted in a variety of ways using CSS. Previous chapters in this part of the book covered the CSS basics—how to write a style definition and how to apply it to various elements within your documents. This chapter begins coverage of the area that surrounds elements and how it can be formatted, including customizing the space around an element and giving it a border. Chapter 16 continues this discussion with colors and background images.

Understanding the CSS Box Formatting Model

Although it is not overtly obvious, all elements in an XHTML document are contained within a box. That box has several properties—margins, padding, and borders—that can be configured to help distinguish the enclosed element from nearby elements.

To illustrate this point, take a look at Figure 15-1. This figure shows a document that isn't overtly boxy.

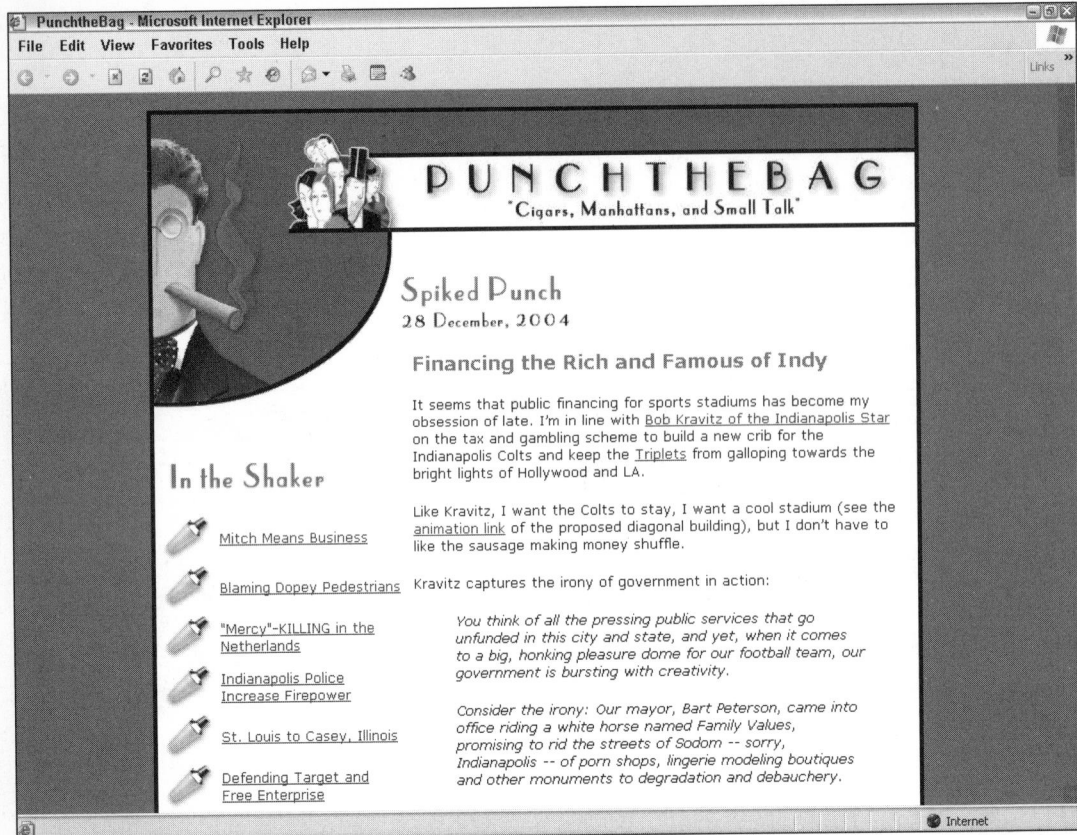

Figure 15-1

The same document is shown in Figure 15-2, but a thin border has been added to all elements, courtesy of the following style:

```
* { border: thin solid black; }
```

Note how all the XHTML elements in the document pick up the border in a rectangular box shape.

As previously mentioned in this part of the book, all elements have a margin, padding, and border property. These properties control the space around the element's contents and the elements around it. These properties stack around elements, as shown in Figure 15-3.

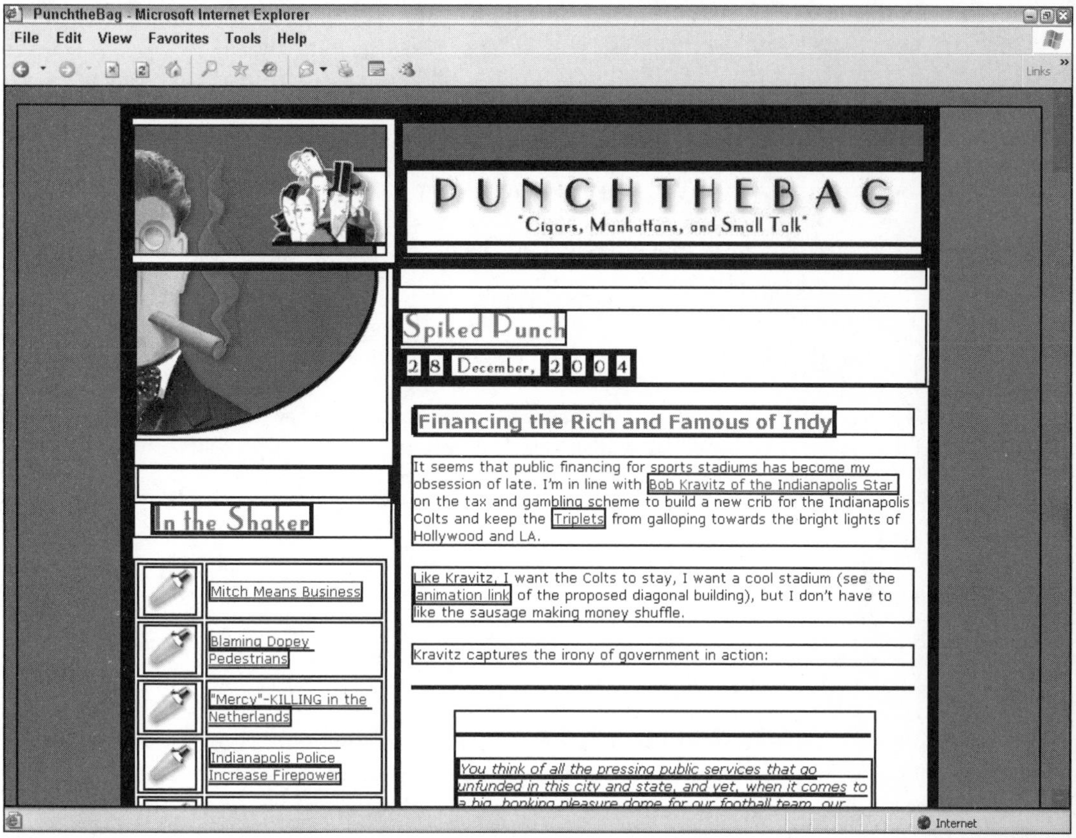

Figure 15-2

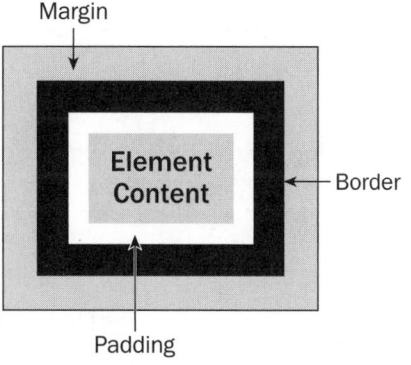

Figure 15-3

The element contents (text, image, and so on) are immediately surrounded by padding. The padding defines the distance between the element's contents and border.

The element's border (if any) is drawn right outside the element's padding.

The element's margin surrounds the element's border, or the space the border would occupy if no border is defined. The margin defines the distance between the element and neighboring elements.

The next few sections cover these properties in more detail.

Element Padding

An element's padding defines the space between the element and the space its border would occupy. This space can be increased or decreased, or set to an absolute value, using the following padding properties:

- `padding-top`
- `padding-right`
- `padding-left`
- `adding-bottom`
- `padding`

The first four properties are predictable in their behavior; for example, `padding-top` will change the padding on the top of the element, `padding-right` will change the padding on the right side of the element, and so forth. The fifth property, `padding`, is a shortcut for all sides; its effect is determined by the number of values provided, as explained in the following table.

Number of Values	The Effect of the Values
One	All sides are set to the value provided.
Two	The top and bottom are set to the first value provided; the left and right are set to the second value provided.
Three	The top is set to the first value provided, the left and right are set to the second value provided, and the bottom is set to the third value provided.
Four	The top is set to the first value provided, the right is set to the second value provided, the bottom is set to the third value provided, and the left is set to the fourth value provided. (In this case, the values are applied in a clockwise order around the element, starting with the top.)

For example, the following style will set the top and bottom padding value to 5 pixels and the right and left padding to 10 pixels:

```
padding:  5px 10px;
```

Although changing an element's padding value will change its distance from neighboring elements, you should use an object's margin property to increase or decrease the distance from neighboring elements.

Note, however, that an element's background color extends to the edge of the element's padding. Therefore, increasing an element's padding can extend the background away from an element. This is one reason to use padding instead of margins to increase space around an element. For more information on backgrounds, see Chapter 16.

As with all CSS properties, you can specify an absolute value (as in the preceding example) or a relative value. When specifying a relative value, the value is applied to the size of the element's content (such as font size, and so on), not to the default value of the padding. For example, the following code would define padding as two times the element's font size:

```
padding:  200%;
```

Element Borders

Borders are among the most versatile CSS properties. As you saw in Figure 15-2, every element in an XHTML document can have a border. However, that figure showed only one type of border, a single, thin, black line around the entire element. Each side of an element can have a different border, all controlled by CSS properties corresponding to width, style (solid, dashed, dotted, and so on), and color of the border. The following sections detail how each of the respective CSS properties can be used to affect borders.

Border Width

The width of an element's border can be specified using the border width properties, which include the following:

- ❏ `border-top-width`
- ❏ `border-right-width`
- ❏ `border-bottom-width`
- ❏ `border-left-width`
- ❏ `border-width`

As with other properties that affect multiple sides of an element, there are border width properties for each side and a shortcut property that can be used for all sides, `border-width`.

*The **border-width** shortcut property accepts one to four values. The way the values are mapped to the individual sides depends on the number of values specified. The rules for this behavior are the same as those used for the **padding** property. See the "Element Padding" section earlier in this chapter for the specific rules.*

As with other properties, the width can be specified in absolutes or relative units. For example, the first style in the following code example sets all of an element's borders to 2 pixels wide. The second style sets all of an element's borders to 50 percent of the element's size (generally font size):

```
p.two-pixel   { border-width: 2px; }

p.fifty-percent { border-width: 50%; }
```

You can also use keywords such as `thin`, `medium`, or `thick` to roughly indicate a border's width. The actual width used when the document is rendered is up to the user agent. However, if you want exact control over a border's width, you should specify it using absolute values.

Border Style

There are 10 different types of predefined border styles. These types are shown in Figure 15-4, generated by the following code:

```
<!DOCTYPE html PUBLIC "-//W3C//DTD XHTML 1.0 Strict//EN"
    "http://www.w3.org/TR/xhtml1/DTD/xhtml1-strict.dtd">
<html>
<head>
  <title>Border Types</title>
  <style type="text/css">
    p { font-size: 12pt; border-width: 6pt;
        text-align: center; padding: 20px;
        margin: 10px; font-weight: bold; }
  </style>
</head>
<body>
<p>
<table width="100%" cellspacing="20px">
<tr><td width="50%">
  <p style="border-style:none ;">None & Hidden</p>
  <p style="border-style:dotted ;">Dotted</p>
  <p style="border-style:dashed ;">Dashed</p>
  <p style="border-style:solid ;">Solid</p>
  <p style="border-style:double ;">Double</p>
</td><td>
<p> </p>
<p style="border-style:groove;">Groove</p>
<p style="border-style:ridge ;">Ridge</p>
<p style="border-style:inset;">Inset</p>
<p style="border-style:outset;">Outset</p>
</td></tr>
</table>
</p>
</body>
</html>
```

The border type **hidden** *is identical to the border type* **none**, *except that the border type* **hidden** *is treated like a border for border conflict resolutions. Border conflicts happen when adjacent elements share a common border (when there is no spacing between the elements). In most cases, the most eye-catching border is used. However, if either conflicting element has the conflicting border set to* **hidden**, *the border between the elements is unconditionally hidden.*

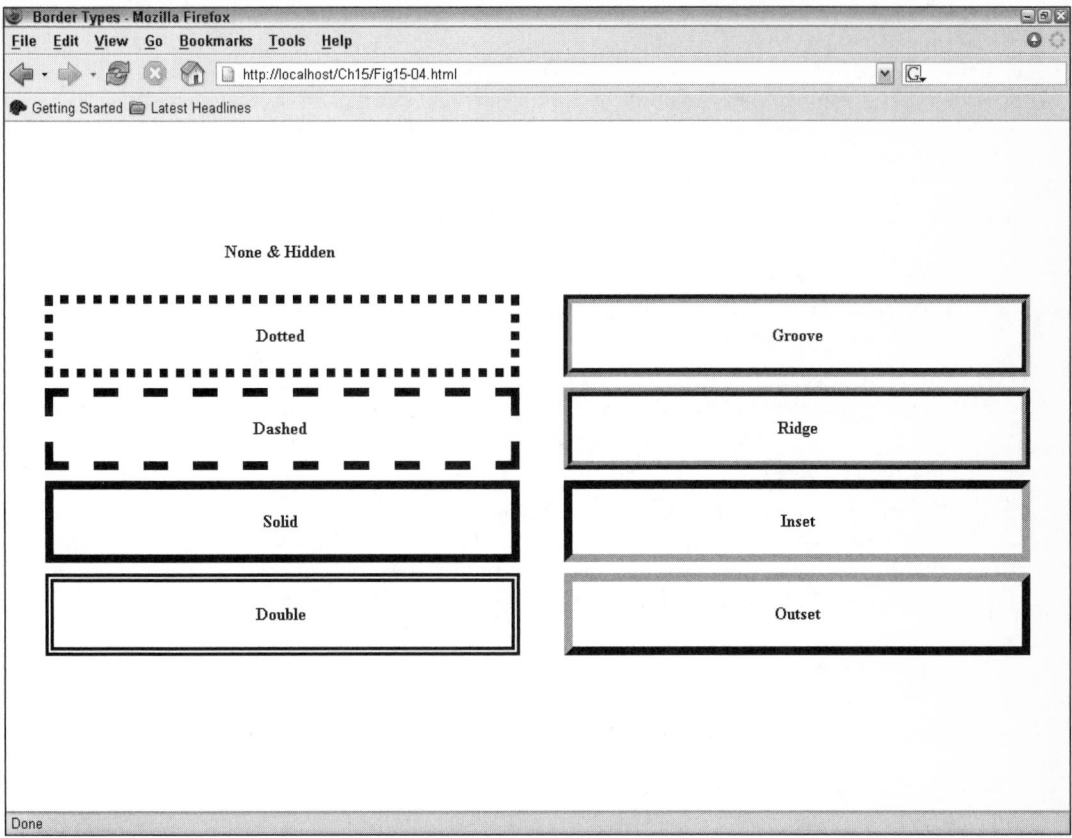

Figure 15-4

As with other properties of this type, there are several different border style properties:

❑   `border-top-style`

❑   `border-right-style`

❑   `border-bottom-style`

❑   `border-left-style`

❑   `border-style`

The first four properties affect the side for which they are named. The last, `border-style`, acts as a shortcut for all sides, following the same rules as other shortcuts covered in this chapter. See the section "Element Padding" for more information.

Border Color

The border color properties allow you to set the color of the element's visible border. As with the other properties in this chapter, there are border color properties for each side of an element (`border-top-color`, `border-right-color`, and so on) as well as a shortcut property (`border-color`) that can affect all sides.

You can choose from three different methods to specify colors in the border colors properties:

❑   **Color keywords** — `Black`, `white`, `maroon`, and so on. Note that the exact color (mix of red, green, and blue) is left up to the browser and its default colors. (See Appendix A for a list of common color keywords.)

❑   **Color hexadecimal values** — Values specified in the form `#rrggbb`, where `rrggbb` is two digits (in hexadecimal notation) for each of the colors red, green, and blue. For example, `#FF0000` specifies red (255 red, 0 green, 0 blue) and `#550055` specifies purple (equal parts of red and blue, no green).

❑   **Color decimal or percentage values** — Values specified using the `rgb()` function. This function takes three values, one each for red, green, and blue. The value can be an integer between 0 and 255 or a percentage. For example, the following specifies the color purple (equal parts red and blue, no green) in integer form and then again in percentages:

```
rgb(100, 0, 100)
rgb(50%, 0, 50%)
```

Most graphic editing programs supply color values in multiple formats, including percentage RGB values and perhaps even HTML-style hexadecimal format. Lynda Weinman's site, **www.lynda.com**, *contains a multitude of information on Web colors, especially the following page:* **http://www.lynda.com/hex.html**.

The Border Property Shortcut

You can use the `border` property as a shortcut when specifying an element's border properties. The `border` property has the following syntax:

```
border:  <border-width>  <border-style>  <border-color>;
```

For example, the following two styles set the same border for different paragraph styles:

```
p.one { border-width: thin;
        border-style: solid;
        border-color: black; }

p.two ( border: thin solid black; }
```

Border Spacing

Two additional border properties bear mentioning here, both of which are primarily used with tables:

❑ border-spacing — This property controls how the user agent renders the space between cells in tables.

❑ border-collapse — This property selects the collapsed method of table borders.

These properties are covered in more depth along with other table properties in Chapter 17.

Element Margins

Margins are the space between an element's border and neighboring elements. Margins are an important property to consider and adjust as necessary within your documents. Most elements have suitable default margins, but sometimes you will find it necessary to increase or decrease an element's margin(s) to suit your unique needs.

For example, consider the image and text shown in Figure 15-5, rendered using the following code:

```
<img src="square.png" style="float: left;"><p>Text next
  to an image using default margins</p>
```

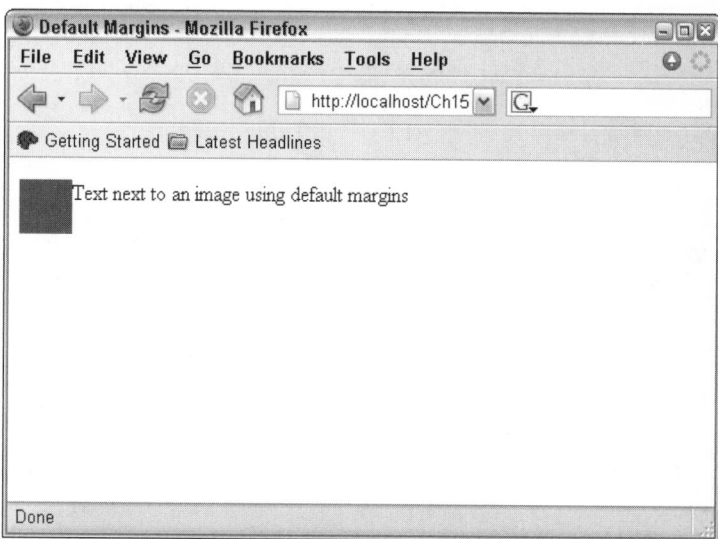

Figure 15-5

Notice how the "T" in "Text" is almost touching the image next to it. In this case, an additional margin would be welcome.

As with other properties in this chapter, margin properties exist for each individual side (`margin-top`, `margin-left`, and so on) as well as a shortcut property to set all sides at once (`margin`). As with the other shortcut properties describe herein, the `margin` property accepts one to four values, and the number of values specified determines how the property is applied to an element. See the "Element Padding" section earlier in this chapter for more information.

For example, you can increase the margins of the image in Figure 15-5 using a style similar to the following:

```
border-right:  5px;
```

This would set the right border of the image (the edge next to the text) to 5 pixels. Likewise, you can change all four margins using a shortcut such as the following:

```
border:  2px  4px  10px  4px;
```

> *There are no guidelines for which margins you should adjust on what elements. However, it's usually best to modify the least number of margins or to be consistent with which margins you do change.*

Dynamic Outlines

Outlines are another layer that exists around an element to allow the user agent to highlight the element, if necessary. This generally happens when a form element receives focus. The position of the outline cannot be moved, but it can be influenced by the position of the element's border. Note that outlines do not occupy any space; the element occupies the same amount of space whether its outline is visible or not.

Figure 15-6 shows an example of a dynamic outline around the Phone label.

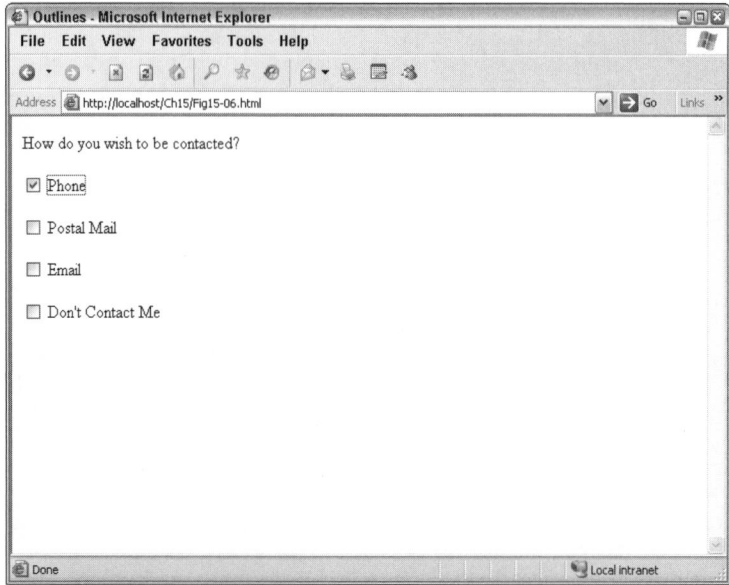

Figure 15-6

Using CSS you can modify the look of outlines. However, unlike other properties covered in this chapter, all sides of an outline must be the same. The CSS properties governing outlines include `outline-color`, `outline-style`, `outline-width`, and the shorthand property `outline`. These properties operate much like the other properties in this chapter, allowing the same values and having the same effects. The format of the `outline` shortcut property is as follows:

```
outline: outline-color  outline-style  outline-width;
```

To use the outline properties dynamically, use the `:focus` and `:active` pseudoelements. These two pseudoelements specify when an element's outline should be visible — when it has focus or when it is active. For example, the following definitions specify a thick green border when form elements have focus and a thin blue border when they are active:

```
form *:focus { outline-width: thick; outline-color: green; }
form *:active { outline-width: thin; outline-color: blue; }
```

However, as of this writing, user agent support for outlines is very inconsistent, when it exists at all. If you intend to use outlines in your documents, you should test your code extensively on all platforms you expect your audience to use.

Summary

This chapter introduced you to the box model of CSS and how you can use various properties of an element's surrounding box to help format your documents. You learned how padding, borders, and margins comprise a layered structure around an element and how each can be manipulated to change how elements render in the document. You learned about the extensive border options and finished with coverage of dynamic outlines. Chapter 16 covers the other customizable pieces of the box model, namely the foreground and background, both colors and images.

16

Colors and Backgrounds

In Chapter 15, you learned about the box-formatting model of CSS and how you can manipulate an element's containing box to format your XHTML documents. This chapter continues that discussion, teaching you about element foreground and background colors and using images for element backgrounds.

Element Colors

Most elements in an XHTML document have two color properties: a foreground property and a background property. Both of these properties can be controlled using CSS styles. The following sections discuss both types of color properties.

Foreground Colors

The foreground color of an element is typically used as the visible portion of an element — in most cases, the color of the font or other visible part of the element. You can control the foreground color of an element using the CSS `color` property, which has the following format:

```
color:  <color_value>;
```

As with other properties using color values, the value can be expressed using one of three methods:

❑ Predefined color names (such as blue, red, black, or green)

❑ Hexadecimal color values in #rrggbb form (#000000 for black, #FF0000 for red, #FF00FF for dark purple, and so on)

❑ An RGB value using the rgb() function (rgb(100%,0,0) or rgb(255,0,0) for red)

More information on color values can be found in the "Border Color" section of Chapter 15.

For example, the following style defines a class of the paragraph element, which will be rendered with a red font:

```
p.redtext { color: red; }
```

The following paragraph, when used with the preceding style, will be rendered with red text:

```
<p class="redtext">This paragraph is important, and as such, appears in
red text. Other paragraphs in this section that are less important, appear
in standard black text.</p>
```

As with all style properties, you are not limited to element-level definitions. As shown in the following code, you can define a generic class that can be used with elements, spans, divisions, and more:

```
.redtext { color: red; }
```

When defining an element's foreground color, you should pay attention to what that element's background color will be, avoiding dark foregrounds on dark backgrounds and light foregrounds on light backgrounds. However, matching foreground and background colors can have its uses — see the note near the end of the following section for an example of this practice.

Keep in mind that the user settings of the user agent can affect the color of elements, as well. If you don't explicitly define an element's color using appropriate styles, the user agent will use its default colors.

Background Colors

An element's background color can be thought of as the color of the virtual page the element is rendered upon. For example, consider Figure 16-1, which shows two paragraphs: the first is rendered against the user agent's default background (in this case, white) and the second against a light-gray background.

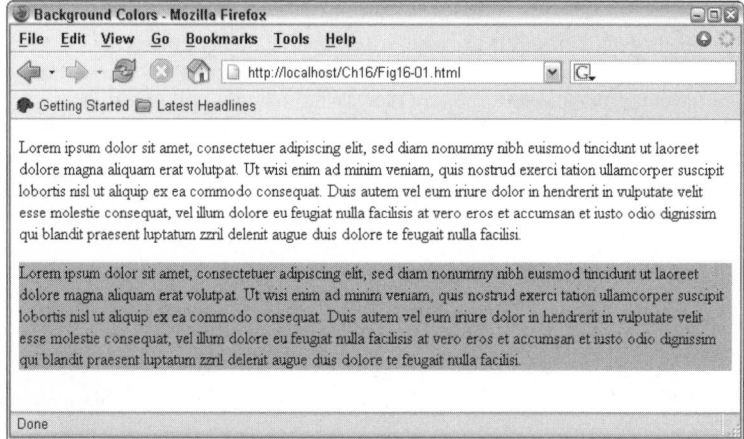

Figure 16-1

Saying that a document has a default color of white is incorrect. The document will have the color specified in the user agent's settings if not otherwise instructed to change it.

You can use the CSS `background-color` property to define a particular color that should be used for an element's background. The `background-color` property's syntax is similar to other element color properties:

```
background-color:  <color_value>
```

For example, you could use this property to define a navy blue background for the entire document (or at least its body section):

```
body { background-color:  navy;
  color: white; }
```

Note that this definition also sets a foreground color so that the default text will be visible against the dark background.

Sometimes it can be advantageous to use similar foreground and background colors together. For example, on a forum that pertains to movie reviews, users may wish to publish spoilers — pieces of the plot that others may not wish to know prior to seeing the movie. On such a site, a style can be defined such that the text cannot be viewed until it is selected in the user agent, as shown in Figure 16-2. The style could be defined as follows:

```
<!DOCTYPE html PUBLIC "-//W3C//DTD XHTML 1.0 Strict//EN"
    "http://www.w3.org/TR/xhtml1/DTD/xhtml1-strict.dtd">
<html>
<head>
  <title>Spoiler Text</title>
  <style type="text/css">
    .spoiler { background-color: gray; color: gray; }
  </style>
</head>
<body>
<p>I was surprised by the ending of <i>Titanic</i>: <span class="spoiler">At
the end of the movie, the boat sinks.</span></p>
</body>
</html>
```

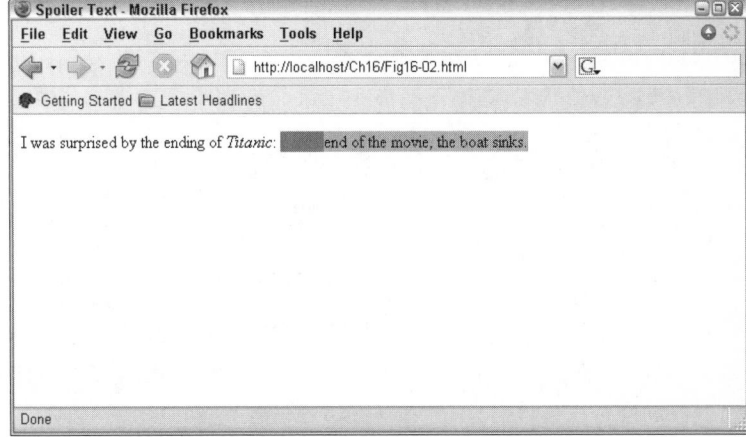

Figure 16-2

Note that an element's background extends to the end of its padding. If you want to enlarge the background of an element, expand its padding accordingly. For example, both paragraphs in Figure 16-3 have a lightly colored background. However, the second paragraph has had its padding expanded, as laid out in the following code:

```
<!DOCTYPE html PUBLIC "-//W3C//DTD XHTML 1.0 Strict//EN"
   "http://www.w3.org/TR/xhtml1/DTD/xhtml1-strict.dtd">
<html>
<head>
  <title>Expanding Backgrounds</title>
  <style type="text/css">
    p { background-color: #CCCCCC; }
    p.larger-background { padding: 20px; }
  </style>
</head>
<body>
<p>Lorem ipsum dolor sit amet, consectetuer adipiscing elit, sed
diam nonummy nibh euismod tincidunt ut laoreet dolore magna
aliquam erat volutpat. Ut wisi enim ad minim veniam, quis nostrud
exerci tation ullamcorper suscipit lobortis nisl ut aliquip ex ea
commodo consequat. Duis autem vel eum iriure dolor in hendrerit in
vulputate velit esse molestie consequat, vel illum dolore eu feugiat
nulla facilisis at vero eros et accumsan et iusto odio dignissim qui
blandit praesent luptatum zzril delenit augue duis dolore te feugait
nulla facilisi.</p>
<p class="larger-background">Lorem ipsum dolor sit amet, consectetuer
adipiscing elit, sed diam nonummy nibh euismod tincidunt ut laoreet
dolore magna aliquam erat volutpat. Ut wisi enim ad minim veniam, quis
nostrud exerci tation ullamcorper suscipit lobortis nisl ut aliquip ex ea
commodo consequat. Duis autem vel eum iriure dolor in hendrerit in
vulputate velit esse molestie consequat, vel illum dolore eu feugiat
nulla facilisis at vero eros et accumsan et iusto odio dignissim qui
blandit praesent luptatum zzril delenit augue duis dolore te feugait
nulla facilisi.</p>
</body>
</html>
```

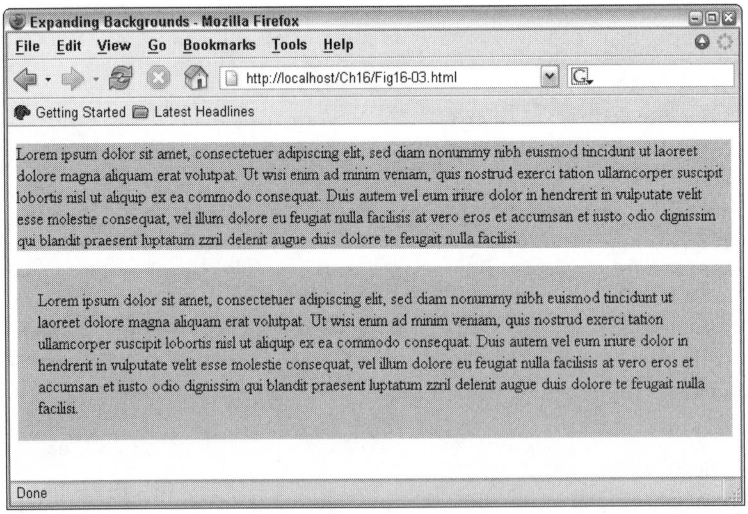

Figure 16-3

Background Images

In addition to solid colors, you can specify that an element use an image as its background. To do so, you use the `background-image` property. This property has the following syntax:

```
background-image: url("<url_to_image>");
```

For example, the following code results in the document rendered in Figure 16-4, where the paragraph is rendered over a light gradient:

```
<!DOCTYPE html PUBLIC "-//W3C//DTD XHTML 1.0 Strict//EN"
    "http://www.w3.org/TR/xhtml1/DTD/xhtml1-strict.dtd">
<html>
<head>
  <title>Background Images</title>
  <style type="text/css">
    p { background-image: url("gradient.gif"); }
  </style>
</head>
<body>
<p>Lorem ipsum dolor sit amet, consectetuer adipiscing elit, sed
diam nonummy nibh euismod tincidunt ut laoreet dolore magna
aliquam erat volutpat. Ut wisi enim ad minim veniam, quis nostrud
exerci tation ullamcorper suscipit lobortis nisl ut aliquip ex ea
commodo consequat. Duis autem vel eum iriure dolor in hendrerit in
vulputate velit esse molestie consequat, vel illum dolore eu feugiat
nulla facilisis at vero eros et accumsan et iusto odio dignissim qui
blandit praesent luptatum zzril delenit augue duis dolore te feugait
nulla facilisi.</p>
<p>Background image:<br />
<img src="gradient.gif" alt="gradient" width="400" height="400" /></p>
</body>
</html>
```

Background images can be used for interesting effects, such as that shown in Figure 16-5, rendered from the following code:

```
<!DOCTYPE html PUBLIC "-//W3C//DTD XHTML 1.0 Strict//EN"
    "http://www.w3.org/TR/xhtml1/DTD/xhtml1-strict.dtd">
<html>
<head>
  <title>Text Frame</title>
  <style type="text/css">
    p.catborder { height: 135px; width: 336px;
       background-image: url("catframe.gif");
       padding: 80px 135px 18px 18px; }
  </style>
</head>
<body>
<p class="catborder">Lorem ipsum dolor sit amet, consectetuer adipiscing elit, sed
diam nonummy nibh euismod tincidunt ut laoreet dolore magna
aliquam erat volutpat. Ut wisi enim ad minim veniam, quis nostrud
exerci tation ullamcorper suscipit lobortis nisl ut aliquip ex ea
commodo consequat. </p>
<p>Background image:<br />
```

231

```
<img src="catframe.gif" alt="gradient" width="490" height="231" /></p>
</body>
</html>
```

Note how the various sides of the paragraph were padded to ensure that the text appears in the correct position relative to the background.

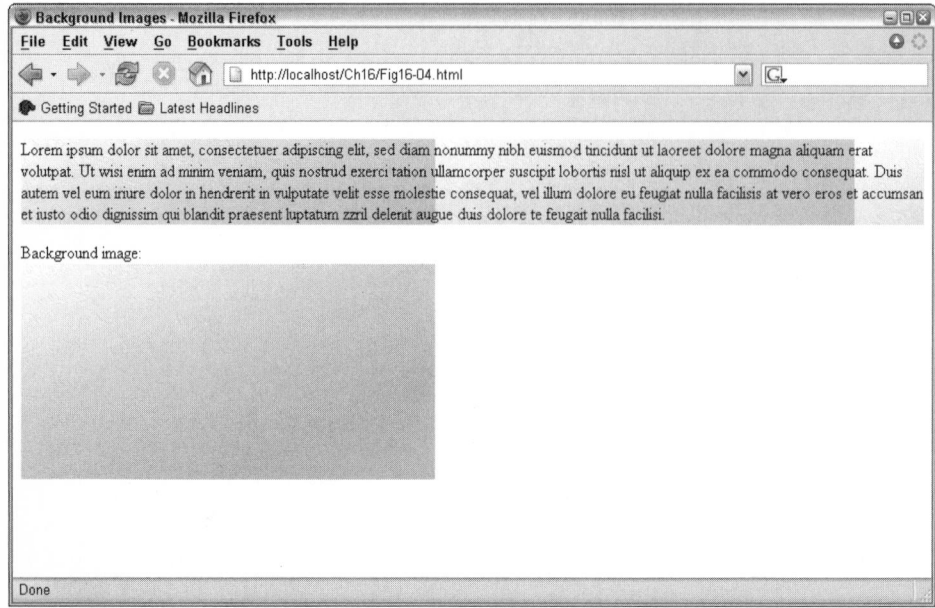

Figure 16-4

Repeating and Scrolling Images

Element background images tile themselves to fill the available space, as you saw in Figure 16-4, where the gradient tiles horizontally to span the width of the paragraph. You can control the scrolling and placement properties of a background image using the `background-repeat` and `background-attachment` properties.

The `background-repeat` property has the following syntax:

```
background-repeat: repeat | repeat-x | repeat-y | no-repeat;
```

The `background-attachment` property has the following format:

```
background-attachment: scroll | fixed;
```

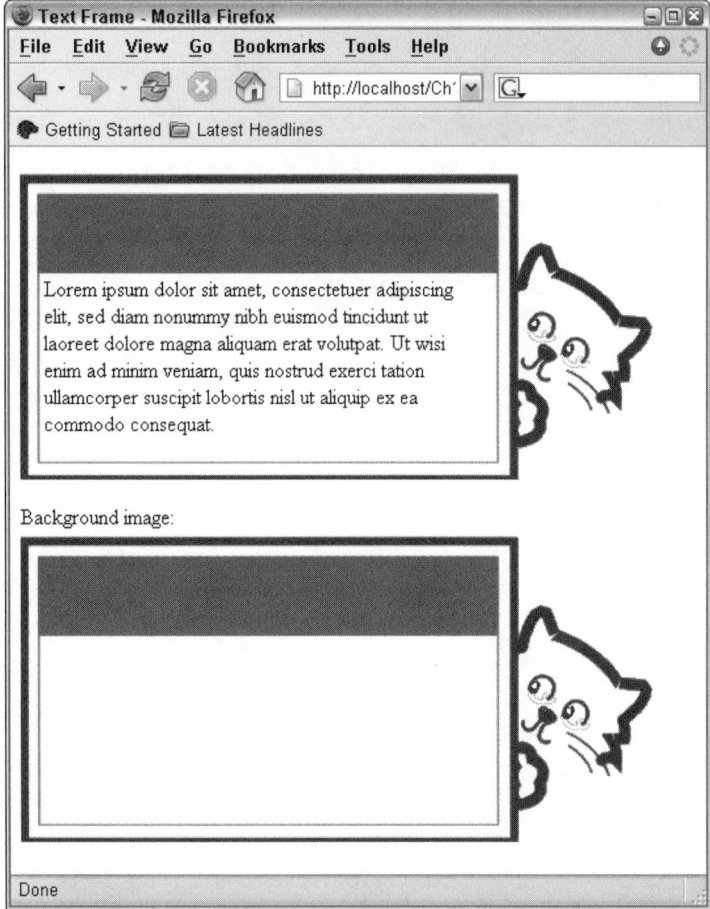

Figure 16-5

Using the `background-repeat` property is straightforward — its values specify how the image repeats. For example, to repeat our smiley face across the top of the paragraph, specify `repeat-x`, as shown in the following definition code and Figure 16-6:

```
p.smiley { background-image: url("smiley.gif");
          background-repeat: repeat-x;
          /* Border to clarity paragraph size */
          border: thin solid black; }
```

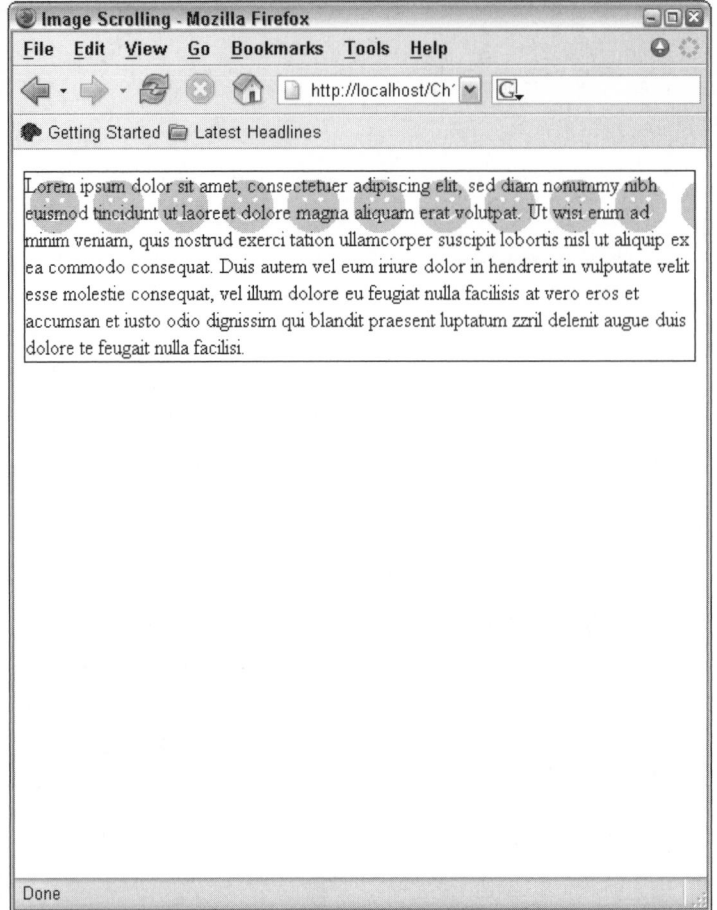

Figure 16-6

Specifying `repeat-y` would repeat the image vertically instead of horizontally. If you specify just `repeat`, the image tiles both horizontally and vertically. Specifying `no-repeat` will cause the image to be placed once only, not repeating in either dimension.

The `background-attachment` property specifies how the background image is attached to the element. Specifying `scroll` allows the image to scroll with the contents of the element, as shown with the second paragraph in Figure 16-7. Both paragraphs were rendered with the following paragraph definition; the second paragraph has been scrolled a bit, vertically shifting both text and image:

```
p.smileyscroll { height: 220px; width: 520px;
       /* Scroll the element's content */
       overflow: scroll;
       /* Define a background image and set
          it to scroll */
```

```
background-image: url("smiley.gif");
background-attachment: scroll;
/* Border for clarity only */
border: thin solid black; }
```

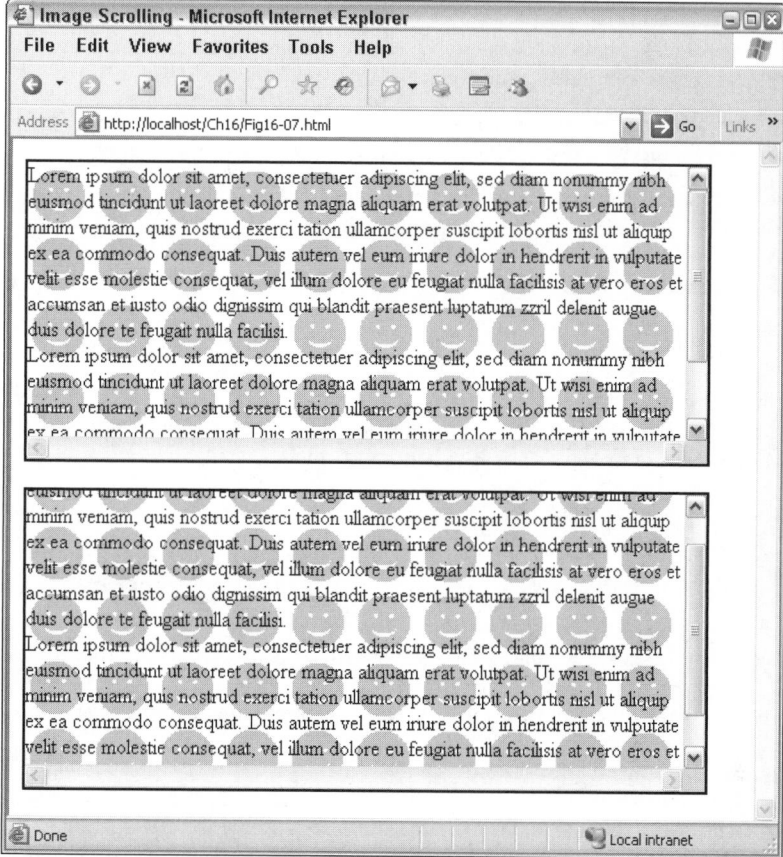

Figure 16-7

Specifying a value of `fixed` for the `background-attachment` property will fix the background image in place, causing it not to scroll if/when the element's content is scrolled. This value is particularly useful for images used as the background for entire documents for a watermark effect.

*The use of the **overflow** property in the code for Figure 16-7 controls what happens when an element's content is larger than its containing box. The **scroll** value enables scroll bars on the element so that the user can scroll to see the entire content. The **overflow** property also supports the values **visible** (which causes the element to be displayed in its entirety, despite its containing box size) and **hidden** (which causes the portion of the element that overflows to be clipped and remain inaccessible to the user).*

Positioning Background Images

You can use the `background-position` property to control where an element's background image is placed in relation to the element's containing box. The `background-position` property's syntax isn't as straightforward as some of the other properties. This property has three different forms for its values:

❑ Two percentages are used to specify where the upper-left corner of the image should be placed in relation to the element's padding area.

❑ Two lengths (in inches, centimeters, pixels, em, and so on) specify where the upper-left corner of the image should be placed in relation to the element's padding area.

❑ Keywords specify absolute measures of the element's padding area. The supported keywords include `top`, `left`, `right`, `bottom`, and `center`.

No matter what format you use for the `background-position` values, the format is as follows:

```
background-position: <horizontal_value> <vertical_value>;
```

If only one value is given, it is used for the horizontal placement and the image is centered vertically. The first two formats can be mixed together (for example, `10px 25%`), but keywords cannot be mixed with other values (for example, `center 30%` is invalid).

For example, to center a background image behind an element, you can use either of the following definitions:

```
background-position: center center;
```

```
background-position: 50% 50%;
```

If you want to specify an absolute position behind the element, you can do so as well:

```
background-position:   10px 10px;
```

You can combine the background image properties to achieve diverse effects. For example, you can use **background-position** *to set an image to appear in the center of the element's padding, and you can specify* **background-attachment: fixed** *to keep it there. Furthermore, you could use* **background-repeat** *to repeat the same image horizontally or vertically, creating striping behind the element.*

Summary

This chapter completed the discussion of the CSS box-formatting model and how you can manipulate the foreground and background of the containing box of elements. You learned about foreground and background colors as well as how to use images as the background for elements. Chapter 17 covers table-formatting properties, and the CSS coverage wraps up in Chapter 18 with an explanation of element positioning.

Tables

In Chapter 8, you learned about all the formatting attributes available for table elements in your XHTML documents. It should come as no surprise that CSS has analogous properties to match each of the table element attributes. However, the various CSS properties do not apply to tables exactly like the element attributes. This chapter breaks down the CSS properties into their respective groups and shows you how to use them to format tables using CSS instead of tag attributes.

CSS Properties and Table Attributes

There are many CSS properties that can be used to control table attributes in your document. The following table lists the basic properties available and how they correspond to table element (`<table>`) attributes.

Purpose	Table Attribute	CSS Property(ies)
Borders	`border`	`border` properties
Spacing inside cell	`cellpadding`	`padding` properties
Spacing between cells	`cellspacing`	`border-spacing`
Width of table	`width`	`width` and `table-layout` properties
Table framing	`frame`	`border` properties
Alignment	`align`, `valign`	`text-align`, `vertical-alignment` properties

Because many of the table element's attributes have not been deprecated in XHTML, you may be tempted to embed all of your document's table formatting within individual table tags. Resist that temptation. Using tag attributes increases the editing difficulty of the document—each table using tag attributes instead of CSS properties must be edited individually. If you use CSS properties instead, you can modify many tables by editing only one style (or a few styles). Furthermore, if you use external style sheets, you can effect changes in multiple documents by editing only a few styles.

The next few sections detail the CSS properties for formatting tables.

Defining Borders

Tables use border properties to control the border of document tables and their subelements. For example, to surround every table and their subelements with a single 1pt border, you could use a style definition similar to the following:

```
/*  Format for tables and their elements */
table, table *  { border:  1pt solid black; }
```

The results of this definition can be seen on the table shown in Figure 17-1.

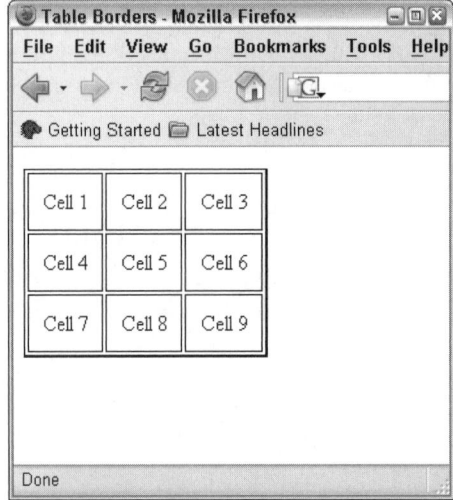

Figure 17-1

Note that the style specifies the table element (`table`) as well as its descendants (`table *`) to ensure that the table itself as well as all of its subelements receive a border. You can define your selectors in creative ways to create unique borders—placing one style around cells, another around the table, a third around the caption, and so on.

To use CSS to create table borders similar to borders created with a `border="1"` attribute, you can use styles similar to those in the following code, whose results are shown in Figure 17-2:

```
<!DOCTYPE html PUBLIC "-//W3C//DTD XHTML 1.0 Strict//EN"
    "http://www.w3.org/TR/xhtml1/DTD/xhtml1-strict.dtd">
<html>
<head>
  <title>Table Borders</title>
```

```
<style type="text/css">
  /* More padding for legibility */
  table td { padding: 5px; }
  /* Formatting similar to border attribute */
  table.attrib-similar { border: outset 1pt; }
  table.attrib-similar td { border: inset 1pt; }
</style>
</head>
<body>
<p><table border="1">
<caption>border="1" attribute</caption>
<tr><td>Cell 1</td><td>Cell 2</td><td>Cell 3</td></tr>
<tr><td>Cell 4</td><td>Cell 5</td><td>Cell 6</td></tr>
</table></p>

<p><table class="attrib-similar">
<caption>CSS styles</caption>
<tr><td>Cell 1</td><td>Cell 2</td><td>Cell 3</td></tr>
<tr><td>Cell 4</td><td>Cell 5</td><td>Cell 6</td></tr>
</table></p>
</body>
</html>
```

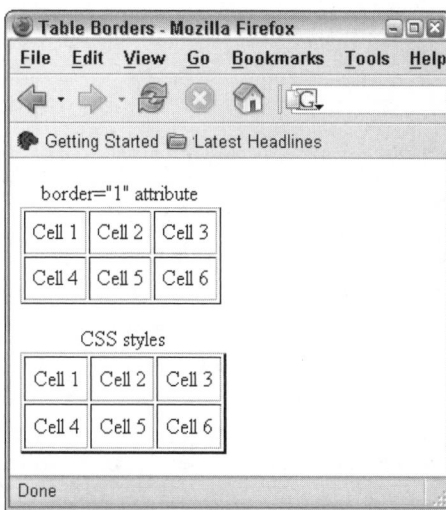

Figure 17-2

Border and Cell Spacing

To adjust the space around table borders, use the border-spacing and padding properties. The border-spacing property adjusts the spacing between element borders much like the table element's cellspacing attribute. The padding properties adjust the space between the table elements' contents and the elements' border, much like these properties do with other elements.

The `border-spacing` property has the following syntax:

```
border-spacing:   horizontal_spacing   vertical_spacing;
```

For example, the following definition will create more space between columns than between rows, as shown in the table in Figure 17-3:

```
table, table * { padding: 5px;
      border-collapse: separate;
      border: thin solid black;
      border-spacing: 5px 15px; }
```

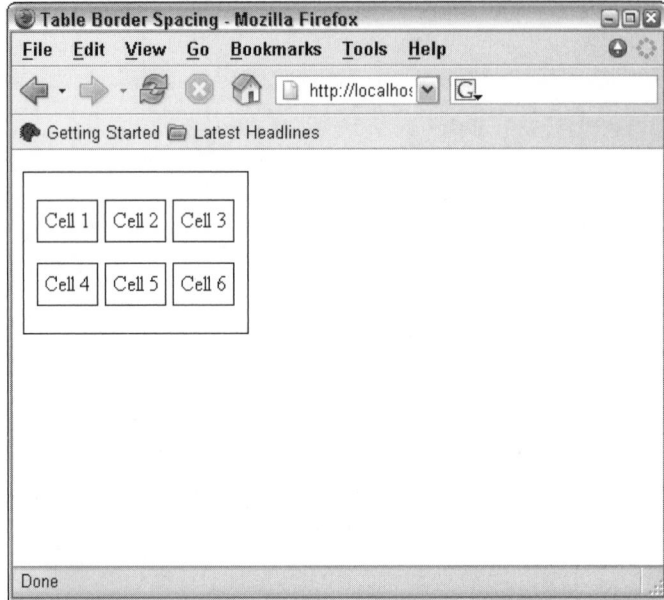

Figure 17-3

*The **border-spacing** property is not supported in current versions of Microsoft Internet Explorer. Also note that this property works only in concert with the **border-collapse** property (described in the next section) set to **separate**.*

The table padding properties function exactly as they do with other elements. For example, to increase the space between a table cell's contents and its border, you could explicitly specify the padding value in an appropriate style:

```
/*  Add more interior space to table cells  */
td.morespace { padding: 10px; }
```

For a full discussion of padding properties, see Chapter 15.

Collapsing Borders

As you may have noticed, the default CSS border handling leaves spaces between the borders of adjacent elements. For example, consider the table in Figure 17-4.

When you want adjacent elements to collapse their borders into one border, you enter the `border-collapse` property, which has the following syntax:

```
border-collapse: separate | collapse;
```

The two values do what you would expect; `separate` causes the borders of each element to be rendered separately, spaced according to the user agent default or the `border-spacing` property's value, while `collapse` causes adjacent elements to be separated by one border. The table in Figure 17-4 is identical to the table in Figure 17-3 except that the `border-collapse` property has been set to `collapse`, as demonstrated in the following code:

```
table, table * { padding: 5px;
     border-collapse: collapse;
     border: thin solid black;
     border-spacing: 5px 15px; }
```

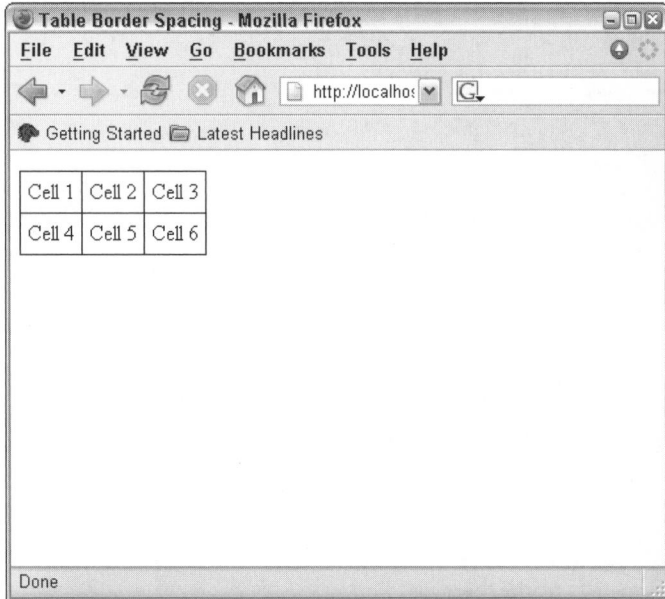

Figure 17-4

Notice how setting `border-collapse` to `collapse` causes the user agent to ignore the `border-spacing` property.

When two adjacent elements have different borders, it is up to the user agent to decide which border to render when the borders are collapsed. Typically, the most ornate border is chosen. For example, consider the following code and the results shown in Figure 17-5:

```
<!DOCTYPE html PUBLIC "-//W3C//DTD XHTML 1.0 Strict//EN"
    "http://www.w3.org/TR/xhtml1/DTD/xhtml1-strict.dtd">
<html>
<head>
  <title>Border Collapse</title>
  <style type="text/css">
    table { width: 400px; }
    table.one, table.one td { border: solid 2pt black; border-collapse: separate;
}
    table.one th { border: inset 3pt; }

    table.two, table.two td { border: solid 2pt black;  border-collapse: collapse;
}
    table.two th { border: inset 3pt; }

  </style>
</head>
<body>
<p><pre>
    table, table td { border: solid 2pt black;
                      border-collapse: separate; }
    table th { border: inset 3pt; }
</pre></p>
<p>
<table class="one">
  <tr><th>Employee</th><th>Start Date</th><th>Next Review</th></tr>
  <tr><td>Vicki S.</td><td>2/15/04</td><td>2/28/04</td></tr>
  <tr><td>Teresa M.</td><td>11/15/03</td><td>3/31/04</td></tr>
  <tr><td>Tamara D.</td><td>8/25/02</td><td>n/a</td></tr>
  <tr><td>Steve H.</td><td>11/02/00</td><td>3/31/04</td></tr>
</table>
</p>

<p><pre>
    table, table td { border: solid 2pt black;
                      border-collapse: collapse; }
    table th { border: inset 3pt; }
</pre></p>
<p>
<table class="two">
  <tr><th>Employee</th><th>Start Date</th><th>Next Review</th></tr>
  <tr><td>Vicki S.</td><td>2/15/04</td><td>2/28/04</td></tr>
  <tr><td>Teresa M.</td><td>11/15/03</td><td>3/31/04</td></tr>
  <tr><td>Tamara D.</td><td>8/25/02</td><td>n/a</td></tr>
  <tr><td>Steve H.</td><td>11/02/00</td><td>3/31/04</td></tr>
</table>
</p>
</body>
</html>
```

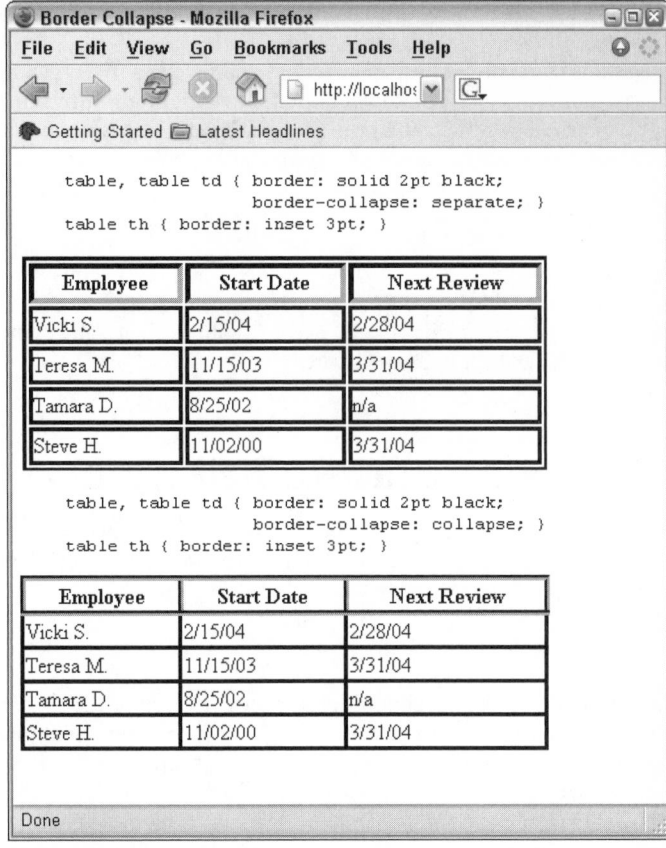

Figure 17-5

Notice how the border between the header row and first data row of the second table (Figure 17-5) is inset. This is because the header row's border was more ornate and won the conflict between the header row and data row borders when collapsed.

The `empty-cells` property controls whether empty cells will have a border rendered for them or not. This property has the following syntax:

```
empty-cells: show | hide;
```

As you would expect, setting the property to `show` (the default) will cause borders to be rendered, while setting the property to `hide` will cause them to be hidden.

*Current versions of Microsoft Internet Explorer disregard this property. To ensure that borders are rendered around "empty" cells in Internet Explorer, you can insert nonbreaking space entities (** **) in each otherwise empty cell.*

Table Layout

Typically, the user agent is in charge of how to render the table to best fit its platform's display based in part on the contents of cells and in part on the default table rendering settings of the platform. You can force the user agent to render the table using only the width values of its elements by using the `table-layout` property. This property has the following syntax:

```
table-layout:  auto | fixed;
```

Setting the property value to `auto` (the default) allows the user agent to consider the contents of the table cells when formatting the table. Setting the property's value to `fixed` causes the user agent to disregard the contents of the table and format it only according to explicit width values given within the document (via CSS) or the table itself (CSS or tag attributes).

Caption Alignment and Positioning

As you saw in Chapter 8, table captions appear centered above the table to which they are attached. However, using the `caption-side` and text alignment properties, you can change this behavior. The `caption-side` property has the following syntax:

```
caption-side:  top | bottom | left | right;
```

Setting the appropriate value will position the caption to the corresponding side of the table. If you wish to change the default alignment (center) of the caption, you can use text alignment properties such as `text-align` or `vertical-align`. The text alignment properties are covered in more depth in Chapter 14.

> Note that you can use the text alignment properties to help control where a table is placed by placing the table within paragraph tags that use appropriate **text-align** properties.

For example, the following definition will position the corresponding table's caption to the right of the table, with a left-justified, horizontal alignment and a top vertical alignment:

```
table { caption-side: right; }
caption { margin-left: 10px;
          text-align: left;
          vertical-align: top; }
```

Summary

This chapter covered the CSS formatting properties of tables. You learned what properties are available and how most of them match up to the table element's attributes. In most cases, you can accomplish the same formatting with either method (CSS or attributes), though the use of CSS is strongly encouraged. Because of the diversity possible with the various combinations of table properties, the examples in this chapter only scratched the surface of formatting possibilities. However, using these examples, you should be able to construct style definitions for just about any table-formatting chore.

Element Positioning

In Chapter 11 you learned how XHTML tables could be used to create document layouts, positioning elements in a grid-like pattern to format a document. The table layout method allows for fairly diverse and complex layouts. However, CSS provides several sizing and positioning properties that allow you much more control over your document. CSS-based document layout has several other advantages, as well, especially when used in conjunction with other technologies (such as Dynamic HTML, covered in Chapters 21 and 22). This chapter covers the various positioning, sizing, and visibility properties available in CSS.

Understanding Positioning Methods

Several element-positioning methods are available via CSS. Which method you choose depends on how you want an element's position to be affected by other elements and changes the user makes to the user agent view port (resizing the view port, moving the view port window, and so on). The positioning model an element uses can be specified using the `position` property. This property has the following syntax:

```
position:   static | relative | absolute | fixed;
```

The following sections detail the various positioning methods (`static`, `relative`, `absolute`, and `fixed`) available via the `position` property.

Not all user agents support all positioning models. If you choose to use a positioning method, you should test your code on all platforms you wish to support.

Static Positioning

Static positioning is the default positioning model used if no other method is specified. This method causes elements to be rendered within their in-line or other containing block, placed in the document as the user agent would normally flow them. The three paragraphs shown in Figure 18-1 are all positioned statically, though the second paragraph has its positioning model explicitly defined with the following style:

```
p.static { width: 400px; height: 200px;
          border: 1pt solid black;
          position: static;
}
```

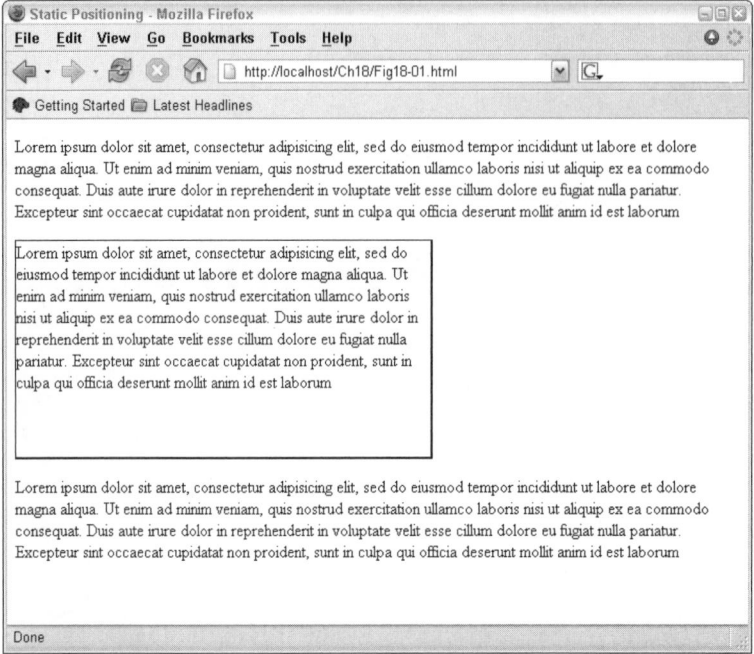

Figure 18-1

Several styles have been added to the demonstration paragraphs within this section to help illustrate the difference in positioning models. Sizing and border properties have been implemented to help visualize the paragraphs' position. Sizing properties are covered later in this chapter, and border properties are covered in Chapter 15.

Other than the sizing and border properties added for clarity, the position of the paragraph is similar to its position using no styles — hence the default static positioning — as shown in Figure 18-2, which has no styles added to the second paragraph.

Relative Positioning

Relative positioning moves an element from its normal position by using measurements *relative* to that normal position. For example, you can nudge an element a bit to the right of its normal position by setting the positioning model to `relative` and specifying a value for the left edge of the element, as in the following example:

```
p.nudge-right { position: relative;  left: 25px; }
```

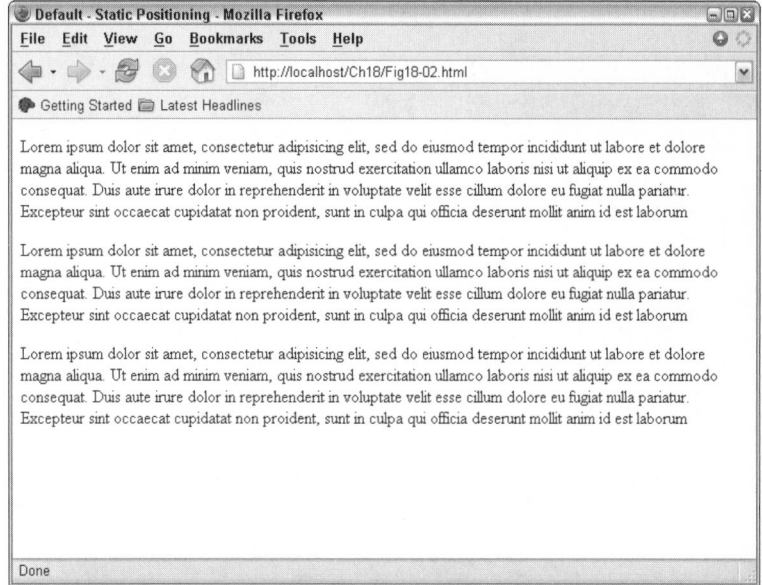

Figure 18-2

This example places the left edge of the paragraph 25 pixels to the right of where it would have been placed using static positioning.

> *When specifying relative measures, you can use the side properties (**top**, **left**, **bottom**, and **right**) to move the corresponding side of the element. Any unspecified sides of the element will be positioned according to other factors affecting their position — their size, margins, neighboring elements, bounding box, and so on.*

Figure 18-3 shows an example of relative positioning; the second paragraph has been moved down and to the right using the following styles:

```
p.relative { width: 400px; height: 200px;
        border: 1pt solid black;
        position: relative;
        top: 50px; left: 50px
}
```

Note that the movement of the second paragraph causes it to overlap (and cover) the text of the third paragraph. Using layer properties, you can control which paragraph ends up on top. (Element layer properties are covered in the "Element Layers" section later in this chapter.) This example also introduces element transparency; without a defined background color, the top element has a transparent background, allowing elements beneath it to show through.

Element repositioned 50 pixels down and to the right

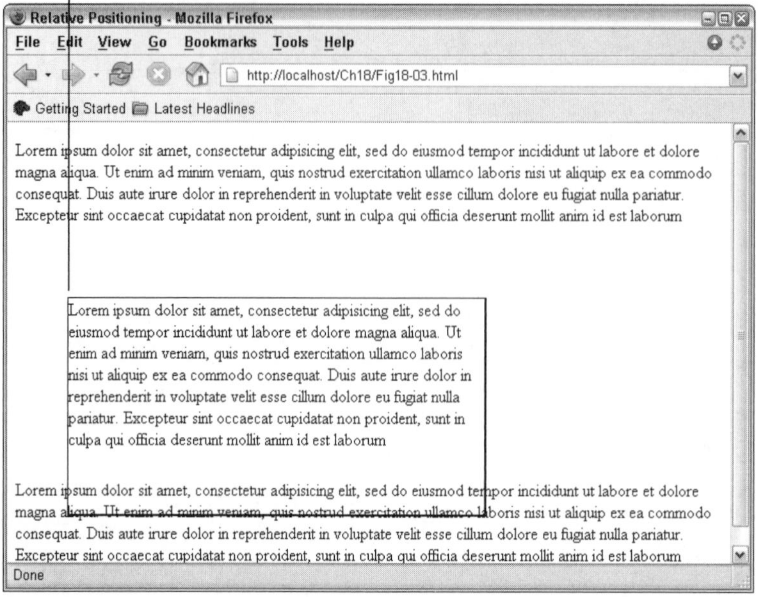

Figure 18-3

Also note that the user agent does not flow elements into the hole created due to the element(s) being repositioned — the third paragraph remains in the position it would occupy had the second paragraph not been repositioned.

Absolute Positioning

Absolute positioning uses absolute measures to position an element in relation to the view port of the user agent. The normal (static) position of the element is not taken into account when this positioning method is used.

The second paragraph in Figure 18-4 has been positioned using absolute positioning with the following styles:

```
p.absolute { width: 400px; height: 200px;
            border: 1pt solid black;
            background-color: white;
            position: absolute;
            top: 50px; left: 50px
}
```

A white background has been added to the demonstration paragraph — overriding the transparent background — to help clarify its position in the document.

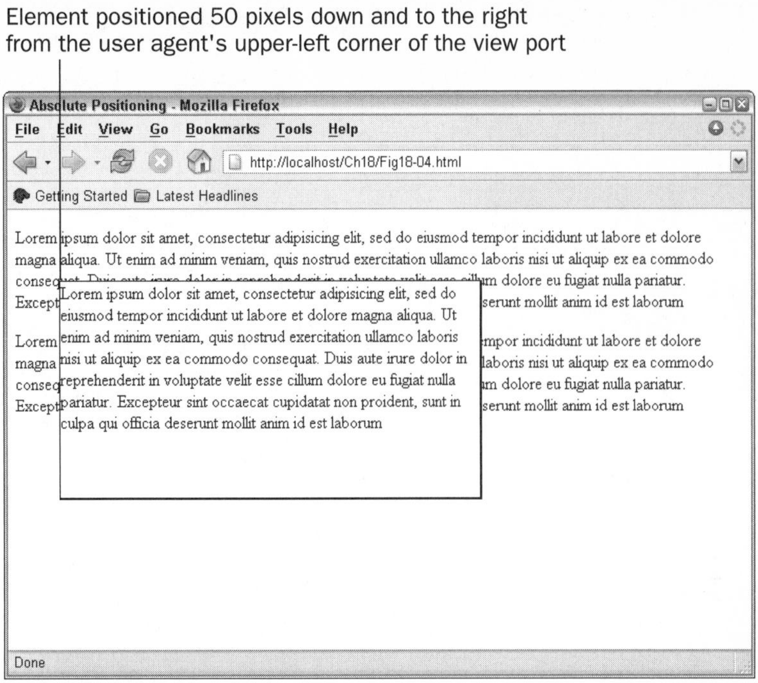

Element positioned 50 pixels down and to the right
from the user agent's upper-left corner of the view port

Figure 18-4

Note that the upper-left corner of the user agent view port is referenced as zero; the preceding code results in the paragraph's upper-left corner being positioned 50 pixels down and to the right from the upper-left corner of the user agent view port. Also note that absolute positioning removes elements from the normal flow of the document; the user agent flows neighboring elements as though the repositioned element did not exist. As with other methods, the repositioned element floats to the top layer of the element stack, overlapping elements below it.

Absolute positioning specifies only the initial position of an element when it is rendered. If the user agent scrolls its view port or the display otherwise changes, the element will move accordingly. See the next section on fixed positioning for a method to fix an element in place.

Fixed Positioning

Although not immediately evident, elements repositioned using other positioning methods are still subject to the flow of the document and scrolling of the user agent's view port. For example, consider Figures 18-5 and 18-6, which both show an element repositioned using absolute positioning. The view port in Figure 18-6 has been scrolled down a bit, causing the repositioned element to scroll accordingly.

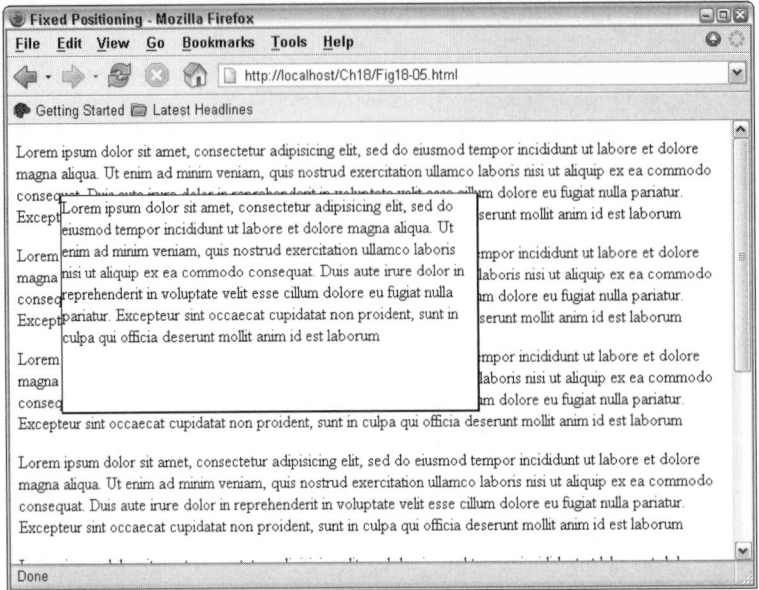

Figure 18-5

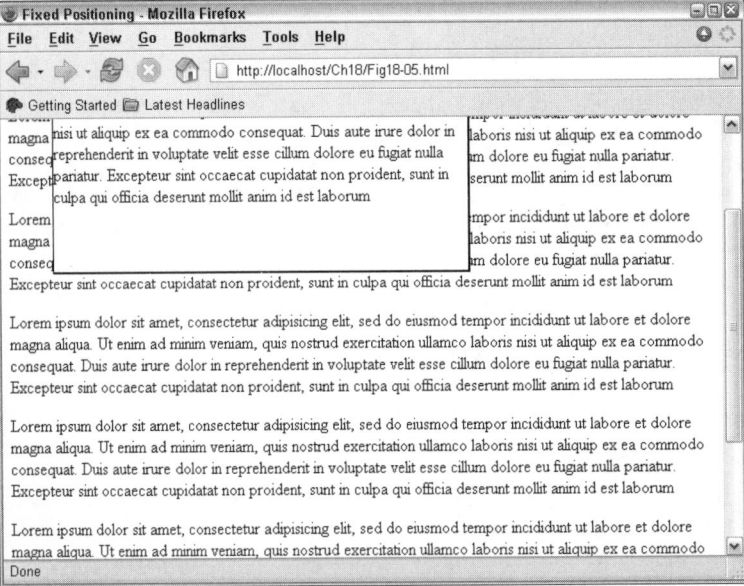

Figure 18-6

Using fixed positioning, you can force an element to retain its initial position despite any movement of the user agent's view port. For example, Figures 18-7 and 18-8 show the same document as the previous two figures (the document has been scrolled a bit in Figure 18-8). However, in the following two figures, the repositioned paragraph uses fixed positioning defined with the following styles:

```
p.fixed { width: 400px; height: 200px;
          border: 1pt solid black;
          background-color: white;
          position: fixed;
          top: 50px; left: 50px
}
```

As you can see in Figure 18-8, despite the document being scrolled in the user agent, the repositioned element retains the position defined by its style thanks to the fixed-positioning method.

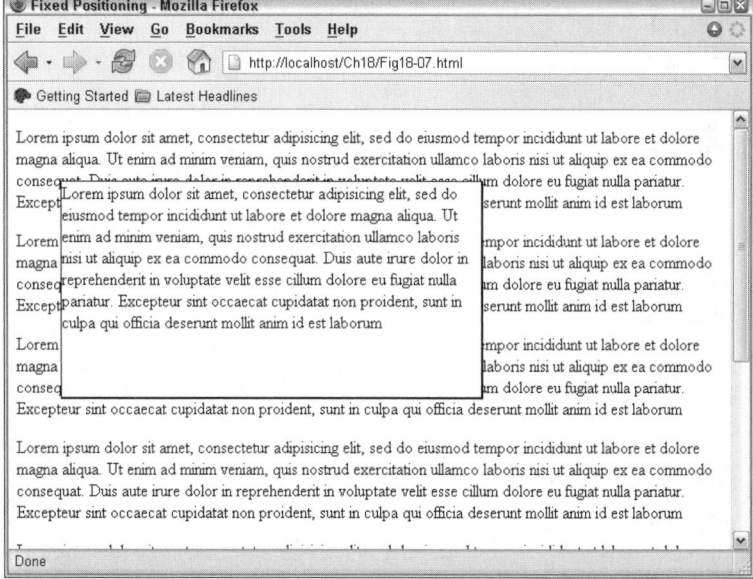

Figure 18-7

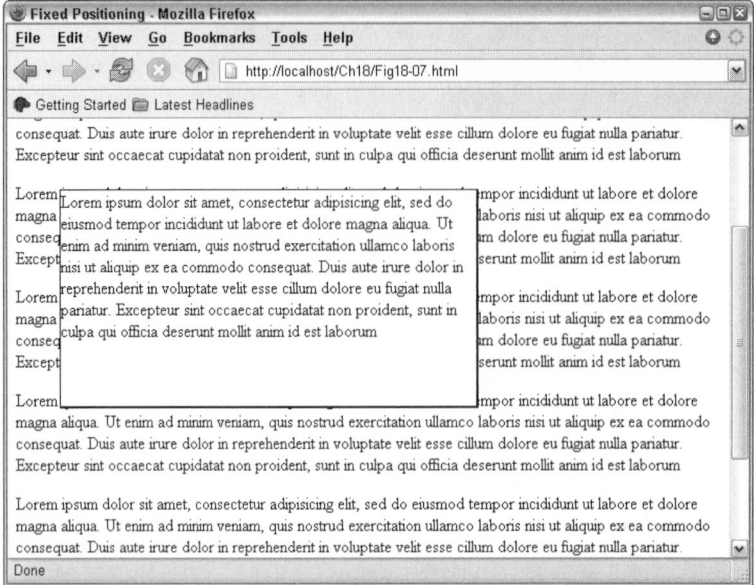

Figure 18-8

Specifying an Element's Position

The `top`, `right`, `bottom`, and `left` CSS properties can be used to position an element. The effect that these properties have on the actual position of the element largely depends on the positioning method being used (positioning methods were covered in the previous section).

The side positioning properties all have the following syntax:

side: <length> | <percentage>;

The specified side of the element (top, right, bottom, or top) is the side used to position the element. The element's other properties (size, borders, and so on) determine the position of the sides not explicitly positioned. The positioning method being employed also plays a role in the actual position of the element (see the previous section).

For absolutely positioned elements, the side values are related to the element's containing block. For relatively positioned elements, the side values are related to the outer edges of the element itself.

For example, the following styles result in positioning an element 50 pixels down from its normal position in the document flow:

```
p.fiftypxdown { position: relative;
           top: 50px; }
```

Using percentages causes the user agent to position an element according to a percentage of its size (or its bounding-box size). For example, to move an element left by 50% of its width, the following style can be used, whose result is shown in Figure 18-9:

```
p.fiftypercentleft   {  border: 1pt solid black;
                        background-color: white;
                        position: relative;
                        right: 50%; }
```

Element repositioned left by 50% of its width

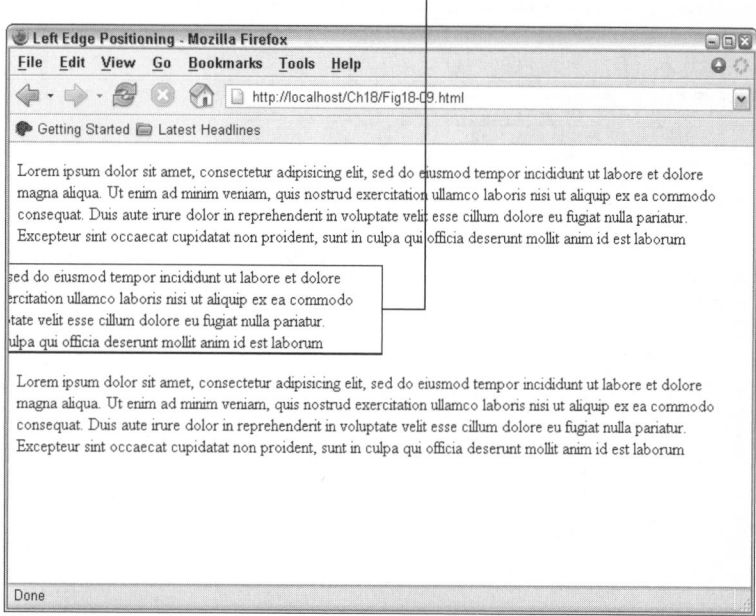

Figure 18-9

As you might expect, changing the positioning model changes the effect of the positioning, as shown with the following code whose result appears in Figure 18-10:

```
p.fiftypercentleft   {  border: 1pt solid black;
                        background-color: white;
                        position: absolute;
                        right: 50%; }
```

In this example, the right side of the element is positioned at the 50% mark (center) of the user agent view port because the positioning method is specified as absolute.

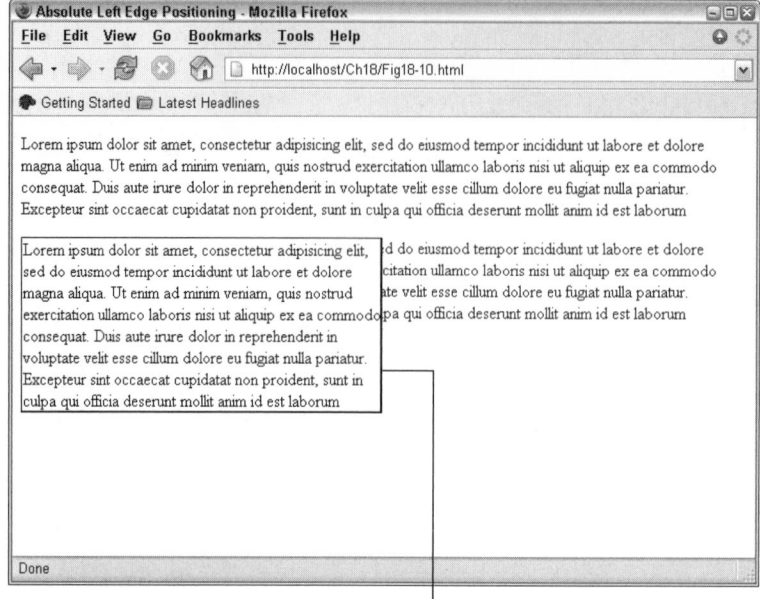

Element's right side repositioned at 50% of user agent's view port

Figure 18-10

Positioning alone can also drive an element's size. For example, the following code will result in paragraph elements being scaled horizontally to 25% of the view port, the left side of each positioned at the 25% horizontal mark, and the right at the 50% horizontal mark.

```
p { position: absolute;
    left: 25%; right: 50%; }
```

However, due to the cascade behavior of CSS, whichever property appears last in the definition drives the final size of the element. So, the following definition will result in paragraph elements that have their left side positioned at the view port's horizontal 25% mark, but each will be 400 pixels wide (despite the size of the view port) because the width property overrides the setting of the right property:

```
p { position: absolute;
    left: 25%; right: 50%;
    width: 400px; }
```

Properties explicitly defining an element's size are covered in the "Controlling an Element's Size" section later in this chapter.

Floating Elements

Occasionally, it is useful to float an element outside of the normal flow of a document's elements. When elements are floated, they are removed from the normal flow and are placed against the specified margin of the user agent's view port.

The `float` property is used to control the floating behavior of elements and has the following syntax:

```
float:  right | left | none;
```

The default behavior of elements is `none` — the element is positioned in the normal flow of elements. If the `float` property is set to `right`, the element is floated to the right margin of the user agent's view port; if the `float` property is set to `left`, the element is floated to the left margin.

For example, the sphere image in Figure 18-11 is not floated; it appears in the position where it is placed in the document's code — in-line with neighboring elements.

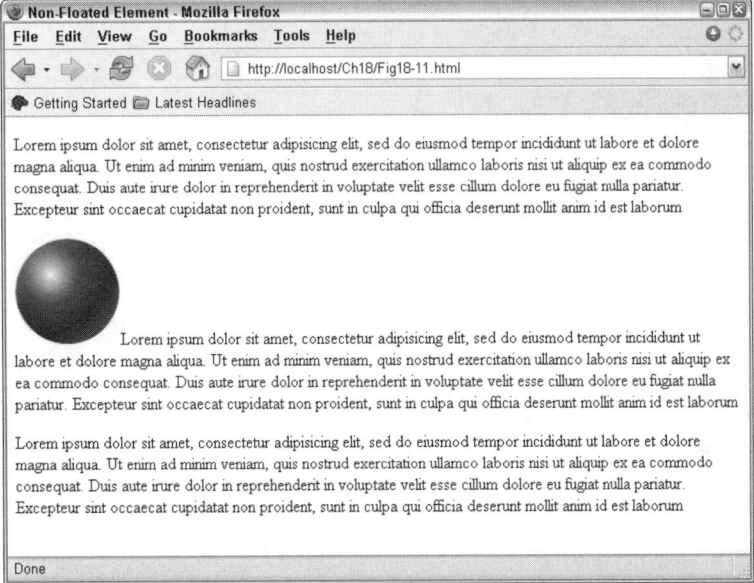

Figure 18-11

The same image appears in Figure 18-12 with the following style applied:

```
img  { float:  left; }
```

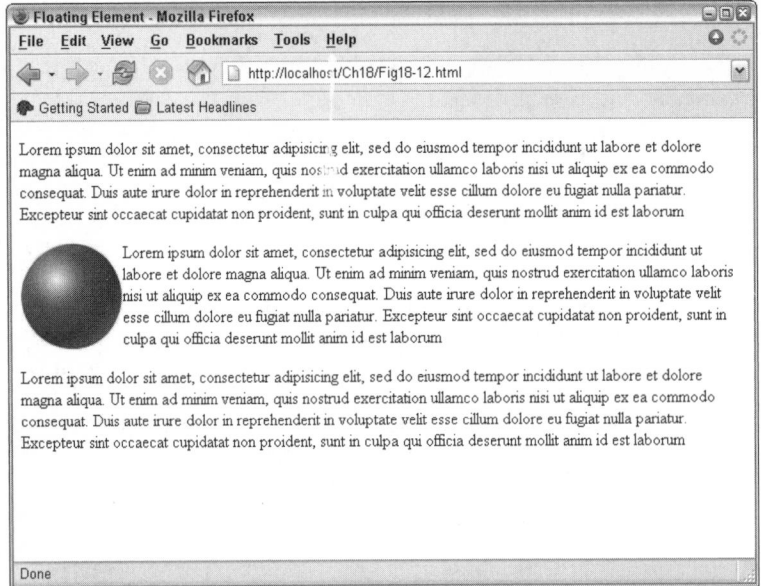

Figure 18-12

Neighboring elements flow around floated elements instead of being rendered in-line with them. The flow is still subject to appropriate margin and other values of the associated elements.

If you do not want elements to flow around neighboring floating elements, you can use the `clear` property to inhibit this behavior. The `clear` property has the following syntax:

```
clear:  left | right | both | none;
```

Setting `clear` to `left` or `right` will ensure that the affected element is positioned after any floated elements on the specified side so that they will not flow around them. Setting `clear` to `both` ensures that both sides of the element are clear of floaters. Setting `clear` to `none` (the default) allows elements to flow normally around floating elements.

Headings are one type of element that can benefit from the `clear` property's setting; typically, you would want headings to avoid flowing around floating elements. You can use the following style to ensure that headings avoid flowing around floating elements:

```
h1, h2, h3, h4, h5, h6  {  float: none; }
```

Controlling an Element's Size

You can control an element's size using CSS. You can specify an exact size for the element to be rendered or specify a minimal size that the element can occupy. You can also control what the user agent should do with any content that doesn't fit in the element. The following sections detail the use of CSS in sizing elements.

Specifying an Exact Size

You can use the `width` and `height` properties to define an element's size. Both properties have a similar syntax:

```
width | height:  <length> | <percentage> | auto;
```

As with most properties, you can use various metrics to specify an element's size. For example, the following style specifies that an element should be rendered 100 pixels square:

```
p.hundredsquare { width: 100px;  height: 100px; }
```

The following code sets an element to 150 percent of its normal width:

```
p.wider { width: 150%; }
```

Specifying `auto` causes the element's dimension (width or height) to be sized according to its contents or other relevant properties.

Specifying a Minimum or Maximum Size

Sometimes you will want to specify the maximum or minimum size an element can be instead of an absolute size. This allows the user agent to size the element using normal parameters for doing so, but within certain constraints. For those purposes, you can use min and max dimension properties:

- ❏ `min-height`
- ❏ `max-height`
- ❏ `min-width`
- ❏ `max-width`

These properties all have the same syntax:

```
property:  <length> | <percentage>;
```

For example, if you want an element to be at least 200px square, you could use the following style:

```
p.atleast200 { min-width:  200px;  min-height:  200px; }
```

Controlling Overflow

Whenever you take the chore of sizing elements away from the user agent, you run the risk of element contents overflowing the size of the element. The `overflow` property can be used to help control what the user agent does when content overflows an element. This property has the following syntax:

```
overflow:  visible | hidden | scroll | auto;
```

This property controls what the user agent should do *with the content that overflows*. The `visible` value ensures that all the content remains visible, even if it must flow outside the bounds of its margins. The `hidden` value causes any content that overflows to be hidden and therefore inaccessible to the user. The `scroll` value causes the element to inherit scroll bars if any content overflows the element. Lastly, the `auto` value allows the user agent to handle the element using the default settings of the user agent.

Figure 18-13 shows an example of the first three values of the `overflow` property.

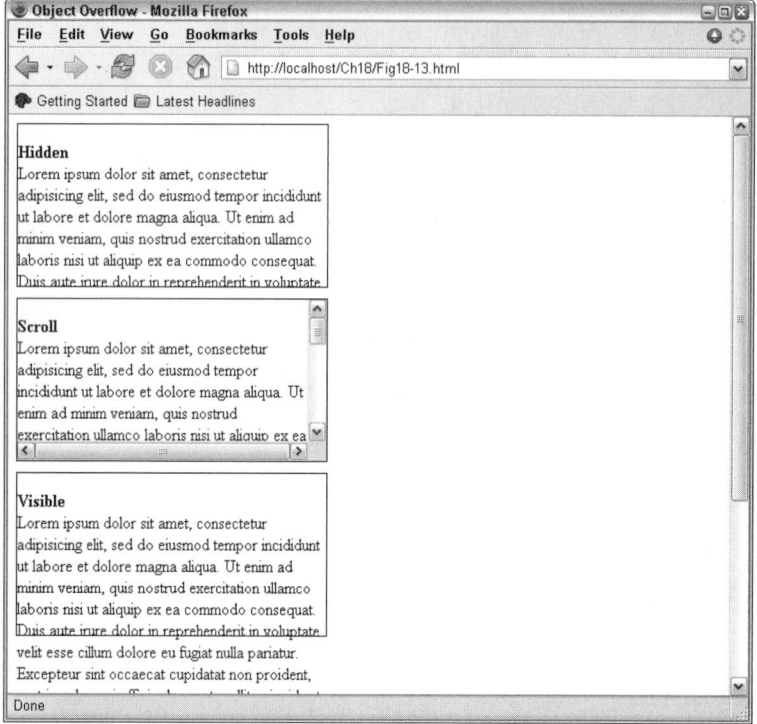

Figure 18-13

*As with many CSS properties, support for the **overflow** property isn't consistent. If you rely on this property in your code, you should test it on all intended platforms.*

Element Layers

CSS also supports a third dimension for elements, allowing you to control what elements are placed on top of what elements. You can usually anticipate how elements will stack and leave control of the stacking up to the user agent. However, if you want more control over the element stack, you can use the `z-index` property to specify an element's position in the stack.

Named for the stacking dimension (z-axis), this property has the following syntax:

```
z-index: <integer> | auto;
```

If an integer is specified as the value for the z-index property, the affected elements will be stacked accordingly — elements with higher z-index values are stacked on top of elements with lower z-index values.

Figure 18-14 provides an illustrative example of how elements stack given different z-index values, using the following code:

```
<!DOCTYPE html PUBLIC "-//W3C//DTD XHTML 1.0 Strict//EN"
   "http://www.w3.org/TR/xhtml1/DTD/xhtml1-strict.dtd"><html>
<head>
<title>Element Stacking</title>
<style type="text/css">
  p { width: 400px;   height: 200px;
      padding: 5px;
      border: 1px solid black;
      background-color: white;
      position: absolute;
      }
   .zlevelone { left: 200px; top: 100px;
                z-index: 1; }
   .zleveltwo { left: 250px; top: 150px;
                z-index: 2; }
   .zlevelthree { left: 300px; top: 200px;
                  z-index: 3; }

</style>
</head>
<body>
<p><b>z-index: 0 (default)</b><br />
Lorem ipsum dolor sit amet, consectetur
adipisicing elit, sed do eiusmod tempor incididunt ut labore et
dolore magna aliqua. Ut enim ad minim veniam, quis nostrud exercitation
ullamco laboris nisi ut aliquip ex ea commodo consequat. Duis
aute irure dolor in reprehenderit in voluptate velit esse
cillum dolore eu fugiat nulla pariatur. Excepteur sint occaecat
cupidatat non proident, sunt in culpa qui officia deserunt
mollit anim id est laborum.</p>

<p class="zlevelone"><b>z-index: 1</b><br />
Lorem ipsum dolor sit amet, consectetur adipisicing elit, sed do
eiusmod tempor incididunt ut labore et dolore magna aliqua. Ut enim
ad minim veniam, quis nostrud exercitation ullamco laboris nisi ut
aliquip ex ea commodo consequat. Duis aute irure dolor in reprehenderit
in voluptate velit esse cillum dolore eu fugiat nulla pariatur.
Excepteur sint occaecat cupidatat non proident, sunt in culpa qui
officia deserunt mollit anim id est laborum.</p>
```

```
<p class="zleveltwo"><b>z-index: 2</b><br />
Lorem ipsum dolor sit amet, consectetur adipisicing elit, sed do
eiusmod tempor incididunt ut labore et dolore magna aliqua. Ut enim
ad minim veniam, quis nostrud exercitation ullamco laboris nisi ut
aliquip ex ea commodo consequat. Duis aute irure dolor in reprehenderit
in voluptate velit esse cillum dolore eu fugiat nulla pariatur.
Excepteur sint occaecat cupidatat non proident, sunt in culpa qui
officia deserunt mollit anim id est laborum.</p>

<p class="zlevelthree"><b>z-index: 3</b><br />
Lorem ipsum dolor sit amet, consectetur adipisicing elit, sed do
eiusmod tempor incididunt ut labore et dolore magna aliqua. Ut enim
ad minim veniam, quis nostrud exercitation ullamco laboris nisi ut
aliquip ex ea commodo consequat. Duis aute irure dolor in reprehenderit
in voluptate velit esse cillum dolore eu fugiat nulla pariatur.
Excepteur sint occaecat cupidatat non proident, sunt in culpa qui
officia deserunt mollit anim id est laborum.</p>
</body>
</html>
```

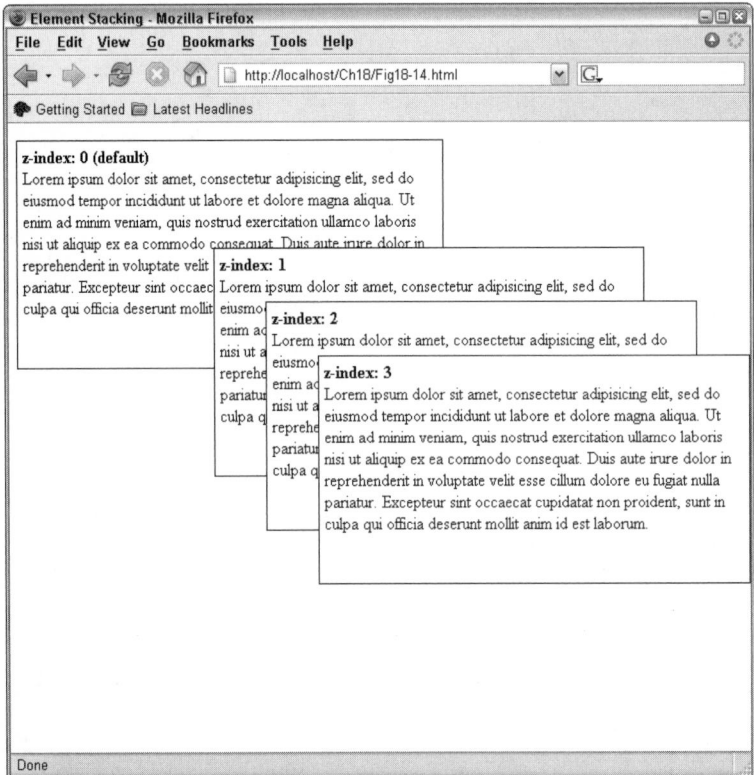

Figure 18-14

Note that the elements have an explicitly coded background color (white). This is because overlapping objects (and, therefore, also those stacked using the z-index property) inherit a transparent background so that elements under them can be seen through the transparency. If the background-color setting is omitted, the document will render similar to that shown in Figure 18-15.

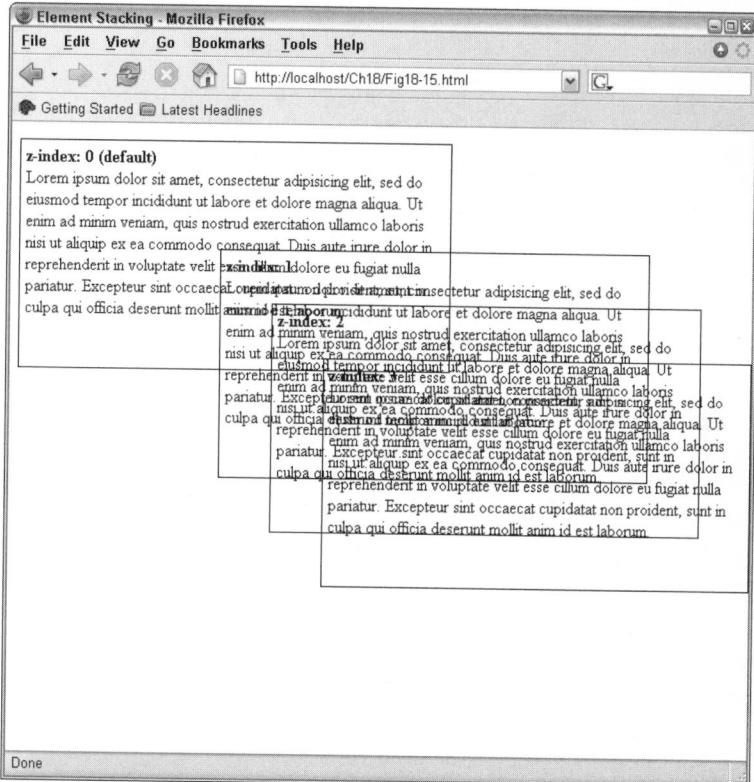

Figure 18-15

Controlling Visibility

You can use the visibility property to control whether an element is visible in the user agent. This property has the following syntax:

```
visibility:  visible | hidden | collapse;
```

The first two values accomplish exactly what their names imply: visible makes the affected element(s) visible in the user agent, and hidden hides them (makes them invisible). Setting this property to the value collapse will have the same effect as hidden on any element except for table columns or rows. If this value is used on a table row or column, the content in that column or row is removed from the table and that space is made available for other content.

You can use positioning, sizing, and visibility properties with JavaScript to create impressive anima-tions in your document. See Chapters 28 and 29 for examples of this and other automation techniques using Dynamic HTML.

Summary

This chapter covered the basics of CSS-based document layout. Using the positioning properties, you can accurately position elements within your documents. Combining the positioning properties with sizing and other visible CSS properties, you can create complex layouts with ease. As you will see in the next section, JavaScript works well with CSS and can be used for further control, automation, and animation of your documents.

JavaScript Basics

Up to this point in the book, you have learned only about static technology for Web documents. Starting in this section, you will learn about technologies that can be used to dynamically deliver content and manipulate content based on various criteria. This section of the book covers JavaScript, a mainstay of XHTML document scripting. This chapter covers the origins of JavaScript, its typical uses, and methods to incorporate scripts into your documents.

History of JavaScript

In the early days of the World Wide Web, it became obvious to the Netscape team that rudimentary scripting would improve the medium greatly. JavaScript was created in 1996, released with Netscape 2.0, to fill that role and is still the most popular scripting language used on the Web. The Netscape team that created JavaScript was the same team that created the Netscape browser — a team that understood the innovations the Web was bringing to the Internet. The scripting language was designed to be integrated into the user agent and to be able to parse details of any document the agent rendered and affect changes in some elements. The parsing was available because of the time the team took to construct the Document Object Model (DOM), a method to access document links, anchors, form and form objects, and other objects.

Shortly after the base language was constructed, it was turned over to the European Computer Manufacturers Association (ECMA) for standardization. The ECMA produced the ECMAscript standard, which embodied most of the features and capabilities of the JavaScript language. Additional capabilities were added to JavaScript over the next few years and matured as other technologies (such as CSS) matured as well.

Despite its naming, JavaScript is not Java. It inherited the moniker "Java" due to many similarities with Sun's Java language. However, the similarities today are slight — noticeable to most programmers, but slight.

> VBScript is an extension of Visual Basic created by Microsoft as a competitor to JavaScript, and it is mostly used to help integrate other Microsoft technologies such as ActiveX. VBScript and other Microsoft technologies are largely proprietary — support for these technologies can be relied on only in versions of Microsoft's user agent, Internet Explorer. As such, this book chooses to cover JavaScript only, which is supported in the majority of user agents (including Internet Explorer).

Different Implementations

Unfortunately, as with many of the Web technologies, development of JavaScript and the DOM fractured over the next few years as other entities adopted and expanded the technologies. The largest gap was created around the DOM, an area of JavaScript long neglected by the Netscape team.

> *Contrary to popular belief, Microsoft did not initially fork the DOM for its own benefit. The DOM that existed in JavaScript around the release of Internet Explorer was plagued with bugs and was poorly implemented. The open source community and other user agent programmers banded together and embraced a DOM guideline constructed by the World Wide Web Consortium. The benefits of forking the DOM from the flawed Netscape implementation were seen and seized by many.*

Despite the existence of a well-known standard, several entities have made subtle changes to their JavaScript implementations. Microsoft, for example, has tweaked its version of JavaScript (JScript), creating quite a few inconsistencies in implementation and use.

Unfortunately, this causes many problems for the scripting programmer who must create code that works on the majority of user agents.

Determining the Document Object Model

The main problem facing programmers is different DOM implementations. Previous implementations of Netscape (prior to the latest Mozilla Firebird release) used the earlier layer implementation. This forces programmers to determine what user agent is being used prior to accessing the DOM.

The following table outlines the Netscape, Internet Explorer, and Mozilla support for the different Document Object Model specifications.

Browser	Level 0 W3C Support	Netscape DOM Support	IE DOM Support	Level 1 W3C Support
Netscape 2.0+	X	X		
Netscape 4	X			
IE 3.0	X		X	
IE 5.0+	X		X	X
Mozilla (Firebird)	X			X

Most user agents report some of their capabilities via their headers. However, this information cannot be relied on—some user agents can be configured as to what information to report and implementations vary. The easiest way to determine a user agent's capabilities is to test for specific capabilities. For example, the following code tests for the layer and W3C DOM so that you can program your scripts accordingly:

```
if (document.all) {
// IE4+ code  (IE4+ uses the document.all collection)
} else if (document.layers) {
```

```
//  NS4+ code   (Older versions of Netscape use the layers collection)
} else if (document.getElementById) {
//  NS6+ code and IE5+ (The latest browsers use getElementById)
}
```

Implicit in the preceding code is the support for the `getElementById` function. This is one break afforded to script programmers; using this one function, you can ascertain the ID assigned to an element and manipulate it using that ID. Of course, only the current crop of browsers (Netscape 6+/Firefox and Internet Explorer 5+) supports `getElementById`.

Uses for JavaScript

It's important to note a few things about JavaScript when deciding when and where you want to use it:

❑ **It is a client-based language.** As such, it has very limited access to server-based resources (databases, and so on) and relies on the client supporting (and allowing) JavaScript to run.

❑ **It is a *scripting* language with definite limitations.** More robust, server-side languages (Perl, Python, and PHP, also covered in this book) should be used for more capable applications.

❑ **JavaScript source code is visible in the documents in which it appears.** Even external script files can usually be browsed with little effort. As such, you should never embed sensitive information in your scripts.

Even with those caveats taken into account, there are still many uses for JavaScript, including the following:

❑ **Form verification.** JavaScript can parse form data prior to the data being submitted to a handler on the server, ensuring that there are no obvious errors (missing or improperly formatted data). Form verification is covered in Chapter 22.

❑ **Document animation and automation.** Accessing element data and properties via the DOM, JavaScript can affect changes in elements' content, appearance, size, position, and so forth. By doing so, simple scripts can create simple animations — menu items that change color, images and text that move, and so on. Rudimentary dynamic content can also be achieved via JavaScript — custom content can be generated according to other behavior initiated by the user. Dynamic HTML (the name for the technology of JavaScript manipulating document objects and elements) is covered in Chapters 23 and 24.

❑ **Basic document intelligence.** As mentioned in the preceding bullet, JavaScript can initiate changes in documents based on other, dynamic criteria. Using JavaScript you can embed a base level of intelligence and an extra layer of user interface in your documents. Elements can be linked to scripts via events (`onclick`, `onmouseover`, and so on) to help the user better use your documents. Sample uses of triggers can be found in Chapter 22.

Incorporating JavaScript in Your Documents

The following sections cover the various ways you can incorporate scripts into your documents and the benefits and detriments of each.

Anatomy of the <script> Tag

The most popular method of incorporating JavaScript in documents is by enclosing the scripts within script (`<script>`) tags. The `<script>` tag has the following syntax:

```
<script type="MIME_type">
    ...script content...
</script>
```

Current versions of XHTML support the following Multipurpose Internet Mail Extensions (MIME) types for the `<script>` tag:

- ❑   text/ecmascript
- ❑   text/javascript
- ❑   text/jscript
- ❑   text/vbscript
- ❑   text/vbs
- ❑   text/xml

Of course, for JavaScript you will want to use the text/javascript MIME type; the rest of the MIME types are for other scripting options and languages.

The `<script>` tag also supports the option attributes listed in the following table:

Attribute	Value(s)	Use
charset	charset code	Defines the character encoding (charset) used in the script
defer	defer	Informs the user agent that the script will not generate content, and document processing (rendering) can continue without waiting to evaluate the script content
src	URL	Instructs the user agent to incorporate the contents of the document found at the specified URL as the script content

Note the versatility inherent in the availability of the src attribute. If you have scripts that you want to make available to several documents, you can place them in an external document and include them via a tag similar to the following:

```
<script type="text/javascript" src="global_scripts.js"></script>
```

Then, whenever you need to change a script used across multiple documents, you have to edit it only once, in the external file.

Placement of the Script Tag

Technically, the script tag should be placed within the <head> section of your document where it can be easily located. However, in practice, you can place the <script> tag anywhere within the document. That said, the <script> tag should always appear within a block element, though it isn't a requirement to be XHTML compliant.

Execution of Scripts

Unless otherwise instructed, user agents execute JavaScript code as soon as it is encountered in a document. The exceptions to this rule include the following:

❑   Scripting being disabled in the user agent

❑   The defer attribute being set in the containing <script> tag

❑   All code being contained within functions that are not explicitly called during the document's rendering

For example, the first code segment in the following code listing will not be executed until an event explicitly calls the function enclosing the code, while the second code segment will be executed as soon as it is encountered by the rendering user agent:

```
<!DOCTYPE html PUBLIC "-//W3C//DTD XHTML 1.0 Strict//EN"
    "http://www.w3.org/TR/xhtml1/DTD/xhtml1-strict.dtd">
<html>
<head>
  <title>Script Execution</title>
  <script type="text/javascript">
    function runmelater() {
     // script code
    }
  </script>
</head>
<body>
<p>
  <script type="text/javascript">
    // script code (not enclosed in function(s))
  </script>
</p>
</body>
</html>
```

Keep in mind that you can force a script to run immediately after the document is loaded by using the onload event in the <body> tag:

```
<body onload="script_function_name">
```

Short scripts can also be embedded directly within event attributes, as in the following example:

```
<input type="button" name="doscript" id="doscript" onclick="short_script_code" />
```

Events are covered in more detail in Chapter 20 and shown in examples in Chapter 21.

Summary

This chapter began the coverage of scripting within this book. This section concentrates on JavaScript, starting with the basics of how JavaScript can be incorporated into your documents and working toward using the language to manipulate a document's object model and using JavaScript for animation and other advanced uses.

The JavaScript Language

The previous chapter introduced you to JavaScript. This chapter dives into the language itself, outlining the language's syntax, structure, functions, objects, and more. Note that this chapter focuses on the ins and outs of the language, not specific uses thereof. Subsequent chapters in this section will introduce you to specific ways to use the language in your documents.

Basic JavaScript Syntax

JavaScript follows a fairly basic syntax that can be outlined with a few simple rules:

❑   All code should appear within appropriate constructs, namely between `<script>` tags or within event attributes. (Events are discussed in the "Event Handling" section later in this chapter.)

❑   With few exceptions, code lines should end with a semicolon (;). Notable exceptions to this rule are lines that end in a block delimiter ({ or }).

❑   Blocks of code (usually under control structures such as `functions`, `if` statements, and so on) are enclosed in braces ({ and }).

❑   Although it is not absolutely necessary, explicit declaration of all variables is a good idea.

❑   The use of functions to delimit code fragments is recommended; it increases the ability to execute those fragments independently from one another and encourages reuse of code. (Functions are discussed in the "User-Defined Functions" section later in this chapter.)

❑   Comments can be inserted in JavaScript code by prefixing the comment with a double-slash (`//`) or surrounding the comment with `/*` and `*/` pairs. In the former case (`//`), the comment ends at the next line break. Use the latter case for multiline comments.

Data Types and Variables

Although JavaScript is somewhat more minimalist than full-fledged programming languages, the language still supports a full roster of data types and variable use. The next two sections detail the data types available in JavaScript and how variables are handled.

Data Types

JavaScript, like most other programming languages, supports a wide range of data types. However, JavaScript employs little data type checking. It doesn't care too much about what you store in variables or how you use the stored data within your scripts. As such, it becomes important to monitor your data types as you write your scripts to ensure that you pass the appropriately typed data to functions and methods.

JavaScript supports the following data types:

- ❏ Booleans
- ❏ Integers
- ❏ Floating-point numbers
- ❏ Strings
- ❏ Arrays

> *JavaScript also supports objects — an unordered container of various data types. Objects are covered in the "Objects" section later in this chapter.*

There is little difference between JavaScript's integer and floating-point data types because numbers are stored in floating-point format. The JavaScript standard specifies an upper/lower bound of floating-point numbers as 1.7976931348623157E+10308, but the user agent implementation may vary. If you need to ensure that a value is an integer, use the parseInt() function accordingly. (Functions are covered later in this chapter — see Appendix C for reference coverage of JavaScript functions.)

JavaScript arrays can contain a mix of the various data types and are declared using the new operator in your declaration statement, as in the following:

```
a = new Array();
```

If you want, you can also define the array's values at declaration time by specifying the values within the Array() declaration, as shown in the following code:

```
months = new Array("January","February","March","April","May","June",
    "July","August","September","October","November","December");
```

You can similarly use the String() and Number() functions within your declarations to ensure that a variable is declared as a specific type. For example, to declare the variable s as a string, you could use the following:

```
s = new String ();
```

Explicitly setting a variable's type helps ensure that it will always contain the data you expect it to. If left to its own devices, JavaScript will adapt a variable's type as needed, perhaps causing rounding errors or more grievous mistakes.

Variables

JavaScript variables are case sensitive and can contain a mix of letters and numbers. You should take care to avoid variable names that use JavaScript reserved words. Unlike some other popular scripting languages, JavaScript does not identify its variables by prefixing them with a special character, such as a dollar sign ($) — its variables are referenced by their names only.

You may wish to use a naming convention for your variables, for example one that describes what sort of data the variable will hold. There are several different naming methods and schemes you can use. Although the preference of which you use is subjective, you would do well to pick one and stick with it. One common method is Hungarian notation, where the beginning of each variable name is a three letter identifier indicating the data type.

Appendix C covers built-in JavaScript operators, functions, objects, and more. This appendix can be used as a source of JavaScript reserved words.

JavaScript uses the `var` statement to explicitly declare variables. As previously mentioned, explicit declaration of variables is not necessary in JavaScript. However, it is good practice to do so.

You can declare multiple variables within one `var` statement by separating the variable declarations with commas. The `var` statement also supports assigning an initial value to the declared variables. The following three lines are all valid `var` statements:

```
var x;
var x = 20;
var x = 20, firstname = "Steve";
```

JavaScript variables have global scope unless they are declared within a function, in which case they have local scope within the function in which they were declared. For example, in the following code the variable x is global while the variable y is local to the function:

```
<script type="text/JavaScript">
var x = 100;
function spacefill(text,amount) {
var y = 0;
...
}
</script>
```

Note that variables with global scope transcend `<script>` sections; that is, variables declared within one `<script>` section are accessible in other `<script>` sections within the document.

Calculations and Operators

JavaScript supports the standard operators for numbers and strings. The following tables outline the basic operators available in JavaScript.

JavaScript Arithmetic Operators

Operator	Use
+	Addition
–	Subtraction
*	Multiplication
/	Division
%	Modulus
++	Increment
––	Decrement

JavaScript Assignment Operators

Operator	Use
=	Assignment
+=	Increment assignment
–=	Decrement assignment
*=	Multiplication assignment
/=	Division assignment
%=	Modulus assignment

JavaScript Comparison Operators

Operator	Use
==	Is equal to
===	Exactly equal to — in value and type
!=	Is not equal to
>	Is greater than
<	Is less than
>=	Is greater than or equal to
<=	Is less than or equal to

JavaScript Logical Operators

Operator	Use
&&	And
||	Or
!	Not

JavaScript Bitwise Operators

Operator	Use
&	And
|	Or
^	Xor
~	Not
<<	Left shift
>>	Right shift
>>>	Zero fill right shift

JavaScript Miscellaneous Operators

Operator	Use
.	Object/property/method separator
?	Condition operator
delete	Delete specified object
new	Create new object
this	Reference current object
typeof	Type of object (number, string, and so on)
void	Evaluate expression without returning a value

String Operators

Operator	Use
+	Concatenation

String Tokens

Token	Character
\\	Backslash
\'	Single quote
\"	Double quote
\b	Backspace
\f	Form Feed
\n	Line Feed
\r	Carriage Return
\t	Horizontal Tab
\v	Vertical Tab

Control Structures

Like many other languages, JavaScript supports many different control structures that can be used to execute particular blocks of code based on decisions or repeat blocks of code while a particular condition is true. The following sections cover the various control structures available in JavaScript.

Do While

The do while loop executes one or more lines of code as long as a specified condition remains true. This structure has the following format:

```
do {
  // statement(s) to execute
} while (<expression>);
```

Due to the expression being evaluated at the end of the structure, statement(s) in a do while loop are executed at least once. The following example will loop a total of 20 times — incrementing the variable x each time until x reaches the value 20:

```
var x = 0;
do {
  x++;  // increment x
} while (x < 20);
```

While

The while loop executes one or more lines of code while a specified expression remains true. The while loop has the following syntax:

```
while (<expression>) {
  // statement(s) to execute
}
```

Because the <expression> is evaluated at the beginning of the loop, the statement(s) will not be executed if the <expression> is false at the beginning of the loop. For example, the following loop will execute 20 times, each iteration of the loop incrementing x until it reaches 20:

```
var x = 0;
while (x <= 20) {  // do until x = 20 (will not execute when x = 21)
  x++;  // increment x
}
```

For and For In

The for loop executes statement(s) a specific number of times governed by two expressions and a condition. It has the following syntax:

```
for (<initial_value>; <condition>; <loop_expression>) {
  // statement(s) to execute
}
```

The <initial_value> expression is evaluated at the beginning of the loop; this event occurs only before the first iteration of the loop. The <condition> is evaluated at the beginning of *each* loop iteration. If the condition returns false, the current iteration is executed; if the condition returns true, the loop exits and the script execution continues after the loop's block. At the end of each loop iteration, the <loop_expression> is evaluated.

Although their usage can vary, for loops are generally used to step through a range of values (such as an array) via a specified increment. For example, the following example begins with the variable x equal to 1 and exits when x equals 20; each loop iteration increments x by 1:

```
for (x = 1; x <= 20; x++ ) {     //  for x = 1 to 20
  //statement(s) to execute
}
```

Note that the <loop_expression> is not limited to an increment expression. The expression should advance the appropriate values toward the exit condition but can be any valid expression. For example, consider the two following snippets of code:

```
for (x = 20; x >= 1; x--) {  // for x = 20 to 1
  // statement(s) to execute
}

for (x = 2; x <= 40; x+=2) {  // for x = 2 to 40, by 2 (even numbers only)
  // statement(s) to execute
}
```

Another variation of the `for` loop is the `for in` loop. The `for in` loop executes statement(s) while assigning a variable to the properties of an object or elements of an array. For example, the following code will assign the variable `i` to each element in the `names` array:

```
names = new array ("Steve","Terri","Sam","Vicki","Bernie","Robin");
for (i in names) {
  // statement(s) to execute
}
```

The following loop code will assign `i` to all the properties of the `document` object:

```
for (i in document) {
  // statement(s) to execute
}
```

If Else

The `if` and `if else` constructs execute a block of code depending on the evaluation (true or false) of an expression. The `if` construct has the following syntax:

```
if (<expression>) {
  // statement(s) to execute if expression is true
} [ else {
  // statement(s) to execute if expression is false
} ]
```

For example, the following code tests if the value stored in `i` is the number 2:

```
if (i == 2) {
  // statement(s) to execute if the value in i is 2
}
```

The following code will execute one block of code if the value of `i` is an odd number, another block of code if the value of `i` is an even number:

```
if ((i % 2) != 0) {
  // statement(s) to execute if i is odd
} else {
  // statement(s) to execute if i is even
}
```

You can also use complex expressions in an `if` loop, as in the following example:

```
if ((i = 2) && (t = 31) && (name = "Panama")) {
  // statement(s) to execute if all three conditions are true
}
```

*Note the use of the parentheses in the previous example. You can use parentheses to explicitly define the precedence in the expression — important when using **or/and** logic.*

In addition, you can create `else if` constructs in JavaScript by nesting `if` statements within one another, as shown in the following code:

```
if ((i % 2) != 0) {
  // statement(s) to execute if i is odd
} else
  if (i == 12) {
  // statement(s) to execute if i is 12
  }
}
```

However, in most cases where you are comparing against one variable, using `switch` (covered in the next section) is a better choice.

Switch

The `switch` construct executes specific block(s) of code based on the value of a particular expression. This structure has the following syntax:

```
switch (<expression>) {
  case <value_1>:  {
    // statement(s) to be executed if <expression> = <value_1>
  break; }
  case <value_2>:  {
    // statement(s) to be executed if <expression> = <value_2>
  break; }
  ...
  default: {
    // statement(s) to be executed if <expression> does not match any other case
  }
}
```

For example, the following structure will perform the appropriate code based on the value of `firstname`:

```
switch (firstname) {
  case "Steve":  {
    // statement(s) to execute if firstname = "Steve"
    break; }
  case "Terri":  {
    // statement(s) to execute if firstname = "Terri"
    break; }
  default: {
    /* statement(s) to execute if firstname does not
       equal "Steve" or "Terri"
  }
}
```

*Note that the **switch** statement is an efficient structure to perform tasks based on the value of one variable—much more efficient than a series of nested **if** statements.*

Note that the `break` statements and the default section are optional. If you omit the `break` statements, each case section after the matching case will be executed. For example, in the preceding code section, if the breaks were removed and `firstname` was equal to "Steve," the code in all sections ("Steve," "Terri," *and* default) would execute.

> The ***break*** *statement is covered in the next section.*

Note that the `switch` construct can only be used to compare against one value. If you need to make decisions based on several different values, use a nested `if` construct instead.

Break and Continue

Occasionally, you need to break out of a loop, either the current iteration or the entire loop structure. The `break` statement causes execution to break out of the current structure; the next code executed is the code following that structure. The `continue` statement breaks out of the current loop iteration to the condition expression of the loop.

For example, the following code will skip processing the number 7, but all other numbers between 1 and 20 will be processed:

```
var x = 1;
while (x <= 20) {
  if (x == 7) continue;  // skip the number 7
  // statement(s) to execute if x does not equal 7
}
```

In the following code, the loop will be exited if the variable x ever equals 100 during the loop's execution:

```
var y = 1;
while (y <= 20) {
  if (x == 100) break;  // if x = 100, leave the loop
  // statement(s) to execute
}
// execution continues here when y > 20 or x = 100
```

The `break` statement can also be used with labels to specify which loop should be broken out of. (See the next section, "Labels," for more information on labels.)

Labels

JavaScript supports labels, which can be used to mark statements for reference by other statements in other sections of a script. Labels have the following format:

```
<label_name>:
```

To use a label, place it before the statement you wish to identify with the label. For example, the following references the `while` loop with the label `code_loop`:

```
var x = 100;
code_loop:
while (x <= 1000) {
  // statement(s)
}
```

You can reference labels using the break statement to exit structures outside of the current structure. For example, both loops in the following code will be broken out of if the variable z ever equals 100:

```
var  x = 0, y = 0;
top_loop:
while (x <= 100) {
  while (y <= 50) {
    ...
    if (z == 100) break top_loop;
  }
}
/* execution resumes here after loops are complete or if
     z = 100 during the loops execution */
```

You can also use labels to mark blocks of code, as in the following example:

```
code_block: {
  // block of code here
}
```

The break statement can then be used to break out of the block, if necessary.

Built-in Functions

JavaScript provides a few built-in functions for data manipulation. Most of the built-in functions exist to convert data between the various data types and to check if data is of a particular type. The following table lists the supported functions:

Function	Use	Returns
escape	Creates portable data — typically used to encode URLs and other information that may, but generally should not, include extended characters. Extended characters (non-alphanumeric) are replaced by their ASCII number equivalent in hexadecimal %xx form. For example, a space (ASCII 32) becomes %20.	Encoded version of supplied argument.
eval	Parses the supplied string for JavaScript code and executes the code if found.	The value of the last valid statement or expression encountered in the supplied argument.

Table continued on following page

Function	Use	Returns
isFinite	Tests an expression or variable to see if it is a valid number.	True if the supplied argument is a valid number, false if the supplied argument is not a valid number.
isNaN	Tests an expression or variable to see if it is not a (valid) number.	Returns true if the argument is not a number and false if the argument is a number.
number	Converts an object (typically string data) to a number.	Returns the supplied argument converted to a number or the value NaN (not a number) if the argument cannot be converted to a valid number.
parseFloat	Parses the given argument for a valid floating-point number. Parsing begins with the first character and ends with the first character that cannot be converted. (If the first character of the argument is not a number, the function returns NaN.)	A floating-point representation of the supplied argument or the value NaN (not a number) if a number cannot be parsed from the argument.
parseInt	Parses the given argument for a valid integer number. Parsing begins with the first character and ends with the first character that cannot be converted. (If the first character of the argument is not a number, the function returns NaN.)	An integer representation of the supplied argument or the value NaN (not a number) if a number cannot be parsed from the argument.
string	Converts the supplied argument to a string representation.	A string representation of the supplied argument.
Unescape	Converts portable data back into its original form (the opposite of the Escape function).	Decoded version of the supplied argument.

User-Defined Functions

JavaScript supports user-defined functions. User-defined functions allow you to better organize your code into discrete, reusable chunks.

User-defined functions have the following syntax:

```
function <function_name> ( <list_of_arguments> ) {
    ...code of function...
    return <value_to_return>;
}
```

For example, the following function will space-fill the string passed to it to 25 characters and return the filled string:

```
function spacefill (text) {
  while ( text.length < 25 ) {
    text = text + " ";
  }
  return text;
}
```

Elsewhere in your code, you can use this function similarly to the following:

```
address = spacefill(address);
```

This would cause the variable `address` to be space-filled to 25 characters and reassigned to itself.

> *Strictly speaking, the* **return** *statement is optional. However, it is usually a good idea to at least include a status code return (success/fail) for all your functions.*

The arguments passed to a function can be of any type. If multiple arguments are passed to the function, separate them with commas in both the calling statement and function definition, as shown in the following examples:

Calling syntax:

```
spacefill(address, 25)
```

Function syntax:

```
function spacefill (text, spaces) {
```

Note that the number of arguments in the calling statement and in the function definition should match. If you supply fewer variables than the number expected by the function, the remaining variables will remain undefined. If you specify more variables than the number expected by the function, the extra values will be discarded.

The variables used by the function for the arguments and any other variables declared and used by the function are considered local variables — they are inaccessible to code outside the function and exist only while the function is executing.

Objects

JavaScript is an object-driven language. As you will see in Chapter 21, "The Document Object Model," the user agent supplies a host of objects that your scripts can reference. However, you will encounter many objects built into JavaScript that are outside of the Document Object Model.

Built-in Objects

JavaScript has several built-in objects. For example, two specific objects exist for manipulating data: one for performing math operations (Math) on numeric data and another for performing operations on string values (String).

These objects have various methods for acting upon data. For example, to find the square root of variable x, you could use the Math.sqrt method:

```
x = Math.sqrt(x);  // square root of x
```

Or, to convert a string to lowercase, you could use the String.toLowerCase() method:

```
s = String.toLowerCase(s);  // convert s to lowercase
```

As with most object-oriented languages, JavaScript supports the with statement. Using the with statement can facilitate using multiple methods of the same object, as shown in the following code:

```
with (Math) {
y = random(200);
x = round(sqrt(y));
}
```

The same code without using the with statement would look like the following code:

```
y = Math.random(200);
x = Math.round(Math.sqrt(y));
```

Although the Math object was referenced only three times in the code, you can see how repeatedly referencing the object could get tedious when constructing complex mathematical operations.

Another very useful object is the Date object. This object has several methods that can be used to manipulate dates and times in various formats. For example, the following code will output the current date (in month, day, year format) wherever it is placed in the document:

```
<script type="text/JavaScript">
   months = new Array ("January","February","March","April","May","June",
      "July","August","September","October","November","December");
   var today = new Date();  // create new date object (with values = today)
   // Set day, month, and year from today's value
   var day = today.getDate();
   var month = today.getMonth();
   var year = today.getYear();
   // Output "month day, year" (month is textual value)
   document.write(months[month]+" "+day+", "+year);
</script>
```

You can use the millisecond methods of the Date object to do calculations on dates—the number of days between two dates or the number of days until a particular date, for example.

Appendix C, "JavaScript Language Reference," lists the available built-in objects, their properties, and methods.

User-Created Objects

The new declaration statement can be used to create new objects based on existing, built-in objects. For example, to create a new array, you could use code similar to the following:

```
employees = new Array ("Steve", "Terri", "Sam", "Vicki", "Bernie");
```

Teaching the concept of objects and object-oriented programming is beyond the scope of this book. As a consequence, this section concentrates only on how to implement objects in JavaScript.

The preceding code creates a new array object, based on the built-in JavaScript array object, and assigns values to the new object.

Creation of new, custom objects requires the existence of an object constructor. This is unnecessary when creating objects based on built-in objects — JavaScript also includes built-in constructors for native objects.

For example, the following function can be used to construct totally new objects of a movie class:

```
function movie(title, genre, releasedate) {
   this.title = title;
   this.genre = genre;
   this.releasedate = releasedate;
}
```

The constructor can then be called via new, as in the following example:

```
mov1 = new movie("Aliens","Scifi","1986-07-18");
```

You can also create a direct instance of an object, bypassing creation and use of a constructor, if you want. For example, the following also creates a movie object, but without use of a constructor:

```
mov1 = new object();
   mov1.title = "Aliens";
   mov1.genre = "Scifi";
   mov1.releasedate = "1986-07-18";
```

You can access the new object's properties via the normal property syntax:

```
if (m.genre == "Horror") {
   // do something if genre is Horror
}
```

Object properties can be objects themselves. For example, you could create a director object that in turn is a property of the movie object:

```
function director(name,age) {
   this.name = name;
   this.age = age;
}
function movie(title, genre, director, releasedate) {
   this.title = title;
```

```
      this.genre = genre;
      this.director = director;
      this.releasedate = releasedate;
   }
   dir1 = new director("James Cameron",51);
   mov1 = new movie("Aliens","Scifi",dir1,"1986-07-18");
   if (mov1.director.name == "James Cameron") // if director of mov1 is Cameron
```

New methods can be assigned to objects via functions. For example, if you have a function named beep that causes the user agent to play the sound of a horn, you could assign that function as a method by using the assignment operator:

```
   car.honk = beep();
```

However, in most cases, you will find that your JavaScript objects fall into the plain old data object model — not needing methods to be manipulated.

> *One very important object available to JavaScript is the Document Object Model (DOM). Using the DOM, your scripts can access a wealth of information about the current document — every element and every attribute is available for reading and manipulation. The Document Object Model is covered in Chapter 21.*

Event Handling

One of the more powerful and often used techniques concerning JavaScript is events. Using event attributes in XHTML tags, such as onmouseover and onclick, you can create interactive documents that respond to the user's actions.

The following table lists the various events supported by JavaScript.

Event	Trigger
onAbort	Abort selected in browser (stop loading of image or document), usually by clicking the Stop button
onBlur	When the object loses focus
onChange	When the object is changed (generally a form element)
onClick	When the object is clicked
onDblClick	When the object is double-clicked
onDragDrop	When an object is dropped into the user agent window (generally a file)
onError	When a JavaScript error occurs (not a browser error — only JavaScript code errors will trigger this event)
onFocus	When an object receives focus
onKeyDown	When the user presses a key
onKeyPress	When the user presses and/or holds down a key

Event	Trigger
onKeyUp	When the user releases a key
onload	When the object is loaded into the user agent (typically used with the `<body>` element to run a script when the document has completed loading)
onMouseDown	When the mouse button is depressed
onMouseMove	When the mouse is moved
onMouseOut	When the mouse pointer moves outside the boundary of an object
onMouseOver	When the mouse pointer moves within the boundary of an object
onMouseUp	When the mouse button is released
onMove	When an object (generally a window or frame) is moved
onReset	When the user selects a reset button
onResize	When an object (generally a window or frame) is resized
onSelect	When the user selects text within the object (generally a form element)
onSubmit	When the user selects a submit button
onUnload	When the object is unloaded from the user agent (generally used with the `<body>` element to run a script when the user navigates away from a document — a favorite tool of pop-up window coders)

For example, table text in the following document will turn red when the user moves the mouse over the table (onmouseover) and back to black when the mouse is moved outside of the table (onmouseout):

```
<!DOCTYPE html PUBLIC "-//W3C//DTD XHTML 1.0 Strict//EN"
    "http://www.w3.org/TR/xhtml1/DTD/xhtml1-strict.dtd">
<html>
<head>
<title>Event Handling</title>
<style type="text/css">
  table { border: thin solid black;
          border-collapse: collapse; }
  td { border: thin solid black;
       padding: 5px; }
</style>
</head>
<body>
  <p>
    <table onmouseover="style.color='red';" onmouseout="style.color='black';" >
      <tr><td>Cell 1</td><td>Cell 2</td></tr>
      <tr><td>Cell 3</td><td>Cell 4</td></tr>
      <tr><td>Cell 5</td><td>Cell 6</td></tr>
    </table>
  </p>
</body>
</html>
```

This technique demonstrates another important technique: incorporating raw code in event attribute values. This technique is useful if the code is unique to the element in which it appears and is a fairly small piece of code. However, in the preceding case, what if you wanted to change other elements' colors as the user moves the mouse over them? In that case, you would be better off defining functions for the color change and calling the functions from within the events, as in the following:

```
<!DOCTYPE html PUBLIC "-//W3C//DTD XHTML 1.0 Strict//EN"
    "http://www.w3.org/TR/xhtml1/DTD/xhtml1-strict.dtd">
<html>
<head>
<title>Event Handling</title>
<script type="text/JavaScript">
function goRed(myobj) {
  myobj.style.color = "red";
}
function goBlack(myobj) {
  myobj.style.color = "black";
}
</script>
<style type="text/css">
  table { border: thin solid black;
          border-collapse: collapse; }
  td { border: thin solid black;
       padding: 5px; }
</style>
</head>
<body>
  <p>
    <table id="tbl1" onmouseover="goRed(tbl1)" onmouseout="goBlack(tbl1)" >
      <tr><td>Cell 1</td><td>Cell 2</td></tr>
      <tr><td>Cell 3</td><td>Cell 4</td></tr>
      <tr><td>Cell 5</td><td>Cell 6</td></tr>
    </table>
  </p>
</body>
</html>
```

Note that the event must pass the object ID to the function to correctly identify the object whose color is to change.

Other methods of identifying objects are covered in Chapters 21–23.

JavaScript Errors and Troubleshooting

Although JavaScript syntax is fairly straightforward, it is incredibly easy to make mistakes that cause your scripts not to function the way you intend. This section will provide some troubleshooting tips to aid you in solving your scripting problems.

Using the Right Tools

First and foremost, using an editor designed to edit code is essential. Although any text editor will work, code-friendly editors offer features such as auto-indenting, syntax highlighting, and regular expression search-and-replace functions.

Some of the tools in the following list are open source and others are commercial. Most of the commercial applications offer free trial versions. Capabilities between the various editors vary—pick an editor that offers the capabilities you need in the price range that works for you.

Windows users should explore tools such as the following:

- ❑ **TextPad**—http://www.textpad.com
- ❑ **PSPad**—http://www.pspad.com/
- ❑ **Homesite**—http://www.macromedia.com/software/homesite/

Linux users should explore tools such as the following:

- ❑ **vim**—http://www.vim.org/
- ❑ **Emacs**—http://www.gnu.org/software/emacs/emacs.html
- ❑ **Bluefish**—http://bluefish.openoffice.nl/

Macintosh users should explore tools such as the following:

- ❑ Many of the editors available for Linux (see preceding list)
- ❑ **BBEdit**—http://www.barebones.com/index.shtml
- ❑ **Dreamweaver**—http://www.macromedia.com/software/dreamweaver/

Common JavaScript Syntactical Mistakes

There are several mistakes that are often made when coding JavaScript. Keep the following in mind when you encounter problems in your scripts:

- ❑ **Matching braces**—Often you might find that a block section of code is missing its beginning or ending brace ({ or }). Adhering to strict syntax formatting will help; it's easier to notice a missing brace if it doesn't appear where it should. For example, consider placing the braces on lines of their own where they are very conspicuous, similar to the following snippet:

```
if (windowName == "menu")
{
  // Conditional code here
}
```

- ❑ **Missing semicolons**—When writing quick and dirty code, it's easy to forget the little things, such as the semicolons on the end of statements. That is one reason why I never treat semicolons as optional; I use them at the end of every statement even when they technically are optional.

❑ **Variable type conflicts** — Because JavaScript allows for loose variable typing, it is easy to make mistakes by assuming a variable contains data of one type when it actually contains data of another type. For example, if you access a numeric variable with a string function, JavaScript will interpret the numeric value as a string, resulting in the original number being rounded, truncated, or otherwise modified.

❑ **Incorrect object references** — You will find that the syntax of referencing objects can sometimes be tricky. What works in one document or user agent may not work in another. It's important to always reference objects starting with the top of the object hierarchy (for example, starting with the `document` object) or use tools such as `getElementID()` to uniquely identify and reference objects.

❑ **Working with noncompliant HTML** — Sometimes the problem is not in the JavaScript but in the XHTML that JavaScript is trying to interact with. It is important to work within the XHTML standards to ensure that elements in your document can be referenced appropriately by your scripts. It is also important to define and adhere to naming conventions for element `id` and `name` attributes, helping avoid typos between your document elements and scripts.

❑ **Your own idiosyncrasies** — After writing several scripts, you may find several personal coding idiosyncrasies that end up constantly biting you. Try to remember those issues and check your code for your consistent problems as you go.

Identifying Problems

One big problem with JavaScript is the lack of feedback when problems do exist. Mozilla Firefox will simply not run a script that has syntactical errors, providing little to no feedback as to what the error is. Internet Explorer will display an error icon in its status bar when a JavaScript syntax error is found; clicking on the icon will usually display a message regarding the error (as shown in Figure 20-1), however cryptic the message might be.

Error icon: Double-click to display error message

Figure 20-1

*The error shown in Figure 20-1, **Object expected**, is a very common error reported by Internet Explorer. In most cases, the error results from an event call (for example, **onClick**) to a function or other external piece of code that failed to compile due to syntax errors. Beginning JavaScript program- mers may spend a lot of time adjusting the syntax of the event call when the problem is actually in the code being called.*

There are several methods you can employ to track down the source of an error. The most common are outlined in the following sections.

Using Alert

The `alert` function is a valuable tool that can be used for basic troubleshooting. You can use this function to display values of variables or to act as simple breakpoints within the script. For example, if you need to track the value of variable x, you could place lines similar to the following in key areas of your script:

```
alert("The value of x is:  " + x);
```

Other `alert` functions can be used to create a kind of breakpoint in your script, letting you know when and where the script enters key areas. For example, the following line could be used before a key loop construct:

```
alert("Entering main FOR loop");
```

When you see the appropriate alert displayed, you know your script has at least executed to that point.

*When using the **alert** function, be sure to include enough information to distinguish the **alert** from other **alerts** of its type. For example, an **alert** reporting simply **Now entering FOR loop** doesn't tell you which **for** loop is actually being reported on.*

Using Try . . . Catch

The `try/catch` construct is meant for troubleshooting scripts by trapping errors. For example, consider the following code:

```
try {
  //code you want to troubleshoot
  // If x<23, there's an error
  if (x < 23) { throw(x); } // Throw value of x
}
catch (err) {
  // Catch the error, and make a decision based on
  //  value passed -- in this case, just report value
  alert("Error: " + err);
}
```

If your code traps an error in the `try` section of the script, you can throw an exception using the `throw` function. Execution of the script moves immediately to the `catch` section where the error can be further diagnosed and reported on. Note that multiple `throws` can be implemented in the `try` section, and the `catch` section can perform more actions than demonstrated in the preceding code. For example, condi- tional statements can be used in the `catch` section to report different messages depending on the value passed by the `throw`.

Using Specialized Tools

There are several additional tools available for troubleshooting your JavaScript scripts. One popular tool is JSUnit (`http://www.edwardh.com/jsunit/`). JSUnit is a port of the popular JUnit (`http://www.junit.org`) testing framework, used to test Java code.

Using JSUnit, you can define assertions and use those assertions to test the functionality of your code. Note that the assertions will not protect you from simple typos and other syntactical errors; assertions will test only for proper values going in and coming out of functions. The JSUnit site has several examples of how assertions can be defined and used. Visit the site for more information.

Summary

This chapter covered the basics of the JavaScript language to familiarize you with its syntax, structure, data objects, and more. After reading this chapter, you should understand how JavaScript compares to other programming languages and be ready to apply that knowledge. The next chapter discusses the Document Object Model, the most powerful data object available to JavaScript. Subsequent chapters cover typical uses of JavaScript as well as using JavaScript with HTML to achieve Dynamic HTML (DHTML).

The Document Object Model

Most Web programmers are familiar with Dynamic HTML (DHTML) and the underlying Document Object Models developed by Netscape and Microsoft for their respective browsers. However, there is a unifying Document Object Model (DOM) developed by the W3C that is less well known and, hence, used less often. The W3C DOM has several advantages over the DHTML DOM—using its node structure it is possible to easily navigate and change documents despite the user agent used to display them. This chapter covers the basics of the W3C DOM and oldChild) teaches you how to use JavaScript to manipulate it.

> *The W3C DOM is much more complex than shown within this chapter. There are several additional methods and properties at your disposal to use in manipulating documents, many more than we have room to address in this chapter. Further reading and information on the standard can be found on the W3C Web site at* **http://www.w3.org/TR/2000/WD-DOM-Level-1-20000929/Overview.html**. *The next chapter covers the details of the DHTML DOM.*

The History of the DOM

The Document Object Model was developed by the World Wide Web Consortium (W3C) to allow programming languages access to the underlying structure of a Web document. Using the DOM a program can access any element in the document, determining and changing attributes and even removing, adding, or rearranging elements at will.

> *It's important to note that the DOM is a type of application program interface (API) allowing any programming language access to the structure of a Web document. The main advantage of using the DOM is the ability to manipulate a document without another trip to the document's server. As such, the DOM is typically accessed and used by client-side technologies, such as JavaScript. Therefore, the coverage of the DOM in this book appears in the JavaScript part of the book and is very JavaScript-centric.*

The first DOM specification (Level 0) was developed at the same time as JavaScript and early browsers. It is supported by Netscape 2 onward.

There were two intermediate DOMs supported by Netscape 4 onward and Microsoft Internet Explorer (IE) versions 4 and 5 onward. These DOMs were proprietary to the two sides of the browser coin—Netscape and Microsoft IE. The former used a collection of elements referenced through a `document.layers` object, while the latter used a `document.all` object. To be truly cross-browser compatible, a script should endeavor to cover both of these DOMs instead of one or the other.

Techniques for accessing these DOMs are covered in Chapter22, "Dynamic HTML."

The latest DOM specification (Level 1) is supported by Mozilla and Microsoft Internet Explorer version 5 onward. Both browser developers participated in the creation of this level of the DOM and as such support it. However, Microsoft chose to continue to support its `document.all` model as well, while Netscape discontinued its `document.layers` model.

Keep in mind also that the DOM was originally intended to allow programs to navigate and change XML, not HTML, documents, so it contains many features a Web developer dealing only with HTML may never need.

Understanding the Document Object Model

The basis of the DOM is to recognize each element of the document as a node connected to other nodes in the document and to the document root itself. The best way to understand the structure is to look at an example. The following code shows an example document that renders as shown in Figure 21-1 and whose resulting DOM is shown in the illustration of Figure 21-2.

```
<html>
<head>
<title>Sample DOM Document</title>

<style type="text/css">

  div.div1 { background-color: #999999; }
  div.div2 { background-color: #BBBBBB; }
  table, table * { border: thin solid black; }
  table { border-collapse: collapse; }
  td { padding: 5px; }

</style>

<script type="text/JavaScript">

</script>

</head>
<body>
<div class="div1">
  <h1>Heading 1</h1>
  <table>
    <tr><td>Cell 1</td><td>Cell 2</td></tr>
    <tr><td>Cell 3</td><td>Cell 4</td></tr>
  </table>
```

```
    <p>Lorem ipsum dolor sit amet, consectetuer adipiscing
    elit, sed diam <b>nonummy nibh euismod</b> tincidunt ut laoreet
    dolore magna aliquam erat volutpat. Ut wisi enim ad minim
    veniam, quis nostrud exerci tation ullamcorper suscipit
    lobortis nisl ut aliquip ex ea commodo consequat.</p>
  </div>
  <div class="div2">
    <h1>Heading 2</h1>
    <p>Lorem ipsum dolor sit amet, consectetuer adipiscing
    elit, sed diam nonummy nibh euismod tincidunt ut laoreet
    dolore magna aliquam erat volutpat. Ut wisi enim ad minim
    veniam, quis nostrud exerci tation ullamcorper suscipit
    lobortis nisl ut aliquip ex ea commodo consequat.</p>
    <ol id="sortme">An ordered list
      <li>Gamma</li>
      <li>Alpha</li>
      <li>Beta</li>
    </ol>
  </div>
  </body>
  </html>
```

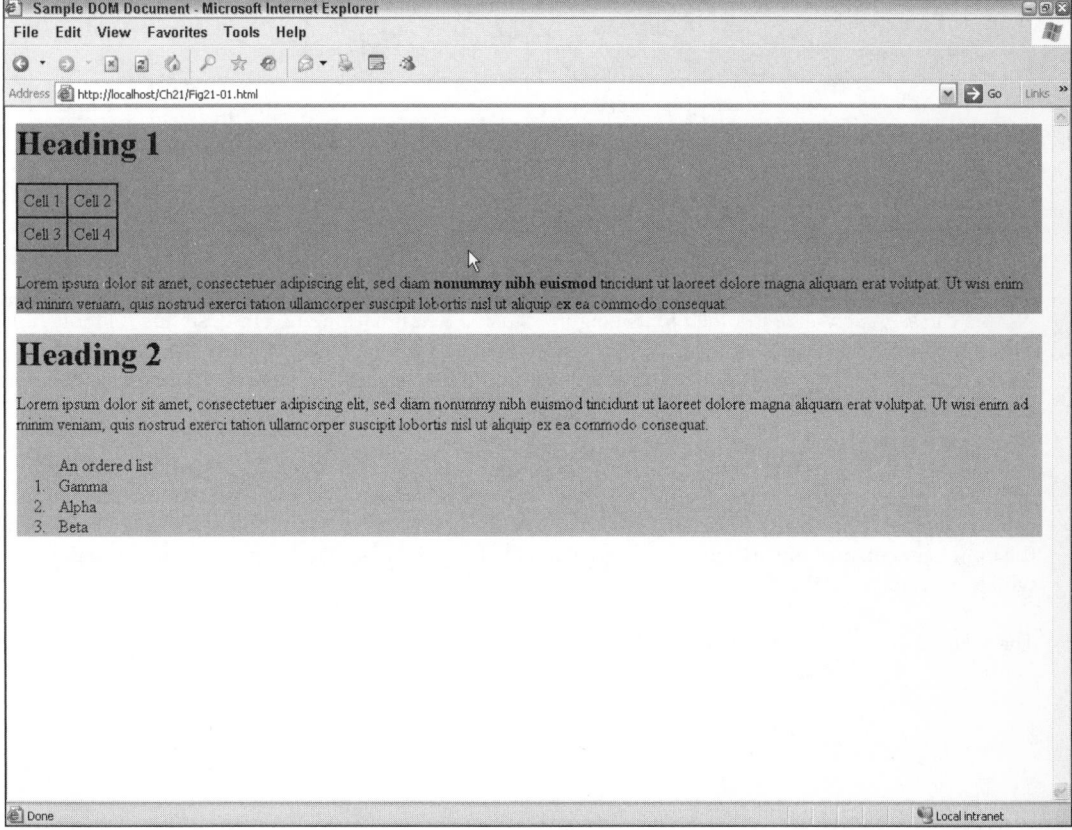

Figure 21-1

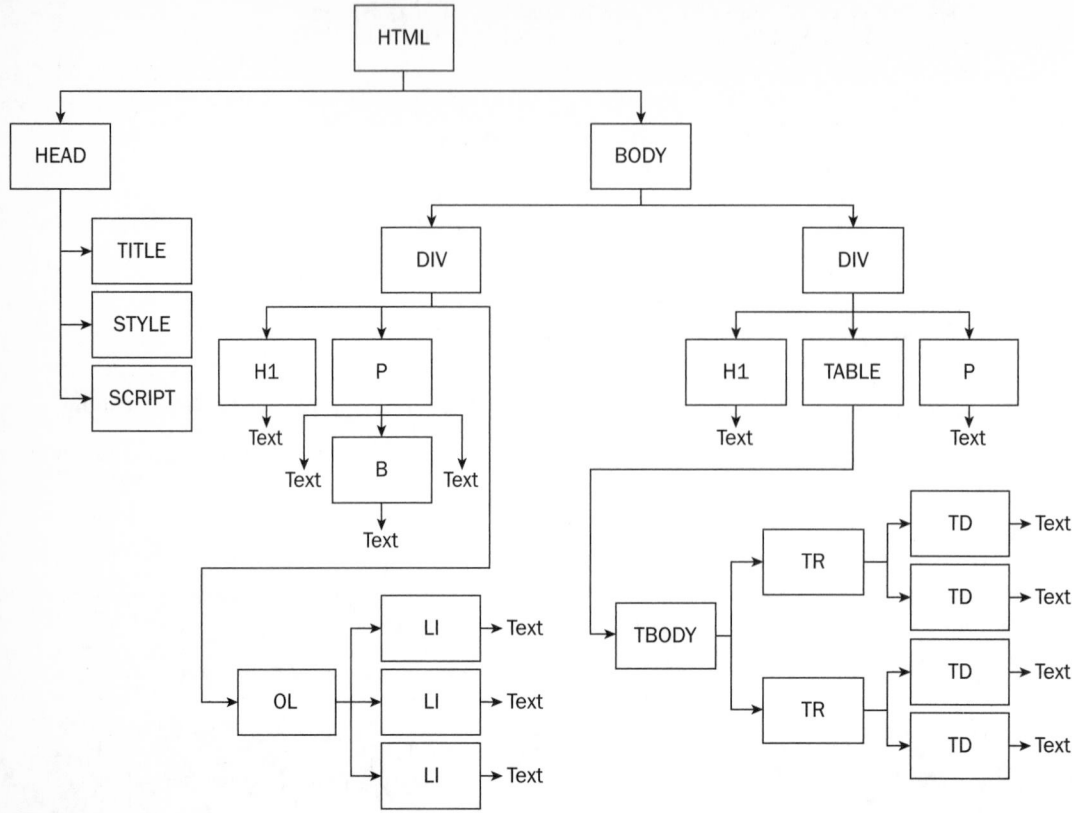

Figure 21-2

As you can see, each node is joined to its neighbors using a familiar parent, child, sibling relationship. For example, the first DIV node is a child of the BODY node, and the DIV node in turn has three children—an H1 node, a P node, and an OL node. Those three children (H1, P, and OL) have a sibling relationship to one another.

Plain text, usually the content of nodes such as paragraphs (P), is referenced as textual nodes and is broken down as necessary to incorporate additional nodes. This can be seen in the first P node, which contains a bold (B) element. The children of the P node include the first bit of text up to the bold element, the bold element, and the text after the bold element. The bold element (B) in turn contains a text child, which contains the bolded text.

The relationships between nodes can be explored and traversed using the DOM JavaScript bindings, as described in the next section.

DOM Node Properties and Methods

The DOM includes several JavaScript bindings that can be used to navigate a document's DOM. A subset of those bindings, used in JavaScript as properties and methods, is listed in the following two tables. The first table describes JavaScript's properties.

A full list of DOM JavaScript bindings can be found on the W3C's Document Object Model Level 1 pages, at **http://www.w3.org/TR/2000/WD-DOM-Level-1-20000929/ecma-script-language-binding.html**.

Property	Description
attributes	This read-only property returns a named node map-NamedNodeMap containing the specified node's attributes.
childNodes	This read-only property returns a node list containing all the children of the specified node.
firstChild	This read-only property returns the first child node of the specified node.
lastChild	This read-only property returns the last child node of the specified node.
nextSibling	This read-only property returns the next sibling of the specified node.
nodeName	This read-only property returns a string containing the name of the node, which is typically the name of the element (P, DIV, TABLE, and so on).
nodeType	This read-only property returns a number corresponding to the node type (1 = element, 2 = text).
nodeValue	This property returns a string containing the contents of the node and is only valid for text nodes.
ownerDocument	This read-only property returns the root document node object of the specified node.
parentNode	This read-only property returns the parent node of the specified node.
previousSibling	This read-only property returns the previous sibling of the specified node. If there is no node, the property returns null.

The second table describes JavaScript's methods.

Method	Description
`appendChild(newChild)`	Given a node, this method inserts the `newChild` node at the end of the children and returns a node.
`cloneNode(deep)`	This method clones the node object. The parameter deep — (a Boolean) — specifies whether the clone should include the source object's attributes and children. The return value is the cloned node(s).
`hasChildNodes()`	This method returns `true` if the node object has children nodes, `false` if the node object has no children nodes.
`insertBefore(newChild, refChild)`	Given two nodes, this method inserts the `newChild` node before the specified `refChild` node and returns a node object.
`removeChild(oldChild)`	Given a node, this method removes the `oldChild` node from the DOM and returns a node object containing the node removed.
`replaceChild(newChild, oldChild)`	Given two nodes, this method replaces the `oldChild` node with the `newChild` node and returns a node object. Note that if the `newChild` is already in the DOM, it is removed from its current location to replace the `oldChild`.

Traversing a Document's Nodes

Using the JavaScript bindings, it is fairly trivial to navigate through a document's nodes, as demonstrated in the examples that follow.

Example: Navigating and Reporting a Document's Object Model

This example navigates through a document's nodes and returns the document's DOM.

Source

This example uses the document example from earlier in the chapter with scripting necessary to navigate the DOM:

```
<!DOCTYPE html PUBLIC "-//W3C//DTD XHTML 1.0 Strict//EN"
    "http://www.w3.org/TR/xhtml1/DTD/xhtml1-strict.dtd">
<html>
<head>
<title>DOM Walk and Display</title>
```

```
   <style type="text/css">

  div.div1 { background-color: #999999; }
  div.div2 { background-color: #BBBBBB; }

  table, table * { border: thin solid black; }
  table { border-collapse: collapse; }
  td { padding: 5px; }

</style>

<script type="text/JavaScript">
var s = new String();

// Add node's children to the listing (String s)
function showChildren(node,lvl) {

  // Only track elements (1), text (3), and the document (9)
  if ( node.nodeType == 1 || node.nodeType == 3 ||
     node.nodeType == 9 ) {
    // Add dashes to represent node level
    for (var x = 0; x < lvl; x++) { s = s + "--"; }
    // Report first 20 chars for text nodes
    if ( node.nodeType == 3 ) {
      mynodeType = node.nodeValue;
      if (mynodeType.length > 20) {
        mynodeType = mynodeType.slice(0,16) + "...";
      }
    } else {
      // Report "Element/Tag" for elements
      mynodeType = "Element/Tag";
    }
    s = s + "+ " + node.nodeName + " (" + mynodeType + ")\n";

    // If the node has children, let's report those too
    if ( node.hasChildNodes() ) {
      var children = node.childNodes;
      for (var i = 0; i < children.length; i++) {
        showChildren(children[i],lvl+1);
      }

    }

  }

}
```

```
function domwalk()
  // Navigate through the DOM and report it in another window
  alert("Click OK to display the document's DOM");
  showChildren(document,0);
  displaywin = window.open("","displaywin",
      "width=400,height=400,scrollbars=yes,resizable=yes");
  displaywin.document.write("<pre>"+s+"</pre>");
}

</script>
</head>
<body onload="domwalk()">
<div class="div1">
  <h1>Heading 1</h1>
  <table>
    <tr><td>Cell 1</td><td>Cell 2</td></tr>
    <tr><td>Cell 3</td><td>Cell 4</td></tr>
  </table>
  <p>Lorem ipsum dolor sit amet, consectetuer adipiscing
  elit, sed diam <b>nonummy nibh euismod</b> tincidunt ut laoreet
  dolore magna aliquam erat volutpat. Ut wisi enim ad minim
  veniam, quis nostrud exerci tation ullamcorper suscipit
  lobortis nisl ut aliquip ex ea commodo consequat.</p>
</div>
<div class="div2">
  <h1>Heading 2</h1>
  <p>Lorem ipsum dolor sit amet, consectetuer adipiscing
  elit, sed diam nonummy nibh euismod tincidunt ut laoreet
  dolore magna aliquam erat volutpat. Ut wisi enim ad minim
  veniam, quis nostrud exerci tation ullamcorper suscipit
  lobortis nisl ut aliquip ex ea commodo consequat.</p>
  <ol id="sortme">An ordered list
    <li>Gamma</li>
    <li>Alpha</li>
    <li>Beta</li>
  </ol>
</div>
</body>

</html>
```

This code works by recursively calling the showChildren() function for each node that has children in the document (identified by the hasChildNodes() property). The nodes are added to a global string (s) until the end of the document is reached (there are no more nodes or children). The script then spawns a new window to display the full DOM as recorded in the string. (Note that your user agent must allow pop-up windows for this code to work.)

Output

The script displays the windows shown in Figure 21-3. The DOM is displayed with representative levels (dashes and pluses) in the new window.

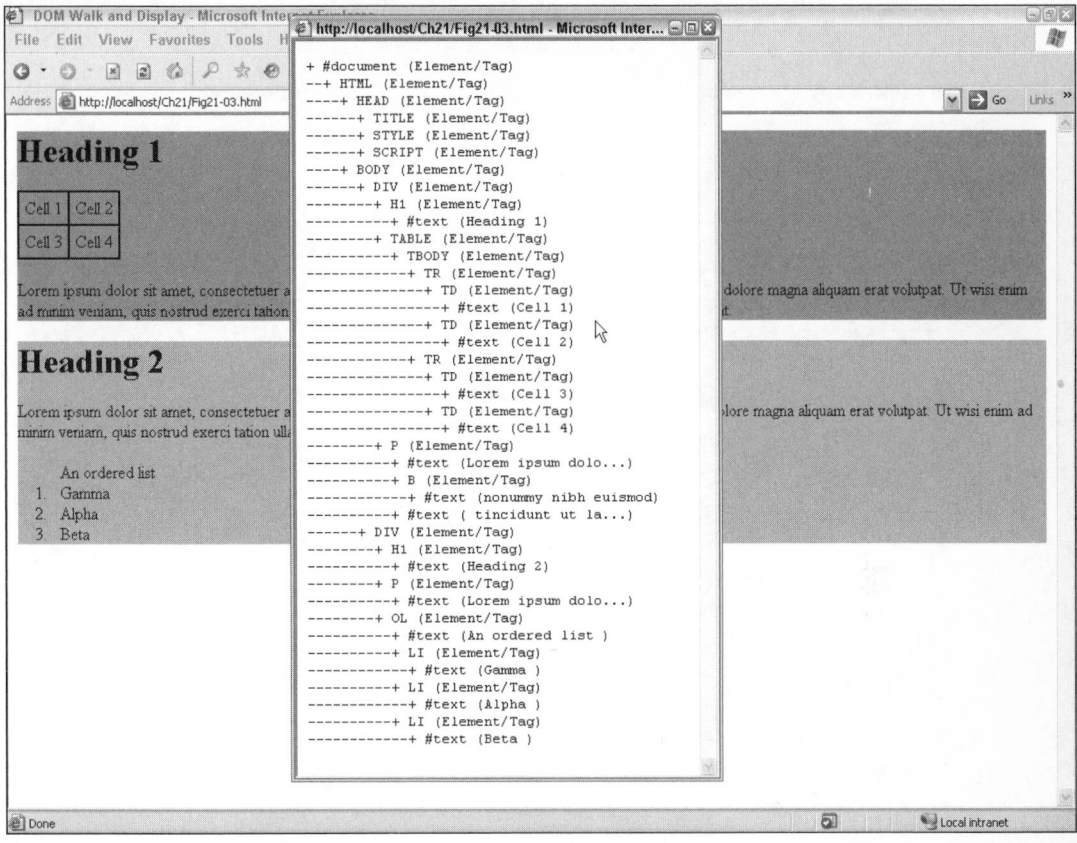

Figure 21-3

You can also use the values and types properties of nodes to effectively search the DOM for nodes, as demonstrated by the next example.

Example: Finding a Particular Node

This example expands upon the previous example by searching for a node with a particular ID in the DOM.

Source

```
    <!DOCTYPE html PUBLIC "-//W3C//DTD XHTML 1.0 Strict//EN"
    "http://www.w3.org/TR/xhtml1/DTD/xhtml1-strict.dtd">
<html>
<head>
<title>DOM Find Node</title>

<style type="text/css">

  div.div1 { background-color: #999999; }
  div.div2 { background-color: #BBBBBB; }

  table, table * { border: thin solid black; }
  table { border-collapse: collapse; }
  td { padding: 5px; }

</style>

<script type="text/JavaScript">

function findNode(startnode,nodename,nodeid) {

  var foundNode = false;

  if ( startnode.nodeName == nodename &&
       startnode.id == nodeid ) {
    foundNode = startnode;
  } else {
    look_thru_children:
    if ( startnode.hasChildNodes() ) {
      var children = startnode.childNodes;
      for (var i = 0; i < children.length; i++) {
        foundNode = findNode(children[i],nodename,nodeid);
          if (foundNode) { break look_thru_children; }
      }
    }
  }
  return foundNode;
}

function dofind() {
  alert("Click OK to find 'sortme' node");
  var node = findNode(document,"OL","sortme");
  alert("Found node: " + node.nodeName);
}

</script>
```

```
      </head>
<body onload="dofind()">
<div class="div1">
  <h1>Heading 1</h1>
  <table>
    <tr><td>Cell 1</td><td>Cell 2</td></tr>
    <tr><td>Cell 3</td><td>Cell 4</td></tr>
  </table>
  <p>Lorem ipsum dolor sit amet, consectetuer adipiscing
  elit, sed diam <b>nonummy nibh euismod</b> tincidunt ut laoreet
  dolore magna aliquam erat volutpat. Ut wisi enim ad minim
  veniam, quis nostrud exerci tation ullamcorper suscipit
  lobortis nisl ut aliquip ex ea commodo consequat.</p>
</div>
<div class="div2">
  <h1>Heading 2</h1>
  <p>Lorem ipsum dolor sit amet, consectetuer adipiscing
  elit, sed diam nonummy nibh euismod tincidunt ut laoreet
  dolore magna aliquam erat volutpat. Ut wisi enim ad minim
  veniam, quis nostrud exerci tation ullamcorper suscipit
  lobortis nisl ut aliquip ex ea commodo consequat.</p>
  <ol id="sortme">An ordered list
    <li>Gamma</li>
    <li>Alpha</li>
    <li>Beta</li>
  </ol>
</div>
</body>

</html>
```

This script works by traversing the DOM (using the same mechanisms from the previous example) looking for a node with the specified name (nodeName) and ID (id). When found, the search stops and the node is reported as found along with the type of node (element name). In this example OL is returned because the node with the ID sortme is an OL element.

*The DOM provides another, easier mechanism to find an element with a particular **id**, namely the **getElementById()** method of the document object. In fact, the entire search function in the preceding script can be replaced with one line:*

```
node = document.getElementById("sortme");
```

The previous method of traversing the DOM was used to illustrate how you can manually search the DOM, if necessary. More information and uses of the getElementById() method can be found in Chapter 22, "Dynamic HTML."

Output

This script simply outputs the alert box shown in Figure 21-4. However, after execution the variable node contains a reference to the node being sought and can be manipulated, as shown in the next section.

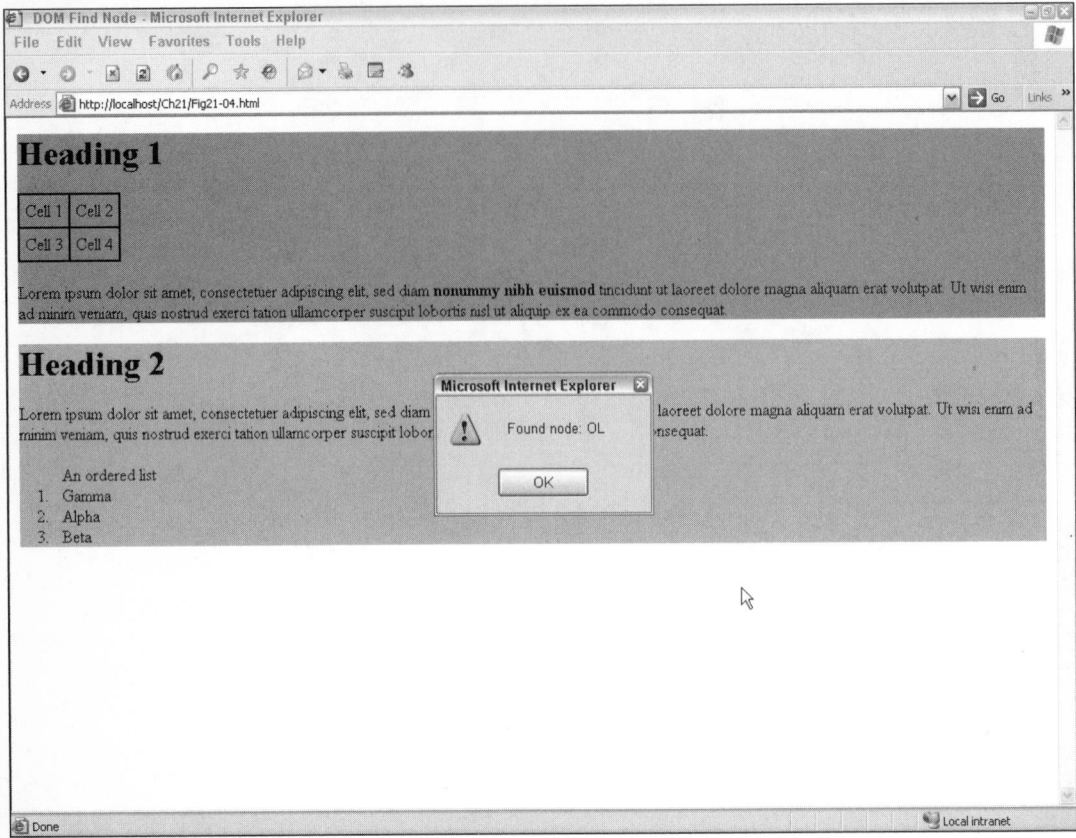

Figure 21-4

Changing Nodes

As previously mentioned, you can manipulate document nodes on the fly, adding, removing, and changing them as needed. The following sections show examples of changing nodes.

Example: Changing a Node's Value

This example shows how a text node's value can be changed.

Source

This example uses previously discussed methods to find and change the text of an OL node.

```
<!DOCTYPE html PUBLIC "-//W3C//DTD XHTML 1.0 Strict//EN"
    "http://www.w3.org/TR/xhtml1/DTD/xhtml1-strict.dtd">
<html>
<head>
<title>DOM Find Node</title>

<style type="text/css">

  div.div1 { background-color: #999999; }
  div.div2 { background-color: #BBBBBB; }

  table, table * { border: thin solid black; }
  table { border-collapse: collapse; }
  td { padding: 5px; }

</style>

<script type="text/JavaScript">

function findNode(startnode,nodename,nodeid) {

  var foundNode = false;

  // Check our starting node for what we are looking for
  if ( startnode.nodeName == nodename &&
       startnode.id == nodeid ) {
    foundNode = startnode;
  } else {
    // If not found, look through children
    look_thru_children:
    if ( startnode.hasChildNodes() ) {
      var children = startnode.childNodes;
      for (var i = 0; i < children.length; i++) {
        foundNode = findNode(children[i],nodename,nodeid);
        // Return when found
        if (foundNode) { break look_thru_children; }
      }
    }
  }
  return foundNode;
}

function dofindNchange() {
  alert("Click OK to change 'sortme' node's text");
  var node = document.getElementById("sortme");
```

```
    if (node.firstChild.nodeType == 3) {
      node.firstChild.nodeValue = "Changed text";
    }
  }

</script>

</head>
<body onload="dofindNchange()">
<div class="div1">
  <h1>Heading 1</h1>
  <table>
    <tr><td>Cell 1</td><td>Cell 2</td></tr>
    <tr><td>Cell 3</td><td>Cell 4</td></tr>
  </table>
  <p>Lorem ipsum dolor sit amet, consectetuer adipiscing
  elit, sed diam <b>nonummy nibh euismod</b> tincidunt ut laoreet
  dolore magna aliquam erat volutpat. Ut wisi enim ad minim
  veniam, quis nostrud exerci tation ullamcorper suscipit
  lobortis nisl ut aliquip ex ea commodo consequat.</p>
</div>
<div class="div2">
  <h1>Heading 2</h1>
  <p>Lorem ipsum dolor sit amet, consectetuer adipiscing
  elit, sed diam nonummy nibh euismod tincidunt ut laoreet
  dolore magna aliquam erat volutpat. Ut wisi enim ad minim
  veniam, quis nostrud exerci tation ullamcorper suscipit
  lobortis nisl ut aliquip ex ea commodo consequat.</p>
  <ol id="sortme">An ordered list
    <li>Gamma</li>
    <li>Alpha</li>
    <li>Beta</li>
  </ol>
</div>
</body>

</html>
```

The change of the node takes place in the `findNchange()` function, after finding the node. The found node's `firstChild` is checked to ensure it is text, and then its value is changed.

Output

Figure 21-5 shows the document after the change; note the OL node's text now reads "Changed text."

Using the DOM, you can also rearrange nodes within the document, as demonstrated in the next example.

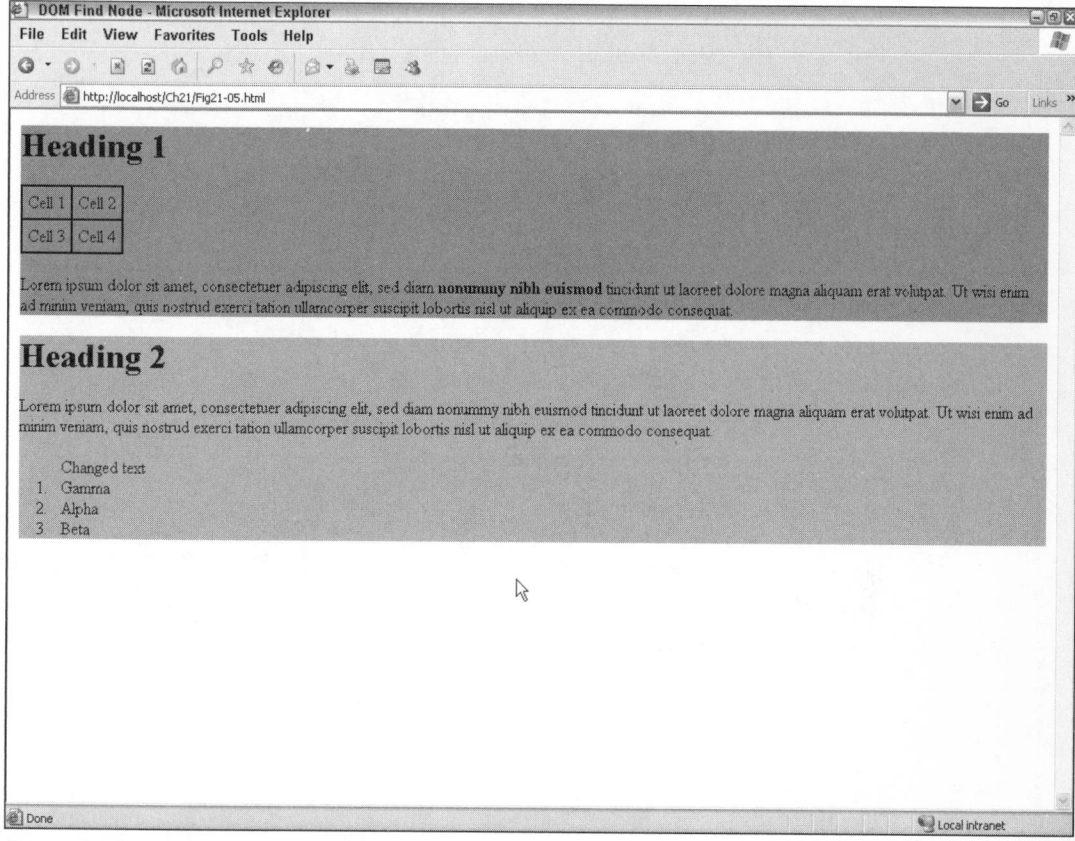

Figure 21-5

Example: Sorting Elements Using the DOM

This example shows how an ordered list (OL node) can have its items (LIs) sorted using the DOM.

Source

This example uses functions used in previous examples but expands upon them by using a sort routine to sort the OL node's children.

```
<!DOCTYPE html PUBLIC "-//W3C//DTD XHTML 1.0 Strict//EN"
    "http://www.w3.org/TR/xhtml1/DTD/xhtml1-strict.dtd">
<html>
<head>
<title>DOM Data Sort</title>

<style type="text/css">
```

```
  div.div1 { background-color: #999999; }
  div.div2 { background-color: #BBBBBB; }

  table, table * { border: thin solid black; }
  table { border-collapse: collapse; }
  td { padding: 5px; }

</style>

<script type="text/JavaScript">

function findNode(startnode,nodename,nodeid) {

  var foundNode = false;

  // Check our starting node for what we are looking for
  if ( startnode.nodeName == nodename &&
       startnode.id == nodeid ) {
    foundNode = startnode;
  } else {
    // If not found, look through children
    look_thru_children:
    if ( startnode.hasChildNodes() ) {
      var children = startnode.childNodes;
      for (var i = 0; i < children.length; i++) {
        foundNode = findNode(children[i],nodename,nodeid);
          // Return when found
          if (foundNode) { break look_thru_children; }
      }
    }
  }
  return foundNode;
}


function sortlist(node) {

  // Does object have at least 2 children?
    if (node.hasChildNodes() && node.firstChild.nextSibling != null) {

    for (i = 1; i < node.childNodes.length; i++) {
      // Only sort LIs
      if (node.childNodes[i].nodeName != "LI") { continue; }

      for (j = i+1; j < node.childNodes.length; j++) {
        // Only sort LIs
        if (node.childNodes[j].nodeName != "LI") { continue; }

        // Sort needed?
        if (node.childNodes[i].firstChild.nodeValue >
            node.childNodes[j].firstChild.nodeValue) {
          // Use temporary nodes to swap nodes
          tempnode_i = node.childNodes[i].cloneNode(true);
```

```
                tempnode_j = node.childNodes[j].cloneNode(true);
                node.replaceChild(tempnode_i, node.childNodes[j]);
                node.replaceChild(tempnode_j, node.childNodes[i]);
              }

          }

        }

      }

    }


    function dofindNsort() {
      alert("Click OK to sort list");
      // Find and sort node
      var node = findNode(document,"OL","sortme");
      sortlist(node);
    }

    </script>

    </head>
    <body onload="dofindNsort()">
    <div class="div1">
      <h1>Heading 1</h1>
      <table>
        <tr><td>Cell 1</td><td>Cell 2</td></tr>
        <tr><td>Cell 3</td><td>Cell 4</td></tr>
      </table>
      <p>Lorem ipsum dolor sit amet, consectetuer adipiscing
      elit, sed diam <b>nonummy nibh euismod</b> tincidunt ut laoreet
      dolore magna aliquam erat volutpat. Ut wisi enim ad minim
      veniam, quis nostrud exerci tation ullamcorper suscipit
      lobortis nisl ut aliquip ex ea commodo consequat.</p>
    </div>
    <div class="div2">
      <h1>Heading 2</h1>
      <p>Lorem ipsum dolor sit amet, consectetuer adipiscing
      elit, sed diam nonummy nibh euismod tincidunt ut laoreet
      dolore magna aliquam erat volutpat. Ut wisi enim ad minim
      veniam, quis nostrud exerci tation ullamcorper suscipit
      lobortis nisl ut aliquip ex ea commodo consequat.</p>
      <ol id="sortme">An ordered list
        <li>Gamma</li>
        <li>Alpha</li>
        <li>Beta</li>
      </ol>
    </div>
    </body>

    </html>
```

This example works similarly to that of previous examples. After the node is found, its LI children are sorted in ascending order. Note the checks built into the sort routine to ensure only the LIs are sorted — the text of the OL and other non-LI children is ignored in the sort routine. This is necessary because you can't always predict the elements a user agent identifies as nodes. For example, compare the DOM from Mozilla's Firefox browser shown in Figure 21-6 to that of Microsoft's Internet Explorer earlier in the chapter (Figure 21-3).

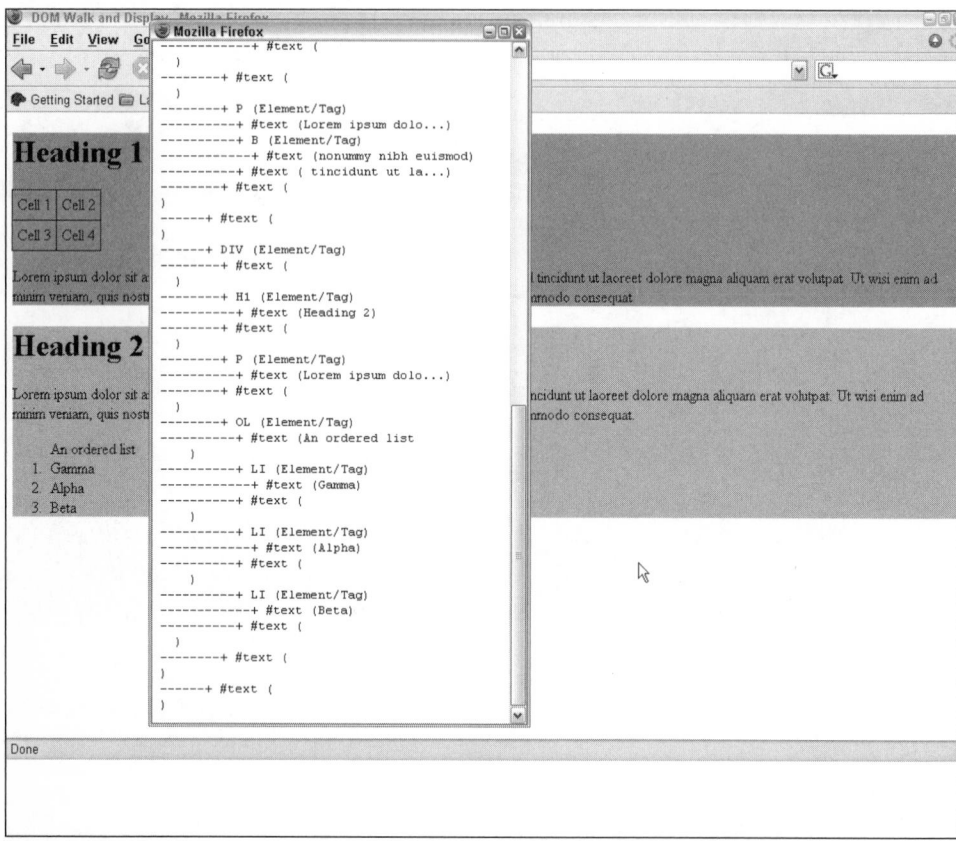

Figure 21-6

Notice the extra text elements scattered throughout the Firefox DOM, especially between elements like the LI nodes. If the script didn't check for valid LI nodeNames, the text nodes would be sorted into the LIs, disrupting the structure.

Also note that temporary nodes are used to swap the node contents. The swap could not be done using traditional methods (one temporary value) using the `replaceChild()` function:

```
tempnode = node.childNodes[j].cloneNode(true);
node.replaceChild(node.childNodes[i], node.childNodes[j]);

node.replaceChild(tempnode, node.childNodes[i]);
```

The second line in the preceding code removes `node.childNodes[i]` from the document to replace `node.childNodes[j]`. Therefore, that node (`[i]`) would not exist for the third line of the code to operate on.

Output

The output of this script is shown in Figure 21-7. Note how the `OL` node's `LI` children have been sorted into ascending order.

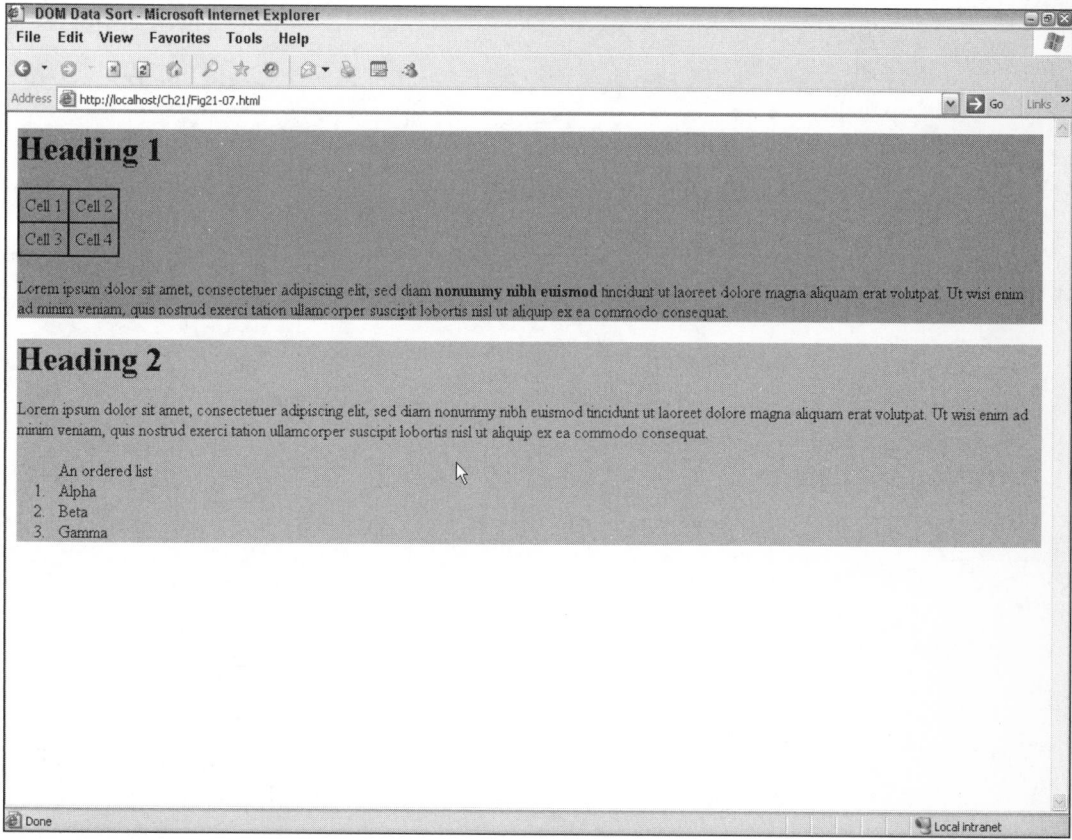

Figure 21-7

Summary

This chapter introduced you to the Document Object Model, its various levels, and how you can use it to manipulate the underlying structure of documents using client-side scripting (JavaScript). You learned how to navigate through the DOM, find nodes of interest, and change the document by manipulating the nodes.

Although the W3C DOM isn't used as much as the DHTML DOM implemented by both major browser developers, the W3C DOM is used by both browser developers and contains much power to manipulate documents using minimal scripting. Chapter 22 delves into Dynamic HTML and the various collections, properties, and methods at the disposal of JavaScript to effect even more changes in your documents.

22

JavaScript Objects and Dynamic HTML

Previous chapters in this part of the book detailed how to program using JavaScript and explained how to hook the language into the W3C Document Object Model. In addition to being a robust language and having access to the document object, JavaScript also has a host of built-in objects that can be accessed and manipulated to achieve a variety of effects, including what has come to be known as Dynamic HTML (DHTML) — the ability to manipulate a document in a dynamic fashion within the client viewing the document. This chapter covers those built-in functions and how they can be used to achieve DTHML.

Built-in JavaScript Objects

As previously mentioned, JavaScript's ability to access a document's structure and elements is perhaps the greatest advantage of using the language. Besides being able to access the Document Object Model (discussed in depth in Chapter 21), JavaScript also has a host of built-in objects that can be used to access the user agent and the document it contains. This section introduces the various objects and how JavaScript can use them.

For in-depth listings of all built-in objects, properties, and methods, see Appendix C. For more examples of how to use JavaScript for Dynamic HTML, see Chapter 23.

Window Object

The `window` object is the top-level object for an XHTML document. It includes properties and methods to manipulate the user agent window. The `window` object is also the top-level object for most other objects.

Using the `window` object, you can not only work with the current user agent window, but you can also open and work with new windows. The following code will open a new window displaying a specific document:

```
NewWin = window.open("example.htm","newWindow",
   "width=400,height=400,scrollbars=no,resizable=no");
```

The `open` method takes three arguments: a URL of the document to open in the window, the name of the new window, and options for the window. For example, the preceding code opens a window named `newWindow` containing the document `example.htm` and will be 400 pixels square, be nonresizable, and have no scrollbars.

The options supported by the `open` method include the following:

❑   `toolbar` = yes|no—Controls whether the new window will have a toolbar

❑   `location` = yes|no—Controls whether the new window will have an address bar

❑   `status` = yes|no—Controls whether the new window will have a status bar

❑   `menubar` = yes|no—Controls whether the new window will have a menu bar

❑   `resizeable` = yes|no—Controls whether the user can resize the new window

❑   `scrollbars` = yes|no—Controls whether the new window will have scrollbars

❑   `width` = *pixels*—Controls the width of the new window

❑   `height` = *pixels*—Controls the height of the new window

Not all user agents support all options.

The `window` object can also be used to size and move a user agent window. One interesting DHTML effect is to shake the current window. The following function can be used to cause the user agent window to visibly shudder:

```
function shudder() {
   // Move the document window up and down 5 times
   for (var i=1; i<= 5; i++) {
     window.moveBy(8,8);
     window.moveBy(-8,-8);
   }
}
```

You can use other methods to scroll a window (`scroll`, `scrollBy`, `scrollTo`) and to resize a window (`resizeBy`, `resizeTo`).

Document Object

You can use the JavaScript `document` object to access and manipulate the current document in the user agent window. Many of the collection objects (`form`, `image`, and so on) are children of the `document` object.

The `document` object supports a `write` and `writeln` method, both of which can be used to write content to the current document. For example, the following code results in the current date being displayed (in `mm/dd/yyyy` format) wherever the code is inserted in the document:

```
<script type="text/JavaScript">
  today = new Date;
  document.write((today.getMonth()+1) + "/" + today.getDate() +
    "/" + today.getFullYear());
</script>
```

The `open` and `close` methods can be used to open and then close a document for writing. Building on the examples in the earlier "Window Object" section, the following code can be used to spawn a new document window and write the current date to the new window:

```
<script type="text/JavaScript">
  today = new Date;
  newWin = window.open("","","width=400,height=400,scrollbars=no,resizable=no");
  newDoc = newWin.document.open();
  newDoc.write((today.getMonth()+1) + "/" + today.getDate() +
    "/" + today.getFullYear());
  newDoc.close();
</script>
```

Form Object

You can use the `form` object to access form elements in a document. The `form` object supports `length` and `elements` properties — the former property returns how many elements (fields) are in the form, and the latter contains an array of form element objects, one per field. You can also access the form elements by their name attribute. For example, the following code will set the size field to the length of the address field using the form name and element names to address the various values:

```
...
<head>
<script type="text/JavaScript">
  function dolength() {
    document.form1.addlength.value =
      document.form1.address.value.length;
  }
</script>
</head>
<body>
<p>
<form name="form1" action="handler.cgi" method="post">
Length: <input type="text" name="addlength" size="5" /><br />
Address: <input type="text" name="address" size="30" onkeyup="dolength();"/>
</form>
</p>
...
```

The `form` object can be used for a variety of form automation techniques. For example, a button can be created to check (or uncheck) all of a series of checkboxes:

```
<head>
<script type="text/JavaScript">

function checkall(field) {
  for (i=0; i<field.length; i++) {
    field[i].checked = true;
  }
}

</script>
</head>
<body>

<p><form name="form1" action="handler.cgi" method="post">
<input type="checkbox" name="list" /> one<br />
<input type="checkbox" name="list" /> two<br />
<input type="checkbox" name="list" /> three<br />
<input type="checkbox" name="list" /> four<br />
<input type="checkbox" name="list" /> five<br />
<input type="checkbox" name="list" /> six<br />
<input type="checkbox" name="list" /> seven<br />
<input type="button" name="x" value="checkall"
  onclick="checkall(document.form1.list);" /><br />
</form>
```

As you can see by the `checkbox` object's `checked` property, JavaScript has built-in properties and methods to manipulate all manner of form fields. A comprehensive list of these properties and methods appears in Appendix C, "JavaScript Language Reference."

Location Object

The `location` object can be used to manipulate the URL information about the current document in the user agent. Various properties of the `location` object are used to store individual pieces of the document's URL (protocol, hostname, port, and so on). For example, you could use the following code to piece the URL back together:

```
with (document.location) {
  var url = protocol + "//";
  url += hostname;
  if (port) { url += ":" + port; }
  url += pathname;
  if (hash) { url += hash; }
}
```

The preceding example is only to illustrate how the various pieces relate to one another — the `location.href` property contains the full URL.

One popular method of using the `location` object is to cause the user agent to load a new page. To do so, your script simply has to set the `document.location` object to the desired URL. For example, the following code will cause the user agent to load the yahoo.com home page:

```
document.location = "http://www.yahoo.com";
```

History Object

The `history` object is tied to the history function of the user agent. Using the `history` object your script can navigate up and down the history list. For example, the following code acts as though the user used the browser's back feature, causing the user agent to load the previous document in the history list:

```
history.back();
```

Other properties and methods of the `history` object allow more control over the history list. For example, the `history.length` property can be used to determine the number of entries in the history list.

As with other objects in this chapter, a full list of properties and methods supported by the object appears in Appendix C.

The Self Object

You can use the `self` object to reference an element making the reference. This object is typically used when calling JavaScript functions, allowing the function to operate on the object initiating the call. For example, the following code passes a reference to the button to the `dosomething()` function:

```
<input type="button" value="Click Me" id="button" onclick="dosomething(self);" />
```

The function can then use that reference to operate on the object that initiated the call:

```
function dosomething(el) {
... // do something with the element referenced by el ...
}
```

For example, the following function can be used to change the color of an element when called with a reference to that element:

```
function changecolorRed(el) {
  el.style.color = "red";
}
```

That function can then be added to an event of any element, similar to the following `onclick` event example:

```
<p onclick="changecolorRed(this);">When clicked, the text will change to red.</p>
```

Accessing an Element by Its ID

One of the surest methods to access a document's elements is to use the `getElementById()` function. This function is supported by any DOM Level 1-compliant user agent, so it can be relied upon to access elements that have a properly assigned ID attribute.

The syntax of the `getElementById()` function is straightforward:

```
element = getElementById("elementID");
```

For example, the following code would assign a reference to the `address` field to the `element` variable:

```
element = getElementById("address");
...
<input type="text" size="30" id="address">
```

Once assigned, the `element` variable can be used to access the referenced field's properties and methods:

```
addlength = element.length;
```

*Before using **getElementById()** you should test the user agent to ensure the function is available. The following **if** statement will generally ensure that the user agent supports the appropriate DOM level and, thus, **getElementById()**:*

```
if (document.all || document.getElementById) {
  ...getElementById should be available, use it...
}
```

Dynamic HTML

Dynamic HTML (DHTML) involves using scripts to manipulate elements within a document. The result is the creation of dynamic content (document automation, animation, and so on). Such manipulation usually involves CSS styles—the manipulation of an element's style is very efficient.

To access and manipulate document elements, you can use either of the two DOMs, the W3C DOM discussed in Chapter 21 or the JavaScript DOM provided via the objects discussed earlier in this chapter.

One popular DHTML technique is to hide or reveal document elements. You can use this to create drop-down text, collapsible outlines, and more.

Example: Using DHTML for Collapsible Lists

This example demonstrates how DHTML can be used to create collapsible lists.

Source

This code uses two classes, one to show the list items, the other to hide the list items.

```
<!DOCTYPE html PUBLIC "-//W3C//DTD XHTML 1.0 Strict//EN"
    "http://www.w3.org/TR/xhtml1/DTD/xhtml1-strict.dtd">
<html>
<head>
<title>Hidden Text</title>
<style type="text/css">
  ul.hidelist li { display: none; }
  ul.showlist li { display: block; }
</style>
<script type="text/JavaScript">

function hideNreveal(list) {
  if (list.className == "hidelist") {
    list.className = "showlist";
  } else {
    list.className = "hidelist";
  }
}

</script>
</head>
<body>

<p>Lorem ipsum dolor sit amet, consectetur adipisicing elit, sed do
eiusmod tempor incididunt ut labore et dolore magna aliqua. Ut enim
ad minim veniam, quis nostrud exercitation ullamco laboris nisi ut
aliquip ex ea commodo consequat. Duis aute irure dolor in reprehenderit
in voluptate velit esse cillum dolore eu fugiat nulla pariatur. Excepteur
sint occaecat cupidatat non proident, sunt in culpa qui officia deserunt
mollit anim id est laborum.</p>
```

```
<p>
<ul id="list1" class="hidelist"
    onclick="hideNreveal(this);">An unordered list.
<li>Item 1</li>
<li>Item 2</li>
<li>Item 3</li>
<li>Item 4</li>
</ul>
</p>
<p>Lorem ipsum dolor sit amet, consectetur adipisicing elit, sed do
eiusmod tempor incididunt ut labore et dolore magna aliqua. Ut enim
ad minim veniam, quis nostrud exercitation ullamco laboris nisi ut
aliquip ex ea commodo consequat. Duis aute irure dolor in reprehenderit
in voluptate velit esse cillum dolore eu fugiat nulla pariatur. Excepteur
sint occaecat cupidatat non proident, sunt in culpa qui officia deserunt
mollit anim id est laborum.</p>
</body>

</html>
```

Output

This example results in a document containing a collapsible list. When the list header (the UL text) is clicked, the list expands or collapses. The two states of the list are shown in Figures 22-1 (collapsed) and 22-2 (expanded).

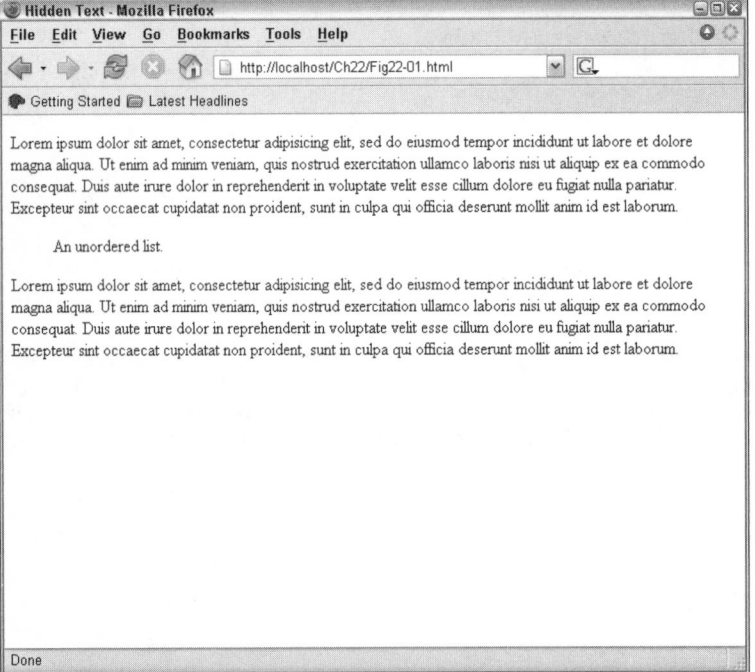

Figure 22-1

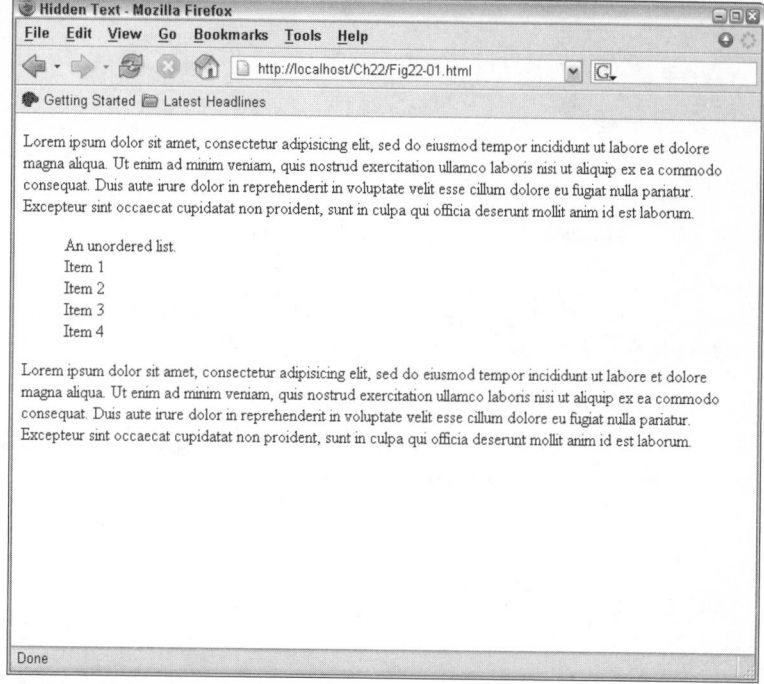

Figure 22-2

Another popular means of manipulating elements is to manipulate their styles directly, changing the values instead of changing the styles applied in a wholesale manner (via `className`). For example, you can move an element by changing its positioning styles, as in the following example.

Example: Moving Elements with JavaScript

This example demonstrates how you can use DHTML to move elements in a document.

Source

This code uses a relative positioned element's top and left values to move an element when it is clicked.

```
<!DOCTYPE html PUBLIC "-//W3C//DTD XHTML 1.0 Strict//EN"
    "http://www.w3.org/TR/xhtml1/DTD/xhtml1-strict.dtd">
<html>
<head>
<title>Moving Text</title>
<style type="text/css">
  p.movable { position: relative; top: 0; left: 0; }
</style>
```

```
<script type="text/JavaScript">
  function moveme(el) {
    if (el.style) { el = el.style; }
    el.top = "-5px"; el.left = "20px";
  }
</script>
</head>
<body>
<p class="movable" onclick="moveme(this);">Lorem ipsum dolor sit amet,
consectetur adipisicing elit, sed do eiusmod tempor incididunt ut labore
et dolore magna aliqua. Ut enim ad minim veniam, quis nostrud exercitation
ullamco laboris nisi ut aliquip ex ea commodo consequat. Duis aute irure
dolor in reprehenderit in voluptate velit esse cillum dolore eu fugiat
nulla pariatur. Excepteur sint occaecat cupidatat non proident, sunt in
culpa qui officia deserunt mollit anim id est laborum.</p>
<p>Lorem ipsum dolor sit amet, consectetur adipisicing elit, sed do
eiusmod tempor incididunt ut labore et dolore magna aliqua. Ut enim
ad minim veniam, quis nostrud exercitation ullamco laboris nisi ut
aliquip ex ea commodo consequat. Duis aute irure dolor in reprehenderit
in voluptate velit esse cillum dolore eu fugiat nulla pariatur. Excepteur
sint occaecat cupidatat non proident, sunt in culpa qui officia deserunt
mollit anim id est laborum.</p>
<p>Lorem ipsum dolor sit amet, consectetur adipisicing elit, sed do
eiusmod tempor incididunt ut labore et dolore magna aliqua. Ut enim
ad minim veniam, quis nostrud exercitation ullamco laboris nisi ut
aliquip ex ea commodo consequat. Duis aute irure dolor in reprehenderit
in voluptate velit esse cillum dolore eu fugiat nulla pariatur. Excepteur
sint occaecat cupidatat non proident, sunt in culpa qui officia deserunt
mollit anim id est laborum.</p>

</body>

</html>
```

This code uses an onclick event to call the moveme function. That function uses the object reference passed to it (this) to access the appropriate object's top and left properties. The properties are changed, creating a dynamic shift in the element (5 pixels up, 20 pixels down).

Output

Figure 22-3 shows the document immediately after loading, and Figure 22-4 shows the document after the first paragraph is clicked and the script modified its position.

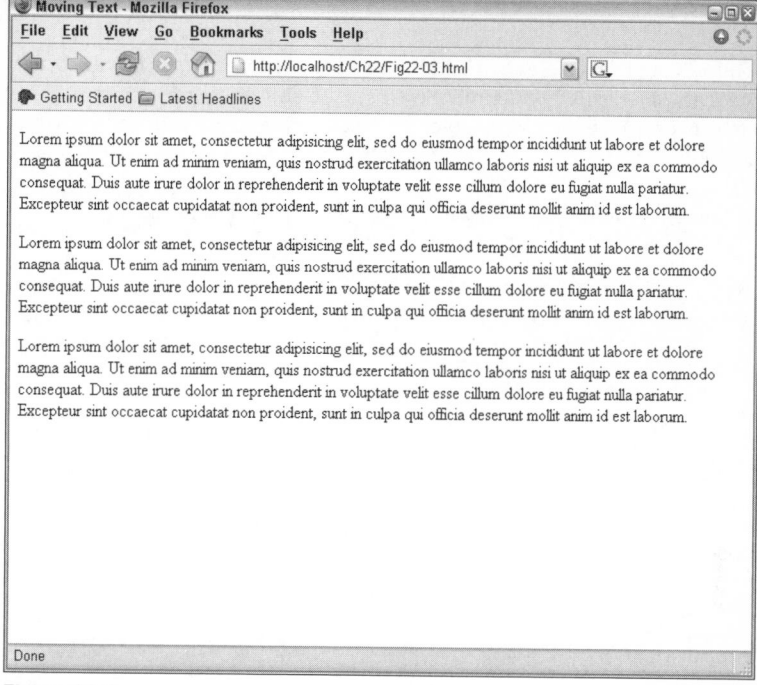

Figure 22-3

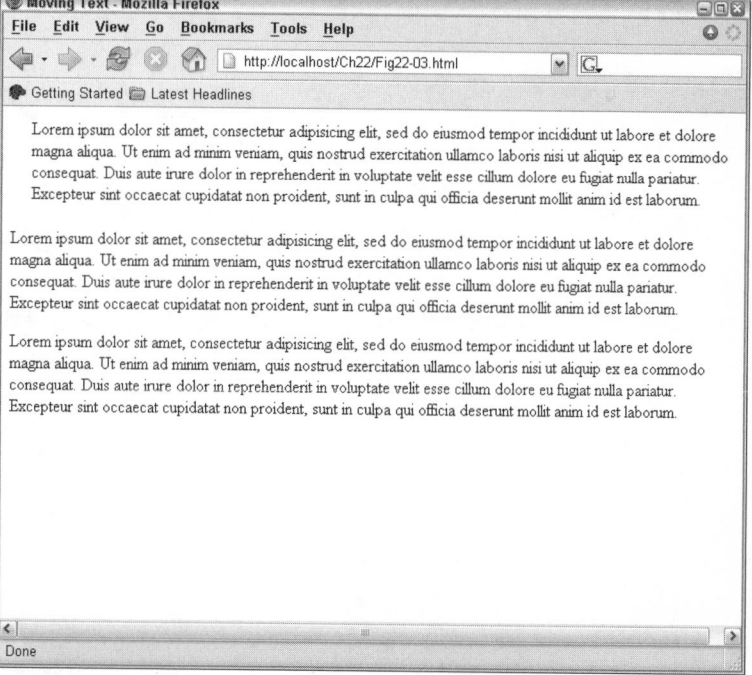

Figure 22-4

Summary

This chapter rounds out the coverage of JavaScript programming, covering the built-in objects that can be used to access and manipulate document elements. Using the information in this chapter and previous chapters in this part, you should be able to construct scripts to perform a variety of useful functions for your documents.

A handful of useful scripts are contained in Chapter 23, "Using JavaScript."

Using JavaScript

An entire section of this book has been dedicated to JavaScript. You learned about the language itself as well as various ways to use it with other technologies. This chapter wraps up that coverage by providing useful examples of JavaScript in action. Feel free to use any of the techniques covered on your own projects.

The code from the examples can be downloaded from this book's companion Web site.

How and When to Use JavaScript

JavaScript is one of the easiest Web programming languages to use — it is built into the client, requiring no server technologies, and is a reasonably easy-to-use language. However, because a technology is accessible isn't always a good reason to use the technology.

The Case Against Using JavaScript

JavaScript is easy to use. It's built into most user agents, runs on the client, and can do miraculous things to documents. However, it's not a foregone conclusion that you should use JavaScript in your documents — there are plenty of data points to consider before automatically jumping in with JavaScript.

Many smaller footprint user agents (cell phones, PDAs, and so on) do not support JavaScript. Many more user agents have JavaScript disabled by default. The net result is that JavaScript is significantly less accessible today than it was in the early days of the Web and graphical user agents.

Those user agents that do support JavaScript cannot be counted on to adhere to any one standard. As previously mentioned in Chapter 21, there are at least four different Document Object Models implemented across the current user agents. Writing code that is truly cross-platform compatible is nearly impossible, very difficult at best.

What this means is that JavaScript cannot be relied on to perform medium- to high-level tasks, and its presence should *never* be relied on to use your documents.

The preceding statement assumes your documents are meant for public consumption where any number of user agents may be employed to access the documents. If you are coding in a known environment where you can control the number and type of user agents in use, you can reasonably rely on JavaScript code.

Also, JavaScript is very limited in scope. It cannot access external information, whether on the client or server. For more complex tasks needing an interface to external resources, you should consider CGI, PHP, or other server-based technology.

Guidelines for Using JavaScript

The following guidelines should be considered before you use JavaScript in your documents:

❑ Is the task JavaScript will perform absolutely necessary? Image rollovers and dynamic text provide cool features to your documents but don't necessarily add functionality.

❑ Can the same thing be accomplished using simpler means (usually straight XHTML code without as many bells and whistles)? If so, you are generally better off using the simpler means.

❑ Can you reasonably code cross-platform scripts? Remember that the more complex the script (for example, DHTML), the more likely the script is not to work properly on some user agents.

❑ Can you offer alternatives to the JavaScript-enabled features? When using JavaScript for fancy navigation menus, for example, can you also include a basic text menu for non-JavaScript-enabled users?

Although it may sound as if I am trying to talk every reader of this book out of using JavaScript, I'm not. I'm simply trying to make the point that because you can easily implement JavaScript doesn't mean you always should use JavaScript — that's all.

JavaScript Resources

Following is a partial list of some of the best JavaScript resources the Web has to offer:

❑ **The ECMA Specification** — The ECMA specification from the ECMA Web site gives the reader an in-depth look at the standards behind JavaScript. It should be kept in mind that not all user agents adhere to the specification, but this background document will help any coder better understand JavaScript. You can find the ECMA specification at `http://www .ecma-international.org/publications/files/ECMA-ST/Ecma-262.pdf`.

❑ **The W3C DOM Specification** — This reference document explains the design and workings of the Document Object Model Level 1. The DOM is described in detail and the bindings specific to ECMA (and therefore, JavaScript) are covered in Appendix D. You can find the W3C DOM Specification at `http://www.w3.org/TR/2000/WD-DOM-Level-1-20000929/Overview.html`.

❑ **The MSDN Web Development Library** — The Web Development section of the MSDN Library (click on the Web Development link in the left pane) has a lot of useful information on the implementation of JavaScript, CSS, and DHTML within Microsoft Internet Explorer. If you need to find out how IE will handle something in particular, this is the source to consult. Find it at `http://msdn.microsoft.com/library/default.asp`.

❑ **The Gecko (Mozilla Firebird) DOM Reference** — This document describes the Gecko DOM implementation. If you need to write code specific to the Gecko browsers, this is the document to consult. Note that many new browsers (many in the mobile arena) are adopting the Gecko browser standard. You can find this reference at `http://www.mozilla.org/docs/dom/domref/`.

❑ **The DevGuru JavaScript Language Index** — DevGuru does an excellent job of providing quick references for various online technologies. Their comprehensive JavaScript Quick Reference is indispensable for quick lookups of JavaScript events, functions, methods, objects, and more. Find this index at `http://www.devguru.com/Technologies/ecmascript/quickref/javascript_index.html`.

❑ **Quirksmode.org** — *The* reference for browser quirks. This site contains information about almost every user agent quirk known to man. Helpful examples and tutorials abound to help even the most inexperienced JavaScript programmer adapt code for cross-platform capability. Find it at `http://www.quirksmode.org/`.

❑ **The getElementById.com Web site** — This site contains many useful DHTML scripts, techniques, and tutorials. Find it at `http://getelementbyid.com/news/index.aspx`.

JavaScript Examples

The following sections provide example documents that include scripts to perform various tasks. Each example is presented with source code, output, an explanation of how the script works, and ways that the script can be extended or improved.

The scripts in this section have been written and verified to run on the two most popular browsers: Mozilla Firefox 1.0 and Microsoft Internet Explorer 6.0+. To keep the examples straightforward and simple, no additional cross-platform coding has been added. However, the scripts should run on any user agent compatible with these two "standards."

Writing Text to a Document

One basic and often used JavaScript function is outputting text to the user agent window. Because JavaScript cannot access external resources, you are limited to the data objects built into JavaScript or otherwise present in the document.

Example 1: Writing the Current Date to the Current Document

This example shows how to output the current date into a document.

Source

```
<!DOCTYPE html PUBLIC "-//W3C//DTD XHTML 1.0 Strict//EN"
    "http://www.w3.org/TR/xhtml1/DTD/xhtml1-strict.dtd">
<html>
<head>
<title>Display Date (Text)</title>
```

```
<script type="text/JavaScript">
 // Set up arrays
  var months = new Array("January","February","March","April",
    "May","June","July","August","September","October",
    "November","December");
  var days = new Array("Sunday","Monday","Tuesday","Wednesday",
    "Thursday","Friday","Saturday");

  function writedate() {
    // Get current values, build output, and display
    var today = new Date;
    var thisMonth = today.getMonth();
    var thisDay = today.getDate();
    var thisYear = today.getFullYear();
    var thisWeekday = today.getDay();
    var datetext = days[thisWeekday] + ", " + months[thisMonth] +
      thisDay + ", " + thisYear;
    document.write(datetext);
  }
</script>
</head>
<body>
  <script type="text/JavaScript">writedate();</script>
</body>
</html>
```

Output

This script simply writes the current date to the user agent window, as shown in Figure 23-1.

Figure 23-1

How It Works

Using the built-in JavaScript date methods, the `writedate()` function assembles the date into a string that is written to the browser via the `document.write` method. Wherever the date is needed in the document, the code to call the `writedate()` function is inserted in lieu of the date:

```
<script type="text/JavaScript">writedate();</script>
```

Improving the Script

Note that this script does not include any error checking. At minimum, it should probably check for the presence of the `document` object if not specifically checking for the `document.write` method. The `writedate()` function could also be extended to support multiple date formats, governed by a format argument.

Example 2: Obscuring an E-mail Address

The current Web environment is a breeding ground for spam of all types. Many e-mail spammers rely on data mining Web pages for e-mail addresses. The spammers use robots that automatically surf the Web and copy anything that resembles an e-mail address to their database. One way to thwart their attempts is by using JavaScript to obscure e-mail addresses in your documents. The following example uses two different means to accomplish this.

Source

```
<!DOCTYPE html PUBLIC "-//W3C//DTD XHTML 1.0 Strict//EN"
    "http://www.w3.org/TR/xhtml1/DTD/xhtml1-strict.dtd">
<html>
<head>
<title>Obscure Email</title>
<script type="text/JavaScript">

// Given domain, address, and text to show as link
//    put email link into document
function eaddr(domain, addr, linktext) {
  if ((linktext.length == 0)) {
    linktext = addr + "@" + domain; }
  document.write("<a href=" + "'mai" + "lto:" + addr + "@" +
      domain + "'>" + linktext + "</a>");
}
</script>
</head>

<body>

<!-- Use an array to break up the address and a for loop to reassemble -->
<p><script type="text/JavaScript">
var a = new Array ("<a h","ref=","'","ma","il","to:",
  "ss","ch","afer","@ex","ampl","e.c","om","'>');
```

```
for (i in a) {
   document.write(a[i]);
}
</script>Email me</a></p>

<!-- Use a function to reassemble domain, address, and link text -->
<p><script type="text/JavaScript">eaddr("example.com","sschafer",
"Email me");</script></p>

</body>
</html>
```

Output

Both methods result in an `Email me` link being displayed in the user agent window, as shown in Figure 23-2.

Figure 23-2

How It Works

The first method builds the script into the body of the document. This script uses an array to break up the e-mail address into chunks that are unrecognizable as an e-mail address, so the spam robots won't recognize it as such:

```
<a h   ref=   '   ma   il   to:   ss   ch   afer   @ex   ampl   e.c   om   '>
```

The script reassembles and writes the address link to the document window.

The second means of obscuring e-mail addresses uses a similar method but encapsulates the code into a reusable function. The function takes the address, domain name, and link text as separate arguments to reassemble and output accordingly.

Improving the Script

The number of ways to obscure an e-mail address using code is unlimited. I've seen examples using fancy encryption, but they yield the same results. One way to improve upon these methods is to avoid them altogether — that is, avoid using JavaScript for all the reasons outlined at the beginning of this chapter. Instead, construct a feedback form to do the contacting, ensuring that your address remains obscured and nonaccessible by bots.

Using forms and CGI or PHP presents other unique challenges. See the chapters in the next two parts of this book for more details on form handling with CGI and PHP.

Using Other Windows

One often-used JavaScript trick is to open and optionally display text in another window. The examples in this section show you how to spawn other user agent windows and how to write to them using JavaScript.

Example 3: Opening Another Window

Using JavaScript, it is trivial to open another user agent window, as shown in the following code.

Opening another user agent window is akin to pop-up windows, which have a very bad reputation in the Web world due to the amount of advertising spam associated with their use. However, pop-up windows can be used for very legitimate reasons; they are used all the time in OS graphical user interfaces (dialog boxes). The key is to use them efficiently, with ample warning so that the user expects them and finds the content (and their use) useful.

Source

```
<!DOCTYPE html PUBLIC "-//W3C//DTD XHTML 1.0 Strict//EN"
    "http://www.w3.org/TR/xhtml1/DTD/xhtml1-strict.dtd">
<html>
<head>
<title>Open New Window</title>

<script type="text/JavaScript">

function newwindow(title,url,options) {
  // options syntax:
  //   width=x,height=y,scrollbars=yes|no,resizable=yes|no
  if (!options) {
    options = "width=650,height=550,scrollbars=yes,resizable=yes";
  }
  return window.open(url,title,options);
}
```

```
</script>
</head>

<body>
<p>
<input type="button" value="Default window"
  onclick="newwindow('NewWindow','','');" />
  
<input type="button" value="Yahoo small"
  onclick="newwindow('YahooWindow','http://www.yahoo.com',
  'width=200,height=200,scrollbars=no,resizable=no');" />
</p>
</body>
</html>
```

Output

The preceding code opens a default, empty window 650 pixels wide by 550 pixels high or a window 200 pixels square displaying the contents of the Yahoo main page, as shown in Figure 23-3.

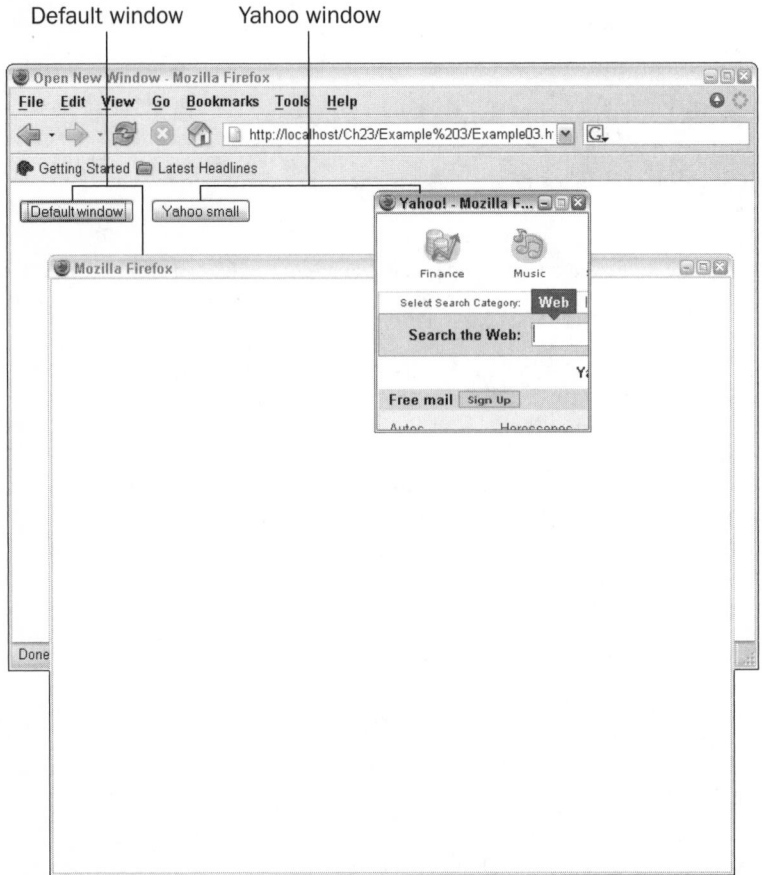

Figure 23-3

How It Works

The script uses input buttons with `onclick()` events to run the `newwindow()` script. The script takes three arguments, specifying the title of the new window, the URL to display in the new window, and options for the new window. If no options are given, the function opens a blank, 650x550, resizable window with scroll bars.

Improving the Script

The `newwindow()` function is fairly complete, allowing arguments to drive the resulting window. It also returns a reference to the new window so that other scripts (like the one in the next example) can write to the window. However, there is no error checking built into the script (the script should probably verify the existence of the `document.open` method before using it) and not all window options are represented in the default operation.

It should be noted (as an exception) that the code in the preceding example is not XHTML compliant, as the input element is not properly contained in a block element. This is done intentionally throughout this section to eliminate XHTML coding overhead, improving the legibility of the examples.

Example 4: Writing Text to Another Window

In addition to opening other windows, JavaScript can also output text to another window if it has a reference to access that window. The following example uses the previous script to open a new window and the resulting reference to the new window to output text to it.

Source

```
<!DOCTYPE html PUBLIC "-//W3C//DTD XHTML 1.0 Strict//EN"
   "http://www.w3.org/TR/xhtml1/DTD/xhtml1-strict.dtd">
<html>
<head>
<title>Write to New Window</title>

<script type="text/JavaScript">

function newwindow(title,url,options) {
  // options syntax:
  //   width=x,height=y,scrollbars=yes|no,resizable=yes|no
  if (!options) {
    options = "width=650,height=550,scrollbars=yes,resizable=yes";
  }
  return window.open(url,title,options);
}

// Create new window and output text to it
function doNewWin() {
  var win = newwindow('NewWin','','');
  win.document.write("<h1>Text to New Window</h1>");
  win.document.close();
}
```

```
      </script>
  </head>

  <body>
  <p>
  <input type="button" value="New window"
    onclick="doNewWin();" />
  </p>
  </body>
  </html>
```

Output

The preceding code opens a default, empty window 650 pixels wide by 550 pixels high and then writes a heading "Text to New Window" in the window, as shown in Figure 23-4.

Figure 23-4

How It Works

This script uses methods similar to the previous script (a button with an `onclick()` handler) to execute a function. That function (`doNewWin()`) uses the `newwindow()` function to open a default window and then uses the reference it returns to access the new window with the `document.write` method:

```
win.document.write("<h1>Text to New Window</h1>");
```

Note the use of the `document.close` method necessary to let the user agent know that the document is complete and no more content is forthcoming.

Improving the Script

As with other simplistic scripts in this chapter, this example lacks sufficient error checking to be truly cross-platform. Another useful change would be to include arguments in the `doNewWin()` function that can be passed to the `newwindow()` function.

Images

JavaScript is also routinely used to manipulate images within a document. The scripts in this section show you several ways to access images using JavaScript.

Example 5: Preloading Images

Occasionally, it is useful to preload images for your documents. This is particularly so in the following cases:

❑ When a site contains a lot of graphics and the user will usually navigate to many of the documents on the site. If a majority of the images can be preloaded, subsequent pages will load more quickly.

❑ When creating animations in a document. Without preloading the images, there will be a delay between image transitions as the new image loads.

❑ When manipulating images using JavaScript. Preloading the images allows your scripts more control over the image data; you know where the image will be stored without needing to navigate the DOM and can perform operations (size the window, change descriptive text, and so on) before displaying the image.

*Preloading images does not cause the images to display; it only causes the user agent to load them into its cache for easy retrieval if and when they are needed for display. Your code can use the images either directly (using **<img>** tags) or indirectly (by changing the **src** attribute of other **<img>** tags).*

Source

```
<!DOCTYPE html PUBLIC "-//W3C//DTD XHTML 1.0 Strict//EN"
    "http://www.w3.org/TR/xhtml1/DTD/xhtml1-strict.dtd">
<html>
<head>
<title>Image Preload</title>
<script type="text/JavaScript">

// If browser supports it, create array
//   and preload images into it
//   Array is global so other routines can
//   later use preloaded array
if (document.images) {
  img = new Array();
  img[0] = new Image;
  img[0].src = "./AboutUs.jpg"
  img[1] = new Image;
  img[1].src = "./AboutUsRO.jpg"
}

</script>
</head>

<body>
</body>
</html>
```

Output

This script produces no visible output.

How It Works

The script works by creating new image objects and loading the specified image files into the objects. This results in a request to the server for the image, which is then cached on the user's system, available to display from local cache instead of across the slower Internet.

To gain the maximum benefit from cached images, it is important to ensure that the URL used in the preload script is identical to the URL used in the document's image (<img>) elements. A URL that is even slightly different may result in the image being requested from the server again, instead of being served from cache.

Note that the image is not displayed using this code, but methods and functions (size, and so on) are available to be used on the image. The image src property can be used to move an image from the cached object to an object in the document using code similar to the following:

```
// Change image src in image tag with id = imgID
document.images[imgID].src = img[1].src;
```

The script has some basic error checking included (it looks for the presence of the document.images collection before preloading).

Improving the Script

One way to improve the script is to incorporate the preload routine into a function that can be called with a URL and returns a reference to the preloaded image. Such a function could then be used globally whenever an image needs preloading. However, this would necessitate explicitly calling the function for each image needing preloading; you couldn't incorporate the script into the head of the document to run at load time.

Additionally, the script container that holds the preload logic should include the `defer` attribute so that the user agent will continue to load the page (because it expects no output from the script within).

Example 6: Image Rollovers

Another graphics trick using JavaScript incorporates the `onmouseover()` and `onmouseout()` events to change an image when the mouse passes over it, and again when the mouse leaves the image. The following script changes the appearance of an "About Us" image using this method.

Source

```
<!DOCTYPE html PUBLIC "-//W3C//DTD XHTML 1.0 Strict//EN"
    "http://www.w3.org/TR/xhtml1/DTD/xhtml1-strict.dtd">
<html>
<head>
<title>Image Rollover</title>
<script type="text/JavaScript">

// Preload the images
if (document.images) {
  img = new Array();
  img[0] = new Image;
  img[0].src = "./AboutUs.jpg"
  img[1] = new Image;
  img[1].src = "./AboutUsRO.jpg"
}

// When rolled over, load the rollover image
function rollover(imgID) {
  if (document.images) {
    document.images[imgID].src = "./" + imgID + "RO.jpg";
  }
}

// When mouse leaves image, revert to normal
function rollout(imgID) {
  if (document.images) {
    document.images[imgID].src = "./" + imgID + ".jpg";
  }
}
```

```
  </script>
  </head>

  <body>
  <p>
  <img src="./AboutUs.jpg" width="200" height="50" alt="About Us"
     id="AboutUs" onmouseover="rollover('AboutUs');"
     onmouseout="rollout('AboutUs');"
     onclick="window.location='./aboutus.htm';" />
  </p>
  </body>
  </html>
```

Output

Figures 23-5 and 23-6 show this script in action. Figure 23-5 shows the image without the mouse over it, while Figure 23-6 shows the image when the mouse is over it. Note that when the mouse leaves the image, it reverts to the image shown in Figure 23-5.

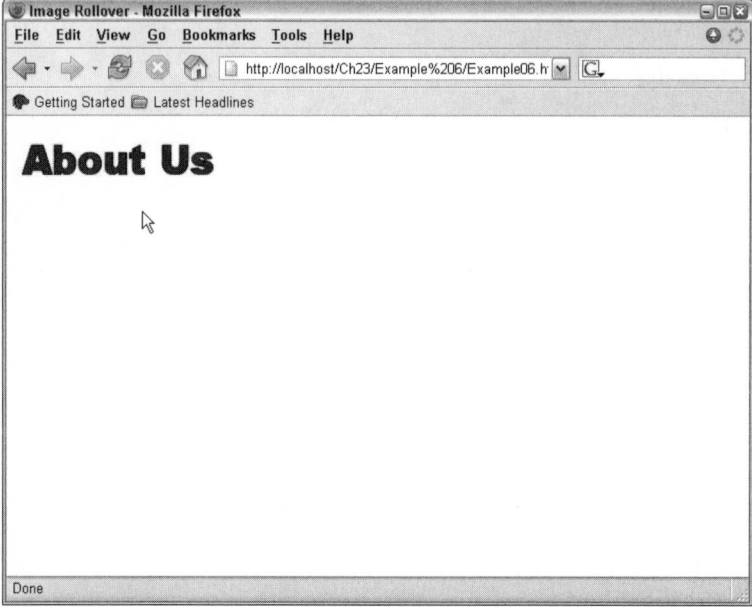

Figure 23-5

How It Works

As previously stated, this script works by tying into the onmouseover() and onmouseout() events of the <img> tag. When the mouse is placed over the image in the document, the onmouseover() event calls the rollover() function, which changes the image element's src property to that of the white-filled text. When the mouse leaves the image, the onmouseout() event calls the rollout() function, which changes the image src back to the original image.

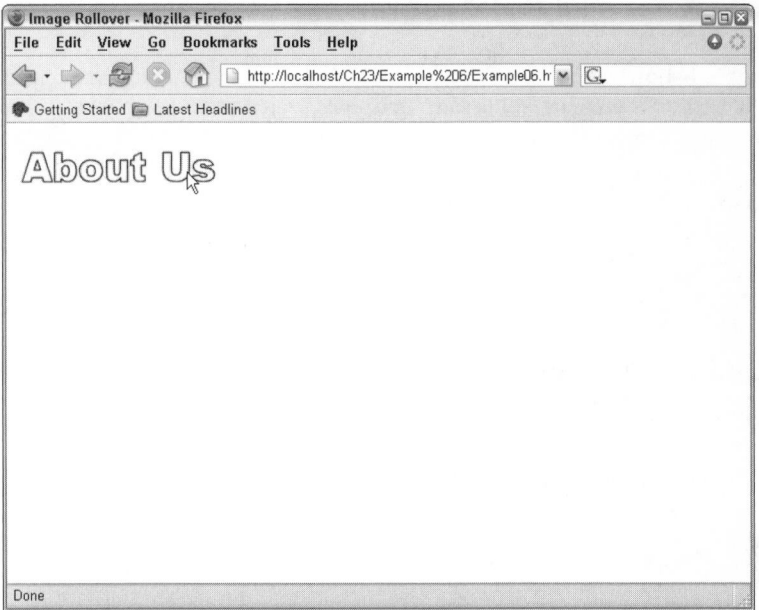

Figure 23-6

The script preloads the images so that they are ready for the rollover. As a result, there should not be a delay when the user rolls over the image the first time.

The result is animated text that responds to the presence of the mouse pointer. The `onclick()` event changes the `window.location` property, making the image act like a hyperlink.

Improving the Script

The preceding script relies on the `onclick()` event for the hyperlink functionality. However, this means that the functionality doesn't work if the user agent isn't JavaScript enabled. Also, the typical visual cues (underline) aren't present to tell the user that the element is a link. A better technique might be to encapsulate the image element within an anchor element, similar to the following:

```
<a href="./aboutus.htm"><img src="./AboutUs.jpg" width="200" height="50"
    alt="About Us" id="AboutUs" onmouseover="rollover('AboutUs');"
    onmouseout="rollout('AboutUs');" style="border: none;" /></a>
```

Notice the addition of the `border` style to the image tag. This removes the pesky border resulting from the encapsulation in the anchor element, giving you a cleaner display.

Example 7: Graphical Date Display

Example 1 showed how to write basic text to the document window. Occasionally, it can be useful to output text in graphic form (graphics prerendered in a particular font) for stylistic consistency. The following example displays the current date built from images instead of text.

Source

```
<!DOCTYPE html PUBLIC "-//W3C//DTD XHTML 1.0 Strict//EN"
    "http://www.w3.org/TR/xhtml1/DTD/xhtml1-strict.dtd">
<html>
<head>
<title>Graphical Date Display</title>
<script type="text/JavaScript">
function ShowDate() {
  // Check for required browser functionality
  if (document.all || document.getElementById) {
    // Set up our variables
    var img = new Array("");
    var today = new Date();
    var date = String(today.getDate());
    var month = String(today.getMonth()+1);
    var year = String(today.getFullYear());
    var date1 = date.charAt(0);
    var date2 = date.charAt(1);
    // Prime the img array
    for (x = 1; x <= 7; x++) {
      img[x] = document.getElementById("img"+String(x));
    }
    // Set src of appropriate images
    // 1&2 = day, 3 = month, 4-7 = year
    if (date2 == "") {
      img[2].src = "./images/dateimgs/" + date1 + ".gif"
      img[1].src = "./images/dateimgs/space.gif"
    } else {
      img[1].src = "./images/dateimgs/" + date1 + ".gif"
      img[2].src = "./images/dateimgs/" + date2 + ".gif"
    }
    img[3].src = "./images/dateimgs/month" + month + ".gif";
    img[4].src = "./images/dateimgs/" + year.charAt(0) + ".gif";
    img[5].src = "./images/dateimgs/" + year.charAt(1) + ".gif";
    img[6].src = "./images/dateimgs/" + year.charAt(2) + ".gif";
    img[7].src = "./images/dateimgs/" + year.charAt(3) + ".gif";
  }
}
</script>
</head>

<body onload="ShowDate()">
<p>
<!-- Simple line table to hold date -->
```

```
<table border="0" cellpadding="0" cellspacing="0">
<tr>
  <td><img id="img1" name="img1" border="0" /></td>
  <td><img id="img2" name="img2" border="0" /></td>
  <td><img id="img3" name="img3" border="0" /></td>
  <td><img id="img4" name="img4" border="0" /></td>
  <td><img id="img5" name="img5" border="0" /></td>
  <td><img id="img6" name="img6" border="0" /></td>
  <td><img id="img7" name="img7" border="0" /></td>
</tr>
</table>
</p>
</body>
</html>
```

Output

This script results in the one-line date display shown in Figure 23-7. The graphics used to display the various elements (numbers, months) are shown within Windows Explorer in Figure 23-8.

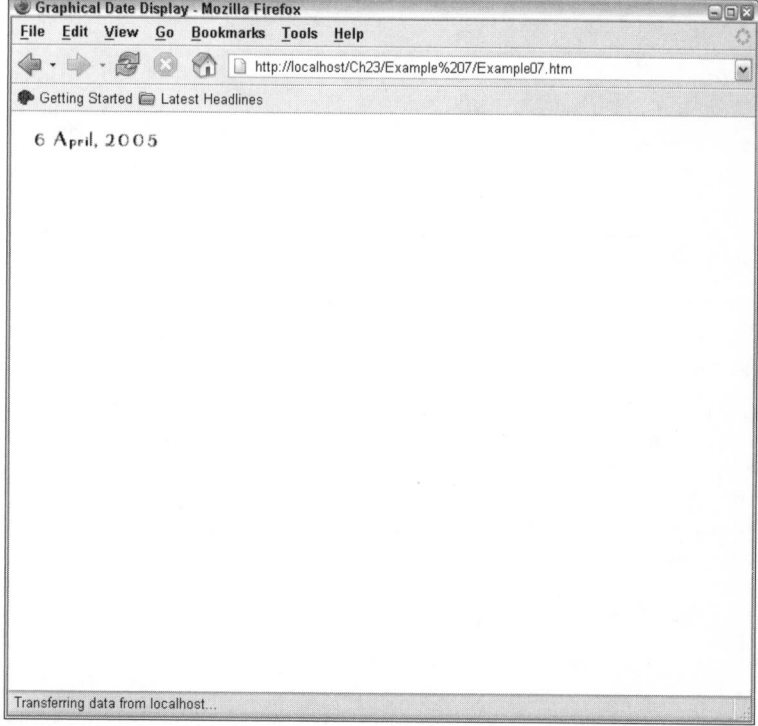

Figure 23-7

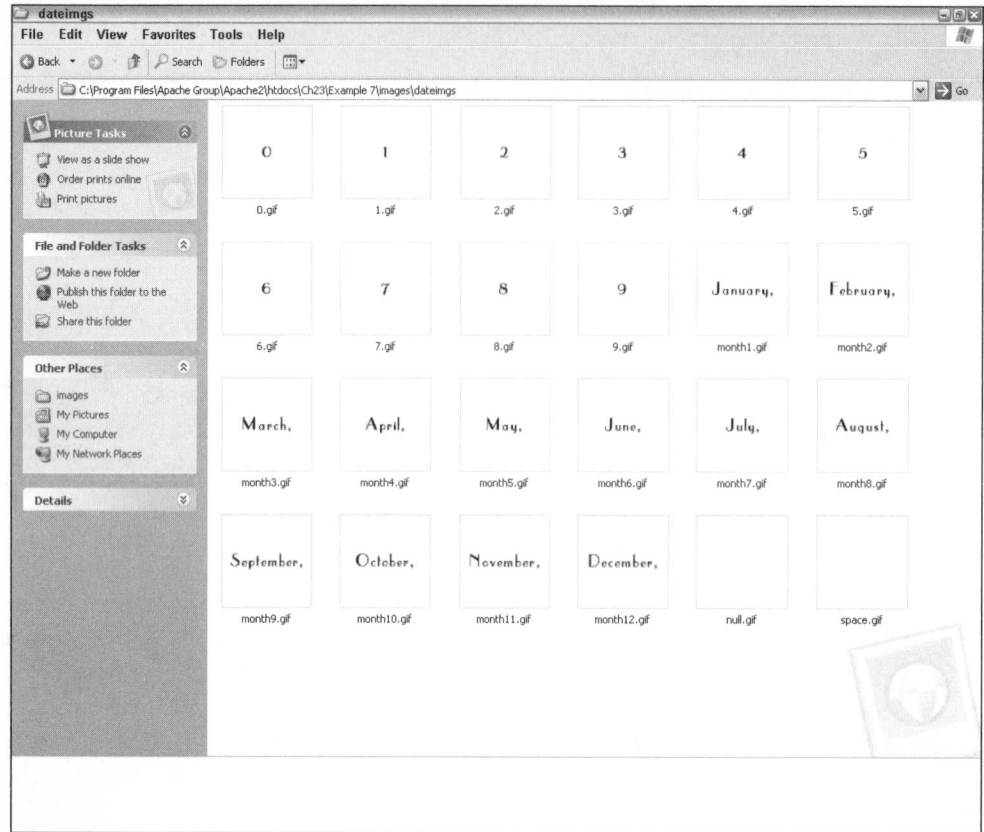

Figure 23-8

How It Works

This script is similar to the script from Example 1; it uses built-in JavaScript functions to ascertain the current date. It then uses premade images for the digits and text of the month — images named to be easy to access (1.gif for the number 1, month1.gif for the month January, and so on). The appropriate image URL(s) are then swapped into the appropriate image elements in the document. In this case, the image elements are encased in a table for formatting purposes.

Improving the Script

This script could be improved in the following ways:

❑   Incorporating a fallback, text-only display if the document.images collection is unavailable for manipulation.

❑   The images could be preloaded to ensure that the pieces of the date appear at the same time. Not doing so can mean that one or more elements load more slowly, causing a broken image link to appear for a second or so.

❑ The script could be modified to display more date formats. The format displayed would be driven by an argument passed to the script. Note that this would mean changing the month images (removing the comma), adding an image or two (comma, dash, slashes, and so on), and perhaps employing a larger table whose elements are used dynamically (not all formats would use all the cells in the table; unused cells would have to be filled by blank images).

Working with Forms

The availability of both the W3C DOM and the standard JavaScript collections allow JavaScript a lot of control over form elements. The examples in this section give you an idea of some of what you can do with forms and JavaScript.

Although it is possible to change default behavior of form elements using JavaScript, resist the temptation. Users are generally used to their platforms' GUI behavior, and unannounced changes (such as automatically moving between fields of a phone number) aren't always welcome.

Example 8: Adding Form Features

Although XHTML's form support is robust enough for most applications, there are times when an additional control or more functionality is welcome. For example, there is no easy, XHTML-only way to limit the number of characters entered into an XHTML text box (`<textarea>` element). This example shows how to create a simple counter so that the user can keep track of the characters entered into a specific text box.

Source

```
<!DOCTYPE html PUBLIC "-//W3C//DTD XHTML 1.0 Strict//EN"
    "http://www.w3.org/TR/xhtml1/DTD/xhtml1-strict.dtd">
<html>
<head>
<title>Form Enhancement</title>

<script type="text/JavaScript">
// Check size (length) of text box and report
//  in another box
function checksize() {
  if (document.all || document.getElementById) {
    var counter = document.getElementById("size");
    var text = document.getElementById("msg");
    counter.value = text.value.length;
  }
}
</script>
</head>

<body onload="checksize()">
<p>
Edit the message below (limited to 120 characters!).<p>
  <form name="form1" id="form1" method="post"
```

```
           action="bogus.htm" onkeyup="checksize()">
       <input type="text" name="size" id="size"
           disabled="disabled" size="6">  Characters
       </p>
       <p>
       <textarea cols="40" rows="3" name="msg" id="msg"
           wrap="virtual"></textarea>
       </p>
       <p>
       <input type="submit" name="submit" value="Submit" />
          
       <input type="reset" name="reset" value="Clear" />
          
       <input type="button" name="close" value="Close"
           onclick="self.close()" />
       </p>
   </form>
 </p>
 </body>
 </html>
```

Output

This example results in a document with two form fields, a text box for text entry and
a smaller text box for tallying the number of characters in the other field, as shown in
Figure 23-9.

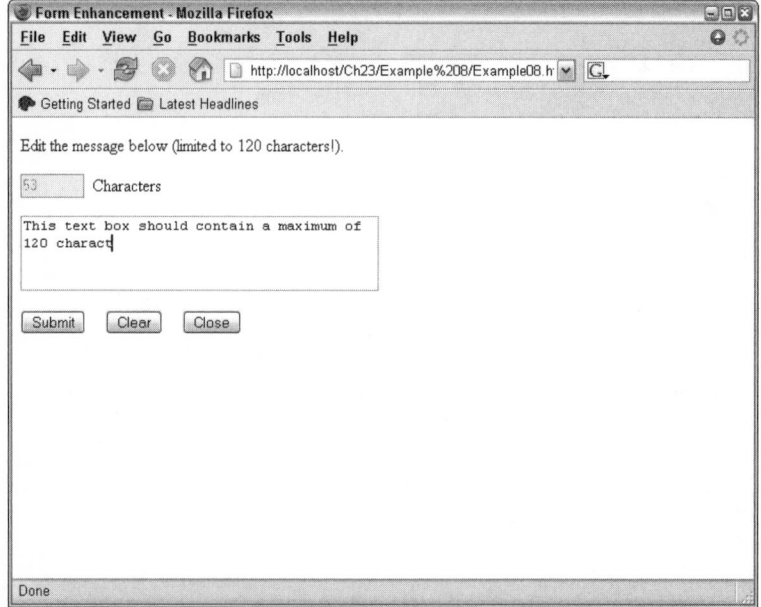

Figure 23-9

How It Works

The script works by accessing the `length` property of the text area and assigning it to the value of the counter box. The script is encapsulated in a function that is called by the `onkeyup()` event handler of the text area element. Every time a keystroke is entered into the text box, the counter is updated. The counter text box is disabled so that it cannot be edited by the user.

Improving the Script

As is, the script is a bit obtrusive. The counter could be moved beside the text area in a less conspicuous place. Additionally, the counter could be contained in a label or other textual XHTML label (where the `innerHTML` property could be used to change its value). The script could also actively constrain the content of the text area; as is, it simply displays how many characters are entered even if the total is over the desired maximum. Active constraint of content would require much more programming to achieve.

Example 9: Form Validation

A popular use of JavaScript is basic form validation. Using simple scripts, you can perform basic validation (data exists, is in a particular format, and so on) before the data is passed to your form handler for processing. The following example shows a basic form validation engine using JavaScript.

Source

```
<!DOCTYPE html PUBLIC "-//W3C//DTD XHTML 1.0 Strict//EN"
    "http://www.w3.org/TR/xhtml1/DTD/xhtml1-strict.dtd">
<html>
<head>
<title>Basic Form Validation</title>
<script type="text/JavaScript">

// Validate email against regex
function FRMcheckEmail(el,name) {
  var err = new String();
  var filter = /^([a-zA-Z0-9_\.\-])+\@(([a-zA-Z0-9\-])+\.)+
([a-zA-Z0-9]{2,4})+$/;

  if (document.all || document.getElementById) {
    elid = document.getElementById(el);
    if (!filter.test(elid.value)) {
      err = "The '" + name + "' field must be a valid email address<br />";
    }
  }
  return err;
}

// Validate that two fields match
function FRMmustMatch(el1,name1,el2,name2) {
```

```
  var err = new String();

  if (document.all || document.getElementById) {
    el1id = document.getElementById(el1);
    el2id = document.getElementById(el2);
    if (el1id.value != el2id.value) {
      err = "The values of '" + name1 + "' and '" + name2 + "' ";
      err += "do not match<br />";
    }
  }
  return err;
}

// Validate length of field
function FRMcheckLength(el,name,minlength,maxlength) {

  var err = new String();

  if (document.all || document.getElementById) {
    elid = document.getElementById(el);
    if ((elid.value.length < minlength) &&
        (minlength != 0)) {
      err = "The '" + name + "' field must be at least ";
      err += minlength + " characters long<br />"
    }
    if ((elid.value.length > maxlength) &&
        (maxlength != 0)) {
      err += "The '" + name + "' field must be less than ";
      err += maxlength + " characters long<br />"
    }
  }
  return err;
}

// Validate field is not blank
function FRMnonBlank(el,name) {

  var err = new String();

  if (document.all || document.getElementById) {
    elid = document.getElementById(el);
    if (elid.value == "") {
      err = "The '" + name + "' field cannot be blank<br />";
    }
  }
  return err;
}

// Validation engine
function FRMvalidate() {

  // Init error string
  var err = new String();
```

```
    // Do validation, building error string as we go
    //  No error = blank string
    err += FRMnonBlank("firstname","First Name");
    err += FRMnonBlank("lastname","Last Name");
    err += FRMcheckEmail("email","Email");
    err += FRMmustMatch("password","Password","confpass","Confirm Password");
    err += FRMcheckLength("password","Password",4,8);

    if (document.all || document.getElementById) {
      if (err.length != 0) {
        errid = document.getElementById("errtext");
        errid.innerHTML = err;
        return(false);
      } else {
        validateid = document.getElementById("validated");
        validateid.value = "true";
      }
    }
    return(true);
}

</script>

<style type="text/css">
 .errtext { color: red; }
 td { padding: 5px; }
</style>

<body>
<p>
<form action="http://www.example.com/handler.cgi" method="GET"
  onsubmit="return FRMvalidate();">

<div id="errtext" name="errtext" class="errtext"></div>

<table border="0">
  <tr>
  <td>First name:</td>
  <td><input type="text" id="firstname" name="firstname" size="20"
    maxlength="20" /></td>
  </tr><tr>
  <td>Last name:</td>
  <td><input type="text" id="lastname" name="lastname" size="20"
    maxlength="20" /></td>
  </tr><tr>
  <td>Email:</td>
  <td><input type="text" id="email" name="email" size="20"
    maxlength="40" /></td>
  </tr><tr>
  <td>Password:</td>
  <td><input type="password" id="password" name="password" size="20"
    maxlength="20" /></td>
  </tr><tr>
```

```
      <td>Confirm Password:</td>
      <td><input type="password" id="confpass" name="confpass" size="20"
         maxlength="20" /></td>
      </tr><tr>
      <td><input type="submit" id="submit" name="submit" value="Submit" /></td>
      <td><input type="reset" id="reset" name="reset"></td>
      </tr>
   </table>

   <input type="hidden" id="validated" name="validated" value="false" />
   </form>
   </p>
   </body>
   </html>
```

Output

This example generates a form with an error section above it, as shown in Figure 23-10. If the user has an error in a field and clicks Submit, the error text appears to help the user identify and fix the problem.

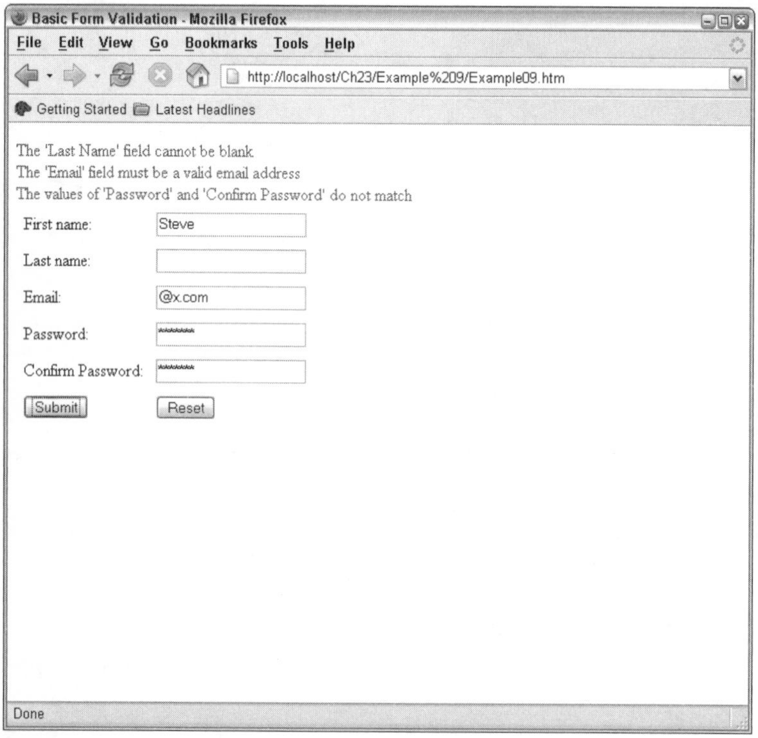

Figure 23-10

How It Works

The example works by tying into the `onsubmit()` event handler of the form element. This handler runs the specified code—in this case calling the `FRMvalidate()` function—when the user tries to submit the form. If the expression of the `onsubmit()` handler (the result of the function) returns true, the form is submitted to the appropriate form handler as defined in the form tag. If the expression evaluates to false, the form is not submitted; it is as if the user never clicked the Submit button.

The `FRMvalidate()` function calls smaller functions to check for specified conditions. For example, the `FRMnonBlank()` function tests to see if the specified field is not blank. Each validation function takes the ID and name of an element to check and returns a string containing the error(s) found, if any. The error text helpfully includes the supplied form element's name. The `FRMvalidate()` function appends each error to a combined error log, which is displayed to the user if necessary. If the error string remains blank after all validation routines have been run, the `FRMvalidate()` function returns true, allowing the form to be submitted. The function also sets the hidden `validated` field to true so that the form handler knows the data has passed the basic validation.

JavaScript validation should never be relied on. Because it is run on the client, it is possible for an unscrupulous user to modify the code to circumvent the validation. It is important that your form handler do its own in-depth validation before doing anything useful with the data. See the chapters in the next two parts of this book for help on writing form handlers in CGI and PHP.

Improving the Script

The form includes basic error handling to ensure that it runs on our two target platforms (Firefox and IE), but additional error handling could be incorporated to include legacy (Netscape, and so on) user agents.

*If the script is run on a nonsupported browser, it will still enable the form data to be passed to the handler, but the **validated** field will remain false.*

Additional validation functions can be added to perform additional validation tasks. Additionally, extra logic can be added to determine the field's name so that less data needs to be passed to each function. Doing so would necessitate using human-readable text for each element's name.

Dynamic HTML Tricks

A hallmark of JavaScript use in the '90s, Dynamic HTML (DHTML) is simply manipulating a document's elements with JavaScript to achieve dynamic content and/or special effects. The examples in this section show you how to accomplish base-level DHTML.

Example 10: Swap Styles

One of the easiest ways to achieve DHTML results is by wholesale swapping of the styles an element uses. This is typically done by manipulating the `className` property of an element, as shown in the following example.

Source

```
<html>
<head>
<title>Swapping Styles</title>

<style type="text/css">
.initialbox { width: 20; height: 20;
              position: absolute;
              top: 200; left: 200;
              visibility: visible;
              border: thick solid black;
              background-color: red;
              overflow: hidden;
              z-index: 3;
              }
.finalbox { width: 200; height: 200;
            top: 200; left: 200;
            position: absolute;
            visibility: visible;
            border: none;
            background-image: url(A45.jpg);
            background-position: center center;
            background-repeat: no-repeat;
            overflow: hidden;
            z-index: 3;
            }
</style>

<script type="text/JavaScript">
// Determine box by id = hiddenbox
//   if browser supports it
function gethiddenbox() {
  if (document.all || document.getElementById) {
    return document.getElementById("hiddenbox");
  } else {
    return false;
  }
}

// Swap style class
function swapStyles() {
  box = gethiddenbox();
  if (box) {
    if (box.className == "initialbox") {
      box.className = "finalbox";
    } else {
```

```
        box.className = "initialbox";
      }
    }
  }
}
</script>

</head>
<body>
<p>Lorem ipsum dolor sit amet, consectetur adipisicing elit, sed
do eiusmod tempor incididunt ut labore et dolore magna aliqua. Ut
enim ad minim veniam, quis nostrud exercitation ullamco laboris
nisi ut aliquip ex ea commodo consequat. Duis aute irure dolor in
reprehenderit in voluptate velit esse cillum dolore eu fugiat nulla
pariatur. Excepteur sint occaecat cupidatat non proident, sunt in
culpa qui officia deserunt mollit anim id est laborum.</p>
<p>Lorem ipsum dolor sit amet, consectetur adipisicing elit, sed
do eiusmod tempor incididunt ut labore et dolore magna aliqua. Ut
enim ad minim veniam, quis nostrud exercitation ullamco laboris
nisi ut aliquip ex ea commodo consequat. Duis aute irure dolor in
reprehenderit in voluptate velit esse cillum dolore eu fugiat nulla
pariatur. Excepteur sint occaecat cupidatat non proident, sunt in
culpa qui officia deserunt mollit anim id est laborum.</p>
<p>Lorem ipsum dolor sit amet, consectetur adipisicing elit, sed
do eiusmod tempor incididunt ut labore et dolore magna aliqua. Ut
enim ad minim veniam, quis nostrud exercitation ullamco laboris
nisi ut aliquip ex ea commodo consequat. Duis aute irure dolor in
reprehenderit in voluptate velit esse cillum dolore eu fugiat nulla
pariatur. Excepteur sint occaecat cupidatat non proident, sunt in
culpa qui officia deserunt mollit anim id est laborum.</p>
<p>Lorem ipsum dolor sit amet, consectetur adipisicing elit, sed
do eiusmod tempor incididunt ut labore et dolore magna aliqua. Ut
enim ad minim veniam, quis nostrud exercitation ullamco laboris
nisi ut aliquip ex ea commodo consequat. Duis aute irure dolor in
reprehenderit in voluptate velit esse cillum dolore eu fugiat nulla
pariatur. Excepteur sint occaecat cupidatat non proident, sunt in
culpa qui officia deserunt mollit anim id est laborum.</p>
<p>
<input type="button" id="swapstyles" value="Swap Styles"
  onclick="swapStyles();">
</p>

<!-- Hidden box -->
<p class="initialbox" name="hiddenbox" id="hiddenbox" onclick="hidebox();"></p>
</body>
</html>
```

*You may have noticed that this example's code does not include a **DOCTYPE** declaration. This, unfortunately, is by design. For some reason unknown to this author, inclusion of the **DOCTYPE** declaration causes this example not to work in Mozilla Firefox or Microsoft Internet Explorer. The **DOCTYPE** declaration is not supposed to affect the operation of code; it is only to inform agents and validation tools of the standard the document is following. However, in this case, the **DOCTYPE** declaration must trigger some unknown (again, to this author) quirk in both user agents.*

Output

This example toggles a paragraph element's attributes each time the button is clicked. The two different styles of the element are shown in Figures 23-11 and 23-12.

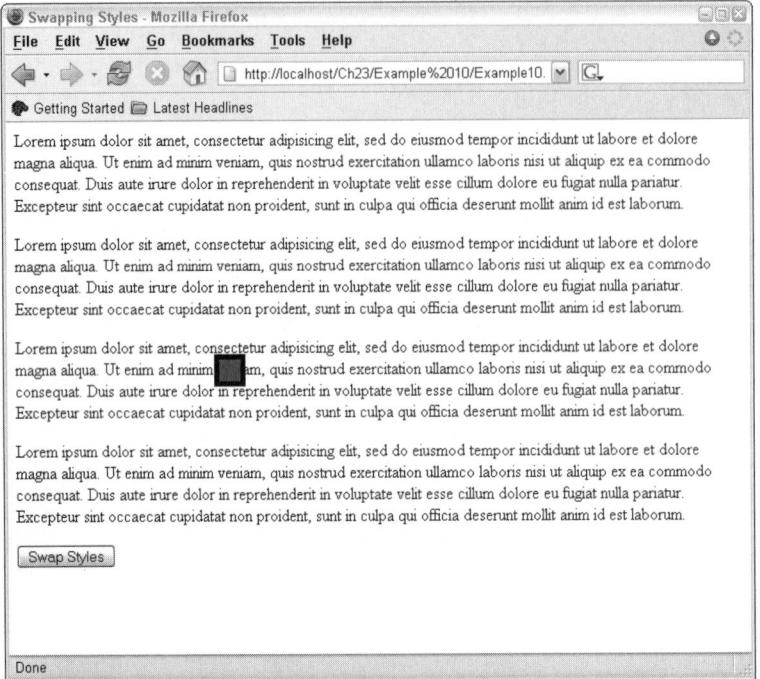

Figure 23-11

How It Works

This example works by examining the current style class assigned to the element and changing it to another, toggling between the two sets of styles. The button's `onclick()` event handler calls the `swapStyle()` function to swap the styles via the `className` property, significantly changing the appearance of the element.

Note that each class needs to include every style necessary for the appropriate state of the paragraph element. This example does not take advantage of style inheritance.

Improving the Script

This technique can be used for any element in a document—changing images, headings, tables, and so on. Additional properties can be added as needed to emphasize the change.

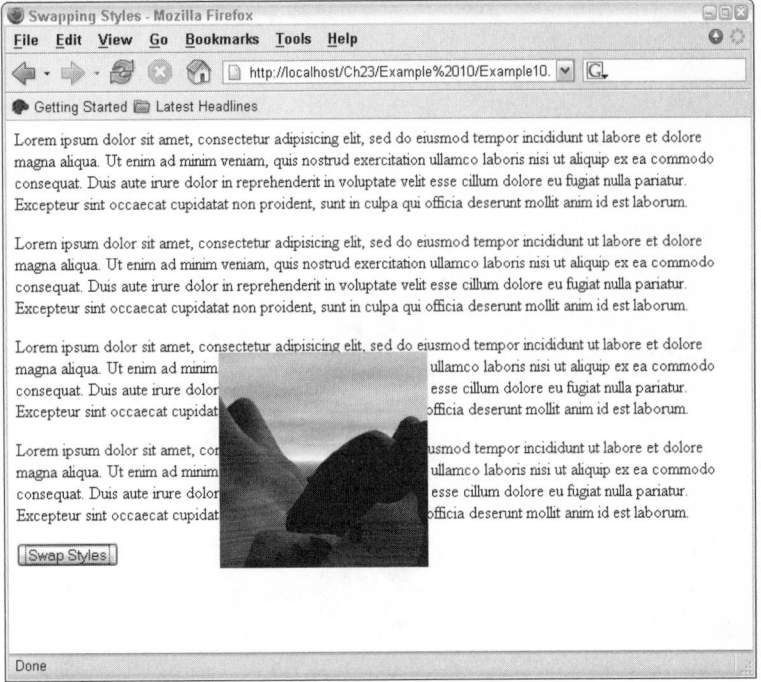

Figure 23-12

Example 11: Animated Menus

Another mainstay of DHTML is animated menus. This example uses the style `display` property to hide and reveal a menu to accomplish a drop-down effect.

Source

```
<!DOCTYPE html PUBLIC "-//W3C//DTD XHTML 1.0 Strict//EN"
    "http://www.w3.org/TR/xhtml1/DTD/xhtml1-strict.dtd">
<html>
<head>
<title>Drop Down Menu</title>

<style type="text/css">

  /* The drop menu container */
  .dropmenu { position: absolute;
            left: 100px; top: 0px;
            background-color: white; }

  /* Table settings for menu */
  table { border-collapse: collapse;
        padding: 0px; }
```

```
      table.menu * { border: thin solid black;
                     margin: 0px;
                     padding: 0px; }
   table td { width: 100px;
              text-align: center;
              padding: 5px; }
   table tr { height: 25px; }

</style>

<script type="text/JavaScript">

// Current state of menu
var menushown = true;

// Determine element by id using
//  appropriate DOM
function getbyID(eID) {

  // Netscape layers
  if( document.layers ) {
      return document.layers[eID];
  }
  // DOM; IE5, NS6, Mozilla, Opera
  if( document.getElementById ) {
      return document.getElementById(eID);
  }
  // Proprietary DOM; IE4
  if( document.all ) {
      return document.all[eID];
  }
  // Netscape alternative
  if( document[eID] ) {
      return document[eID];
  }
  return false;
}

// Set display to none (hide menu items)
function hideitems() {
  if (!menushown) { return; }
  var div = getbyID("menuitems");
  if (div) {
    if (div.style) { div = div.style; }
    div.display = "none";
    menushown = false;
  }
}

// Set display to inline (show menu items)
function revealitems() {
  if (menushown) { return; }
  var div = getbyID("menuitems");
  if (div) {
```

```
      if (div.style) { div = div.style; }
      div.display = "inline";
      menushown = true;
   }
}

// Initialize menu (hide it)
function initmenu() {
  hideitems();
}

</script>
</head>

<body onload="initmenu();">
<div class="main">

  <!-- Div for menu -->
  <div class="dropmenu" id="dropmenu" onmouseover="revealitems();"
    onmouseout="hideitems();" >
  <p>
  <table border="0" class="menu" id="menuitems">
    <tr><td><a href="/page1.htm">Item 1</a></td></tr>
    <tr><td><a href="/page2.htm">Item 2</a></td></tr>
    <tr><td><a href="/page3.htm">Item 3</a></td></tr>
  </table>
  <!-- Menu tab must override display setting -->
  <table border="0" class="menu" style="display:block;">
    <tr><td>MENU</td></tr>
  </table>
  </p>
  </div>

<p style="height: 50px;"></p>
<!-- Main page content below -->
<p>Lorem ipsum dolor sit amet, consectetur adipisicing elit, sed do eiusmod
tempor incididunt ut labore et dolore magna aliqua. Ut enim ad minim veniam,
quis nostrud exercitation ullamco laboris nisi ut aliquip ex ea commodo
consequat.
Duis aute irure dolor in reprehenderit in voluptate velit esse cillum dolore eu
fugiat nulla pariatur. Excepteur sint occaecat cupidatat non proident, sunt in
culpa qui officia deserunt mollit anim id est laborum.</p>
<p>Lorem ipsum dolor sit amet, consectetur adipisicing elit, sed do eiusmod
tempor incididunt ut labore et dolore magna aliqua. Ut enim ad minim veniam,
quis nostrud exercitation ullamco laboris nisi ut aliquip ex ea commodo
consequat.
Duis aute irure dolor in reprehenderit in voluptate velit esse cillum dolore eu
fugiat nulla pariatur. Excepteur sint occaecat cupidatat non proident, sunt in
culpa qui officia deserunt mollit anim id est laborum.</p>
<p>Lorem ipsum dolor sit amet, consectetur adipisicing elit, sed do eiusmod
tempor incididunt ut labore et dolore magna aliqua. Ut enim ad minim veniam,
quis nostrud exercitation ullamco laboris nisi ut aliquip ex ea commodo
consequat.
```

```
Duis aute irure dolor in reprehenderit in voluptate velit esse cillum dolore eu
fugiat nulla pariatur. Excepteur sint occaecat cupidatat non proident, sunt in
culpa qui officia deserunt mollit anim id est laborum.</p>

</div>
</body>
</html>
```

Output

This document displays a MENU tab at the top of the screen that, when moused over, drops down a menu of links. The tab is shown in Figure 23-13 and the full menu is shown in Figure 23-14.

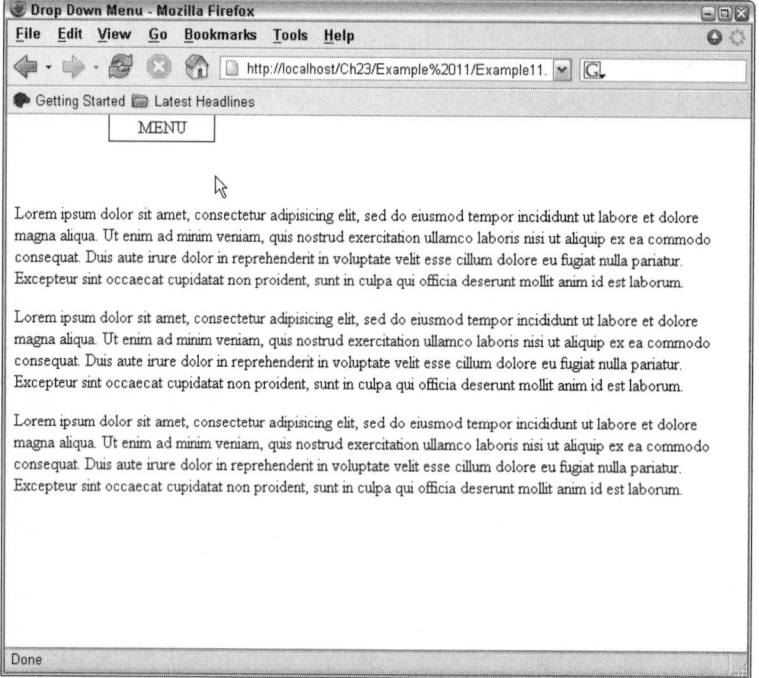

Figure 23-13

How It Works

The script works by placing the tab and menu tables within a division (<div>) that incorporates onmouseover() and onmouseout() event handlers. When the mouse moves appropriately, the corresponding function is called to drop down or roll up the menu. The menu animation is accomplished by toggling the display property of the menu table. The current state of the menu is kept in the menushown variable to keep the functions from performing unnecessary work (showing the menu when it is already shown, and vice versa).

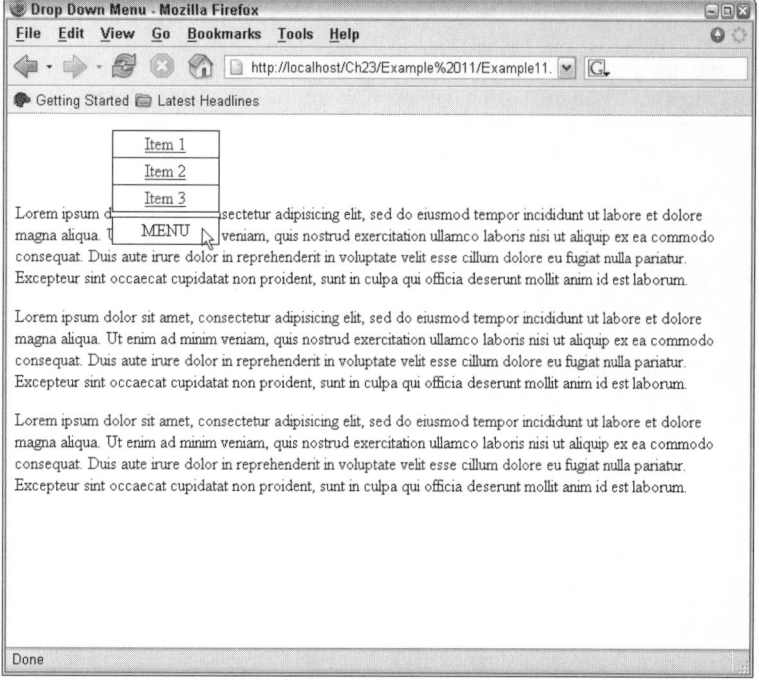

Figure 23-14

Improving the Script

This example uses the `display` property to achieve the desired effect. However, there are many other ways to achieve this effect, including the following:

❑   Actually moving the menu using positioning properties (`top`, `left`, and so on).

❑   Resizing the menu's containing block using size properties (`width`, `height`).

❑   Using the `hidden` property instead of the `display` property (hiding the menu by making it invisible instead of moving it off-screen). Note that using the `display` property would require a change in the `position` properties, as well — positioning the menu permanently in the visible position.

The mechanism for dropping down or rolling up the menu can be changed, as well. Although the current mechanism is quite fluid in Microsoft Internet Explorer, it is a bit erratic in Mozilla Firefox. An alternative would be to use an `onclick()` event handler on the MENU tab table that toggles the state of the menu.

Example 12: Moving Elements

Another popular DHTML technique is animating entire blocks of code. Visit a popular site such as MSN and you are sure to see such an animation, usually in the form of an ad that opens on top of the window content or slides in from off-screen. This example shows you how to animate a division of a document.

Source

```
<!DOCTYPE html PUBLIC "-//W3C//DTD XHTML 1.0 Strict//EN"
    "http://www.w3.org/TR/xhtml1/DTD/xhtml1-strict.dtd">
<html>
<head>
<title>Div Movement</title>

<style type="text/css">
/* Set initial styles for div */
.hiddendiv { width: 0px; height: 0px;
            position: absolute;
            top: 0px; left: 1px;
            color: white;
            visibility: hidden;
            border: thin dotted black;
            background-image: url(A45.jpg);
            background-position: center center;
            background-repeat: no-repeat;
            overflow: hidden;
            z-index: 3;
            }

</style>

<script type="text/JavaScript">

// Determine div by divID using
//   appropriate DOM
function getdivID(divID) {

  // Netscape layers
  if( document.layers ) {
     return document.layers[divID];
  }
  // DOM; IE5, NS6, Mozilla, Opera
  if( document.getElementById ) {
     return document.getElementById(divID);
  }
  // Proprietary DOM; IE4
  if( document.all ) {
     return document.all[divID];
  }
  // Netscape alternative
```

```
        if( document[divID] ) {
            return document[divID];
        }
        return false;
    }


    // Make div visible
    function showdiv() {
      var div = getdivID("hiddendiv");

      //DOM & proprietary DOM
      if(div.style) {
          div.style.visibility = 'visible';
      } else {
        //Netscape
        if(div.visibility) {
          div.visibility = 'show';
        }
      }
    }


    // Make div invisible
    function hidediv() {
      var div = getdivID("hiddendiv");

      // DOM & proprietary DOM
      if(div.style) {
          div.style.visibility = 'hidden';
      } else {
        // Netscape
        if(div.visibility) {
          div.visibility = 'hide';
        }
      }
    }


    function movediv() {

      // Set up measurements
      var noPx = document.childNodes ? 'px' : 0;
      var div = getdivID("hiddendiv");

      if (div.style) { div = div.style; }

      // Move div until it reaches 200px from left edge
      if (parseInt(div.left) < 200) {

        div.width = (parseInt(div.width) + 25) + noPx;
        if (parseInt(div.width) > 400) { div.width = 400 + noPx; }
```

```
            div.height = (parseInt(div.height) + 20) + noPx;
            if (parseInt(div.height) > 300) { div.height = 300 + noPx; }

            div.left = (parseInt(div.left) + 10) + noPx;
            div.top = (parseInt(div.top) + 10) + noPx;

            // Movement is every 20ms
            movetimeID = setTimeout('movediv()',20);
        }
    }


// Reveal and move the div
function revealdiv() {
    var div = getdivID("hiddendiv");
    // Reveal the div
    showdiv();
    // Set initial values for browsers that don't
    // support reading from style set values
    if( div.style ) { div = div.style; }
    div.left = "0px";
    div.top = "0px";
    div.width = "0px";
    div.height = "0px";
    // Do movement
    movediv();
}
</script>

</head>
<body>
<div>
<p>Lorem ipsum dolor sit amet, consectetur adipisicing elit, sed
do eiusmod tempor incididunt ut labore et dolore magna aliqua. Ut
enim ad minim veniam, quis nostrud exercitation ullamco laboris
nisi ut aliquip ex ea commodo consequat. Duis aute irure dolor in
reprehenderit in voluptate velit esse cillum dolore eu fugiat nulla
pariatur. Excepteur sint occaecat cupidatat non proident, sunt in
culpa qui officia deserunt mollit anim id est laborum.</p>
<p>Lorem ipsum dolor sit amet, consectetur adipisicing elit, sed
do eiusmod tempor incididunt ut labore et dolore magna aliqua. Ut
enim ad minim veniam, quis nostrud exercitation ullamco laboris
nisi ut aliquip ex ea commodo consequat. Duis aute irure dolor in
reprehenderit in voluptate velit esse cillum dolore eu fugiat nulla
pariatur. Excepteur sint occaecat cupidatat non proident, sunt in
culpa qui officia deserunt mollit anim id est laborum.</p>
<p>Lorem ipsum dolor sit amet, consectetur adipisicing elit, sed
do eiusmod tempor incididunt ut labore et dolore magna aliqua. Ut
enim ad minim veniam, quis nostrud exercitation ullamco laboris
nisi ut aliquip ex ea commodo consequat. Duis aute irure dolor in
reprehenderit in voluptate velit esse cillum dolore eu fugiat nulla
pariatur. Excepteur sint occaecat cupidatat non proident, sunt in
culpa qui officia deserunt mollit anim id est laborum.</p>
```

```
<p><form>
<input type="button" id="reveal" value="Reveal Div"
  onclick="revealdiv();">
</form></p>
</div>

<!-- Hidden box -->
<div class="hiddendiv" name="hiddendiv" id="hiddendiv"
  onclick="hidediv();"></div>
</body>
</html>
```

Output

This example animates a division (`<div>`), moving it from the upper-left corner of the screen to a position in the middle of the document while it grows from a small size to its normal size. Figures 23-15, 23-16, and 23-17 illustrate the animation in progress.

How It Works

This example incorporates more error checking and cross-platform code than any other example in this chapter. The initial state of the division is set via the `hiddendiv` style class; the element is hidden, set to a size of 10 pixels square, and placed in the upper-left corner of the document's display.

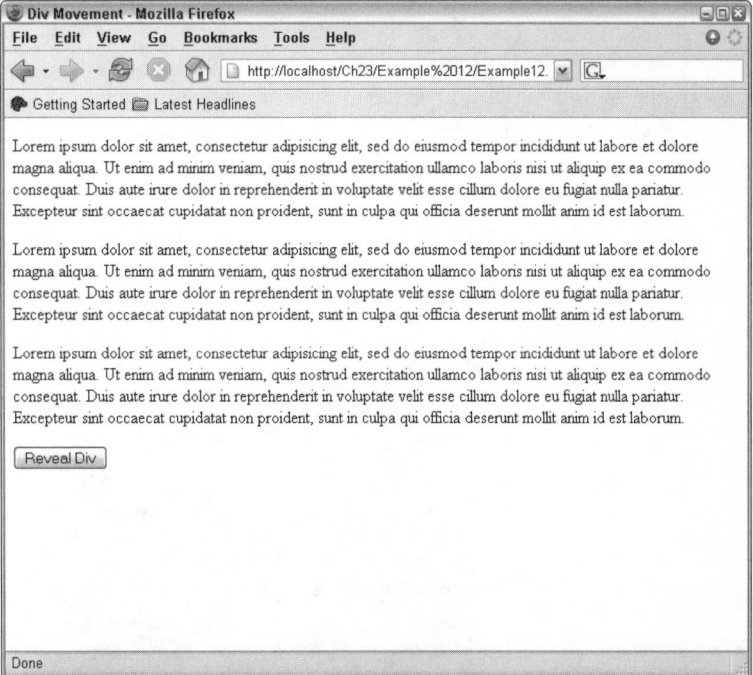

Figure 23-15

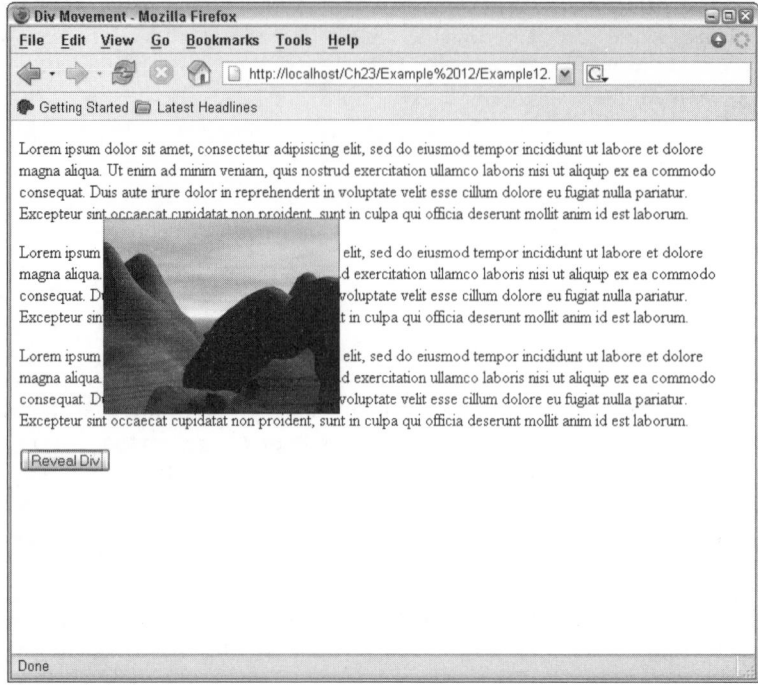

Figure 23-16

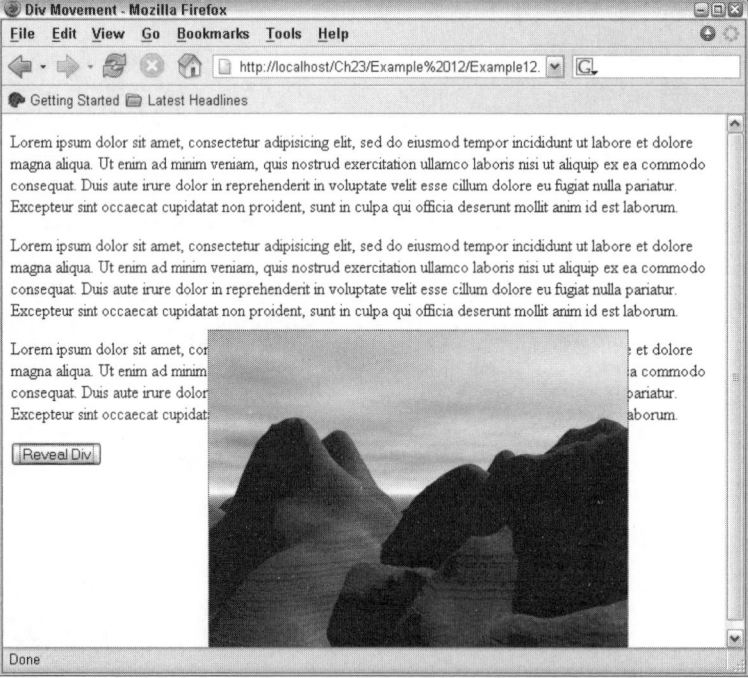

Figure 23-17

The button's onclick() event handler calls the revealdiv() function that prepares the division for movement (makes the element visible, sets initial size and position values) and then calls the movement function, movediv().

The movediv() function increases the size of the element and moves it 10 pixels right and down each time it is called. A timer is used to call the movediv() function every 20 milliseconds until the element reaches the specified location on-screen (200 pixels from the left margin). Once the element arrives at its destination, the function stops calling itself and the operation is done.

Most of the error checking built into the script centers around the getdivID() function that returns an element's ID despite the DOM that the user agent might be using. Note that this function supports far more diverse user agents than previous examples and can be retrofitted into other scripts needing more than Firefox and IE compatibility.

Additional error checking is built into checking for appropriate use of the style property (for example, using div.width or div.style.width) and appropriate values for the visibility style. Also, because of a quirk in Firefox you must set the initial values of the division element using JavaScript; Firefox seems incapable of reading the size and position values from the style class set by XHTML.

Lastly, the appropriate measures (pixels or more specifically px) must be used and worked around when present. The initial assignment of the noPx variable is done according to the user agent capabilities. Just in case px appears in the values, parseInt is used to parse the integer values out of the appropriate properties before calculations are performed.

Improving the Script

This script can be adapted in a variety of ways for other uses. The content of the division in the example is simple (a static image), but it doesn't have to be. You can place text or any other valid XHTML element within the division. The initial and final destinations can be tweaked, as well as the movement frequency or amplitude.

This example can also be combined with other examples in this chapter. The division can have content appear after being moved and/or the error checking routines present in this example can be used for effect in other examples.

Summary

This chapter wraps up the book's coverage of JavaScript. Using the examples and resources within this chapter, you should be able to utilize JavaScript to the best of its potential.

CGI Basics

The Common Gateway Interface (CGI) is an important tool in a Web programmer's bag of tricks. When HTTP was created, it was introduced as a simple way to receive and respond to queries for documents. As the Web grew, it became important that the protocol be able to interface with additional resources beyond those of simple textual documents. This chapter introduces CGI as a concept along with the techniques and technology involved in its operation.

CGI History and Operation

CGI has been around almost as long as the Web. It was developed as a means to extend early HTTP servers, allowing users to submit data to the server and receive appropriate content based on that submission.

Perl was perhaps the earliest means of accomplishing CGI, although any programming language capable of reading from standard input (STDIN) and writing to standard output (STDOUT) can be used for CGI purposes.

Understanding HTTP Request and Response

At its simplest, the HTTP protocol works by the server taking a *request* from a client and returning a *response* to that request. In most cases, the request is for a document whose content is sent in the server's response. A variety of other operations are possible between client and server, but we will concentrate on this simple "I want a document" request and "here it is" response. This operation is diagrammed in Figure 24-1.

The client request typically resembles the following:

```
GET  somepath/somedocument  HTTP/1.1
```

Note that this section provides the bare essentials regarding HTTP requests and responses. More detail on this subject is covered in Chapter 1 in the section "The Web Protocol."

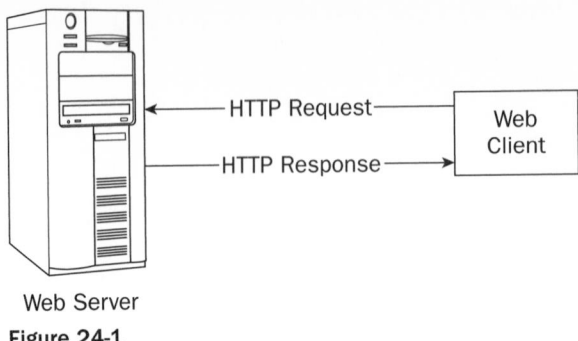

Figure 24-1

This request asks for a document in a particular directory (governed by `somepath`) and tells the server that the client speaks HTTP version 1.1. For example, to request the top-level page from a server, a client might use the following:

```
GET   /index.html   HTTP/1.1
```

This request asks for the `index.html` file from the server's root directory.

The server then responds with a header indicating the success or failure of the request. When the request can be fulfilled, the server usually responds with the following header:

```
HTTP/1.1   200   OK
```

This header indicates it is in HTTP 1.1 format and includes the status code in both numeric (`200`) and textual (`OK`) form. If appropriate, the header is followed by the content requested. If the request cannot be fulfilled, the server instead sends an error code in the status reply, such as the familiar "404 document not found" error:

```
HTTP/1.1   404   Not Found
```

In some cases, such as the preceding 404 error, the server is configured to perform other actions besides simply returning an error. For example, most Web servers are configured to send a special page to a client along with the 404 error, as shown in Figure 24-2.

HTTP Data Encapsulation

There are two ways CGI scripts can receive data: via information embedded in the requested URL (`GET`) or via data embedded in the HTTP headers (`POST`).

Using the first method (GET), data is embedded in the URL by separating the request info and the data with a question mark (`?`). The data is then contained in name/value pairs, separated by ampersands (`&`). For example, to pass my first and last name in a URL, I could use the following:

```
http://www.example.com/index.html?firstname=Steve&lastname=Schafer
```

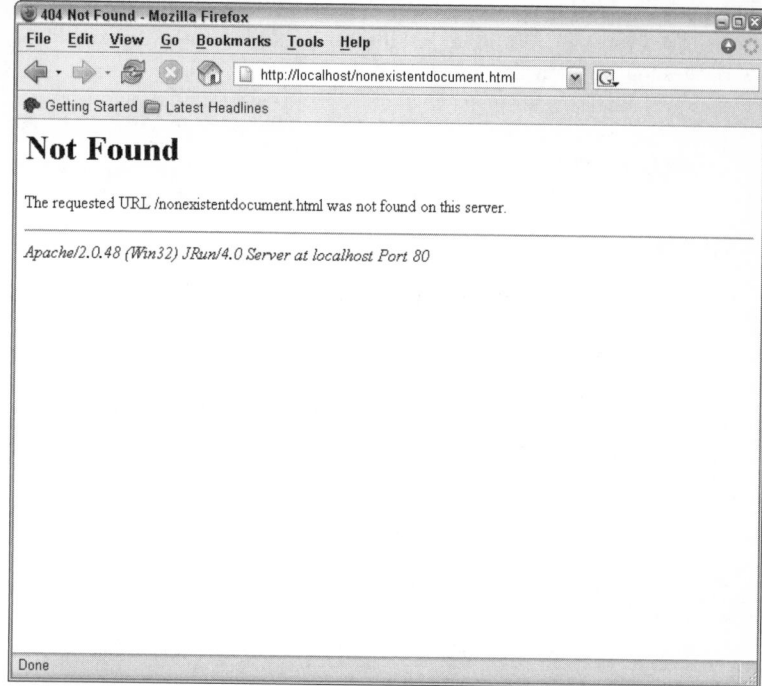

Figure 24-2

This URL breaks down as follows:

- ❏ `http://www.example.com/index.html` — The document being requested
- ❏ `?` — The document/data separator
- ❏ `firstname` — The first of the two data fields
- ❏ `=` — The assignment operator for the first data field
- ❏ `Steve` — The value for the first data field
- ❏ `&` — The separator for data fields
- ❏ `lastname=Schafer` — The second data field (`lastname`) and its data (`Schafer`)

Using the second method (POST), the data is sent back to the server embedded in HTTP headers. For example, the following headers encapsulate the same data as in the preceding GET example:

```
POST   /URL-TO-SCRIPT-OR-DOCUMENT  HTTP/1.1
Host:  www.example.com
Content-Length: 32
Content-Type: application/x-www-form-urlencoded

firstname=Steve&lastname=Schafer
```

The minimal headers tell the destination (script or page) that the incoming data is encoded; the actual data is passed as name/value pairs after the headers (and the end-header blank line).

In either case, the data is available to the CGI script. In most cases, dedicated libraries or variables exist to address the data. For example, Perl has a CGI library for addressing GET and POST data while PHP has _SERVER variables that contain GET or POST data.

The individual means of handling GET and POST data are covered in the respective script language chapters in this part of the book.

How CGI Works

CGI works by mimicking the standard request/response operation of HTTP. CGI scripts cause the server to bypass its internal request and response handling. Instead, the task is performed directly by the appropriate (usually the requested) script — that is, of course, if the request for the script can be fulfilled to begin with.

This is best seen with an example. Suppose that a client submits the following request:

```
GET  /cgi-bin/somescript.cgi  HTTP/1.1
```

If the server can find the script /cgi-bin/somescript.cgi, the script is executed according to local system policies — usually allowing the script to communicate directly with the client. This process resembles that shown in Figure 24-3.

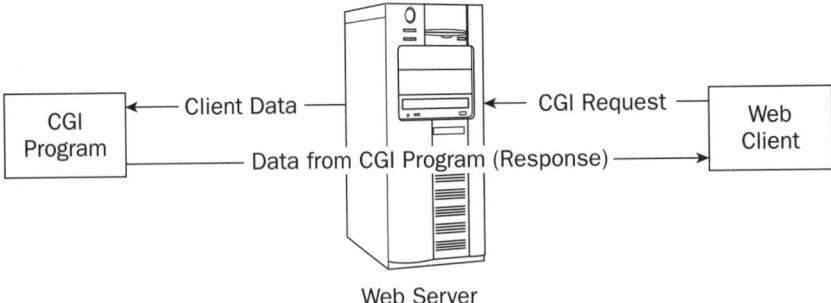

Figure 24-3

The best thing about CGI is that most of the communication sent back to the client can be handled directly through the standard output (STOUT) device. For example, this simple Perl script sends a short, concise document to any client requesting it:

```
#!/usr/bin/perl -w

print "Content-type: text/html\n\n";
print "<html><body><p>Hello world!</p></body></html>";
```

Note, however, that the burden of HTTP protocol adherence is now the script's responsibility. It has to send the appropriate header(s), as necessary, so that the client can appropriately understand the data.

The following script shows how easy it can be to handle data passed to a script:

example.pl

```
#!/usr/bin/perl -w

use CGI qw(:standard);
my $firstname = param('firstname') || "unknown";
my $lastname = param('lastname') || "unknown";

print "Content-type: text/html\n\n";
print "<html><body>";
print "<p>Hello $firstname $lastname!</p>";
print "</body></html>";
```

As previously mentioned, Perl has several libraries that make dealing with CGI tasks easier. In the preceding example, the CGI library is used to access the data passed via GET.

Figure 24-4 shows the result when this script is accessed using the URL `test.pl?firstname=Steve&lastname=Schafer`.

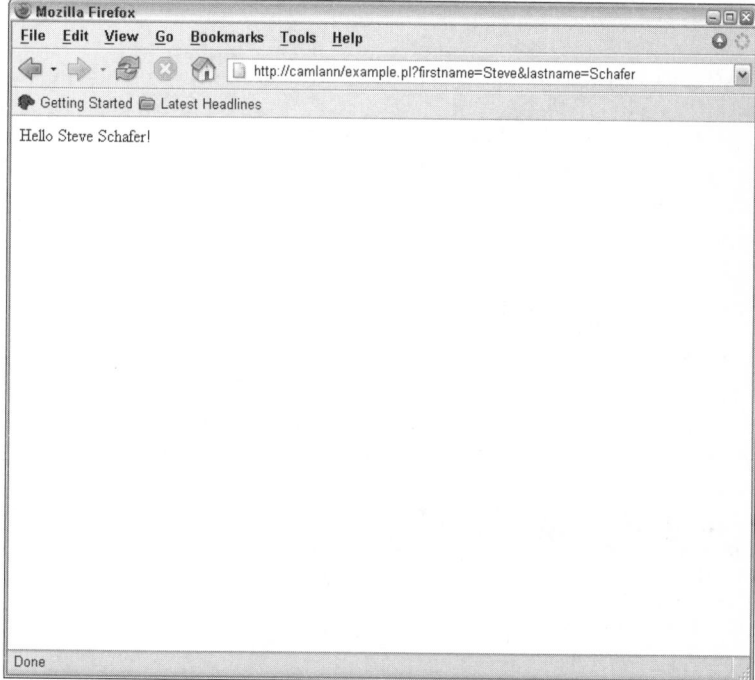

Figure 24-4

Serving CGI

Not all Web servers are capable of serving CGI scripts. To do so requires that the server be configured accordingly. This includes fulfilling the following requirements:

❑ Having the required scripting language installed

❑ Being configured to allow CGI scripts to run (usually restricted to certain directories on the server)

❑ Having appropriate permissions to execute the script(s)

The real power of CGI comes from the capabilities of the scripting language, which is usually capable of the following:

❑ Reading and writing to the file system on the server

❑ Accessing data via the network or Internet

❑ Accessing server hardware or hardware otherwise connected to the server

❑ Accessing other resources such as databases

Due to the power inherent in such actions, many system administrators do not have CGI enabled on their servers or choose to restrict its usage.

> *Another risk of CGI scripting is the load such scripts can put on the server. Improperly written scripts can use too many resources, bringing a server to its knees.*

It is also imperative that script authors take all necessary actions to ensure that their scripts are well written, well behaved, and pose no serious security risks to the server on which they are run.

> *The separate scripting chapters in this part of the book contain tips and techniques that can be employed to help write safe and secure scripts.*

A Simple CGI Example

It's important to wrap up this discussion by showing a simple, but working, CGI script. Don't be too concerned about understanding how the script works at this point. Subsequent chapters will explain more about accomplishing CGI using particular languages. Right now, just be conscious of the various sections of the script (outlined by comments) and what those sections contain.

Example: A Perl CGI Script

This script outputs a simple XHTML document containing one paragraph that includes a parameter passed via GET.

Source

```
#!/usr/bin/perl

# Use CGI methods to get parameters
use CGI;
my $cgi = CGI->new();
my %params = $cgi->Vars;


# Print document header
```

```
print "Content-type: text/html\n\n";
print <<HTML;
<!DOCTYPE html PUBLIC "-//W3C//DTD XHTML 1.0 Strict//EN"
    "http://www.w3.org/TR/xhtml1/DTD/xhtml1-strict.dtd">
<html>
<head>
  <title>CGI Example</title>
</head>
<body>

HTML

# Print "Hello name" where name is from GET data
print "Hello ", $cgi->{'name'}[0], "</p>\n";

# Close document
print "</body>\n</html>";
```

Output

The output of this script is shown in Figure 24-5. Note that the parameter (name), passed via GET, appears on the address line (appended to the URL).

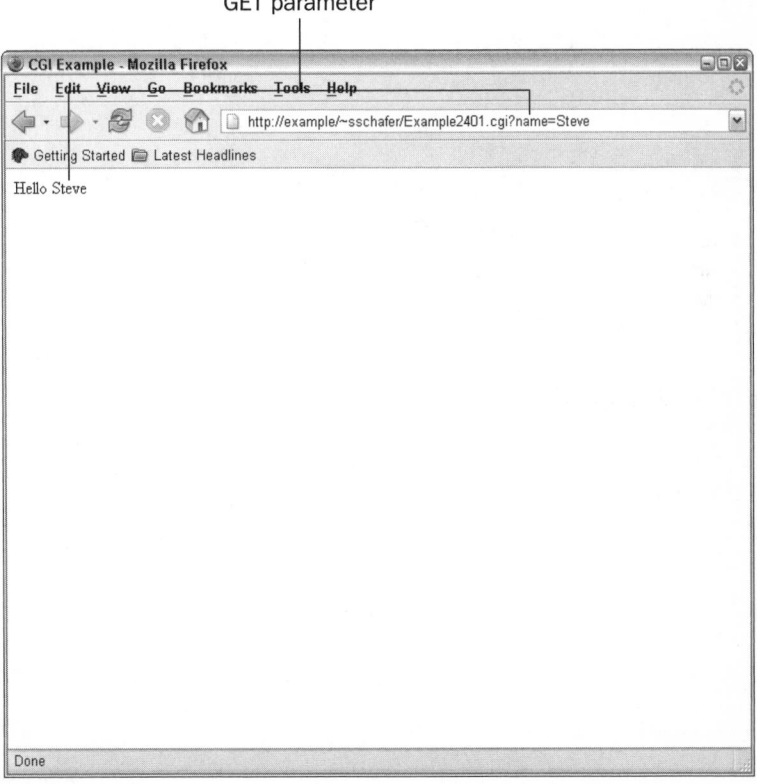

Figure 24-5

Summary

This chapter introduced CGI and showed the basics of how the technology works. Subsequent chapters in this part of the book cover the specifics of particular scripting languages. Useful examples are covered in each chapter and compiled in Chapter 28, "Using CGI."

Perl Language

Perl is one of the mainstays of CGI scripting. Originally conceived as a simple reporting language, it has grown to be one of the most popular Web and system scripting languages. Although somewhat quirky in nature, the community around Perl has created many additional resources and code to help even the neophyte programmer tap its capabilities.

The History of Perl

The Practical Extraction and Report Language (Perl) was created in 1987 by Larry Wall. Perl was originally created as a means to access and report on file contents. Perl has grown considerably from its humble beginnings and is used extensively on the Web and as a system scripting language. One of the reasons Perl is so popular is circular in nature — its popularity spawns more (community) development, which increases its popularity, and so forth.

The Perl community has created hundreds of modules, constructs that can easily be added to your scripts to increase their capabilities without having to code the capabilities yourself. There are modules to access other application data (databases, and so on), emulate protocol stacks, communicate with hardware, and more.

However, rapid growth from humble beginnings brings with it some growing pains. Perl is quirky and somewhat dated; although powerful, a lot of Perl's power comes in the form of patches and hacks. Still, Perl is one of the most powerful and versatile scripting solutions available.

Additional Perl Resources

This chapter provides an overview of Perl, but due to the scope of this book, it is simply an overview. For more information on Perl, consult the following resources.

❑   **The Perl.org Web site** (`http://www.perl.org`) — The main site for information and documentation on Perl. Download Perl, read online documentation, and follow Perl's development here.

❑ **The Perl.com O'Reilly Web site** (http://www.perl.com) — A great resource for Perl documentation, code examples, and so on.

❑ **The Comprehensive Perl Archive Network (CPAN)** (http://www.cpan.org) — The one and only comprehensive resource for Perl modules. Search the module archive based on keywords, capabilities, or module names. The archive includes entries for almost all previous versions of modules as well as the most current.

Basic Perl Syntax

Perl follows a syntax similar to that of the C programming language. Perl syntax can be summed up with a few simple rules:

❑ With few exceptions, code lines should end with a semicolon (;). Notable exceptions to the semicolon rule are lines that end in a block delimiter ({ or }).

❑ Blocks of code (usually under control structures such as functions, if statements, and so on) are enclosed in braces ({ and }).

❑ Explicit declaration of all variables is a good idea, and necessary if using strict data declarations.

❑ The use of functions to delimit code fragments is recommended and increases the ability to execute those fragments independently from one another. (Functions are discussed in the "User-Defined Functions" section, later in this chapter.)

❑ Comments can be inserted in Perl code by prefixing the comment with a pound sign (#) or surrounding the comment with /* and */ pairs. In the former case (#), the comment ends at the next line break. Use the latter case for multiline comments.

Data Types and Variables

Perl supports the usual range of data types — numeric and string. The next two sections detail the data types available in Perl and how variables are handled.

Data Types

Perl supports three types of data:

❑ Scalars

❑ Arrays

❑ Associative arrays

Perl also supports objects — an unordered container of various data types. Objects are covered in the "Objects" section later in this chapter.

Scalar values are individual numeric, string, or Boolean values. Example scalar values include 3, 3.14159, TRUE, and "character data."

Arrays are collections of scalars. Individual elements in an array are referenced by an index relating to their position in the array with a zero index. For example, in the following string array, "Steve" is element number 3:

```
"Terri","Ian","Branden","Steve","Tammy"
```

Associative arrays are arrays that use string identifiers instead of numeric identifiers for elements of the array. Associative arrays are generally used to store data associated with a particular identifier. For example, you could define an associative array to store anniversary dates of employees so that accessing the array with an index of "Steve" would return the date associated with Steve.

Variables

Perl variables are largely untyped; you can use the same variable to contain different scalar values at different times in your scripts. Of course, doing so is generally frowned upon — the point is that variable typing in Perl is left up to the programmer.

Perl variable names are prefixed with a specific character depending on the use of the variable, as shown in the following table:

Character	Use
$	Individual scalar value, individual value in an array or associative array
@	Entire array or slice of an array
%	Entire associative array or slice of an associative array

The index delimiter of normal arrays is the square bracket ([and]) while the index delimiter of associative arrays is the curly bracket ({ and }). For example, the first following print statement prints the third value of array **name** *while the second prints the "Steve" value of the associative array* **birthdate***:*

```
print $name[3];
print $birthdate{'Steve'};
```

Variables in Perl are declared using standard programming nomenclature (that is, variable name and equal sign and then the desired value). It is recommended that each variable declaration include the generic variable constructor (my), as shown in the following examples:

```
use strict; # See note below
my $name="Steve";  # Scalar string
my %birthdates;  # Empty associative array, followed by two element declarations
   $birthdates{'Steve'} = "5/10";
   $birthdates{'Angela'} = "8/2";
my %cars = ("Steve" => "S2000",
    "Angela" => "MiniCooper"); # Associative array with two elements
my pi = 3.1415926;  # Scalar numeric
```

The use of **strict** *pragma (***use strict***) causes Perl to require explicit variable declarations (before use), enforces local variable scope, and requires explicit references. All three aspects of the* **strict** *pragma help enforce good programming practices and should be enabled in all of your Perl scripts.*

Special Variables

Perl has many special variables to contain internal data, specific to the script being run. Special variables can be used to hold results of searches, values of environment variables, debugging flags, and more. The following table details most of these variables.

More information on these variables can be found in the **perlvar** *documentation that comes with Perl distributions. The format and the location of this documentation depend on your platform and the Perl distribution you are using. Generally speaking, Linux users can access the* **perlvar** *docs by using* **man perlvar***.*

Variable	Use
$_	The default parameter for a lot of functions.
$.	Holds the current record or line number of the file handle that was last read. It is read-only and will be reset to 0 when the file handle is closed.
$/	Holds the input record separator. The record separator is usually the newline character. However, if $/ is set to an empty string, two or more newlines in the input file will be treated as one.
$,	The output separator for the print() function. Normally, this variable is an empty string. However, setting $, to a newline might be useful if you need to print each element in the parameter list on a separate line.
$\	Added as an invisible last element to the parameters passed to the print() function. Normally, an empty string, but if you want to add a newline or some other suffix to everything that is printed, you can assign the suffix to $.
$#	The default format for printed numbers. Normally, it's set to %.20g, but you can use the format specifiers covered in the section "Example: Printing Revisited" in Chapter 9 to specify your own default format.
$%	Holds the current page number for the default file handle. If you use select() to change the default file handle, $% will change to reflect the page number of the newly selected file handle.
$=	Holds the current page length for the default file handle. Changing the default file handle will change $= to reflect the page length of the new file handle.
$-	Holds the number of lines left to print for the default file handle. Changing the default file handle will change $- to reflect the number of lines left to print for the new file handle.
$~	Holds the name of the default line format for the default file handle. Normally, it is equal to the file handle's name.
$^	Holds the name of the default heading format for the default file handle. Normally, it is equal to the file handle's name with _TOP appended to it.
$|	If nonzero, will flush the output buffer after every write() or print() function. Normally, it is set to 0.

Variable	Use
$$	This UNIX-based variable holds the process number of the process running the Perl interpreter.
$?	Holds the status of the last pipe close, back-quote string, or `system()` function.
$&	Holds the string that was matched by the last successful pattern match.
$`	Holds the string that preceded whatever was matched by the last successful pattern match.
$'	Holds the string that followed whatever was matched by the last successful pattern match.
$+	Holds the string matched by the last bracket in the last successful pattern match. For example, the statement `/Fieldname: (.*)|Fldname: (.*)/ && ($fName = $+);` will find the name of a field even if you don't know which of the two possible spellings will be used.
$*	Changes the interpretation of the ^ and $ pattern anchors. Setting $* to 1 is the same as using the /m option with the regular expression matching and substitution operators. Normally, $* is equal to 0.
$0	Holds the name of the file containing the Perl script being executed.
$<number>	This group of variables ($1, $2, $3, and so on) holds the regular expression pattern memory. Each set of parentheses in a pattern stores the string that matches the components surrounded by the parentheses into one of the $<number> variables.
$[	Holds the base array index. Normally, it's set to 0. Most Perl authors recommend against changing it without a very good reason.
$]	Holds a string that identifies which version of Perl you are using. When used in a numeric context, it will be equal to the version number plus the patch level divided by 1000.
$"	This is the separator used between list elements when an array variable is interpolated into a double-quoted string. Normally, its value is a space character.
$;	Holds the subscript separator for multidimensional array emulation. Its use is beyond the scope of this book.
$!	When used in a numeric context, holds the current value of `errno`. If used in a string context, will hold the error string associated with `errno`.
$@	Holds the syntax error message, if any, from the last `eval()` function call.
$<	This UNIX-based variable holds the read `uid` of the current process.
$>	This UNIX-based variable holds the effective `uid` of the current process.
$)	This UNIX-based variable holds the read `gid` of the current process. If the process belongs to multiple groups, $) will hold a string consisting of the group names separated by spaces.

Table continued on following page

Variable	Use
`$:`	Holds a string that consists of the characters that can be used to end a word when word wrapping is performed by the ^ report formatting character. Normally, the string consists of the space, newline, and dash characters.
`$^D`	Holds the current value of the debugging flags.
`$^F`	Holds the value of the maximum system file description. Normally, it's set to 2. The use of this variable is beyond the scope of this book.
`$^I`	Holds the file extension used to create a backup file for the in-place editing specified by the -i command line option. For example, it could be equal to ".bak."
`$^L`	Holds the string used to eject a page for report printing.
`$^P`	This variable is an internal flag that the debugger clears so that it will not debug itself.
`$^T`	Holds the time, in seconds, at which the script begins running.
`$^W`	Holds the current value of the -w command line option.
`$^X`	Holds the full pathname of the Perl interpreter being used to run the current script.
`$ARGV`	Holds the name of the current file being read when using the diamond operator (<>).
`@ARGV`	This array variable holds a list of the command line arguments. You can use `$#ARGV` to determine the number of arguments minus one.
`@F`	This array variable holds the list returned from autosplit mode. Autosplit mode is associated with the -a command line option.
`@Inc`	This array variable holds a list of directories where Perl can look for scripts to execute. The list is mainly used by the `require` statement.
`%Inc`	This hash variable has entries for each filename included by do or `require` statements. The keys of the hash entries are the filenames, and the values are the paths where the files were found.
`%ENV`	This hash variable contains entries for your current environment variables. Changing or adding an entry affects only the current process or a child process, never the parent process. See the section "Example: Using the %ENV Variable" later in this chapter.
`%SIG`	This hash variable contains entries for signal handlers.
`_`	This file handle (the underscore) can be used when testing files. If used, the information about the last file tested will be used to evaluate the new test.
`DATA`	This file handle refers to any data following __END__.
`STDERR`	This file handle is used to send output to the standard error file. Normally, this is connected to the display, but it can be redirected if needed.

Variable	Use
STDIN	This file handle is used to read input from the standard input file. Normally, this is connected to the keyboard, but it can be changed.
STDOUT	This file handle is used to send output to the standard output file. Normally, this is the display, but it can be changed.

Calculations and Operators

Perl supports the standard operators for its various data types. The following tables outline the basic operators available in Perl.

Perl Arithmetic Operators

Operator	Use
+	Addition
-	Subtraction
*	Multiplication
/	Division
%	Modulus
**	Exponent
++	Increment
--	Decrement

Perl Assignment Operators

Operator	Use
=	Assignment
+=	Increment assignment
-=	Decrement assignment
*=	Multiplication assignment
/=	Division assignment
%=	Modulus assignment
**=	Exponential assignment
.=	String concatenation assignment

Perl Comparison Operators

Operator	Use
==	Numeric is equal to
!=	Numeric is not equal to
>	Numeric is greater than
<	Numeric is less than
>=	Numeric is greater than or equal to
<=	Numeric is less than or equal to
eq	String equality
ne	String nonequality
gt	String greater than
lt	String less than
ge	String greater than or equal to
le	String less than or equal to

Perl Logical Operators

Operator	Use
&&	And
||	Or
!	Not

Perl Bitwise Operators

Operator	Use
&	And
|	Or
^	Xor
~	Not
<<	Left shift
>>	Right shift

Perl Miscellaneous Operators

Operator	Use
.	Object/property/method separator
?	Condition operator
delete	Delete specified object
new	Create new object
this	Reference current object
ref	Type of object (number, string, and so on)
void	Evaluate expression without return value

String Operators

Operator	Use
.	Concatenation
x	Repetition

String Tokens

Token	Character
\b	Backspace
\e	Escape
\t	Horizontal Tab
\n	Line feed
\v	Vertical Tab
\f	Form feed
\r	Carriage return
\"	Double quote
\'	Single quote
\$	Dollar sign
\@	At sign
\\	Backslash

Control Structures

Like other languages, Perl supports many different control structures that can be used to execute particular blocks of code based on decisions or repeat blocks of code while a particular condition is true. The
following sections cover the various control structures available in Perl.

While and Until

The `while` loop executes one or more lines of code while a specified expression remains true. The `while`
loop has the following syntax:

```
while (<expression>) {
    # statement(s) to execute
}
```

Because the `<expression>` is evaluated at the beginning of the loop, the statement(s) will not be executed if the `<expression>` is false at the beginning of the loop. For example, the following loop will
execute 20 times, each iteration of the loop incrementing x until it reaches 20:

```
my $x = 0;
while ($x <= 20) {   # do until $x = 20 (will not execute when x = 21)
  $x++;   # increment x
}
```

The `until` loop is similar to the `while` loop except that the loop is executed until the expression is false:

```
until (<expression>) {
   # statement(s) to execute while expression is true
}
```

For

The `for` loop executes statement(s) a specific number of times and is governed by two expressions and a
condition:

```
for (<initial_value>; <condition>; <loop_expression>) {
  # statement(s) to execute
}
```

The `<initial_value>` expression is evaluated at the beginning of the loop; this event occurs only
before the first iteration of the loop. The `<condition>` is evaluated at the beginning of *each* loop iteration. If the condition returns false, the current iteration is executed; if the condition returns true, the loop
exits and the script execution continues after the loop's block. At the end of each loop iteration, the
`<loop_expression>` is evaluated.

Although their usage can vary, `for` loops are generally used to step through a range of values via a specified increment. For example, the following example begins with the variable x equal to 1 and exits when
x equals 20 — each loop iteration increments x by 1:

```
for ($x = 1; $x <= 20; $x++ ) {    #  for $x = 1 to 20
  # statement(s) to execute
}
```

Note that the `<loop_expression>` is not limited to an increment expression; the expression should advance the appropriate values toward the exit condition but can be any valid expression. For example, consider the two following snippets of code:

```
for ($x = 20; $x >= 1; $x--) {   # for $x = 20 to 1
  # statement(s) to execute
}

for ($x = 2; $x <= 40; $x+=2) {   # for $x = 2 to 40, by 2 (even numbers only)
  # statement(s) to execute
}
```

Foreach

The `foreach` loop is similar to that of a normal `for`, but it assigns values to the controlling variable from a list, one after another, until all values have been assigned. This loop is handy for finding the largest element, printing all the elements (or performing a particular task on all elements), or simply seeing if a given value is a member of a list. The `foreach` structure has the following syntax:

```
foreach $<variable> (@<array/list>) {
  # statement(s) to execute with $<variable>
}
```

For example, the following code would print all the values in the `$names` array, each followed by a new-line (`\n`):

```
my @names = ("Steve","Terri","Ian","Angie","Branden");
foreach $name (@names) {
  print $name."\n";   # Will print all values from the names array
}
```

You can also use `foreach` with a static list:

```
foreach $name ("Steve","Terri","Ian","Angie","Branden") {
  print $name."\n";   # Will print all values from the list
}
```

If Else

The `if` and `if else` constructs execute a block of code depending on the evaluation (true or false) of an expression. The `if` construct has the following syntax:

```
if (<expression>) {
  # statement(s) to execute if expression is true
} [ else {
  # statement(s) to execute if expression is false
} ]
```

For example, the following code tests if the value stored in `i` is the number 2:

```
if (i == 2) {
  # statement(s) to execute if the value in i is 2
}
```

The following code will execute one block of code if the value of i is an odd number, another block of code if the value of i is an even number:

```
if ((i % 2) != 0) {
    # statement(s) to execute if i is odd
} else {
    # statement(s) to execute if i is even
}
```

You can also use complex expressions in an if loop, as in the following example:

```
if ((i = 2) && (t = 31) && (name = "Panama")) {
    # statement(s) to execute if all three conditions are true
}
```

You can also create else if constructs in JavaScript by nesting if statements within one another, as shown in the following code:

```
if ((i % 2) != 0) {
    # statement(s) to execute if i is odd
} else
    if (i == 12) {
    # statement(s) to execute if i is 12
    }
}
```

However, Perl provides the elsif directive for just this purpose:

```
if ((i % 2) != 0) {
    # statement(s) to execute if i is odd
} elsif (i == 12) {
    # statement(s) to execute if i is 12
    }
}
```

More Loop Control — Continue, Next, Last, Redo

Perl offers more loop control mechanisms than standard languages. The following table summarizes the control words and their effect on a loop:

Control	Use
continue	Performs additional statements at the end of each loop iteration (see notes after this table).
next	Skip immediately to the conditional statement, bypassing any other statements.
last	Exit the current loop as though the condition had been met.
redo	Repeat the current iteration of the loop. (Note that neither the increment/ decrement expression nor the conditional expression is evaluated before restarting the block.)

The `continue` statement creates a special block of code that is executed at the end of each loop iteration, immediately before the loop condition expression is evaluated. A `continue` block is executed even in the event that the loop does a `next` or `redo` but not a `last` (`last` skips the `continue` block). A `while` loop with a `continue` block would resemble the following:

```
while (<expression>) {
     # redo jumps to here
     # statements;
} continue {
     # next jumps to here
     # statements;
     # standard loop jumps back to <expression>
}
# last jumps to here
```

A loop without a `continue` block is assumed to have an empty `continue` block.

Regular Expressions

One technology that Perl is renowned for is regular expressions (commonly abbreviated regex). Regular expressions are special strings used as a template to match content, a kind of search expression in a way. Regular expressions are used in one of three ways: to match, to substitute, and to translate. Using regular expressions, you can construct advanced pattern-matching algorithms. The following sections cover the basics of Perl regular expressions.

Coverage of regular expressions can fill a book in itself. This section serves only as an introduction to the subject.

Regular Expression Operations

Regular expressions have three main operations in Perl: matching, substitution, and translation. In Perl you delimit regular expressions with forward slashes, prefixing the expression with the operator. An example of each operator's syntax is shown in the following code:

```
m/<expression>/  # match expression
s/<expression1>/<expression2>/   # substitute expression2 for expression1
tr/<expression>/  # translate expression
```

By default, Perl uses the built-in variable $_ as the space to be searched/matched by a regular expression and the variables $n ($1, $2, and so on) as variables to store data returned from regular expression operations. You can also use the regex assignment operator (=~) to perform a regex operation on any variable's content. For example, to perform a regex operation on the text stored in the string variable $content, you could use the following code:

```
$content =~ /<regex_pattern>/;
```

If the pattern matches content in the searched variable, the expression will return TRUE. Therefore, you can also use regular expressions within control structures, as in the following code example:

```
if ($content =~ /^Yabba(.*)Doo!$/) {
   # do something if regex found in $content
}
```

Regex Special Characters

The following table describes some of the more popular special characters used in regular expressions.

Character	Use
^	Match beginning of line
$	Match end of line
.	Match any character (except newline)
|	Specify alternatives to match
[ ]	Specify group or range to match
\	Escape the next character
Other character	Match literal character

You can modify each matching character or expression with a matching quantifier, specifying how many matches should be found. The valid quantifiers are described in the following table.

Quantifier	Meaning
*	Match 0 or more times
+	Match 1 or more times
?	Match 0 or 1 times
{n}	Match exactly n times
{n,}	Match at least n times
{n,m}	Match between n and m times (inclusive)

Perl regular expressions also have meta and control characters that can be used in expressions. The meta and control characters are described in the next table.

Character	Meaning
\t	Tab
\n	Newline
\r	Carriage return
\f	Form feed

Character	Meaning
\d and \D	Digit and nondigit
\s and \S	Space and nonspace (white space and non–white space)
\w and \W	Word and nonword
\b and \B	Word and nonword boundary

Example Expressions

Before moving on to how regular expressions can be used in Perl, it is important to understand how the pattern-matching strings are constructed and what they match.

As mentioned in the previous section, an asterisk quantifier (*) is used to match 0 or more of a particular character. Consider the following expression:

```
ba*h
```

This expression would match bah, baah, baaah, and so on, as well as bh. The * quantifies that the a should be matched 0 (bh) or more (baaaaah) times.

If the + quantifier were used instead of * (for example, ba+h), bh would not be matched because the a would have to be matched at least once.

Using the group/range construct ([and]), you can specify a group of characters or a contiguous range of characters to match. To specify a group of characters, you simply list them in between the brackets. For example, consider the following expression:

```
b[uo]t
```

This expression would match but and bot (either a u or an o between the b and t). To specify a range, you list the beginning and ending character separated by a dash (-). Ranges can be included in groups simply by listing them next to other elements. For example, consider the following expressions and comments indicating what they would match:

```
[a-z]  #  any single lowercase letter
[a-zA-Z]  #  any single letter
[0123456789]  or  [0-9]  # any single number
[0-9A-CZ]  #  any single number, a capital letter A-C, or a capital letter Z
```

A caret (^) can be used within a group/range construct to negate it. For example, the following expression would match anything *except* a single number:

```
[^0-9]
```

Modifying Expressions

There are a few characters that can be appended after the regular expression (after the closing /), modifying how the regular expression is applied. The modifiers are listed in the following table:

Modifier	Meaning
i	Case-insensitive match
g	Global match (useful mainly with substitutions)
m	Match across multiple lines
s	Treat string as one line (. will then match newlines)

For example, the global switch (g) can be used so that a match will replace *all* substrings matched, not just the first substring (as is the default):

```
$_ = "Yabba Dabba Doo!";
s/abba/xxxx/;    #  Yields "Yxxxx Dabba Doo!"
$_ = "Yabba Dabba Doo!";
s/abba/xxxx/g;   #  Yields "Yxxxx Dxxxx Doo!"
```

Memorizing Substrings

If you enclose parts of an expression in parenthesis, whatever is matched by the parenthetical pattern will be returned in the appropriate $n variable (first parenthetical in $1, second parenthetical in $2, and so forth). For example, the following code would print "abba" and "Doo!":

```
#!/usr/bin/perl

$_ = "Yabba Dabba Doo!";
# match everything between "Y" and "<space>Dabba"
#    and everything after "Dabba"
/^Y(.*)\sDabba(.*)$/;

print $1."\n".$2."\n";
```

The parentheticals can also be used in the expression as shorthand match expressions by prefixing the appropriate number with a backslash (\1 for the first parenthetical, and so on). Of course, the shorthand must come *after* the parenthetical for which it is a match. For example, the following expression matches the earlier "Yabba Dabba Doo!" example:

```
/^Y(.*)\sD\1.*/   # match first Y"abba" and use shorthand (\1) for second D"abba"
```

Built-in Functions

Perl has a host of built-in functions for manipulating data. The functions are accessed in typical fashion for programming languages:

```
function_name(<argument(s)>)
```

Most functions return values; therefore, you can use functions to make assignments, use them as/in expressions in loop statements, and so on.

Strictly speaking, all functions return values. However, not all functions can be relied on to return mean-ingful values.

A fairly comprehensive list of the more popular built-in Perl functions can be found in Appendix D, "Perl Language Reference."

User-Defined Functions

You can create your own functions by using the `sub` directive. User-defined functions have the following syntax:

```
sub <function_name> {
  #  function statements
  return <value>;
}
```

Note that Perl does not include function arguments in the function definition as in most other languages. That is because the arguments sent to the function are automatically stored in the $_ variable array. The first argument is stored in $_[0], the second argument is stored in $_[1], and so forth. Within the function, it is the programmer's duty to distill the array into useful variables. For example, to create a function to find the area of a circle, you could use code similar to the following:

```
sub areaofcircle {
  my $radius = $_[0];
  # area = pi * (r squared)
  my $area = 3.1415 * ($radius ** 2);
  return $area;
}
```

A popular and efficient way of distilling function parameters is to use code similar to the following:

```
my(
  $firstparam,
  $secondparam,
  $thirdparam,
  $fourthparam,
) = @_;
```

This code transfers the contents of the $_ array (referenced in its entirety by @_) to the variables speci-fied. (Of course, you would want to use variable names that are more meaningful to your function.)

It is worth noting that use of the `return` function is not necessary if the last expression evaluated con-tains the desired return value (as is the case in the `areaofcircle()` function example). However, it is usually best to be explicit with your code and always use the `return` function.

File Operations

One of the advantages of using CGI programs is that they can read and write to the filesystem, and Perl is no exception. Perl includes quite a few functions for dealing with file IO, covered in the following sections.

Standard Operating Procedure

To access files, there are three operations that you need to perform:

- ❑ Open the file and assign a file handle.
- ❑ Perform file operations (read/write).
- ❑ Close file handle, thereby closing the open file.

In an effort to make programs more uniform, there are three connections that always exist when your program starts. These are STDIN, STDOUT, and SDTERR (these variable names are open file handles).

Opening a File

To open a file, Perl uses (strangely enough) the open function. The open function has the following syntax:

```
open(FILEHANDLE, "<filename>")
```

For example, to open the file test.txt you would use code similar to the following:

```
open(FILEHANDLE,"test.txt") || die "cannot open file";
```

*The preceding syntax will result in the script exiting and displaying "cannot open file" if the **open** function does not succeed.*

The FILEHANDLE can be any valid variable name but should be descriptive to be easily identified as a file handle. One standard practice is to capitalize the file handle variables.

The default operation of the open function is to open a file for reading. To open a file for writing, you need to preface the filename with a >; to append to a file, you would preface the name with >>. Both of these conventions are standard input redirectors.

```
open(FILETOWRITE,">test.txt")
```

```
open(FILETOAPPEND,">>test.txt")
```

Reading from a Text File

To read from a text file, Perl uses the diamond operator, angle brackets (< >) enclosing the file handle. Each call by the diamond operator reads a line from the linked file, which is stored in the default variable ($_).

For example, the following snippet of code will read all lines from the file test.txt:

```
...
open (FILE,"test.txt) || die "cannot open file";
while (<FILE>) {
  # do something useful with input
}
...
```

Writing to a Text File

To write to a text file, Perl uses the standard `print` functions, simply redirected to the appropriate file handle. To redirect the print output, the file handle is specified after the `print` command but before the output:

```
print FILEHANDLE <output>;
```

For example, the following code snippet will write the value of the `$contents` variable to the file `test.txt`:

```
...
my $contents = "This is a line to write to a file";
open (FILE,">test.txt")  ||  die "cannot open file";
print FILE $contents;
...
```

The `select` function can be used to change the standard output handle from STDOUT to the specified file handle. For example, both of the following code snippets accomplish the same thing, directing the `print` function's output to the file handled by the file handle `FILE`:

```
print FILE "output string";

select(FILE);
print "output string";
```

Note that the `select` function also returns the current file handle so you can reset it later if you would like.

Closing a File

To close a file, you simply use the `close` function with the appropriate file handle. For example, to close a file opened with the `FILE` file handle, you would use the following code:

```
close(FILE);
```

Once a file has been closed, it cannot be read from or written to. However, until a written file is closed, its contents cannot be relied on — the operating system may not write its buffers until the file is closed.

Working with Binary Files

Binary files are handled by a similar method as text files, but the content is handled differently. Each character in a binary file is handled separately. In text files, for example, the end of a line is handled as one character even if (in DOS/Windows format) it is indeed two characters (line feed and carriage return).

One important difference in using the `read` function with binary files is the addition of a buffer and length parameters within the function. When used with binary files, the `read` function has the following syntax:

```
read(FILEHANDLE, $<buffer_var>, byte_length)
```

The buffer variable can be any scalar variable, but it must be declared before being used.

For example, the following code snippet will read a binary file in 4K chunks:

```
...
my $buffer = "";
open(FILE,"test.bin")  ||  die "cannot open file";
while ( read(FILE, $buffer, 4096) ) {
  # do something useful with contents ($buffer)
}
...
```

This code reads 4K chunks until the read fails, at which time the while statement exists.

Writing to binary files in Perl is no different from writing to text files.

Getting File Information

There are many functions in Perl to get extra information about files on the filesystem. The following table lists the tests available to be performed on files and the data they return.

Operator	Meaning
-A	Returns time of last access
-b	Is a block device
-B	Is a binary file
-c	Is a character device
-C	Returns the time of last change
-d	Is a directory
-e	Exists
-f	Is a regular file
-g	Is setgid bit set
-k	Is sticky bit set
-l	Is a symbolic link
-M	Returns age of file
-o	Is owned by current user
-O	Is owned by the read user
-p	Is a named pipe
-r	Can be read from
-R	Can be read by the current user

Operator	Meaning
-s	Returns size of file
-S	Is a socket
-t	Is open to a tty
-T	Is a text file
-u	Is setuid bit set
-w	Can be written to
-W	Can be written to by the current user
-x	Can be executed
-X	Can be executed by the current user
-z	Is size zero

For example, the following code tests if a file exists and can be written to:

```
$_ = "test.txt";
if ((-f) && (-w)) {
  print "File exists and can be written to";
}
```

Other File Functions

Many other functions are available in Perl to deal with files. There are functions to create and remove directories, read directory contents, change file permissions, and more. A comprehensive list appears in Appendix D, "Perl Language Reference."

Objects

Perl has robust support for object data types. Although a full description of object-oriented programming is beyond the scope of this book, the following sections provide a primer on Perl's handling of objects.

Perl's Object Nomenclature

As with all things Perl, there are several ways (and related syntax) to achieve a desired goal. In this case, there are several ways to work with objects. We will stick with the standard -> separator syntax familiar to most object-oriented programmers.

This syntax uses -> to separate objects and methods. For example, when creating a new object of class dog, you use the new() method similarly to the following:

```
doberman = dog_object->new();
```

Object properties are assigned using the associative assignment operator, =>. This creates the properties as hashes (associative arrays) and has the benefit of providing a ready-made method for accessing property values using simple statements such as the following:

```
print %{doberman}->{'color'};
```

Perl Constructors

One easy way to create constructors is to use a separate namespace in Perl to create a new() function and associated initialization routines. For example, to create a constructor for the dog class, you could use code similar to the following:

```
package dog_object;
   sub new {

      my $class = shift;
      my %params = @_;

      bless {
         "color"  => $params{"color"},
         "size"   => $params{"size"}
      }, $class;

   }
```

This code defines a new namespace (dog_object) where the new() function can be initialized and distinguished from other new() functions in the script. The new() function itself shifts the class name off the parameter stack and assigns the rest of the parameters to the params associative array. This array is then used to initialize the object's properties, and the object is reassigned as a data type of $class.

Accessing Property Values

As previously mentioned, using the methods outlined in this chapter, you can access an object's properties using associative array methods. For example, let's expand upon the dog object example and create a full script that creates an object and outputs its properties:

```
#!/usr/bin/perl

# dog object constructor
package dog_object;
   sub new {

      my $class  = shift;
      my %params = @_;

      bless {
         "color"  => $params{"color"},
         "size"   => $params{"size"}
      }, $class;
   }
```

```
# back to normal namespace
package main;

# create a new dog object (doberman: color brown, size large)
$doberman = dog_object->new("color" => "brown", "size" => "large");

# print the new object's properties
print "A doberman is a " . %{$doberman}->{'size'} . ", ";
print %{$doberman}->{'color'} . " dog.\n";
```

Modules

As mentioned early in this chapter, a lot of Perl's power comes from the abundance of prefab modules available for use with your scripts. Many of these scripts are available in CPAN (www.cpan.org).

To use a module, you must install it into your Perl modules directory and then declare the module within your script. You can employ the use directive to import a module, its classes, variables, and methods for use in your script. The syntax for the use directive is as follows:

```
use <module_name> qw (<list of exports>);
```

For example, to use the popular CGI module in your scripts, you could use the following at the beginning of your script:

```
use CGI qw/:standard/;
```

*The **qw** function (quote words) is used to quickly expand a list into single-quoted words. Most Perl modules have functions bundled into lists such as* **:standard**; *specifying* **qw(:standard)** *in a* **use** *statement will expand the list into the individual single-quoted functions to include. Alternatively, you could specify the individual functions (comma-separated as single words if using **qw** or comma-separated single-quoted names if not using **qw**). Note that you shouldn't use commas inside a **qw** with slashes as delimiters (**qw//**). Doing so will cause an error.*

Using Perl for CGI

Perl is very popular for CGI use due to its simple structure, speed, stability, unrivaled text handling, and number of available modules. Using various modules, you can tie Perl, and therefore your Web content, into almost any data or technology.

Perl has the same requirements for CGI as any other scripting language:

❑   Your script must be able to output to standard output.

❑   Your script must supply HTTP headers.

❑   Your script must supply compliant HTML (or whatever content dictated by the headers it supplies).

By itself, Perl can accomplish a lot of system integration with Web documents — directory listings, reading/writing files, and so on. However, to truly utilize the CGI power of Perl, it is highly suggested that you use the CGI.pm module.

This module, available via CPAN (www.cpan.org) or packaged specifically for most Linux distributions, provides the interface for receiving POST and GET data, as well as outputting most XHTML tags and related data. The latest version of CGI.pm operates using the Perl object model — a new CGI object is created and acted upon to output the appropriate XHTML.

A quick example of how easy CGI.pm can make your CGI work is shown in the following code:

```perl
#!/usr/bin/perl -w

# Use CGI routines
use CGI;
# Create CGI object
$q = new CGI;
# Output HTTP header
print $q->header;
# Start the document, specifying the document title
print $q->start_html('Document Title');
# Output a H1 Tag (containing "Header Text"
print $q->h1('Header Text');
# End the document
$q->end_html;
```

Retrieving data sent via POST or GET is equally simple by accessing the passed data via the Vars parameter of the CGI object ($cgi->Vars). The type of data (GET/POST) can be ascertained by examining the Request Method environment variable ($ENV{REQUEST_METHOD}, which will contain GET or POST).

Example 2 in Chapter 28 shows how to parse GET and POST data using the CGI module.

Perl Errors and Troubleshooting

You are bound to encounter problems when programming CGI applications in Perl. This section gives you a few examples of how to troubleshoot and fix problems you encounter.

Maximum Error Reporting

The first thing you should do to help troubleshoot errors is maximize the information Perl reports when it encounters an error. There are two methods to help increase the error text reported by Perl.

The first way is to use the w flag when running Perl. In your scripts, you simply add the flag to the interpreter line at the top of the script:

```perl
#!/usr/bin/perl -w
```

The second way to increase data reporting is to use the `CGI::Carp fatalsToBrowser` routine. Including this function causes Perl to attempt to output any errors to the browser window. This directive can be specified using the following line in your scripts:

```
use CGI::Carp qw(fatalsToBrowser);
```

For example, the following script will output the error in the `die` function, in this case `---An error occurred here---`, as shown in Figure 25-1:

```
#!/usr/bin/perl -w
use CGI::Carp qw(fatalsToBrowser);
die "---An error occurred here---";
```

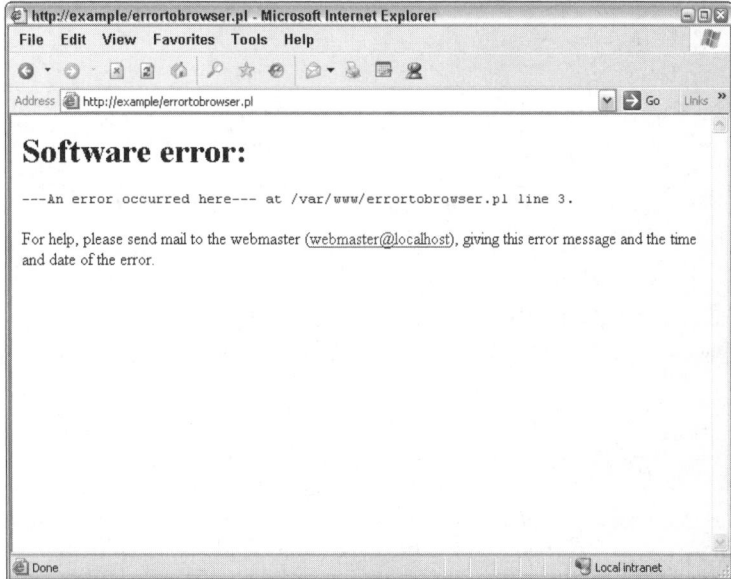

Figure 25-1

*The **fatalsToBrowser** directive helps avoid the problem described in the next section—the dreaded Apache Internal Server Error message.*

If you want to, change the default message supplied by the `fatalsToBrowser` routine by also importing the `CGI::Carp set_message` function and use it to define a more appropriate message, as in the following sample:

```
#!/usr/bin/perl -w
use CGI::Carp qw(fatalsToBrowser);
set_message("This is a custom error message.");
```

The Apache Internal Server Error Message

The most prevalent message you will encounter with Perl CGI scripts is shown in Figure 25-2:

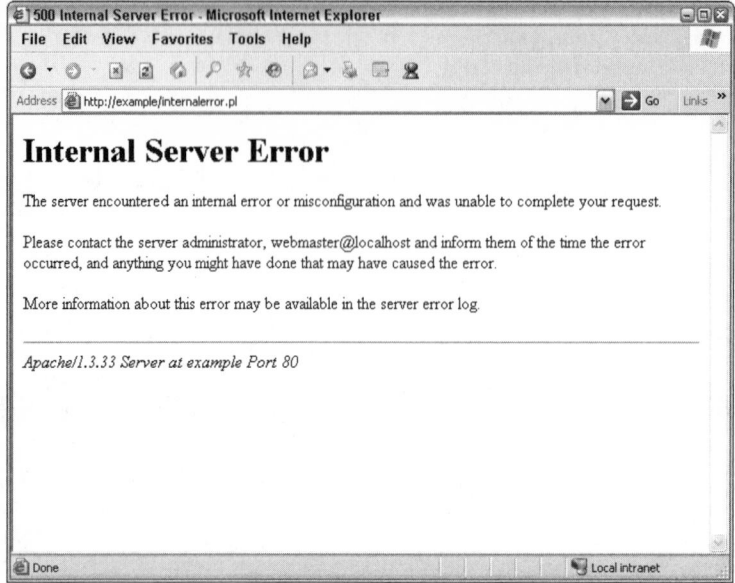

Figure 25-2

This error doesn't include a lot of useful information, but it does throw up a flag that should cause you to check the Apache error log. The following error typically accompanies the Internal Server browser message:

```
[Sun Apr 17 15:26:23 2005] [error] [client 192.168.1.13] Premature end of
script headers: /var/www/errortobrowser.pl
```

The root of the actual problem is that Perl script spit out an error message *before* it sent appropriate HTTP headers allowing the Web server and browser to communicate properly. One way to troubleshoot the actual error is to run the script from the command line and see what error the interpreter is reporting.

Summary

This chapter provided a primer to the Perl scripting language. Chapter 26 covers the basics of Python, another popular scripting language used on the Web. Insight into using other executable code for CGI purposes is covered in Chapter 27, and practical examples using all forms of CGI are presented in Chapter 28.

The Python Language

Python is a rising star in CGI scripting. Touted for its uncomplicated nature, readability, and robustness, it has grown to be one of the most widely used Web and system scripting languages. Python is interpreted and object oriented. Python has more features than Perl or Tcl and is easier to learn and use. The documentation and tutorials available to aid in the learning process are much clearer than those available for PHP. Python also edges out PHP in the elegant way it handles namespaces. Python has a wide variety of uses, including the following:

- ❑ Command-line tools development
- ❑ Web development
- ❑ Component integration
- ❑ Database access and manipulation
- ❑ Distributed programming
- ❑ Parsing
- ❑ Image processing
- ❑ Scientific programming

The History of Python

Python was invented by Guido van Rossum; development began in the late 1980s. Van Rossum began work on Python in the Netherlands at the National Research Institute for Mathematics and Computer Science or Centrum voor Wiskunde en Informatica (CWI), as it is known in Dutch. He got assigned to a project called the Amoeba Project, which needed a scripting language that he was assigned to develop. That scripting language was the beginning of Python, which van Rossum originally intended to be a second language for C and C++ developers to use when a powerful shell-scripting language was needed to script something written for a single, particular use. Since then, Python, now owned by the Python Software Foundation, has developed a reputation for clean syntax and productivity. Guido van Rossum describes Python as sharing some characteristics with scripting languages, but also sharing some characteristics with more traditional programming languages.

Additional Python Resources

This chapter provides an overview of Python, but due to the scope of this book, it is simply an overview. For more information on Python, consult the following resources:

❑ **The Python.org Web site** (http://www.python.org) — The main site for information and documentation on Python, downloading Python, reading online documentation to include a detailed Module index, and following Python's development.

❑ **The Starship Python Web site** (http://starship.python.net/) — A pretty good resource for Python documentation, code examples, and so on, especially the search engine at http://starship.python.net/crew/theller/pyhelp.cgi.

❑ **Pythonware.com Web site** (http://www.pythonware.com/) — A good source for Python news, including a daily updated news log.

❑ **The Zope Project** (http://www.zope.org) — Zope is an Open Source Web applications server primarily written in Python.

❑ **The Graphical User Interface sites** — There is not one single library for creating graphical user interfaces with Python. Tkinter has the edge time-wise, although Python users often question why wxPython is not the recommended library. If you are considering doing graphical user interfaces with Python, consider both these sites:

   ❑ **Tkinter** (http://www.pythonware.com/library/) — The Tkinter library is based on Tcl/Tk. It is the de facto standard for GUIs.

   ❑ **WxPython** (http://www.wxpython.org/) — An up-and-coming library, WxPython is a cross between the wxWindows class library for C++ and Python.

Modules

A lot of Python's functionality comes from the availability of prefab modules available for use with your scripts. Many of these modules are listed in Appendix E, "Python Language Reference." A more complete list of modules for the current python version is available at http://docs.python.org/modindex.html. Many modules are available, but if you don't find one you need, you can write it yourself. The distutils package provides support for building and installing your own modules. The new modules may be written purely in Python or may be written as extension modules in C. You can also build them from a combination of Python and C.

Python Interpreter

On a UNIX system, the Python interpreter is called an Integrated DeveLopment Environment (IDLE) but is usually thought to be named after a character in the Monty Python comedy troop for which Python itself was named. IDLE is usually installed as /usr/local/bin/python or /usr/bin/python. If its location is in your PATH, you can start it by typing the following command: **python**.

On a Windows system, the Python IDE is GUI-based and is called PythonWin. PythonWin is usually installed in the same directory as Python. The executable is called pythonwin.exe.

Python is available for Mac, too. That project is called MacPython, and it contains the Mac version of IDLE.

Whichever operating system you choose, you will find that, in interactive mode, the interpreter will display a prompt of >>>. This prompt allows you to type in your Python commands. If any of these commands are not built in, you must first import the module that contains that command, like this:

```
>>> import re
```

To exit the Python interpreter, type an end-of-file character (Control+D on UNIX, Control+Z on Windows) at the primary prompt. The interpreter will exit with a zero exit status.

You can also invoke a Python script directly by making the first line of the script look like this,

```
#!/usr/local/bin/python
```

with the path representing the path to the Python interpreter. Although the preceding hard-coded method works, on UNIX systems the preferred method is to use the env command, which will look for the Python interpreter in your PATH. The env command is usually found in /bin or /usr/bin. In this case, the first line of your script would look like this:

```
#! /usr/bin/env python
```

The names of Python scripts usually end with the extension .py. The script must have the executable attribute set and may be called like this:

```
python file2execute
```

Or if it has the executable attribute set, it may simply be executed like this:

```
/path2script/file2execute
```

If you are planning to use Tkinter, you might need to set some environmental variables if Tcl/Tk is not in a standard location. Set TK_LIBRARY and TCL_LIBRARY variables to point to the local Tcl and Tk library file destinations. In some instances, the PYTHONPATH environment variable is used to specify possible module locations. In Windows, the PYTHONPATH variable is stored in the Registry.

The os module's environ function is used to turn the shell environment into a simple Python object. The os.environ function will list the environment variables as follows:

```
>>> import os
>>> os.environ.keys()
['LESS', 'MINICOM', 'LESSOPEN', 'SSH_CLIENT', 'LOGNAME', 'USER', 'INPUTRC',
'QTDIR', 'PS2', 'PATH', 'PS1', 'LANG', 'KDEDIR', 'TERM', 'SHELL', 'XAUTHORITY',
'SHLVL', 'EDITOR', 'MANPATH', 'JAVA_HOME', 'HOME', 'PYTHONPATH', 'T1LIB_CONFIG',
'LS_OPTIONS', '_', 'SSH_CONNECTION', 'WINDOW_MANAGER', 'GDK_USE_XFT', 'SSH_TTY',
'LC_COLLATE', 'HOSTNAME', 'CPLUS_INCLUDE_PATH', 'PWD', 'MAIL', 'LS_COLORS']
```

Because the PYTHONPATH previously looked at is listed, let's look to see what it is set to with the environ function, as follows:

```
>>> import os
>>> os.environ['PYTHONPATH']
'/usr/lib/python2.4/;/usr/local/lib/mylib'
```

If the PYTHONPATH variable is not set, the sys.path is searched. Typically, developers will add their own modules to the site-packages of the Python installation.

In recent Python versions, you can also use this functionality to set or change the PYTHONPATH like this:

```
>>> os.environ['PYTHONPATH']="/usr/lib/python2.4"
>>> os.environ['PYTHONPATH']
'/usr/lib/python2.4'
```

Basic Python Syntax

Python follows a syntax that can be summed up with a few simple rules:

❑   Comments are preceded by hash marks (#) and can begin anywhere in a line, although no active code may follow it on the same line. Multiline comments should also be indented, with each line preceded by a hash mark.

❑   Blocks of code, called *suites*, are delimited with indentation, typically four spaces. Spaces and tabs should not be intermixed. Each time the level of indentation is increased, a new code block begins. The end of that code block is marked by the reduction of indentation to match the previous level.

❑   A colon (:) separates the header of a code block from the rest of the suite.

❑   Newline (\n) is the standard line separator.

❑   Python statements are delimited by newlines, but single statements can be broken into multiple lines by using backslashes (\) to continue a line.

❑   Functions are organized as importable modules. Each module is a separate Python file.

Data Types and Variables

Python uses dynamic data typing. This means that the Python compiler doesn't assign a type to the objects that it uses. The virtual machine instead does the assignment at run-time. This adds a great deal of flexibility to Python, but it can also create errors that are difficult to find. For example, if a typographical error is made when typing the variable name, it will be recognized as a new variable, which may not be immediately obvious to the person executing the code.

Data Types

Python supports the following five types of data:

❑   Numbers

❑   Strings

- ❏ Lists
- ❏ Dictionaries
- ❏ Tuples

Numbers

Python supports four numerical types:

- ❏ **int** (signed integers) — Most 32-bit computers will offer an integer range from –231 to 231–1 (–2,147,483,648 to 2,147,483,647).

- ❏ **long** (long integers) — The range of Python longs are limited only by the amount of virtual memory a system has. Longs may be represented in decimal, octal, or hexadecimal notation. As in most other languages, long integers in decimal form are denoted by an uppercase L or a lowercase l. Some examples follow:

  - ❏ 99999999999L

  - ❏ –234561

  - ❏ 0xD34F867CA0

- ❏ **float** (floating-point real values) — Floating-point numbers in Python are denoted by a decimal point and either a lowercase e or an uppercase E and a positive (+) or negative (–) sign. Examples follow:

  - ❏ 0.99

  - ❏ –953.234

  - ❏ 96.7e3

  - ❏ –1.609E-19

- ❏ **complex** (complex numbers) — Complex numbers have real and imaginary components. Complex number attributes are accessible like this:

```
>>>myComplex = -7.345-1.53j
>>>myComplex
(-7.345-1.53j)
```

- ❏ If you want to see only the real portion of the number, it may be returned this way:

```
>>>myComplex.real
-7.345
```

- ❏ Likewise, to see only the imaginary portion, use the imag functionality, as follows:

```
>>>myComplex.imag
-1.53
```

- ❏ The conjugate function shows both:

```
>>>myComplex.conjugate()
(-7.345+1.53j)
```

Chapter 26

Strings

Strings are immutable sequences of alphanumeric characters. The elements of a Python string may be contained either within single quotes (tic marks) or double quotes. A single-quoted string may contain double quotes and vice versa. Strings can also be contained in triple quotes. Because strings are immutable, string functions do not change the string passed to it but instead return a new string. Due to Python's memory management capabilities, you might not notice when this happens. Consider the following example where two strings are added together:

```
>>> string = "abcdef"
>>> id(string)
1077882912
>>> string = string + "ghi"
>>> string
'abcdefghi'
>>> id(string)
1077879296
```

You can see from this example that the resulting string is not the same string that we started with. Because strings are immutable, a new string with a new identity is created. Still, you'll most likely refer to it primarily by its variable name of string, so the fact that it is not the original string might be transparent to you.

String Operators

Operator	Use
+	Concatenation
%	Format
*	Repetition
r or R	Raw string
u or U	Unicode string

A string can be preceded by the character r, which means to take escape characters literally. They can also be preceded by u to indicate that the string is of type Unicode. Here are some examples:

```
"Python is the bomb!"
'I said, "Do it in Python!"'
'Here is a string with a \n newline in it.'
r'Here is another string where the \n just means a slash and the letter n.'
 u'Here is a unicode string.'
'''triple quotes'''
```

Strings can be added together like this:

```
>>> string1 = "pre"
>>> string2 = "post"
>>> string1+string2
'prepost'
```

The repetition operator can be used to create a new string with multiple instances of the specified string. Here is an example using `string1`, which we set in the preceding code to "pre":

```
>>> string1*3
'preprepre'
```

Strings can also be compared by numeric value.

```
>>> "hello" < "mellow"
True
```

String Methods

Operator	Use
string.capitalize()	Returns string with first character capitalized. For example, `'string'.capitalize` returns "String".
string.center(width[,fillchar])	Returns string centered in a new string padded with `fillchar` on each side to length `width`. For example, `'string'.center(10)` returns " string ".
string.count(sub[,start][,end])	Returns the number of times that `sub` appears in string. Arguments start and end, if specified, and are interpreted as slice notation. For example, `'feroferofero'.count(fer)` returns 3.
string.decode([encoding[,errors]])	Decodes the string using the codec registered for encoding and using the error-handling scheme specified by `errors`. For example, `'string'.decode()` returns u'string'.
string.encode([encoding[,errors]])	Returns the encoded string using the codec registered by encoding and the error-handling scheme specified by `errors`. For example, `'string'.encode()` returns 'string'.
string.endswith(suffix[,start[,end]])	Returns `True` if the string ends with the specified suffix, otherwise returns `False`. The start and end parameters limit where to search for `string`. For example `'string'.endswith('ing')` returns True. `'string'.endswith('foo')` returns False.
string.expandtabs([tabsize])	Returns `string` with each tab replaced by a number of spaces, as specified by `tabsize`.
string.find(sub[start[,end]])	Returns lowest index where `sub` can be found in `string`. If start and end are specified, they limit where to search for the substring. For example: `'stringstringstring'.find('ing',8,12)` returns 9.
string.lower()	Returns `string` in lowercase letters. For example, `'STRING'.lower()` returns 'string'.

Table continued on following page

Operator	Use
string.join(words)	Concatenates specified words with separator of `string`. For example, `'foo'.join(['str','ing','str','ing'])` returns 'strfooingfoostrfooing'.
string.split(sep)	Returns `string` as separated at the specified separator. For example, `'string'.split('i')` returns 'str' and 'ng'.

Python provides a powerful tool that is similar to the `printf` function in C. Strings may be formatted using these format operators as in the following example:

```
>>> "Hello %s. You are number %i." %   ("Jake", 77)
'Hello Jake. You are number 77.'
```

The preceding is only one example. The following table illustrates some other options:

String Format Operators

Symbol	Conversion
%c	Character
%s	String
%i	Signed decimal integer
%d	Signed decimal integer
%u	Unsigned decimal integer
%o	Octal integer
%x	Hexadecimal integer
%X	Hexadecimal integer
%e	Exponential notation
%E	Exponential notation
%f	Float point real number
%g	The shorter of %f and %e
%G	The shorter of %f and %E

Lists

Python lists are zero-based, mutable sequences of elements, which might be numeric, strings, or something else.

Lists are denoted by square brackets, and their elements are comma delimited. They look something like this:

```
[1,2,3,4]
[`first`,`second`,`third`]
```

A number of methods are associated with a list instance: new, append, extend, insert, remove, sort, reverse, and so on.

```
>>>mylist = [] #Create an empty list
>>>mylist
[]
>>>myotherlist = [1, `two` ,3] #Creates a list with initial values.
>>>mylist
[1, `two`, 3]
>>>mylist.append(`four`) #Add a new value to the end of the list.
>>>mylist
[1,` two`, 3, `four`]
>>>mylist.extend(`another`) #Adds each element of the list "another" as a separate
member of mylist.
>>>mylist
[1, `two`, 3, `four`, `a`, `n`, `o`, `t`, `h`, `e`, `r`]
```

Passing a list as a parameter to the append *function causes the list to be seen as one member.*

Another way to add items to a list is to add two lists, as follows:

```
>>>mylist+myotherlist
[1, `two`, 3, `four`, `a`, `n`, `o`, `t`, `h`, `e`, `r`, 1, `two`, 3]
```

Lists may be accessed by index, as well.

```
>>>mylist[0]
1
```

A negative index indicates that the count is to begin with the last element in the list.

```
>>>mylist[-2]
'e'
```

A list can even be treated as a stack with the pop method, which would return the last member of the list.

```
>>>mylist.pop()
`r`
```

Dictionaries

Dictionaries are arrays of key-value pairs, each having a one-to-one relationship. The keys and values may be nearly any type of Python object. Dictionaries are declared like this:

```
myDictionary={'name':'Jacob','hobby':'Pokemon','sport':'basketball'}
```

There are several ways to access the information in a dictionary. Among the most common are the following:

```
hisHobby = myDictionary['hobby'] #Retrieves the value associated with hobby from
myDictionary and associates it with the variable hisHobby.
myDictionary['newfield'] = 'value' #Creates new dictionary key-value pair
('newfield':'value')
```

Tuples

Tuples are sequences of values similar to lists, except that tuples are immutable. A tuple is declared like so:

```
>>>vegetables = ('carrot','potato','broccoli','celery','cauliflower')
```

To get the third value of this (zero-indexed) tuple, use the following:

```
>>>vegetables[2]
'broccoli'
```

However, because tuples are immutable, overwriting the third value with another value cannot be done directly with the following:

```
>>>vegetables[2] = 'newvalue'
```

This generates an error:

```
TypeError: object does not support item assignment
```

Instead, you can use slicing and concatenation to simulate the same thing. You make a new tuple by slicing and concatenation, but it does not have the same identifier as the original tuple, because the original tuple isn't changed; simply bind the result to the same name as the old tuple.

```
>>> v = t = (1,2,3,4)
>>> t
(1, 2, 3, 4)
id(t)
1077685140
>>> v
(1, 2, 3, 4)
id(v)
1077685140
```

At this point, the two tuples are still the same. Now let's do some slicing and concatenating of t, leaving v alone. To do this, we rebind the return value to t in each step.

```
>>> t = t[:3]
>>> t
(1, 2, 3)
id(t)
1077858988
>>> t = t[:2]
```

```
>>> t
(1, 2)
id(t)
1077883052
>>> t = t + (3,4)
>>> t
(1, 2, 3, 4)
id(t)
1077879348
```

In rechecking the value of tuple v and its identifier, you see that they haven't changed.

```
>>> v
(1, 2, 3, 4)
id(v)
```

1077685140Variables

Python variables are untyped. You can use the same variable to contain different Python data types at different times in your scripts. Of course, doing so can be quite confusing and is generally not considered good programming practice. Python takes care of typing issues behind the scenes, so no errors will be generated by such a practice.

Another difference between Python variables and those of some other programming languages is that Python variables don't have to be declared. Just start using the variable and it exists. The type will be assigned at run-time.

Variable Scope

The scope of a variable may be defined as the area of a program in which a variable is visible and the length of time that variable is accessible for. There are three scopes in Python, shown here in the order resolved by Python:

1. Local scope — Defined within a function or a class method

2. Module scope — Defined within a file

3. Built-in scope — Always available; defined within Python itself

Accessing objects not in the local scope

To access an object (a variable or a function) not in the local scope, it must be imported. You can import the entire module and then use the variable name prefaced with the module name and a period, as in the following example:

```
import sys
sys.exit()
```

The privilege of not having to declare variables is not without some cost. With Python, if you accidentally reuse a variable name within the same scope, the first will be overwritten by the second. This can lead to program bugs that are difficult to find and fix.

Another common mistake is to accidentally misspell a variable name in one place and spell it correctly in another, again within the same scope. This causes the misspelled variable to be seen as a new variable name and does not generate an error as it would if Python were more strongly typed.

Calculations and Operators

Python supports the standard mathematical operators for its various data types, and they work pretty much the same as in other languages. The following tables outline the arithmetic operators available in Python.

Python Arithmetic Operators

Operator	Use
+	Addition
-	Subtraction
*	Multiplication
/	Division
%	Modulus
**	Exponent
++???	Legal in Python but doesn't act as in other languages. Instead because + is a unary prefix, ++x parses to +(+(x)), which for numbers results in x.

Although Python's primary assignment operator is the equal sign, Python supports a number of others, as shown in the following table. It is worth noting that Python supports multiple assignment, whereby all objects are assigned the same value, as in this example:

```
a = b = c = 11
```

Python Assignment Operators

Operator	Use
=	Assignment
+=	Increment assignment
-=	Decrement assignment
*=	Multiplication assignment
/=	Division assignment

Operator	Use
%=	Modulus assignment
**=	Exponential assignment
<<=	Left shift assignment
>>=	Right shift assignment
&=	And assignment
^=	Xor assignment
|=	Or assignment

Python supports a pretty standard set of comparison operators. They behave much as expected, except in the case of the < or >, which may be used in combination. The following sequence

```
>>> 3 > 2 > 1
```

is invalid in many languages, and actually means (3 > 2) and (2 > 1).

Python Comparison Operators

Operator	Use
==	Numeric is equal to
!=	Numeric is not equal to
<>	Alternate numeric is not equal to
>	Numeric is greater than
<	Numeric is less than
>=	Numeric is greater than or equal to
<=	Numeric is less than or equal to

Python Logical Operators

Operator	Use
and	And
or	Or
not	Not

Python Bitwise Operators

Operator	Use
&	And
|	Or
^	Xor
>>	Right Shift
<<	Left Shift

Python Miscellaneous Operators

Operator	Use
.	Object/property/method separator
*	Width or precision specifier
-	Left justifier
+	Display the sign
<sp>	Leave blank space before positive number
#	Add the octal leading zero '0' or hexadecimal leading '0x' or '0X'
0	Pad from left with zeroes instead of spaces
%	'%%' yields single literal '%'

Control Structures

Like many other languages, Python supports many different control structures that can be used to execute particular blocks of code based on decisions or repeat blocks of code while a particular condition is true. The following sections cover the various control structures available in Python.

While Loop

The `while` loop executes one or more lines of code while a specified expression remains true. The expression is tested prior to execution of the code stanza and again when the flow returns to the top of the stanza. This loop has the following syntax:

```
while expression;
    executeMe    #executes if the while expression evaluates to True.
```

Because the expression is evaluated at the beginning of the loop, the statement(s) will not be executed at all if the expression evaluates to false at the beginning of the loop. For example, the following loop will execute 20 times, each iteration of the loop incrementing x = 20:

```
x = 0;
while x <= 20
    x += 1;  # increment x if the while expression evaluates to True.
```

For Loop

The Python `for` loop is a bit different than the same loop in C or Perl. Whereas these languages execute their loop based on the specified step and halting condition, in Python the `for` loop iterates its loop over a sequence such as a list or a string. The statement(s) are executed a specific number of times depending on the number of members in the sequence or the range of values passed to it:

```
>>> for each in [`first.txt`,`second.txt`,`third.txt`,`fourth.txt`]:
...        print each, len(each)
...
one 3
two 3
three 5
four 4
```

Or using the range function:

```
>>> for each in range(4):
...        print each
...
0
1
2
3
```

The loop iterates for each member in the specified range. In the first case, the range is determined by the quantity of elements in the array. In the second case, the `range()` built-in function passes the array of [0,1,2,3] with exactly four elements, causing the loop to execute exactly four times.

If Statement

The `if` and `elif` constructs execute a block of code depending on the evaluation (`true` or `false`) of the specified expression. The `if` construct has the following syntax:

```
if expression:
    executeMeifTrue
else:
    executeMeifFalse
```

The `else` clause is optional.

Also available is the `elif` clause, of which there may be zero or more. An `elif` is used to mean execute the code block following it only if the primary expression evaluates to False and the expression following the `elif` evaluates to True.

```
if x==0:
    print `zero'
elif x==1:
    print 'one'
```

The `elif` and `else` clauses may be used in the same `if` clause as long as the `else` is last:

```
if x==0:
    print `zero'
elif x==1:
    print 'one'
else:
    print 'neither'
```

In the preceding code, if x is 0, the string 'zero' would be printed; if x is 1, the string 'one' would be printed; and if x is something else, the string 'neither' would be printed.

Try Statement

Python provides a rather unique statement to allow for the specification of error handlers for a group of statements. The `try` statement with an `except` clause is commonly used when a file is being opened so that an error that prevents the file from being accessed allows you to gracefully break out of the block of code intended to process that file's contents.

```
try:
    file = open(`/tmp/filename.txt', `r')
    line = file.readfile()
except IOError:
    print `Error opening the file.'
```

Multiple `except` clauses are allowed to test for different conditions, as follows:

```
try:
    file = open(`/tmp/filename.txt', `r')
    line = file.readfile()
except IOError:
    print `Error opening the file.'
except SystemError:
    print `System error while opening the file.'
```

Another form of the `try` statement allows some functionality to be specified as a way out. The `try` clause is executed, and when no exception occurs, the `finally` clause is executed. If an exception occurs in the `try` clause, the exception is temporarily saved while the `finally` clause is executed and then reraised. If the `finally` clause raises another exception or executes a return or `break` statement, the saved exception is lost.

```
try:
    file = open(`/tmp/filename.txt', `r')
    line = file.readfile()
finally:
    line = ''
```

More Loop Control — Continue, Break

Python has two additional loop control mechanisms: `continue` and `break`. The following table summarized these control mechanisms and their effect on a loop:

Control	Use
continue	Continues with next iteration of the loop
break	Breaks out of the closest `for` or `while` loop
pass	Indicates "do nothing"

The `continue` statement must be nested in a `for` or `while` loop but not in a function or class definition or `try` statement within that loop. It continues with the next cycle of the nearest enclosing loop.

A `break` is used to terminate the current loop and continue execution at the next statement. It may be found in either `while` or `for` loops.

A `while` loop with a `continue` block and a `break` statement would look like this:

```
while count > 0:
    input = raw_input("Type your password:")
    for each in passwdList:
        if input == thisPasswd:
    accepted = 1
            break
    if not accepted:
        print "Password not accepted."
        count = count - 1
        continue
    else:
        break
```

The `pass` statement is necessary in Python when a statement expects a block of code and one is not present, as follows:

```
if user != "Jacob":
    print "That's not him."
else:
    pass
```

Regular Expressions

For text analysis, Python provides the `regex` and the `re` modules. The `regex` module is old and somewhat deprecated, although still available. The `regex` module uses an emacs-style format, which some users find difficult to read. Using regular expressions from the `re` module, you can construct advanced pattern-matching algorithms in a less arcane syntax. Regular expressions are handled via a small, highly specialized programming language embedded in Python and are made available through the `re` module. Using the `re` module, you specify the rules for the set of possible strings that you want to match. You can use it to determine whether the string matches the pattern or whether there is a match for the pattern anywhere in the string. You can also use the `re` module to modify a string or to split it apart in various ways. The following sections cover basic Python regular expressions.

Regular Expression Operations

In Python, string methods are typically used for searching, replacing, and parsing. Regular expressions are used for matching and are delimited with forward slashes. Regular expressions are compiled into RegexObject instances, which have methods for various operations such as searching for pattern matches or performing string substitutions.

```
>>> import re
>>> reobj = re.compile('foo*')
>>> print reobj
<_sre.SRE_Pattern object at 0x403c38c0>
```

Regex Special Characters

The following table describes some of the more popular special characters used in regular expressions.

Character	Use
^	Match beginning of line.
$	Match end of line.
.	Match any character. Match newline only if DOTALL flag is specified.
\	Escape the next character.
\\	Match a literal \.
[ ]	Specify group of characters to match.
[^]	Match character not in set.
Other character	Match literal character.

The following regular expressions are commonly used to represent the indicated classes of characters or numbers:

```
[a-z]      #  any single lowercase letter
[a-zA-Z]   #  any single letter
[0123456789]  or  [0-9]  # any single number
[0-9A-CZ]  #  any single number, a capital letter A-C, or a capital letter Z
```

A caret (^) can be used within a group/range construct to negate it. For example, the following expression would match anything except a single digit:

```
[^0-9]
```

Each matching character or expression can be modified by a matching quantifier, specifying how many matches should be found. The valid quantifiers are described in the following table:

Quantifier	Meaning
*	Match 0 or more times
+	Match 1 or more times
?	Match 0 or 1 times
{n}	Match exactly n times
{m,n}	Match between m and n times (inclusive)

The * quantifier works like it does in most languages. For example, foo* will match fo, foo, or fooooooo. (In fact, it would match fo followed by any number of the letter o.)

The + quantifier is very similar to the * except that it doesn't match if the character preceding the star doesn't exist. In contrast to the preceding example, which matches fo even though it has zero instances of the second o, foo+ will match only foo or foo followed by any number of the letter o.

The ? quantifier acts just as the * quantifier previously shown.

The {n} quantifier matches the preceding character 0 or 1 times. So bar? will match either ba or bar.

The most complicated quantifier is {m,n}, where m and n are decimal integers. This quantifier means there must be at least m repetitions, and at most n. For example, a/{1,3}b will match a/b, a//b, and a///b. It won't match ab, which has no slashes, or a////b, which has four.

Python regular expressions also have meta and control characters that can be used in expressions. The meta and control characters are described in the next table.

Character	Meaning
\A	Matches only at start of string
\d and \D	Digit and nondigit
\s and \S	Space and nonspace
\w and \W	Alphanumeric character and nonalphanumeric character
\b and \B	Word and nonword boundary

Built-in Functions

Python has many built-in functions that are accessible from any namespace. Two of the most common are explained here:

The __init__ function is one of the most widely used functions in Python. Its purpose is to define what should be done when the class is instantiated.

```
__init__(self)
```

The built-in function `dir()` returns a list of strings representing the functions and attributes that the module defines. It is called like this:

```
>>> import sys
>>> dir(sys)
['__displayhook__', '__doc__', '__excepthook__', '__name__', '__stderr__',
'__stdin__', '__stdout__', '_getframe', 'api_version', 'argv',
'builtin_module_names', 'byteorder', 'call_tracing', 'callstats', 'copyright',
'displayhook', 'exc_clear', 'exc_info', 'exc_type', 'excepthook', 'exec_prefix',
'executable', 'exit', 'getcheckinterval', 'getdefaultencoding', 'getdlopenflags',
'getfilesystemencoding', 'getrecursionlimit', 'getrefcount', 'hexversion',
'maxint', 'maxunicode', 'meta_path', 'modules', 'path', 'path_hooks',
'path_importer_cache', 'platform', 'prefix', 'ps1', 'ps2', 'setcheckinterval',
'setdlopenflags', 'setprofile', 'setrecursionlimit', 'settrace', 'stderr', 'stdin',
'stdout', 'version', 'version_info', 'warnoptions']
```

After importing the `sys` module, any of these items may be called by the item name prefaced with `sys` and a period.

A more comprehensive list of the more popular built-in Python functions can be found in Appendix E, "Python Language Reference."

User-Defined Functions

You can create your own functions by using the `def` directive. User-defined functions have the following syntax:

```
def function_name(parameters):
    #  function statements
```

For example, to create a function to find the area of a circle you could use code similar to the following:

```
def areaofcircle()
    radius = input("Please enter the radius: ")
    area = 3.14+(radius**2)
    print "The area of the circle is", area
```

User-defined functions have the following attributes:

Attribute	Description
__doc__	documentation string
__name__	string version of function name
func_code	byte-compiled code object
func_defaults	default argument tuple
func_globals	global namespace dictionary

```
>>> areaofcircle.__doc__
>>> areaofcircle.__name__
'areaofcircle'
>>> areaofcircle.func_code
<code object areaofcircle at 0x403eab60, file "<stdin>", line 1>
>>> areaofcircle.func_defaults
>>> areaofcircle.func_globals
{'lambdaFunc': <function <lambda> at 0x403ebbfc>, '__builtins__': <module
'__builtin__' (built-in)>, 'areaofcircle': <function areaofcircle at 0x403ebd4c>,
'datetime': <module 'datetime' from '/usr/lib/python2.4/lib-dynload/datetime.so'>,
'sys': <module 'sys' (built-in)>, 'time': <module 'time' from '/usr/lib/python2.4/
lib-dynload/time.so'>, '__name__': '__main__', 'os': <module 'os' from '/usr/lib/
python2.4/os.pyc'>, '__doc__': None}
```

Lamda Functions

Python allows for the creation of anonymous functions using the lamda keyword. Lamda expressions are similar to user-defined functions without the __name__ (actually the __name__ when invoked from a lambda function returns the string '<lambda>'). An example of a lambda function follows:

```
>>> lambdaFunc = lambda x: x/3
>>> lambdaFunc(3)
1
```

File Operations

One of the advantages of using CGI programs is that they can read and write to the filesystem, and Python is no exception. Python includes quite a few functions for dealing with file IO, which are covered in the following sections.

Standard Operating Procedure

To access files, there are three operations that you need to perform:

1. Open the file and assign a file handle.

2. Perform file operations (read/write/append).

3. Close the file handle, thereby closing the open file.

Opening a File

To open a file, Python uses the open function. The open function has the following syntax:

```
FILEHANDLE=open("filename",mode)
```

For example, to open the file test.txt, you would use code similar to the following:

```
try:
    FILEHANDLE = open(`/tmp/filename.txt', `r')
except IOError:
    print `cannot open file.'
```

The preceding syntax will result in the script exiting and displaying "cannot open file" if the open function does not succeed.

The preceding syntax will result in the script exiting and displaying "cannot open file" if the open function does not succeed. The `FILEHANDLE` can be any valid variable name but should be descriptive enough to be easily identified as a file handle. One standard practice is to capitalize the file handle variables.

The default operation of the `open` function is to open a file for reading. To open a file for writing you need to specify a mode of 'w'; to append to a file you would specify a mode of 'a'; to open the file read-only you would specify a mode of 'r'.

Reading From a Text File

To read from a text file, Python uses the built-in `file` class. This class currently has an alias class called `open`, although Guido van Rossum states, "In the future, I could see `open()` become a factory function again that could return an instance of a different class depending on the mode argument, the default encoding for files, or who knows what; but `file` will always remain a class." Currently, you can use `open` and `file` interchangeably, but who knows what the future holds? For this reason, you might choose to use the `file` class exclusively.

For example, the following snippet of code will read all lines from the file `filename.txt` into a buffer where it can be acted upon:

```
    ...
    try:
        FILEHANDLE = file(`/tmp/filename.txt', `r')
        data = FILEHANDLE.readlines()
        #Do something useful with data.
    except IOError:
        print `cannot open file.'
    ...
```

After a file is opened, the file object maintains state information about the file it has opened: `<open file '/tmp/filename.txt', mode 'r' at 0x403e73c8>`. The `file` object supports the following methods:

Methods	Meaning
close()	Closes the file, preventing reading and writing. Can be called more than once.
flush()	Flushes the internal buffer.
fileno()	Returns the integer "file descriptor" that is used by the underlying implementation to request I/O operations from the operating system.

Methods	Meaning
isatty()	Returns `True` if the file is connected to a tty-like device; otherwise returns `False`.
next()	Returns the next line of the file.
read([*size*])	Returns size characters from file at current position.
readline([*size*])	Returns one line from file or size characters, which might be a partial line. Returns empty string if first character read is EOF.
readlines([*sizehint*])	Returns a list of all the lines in the file.
seek(*offset*[,*whence*])	Sets the file's current position.
tell()	Tells the file's current position.
truncate([*size*])	Truncates the file as represented in the buffer to the current position or to the location represented by *size*.
write(*str*)	Writes *str* to the fileptr to be flushed.
writelines(*sequence*)	Writes lines represented by *sequence* to the fileptr to be flushed.

The file class also includes the following attributes.

Attributes	Usage
closed	Returns True if the file is closed; otherwise returns False.
encoding	Returns the encoding method for the file.
mode	Returns the mode that the file was opened in.
name	Returns the file name.
newlines	If Python was configured with the `--with-universal-newlines` option, it returns the number of newlines in the file.
softspace	Returns a Boolean that indicates whether a space character needs to be printed before another value when using the `print` statement.

Writing to a Text File

To write to a text file, Python uses the `write` method of the file class. For example, the following code snippet will set up a list and then write it to a file:

```
>>> myList=["one","two","three"]
>>> OutputFile=file("/tmp/outputfile.txt","w")
>>> for item in myList:
>>>     OutputFile.write(item)
```

Closing a File

To close the file, you use the `close` method from the instance of the file class representing the file to be closed.

```
>>> OutputFile.close()
>>> OutputFile=file("/tmp/outputfile.txt","r")
>>> OutputFile.readlines()
['onetwothree']
```

Once a file has been closed, it cannot be read from or written to. However, until a written file is closed, its contents cannot be relied upon — the operating system may not write its buffers until the file is closed.

Working with Binary Files

Binary files are handled in a similar method as text files, but the content is handled differently. Each character in a binary file is handled separately; in text files, for example, the end of line is handled as one character even if (in DOS/Windows format) it is indeed two characters (line feed and carriage return).

One important difference in instantiating a file class for a binary file is the addition of a b in the mode for that file. When used with binary files, the file function has the following syntax:

```
OutputFile=file("/tmp/outputfile.txt","rb")
```

Writing to binary files in Python is no different from writing to text files.

Objects

Python has robust support for object data types. Although a full description of object-oriented programming is beyond the scope of this book, the following sections provide an introduction to Python's handling of objects.

Python is classified as an object-oriented programming language, although you can write useful Python code without using classes and instances. Many Python programmers make good use of Python without taking advantage of its object-oriented features. In Python, everything is an object: list, tuple, string, class, or instance of class.

Python classes are instantiated in the following way. First, define the class like this:

```
class MyClass:
    def __init__(self):
        #code to execute
    def function1(self,args):
        #code to execute
```

Then instantiate it like this:

```
if __name__ == '__main__':
    results = MyClass()
```

Python Errors and Exception Handling

Python signals errors by throwing exceptions. Unless redirected, all error messages are written to the standard error stream; normal output from the executed commands is written to standard output. Some types of errors are unconditionally fatal and cause the Python program to exit with a nonzero exit status; these errors typically are due to internal system inconsistencies or are sometimes the result of running out of memory. Python error handling includes two phases: exception detection and exception handling. Python developers are allowed a great deal of control in error handling. To add error detection, simply wrap the code in a `try-except` statement. The code that follows the `except` statement will execute upon exception. Anticipating which errors your code might encounter is important because any exception not handled directly in your code will be fatal. You can find a hierarchy of standard exceptions at `http://docs.python.org/lib/module-exceptions.html`.

In the following code, Python attempts to execute the statements between the `try` and the first `except` statement. If an error is encountered, execution of the `try` statements stops and the error is checked against the `except` statements. Execution progresses through each `except` statement until it finds one that matches the generated exception. If a matching `except` statement is found, the code block for that exception is executed. If there is no matching `except` statement in the `try` block, the final `else` block is executed. In practice, the `else` statement is not often used.

```
try:
    # program statements
except ExceptionType:
    # exception processing for named exception
except AnotherType:
    # exception processing for a different exception
else:
    # clean up if no exceptions are raised
```

Troubleshooting in Python

There are several methods to diagnose problematic Python code. The methods most commonly used for diagnosing CGI code are listed in order from least to most robust in the following section.

Run the Code in the Interpreter

Any Python code can be run from the interpreter if you import the modules you need. If you try to run CGI code in the interpreter, it will simply print the HTML code to the screen. This is sometimes useful, however, in finding the problem with your code. Running your code in the interpreter allows you to readily see if you are missing any module imports or have syntax errors.

Using the cgitb Module

Python's `cgitb` module provides an exception handler for Python CGI scripts. If an uncaught exception occurs after the `cgitb` module has been enabled, extensive traceback information is displayed as HTML sent to your browser to help you troubleshoot the problem. This is an invaluable tool in CGI script development. To use this feature, import the module and enable `cgitb`, as follows:

```
import cgitb
cgitb.enable()
```

Redirecting the Error Stream

A more robust approach to examining traceback information uses only built-in modules and sets the content type of the output to plain text, which disables all HTML processing. As previously mentioned, if your script works, the HTML code will be displayed by your client. If an exception is raised, a traceback will be displayed to help you track down the problem. Employ the following to use this method:

```
import sys
sys.stderr = sys.stdout
print "Content-Type: text/plain"
print
...your code here...
```

Because no HTML interpretation is going on, the traceback will be more readable, not requiring you to wade through HTML code to get to the important stack trace.

These are not the only troubleshooting techniques available to you, but these are the most commonly used with regard to CGI code.

Summary

This chapter provided a primer to the Python scripting language. It discussed the basics of Python syntax, how to implement Python on your system, Python's object-oriented nature, and how to troubleshoot CGI code written in Python. That, put together with previous chapters, gives you an idea how to create CGI code in Perl and Python. Chapter 27 covers using other languages for CGI, and Chapter 28 gives you several examples of Perl and Python CGI scripts.

Scripting with Other Executable Code

This book concentrates on the programming/scripting languages that are most used for CGI on the Web. However, you can effectively use any program, interpreted script, or other executable supported by the platform that is running the Web server. This chapter demonstrates some techniques that can be used with other programming and scripting languages to accomplish CGI.

Requirements for CGI

There are some basic requirements for any program or script used for CGI:

❑ The OS must be able to execute the program or script.

❑ The program or script must be accessible by the Web server. This means it must exist in a directory the server can access and must be a file type that the Web server recognizes as deliverable.

❑ The program or script must have sufficient rights or privileges to perform the tasks required of it (permission to access files it depends on, and so on).

❑ The program or script must adhere to HTTP standards for any output it produces, including passing any appropriate headers as required (for example, a Content-type header before the content, and so on). To that end, the program or script should be in a language that provides robust output options, allowing for the output of special characters (line breaks, and so on).

❑ The program or script must adhere to the guidelines governing the type of content it delivers. For example, if delivering HTML content, the program or script should endeavor to provide standards-compliant markup.

❑ The program or script should also adhere to any standards dictated by the Web server delivering the script to end users.

There is a method of CGI known as Non-parsed Headers (NPH) scripting that allows a program or script to bypass the Web server entirely, taking on the entire burden of the headers itself. To accomplish NPH, you will need a Web server with NPH enabled, and you should name your NPH scripts starting with **nph-** *(nph and a dash, for example,* **nph-myscript.cgi***). This naming convention identifies the script as an NPH script, causing the server to forgo supplying any headers itself. NPH provides a useful technique for processing data in real time. However, using NPH techniques is not without unique hazards — such as assuring that NPH scripts do not run endlessly; without the intervention of a Web server, runaway scripts can quickly consume resources.*

Of course, just because a program or script can fulfill the requirements for CGI doesn't mean that it should be used for CGI purposes. Due to the fact that CGI scripts can access privileged areas of the operating and file systems, CGI scripts pose security risks usually not inherent in the Web server itself.

Scripting languages such as Perl and Python have been tailored for CGI use and, as such, have dealt with several of the security issues relating to CGI. Therefore, using more standard languages for CGI should be encouraged.

Sample CGI Using Bash Shell Scripting

This section demonstrates how to perform CGI tasks using standard Linux Bash shell scripts. The same methods outlined in this section can be applied to most other programming and scripting languages.

The examples in this section were created on a GNU/Debian Linux system and may need to be modified to run on other versions of Linux.

Configuring Apache to Deliver Bash Scripts

Configuring Apache to deliver other scripts is fairly straightforward, involving making it aware that a particular file type should be handled like a script.

It is possible to cheat and simply name your scripts using filenames representative of other scripting languages. For example, if the Web server is already configured to deliver **.cgi** *files as scripts, you can simply name your Bash scripts using the* **.cgi** *extension. However, it is usually advisable to appropriately name your scripts following conventions for the language being used and to configure Apache appropriately for that language. For example, use* **.sh** *extensions for shell scripts,* **.py** *extensions for Python scripts, and so on.*

The essential steps to configure Apache to deliver shell scripts are as follows:

1. Ensure that the Apache CGI module is installed and active. The module should be compiled into Apache or appear in a `LoadModule` line within the Apache configuration file similar to the following:

```
LoadModule cgi_module /usr/lib/apache/1.3/mod_cgi.so
```

2. Enable CGI scripting in the directory(ies) where you will place your scripts. This is typically accomplished by adding the `ExecCGI` option to the appropriate directory configuration sections of the Apache configuration file. Such configuration sections resemble the following:

```
<Directory /usr/lib/cgi-bin/>
    AllowOverride None
    Options ExecCGI
    Order allow,deny
    Allow from all
</Directory>
```

3. Add an appropriate handler for an `.sh` file type. If you have a handler defined for CGI scripts, simply add the `.sh` extension to the existing list of extensions:

```
AddHandler cgi-script .cgi .pl .sh
```

After making changes to the Apache configuration file, don't forget to restart Apache for the changes to take effect.

*It is highly recommended to restrict shell script CGI as much as possible. If you wish to try out the examples in this section, you would do well to allow shell scripting only in the directory containing the examples and perhaps should protect that directly with an **.htaccess** or other protection scheme to ensure the scripts cannot be accessed by unscrupulous users of your Web server.*

Getting Data into the Script

Unless the program or scripting language provides CGI libraries capable of dealing with GET or POST data, you will be limited to using command line arguments with your program or script.

To pass data to a script, you would use the standard URL GET encoding; that is, following the URL to the script with a question mark and then the arguments to pass to the script:

```
<url-to-script>?<command-line-argument(s)>
```

The script would then use its standard methods for dealing with command line arguments. In the case of the Bash shell, the methods are in the form of the variables listed in the following table:

Variable	Use
$@	The full list of arguments passed to the script.
$1 - $9	The first nine arguments passed to the script. The first argument is stored in $1, the second in $2, and so on.
$_	The full path to the root program being run (in this case, the Bash shell because it is interpreting the script).
$0	The full path to the script.
$#	The number of arguments passed to the script.

To illustrate how these variables work with the command line, consider the following script:

cmdline.sh

```
#!/bin/bash

# Echo the command being run
echo -e "Command:   $0"

# Echo parameter heading
echo -e "Parameters: "

# While parameters exist
while [ "$1" != "" ]
do
   # Echo it to console
   echo -e "$1"
   # Shift to next parameter
   shift
done
```

When executed with the following command line, the script provides the output shown here:

```
$ ./cmdline.sh this is a series of parameters passed on the command line
Command:   ./cmdline.sh
Parameters:
this
is
a
series
of
parameters
passed
on
the
command
line
```

Scripts that are not enabled with specific CGI libraries and methods will be bound to the limits of their respective command lines. For example, Bash command line arguments cannot contain certain characters unless they are quoted because those characters mean special things to the Bash shell. Still, the Web server may censor other characters prior to their arriving at the script. As such, it's important to keep your parameter-passing simple when working with non–CGI-enabled scripts.

Getting Data Out of the Script

The following is an example of a Bash script that simply echoes the command line it was given:

echocmdline.sh

```
#!/bin/bash

# Echo the command line
echo -e "$0 $@ \n\n"
```

This script will run from a command line just fine:

```
$ ./echocmdline.sh these are arguments
```

```
./echocmdline.sh these are arguments
```

However, if accessed via a Web server, it will generate the error shown in Figure 27-1.

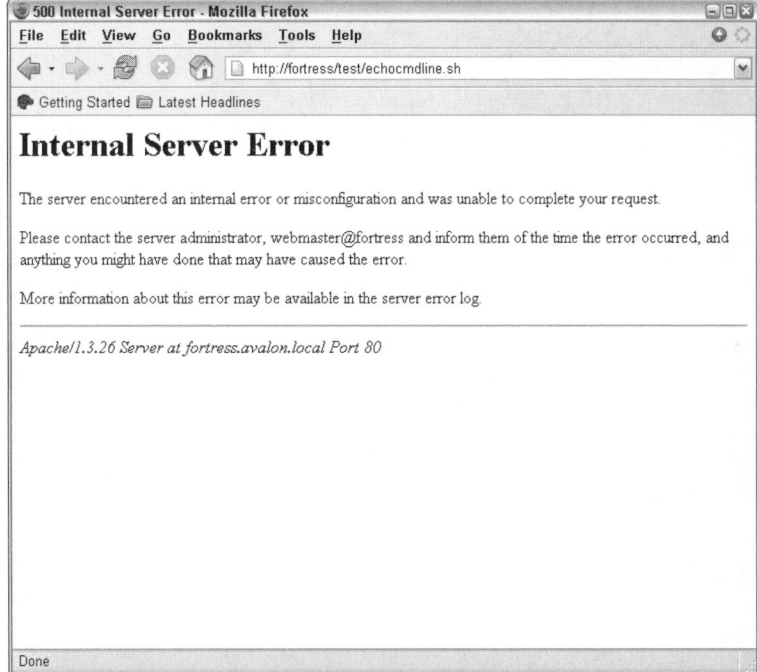

Figure 27-1

This error is a typical response if the Web server doesn't detect that the script has provided adequate header information. If you examine the Apache error log, you can immediately see the root cause of the problem; the script didn't provide adequate headers:

```
[Wed Mar  9 03:43:16 2005] [error] [client 192.168.3.141] malformed header from
    script. Bad header=/var/www/test/echocmdline.sh  : /var/www/test/echocmdline.sh
```

To correct this error, you must include appropriate headers in the output from your script. In the case of this simple example script, the output can be plain text, so adding a Content-type header is all that is required:

echocmdline.sh

```
#!/bin/bash
```

```
# Provide the content-type header
echo -e "Content-type: text/plain \n"
```

```
# Echo the command line
echo -e "$0 $@ \n\n"
```

Notice the newline (\n) at the end of the content-type echo statement. This provides a blank line after the **Content-type** *header, which is required to let the user agent know that the end of the headers has been reached.*

The script now operates correctly, as shown in Figure 27-2.

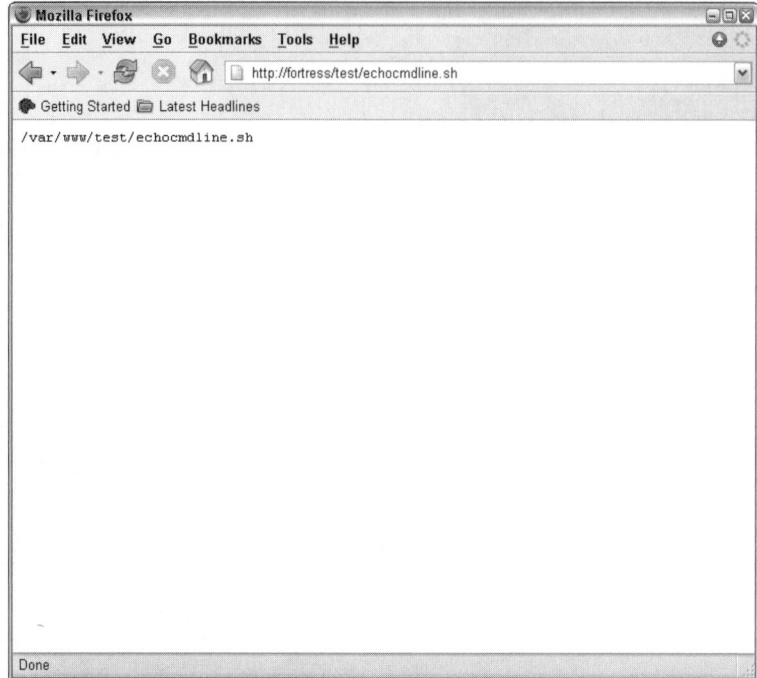

Figure 27-2

Keep in mind that a script doesn't always have to provide output.

Doing Useful Things

Because the Bash shell has access to various OS features, other programs, and the file system, it can be a powerful tool when used with CGI. The following sections provide some simple tasks possible with Bash CGI.

Shell scripting is quite powerful. This chapter covers only the basic input/output CGI functionality. Using the full power of a shell scripting, however, you can accomplish some truly amazing things.

Listing a File

The following script will list the file passed to it via GET by using the Linux cat command.

```
#!/bin/bash

# Echo content-type header
echo -e "Content-type: text/plain\n"

# If parameter exists (was given), try to cat the file
if [ "$1" != "" ]; then
  # If file exists
  if [ -f "$@" ]; then
    cat $@
  else
    echo -e "Cannot CAT file: $@\n"
  fi
else
  echo -e "Nothing to do!\n"
fi
```

Toggling a State

The following script will simply toggle a state, in this case alternately creating or deleting a lock file on the file system. This simplistic example can be extended to allow a server to be started and stopped, a process to be paused, and so on, using Web access.

```
#!/bin/bash

# File to toggle
FILE="/var/www/file.lock"

# Echo content-type header
echo -e "Content-type: text/plain\n"

# If file exists remove it
# If file doesn't exist, create it
if [ -f $FILE ]; then
  rm -rf $FILE
  echo -e "Lock file removed.\n"
else
  touch $FILE
  echo -e "Lock file created.\n"
fi
```

Running a User-Specified Command

The following script will execute the command line passed to it via GET by using the Linux `eval` command to evaluate the arguments. The output of the command is displayed in the user agent.

```
#!/bin/bash

# Echo content-type header
echo -e "Content-type: text/plain\n"

# If parameter exists, try to cat the file
if [ "$1" != "" ]; then
  echo -e "Executing command:  $@"
```

```
    echo -e "------------------------------\n"
    eval $@
else
    echo -e "Nothing to do!\n"
fi
```

This example is shown only to illustrate the extreme danger that scripts can pose to a system. In most cases, the script will be run as the same user the Web server is running as, which can limit the damage that can be done by such scripts. However, never underestimate the power of allowing command line access to a system.

Summary

As you can see by the examples in this chapter, providing basic CGI functionality via any executable code is trivial. However, it is difficult to pass complex data to scripts that do not have CGI libraries or modules to handle HTTP GET or POST operations. Also, scripting using native OS tools (such as shell scripts) can pose hazards that are typically mitigated with the CGI functions of more robust programming and scripting languages.

28

Using CGI

The previous chapters in this part demonstrated how CGI works behind the scenes — the syntax and functionality of Perl, Python, and other CGI-enabled technologies. This chapter rounds out the CGI coverage by showing some basic but useful examples of CGI in action.

How and When to Use CGI

CGI is a powerful tool for any Web developer. Unfortunately, it can also be a powerful tool for a hacker looking to exploit your site. CGI can also be a source of server load; using CGI to deliver all of a site's content increases the load on its server considerably.

Here are some reasons to consider using CGI:

❑   You need documents to provide dynamic content or interactive functions to your static documents.

❑   You need content from other resources, databases, hardware, and so on.

❑   You need more interactivity between your documents and their audience than straight XHTML technologies can provide.

That said, you should also consider the following before deploying a CGI solution:

❑   Can client-side technologies (such as JavaScript) provide what you need?

❑   Weigh the overall load on the server versus the need for the script. (Keep in mind that because most scripts are accessed via HTTP URLs, you can host the scripts on a server separate from the server delivering the XHTML documents.)

❑   Using CGI presents an inherent security risk — even well-written scripts can contain vulnerabilities that leave your server exposed to hackers.

All that said, CGI provides a great resource to infuse your documents with interactivity and dynamic content.

One popular CGI technique to decrease server load is the use of Server Side Includes (SSI). SSI lets you to embed scripts in static documents, allowing the script to deliver the dynamic portion of the document but relying upon the standard HTTP server to deliver the static content. SSI coverage is beyond the scope of this book, but for more information on SSI, I'd suggest visiting the Apache Web site, specifically the SSI tutorial at http://httpd.apache.org/docs-2.0/howto/ssi.html.

Sample Data

This section details the sample data used in this chapter and in Chapter 31, "Using PHP." Note that the code listed in this section is available on the book's companion Web site, but it is also listed here for immediate reference.

Sample Form

The following form is used in the form examples — data from this form is sent to the form handler.

```
<!DOCTYPE html PUBLIC "-//W3C//DTD XHTML 1.1//EN"
    "http://www.w3.org/TR/xhtml11/DTD/xhtml11.dtd">
<html>
  <head>
    <title>Sample Form</title>
  </head>
  <body>
    <form action="FORM_HANDLER" method="post">
    <table cellspacing="20">
    <tr><td>

      <!-- Text boxes -->
      <p>
      First Name: <input type="text" name="fname" id="fname" size="20" /><br />
      Last Name: <input type="text" name="lname" id="lname" size="20" />
      </p>

      <!-- Text area -->
      <p>
      Address:<br />
        <textarea name="addr" id="addr" cols="20" rows="4"></textarea>
      </p>

      <!-- Password -->
      <p>
      Password: <input type="password" name="pwd" id="pwd" size="20" />
      </p>
      </td><td>

      <!-- Select list -->
      <p>
      What product(s) are you<br />
```

```
              interested in? <br />
              <select name="prod" id="prod" multiple="multiple" size="4">
                <option id="MB">Motherboards</option>
                <option id="CPU">Processors</option>
                <option id="Case">Cases</option>
                <option id="Power">Power Supplies</option>
                <option id="Mem">Memory</option>
                <option id="HD">Hard Drives</option>
                <option id="Periph">Peripherals</option>
              </select>
              </p>

              <!-- Check boxes -->
              <p>
              How should we contact you?<br />
                <input type="checkbox" name="email" id="email"
                  checked="checked" /> Email<br />
                <input type="checkbox" name="postal" id="postal" /> Postal Mail<br />
              </p>

              </td></tr>
              <tr><td>

              <!-- Radio buttons -->
              <p>
              How soon will you be buying hardware?<br />
              <input type="radio" name="buy" id="buyASAP" value="ASAP" />ASAP<br />
              <input type="radio" name="buy" id="buyDays"
                 value="10" />Within 10 business days<br />
              <input type="radio" name="buy" id="buyMonth"
                 value="30" />Within the month<br />
              <input type="radio" name="buy" id="buyNever" value="Never" />Never!
              </p>
              </td><td>

              <!-- Submit and Reset buttons -->
              <p>
              <input type="submit" name="submit" id="submit"
                 value="Submit" />   <input type="reset"
                 name="reset" id="reset" />

              <!-- Hidden field -->
              <input type="hidden" name="referredby" id="referredby" value="Google" />
              </p>

          </td></tr>
          </table>
          </form>
        </body>
      </html>
```

This form will be filled out as shown in Figure 28-1, and the resulting data will be passed to the example script.

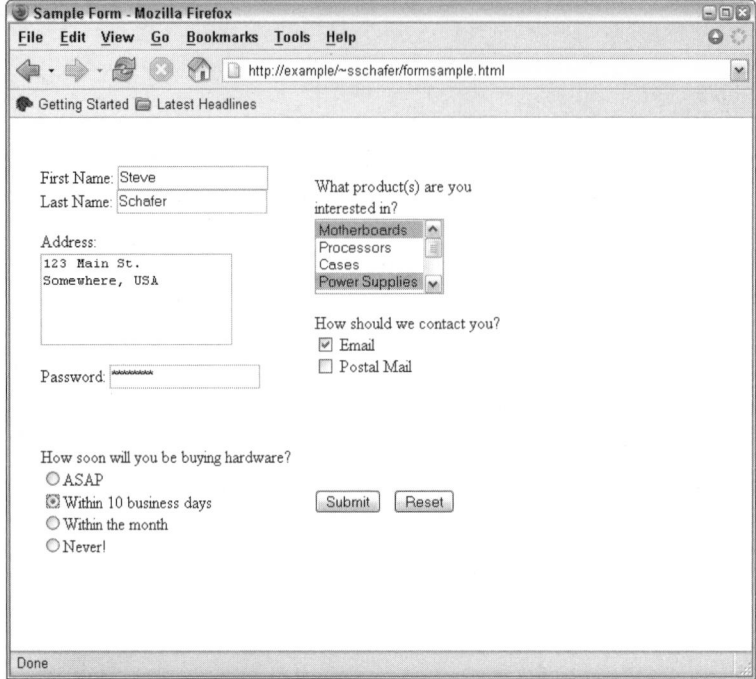

Figure 28-1

Sample MySQL Data

The following listings detail the data contained in the MySQL database used in the MySQL example scripts. The first listing shows the statements used to create the database and tables and to populate the tables with data.

MySQL Database, Tables, and Data

```
CREATE DATABASE mysqlsamp;

USE mysqlsamp;

--
-- Table structure for table 'computers'
--

CREATE TABLE computers (
  comp_id int(5) unsigned zerofill NOT NULL default '00000',
  comp_make varchar(25) default NULL,
  comp_model varchar(10) default NULL,
  comp_cpu char(2) NOT NULL default '',
  comp_speed int(4) NOT NULL default '0',
  comp_mem int(4) NOT NULL default '0',
  comp_HD int(4) NOT NULL default '0',
```

```
    comp_CD enum('CD','DVD','CDRW','CDR','CDRW/DVD') default NULL,
    comp_location varchar(10) default NULL,
    comp_ts timestamp(10) NOT NULL,
    PRIMARY KEY  (comp_id)
) TYPE=MyISAM;


--
-- Dumping data for table 'computers'
--

INSERT INTO computers VALUES
    (02210,'Compumate','A','P3',1600,512,40,'DVD','C124','0000000000');
INSERT INTO computers VALUES
    (01347,'Compumate','A','P3',1600,512,40,'DVD','C033','0000000000');
INSERT INTO computers VALUES
    (06073,'Compumate','A','P3',1600,512,40,'DVD','C224','0000000000');
INSERT INTO computers VALUES
    (09307,'Compumate','A','P3',1600,512,40,'DVD','C224','0000000000');
INSERT INTO computers VALUES
    (01523,'Compumate','A','P3',1600,512,40,'DVD','A125','0000000000');
INSERT INTO computers VALUES
    (07065,'Compumate','B','P3',1000,256,30,'CD','A003','0000000000');
INSERT INTO computers VALUES
    (07185,'Compumate','B','P3',1400,256,30,'CD','A122','0000000000');
INSERT INTO computers VALUES
    (09894,'Compumate','C','P3',1000,128,30,'CD','B022','0000000000');
INSERT INTO computers VALUES
    (09569,'Compumate','C','P3',1000,128,30,'CD','B022','0000000000');
INSERT INTO computers VALUES
    (08036,'Compumate','A','P3',1600,512,40,'DVD','C250','0000000000');
INSERT INTO computers VALUES
    (08057,'Compumate','B','P3',1400,256,30,'DVD','A021','0000000000');
INSERT INTO computers VALUES
    (05654,'Custom','3','C',500,128,30,'CD','A122','0000000000');
INSERT INTO computers VALUES
    (09834,'Custom','1','P3',900,512,60,'CD','C200','0000000000');
INSERT INTO computers VALUES
    (07743,'Custom','1','P3',866,384,60,'CDRW','C200','0000000000');
INSERT INTO computers VALUES
    (02559,'Custom','3','P3',733,256,60,'CDRW','A010','0000000000');
INSERT INTO computers VALUES
    (08316,'Custom','3','P3',733,256,60,'CDRW','B125','0000000000');
INSERT INTO computers VALUES
    (09499,'Custom','1','P3',866,512,60,'CDR','B126','0000000000');
INSERT INTO computers VALUES
    (00946,'Super-puter','XL','P4',2400,1000,180,'CDRW/DVD','LAB05','0000000000');
INSERT INTO computers VALUES
    (04070,'Super-puter','XL','P4',2400,1000,180,'CDRW/DVD','LAB06','0000000000');
INSERT INTO computers VALUES
    (09144,'Super-puter','XL','P4',2400,1000,180,'CDRW/DVD','LAB07','0000000000');
INSERT INTO computers VALUES
    (05212,'Super-puter','SE','P4',2000,512,80,'CDRW/DVD','A300','0000000000');
INSERT INTO computers VALUES
    (03663,'Super-puter','SE','P4',2000,512,80,'CDRW','A310','0000000000');
```

```
INSERT INTO computers VALUES
   (05295,'Super-puter','XL','P4',2400,1000,180,'CDRW/DVD','ITLAB','0000000000');
INSERT INTO computers VALUES
   (04780,'Super-puter','XS','P4',2400,1000,180,'CDRW','LAB01','0000000000');
INSERT INTO computers VALUES
   (05021,'Custom','3','P3',1000,512,0,'CD','ITLAB','0000000000');


--
-- Table structure for table 'keyboards'
--

CREATE TABLE keyboards (
   kbd_id int(5) unsigned zerofill NOT NULL default '00000',
   kbd_type char(3) NOT NULL default 'PS2',
   kbd_model varchar(5) NOT NULL default '104',
   kbd_comp int(5) unsigned zerofill NOT NULL default '00000',
   kbd_ts timestamp(10) NOT NULL,
   PRIMARY KEY  (kbd_id)
) TYPE=MyISAM;


--
-- Dumping data for table 'keyboards'
--


INSERT INTO keyboards VALUES (00684,'USB','102',02210,'0000000000');
INSERT INTO keyboards VALUES (00245,'PS2','102',01347,'0000000000');
INSERT INTO keyboards VALUES (00149,'PS2','104',06073,'0000000000');
INSERT INTO keyboards VALUES (00278,'PS2','102',09307,'0000000000');
INSERT INTO keyboards VALUES (00011,'PS2','102',01523,'0000000000');
INSERT INTO keyboards VALUES (00527,'PS2','102',07065,'0000000000');
INSERT INTO keyboards VALUES (00660,'PS2','102',07185,'0000000000');
INSERT INTO keyboards VALUES (00143,'PS2','102',09894,'0000000000');
INSERT INTO keyboards VALUES (00656,'USB','104MM',09569,'0000000000');
INSERT INTO keyboards VALUES (00854,'PS2','102',08036,'0000000000');
INSERT INTO keyboards VALUES (00007,'PS2','102',08057,'0000000000');
INSERT INTO keyboards VALUES (00643,'PS2','102',05654,'0000000000');
INSERT INTO keyboards VALUES (00129,'USB','102',09834,'0000000000');
INSERT INTO keyboards VALUES (00250,'PS2','102',07743,'0000000000');
INSERT INTO keyboards VALUES (00232,'PS2','102',02559,'0000000000');
INSERT INTO keyboards VALUES (00920,'PS2','104MM',08316,'0000000000');
INSERT INTO keyboards VALUES (00469,'PS2','102',09499,'0000000000');
INSERT INTO keyboards VALUES (00103,'PS2','102',00946,'0000000000');
INSERT INTO keyboards VALUES (00859,'USB','102',04070,'0000000000');
INSERT INTO keyboards VALUES (00976,'PS2','102',09144,'0000000000');
INSERT INTO keyboards VALUES (00500,'PS2','102',05212,'0000000000');
INSERT INTO keyboards VALUES (00598,'PS2','104',03663,'0000000000');
INSERT INTO keyboards VALUES (00967,'USB','104',05295,'0000000000');
INSERT INTO keyboards VALUES (00466,'USB','104',04780,'0000000000');
INSERT INTO keyboards VALUES (00089,'USB','104MM',00000,'0000000000');
INSERT INTO keyboards VALUES (00377,'PS2','102',00000,'0000000000');
INSERT INTO keyboards VALUES (00444,'USB','102',00000,'0000000000');


--
-- Table structure for table 'mice'
--
```

```
CREATE TABLE mice (
  mouse_id int(5) unsigned zerofill NOT NULL default '00000',
  mouse_type char(3) NOT NULL default 'PS2',
  mouse_model varchar(5) NOT NULL default '2BS',
  mouse_comp int(5) unsigned zerofill NOT NULL default '00000',
  mouse_ts timestamp(10) NOT NULL,
  PRIMARY KEY  (mouse_id)
) TYPE=MyISAM;

--
-- Dumping data for table 'mice'
--

INSERT INTO mice VALUES (00400,'USB','2B',02210,'0000000000');
INSERT INTO mice VALUES (00543,'PS2','2BS',01347,'0000000000');
INSERT INTO mice VALUES (00345,'PS2','3B',06073,'0000000000');
INSERT INTO mice VALUES (00961,'USB','2BS',09307,'0000000000');
INSERT INTO mice VALUES (00693,'PS2','2BS',01523,'0000000000');
INSERT INTO mice VALUES (00579,'PS2','2BS',07065,'0000000000');
INSERT INTO mice VALUES (00702,'PS2','2BS',07185,'0000000000');
INSERT INTO mice VALUES (00710,'USB','2B',09894,'0000000000');
INSERT INTO mice VALUES (00558,'PS2','2BS',09569,'0000000000');
INSERT INTO mice VALUES (00769,'PS2','2BS',08036,'0000000000');
INSERT INTO mice VALUES (00303,'PS2','3B',08057,'0000000000');
INSERT INTO mice VALUES (00142,'USB','2BS',05654,'0000000000');
INSERT INTO mice VALUES (00536,'PS2','2BS',09834,'0000000000');
INSERT INTO mice VALUES (00411,'PS2','2BS',07743,'0000000000');
INSERT INTO mice VALUES (00984,'PS2','2BS',02559,'0000000000');
INSERT INTO mice VALUES (00356,'USB','3B',08316,'0000000000');
INSERT INTO mice VALUES (00807,'PS2','2BS',09499,'0000000000');
INSERT INTO mice VALUES (00562,'PS2','2BS',00946,'0000000000');
INSERT INTO mice VALUES (00432,'PS2','2BS',04070,'0000000000');
INSERT INTO mice VALUES (00553,'USB','L2BS',09144,'0000000000');
INSERT INTO mice VALUES (00648,'USB','2BS',05212,'0000000000');
INSERT INTO mice VALUES (00067,'USB','2BS',03663,'0000000000');
INSERT INTO mice VALUES (00944,'USB','3B',05295,'0000000000');
INSERT INTO mice VALUES (00670,'PS2','3B',04780,'0000000000');
INSERT INTO mice VALUES (00444,'PS2','2BS',00000,'0000000000');
INSERT INTO mice VALUES (00324,'USB','3B',00000,'0000000000');

--
-- Table structure for table 'mice_type'
--

CREATE TABLE mice_type (
  mouse_type_id int(5) unsigned zerofill NOT NULL auto_increment,
  mouse_interface enum('USB','PS2') default 'PS2',
  mouse_buttons tinyint(2) NOT NULL default '2',
  mouse_scroll enum('Y','N') default 'Y',
  mouse_manufacture varchar(20) NOT NULL default '',
  PRIMARY KEY  (mouse_type_id)
) TYPE=MyISAM;
```

```
--
-- Dumping data for table 'mice_type'
--


--
-- Table structure for table 'monitors'
--

CREATE TABLE monitors (
  mon_id int(5) unsigned zerofill NOT NULL default '00000',
  mon_size tinyint(2) NOT NULL default '0',
  mon_features varchar(40) default NULL,
  mon_comp int(5) unsigned zerofill NOT NULL default '00000',
  mon_ts timestamp(10) NOT NULL,
  PRIMARY KEY  (mon_id)
) TYPE=MyISAM;


--
-- Dumping data for table 'monitors'
--

INSERT INTO monitors VALUES (00461,17,'',02210,'0000000000');
INSERT INTO monitors VALUES (00436,17,'',01347,'0000000000');
INSERT INTO monitors VALUES (00499,15,'',06073,'0000000000');
INSERT INTO monitors VALUES (00656,17,'LCD',09307,'0000000000');
INSERT INTO monitors VALUES (00236,20,'DUAL',01523,'0000000000');
INSERT INTO monitors VALUES (00428,17,'',07065,'0000000000');
INSERT INTO monitors VALUES (00007,20,'',07185,'0000000000');
INSERT INTO monitors VALUES (00603,15,'',09894,'0000000000');
INSERT INTO monitors VALUES (00184,20,'',09569,'0000000000');
INSERT INTO monitors VALUES (00239,21,'',08036,'0000000000');
INSERT INTO monitors VALUES (00255,17,'',08057,'0000000000');
INSERT INTO monitors VALUES (00851,15,'LCD',05654,'0000000000');
INSERT INTO monitors VALUES (00417,20,'DUAL',09834,'0000000000');
INSERT INTO monitors VALUES (00887,17,'',07743,'0000000000');
INSERT INTO monitors VALUES (00578,17,'',02559,'0000000000');
INSERT INTO monitors VALUES (00355,15,'',08316,'0000000000');
INSERT INTO monitors VALUES (00214,17,'',09499,'0000000000');
INSERT INTO monitors VALUES (00795,20,'',00946,'0000000000');
INSERT INTO monitors VALUES (00448,21,'',04070,'0000000000');
INSERT INTO monitors VALUES (00058,20,'DUAL',09144,'0000000000');
INSERT INTO monitors VALUES (00167,22,'',05212,'0000000000');
INSERT INTO monitors VALUES (00741,21,'',03663,'0000000000');
INSERT INTO monitors VALUES (00605,22,'',05295,'0000000000');
INSERT INTO monitors VALUES (00300,19,'LCD',04780,'0000000000');
INSERT INTO monitors VALUES (00450,19,'LCD',00000,'0000000000');
```

The following listing shows the permission statement used to create the sample user in the MySQL examples:

User and Permission Setup

```
grant all on mysqlsamp.* to webuser@localhost identified by "password99";
flush privileges;
```

Perl Examples

This section demonstrates a few examples of how Perl can be used for CGI. The examples show how you can leverage Perl's capabilities and add-on modules to deliver dynamic document content.

Date and Time Handling

When using Perl you have a ton of modules and libraries available to extend the language to interact with a variety of technologies and to perform a variety of calculations. One important and often-used segment of the libraries is time and date handling. This example shows a simple use of the extensive `Time::Piece` library.

For a more dynamic calendar example, see Example 3 in this chapter.

Example 1: A Simple Calendar

Source — Perl-Example01.cgi

```perl
#!/usr/bin/perl

# Use the Time::Piece library for our date/time needs
use Time::Piece;

# Set up the variables (today, month, year)
#   today = m/d/y
sub setvars() {

  # Default is today
  my $day = localtime->mday();
  my $month = localtime->mon();
  my $year = localtime->year();
  my $today = $month."/".$day."/".$year;

  # Return vars in a hash
  my %t = ("today" => $today,
           "month" => $month,
           "year" => $year);
  return %t;
}  # End setvars()


# Do the document header
sub docheader($$) {

  my $month = shift;
  my $year = shift;

my $t = Time::Piece->strptime($month,"%m");
$month_text = $t->strftime("%B");
```

```
# Print the document header (up to first date row)
print <<HTML;
Content-type: text/html

<!DOCTYPE html PUBLIC "-//W3C//DTD XHTML 1.0//EN"
   "http://www.w3.org/TR/xhtml11/DTD/xhtml1.dtd">
<html>
<head>
  <title>Calendar - $month_text $year</title>
  <style type="text/css">
    tr.weekdays td { width: 100px;
                      text-align: center;
                    }
    tr.week td { width: 100px;
                  height: 100px;
                  color: black;  }
  </style>
</head>
<body>
<table border="1">

<!-- Controls and calendar title (month) -->
<tr>
  <td colspan="7" align="center">
    <strong>
      $month_text $year
    </strong>
  </td>
</tr>

<!-- Day of week header row -->
<tr class="weekdays">
  <th>Sunday</th>
  <th>Monday</th>
  <th>Tuesday</th>
  <th>Wednesday</th>
  <th>Thursday</th>
  <th>Friday</th>
  <th>Saturday</th>
</tr>

<!-- Calendar (days) start here -->

HTML

}  # End docheader()


# Do the document footer (close tags, end doc)
sub docfooter() {

print <<HTML;
<!-- Close all open tags, end document -->
```

```perl
</table>
</body>
</html>

HTML

} # End docfooter()


# Print an empty day (cell)
sub emptyday() {

print <<HTML;
  <td align="right" valign="top"> </td>

HTML

} # End emptyday()


# Print a day cell
sub day($$$$) {

  my $today = shift;
  my $month = shift;
  my $day = shift;
  my $year = shift;
  my $font = "";

  my $curday = $month."/".$day."/".$year;
  if ( $curday eq $today ) {
    $font = " style=\"color: red;\"";
  }

print <<HTML;
  <td align="right" valign="top" $font>$day</td>

HTML

} # End day()


# Open or close a row
sub weekrow($) {

  my $cmd = shift;

  if ($cmd eq "open") {
    print "<tr class=\"week\">\n";
  }
  if ($cmd eq "close") {
      print "</tr>\n";
  }
```

```
}   # End weekrow()


# Main program body
sub main() {

  # Set the date vars
  my %vars = setvars();
  my $today = $vars{'today'};
  my $month = $vars{'month'};
  my $year = $vars{'year'};

  # Do the header and open first row
  docheader($month,$year);
  weekrow("open");

  # Set up first weekday and 1st day (m/1/y)
  my $t = Time::Piece->strptime($month."/1/".$year,
                                "%m/%d/%Y");

  my $first_weekday = $t->strftime("%w") + 1;
  my $day = 1;

  # Print empty days up to the first weekday of month
  for ($weekday = 1; $weekday < $first_weekday; $weekday++) {
    emptyday();
  }

  my $last_day = $t->month_last_day;

  # Do rest of month while we have a valid date
  while ($day <= $last_day) {
    # If SUN, open the row
    if ($weekday == 1) {
      weekrow("open");
    }
    # Print day and increment
    day($today,$month,$day,$year);
    $weekday++;
    $day++;
    # If SAT, close row reset weekday
    if ($weekday > 7) {
      weekrow("close");
      $weekday = 1;
    }
  }


  # Close current week
  while ($weekday != 1 && $weekday <= 7) {
    emptyday();
    $weekday++;
  }
```

```
    # Close document
    docfooter();

} # End main();


# Kick it all off
main();
```

Output

This script outputs an XHTML table similar to that shown in Figure 28-2.

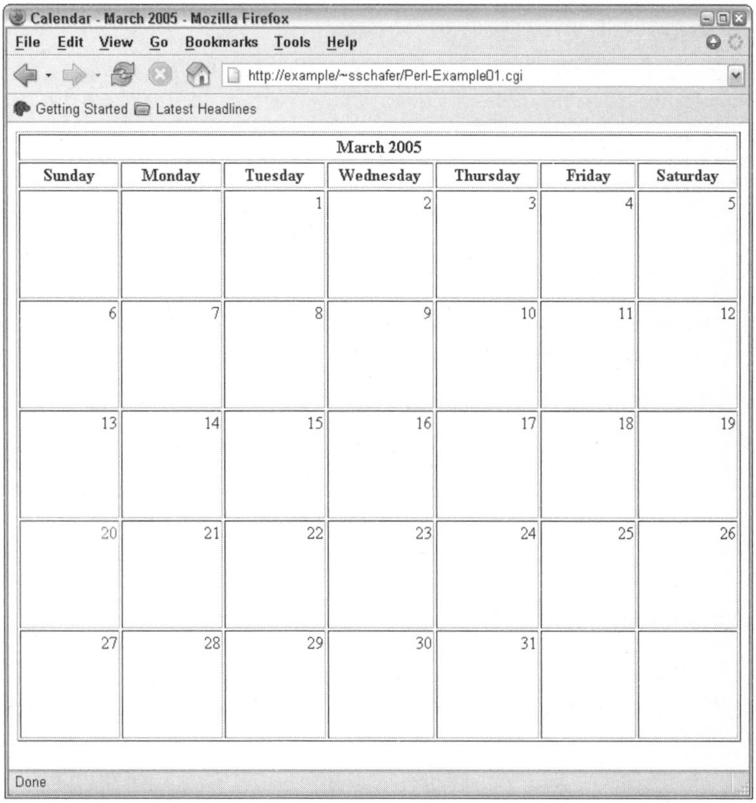

Figure 28-2

How It Works

This script uses the date and time functions in the `Time::Piece` library (found on CPAN) to determine these parameters about the current month:

❑ First weekday of the month

❑ Current day (for highlighting purposes)

❑ Number of days in the month

Using those parameters, the script can create a calendar for any month — past, present, or future. The rest of the script is fairly straightforward:

1. Output the document header (Content-type, doctype, head tags, and so on).

2. Determine the first weekday of the month.

3. Output blank cells for weekdays up to the first day of the month.

4. Output cells for each day of the month.

5. Close the month by outputting blank cells to fill the last week.

Improving the Script

This script simply shows how Perl can be extended with libraries to perform complex calculations such as functions on dates and times. Besides changing the format of the output (for example, a smaller table for a smaller calendar), the script could do many other time/date functions, as reflected in the following list:

❑ Thumbnail calendars for the months on either side of the current month could be displayed in the calendar header, much like paper calendars.

❑ Multiple months could be assembled into a longer calendar.

❑ The calendar functions could be applied to other Web-enabled features.

❑ The calendar could be extended to be dynamic, able to output any month. An example of a more dynamic calendar appears in Example 3 in this chapter.

Handling Form Data

The most popular use for CGI is probably XHTML form handling (that is, taking data from an XHTML form and doing something useful with the submitted data). This example shows how to decipher data passed to a Perl script. This script simply lists the GET and POST data passed to it.

Example 2: Deciphering and Dealing with Form-Submitted Data

Source — Perl-Example02.cgi

```
#!/usr/bin/perl

# Use CGI methods to get parameters
use CGI;
my $cgi = CGI->new();
```

```perl
my %params = $cgi->Vars;


# Print document header
print "Content-type: text/html\n\n";
print <<HTML;
<!DOCTYPE html PUBLIC "-//W3C//DTD XHTML 1.0 Strict//EN"
   "http://www.w3.org/TR/xhtml1/DTD/xhtml1-strict.dtd">
<html>
<head>
  <title>POST/GET Variable Dump</title>
</head>
<body>

HTML


# If there is POST data, dump it
#   else display "No Data"
if ($ENV{REQUEST_METHOD} eq "POST" ) {

  # Header for data
  print "<h2>POST Data</h2>\n";
  print "<pre>\n<p>\n";

  # Walk through data
  foreach my $key (sort keys %params) {

    # If multiple values, display as such
    my $size = @{$cgi->{$key}};
    if ($size > 1) {
      my $count = 0;
      for (@{$cgi->{$key}}) {
        print "  $key\[$count\] => ", $cgi->{$key}[$count], "\n";
        $count++;
      }
    } else {
      # Display single value
      print "  $key => $cgi->{$key}[0]", "\n";
    }
    print "\n";
  }
  print "</pre>\n</p>\n";
} else {
  print "<h2>No POST Data</h2>\n";
}

# If there is GET data, dump it
#   else display "No Data"
if ($ENV{REQUEST_METHOD} eq "GET" ) {

  # Header for data
```

```
      print "<h2>GET Data</h2>\n";
      print "<pre>\n<p>\n";

      # Walk through data
      foreach my $key (sort keys %params) {

      # If multiple values, display as such
        my $size = @{$cgi->{$key}};
        if ($size > 1) {
          my $count = 0;
          for (@{$cgi->{$key}}) {
            print "  $key\[$count\] => ", $cgi->{$key}[$count], "\n";
            $count++;
          }
        } else {
          # Display single value
          print "  $key => $cgi->{$key}[0]", "\n";
        }
        print "\n";
      }
      print "</pre>\n</p>\n";
    } else {
      print "<h2>No GET Data</h2>\n";
    }


    # Close document
    print "</body>\n</html>";
```

Output

This script, when passed the example data outlined in the "Sample Data" section earlier in this chapter, displays the document shown in Figure 28-3.

How It Works

This script uses the CGI.pm module to access the HTTP information passed to the script. The Request-Method header (accessed by the $ENV{REQUEST_METHOD} variable) contains the method used to send the data to the script (GET or POST), while the param() method is used to return the data itself. If the data contains multiple values (such as from a select form element), each value is displayed.

Improving the Script

This script simply outputs the form data it is given; it doesn't do anything useful with the data. However, you can combine these methods to access form data with other CGI functionality (accessing databases, for example).

*This script can be used to troubleshoot XHTML form data. Simply specify it as the form handler (in the **action** property of the **form** tag).*

Figure 28-3

Using Form Data

The preceding example showed how to parse the data passed to the script via HTTP. This example builds on that concept and Example 1 to create a dynamic calendar—a calendar with controls to move the month displayed forward and backward.

Example 3: Creating a Dynamic Calendar

Source — Perl-Example03.cgi

```perl
#!/usr/bin/perl

use Time::Piece;
use CGI;

# Set up the variables (today, month, year)
#   today = m/d/y
sub setvars() {
```

```
  # Default is today
  my $day = localtime->mday();
  my $month = localtime->mon();
  my $year = localtime->year();
  my $today = $month."/".$day."/".$year;

  my $cgi = CGI->new();
  my %params = $cgi->Vars;
  my $cmd = 0;

  if (exists($params{month})) {
    $month = $params{month};
  }
  if (exists($params{year})) {
    $year = $params{year};
  }
  if (exists($params{next})) {
    $cmd = 1;
  }
  if (exists($params{prev})) {
    $cmd = -1;
  }

  if ($cmd != 0) {
    $month += $cmd;
    # Adjust month over or underrun
    if ($month >= 13) {
      $month = 1;
      $year += 1;
    } else {
      if ($month <= 0) {
        $month = 12;
        $year -= 1;
      }
    }
  }

  # Return vars in a hash
  my %t = ("today" => $today,
           "month" => $month,
           "year" => $year);
  return %t;
}  # End setvars()


# Do the document header
sub docheader($$) {

  my $month = shift;
  my $year = shift;

my $t = Time::Piece->strptime($month,"%m");
$month_text = $t->strftime("%B");
```

```
# Print the document header (up to first date row)
print <<HTML;
Content-type: text/html

<!DOCTYPE html PUBLIC "-//W3C//DTD XHTML 1.0//EN"
   "http://www.w3.org/TR/xhtml11/DTD/xhtml1.dtd">
<html>
<head>
  <title>Calendar - $month_text $year</title>
  <style type="text/css">
    tr.weekdays td { width: 100px;
                     text-align: center;
                   }
    tr.week td { width: 100px;
                 height: 100px;
                 color: black;  }
  </style>
</head>
<body>
<form action="$this_script" method="post">
<table border="1">

<!-- Controls and calendar title (month) -->
<tr>
  <td colspan="1" align="left">
    <input type="submit" name="prev" value="&lt;&lt;" />
  </td>
  <td colspan="5" align="center">
    <strong>
      $month_text $year
    </strong>
    <input type="hidden" name="month" value="$month" />
    <input type="hidden" name="year" value="$year" />
  </td>
  <td colspan="1" align="right">
    <input type="submit" name="next" value="&gt;&gt;" />
  </td>
</tr>

<!-- Day of week header row -->
<tr class="weekdays">
  <th>Sunday</th>
  <th>Monday</th>
  <th>Tuesday</th>
  <th>Wednesday</th>
  <th>Thursday</th>
  <th>Friday</th>
  <th>Saturday</th>
</tr>

<!-- Calendar (days) start here -->

HTML
```

```perl
}   # End docheader()


# Do the document footer (close tags, end doc)
sub docfooter() {

print <<HTML;
<!-- Close all open tags, end document -->
</table>
</form>
</body>
</html>

HTML

} # End docfooter()


# Print an empty day (cell)
sub emptyday() {

print <<HTML;
  <td align="right" valign="top"> </td>

HTML

} # End emptyday()


# Print a day cell
sub day($$$$) {

  my $today = shift;
  my $month = shift;
  my $day = shift;
  my $year = shift;
  my $font = "";

  my $curday = $month."/".$day."/".$year;
  if ( $curday eq $today ) {
    $font = " style=\"color: red;\"";
  }

print <<HTML;
  <td align="right" valign="top" $font>$day</td>

HTML

} # End day()


# Open or close a row
sub weekrow($) {
```

```perl
  my $cmd = shift;

  if ($cmd eq "open") {
    print "<tr class=\"week\">\n";
  }
  if ($cmd eq "close") {
      print "</tr>\n";
  }

}  # End weekrow()


# Main program body
sub main() {

  # Set the date vars
  my %vars = setvars();
  my $today = $vars{'today'};
  my $month = $vars{'month'};
  my $year = $vars{'year'};

  # Do the header and open first row
  docheader($month,$year);
  weekrow("open");

  # Set up first weekday and 1st day (m/1/y)
  my $t = Time::Piece->strptime($month."/1/".$year,
                                "%m/%d/%Y");

  my $first_weekday = $t->strftime("%w") + 1;
  my $day = 1;

  # Print empty days up to the first weekday of month
  for ($weekday = 1; $weekday < $first_weekday; $weekday++) {
    emptyday();
  }

  my $last_day = $t->month_last_day;

  # Do rest of month while we have a valid date
  while ($day <= $last_day) {
    # If SUN, open the row
    if ($weekday == 1) {
      weekrow("open");
    }
    # Print day and increment
    day($today,$month,$day,$year);
    $weekday++;
    $day++;
    # If SAT, close row reset weekday
    if ($weekday > 7) {
      weekrow("close");
      $weekday = 1;
    }
```

```
  }

  # Close current week
  while ($weekday != 1 && $weekday <= 7) {
    emptyday();
    $weekday++;
  }

  # Close document
  docfooter();

} # End main();


# Kick it all off
main();
```

Output

This script results in a document that displays a monthly calendar, as shown in Figure 28-4.

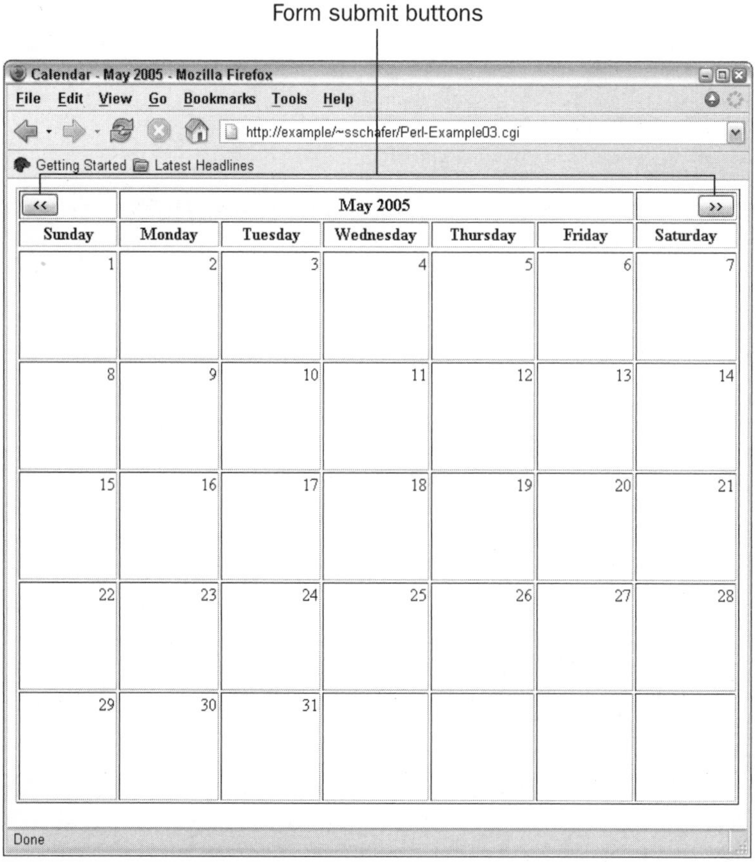

Figure 28-4

How It Works

This script utilizes the same concepts as in Example 2, earlier in this chapter, to parse the data provided via HTTP. The hidden fields `month` and `year` tell the script which month was displayed in the last run. The user clicking the `prev` or `next` submit button tells the script to subtract or add a month to display the month currently called for.

Once the month and year are determined, the script uses the same logic as shown in Example 1 to display the month, embedding the new month and year in the appropriate hidden fields.

This script can also be used to display an arbitrary month by passing the month and year values via GET (embedded in the URL). For example, calling this script with the following URL will result in it displaying the month March 2006: calendar.cgi?month=3&year=2006.

Improving the Script

This script shows a basic example of displaying a dynamic calendar. This capability can be used with a variety of other Perl extensions to interact with other technologies, using the form data to control software and hardware.

Accessing Databases

Another popular Web technique is to extend standard XHTML documents using data from other technologies, such as databases. This example shows how Perl can be used to access a MySQL database.

Example 4: Performing a Query and Reporting Data

Source — Perl-Example04.cgi

```perl
#!/usr/bin/perl

# Use the DBI library with the MySQL DBD
use DBI;
use Mysql;


# Document header (doctype -> body tag)
sub docheader() {

print <<HTML;
Content-type: text/html

<!DOCTYPE html PUBLIC "-//W3C//DTD XHTML 1.0//EN"
    "http://www.w3.org/TR/xhtml11/DTD/xhtml11.dtd">
<html>
<head>
  <title>MySQL Query Result</title>
</head>
<body>
```

```
HTML

} # End docheader()


# Connect the DB with the given creds
sub connectDB($$$$) {

  my $host = shift;
  my $user = shift;
  my $password = shift;
  my $database = shift;

  $dblink = Mysql->connect($host, $database, $user, $password);

  return $dblink;

}   # End connectDB()


# Do the query, return the result
sub doquery($$) {

  my $dblink = shift;
  my $sql_statement = shift;

  $result = $dblink->query($sql_statement);

  return $result;

} # End doquery()


# Output the results of the query in a table
sub dotable($) {

  my $result = shift;

print <<HTML;
<table border="1" cellpadding="5">
<tr>

HTML

  my $ttl_rows = $result->affectedrows;
  my @col_names = $result->name;

  for ($i=0; $i <= $ttl_rows - 1; $i++) {
    print "  <th>".$col_names[$i]."</th>\n";
  }

  print "</tr>\n";
```

```
  for ($rows = 1; $rows <= $ttl_rows; $rows++) {
    print "<tr>\n";
    @rowdata = $result->fetchrow;
    foreach $data (@rowdata) {
      print "  <td>".$data."</td>\n";
    }
    print "</tr>\n";
  }

  print "</table>\n";

} # End dotable()


# Document footer (close tags and end document)
sub docfooter() {

print <<HTML;
</body>
</html>

HTML

}  # End docfooter()


sub main() {

  # Set up DB access vars
  my $host = "localhost";
  my $database = "mysqlsamp";
  my $user = "webuser";
  my $password = "password99";

  # Connect the DB
  $link = connectDB("localhost","webuser","password99","mysqlsamp");

# Set up and perform query
$query = <<HTML;
SELECT computers.comp_id as computer_id,
       mice.mouse_model as mouse_model,
       computers.comp_location as location
  FROM computers, mice
  WHERE mice.mouse_type = "USB"
  AND computers.comp_location like "A%"
  AND mice.mouse_comp = computers.comp_id

HTML

  $result = doquery($link,$query);

  # Do document header
  docheader();
```

```
        # Do results in table
        dotable($result);

        # Do document footer
        docfooter();


    }   # End main()


    # Kick it all off
    main();
```

Output

This script produces the document shown in Figure 28-5.

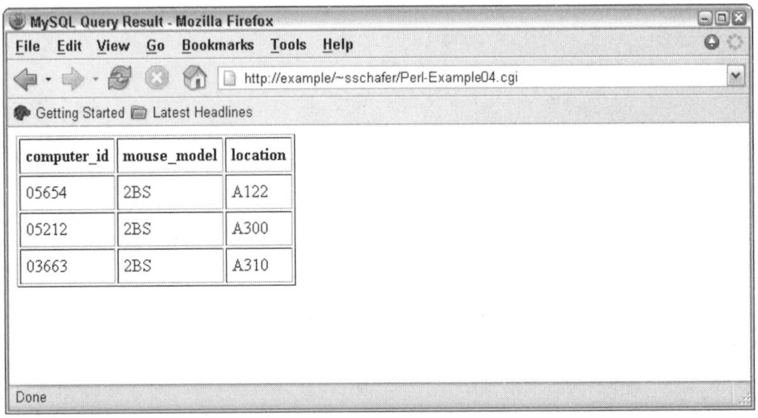

Figure 28-5

How It Works

This script uses the Perl DBI module for basic database access and the MySQL DBD module for specific MySQL connectivity. Using methods built into the modules, the script connects to the database (using `Mysql->connect()`), performs the query (using `$dblink->query()`), and accesses the returned data set (using `$result->affectedrows()`, `$result->name()`, and `$result->fetchrow()`) for output in a document.

Improving the Script

This script shows the most basic use of MySQL connectivity—querying a database and returning the dataset. Similar methods can be used to create more advanced documents, returning the entire content for a document, individual articles for use in a larger document, or other pieces of content for use in documents.

This script is generalized and will work with any database and any query. The resulting table will have a column for each column in the dataset returned by the query and a row for each row returned.

Python Examples

This section demonstrates a few examples of how Python can be used for CGI. The examples show how you can leverage Python's capabilities and add-on modules to deliver dynamic document content.

Date and Time Handling

Data and time handling functions are useful in everyday system administration scripts all the way up to an actual calendar application. Python offers the `time` module, the `datetime` module, and the `calendar` module. The `time` module provides functionality for accessing and formatting time/date strings by calling platform C functions that perform the desired task. The `datetime` module, new in Python 2.3, supplies classes for manipulating dates and times either simply or in a more complex way. Typically, `datetime` functions are considered to be improvements over the older `time` module functionality. The `calendar` module completes the date and time handling functions, giving Python everything it needs for simple and complex date and time operations.

Example 5: A Simple Calendar

Source — Python-Example05.py

```python
#!/usr/bin/python

import os, sys
import cgi
import time
import calendar

from datetime import datetime

#Set up date variables
date = datetime.now().date()
today= date.strftime("%m %Y")
thisyear = date.strftime("%Y")
thismonth = date.strftime("%m")
thisday = date.strftime("%d")

#Write out the document header
def docheader(month, year):
    ''' month is a string with the month number
        year is a string with the year '''

    t = time.strptime(month, '%m')
    month_text = time.strftime('%B', t)

    data = '''Content-type: text/html

<!DOCTYPE html PUBLIC "-//W3C//DTD XHTML 1.0//EN"
    "http://www.w3.org/TR/xhtml11/DTD/xhtml1.dtd">
<html>
<head>
    <title>Calendar - %(month)s %(year)s</title>
```

```
            <style type="text/css">
              tr.weekdays td { width: 100px;
                            text-align: center;
                         }
              tr.week td { width: 100px;
                        height: 100px;
                        color: black; }
            </style>
        </head>
        <body>
        <table border="1">

        <!-- Calendar title (month) -->
        <tr>
            <td colspan="7" align="center">
              <strong>
                %(month)s %(year)s
              </strong>
            </td>
        </tr>

        <!-- Day of week header row -->
        <tr class="weekdays">
            <th>Sunday</th>
            <th>Monday</th>
            <th>Tuesday</th>
            <th>Wednesday</th>
            <th>Thursday</th>
            <th>Friday</th>
            <th>Saturday</th>
        </tr>

        <!-- Calendar (days) start here -->
        ''' %  { 'month':month_text, 'year':year }
        return data

def do_calendar(thismonth, thisyear):

    calendar.setfirstweekday(6) #Set first day of week to Sunday
    month = calendar.monthcalendar(int(thisyear),int(thismonth))
    print docheader(thismonth, thisyear)
    for week in month:
        i=0
        print '<tr class="week">'
        for day in week:
            if int(day) == int(thisday):
                print '   <td align="right" valign="top" style="color: red">'
                print '      <b>',day,'</b>'
            elif int(day):
                print '   <td align="right" valign="top">'
                print '      <b>',day,'</b>'
            else:
                print '   <td align="right" valign="top">'
                print '     </td>'
```

```
        print '</tr>'
    print '</table>'
    print '</body></html>'

do_calendar(thismonth, thisyear)
```

Output

This script outputs an XHTML table similar to that shown in Figure 28-6.

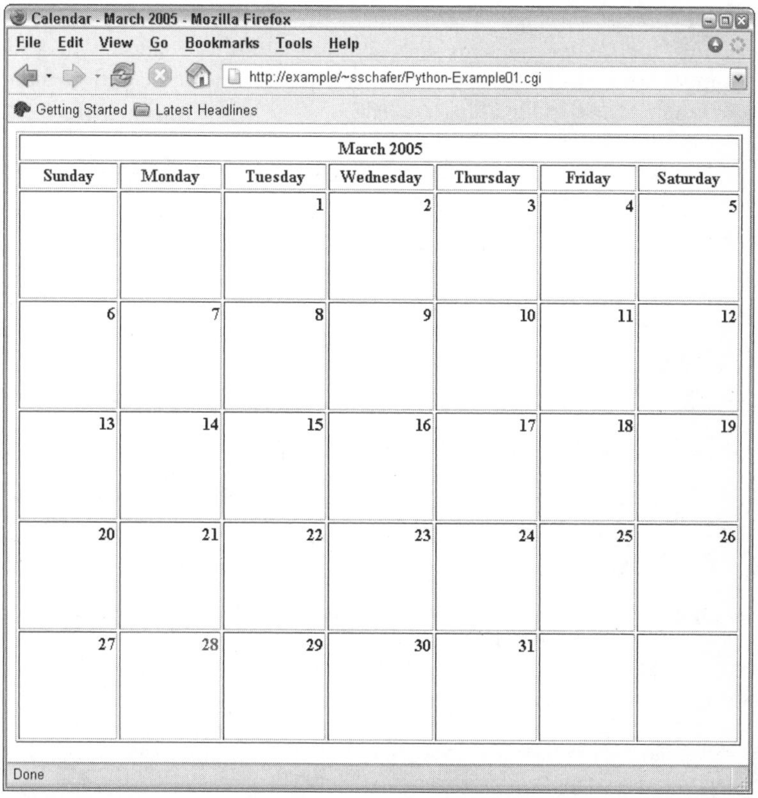

Figure 28-6

How it Works

This script uses the date and time functions in the `datetime` and `calendar` modules to determine these parameters about the current month:

- ❑ First weekday of the month
- ❑ Current year, month, and day (for highlighting purposes)
- ❑ Number of days in the month

Using those parameters, the script can create a calendar for any month — past, present, or future. The rest of the script is fairly straightforward:

1. Output the document header (Content-type, doctype, head tags, and so on).

2. Determine the first weekday of the month.

3. Output calendar data, adding a blank when the date cell should be empty.

Improving the Script

This script simply shows how Python can be extended with modules to perform complex calculations, such as functions on dates and times. Besides changing the format of the output (for example, a smaller table for a smaller calendar), the script could do many other time/date functions, as reflected in the following list:

❑   Thumbnail calendars for the months on either side of the current month could be displayed in the calendar header, much like paper calendars.

❑   Multiple months could be assembled into a longer calendar.

❑   The calendar functions could be applied to other Web-enabled features.

❑   The calendar could be extended to be dynamic, able to output any month. An example of a more dynamic calendar appears in Example 7.

❑   Appointment-keeping capability could be built into the calendar.

❑   Certain days could be different colors to enhance them (such as weekends).

Handling Form Data

The ability to create a form in HTML and gather data from it via a Python script is very commonly used. The Python portion can gather the data and manipulate it in a number of useful ways. Here is a simple example that takes data from an HTML form and outputs it to your screen. The example is written to use both POST and GET data.

Example 6: Deciphering and Dealing with Form-Submitted Data

Source — Python-Example06.py

```
#! /usr/bin/python
import os, sys
import cgi

print '''Content-type: text/html

    <!DOCTYPE html PUBLIC "-//W3C//DTD XHTML 1.0//EN"
    "http://www.w3.org/TR/xhtml11/DTD/xhtml1.dtd">
    <html> <head> <title>MySQL Query Result</title> </head>
```

```
<body>
<table border="1" cellpadding="5"><form>'''


#Initialize found_post_data variable
found_post_data = False
#Check whether there is POST data
if ( os.environ['REQUEST_METHOD'] == 'POST' ):
    form = cgi.FieldStorage()
    #If the form filled in by cgi.FieldStorage isn't empty
    if form.list != []:
        found_post_data = True
        print "<b>POST DATA</b><br><br>"
        #Iterate over all the keys printing the key and it's value
        for key in form:
            datalist = form.getlist(key)
            if len(datalist) == 1:
                print "%s => %s<br>" % (key,datalist[0])
            else:
                for i, item in enumerate(datalist):
                    print "%s[][%d]=> %s<br>" % (key, i, item)

#If there is no post data, say so.
if not found_post_data:
    print "<b>No POST data.</b><br>"

print '<br>'

# Get a dict with all the query parameters
query_params = os.environ.has_key('QUERY_STRING') \
    and cgi.parse_qs(os.environ['QUERY_STRING'], keep_blank_values=True)

if query_params:
    print "<b>GET DATA</b><br><br>"
    for key, value in query_params.iteritems():
        if len(value) == 1:
            print "%s => %s<br>" % (key,value[0])
        else:
            for i, item in enumerate(value):
                print "%s[][%d]=> %s<br>" % (key, i, item)
else:
    #If there is no GET data,say so.
    print "<b>No GET data.</b><br>"


print "</form></table></body></html>"
```

Output

This script, when passed the example data outlined in the "Sample Data" section earlier in this chapter, displays the document shown in Figure 28-7.

Figure 28-7

How It Works

This script uses the CGI module's FieldStorage class to access the HTTP POST data information passed to the script. The Request-Method header (accessed by the os module's environ method) contains the method used to send the POST data to the script, while the FieldStorage class is used to return the data itself. If the data contains multiple values (such as from a select form element), each value is displayed. After obtaining the POST data, we parse the parameters to see if there is any GET data. If we find some, we print it out; otherwise we print that there is none.

Improving the Script

This script simply outputs the form data it is given; it doesn't do anything useful with the data. However, you can combine these methods to access form data with other CGI functionality (accessing databases, for example).

Using Form Data

The static calendar created in Example 5 is only minimally useful due to its static nature. You can also use Python to make it a bit more dynamic, allowing you to specify which month to create the calendar for and to change from one to another.

Example 7: Creating a Dynamic Calendar

Source — Python-Example07.py

```python
#!/usr/bin/python

import cgitb, os, sys
cgitb.enable()
sys.stderr = sys.stdout

import cgi
import time
import calendar

from datetime import date

def decrement_month(month, year):
    prev_month = month - 1
    if prev_month <= 0:
        prev_month = 12
        prev_year = year -1
    else:
        prev_year = year
    return prev_month, prev_year

def increment_month(month, year):
    next_month = month + 1
    if next_month > 12:
        next_month = 1
        next_year = year +1
    else:
        next_year = year
    return next_month, next_year


print '''Content-Type: text/html\n\n

    <!DOCTYPE html PUBLIC "-//W3C//DTD XHTML 1.0//EN"
        "http://www.w3.org/TR/xhtml11/DTD/xhtml1.dtd">'''

form = cgi.FieldStorage()

today = date.today()

if form.has_key('month') and form.has_key('year'):
    # Use month and year from form submission
```

```
        thisyear = int(form.getvalue('year'))
        thismonth = int(form.getvalue('month'))

        if form.has_key('next'):
            thismonth, thisyear = increment_month(thismonth, thisyear)
        elif form.has_key('prev'):
            thismonth, thisyear = decrement_month(thismonth, thisyear)

        if thisyear == today.year and thismonth == today.month:
            thisday = today.day
        else:
            thisday = -1
    else:
        # Use today
        thisyear = today.year
        thismonth = today.month
        thisday = today.day


def docheader(month, year):
    ''' month is an integer month number
        year is an integer year '''

    t = time.strptime(str(month), '%m')
    month_text = time.strftime('%B', t)

    my_name = os.environ['SCRIPT_NAME']

    data = '''<html>
    <head>
        <title>Calendar - %(month_text)s %(year)s</title>
        <style type="text/css">
          tr.weekdays td { width: 100px;
                      text-align: center;
                  }
          tr.week td { width: 100px;
                  height: 100px;
                  color: black; }
        </style>
    </head>

    <body>
    <form method="POST" action="%(my_name)s">
    <table border="1">

    <!-- Controls and calendar title (month) -->
    <tr>
    <td colspan="1" align="left">
    <input type="submit" name="prev" value="&lt;&lt;" />
    <input type="hidden" name="month" value="%(month)d" />
    <input type="hidden" name="year" value="%(year)d" />
    </td>
    <td colspan="5" align="center">
```

```
           <strong>
           %(month_text)s %(year)s
           </strong>
           </td>
           <td colspan="1" align="right">
           <input type="submit" name="next" value="&gt;&gt;" />
           </td>
           </tr>
           </form>

           <!-- Day of week header row -->
           <tr class="weekdays">
              <th>Sunday</th>
              <th>Monday</th>
              <th>Tuesday</th>
              <th>Wednesday</th>
              <th>Thursday</th>
              <th>Friday</th>
              <th>Saturday</th>
           </tr>

           <!-- Calendar (days) start here -->
           ''' %  locals()

           return data

   def do_calendar(thismonth, thisyear, thisday):

           calendar.setfirstweekday(6) #Set first day of week to Sunday
           month = calendar.monthcalendar(thisyear, thismonth)
           print docheader(thismonth, thisyear)
           for week in month:
               i=0
               print '<tr class="week">'
               for day in week:
                   if int(day) == int(thisday):
                           print '    <td align="right" valign="top" style="color: red">'
                           print '      <b>',day,'</b>'
                   elif int(day):
                           print '    <td align="right" valign="top">'
                           print '      <b>',day,'</b>'
                   else:
                           print '    <td align="right" valign="top">'
                           print '       </td>'
               print '</tr>'
           print '</table>'
           print '</body></html>'

   do_calendar(thismonth, thisyear, thisday)
```

Output

This script results in a document that displays a monthly calendar, as shown in Figure 28-8.

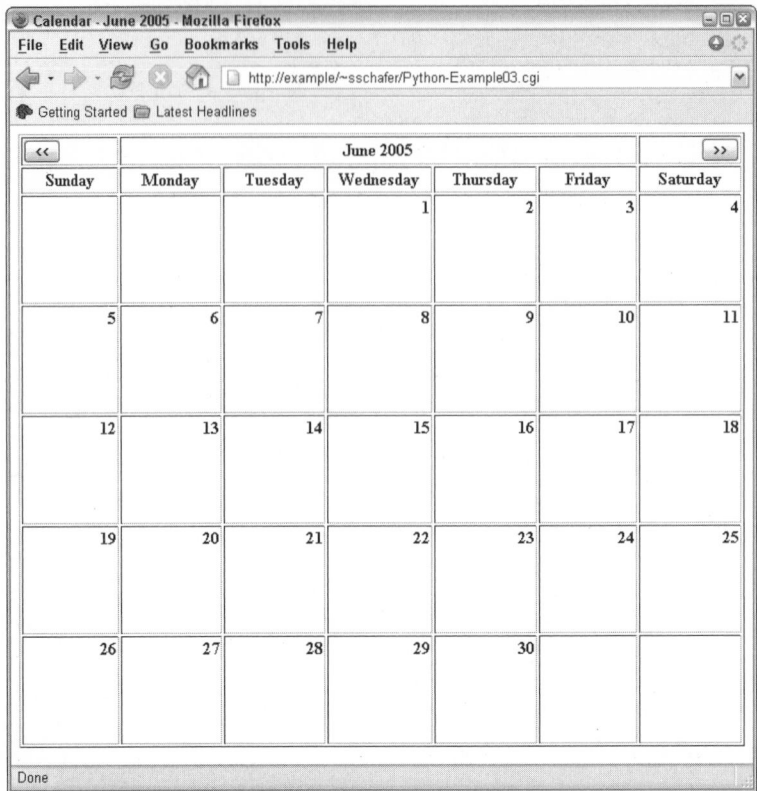

Figure 28-8

How It Works

This script utilizes the same concepts as the previous static example in this section to parse the data provided via HTTP. The hidden fields month and year tell the script which month was displayed in the last run. The user clicking the prev or next submit button tells the script to subtract or add a month to display the month currently called for.

Once the month and year are determined, the script uses the same logic as shown in Example 5 to display the month, embedding the new month and year in the appropriate hidden fields.

This script can also be used to display an arbitrary month by passing the month and year values via GET (embedded in the URL). For example, calling this script with the following URL will result in it displaying the month March 2006: calendar.cgi?month=3&year=2006.

Improving the Script

This script shows a basic example of acting on form data and using it recursively to display a dynamic calendar. This capability can be used with a variety of other Python extensions to interact with other technologies, using the form data to control software and hardware.

Accessing Databases

The ability to access a database in Python is widely used. Think how much more powerful a script that gathers data from a database would be. The next example does just that.

Example 8: Performing a Query and Reporting Data

Source — Python-Example08.py

```python
#!/usr/bin/python

import MySQLdb
import MySQLdb.cursors
import cgi

def printheader():
    print """Content-Type: text/html

    <!DOCTYPE html PUBLIC "-//W3C//DTD XHTML 1.0 Strict//EN"
        "http://www.w3.org/TR/xhtml1/DTD/xhtml1-strict.dtd">
    <html>
      <head>
       <title>MySQL Query Result</title>
      </head>
    <body>\n\n"""

def getdata():
    conn = MySQLdb.Connect(
        host='localhost', user='webuser',
        passwd='password99', db='mysqlsamp',compress=1)
    cursor = conn.cursor()
    cursor.execute("""SELECT computers.comp_id as computer_id,
        mice.mouse_model as mouse_model,
        computers.comp_location as location
        FROM computers, mice
        WHERE mice.mouse_type = "USB"
        AND computers.comp_location like "A%"
        AND mice.mouse_comp = computers.comp_id;""")

    print '''
    <table border="1" cellpadding="5">
    '''
    rows = cursor.fetchall()

    print "<tr>"
    for col in cursor.description:
        print '<td>%s</td>' % col[0]
    print "</tr>"

    for row in rows:
        print "<tr>"
        for cell in row:
            print "<td> %s </td>" % cell
        print "</tr>"
```

467

```
        cursor.close()
        conn.close()

# Document footer (close tags and end document)
def docfooter():

        print '''
        </body>
        </html>

        '''

# End docfooter()

printheader()
getdata()
docfooter()
```

Output

This script produces the document shown in Figure 28-9.

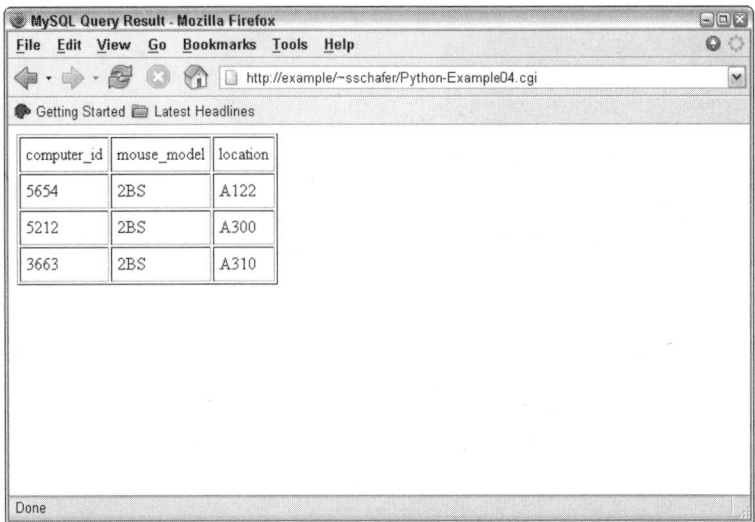

Figure 28-9

How It Works

This script uses the Python MySQLdb module for MySQL database access. Using methods built into the modules, the script connects to the database (using MySQLdb.Connect ()), performs the query (using MySQLdb.cursors), and accesses the returned data set (using cursor.fetchall(), cursor.description, and standard for statements) for output in a document.

Improving the Script

This script is written to adapt its output to whatever data is returned from the MySQL query. It is commonly thought safer to know the database schema and hard code the headers rather than use the ones returned from the cursor. Additionally, this allows you to label the output something less cryptic than the description returned from the cursor. This script can be adapted to use some database other than a MySQL database, if desired (for example, Postgres).

Summary

This chapter demonstrated many popular techniques used with Perl and Python scripts to deliver dynamic content. Although the examples presented here are fairly simplistic by necessity, they provide a solid foundation for utilizing common techniques in CGI and provide building blocks you can use to create more robust applications.

29

PHP Basics

PHP is a relative newcomer to the Web-scripting scene, but it is a revolutionary step for online scripting. PHP was built to deliver markup content (HTML, XHTML, and so on) over the Web. As such, it contains many native features that make that task easier. With a syntax that is easy to understand and use, PHP provides an excellent tool for delivering dynamic content. This chapter introduces PHP.

The History of PHP

PHP was originally conceived and created by Rasmus Lerdorf in 1995. Dubbed Personal Home Page/Forms Interpreter (or PHP/FI), the original scripting language was created to track how many times a particular page was accessed. As the needs for the scripting system grew, so did the language. By 1997, the small, personal scripting project was used by thousands of people worldwide.

In 1997 Andi Gutmans and Zeev Suraski did a complete rewrite of PHP/FI when they found it underpowered for a particular task. This new version included powerful extensibility features that allowed it to interface with many other programs, applications, data structures, and APIs. Version 3.0 was officially released in June 1998. It is estimated that PHP 3.0 was installed on 10 percent of Internet servers at its peak.

Version 4.0 with the Zend engine—a notable performance enhancement named for its creators, Zeev Suraski and Andi Gutmans—was released in May 2000.

PHP is now in version 5 (released in July 2004) and is a much more powerful language, but it provides the same extensibility features.

> *Upon the release of version 3.0 the decision was made to keep the PHP part of the name but drop the FI. The meaning of PHP was also changed to a recursive acronym: PHP: Hypertext Preprocessor.*

PHP provides the following advantages as a scripting language:

❑   A familiar Perl-like structure and syntax

❑   Robust HTTP-handling capabilities

❑   The capability to coexist with raw HTML in the same file

❑   Modules for interacting with other technologies, such as MySQL

However, being a relative newcomer to the Internet, PHP has a few disadvantages as well, the most prevalent being security. Earlier versions of PHP were plagued by several security vulnerabilities. Other scripting languages, such as Perl, have been around longer and have had most of their security bugs ironed out over time. That said, the current version of PHP provides a stable, secure language suitable for almost any Web task. The main purpose for PHP on the Web is delivering dynamic content, utilizing its rich function set and interoperability with other resources.

Like the Apache HTTP server, PHP is a project of the Apache Software Foundation.

Requirements for PHP

PHP can run in two modes: as a module on the server or in CGI mode as an external script (similar to Perl and Python scripts). Running PHP as a CGI script requires the appropriate interpreter line at the beginning of the script on Linux (usually `#!/usr/bin/php`) or associating the php extension with the PHP interpreter on Windows.

Running PHP as a module is a better choice for performance and security reasons but requires the appropriate module being compiled into or loaded on the Web server.

In the case of Apache, you can usually add a line to the Apache configuration file similar to the following to load the PHP module:

```
LoadModule php5_module modules/libphp5.so
```

You must also add an appropriate type to Apache so it knows how to handle PHP files. This can be done with a line in the Apache configuration file similar to the following:

```
AddType application/x-httpd-php .php
```

To test whether PHP is correctly installed on your server, place the following script in your Web server's root directory and access it with a browser:

```
<?php
  phpinfo();
?>
```

The browser should display something similar to that shown in Figure 29-1.

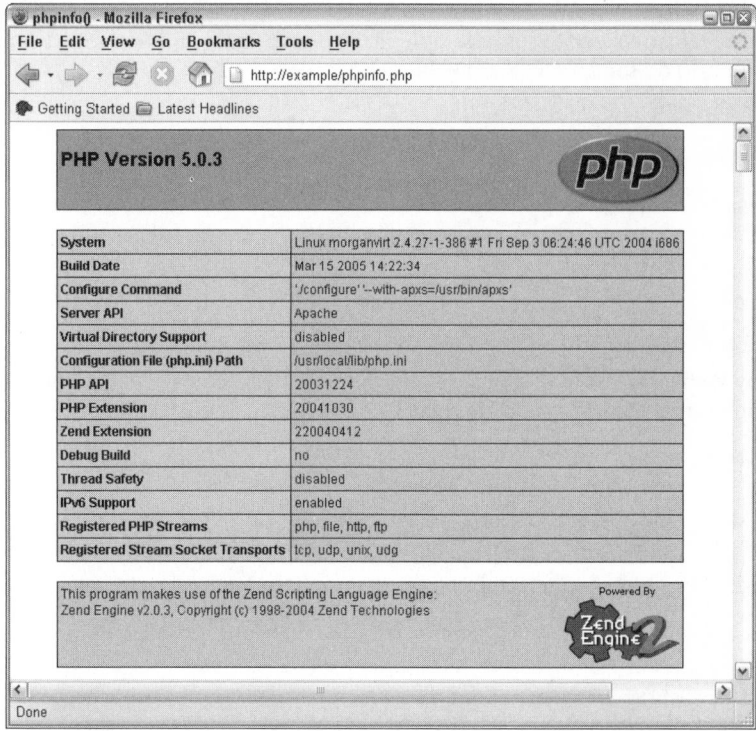

Figure 29-1

PHP Fundamentals

PHP scripts are stored in plaintext format and follow a specific syntax. The following sections introduce you to PHP's scripting structure and syntax.

PHP Beginning and Ending Tags

All PHP code needs to be enclosed within beginning and ending tags. The PHP beginning tag is `<?php` and the ending tag is `?>`. For example, examine the following basic PHP script:

```php
<?php
  print "Hello world. \n";
?>
```

Notice how the first line contains the beginning tag and the last line contains the ending tag. Because of PHP's interpretation of white space (generally ignored), you could just as easily use the following:

```php
<?php  echo "Hello world. \n";  ?>
```

You can turn PHP processing on and off within a script by closing and reopening the PHP tags. For example, if you wanted to embed some complex HTML within a script (or embed simple scripts within XHTML), you could do something like the following:

```
<?php
   [php code here]
?>
   [XHTML code here]
<?php
   [more php code here]
?>...
```

Likewise, you can use PHP only where absolutely necessary in a document:

```
[XHTML code here]
<?php  [minimal php code here]   ?>
[XHTML code here]
```

Command Termination Character and Blocks of Code

PHP uses the semicolon character as the end marker for commands. The language also recognizes braces as the delimiter for blocks of code. For example, consider the following if construct:

```
if (condition) {
   [lines to execute if condition is true]
} else {
   [lines to execute if condition is false]
}
```

The braces in the preceding example delimit the code blocks for the if and else constructs.

PHP's Use of White Space

As with most scripting languages, PHP ignores white space, treating all manner of white space as the equivalent of a single space. As such, you can use white space liberally to improve the legibility of your PHP scripts.

Commenting Code

PHP supports several methods of adding comments to your scripts, including the following:

❑ Any text following a pound sign (#) or a double-slash (//) is treated as a comment and ignored up to the next line break.

❑ Multiline comments can be inserted between /* and */ tags. This is useful when using large blocks of text in comments.

PHP Variables

Unlike Perl, in PHP you need to prefix variables with a dollar sign. Variable names can be any length and contain numbers, letters, or underscores. However, variable names must start with a letter or an underscore — they cannot start with a number. Examples of valid variables include the following:

```
$name
$_code_ptr
$first_and_last_name
$SubTotal
$log99
```

You can use variables to store text, integers, floating-point values, objects, resources, or arrays of other variables. Because PHP variables are untyped, you can store any type of data in any variable. You can even store multiple types of data in the variable arrays. For example, any of the following values can be stored in a variable:

```
"Amy Libler"  (text)
123  (integer)
49.95  (floating point)
"$99.95"  (text, due to non-number character "$")
```

PHP includes a multitude of built-in functions to determine the type of a particular variable and to transfer a variable's value from one type to another.

PHP supports the following data types:

- ❑ **Booleans** — True or False (case insensitive).
- ❑ **Integers** — Such as 0, 1, 2, -5, and so on.
- ❑ **Floating-point numbers** — The maximum size of a floating-point type in PHP is platform-dependent (a maximum of ~1.8e308 with a precision of roughly 14 decimal digits is common).
- ❑ **Strings** — PHP supports single-quoted, double-quoted, and heredoc strings (long strings delimited by special characters, as shown in the example in the next section).
- ❑ **Arrays** — PHP supports arrays of all and multiple data types. All arrays in PHP are ordered maps and can be used as traditional (numerical index) arrays, lists, or hashes.
- ❑ **Objects** — Up until version 5.0, PHP object support was relatively weak. PHP version 5 included more robust object handling.
- ❑ **Resource** — PHP uses resource variables to reference external resources (files, and so on).

A Sample PHP Script

It usually helps to see a practical example to get a grip on a new language. Therefore, this section demonstrates outputting a document with the current date embedded in the document.

Example: A Simple PHP Script

This example creates a simple document with the current date and time embedded in a header.

Source

```php
<?php

// Print document header  (using heredoc syntax)
print <<<HTML
<!DOCTYPE html PUBLIC "-//W3C//DTD XHTML 1.0 Strict//EN"
   "http://www.w3.org/TR/xhtml1/DTD/xhtml1-strict.dtd">
<html>
  <head>
    <title>Sample PHP Script</title>
  </head>
<body>
  <p>

HTML;

// Assemble the date in format:
//   Weekday, Month DD, YYYY
$curdate = date("l, F j, Y");
print "     <h1>$curdate</h1>\n";

// Close the html document
print <<<HTML
  </p>
</body>
</html>

HTML;

?>
```

Output

This script renders a simple document in the user agent, as shown in Figure 29-2.

This example used PHP to output the entire document for example purposes. It could easily have been entirely XHTML except for the section that determines the date and embeds it in the header:

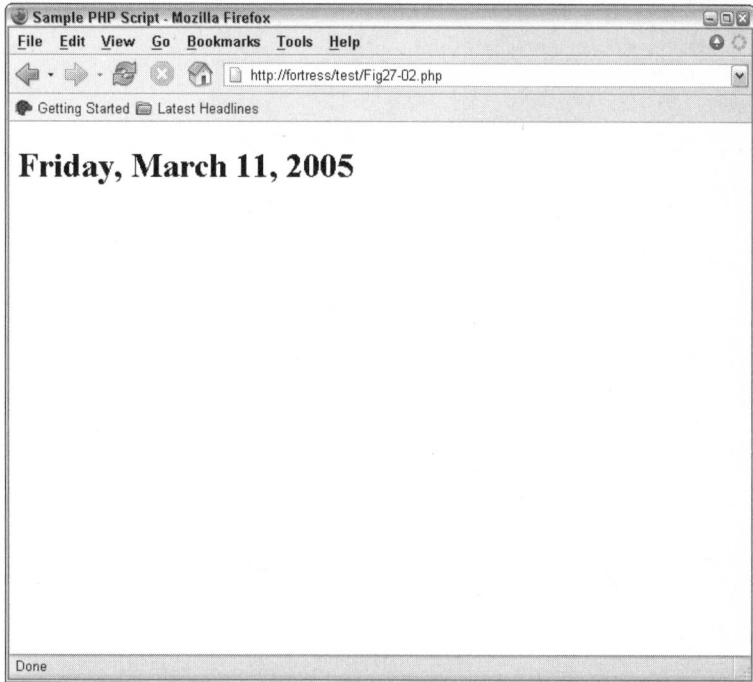

Figure 29-2

```
<!DOCTYPE html PUBLIC "-//W3C//DTD XHTML 1.0 Strict//EN"
   "http://www.w3.org/TR/xhtml1/DTD/xhtml1-strict.dtd">
<html>
  <head>
    <title>Sample PHP Script</title>
  </head>
<body>
  <p>
<?php
  $curdate = date("l, F j, Y");
  print "    <h1>$curdate</h1>\n";
?>
  </p>
</body>
</html>
```

Summary

This chapter introduced PHP, its history, advantages, basic syntax, and methods for delivering content. PHP coverage continues in the next two chapters: Chapter 30 provides in-depth coverage of PHP's features, and Chapter 31 contains several useful examples.

The PHP Language

Chapter 29 introduced you to the PHP scripting language and gave you a preview of its complexity and power. This chapter delves deeper into PHP and gives you specifics on the various language constructs at your disposal when using PHP.

Calculations and Operators

PHP supports the usual collection of standard operators, as shown in the following table:

PHP Arithmetic Operators

Operator	Use
+	Addition
-	Subtraction
*	Multiplication
/	Division
%	Modulus
++	Increment
--	Decrement

PHP supports C-style pre and post types of increment and decrement operators. The pre operators (designated by placing the operators prior to the variable, for example, --$a) perform the operation and then return the value of the variable. The post operators (designated by placing the operators after the variable, for example, $a--) return the value of the variable and then perform the operation.

PHP Assignment Operators

Operator	Use
=	Assignment
+=	Increment assignment
-=	Decrement assignment
*=	Multiplication assignment
/=	Division assignment
%=	Modulus assignment

PHP Comparison Operators

Operator	Use
==	Is equal to
===	Exactly identical, in value and type
!=	Is not equal to
!==	Is not identical
>	Is greater than
<	Is less than
>=	Is greater than or equal to
<=	Is less than or equal to

PHP Logical Operators

Operator	Use
&& or and	And
|| or or	Or
!	Not
xor	Xor

PHP Bitwise Operators

Operator	Use
&	And
|	Or

Operator	Use
^	Xor
~	Not
<<	Left shift
>>	Right shift

PHP Miscellaneous Operators

Operator	Use
? :	Condition operator

PHP String Operators

Operator	Use
.	Concatenation
. =	Concatenation assignment

PHP Array Operators

Operator	Use
+	Union

PHP String Tokens

Token	Character
\b	Backspace
\t	Horizontal tab
\n	Line feed
\v	Vertical tab
\f	Form teed
\r	Carriage return
\"	Double-quote
\'	Single-quote
\\	Backslash

Control Structures

Like many other languages, PHP supports many different control structures that can be used to execute particular blocks of code based on decisions or repeat blocks of code while a particular condition is true. The following sections cover the various control structures available in PHP.

Do-while

The do-while loop executes one or more lines of code as long as a specified condition remains true. This structure has the following format:

```
do {
    // statement(s) to execute
} while (<expression>);
```

Due to the expression being evaluated at the end of the structure, statement(s) in a do-while loop are executed at least once. The following example will loop a total of 20 times — incrementing the variable $x each time until $x reaches the value 20:

```
$x = 0;
do {
    $x++;   // increment x
} while ($x < 20);
```

While

The while loop executes one or more lines of code while a specified expression remains true. The while loop has the following syntax:

```
while (<expression>) {
    // statement(s) to execute
}
```

Because the <expression> is evaluated at the beginning of the loop, the statement(s) will not be executed if the <expression> is false at the beginning of the loop. For example, the following loop will execute 20 times, each iteration of the loop incrementing $x until it reaches 20:

```
$x = 1;
while ($x <= 20) {   // do until $x = 20 (will not execute when x = 21)
    $x++;   // increment $x
}
```

For

The for loop executes statement(s) a specific number of times, governed by two expressions and a condition:

```
for (<initial_value>; <condition>; <loop_expression>) {
    // statement(s) to execute
}
```

The `<initial_value>` expression is evaluated at the beginning of the loop; this event occurs only before the first iteration of the loop. The `<condition>` is evaluated at the beginning of *each* loop iteration: If the condition returns false, the current iteration is executed, and if the condition returns true, the loop exits and the script execution continues after the loop's block. At the end of each loop iteration, the `<loop_expression>` is evaluated.

Although their usage can vary, for loops are generally used to step through a range of values via a specified increment. For example, the following example begins with the variable $x equal to 1 and exits when $x equals 20; each loop iteration increments $x by 1:

```
for ($x = 1; $x <= 20; $x++ ) {     //  for $x = 1 to 20
  //statement(s) to execute
}
```

Note that the `<loop_expression>` is not limited to an increment expression; the expression should advance the appropriate values toward the exit condition but can be any valid expression. For example, consider the two following snippets of code:

```
for ($x = 20; $x >= 1; $x--) {  // for $x = 20 to 1
  // statement(s) to execute
}
```

```
for ($x = 2; $x <= 40; $x+=2) {  // for $x = 2 to 40, by 2 (even numbers only)
  // statement(s) to execute
}
```

Foreach

The PHP foreach construct is much like the Perl foreach, allowing an easy way to iterate over arrays. The foreach construct has the following two forms of syntax:

```
// For non-associative arrays
foreach (<array_expression> as $value) {
  // statement(s) to execute
}

// For associative arrays
foreach (<array_expression> as $key => $value) {
  // statement(s) to execute
}
```

The first form of the foreach construct allows you to move through a nonassociative array. For example, the following code will print all the elements in the $names array:

```
$names = array ("Terri","Amy","Steve","Jeff","Rose","Ben");
foreach ($names as $value) {
  print $value . "\n";
}
```

The second form of the foreach construct allows you to move through associative arrays, accessing the keys and values of that array. For example, consider the following code, which accesses and prints the keys and values of the associative array $parts:

```
$parts = array (
   "X37-22"  =>  "cogwheel",
   "T33-99"  =>  "capacitor",
   "L45-09"  =>  "large lever",
   "Y66-7B"  =>  "updated LED");
foreach ($names as $key => $value) {
   print "Key: " . $key . "   Value: ". $value . "\n";
}
```

If Else

Predictably, PHP has a robust if/else construct. The if and if/else constructs execute a block of code depending on the evaluation (true or false) of an expression. The if construct has the following syntax:

```
if (<expression>) {
   // statement(s) to execute if expression is true
} [ else {
   // statement(s) to execute if expression is false
} ]
```

For example, the following code tests whether the value stored in $i is the number 2:

```
if ($i == 2) {
   // statement(s) to execute if the value in $i is 2
}
```

The following code will execute one block of code if the value of $i is an odd number, another block of code if the value of $i is an even number:

```
if (($i % 2) != 0) {
   // statement(s) to execute if $i is odd
} else {
   // statement(s) to execute if $i is even
}
```

You can also use more complicated expressions in an if construct, as in the following example:

```
if (($i = 2) && ($t = 31) && ($name = "Panama")) {
   // statement(s) to execute if all three conditions are true
}
```

In addition, you can create constructs in PHP by nesting if statements within one another, as shown in the following code:

```
if (($i % 2) != 0) {
   // statement(s) to execute if $i is odd
```

```
  } else
    if ($i == 12) {
    // statement(s) to execute if $i is 12
    }
  }
```

However, in many cases, using **switch** (covered in the next section) to handle multiple possible values is a better choice.

PHP also supports the `elseif` construct, which can be used instead of nested `if` statements:

```
if (($i % 2) != 0) {
  // statement(s) to execute if $i is odd
} elseif ($i == 12) {
  // statement(s) to execute if $i is 12
  }
}
```

Switch

The `switch` construct executes specific block(s) of code based on the value of a particular expression. This structure has the following syntax:

```
switch (<expression>) {
  case <value_1>:
    // statement(s) to be executed if <expression> = <value_1>
  break;
  case <value_2>:
    // statement(s) to be executed if <expression> = <value_2>
  break;
...
  [default:
    // statement(s) to be executed if <expression> does not match any other case
  ]
}
```

For example, the following structure will perform the appropriate code based on the value of `$firstname`:

```
switch ($firstname) {
  case "Steve":
    // statement(s) to execute if $firstname = "Steve"
    break;

  case "Terri":
    // statement(s) to execute if $firstname = "Terri"
    break;

  default:
    /* statement(s) to execute if $firstname does not
       equal "Steve" or "Terri" */

}
```

Note that the break statements and the default section are optional. If you omit the break statements, each case section after the matching case will be executed. For example, in the preceding code section, if the breaks were removed and firstname were equal to "Steve", the code in all sections ("Steve", "Terri", and default) would execute.

*The **break** statement is covered in the next section.*

Break and Continue

Occasionally, you need to break out of a loop, either the current iteration or the entire loop structure. The break statement causes execution to break out of the current structure; the next code executed is the code following that structure. The continue statement breaks out of the current loop iteration to the condition expression of the loop.

For example, the following code will skip processing the number 7, but all other numbers between 1 and 20 will be processed:

```
$x = 1;
while ($x <= 20) {
  if ($x == 7) continue;   // skip the number 7
  // statement(s) to execute if $x does not equal 7
}
```

In the following code, the loop will be exited if the variable $x ever equals 100 during the loop's execution:

```
$y = 1;
while ($y <= 20) {
  if ($x == 100) break;   // if $x = 100, leave the loop
  // statement(s) to execute
}
// execution continues here when $y > 20 or if $x = 100
```

Note that both break and continue can be used with an optional numeric argument to break or continue more than one loop. For example, the following code shows how to break out of multiple loops:

```
for ($i = 1; $i <= 100; $i++) {
  for ($j = 1; $j <= 10; $j++) {
    // statement(s) to perform
    if ($x == 20) { break 2; }   // if $x = 20, break out of both for loops
  }
}
```

Built-in PHP Functions

One of the many features that make PHP so popular is its multitude of available functions—over 140 categories. Many of the functions are available within the PHP core, but others require support for those features to be compiled into the version of PHP you are using.

The following list shows the categories of built-in functions according to the PHP documentation available at: http://www.php.net/manual/en/funcref.php.

Advanced PHP debugger	Apache-specific Functions
Array Functions	Aspell functions [deprecated]
BCMath Arbitrary Precision Mathematics Functions	PHP bytecode Compiler
Bzip2 Compression Functions	Calendar Functions
CCVS API Functions [deprecated]	Classkit Functions
Class/Object Functions	COM and .Net (Windows)
ClibPDF Functions	Crack Functions
Character Type Functions	CURL, Client URL Library Functions
Cybercash Payment Functions	Cyrus IMAP administration Functions
Date and Time Functions	Database (dbm-style) Abstraction Layer Functions
dBase Functions	DBM Functions [deprecated]
DB++ Functions	dbx Functions
Direct IO Functions	Directory Functions
DOM Functions	DOM XML Functions
.NET Functions	Error Handling and Logging Functions
Program Execution Functions	Exif Functions
File Alteration Monitor Functions	FrontBase Functions
Forms Data Format Functions	filePro Functions
Filesystem Functions	FriBiDi Functions
FTP Functions	Function Handling Functions
Gettext	GMP Functions
HTTP Functions	Hyperwave Functions
Hyperwave API Functions	Firebird/InterBase Functions
ICAP Functions [deprecated]	iconv Functions
ID3 Functions	Informix Functions
IIS Administration Functions	Image Functions
IMAP, POP3, and NNTP Functions	PHP Options & Information
Ingres II Functions	IRC Gateway Functions
PHP / Java Integration	LDAP Functions

LZF Functions

mailparse Functions

MaxDB PHP Extension

MCAL Functions

MCVE Payment Functions

Mhash Functions

Ming functions for Flash

mnoGoSearch Functions

mSQL Functions

muscat Functions

Improved MySQL Extension

Network Functions

Lotus Notes Functions

Object Aggregation/Composition Functions

OpenAL Audio Bindings

Oracle Functions

Object property and method call overloading

Parsekit Functions

Regular Expression Functions (Perl-Compatible)

PDO Functions

PostgreSQL Functions

Printer Functions

qtdom Functions

GNU Readline

Regular Expression Functions (POSIX Extended)

SESAM Database Functions

Shared Memory Functions

SNMP Functions

Socket Functions

Mail Functions

Mathematical Functions

Multibyte String Functions

Mcrypt Encryption Functions

Memcache Functions

Mimetype Functions

Miscellaneous Functions

Mohawk Software Session Handler Functions

Microsoft SQL Server Functions

MySQL Functions

Ncurses Terminal Screen Control Functions

YP/NIS Functions

NSAPI-specific Functions

Oracle 8 functions

OpenSSL Functions

Output Control Functions

Ovrimos SQL Functions

Process Control Functions

PDF functions

Verisign Payflow Pro Functions

POSIX Functions

Pspell Functions

Rar Functions

GNU Recode Functions

Semaphore, Shared Memory and IPC Functions

Session Handling Functions

SimpleXML functions

SOAP Functions

Standard PHP Library (SPL) Functions

SQLite Functions

Stream Functions

Shockwave Flash Functions

TCP Wrappers Functions

Tokenizer Functions

URL Functions

vpopmail Functions

WDDX Functions

xdiff Functions

XML-RPC Functions

XSLT Functions

Zip File Functions (Read Only Access)

Secure Shell2 Functions

String Functions

Sybase Functions

Tidy Functions

Unified ODBC Functions

Variable Handling Functions

W32api Functions

xattr Functions

XML Parser Functions

XSL functions

YAZ Functions

Zlib Compression Functions

A comprehensive list of functions and their usage appears in Appendix F.

As you can see from the list, PHP can interface with many technologies. For example, the following script will show details about the contents of the zip file `test.zip`:

```php
<?php

print <<<HTML
<!DOCTYPE html PUBLIC "-//W3C//DTD XHTML 1.0 Strict//EN"
    "http://www.w3.org/TR/xhtml1/DTD/xhtml1-strict.dtd">
<html>
<head>
<title>Zip Contents</title>
</head>
<body>
<p>

HTML;

$zip = zip_open("test.zip");

if ($zip) {
  print "<h2>Zip File Contents</h2> \n";
  print "<pre> \n";
  while ($zip_entry = zip_read($zip)) {
    print " Name:              " . zip_entry_name($zip_entry) . "\n";
    print " Actual Filesize:   " . zip_entry_filesize($zip_entry) . "\n";
    print " Compressed Size:   " . zip_entry_compressedsize($zip_entry) . "\n";
    print " Compression Method: " . zip_entry_compressionmethod($zip_entry);
    print "\n";
  }
  zip_close($zip);
```

```
    print "</pre> \n";
}

print <<<HTML
</p>
</body>
</html>

HTML;

?>
```

Some of the features are available only on certain platforms. For example, the printer functions are available only on Windows platforms (as opposed to the language construct print, which is available on all platforms).

User-Defined Functions

PHP has standard support for user-defined functions. The syntax for defining a function in PHP is as follows:

```
function <function_name>([<argument1>, <argument2>...]) {
   // code of the function;
   return(<value>);
}
```

The code for the function is delimited by the braces.

Return Values

The function's return value is determined by the value supplied to the return construct within the user-defined function. Multiple return constructs can be used within the same function; when the function encounters a return construct, the function terminates and returns the appropriate value. A function can return any type of value. The same function can even return several types of values via several return constructs in the same function (although that is generally a bad programming technique).

Arguments

PHP functions support one or more arguments passed to the function. Typically, the number of articles supplied to the function must match the number of arguments defined in the function itself. Supplying more arguments causes the function to simply ignore the extra arguments, but supplying fewer causes an error.

However, sometimes it is useful to define optional arguments — arguments that are replaced by defaults if they are not given when a function is called. For example, suppose you had a function to print a date and need to occasionally specify a particular format for the date but usually want the same format. You could define the function as follows:

```
function printdate ($date, $format="m d, y") {
  // code of function
}
```

The function would always need to be called with one argument, `date`. However, the `format` argument is optional. If not supplied in the function call, the default value ("m d, y") is used. Because PHP assigns parameters in the order they appear in the function definition, optional functions should appear at the end of the argument list, where their omission won't cause other problems.

Variable Scope

As with most languages, variables in PHP retain local scope — that is, they are recognized only in the scope where they are defined. For example, a variable declared in a function is valid only within that function. If you wish a variable to be recognized outside of its defined scope, you will need to define the variable using the `global` keyword:

```
global $a, $b, $c;    // Global variables
```

Objects

Versions of PHP prior to version 5.0 had lackluster object support. PHP version 5.0 added more object-oriented support, placing PHP more in line with other modern programming languages. This section gives an overview of PHP's object features.

Class Definitions

Class definitions in PHP begin with the `class` keyword and enclose the class definition within curly braces (as with most other structures in PHP). A typical class definition would resemble the following:

```
class <class_name> {
  // Class definition
}
```

The class name can be any nonreserved word in PHP. Class naming rules are similar to PHP variable naming rules.

Constructors and Destructors

PHP version 5.0 uses a new type of constructor that previous versions don't have. The new format recognizes a function named `__construct()` in the class definition as the object's constructor. For example, consider the following example object:

```
class myClass {
  function __construct() {
    // Construction of object
  }
}
```

For backward-compatibility, PHP version 5.0 will check for the prior versions' constructor format — a function within the class definition named the same as the class. If such a function is not found, PHP version 5.0 will then look for the __construct() function.

An object's constructor is typically used to initialize the object's properties. See the "Methods and Properties" section later in this chapter for more information on object properties. To create a new object (and hence run the class' constructor), you declare the new object with the new function:

```
newObject = new myClass();
```

PHP version 5.0 also adds a destructor that you can use to perform tasks when discarding an object. Following the new constructor format, the destructor is contained in a function named __destruct(). A code example of a class definition with both a constructor and destructor follows:

```
class myClass {
  function __construct() {
    // Tasks to perform on construction of object
  }
  function __destruct() {
    // Tasks to perform on destruction of object
  }
}
```

The destructor is typically used to save changes to objects, related data, or states pertaining to an object before it is destroyed and the data is lost. For example, you could load data into an object from a database or other source, manipulate it within the object, and then destroy the object, letting the object's destructor take care of saving the object's data back into the database.

Methods and Properties

Object methods are defined as functions within the class definition. For example, consider the following code, which defines an object with a method:

```
class myClass {
  function __construct() {
    // Tasks to perform on construction of object
  }

  function myMethod () {
    // Tasks to perform when method is called
  }
}
```

To call an object's method you use the object name and the method, separated by the -> connector. For example, to call the method described in the preceding code, you could use code similar to the following, which creates a new object of the myClass class and calls the myMethod method:

```
newObject = new myClass();
newObject->myMethod();
```

In PHP, properties are simply variables declared within the class definition. For example, the following declares a property within the familiar class definition:

```
class myClass {

  public $myProperty;

  function __construct() {
    // Tasks to perform on construction of object
  }
}
```

*As you might have noticed in the preceding code, you can define variables and other structures in the class definition as public or private by prefacing the definition with the appropriate keyword (**public** or **private**). Resources defined as private are accessible only to the class itself.*

Accessing public properties outside the definition is accomplished similarly to accessing an object's methods: you specify the object name and the property name separated by ->:

```
newObject = new myClass();
newObject->myProperty = 152;
```

Working with Objects

This section shows a practical example of PHP objects.

Creating Objects for Storing Movie Data

This example creates two classes to store movie data:

❑   A director class for storing the name and age of a director

❑   A movie class for storing the name, genre, director, and release date of a movie

The example also creates a simple method for the director class, a method to return the formal name (last name, comma, first name) of a director.

Source

```
<?php

  class director {

    public $name;
    public $age;

    function __construct($name, $age) {
      $this->name = $name;
      $this->age = $age;
    }
```

```
      // Given name (John Doe), return last name-comma-first name
      //   (Doe, John)
      function getFormalName() {
        $name = array();
        $name = explode(" ",$this->name);
        $fname = $name[0];
        array_shift($name);
        $name[count($name)-1] .= ",";
        array_push($name,$fname);

        return implode(" ",$name);
      }
    }


    class movie {

      public $title;
      public $genre;
      public $director;
      public $releasedate;

      function __construct($title, $genre, $director, $releasedate) {
        $this->title = $title;
        $this->genre = $genre;
        $this->director = $director;
        $this->releasedate = $releasedate;
      }
    }

$myDirector = new director("James Cameron",51);
$myMovie = new movie("Aliens","Scifi",$myDirector,"1986-07-18");

if ($myMovie->director->name == "James Cameron") {
  print "King of the world!";
}

?>
```

Output

This code would output King of the world! because the name of the movie's director is James Cameron.

Additional Object Conventions

PHP version 5.0 supports many other traditional conventions for dealing with objects. For example, you can add the suffix extends <classname> to a class definition to designate that definition as an extension to another class.

A full discussion of PHP's object handling is outside the scope of this chapter, but a good overview can be found in the PHP documentation at `http://www.php.net/manual/en/language.oop5.php`.

Basic syntax for many of the object-related functions can be found in Appendix F.

File Operations

As with other areas of functionality, PHP includes many functions for dealing with files. This section covers the basics of file operations and functions in PHP.

Opening a File

PHP uses the `fopen()` function for opening files. The syntax of this function is as follows:

```
fopen(<filename>,<mode>)
```

The `fopen()` function returns a resource pointer to the file or the value `false` if the file could not be opened.

The various values that can be used for `<mode>` are shown in the following table:

Mode	Meaning
r	Open the file for reading *only* and place the file pointer at the beginning of the file.
r+	Open the file for reading *and* writing and place the file pointer at the beginning of the file.
w	Open the file for writing *only*, zero (erase) the file if it exists, or attempt to create the file if it does not exist.
w+	Open the file for reading *and* writing, zero (erase) the file if it exists, or attempt to create the file if it does not exist.
a	Open the file for writing *only* and place the file pointer at the *end* of the file. If the file does not exist, attempt to create it.
a+	Open the file for reading *and* writing and place the file pointer at the *end* of the file. If the file does not exist, attempt to create it.
x	*Create* and open the file for writing *only*, placing the file pointer at the beginning of the file. If the file already exists, return `false`.
x+	*Create* and open the file for reading *and* writing, placing the file pointer at the beginning of the file. If the file already exists, return `false`.

A common syntax for using the `fopen()` function follows:

```
// Open a text file for reading and writing
$file = fopen("somefile.txt","r+")
    or die("Could not open file!");
```

If the file open was successful, the variable $file would then contain a reference to the file somefile.txt and could be used by other file functions (as described in the following sections).

The fopen() function supports two additional mode switches: b (binary) and t (translate). The binary switch ensures that the file will be opened in binary mode and is designed to be used with the binary safe read and write functions. The translate switch is available only on Windows and causes line breaks (/n) written to files to be transparently translated to line break-return pairs (/n/r).

Both of these switches must be used at the end of the mode string. For example, to open an existing binary file for read-write access, you could use the following code:

```
// Open a text file for binary safe reading and writing
$file = fopen("somefile.bin","r+b")
    or die("Could not open file!");
```

Reading Text from a File

PHP has several functions available for reading data from a file. The two most popular functions are fgets() (file get string) and fgetc() (file get character). The functions read their respective amount of data — string/line or character — from the file resource specified. The syntax for both functions appears here:

```
fgets(<resource>[,<length>])
```

```
fgetc(<resource>)
```

Note that the fgets() function reads up to the <length> (byte wise) specified, up to the next line break, or to the end of the file, whichever comes first. If the <length> is not specified, the function will read up to 1024 bytes (1K). The fgetc() function returns false if the end of the file is encountered; the fgets() function returns false only on an error.

A common PHP construct for reading and printing the entire contents of a file, line by line, follows:

```
$file = fopen("somefile.txt","r")
   or die ("Could not open file!");
// Read the file, line by line (in max 4K chunks)
while (!feof($file)) {
  $line = fgets($file,4096);
  print $line;
}
```

*The **feof()** function tests for the end of the file and is covered in the "Other File Functions" section of this chapter.*

The following table lists several other functions that can be used for reading data from a file:

Function	Returns	Use

`fgetcsv ( resource handle`
`[, int length [,`
`string delimiter`
`[, string enclosure]]] )`
	array	Reads values from a comma-separated value file into an array

`fgetss ( resource handle`
`[, int length [, string`
`allowable_tags]] )`
	string	Reads a string from a file, stripping HTML tags before returning the string

`fread ( resource handle,` `int length )`	string	Binary-safe file reading function
`fscanf ( resource handle,` `string format [, mixed &...] )`	mixed	Parses input from a file according to the format given in the function call (similar to the PHP `sscanf()` function)

Writing Text to a File

Unlike the many functions to read from a file, PHP has only one main function to write to a file — `fwrite()`. The syntax for `fwrite()` is as follows:

```
fwrite(<resource>,<string>[,<length>])
```

The `fwrite()` function will return the number of bytes written to the file or `false` if an error occurs. If the `<length>` parameter is specified, the function will write the number of bytes specified or to the end of the string, whichever comes first.

On systems that differentiate between text and binary files (such as Windows), it is important to use the b mode flag when opening the file. For more information, see the "Opening a File" section earlier in this chapter.

Closing a File

To close a file, PHP uses the `fclose()` function. This function is straightforward, taking the file resource variable as its only parameter:

```
fclose($file)
```

This function returns `true` or `false` depending on the results of the operation.

Working with Binary Files

The `fseek()` function is the missing piece of working with binary files. Using `fread()` and `fwrite()`, you can read and write data to binary files, but you need `fseek()` to accurately position the file pointer before you perform either operation. The `fseek()` function has the following syntax:

```
fseek(<resource>,<offset>[,<whence_key>])
```

This function returns 0 on success and -1 on failure. Note that seeking past the end of the file is not considered an error.

> *The **ftell()** function can be used to determine the current position of the file pointer. Using the **ftell()** function with the **filesize()** function (which returns the size of a file) gives you the ability to discern where the file pointer currently is in regards to the end of a file.*

The <offset> parameter is in bytes and the <whence_key> parameter is one of the constants shown in the following table:

Constant	Meaning
SEEK_SET	Set the file pointer to the offset given in bytes. This is the default option and is assumed if no other option is specified.
SEEK_CUR	Set the file pointer to the current position plus the offset given in bytes.
SEEK_END	Set the file pointer to the end of the file plus the offset given in bytes. Note that giving a negative offset with this option will seek to the offset *before* the end of the file.

The following code snippet shows an example of writing a 1K string of spaces in alternating 1K chunks throughout an existing file:

```
// Set up the file info and our 1K string
$filename = "somefile.bin";
$filesize = filesize($filename);
$oneK = str_pad($oneK,1024);

// Open the file
$file = fopen($filename,"r+b")
    or die("Cannot open file!");

// Do until loop is broken
while (true) {

  // Write the 1K stripe
  if (fwrite($file, $oneK) === FALSE) {
    die ("Cannot write to file!");
  }

  // Determine if we have room for another stripe
  //   (skip 1K and write 1K)
  // If not, break loop
  if ( (ftell($file) + 2048) < $filesize) ) {
    break;
  }

  // Skip 1K in preparation for another stripe
  if (fseek($file,1024,SEEK_CUR) === FALSE) {
    die ("Could not seek on file!");
  }
}
```

Locking Files

The `flock()` is a function that can be used to lock a file for access. The function has the following syntax:

```
flock(<resource>, <operation>)
```

The `<operation>` parameter is one of the constants shown in the following table:

Constant	Use
LOCK_SH	Lock the file using a shared lock (usually for read only access).
LOCK_EX	Lock the file using an exclusive lock (usually for writing access).
LOCK_UN	Release a lock on a file.
LOCK_NB	Lock the file without blocking.

The `flock()` function returns true on success or false on failure. Note that file locking with the `flock()` function is mandatory on the Windows platform.

Other File Functions

PHP has several additional file functions, some of which are listed in the following table:

Function	Use
feof(<resource>)	Test for the end of the file (file pointer at or exceeding the end of the file). Returns `true` or `false` depending on the end of the file being reached.
file_exists(<filename>)	Test whether a file exists. Returns `true` if the file exists or `false` if the file does not exist.
fileatime(<filename>)	Returns a timestamp of the last time a file was accessed or `false` on an error.
filectime(<filename>)	Returns a timestamp of the last time a file was changed or `false` on an error.
fileinode(<filename>)	Returns the inode number of the file or `false` on an error.
filemtime (<filename>)	Returns a timestamp of the last time a file was modified or `false` on an error.
fileowner(<filename>)	Returns the user ID of the owner of the file or `false` on an error.
fileperms(<filename>)	Returns the permission on the file or `false` on an error.
filesize(<filename>)	Returns the size (in bytes) of the file or `false` on an error.
filetype(<filename>)	Returns the type of a file (for example: `fifo`, `char`, `dir`, `block`, `link`, `file`, and `unknown`) or `false` on an error.

Table continued on following page

Function	Use
`fputcsv(<resource>, <data_array>[, <char_delimiter>, <char_separator>])`	Writes an array to a file in CSV format. Returns the length of the data written or `false` on an error.
`fstat(<resource>)`	Returns an array of statistical information on the file specified.
`is_dir(<filename>)`	Returns `true` if the file is a directory or `false` if the file is not.
`is_executable(<filename>)`	Returns `true` if the file is executable or `false` if the file is not.
`is_file(<filename>)`	Returns `true` if the file is a regular file or `false` if the file is not.
`is_link(<filename>)`	Returns `true` if the file is a link or `false` if the file is not.
`is_readable(<filename>)`	Returns `true` if the file is readable or `false` if the file is not.
`is_writeable(<filename>)`	Returns `true` if the file is writeable or `false` if the file is not.
`tmpfile()`	Creates a file with a unique name in read-write (`w+`) mode and returns a resource handle to the created file.
`unlink(<filename>)`	Deletes the specified file, returning `true` on success or `false` on failure.

There are many other file functions in PHP; the list is too exhaustive to cover in this format. See Appendix F for more information on PHP functions.

PHP Errors and Troubleshooting

You are sure to encounter problems while coding your PHP scripts. This section provides some guidance on how to best avoid and troubleshoot errors encountered in your scripts.

Use the Right Tools

It's important to use the right tools while coding PHP. First and foremost, use a code-friendly editor. Although any text editor can be used to construct PHP scripts, code-friendly editors offer features such as auto-indenting, syntax highlighting, and regular expression search and replace functions.

Some of the tools in the following lists are Open Source and others are commercial. Most of the commercial applications offer free trial versions. Capabilities between the various editors vary; pick an editor that offers the capabilities you need in the price range that works for you.

Windows users should explore tools such as the following:

❏ **TextPad** — http://www.textpad.com

❏ **PSPad** — http://www.pspad.com/

❏ **Homesite** — http://www.macromedia.com/software/homesite/

Linux users should explore tools such as the following:

- ❑ **vim** — http://www.vim.org/
- ❑ **Emacs** — http://www.gnu.org/software/emacs/emacs.html
- ❑ **Bluefish** — http://bluefish.openoffice.nl/

Macintosh users should explore tools such as the following:

- ❑ Many of the editors available for Linux (see preceding list)
- ❑ **BBEdit** — http://www.barebones.com/index.shtml
- ❑ **Dreamweaver** — http://www.macromedia.com/software/dreamweaver/

If you want to use a fully integrated development environment (IDE) or dedicated PHP editor rather than a universal code editor, check out the listings, reviews, and links at the PHP-Editors Web site: http://www.php-editors.com/.

> *For a truly professional IDE product, check out Zend Studio, available at* http://www.zend.com/store/products/zend-studio/index.php.

Avoiding Common Syntactical Mistakes

There are several mistakes often made when coding PHP. Keep the following in mind when you encounter problems in your scripts:

- ❑ **Matching braces** — Often you might find that a block section of code is missing its beginning or ending brace ({ or }). Adhering to strict syntax formatting will help; it's easier to notice a missing brace if it doesn't appear where it should.

- ❑ **Missing semicolons** — When writing quick and dirty code, it's easy to forget the little things, such as the semicolons on the end of statements. That is one reason why I never treat semicolons as optional; I use them at the end of every statement even when they are technically optional.

- ❑ **Variable type conflicts** — Because PHP allows for loose variable typing, it is easy to make mistakes by assuming a variable contains data of one type when it actually contains data of another type. For example, if you access a numeric variable with a string function, PHP will interpret the numeric value as a string, resulting in the original number being rounded, truncated, or otherwise modified.

- ❑ **Working with noncompliant HTML** — Sometimes the problem is not in the PHP but in the XHTML that is output by PHP. It is important to work within the XHTML standards to ensure that your documents render the way you intend in the most user agents possible.

- ❑ **Your own idiosyncrasies** — After writing several scripts, you will find personal coding idiosyncrasies that end up constantly biting you. Try to remember those issues and check your code for your consistent problems as you go.

Identifying Problems

One of the things that PHP is fairly good at is reporting errors. Generally, when an error is encountered in a script, the interpreter reports a useful message that can be used to quickly identify and fix the problem. For example, a missing semicolon in the following code results in a message similar to that shown in Figure 30-1.

```
function doquery($link,$query) {

    $result = mysql_query($query,$link)
      or die("Could not perform query!")

    return $result;

} // End doquery()
```

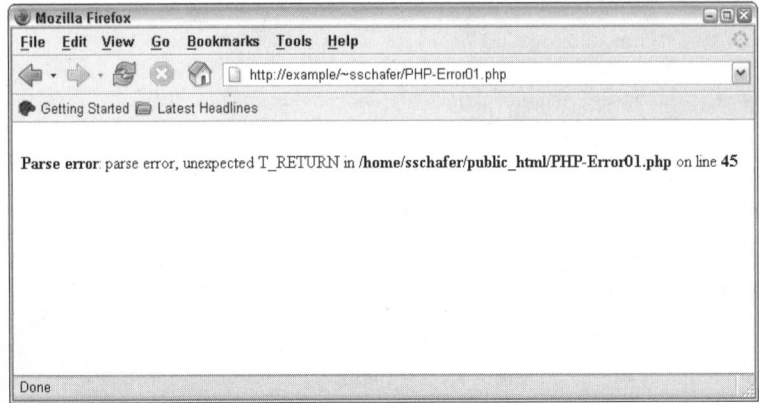

Figure 30-1

The error reports an unexpected `return` statement, which isn't the actual error. However, the line number leads you directly to the problem area and the missing semicolon is readily identified as the actual problem.

However, some PHP errors are too cryptic to be useful. For example, Figure 30-2 shows an error from a script that has 308 lines.

In such cases, additional troubleshooting and error handling can help. The next section provides some guidance in that area.

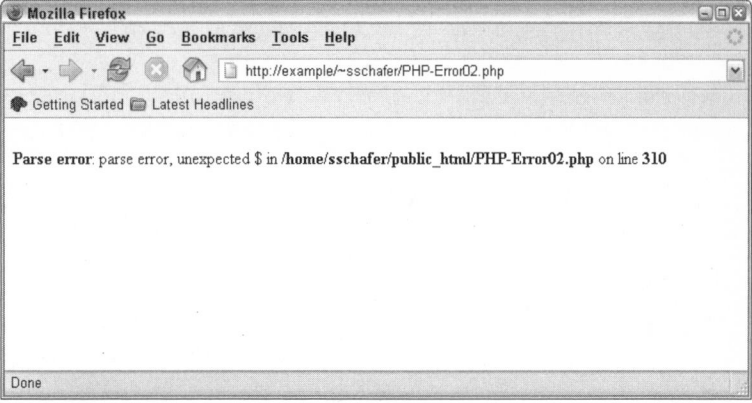

Figure 30-2

Error Control and Processing

PHP has a host of functions and other constructs to help control how errors are handled in your code. By using these functions, you can control the level of errors reported, intercept errors, and more.

Controlling the Error Level

The PHP `error_reporting()` function controls the level of errors reported at run time. This function takes one argument, either a bitmapped value or named constant, corresponding to the error levels you want returned. The following table lists the bitmapped values and their named constant counterparts.

Value	Constant
1	E_ERROR
2	E_WARNING
4	E_PARSE
8	E_NOTICE
16	E_CORE_ERROR
32	E_CORE_WARNING
64	E_COMPILE_ERROR
128	E_COMPILE_WARNING
256	E_USER_ERROR
512	E_USER_WARNING
1024	E_USER_NOTICE
2047	E_ALL

See the PHP documentation on error code constants (www.php.net/manual/en/ref.errorfunc.php#errorfunc .constants) for more information on what kinds of errors fall into each category.

For example, if you wanted to report runtime errors and warnings, you could use either of the following two formats:

```
// Bitmapped number
//  Note that level 3 = level 2 + level 1
error_reporting(3);

// Note each error level constant should be listed,
//  separated by a vertical bar (|)
error_reporting(E_ERROR | E_WARNING);
```

If you do not want any errors reported, use a zero with the `error_reporting()` function call:

```
// No error reporting
error_reporting(0);
```

Robust error reporting through the user agent can be a liability for production scripts; the error text often contains filenames, user names, database names, and more. Instead of disabling errors to protect such information, redirect the errors to another source, as covered in the next section.

Sending Errors to a File or E-mail Address

The `error_log()` function can be used to send specific information regarding an error to a file or e-mail address. This function is most useful for production scripts where the end-user, not the programmer, experiences the error messages. Using the `error_log()` function, you can ensure that your scripts pass their errors on to you to troubleshoot. The `error_log()` function has the following syntax:

```
error_log(error_message[, message_type[, message_destination[, extra_headers]]]);
```

The first argument, `error_message`, is a string containing the type and description of the error. For example, you could send the text, `Unable to open file filename`, replacing *filename* with the name of the file that could not be opened.

The second argument, `message_type`, tells the `error_log()` function where to send the error (file or e-mail). This argument supports the values contained in the following table:

Value	Meaning
0	Sends the error text to the system's logger or the filename in the `error_log` directive (contained in the `php.ini` file).
1	Sends the error text via e-mail to the address specified in the `message_destination` argument. This function uses the same routines as the `mail()` function to send the e-mail.
2	Sends the text through the remote debugging interface. This operation requires that remote debugging be enabled. The `message_destination` argument should specify the IP address (and, optionally, the port) where the information should be sent.

Value	Meaning
3	Appends the error text to the filename specified in the message_destination argument.

*Note that the error-reporting functions are influenced by the **log_errors** and **error_reporting** directives. Remember that you can use the **ini_set()** function or specific error functions (for example, **error_reporting()**) to change these directives at run time.*

Custom Error Handling

The real power of PHP's error functions comes from the set_error_handler() function. This function enables you to define your own error-handling function, giving you ultimate control over how errors are reported and handled. Custom error handlers are critical for creating recovery code for otherwise catastrophic errors.

The set_error_handler() function has the following syntax:

```
set_error_handler(function_name);
```

For example, the following code defines the function err_handler() as the de facto error-handling function:

```
set_error_handler("err_handler");
```

The set_error_handler() function returns the previous error handler. Your scripts can use that value when reporting errors; knowing what error handler didn't report errors can be as valuable as knowing those that do. The complementary restore_error_handler() function reinstates the previous error handler, whether it is the internal PHP handler or a user-defined handler. Note that the restore_error_handler() function takes no arguments: PHP remembers and reinstates the previous handler automatically.

Any error-handling function should accept at least the first two of the following arguments, preferably all five:

❑ The code of the error that was generated

❑ The text of the error that was generated

❑ The filename of the script in which the error occurred

❑ The line number on which the error occurred

❑ An array that points to the active symbol table at the time the error occurred

*User-defined error handlers cannot be used to handle the following types of errors: **E_ERROR**, **E_PARSE**, **E_CORE_ERROR**, **E_CORE_WARNING**, **E_COMPILE_ERROR**, and **E_COMPILE_WARNING**. See the PHP documentation for more information on these errors.*

What you do inside the error-handling function is completely arbitrary. You can perform different actions based on the type of error, do additional checking of values, and more. However, your function is now solely responsible for handling the error — at minimum, you should be sure to capture as much useful information about the error as possible and attempt to gracefully exit the script.

Summary

This chapter covered the details of various PHP operations and the functions and conventions behind their use. This chapter, combined with the listings in Appendix F, should give you the information necessary to become proficient in writing useful PHP scripts.

Chapter 31 provides a handful of complete scripts that you can use to build your own scripts.

Using PHP

The previous chapters in this section demonstrated how PHP works behind the scenes, describing the syntax and functionality of the language and its ability to interface with other technologies. This chapter rounds out the PHP coverage by showing some basic but useful examples of PHP in action.

How and When to Use PHP

PHP is a great choice for any online document needing dynamic content. The rich language combined with the interoperability with other technologies allows your documents to incorporate data from many sources — data that can be manipulated in various ways prior to being displayed.

However, PHP isn't a magic bullet for XHTML content and shouldn't be used indiscriminately to deliver content. Consider using PHP for the following purposes:

❑   When interfacing with other technologies accessible from the Web server (databases, specific hardware, and so on)

❑   When the content on a Web page needs to be dynamic, taking into account input from other resources

❑   When complex documents need to interact with the user via XHTML forms or other means

However, consider using other technologies when the following conditions apply:

❑   The capabilities you need in a document can be found in client technologies such as JavaScript.

❑   The documents delivered will be accessed by many clients simultaneously every day.

❑   The machines performing the delivery contain very sensitive data and need to remain highly secure.

The first two conditions take into account the implicit load running constant PHP scripting can put on a server. If you can distribute the load to the clients (using JavaScript or other client-centric technology), you usually should. And the third condition listed is not meant as a slap in the face of PHP in particular; adding any additional technology to Web-delivered content increases the risk of introducing security vulnerabilities into the mix. Consider that tradeoff against what PHP can add to your documents when deciding whether to employ PHP.

> *You may want to investigate the use of the **expose_php** setting in the **php.ini** file (or via scripting commands). This setting determines whether PHP should expose itself as running via document headers and the like. It's advisable to set **expose_php** to 0 if you are concerned about security. Neither setting poses an inherent security risk, but if hackers can determine the version of PHP in use, they could conceivably target particular exploits contained in that version.*

One popular technique often employed when using PHP is to build the documents statically, running PHP scripts in the background, usually on separate machines from the Web server(s). The documents are built using dynamic techniques and then made accessible to the servers doing the actual document delivery. This, of course, does not work for documents that must reflect up-to-the-minute data but can work for newsletters or other documents that change only on a regular schedule.

PHP Resources

Several online resources can help you with your PHP tasks. Some of the most popular resources are listed here:

❑ **The Official PHP Web Site** (http://www.php.net) — The home of PHP provides a wealth of information on the language including comprehensive documentation, information on specific language features, and security updates. The search function at the top of the main page is invaluable for quickly looking up information in the function list or main documentation.

❑ **PHP Extension and Application Repository (PEAR)** (http://pear.php.net) — PEAR provides a "framework and distribution system for reusable PHP components." The repository contains many prefab components that you can use to build your PHP applications. In a way, PEAR is the CPAN of PHP. (See Chapter 28 for more information about CPAN.) You can find components to perform just about any task.

Note that current versions of PHP (5+) from the PHP site include PEAR in the installation of the base PHP system. However, you should consult the documentation in your platform's implementation for details on how to install and utilize PEAR.

❑ **<?PHPBuilder?>** (http://www.phpbuilder.com/) — The PHPBuilder site is a third-party repository of PHP news, articles, tips, and code. It is an invaluable resource for communicating with the rest of the PHP community and for finding interesting code implementations (*snippets*) to help in programming your own applications.

PHP Examples

This section provides four examples of how PHP can be used with XHTML to provide dynamic content. Using the examples in this section, you should be able to construct a solid foundation of PHP skills to interact with other technologies and create rich content for delivery over the Web.

This section uses the same sample data outlined in Chapter 28, "Using CGI." See the "Sample Data" section in that chapter for more details on the sample data used for the examples here.

Date and Time Handling

This example shows how the PHP date and time routines can be used to create a simple XHTML calendar. This example displays the current month, with the current day in red.

For a more dynamic calendar example, see the third example in this section.

Example 1: A Simple Calendar

Source

```php
<?php

// Set up the variables (today, month, year, cmd)
//   today = m/d/y
function setvars() {

  // Default is today
  $today = getdate();
  $month = $today['mon'];
  $year = $today['year'];
  $today = $month."/".$today['mday']."/".$year;

  // Return vars in an array
  return array("today" => $today,
               "month" => $month,
               "year" => $year);

}  // End setvars()


// Do the document header
function docheader($month,$year) {

  $month_text =  date("F",strtotime($month."/1/".$year));

  // If content header has not been sent,
  //   send it
  if (!headers_sent()) {
    header('Content-type: text/html');
  }

// Print the document header (up to first date row)
```

```
print <<<HTML
<!DOCTYPE html PUBLIC "-//W3C//DTD XHTML 1.0//EN"
    "http://www.w3.org/TR/xhtml11/DTD/xhtml1.dtd">
<html>
<head>
  <title>Calendar - $Month $Year</title>
  <style type="text/css">
    tr.weekdays td { width: 100px;
                     text-align: center;
                   }
    tr.week td { width: 100px;
                 height: 100px;
                 color: black;  }
  </style>
</head>
<body>
<table border="1">

<!-- Controls and calendar title (month) -->
<tr>
  <td colspan="7" align="center">
    <strong>
      $month_text $year
    </strong>
  </td>
</tr>

<!-- Day of week header row -->
<tr class="weekdays">
  <th>Sunday</th>
  <th>Monday</th>
  <th>Tuesday</th>
  <th>Wednesday</th>
  <th>Thursday</th>
  <th>Friday</th>
  <th>Saturday</th>
</tr>

<!-- Calendar (days) start here -->

HTML;

}  // End docheader()


// Do the document footer (close tags, end doc)
function docfooter() {

print <<<HTML
<!-- Close all open tags, end document -->
</table>
</body>
```

```php
</html>

HTML;

} // End docfooter()


// Print an empty day (cell)
function emptyday() {

print <<<HTML
  <td align="right" valign="top"> </td>

HTML;

} // End emptyday()


// Print a day cell
function day($today,$month,$day,$year) {

  $curday = $month."/".$day."/".$year;
  if ($curday == $today) {
    $font = " style=\"color: red;\"";
  } else {
    $font = "";
  }

print <<< HTML
  <td align="right" valign="top" $font>$day</td>

HTML;

} // End day()


// Open or close a row
function weekrow($cmd) {

  switch ($cmd) {
    case "open":
      print "<tr class=\"week\">\n";
      break;
    case "close":
      print "</tr>\n";
      break;
  }

}  // End weekrow()


// Main program body
function main() {

  // Set the date vars
```

```php
    $vars = setvars();
    $today = $vars['today'];
    $month = $vars['month'];
    $year = $vars['year'];

    // Do the header and open first row
    docheader($month,$year);
    weekrow("open");

    // Set up first weekday and 1st day (m/1/y)
    $first_weekday = date("w",strtotime($month."/1/".$year)) + 1;
    $day = 1;

    // Print empty days up to the first weekday of month
    for ($weekday = 1; $weekday < $first_weekday; $weekday++) {
      emptyday();
    }

    // Do rest of month while we have a valid date
    while (checkdate($month,$day,$year)) {
      // If SUN, open the row
      if ($weekday == 1) {
        weekrow("open");
      }
      // Print day and increment
      day($today,$month,$day,$year);
      $weekday++;
      $day++;
      // If SAT, close row reset weekday
      if ($weekday > 7) {
        weekrow("close");
        $weekday = 1;
      }

    }

    // Close current week
    while ($weekday != 1 && $weekday <= 7) {
      emptyday();
      $weekday++;
    }

    // Close document
    docfooter();

} // End main();


// Kick it all off
main();

?>
```

This script outputs an XHTML table similar to that shown in Figure 31-1.

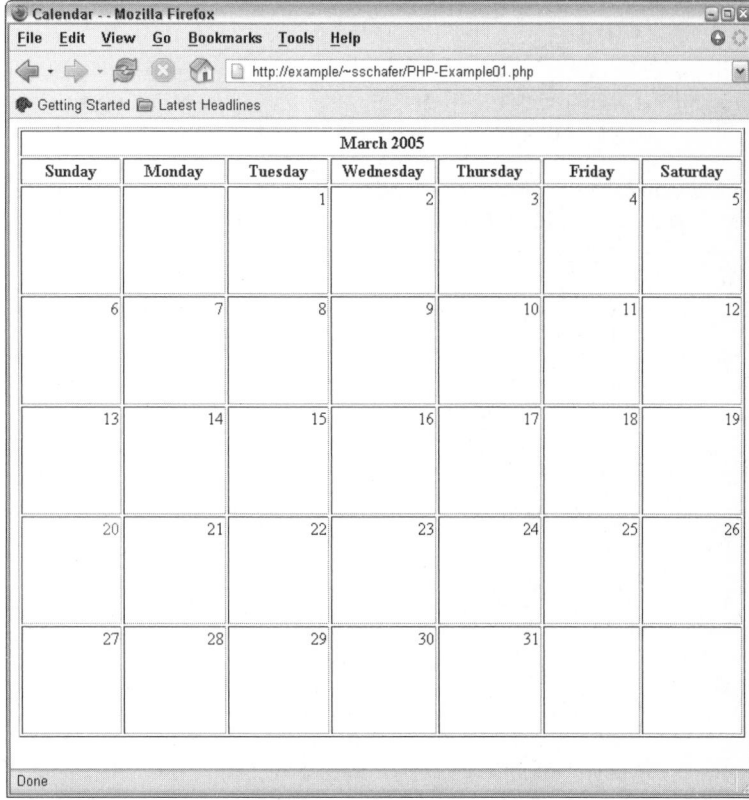

Figure 31-1

How It Works

This script uses the basic PHP date- and time-handling functions to determine the following:

❑ First weekday of the month

❑ Current day (for highlighting purposes)

❑ Number of days in the month

Using those parameters, the script can create a calendar for any month, past, present, or future. The rest of the script is fairly straightforward:

1. Output the document header (Content-type, doctype, head tags, and so on).

2. Determine the first weekday of the month.

3. Output blank cells for weekdays up to the first day of the month.

4. Output cells for each day of the month.

5. Close the month by outputting blank cells to fill the last week.

Improving the Script

This script simply shows how PHP can handle complex calculations such as functions on dates and times. Besides changing the format of the output (for example, a smaller table for a smaller calendar), the script could perform many other time/date functions:

❑ Thumbnail calendars for the months on either side of the current month could be displayed in the calendar header, much like paper calendars.

❑ Multiple months could be assembled into a longer calendar.

❑ The calendar functions could be applied to other Web-enabled features.

❑ The calendar could be extended to be dynamic, able to output any month. (An example of a more dynamic calendar appears in the third example in this section.)

Handling Form Data

This example shows how to decipher data passed to a PHP script. This script simply lists the GET and POST data passed to it.

Example 2: Deciphering and Dealing with Form-Submitted Data

Source

```php
<?php

// Print document header

  // If content header has not been sent,
  //   send it
  if (!headers_sent()) {
    header('Content-type: text/html');
  }

print <<<HTML
<!DOCTYPE html PUBLIC "-//W3C//DTD XHTML 1.1 Strict//EN"
    "http://www.w3.org/TR/xhtml1/DTD/xhtml11-strict.dtd">
<html>
<head>
```

```
  <title>POST/GET Variable Dump</title>
</head>
<body>

HTML;

// If there is POST data, dump it
//  else display "No Data"
if (isset($_POST) && count($_POST) != 0) {
  print "<h2>POST Data</h2>\n";
  print "<pre>\n<p>\n";

  var_dump($_POST);

  print "</pre>\n</p>\n";
} else {
  print "<h2>No POST Data</h2>\n";
}

// If there is GET data, dump it
//  else display "No Data"
if (isset($_GET) && count($_GET) != 0) {
  print "<h2>GET Data</h2>\n";
  print "<pre>\n<p>\n";

  var_dump($_GET);

  print "</pre>\n</p>\n";
}  else {
  print "<h2>No GET Data</h2>\n";
}

// Close document
print <<<HTML
</body>
</html>

HTML;

?>
```

Output

This script, when passed the data specified in the "Sample Data" section of Chapter 28, results in the document shown in Figure 31-2.

```
POST/GET Variable Dump - Mozilla Firefox
File  Edit  View  Go  Bookmarks  Tools  Help
    http://example/~sschafer/PHP-Example02.php
Getting Started   Latest Headlines

POST Data

array(9) {
  ["fname"]=>
  string(5) "Steve"
  ["lname"]=>
  string(7) "Schafer"
  ["addr"]=>
  string(28) "123 Main St.
Somewhere, USA"
  ["pwd"]=>
  string(8) "password"
  ["prod"]=>
  array(2) {
    [0]=>
    string(12) "Motherboards"
    [1]=>
    string(14) "Power Supplies"
  }
  ["email"]=>
  string(2) "on"
  ["buy"]=>
  string(2) "10"
  ["submit"]=>
  string(6) "Submit"
  ["referredby"]=>
  string(6) "Google"
}

No GET Data

Done
```

Figure 31-2

How It Works

This script makes use of the built-in $_POST and $_GET variables to parse the appropriate HTTP-passed data. Both variables return an associative array containing the variable names (as keys in the array) and the variable values (as values in the array). You can test for the existence of GET or POST data by accessing the size of the appropriate array and then accessing each value individually.

The handy PHP (print human readable) function, print_r(), is used to output the arrays in human-readable format within a <pre> block to preserve the formatting.

Improving the Script

This script handles HTTP-passed data at its simplest level, merely displaying what it was passed. The methods for making use of said data are endless, driven only by your needs. You could simply store the data as-is in a database, perform calculations and make decisions based on the data, or discard it as needed. The next example shows how a script can make decisions based on form data.

PHP offers many functions for aiding in dealing with HTTP-passed data. For example, see Chapter 38 in the PHP Manual, "Handling file uploads," at http://www.php.net/manual/en/features .file-upload.php.

Using Form Data

This example shows how a script can act upon the HTTP-supplied data. In this case, the calendar script from earlier in this chapter is extended to allow the user to move the calendar forward or backward by a month at a time using simple XHTML form `submit` buttons.

Example 3: Creating a Dynamic Calendar

Source

```php
<?php

// Set up the variables (today, month, year, cmd)
//   today = m/d/y
//   cmd = 1 (add month) or -1 (sub month)
function setvars() {

  // Default is today
  $today = getdate();
  $month = $today['mon'];
  $year = $today['year'];
  $today = $month."/".$today['mday']."/".$year;

  // Get POST data
  if (isset($_POST) && count($_POST) != 0) {
    if (isset($_POST['month'])) {
      $month = $_POST['month']; }
    if (isset($_POST['year'])) {
      $year = $_POST['year']; }
    if (isset($_POST['next'])) {
      $cmd = 1; }
    if (isset($_POST['prev'])) {
      $cmd = -1; }
  }

  // Get GET data
  if (isset($_GET) && count($_GET) != 0) {
    if (isset($_GET['month'])) {
      $month = $_GET['month']; }
    if (isset($_GET['year'])) {
      $year = $_GET['year']; }
    if (isset($_GET['next'])) {
      $cmd = 1; }
    if (isset($_GET['prev'])) {
      $cmd = -1; }
  }

  // If given a command (move month)
  //   act on it
  if (isset($cmd)) {
    $month += $cmd;
    // Adjust month over or underrun
    if ($month >= 13) {
```

```php
        $month = 1;
        $year += 1;
    } elseif ($month <= 0) {
        $month = 12;
        $year -= 1;
    }
  }

  // Return vars in an array
  return array("today" => $today,
               "month" => $month,
               "year" => $year,
               "cmd" => $cmd);

}  // End setvars()


// Do the document header
function docheader($month,$year) {

  // Set script to return to (form action)
  $this_script = $_SERVER['PHP_SELF'];
  $month_text =  date("F",strtotime($month."/1/".$year));

  // If content header has not been sent,
  //   send it
  if (!headers_sent()) {
    header('Content-type: text/html');
  }

// Print the document header (up to first date row)
print <<<HTML
<!DOCTYPE html PUBLIC "-//W3C//DTD XHTML 1.1//EN"
    "http://www.w3.org/TR/xhtml11/DTD/xhtml11.dtd">
<html>
<head>
  <title>Calendar - $Month $Year</title>
  <style type="text/css">
    tr.weekdays td { width: 100px;
                     text-align: center;
                   }
    tr.week td { width: 100px;
                 height: 100px;
                 color: black;  }
  </style>
</head>
<body>
<form action="$this_script" method="post">
<table border="1">

<!-- Controls and calendar title (month) -->
<tr>
  <td colspan="1" align="left">
    <input type="submit" name="prev" value="&lt;&lt;" />
```

```
      </td>
      <td colspan="5" align="center">
        <strong>
          $month_text $year
        </strong>
        <input type="hidden" name="month" value="$month" />
        <input type="hidden" name="year" value="$year" />
      </td>
      <td colspan="1" align="right">
        <input type="submit" name="next" value="&gt;&gt;" />
      </td>
    </tr>

    <!-- Day of week header row -->
    <tr class="weekdays">
      <th>Sunday</th>
      <th>Monday</th>
      <th>Tuesday</th>
      <th>Wednesday</th>
      <th>Thursday</th>
      <th>Friday</th>
      <th>Saturday</th>
    </tr>

    <!-- Calendar (days) start here -->

HTML;

}  // End docheader()


// Do the document footer (close tags, end doc)
function docfooter() {

print <<<HTML
<!-- Close all open tags, end document -->
</table>
</form>
</body>
</html>

HTML;

} // End docfooter()


// Print an empty day (cell)
function emptyday() {

print <<<HTML
```

```
      <td align="right" valign="top"> </td>

HTML;

} // End emptyday()


// Print a day cell
function day($today,$month,$day,$year) {

  $curday = $month."/".$day."/".$year;
  if ($curday == $today) {
    $font = " style=\"color: red;\"";
  } else {
    $font = "";
  }

print <<< HTML
  <td align="right" valign="top" $font>$day</td>

HTML;

} // End day()


// Open or close a row
function weekrow($cmd) {

  switch ($cmd) {
    case "open":
      print "<tr class=\"week\">\n";
      break;
    case "close":
      print "</tr>\n";
      break;
  }

}  // End weekrow()


// Main program body
function main() {

  // Set the date vars by default, POST, or GET
  $vars = setvars();
  $today = $vars['today'];
  $month = $vars['month'];
  $year = $vars['year'];
  $cmd = $vars['cmd'];

  // Do the header and open first row
  docheader($month,$year);
```

```php
  weekrow("open");

  // Set up first weekday and 1st day (m/1/y)
  $first_weekday = date("w",strtotime($month."/1/".$year)) + 1;
  $day = 1;

  // Print empty days up to the first weekday of month
  for ($weekday = 1; $weekday < $first_weekday; $weekday++) {
    emptyday();
  }

  // Do rest of month while we have a valid date
  while (checkdate($month,$day,$year)) {
    // If SUN, open the row
    if ($weekday == 1) {
      weekrow("open");
    }
    // Print day and increment
    day($today,$month,$day,$year);
    $weekday++;
    $day++;
    // If SAT, close row reset weekday
    if ($weekday > 7) {
      weekrow("close");
      $weekday = 1;
    }

  }

  // Close current week
  while ($weekday != 1 && $weekday <= 7) {
    emptyday();
    $weekday++;
  }

  // Close document
  docfooter();

} // End main();


// Kick it all off
main();

?>
```

Output

This script displays a calendar similar to that shown in Figure 31-3, complete with buttons to move forward and backward month by month.

Form submit buttons

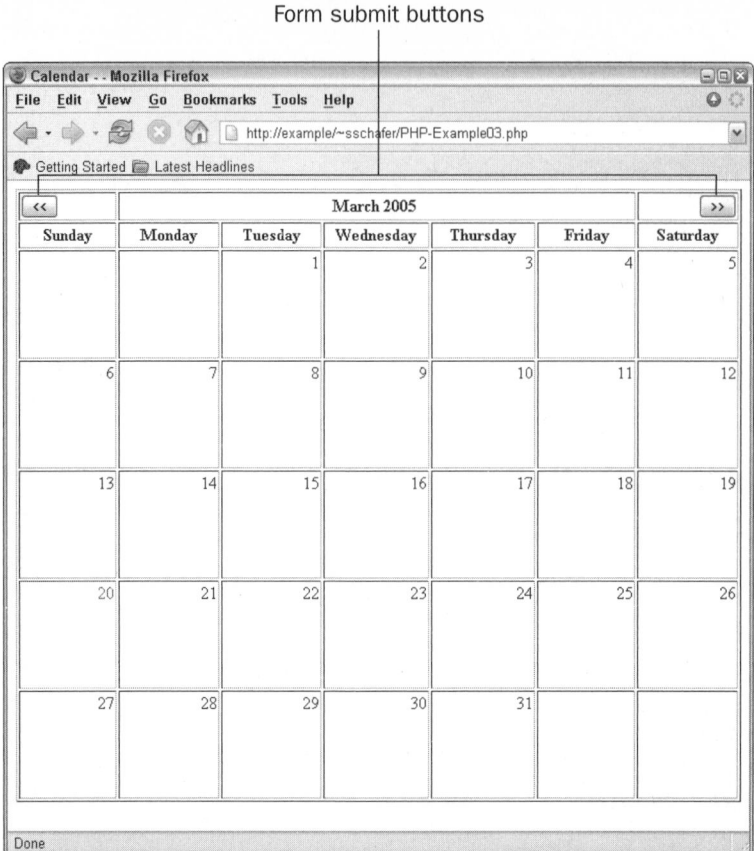

Figure 31-3

How It Works

This script combines the concepts shown in the previous two examples in this chapter, parsing HTTP-supplied data and displaying a calendar. The hidden fields month and year tell the script which month was displayed in the last run; the user clicking the prev or next submit button tells the script to subtract or add a month to display the month currently called for.

Once the month and year are determined, the script uses the same logic as shown in Example 1 to display the month, embedding the new month and year in the appropriate hidden fields.

This script can also be used to display an arbitrary month by passing the month and year values via GET (embedded in the URL). For example, calling this script with the following URL will result in it displaying the month March 2006:

```
calendar.php?month=3&year=2006
```

Improving the Script

This script shows a basic example of acting on form data and using it recursively to display a dynamic calendar. This capability can be used with a variety of other PHP functions to interact with other technologies, using the form data to control software and/or hardware.

This script is subject to the vulnerabilities with respect to the year 2038, as values outside the range of the UNIX calendar may not work on Linux and UNIX systems.

Accessing Databases

One important feature of dynamically generated content is the ability to interface with storage solutions, such as relational databases. Using relational database interoperability, scripts can perform complex queries against datasets and return the resulting data to the end user. This script performs a query against the sample database (detailed in the "Sample Data" section of Chapter 28) and returns the results in an XHTML table.

Example 4: Performing a Query and Reporting Data

Source

```php
<?php

// Document header (doctype -> body tag)
function docheader() {

  // If content header has not been sent,
  //   send it
  if (!headers_sent()) {
    header('Content-type: text/html');
  }

print <<<HTML
<!DOCTYPE html PUBLIC "-//W3C//DTD XHTML 1.1//EN"
    "http://www.w3.org/TR/xhtml11/DTD/xhtml11.dtd">
<html>
<head>
  <title>MySQL Query Result</title>
</head>
<body>

HTML;

} // End docheader()


// Connect the DB with the given creds
function connectDB($server,$user,$password,$dbname) {

  $link = mysql_connect($server, $user, $password)
    or die("Could not connect to server!");
```

```
    mysql_select_db($dbname)
      or die("Could not select database!");

    return $link;

}  // End connectDB()


// Do the query, return the result
function doquery($link,$query) {

  $result = mysql_query($query,$link)
    or die("Could not perform query!");

  return $result;

} // End doquery()


// Output the results of the query in a table
function dotable($result) {

print <<<HTML
<table border="1" cellpadding="5">
<tr>

HTML;

  $line = mysql_fetch_array($result, MYSQL_ASSOC);
  $headers = array_keys($line);

  for ($i=0; $i <= count($headers) - 1; $i++) {
    print "  <th>".$headers[$i]."</th>\n";
  }

  print "</tr>\n";

  mysql_data_seek($result,0);
  while ($line = mysql_fetch_array($result, MYSQL_ASSOC)) {
    print "<tr>\n";
    foreach ($line as $key => $value) {
      print "  <td>".$value."</td>\n";
    }
    print "</tr>\n";
  }

  print "</table>\n";

} // End dotable()


// Document footer (close tags and end document)
```

```php
function docfooter() {

print <<<HTML
</body>
</html>

HTML;

} // End docfooter()



// Main function
function main() {

  // Connect the DB
  $link = connectDB("localhost","webuser","password99","mysqlsamp");

// Set up and perform query
$query = <<<HTML
SELECT computers.comp_id as computer_id,
       mice.mouse_model as mouse_model,
       computers.comp_location as location
  FROM computers, mice
  WHERE mice.mouse_type = "USB"
  AND computers.comp_location like "A%"
  AND mice.mouse_comp = computers.comp_id

HTML;

  $result = doquery($link,$query);

  // Do document header
  docheader();

  // Do results in table
  dotable($result);

  // Do document footer
  docfooter();


}  // End main()


// Kick it all off
main();

?>
```

Output

This script results in a document with a table containing the results of the SQL query specified in the script, as shown in Figure 31-4.

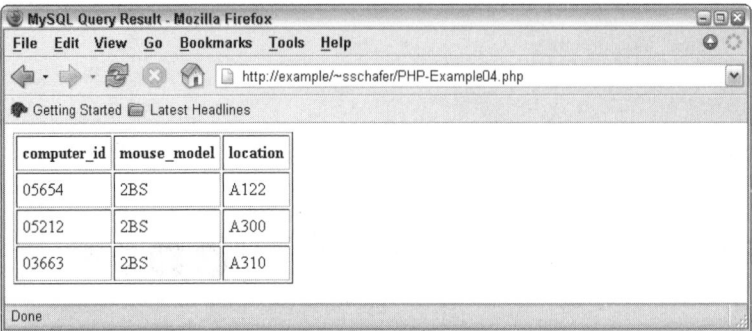

Figure 31-4

How It Works

This script uses the built-in PHP MySQL modules for the basic MySQL database. Using standard methods, the script connects to the database (using `mysql_connect()`), performs the query (using `mysql_query()`), and accesses the returned dataset (using `mysql_fetch_array()`, `mysql_data_seek()`, and `mysql_fetch_array()`) for output in a document.

PHP must be compiled with MySQL support and must have the MySQL library included in the **php.ini** *file to access the MySQL functions.*

Improving the Script

This script shows the most basic use of PHP's MySQL connectivity, querying a database and returning the dataset. Similar methods can be used to create more advanced documents — returning the entire content of a document, individual articles for use in a larger document, or other pieces of content for use in documents.

This script is generalized and will work with any database and any query. The resulting table will have a column for each column in the dataset returned by the query and a row for each row returned.

Summary

This chapter demonstrated a number of popular techniques used with PHP scripts to deliver dynamic content. Although the examples presented here are fairly simplistic by necessity, they provide a solid foundation for utilizing common techniques in PHP and provide building blocks you can use to create more robust applications.

XHTML Reference

Due to its XML heritage, XHTML is much less forgiving than HTML has historically been (or perhaps more accurately, than HTML browsers have been). You cannot leave out closing tags or place `<i>` inside `<a>`. Attribute values must be quoted, and minimized attributes are disallowed, leading to odd constructs such as `<select multiple="multiple">`.

Here are some tips to keep in mind when working with XHTML:

- ❑ XHTML documents must be well formed (closing tags required; no overlapping tags allowed).

- ❑ Empty elements can be both opened and closed with one tag: `<img src="foo"/>`.

- ❑ All elements and tags must be in lowercase.

- ❑ Attribute values must be quoted (either with single or double quotes).

- ❑ Attributes cannot be minimized. As an illustration, `<textarea>` supports a `readonly` attribute; in HTML 4, it would look like `<textarea readonly>`, but because XML does not support this syntax, with XHTML it would be `<textarea readonly="readonly">`.

In the element listings that follow, the location within a document in which each element may reside is indicated through one of two mechanisms. If the element has a very limited number of valid parent elements, those will be listed. Otherwise, the placement will be described as either "inline" or "block."

In turn, unless there are a limited number of valid children for a nonempty element, the content will be documented as some combination of block, inline, or text.

If an element is listed as having a block placement, it may reside directly within any other element that is listed as having block contents (and nowhere else). Most block elements will render as such, and most inline elements will render inline, but that is not always true.

For a list of the core, internationalization, and standard-event attributes, see the end of this appendix.

Element Listings

This section lists all of the elements defined in the strict DTD of XHTML 1.0.

\<a\>

Specify either the inclusion or terminating point of a hyperlink.

Context

Placement	Inline
Content	Inline and text

Attributes

Optional

```
accesskey="<character>"
charset="<character encoding>"
coords="<length (pixels or percentage),...>"
href="<URL>"
hreflang="<language code>"
name="<anchor>"
onblur="<script>"
onfocus="<script>"
rel="<linktype ...>"
rev="<linktype ...>"
shape="rect|circle|poly|default"
tabindex="<number>"
type="<MIME type>"
```
Core
Internationalization
Standard events

Usage Example

```
<p><a name="lincoln-anchor">Lincoln's</a>
<a href="http://en.wikipedia.org/wiki/Gettysburg_Address">Gettysburg
Address</a> has both been widely noted and long remembered.</p>
```

Using **\<a\>** *as an anchor point with the* **name** *attribute is frequently seen with machine-generated HTML that includes a table of contents or an index.*

\<abbr\>

Demarcate the enclosed text as an abbreviation.

Context

Placement	Inline
Content	Inline and text

Attributes

Optional

Core
Internationalization
Standard events

Usage Example

```
<p>If you're old enough to remember using <abbr>Fla</abbr> to send mail to
Florida, you're getting up there.  Of course, if you're old enough to remember
sending letters at all&hellip;</p>
```

The W3C refers to acronyms such as HTTP as abbreviations, so the distinction between **<abbr>** *and*
<acronym> *seems to be pretty fuzzy.*

<acronym>

Demarcate the enclosed text as an acronym.

Context

Placement	Inline
Content	Inline and text

Attributes

Optional

Core
Internationalization
Standard events

Usage Example

```
<p>The <acronym title="World Wide Web Consortium">W3C</acronym> is the organization
responsible for guiding <acronym title="HyperText Markup Language">HTML</acronym>
and many related standards.</p>
```

*When combined with the title attribute and CSS, this tag can be used to edify the reader. For example, if
the preceding paragraph is combined with a stylesheet that indicates that the browser should render
acronyms as underlined or boxed, the browser will render the acronyms in a way that indicates that the
user can interact with them, and placing the mouse over one of them will display a tooltip (assuming a
graphical Web browser).*

<address>

Demarcate the enclosed content as the address of an individual or organization.

Context

Placement	Block
Content	<p>, inline, and text

Attributes

Optional
Core
Internationalization
Standard events

Usage Example

```
<p>Sincerely, John Doe.</p>
<address>
  <p>1234 Main St.</p>
  <p>Springfield, U.S.  101010</p>
</address>
```

Infrequently used.

<area>

Describe the physical layout of an image map.

Context

Parent	<map>

Attributes

Required	Optional
alt="<text>"	accesskey="<character>"
	coords="<length (pixels or percentage),...>"
	href="<URL>"
	nohref="nohref"
	onblur="<script>"
	onfocus="<script>"
	shape="rect|circle|poly|default"
	tabindex="<number>"
	Core
	Internationalization
	Standard events

Usage Example

See <map>.

<b>

Indicate that the enclosed text should be rendered in a bold typeface.

Context

Placement	Inline
Content	Inline and text

Attributes

Optional

Core
Internationalization
Standard events

Usage Example

```
<p>Do <b>not</b> press the red button!</p>
```

*Whenever feasible, try describing the semantic meaning of the text instead of the rendering properties; for example, use **<em>** instead of **<b>**. CSS is the most flexible mechanism for specifying the appropriate rendering for semantic content.*

*See **<em>** and **<strong>**.*

<base>

Define the original/desired location for the document.

Context

Parent	<head>

Attributes

Required

```
href="<URL>"
```

Usage Example

```
<head>
  <base href="http://www.w3.org/TR/html401/index/elements.html"/>
  <title>Index of the HTML 4 Elements</title>
</head>
```

Used so that relative links within the document are evaluated with respect to the base location rather than wherever it may currently reside.

<bdo>

Indicate that the enclosed text should be rendered in a specific direction (left to right or right to left) that may be different from its environment.

Context

Placement	Inline
Content	Inline and text

Attributes

Required	Optional

`dir="ltr|rtl"`
`xml:lang="<language code>"`
Core
Standard events
	`lang="<language code>"`

Usage Example

```
<p><bdo dir="rtl">Quite a dramatic cultural difference to read text right to
left.</bdo></p>
```

Internationalization is a complex issue; the directionality in which a language is rendered is just one of many issues to consider. Most Web content ignores the issue, assuming that most readers will understand English, but it is unclear how long that assumption will hold true.

<big>

Indicate that the enclosed text should be rendered in a larger font.

Context

Placement	Inline
Content	Inline and text

Attributes

Optional
Core *Internationalization* *Standard events*

Usage Example

```
<p>Last week I nearly caught a <big>really big</big> fish, but it got
away.</p>
```

CSS provides more flexible font resizing.

See also **<small>**.

<blockquote>

Enclose a long quotation.

Context

Placement	Block
Content	Block, <form>, <noscript>, <ins>, <del>

Attributes

Optional

```
cite="<URL>"
```
Core
Internationalization
Standard events

Usage Example

```
<blockquote cite="htt ://wikisource.org/wiki/Gettysburg_Address">Four score
and seven years ago our fathers brought forth on this continent, a new nation,
conceived in Liberty, and dedicated to the proposition that all men are
created equal.</blockquote>
```

This should not be used as a mechanism for indenting arbitrary text. Instead, use a **<p>** *or* **<div>** *tag with CSS.*

See **<q>** *for the inline equivalent to this tag.*

<body>

All content visible on a Web page is contained within this tag.

Context

Parent	<html>
Content	Block, inline, and text

Attributes

Optional

```
onload="<script>"
onunload="<script>"
```
Core
Internationalization
Standard events

Usage Example

```
<html>
  <head><title>Just another web page</title></head>
  <body><h1>Just another web page</h1>
...
  </body>
</html>
```

Once upon a time, the body tag was optional. This is no longer true.

Force a newline between text or inline elements.

Context

Placement	Inline

Attributes

Optional

Core

Usage Example

```
<p>Down by the salley gardens my love and I did meet;<br/>
She passed the salley gardens with little snow-white feet.<br/>
She bid me take love easy, as the leaves grow on the tree;<br/>
But I, being young and foolish, with her would not agree.</p>
```

Use this tag sparingly. It should not be used as a substitute for paragraph tags.

See also **<pre>**.

<button>

Define a button in a form. Any content will be superimposed on the button.

Context

Placement	Inline
Content	Block, inline, and text

Attributes

Optional

```
accesskey="<character>"
disabled="disabled"
name="<button name>"
onblur="<script>"
onfocus="<script>"
tabindex="<number>"
type="button|submit|rese "
value="<application value "
```
Core
Internationalization
Standard events

Usage Example

```
<form action="/cgi-bin/post" method="post">
<p>...
<button value="submit"><img src="/images/submit.gif"/></button>
</p></form>
```

This is similar to the **<input type='button'>** *element but allows content.*

<caption>

Define a caption for a table.

Context

Parent	<table>
Content	Inline and text

Attributes

Optional

Core
Internationalization
Standard events

Usage Example

See `<table>`.

Contrary to what one might expect, by default a table caption is not rendered with any particular emphasis. Use CSS to highlight the caption, such as through use of a larger font or bold typeface.

<cite>

Demarcate a source citation.

Context

Placement	Inline
Content	Inline and text

Attributes

Optional
Core *Internationalization* *Standard events*

Usage Example

```
<p>The population of Freedonia in 1803 was larger than that of Malta.
(<cite>Williams 1953, p. 42</cite>)</p>
```

<code>

Demarcate inline code snippets.

Context

Placement	Inline
Content	Inline and text

Attributes

Optional
Core *Internationalization* *Standard events*

Usage Example

```
<p>In Perl, iterating over a list can easily be achieved with
<code>foreach</code>: <code>foreach my $value (sort @keys) { ... }</code>.</p>
```

*For longer blocks of code, use the **<pre>** element.*

<col>

Specify attributes for a full column in a table.

Context

Parents	<colgroup>
	<table>

Attributes

Optional

```
align="left|center|right|justify|char"
char="<character>"
charoff="<length (pixels or percentage)>"
span="<number>"
valign="top|middle|bottom|baseline"
width="<length (pixels, percentage, relative)>"
```
Core
Internationalization
Standard events

Usage Example

See <table>.

Support for this element is limited in many browsers.

<colgroup>

Group columns in a table for assigning attributes.

Context

Parent	<table>
Content	<col>

Attributes

Optional
align="left|center|right|justify|char" char="<character>" charoff="<length (pixels or percentage)>" span="<number>" valign="top|middle|bottom|baseline" width="<length (pixels, percentage, relative)>" *Core* *Internationalization* *Standard events*

Usage Example

See <table>.

As with **<col>**, *full support for this element is not widespread.*

<dd>

Wrap the definition of a term in a definition list.

Context

Parent	<dl>
Content	Inline and text

Attributes

Optional
Core *Internationalization* *Standard events*

Usage Example

See <dl>.

<del>

Demarcate content that has been deleted from a document.

Context

Placement	Anywhere inside <body> or its children
Content	Inline and textBlock permissible when not functioning as an inline

Attributes

Optional

```
cite="<URL>"
datetime="<ISO Date/Time>"
```
Core
Internationalization
Standard events

Usage Example

```
<p>Four score and seven years ago <del>when the British held sway over these
lands</del> our fathers brought forth, on this continent...
```

The inverse of this tag is **<ins>**.

<dfn>

Indicate that a term is defined in this location.

Context

Placement	Inline
Content	Inline and text

Attributes

Optional

Core
Internationalization
Standard events

Usage Example

```
<p><dfn>UNIX</dfn> is a widespread operating system that originated at Bell
Labs.</p>
```

This element is useful for machine-generated indices.

<div>

Enclose a block of content for structural or style purposes.

Context

Placement	Block
Content	Block, inline, and text

Attributes

Optional

Core
Internationalization
Standard events

Usage Example

```
<div class="blockquote">With CSS, this block of text can be rendered like a
&lt;blockquote&gt;.</div>
```

The inline equivalent is **\<span***:*

\<dl>

Enclose a list of terms and definitions.

Context

Placement	Block
Content	\<dt>
	\<dd>

Attributes

Optional

Core
Internationalization
Standard events

Usage Example

```
<dl><dt>molecule</dt>
<dd><cite>Webster's Revised Unabridged Dictionary (1913)</cite>: One of the
very small invisible particles of which all matter is supposed to consist.</dd>
</dl>
```

\<dt>

Wrap a term defined in a definition list.

Context

Parent	\<dl>
Content	Inline and text

Attributes

Optional

Core
Internationalization
Standard events

Usage Example

See `<dl>`.

`<em>`

Demarcate text that should be emphasized.

Context

Placement	Inline
Content	Inline and text

Attributes

Optional

Core
Internationalization
Standard events

Usage Example

```
<p>There is <em>no</em> substitute for catsup.</p>
```

See also **`<strong>`**, **`<i>`** *and* **`<b>`**.

`<fieldset>`

Wrap a group of related labels and controls in a form.

Context

Placement	Block
Content	First child: `<legend>` Remainder: Block, inline, and text

Attributes

Optional

Core
Internationalization
Standard events

Usage Example

See `<form>`.

*This element is useful for accessibility purposes. See **`<label>`** for another form element that is courteous to include to assist those who are using a nonvisual mechanism for "viewing" a form.*

`<form>`

Define a collection of controls used to gather and submit information to a Web application.

Context

Placement	Block
Content	Block (except nested `<form>` elements) Can also contain `<script>`

Attributes

Required	Optional
`action="<URL>"`	`accept-charset="<character encoding ...>"` `accept="<MIME type, ...>"` `enctype="<MIME type>"` `method="get|post"` `onreset="<script>"` `onsubmit="<script>"` *Core* *Internationalization* *Standard events*

Usage Example

```
<form action="https://www.example.com/cgi-bin/do-something.cgi"
onsubmit="validate()">
  <fieldset><legend>Shipping address</legend>
    <label>Name: <input type="text" name="name"/></label>
    <label>Street address: <input type="text" name="street"/></label>
  </fieldset>
  <p>
```

```
          <input type="submit" value="Ship it!"/>
          <input type="reset" value="Oops, start over"/>
     </p>
  </form>
```

Many HTML documents use inline elements such as `<input>` directly underneath a `<form>` tag, so the failure to use only block elements (not counting `<script>`) inside `<form>` is a common validation error when writing XHTML Strict DTD documents.

See also: `<input>`, `<button>`, `<textarea>`, `<select>`, `<label>`, and `<fieldset>`.

`<h1>`, `<h2>`, `<h3>`, `<h4>`, `<h5>`, `<h6>`

Header tags provide some structure to a document.

Context

Placement	Block
Content	Inline and text

Attributes

Optional

Core
Internationalization
Standard events

Usage Example

```
<body>
<h1>Analysis of the price of wheat in 17th century Freedonia</h1>
...
  <h2>Inflation between 1620 and 1640</h2>
...
    <h3>The great price spike of 1623</h3>
...
      <h4>Maltese shipping embargo: fact or political fiction?</h4>
...
  <h2>Price controls .n the latter half of the century</h2>
```

If you are unhappy with the way different header tags are rendered, you can use CSS to correct the problem without changing the tags.

`<head>`

Wrap the important metadata for a document.

Context

Parent	<html>	
Content	<base>	<script>
	<link>	<style>
	<meta>	<title>
	<object>	

Attributes

Optional

```
id="<ID>"
profile="<URL>"
```
Internationalization

Usage Example

```
<html>
  <head>
    <title>Freedonia through the ages</title>
    <meta name="author" content="John Q. Publique"/>
    <meta name="keywords" content="freedonia history europe"/>
    <style type="text/css"> ... </style>
  </head>
```

<hr>

Define the location for a horizontal rule in the document.

Context

Placement	Block

Attributes

Optional

Core
Internationalization
Standard events

Usage Example

```
<p>...</p>
<hr/>
<h3>Constitutional crisis of 1901: Freedonia's last stand</h3>
```

Styling horizontal rules with CSS is challenging due to inconsistencies between browsers.

<html>

This is the master element for most XHTML documents.

Context

Content	<head>
	<body>

Attributes

Optional

```
id="<ID>"
xmlns="<URI>"
Internationalization
```

Usage Example

```
<html>
  <head>
    <!-- Metadata here -->
  </head>
  <body>
    <!-- Content here -->
  </body>
</html>
```

The namespace URI for the **xmlns** *attribute for XHTML 1.0 is* `http://www.w3.org/1999/xhtml`.

<i>

Indicate that the contained text should be rendered with italics.

Context

Placement	Inline
Content	Inline and text

Attributes

Optional

Core
Internationalization
Standard events

Usage Example

```
<p><i>I thought they were finished,</i> she thought to herself.</p>
```

In many instances, the semantics behind the italics can be conveyed through tags such as **`<cite>`** *or* **`<em>`** *instead of using* **`<i>`**.

\<img>

Denote via a hyperlink an image to incorporate into the document.

Context

Placement	Inline

Attributes

Required	Optional

`alt="<text>"`
`src="<URL>"`
	`height="<length (pixels or percentage)>"`
	`ismap="ismap"`
	`longdesc="<URL>"`
	`usemap="<URL>"`
	`width="<length (pixels or percentage)>"`
	Core
	Internationalization
	Standard events

Usage Example

```
<img alt="Sleeping polar bear"
   src="http://www.example.com/images/polarbear.jpg"/>
```

Notes

See also **`<object>`**. *This tag is now redundant.*

\<input>

Define a mechanism for form input.

Context

Placement	Inline

Attributes

Optional

`accept="<MIME type, ...>"`
`accesskey="<character>"`
`alt="<short description>"`
`checked="checked"`
`disabled="disabled"`
`maxlength="<number>"`
`name="<input name>"`

```
onblur="<script>"
onchange="<script>"
onfocus="<script>"
onselect="<script>"
readonly="readonly"
size="<length (characters or pixels)>"
src="<URL>"
tabindex="<number>"
type="<input type>" (see Notes below)
usemap="<URL>"
value="<application value>"
```
Core
Internationalization
Standard events

Usage Example

See `<form>`.

The valid type attributes: text, password, checkbox, radio, submit, reset, file, hidden, image, button.

*See also: **`<button>`**, **`<textarea>`**, **`<select>`**, **`<label>`**, and **`<fieldset>`**.*

<ins>

Demarcate text or content that has been inserted into a document.

Context

Placement	Anywhere inside `<body>`
Content	Inline and text Block permissible when not functioning as an inline

Attributes

Optional

```
cite="<URL>"
datetime="<ISO Date/Time>"
```
Core
Internationalization
Standard events

Usage Example

```
<h2>Freedonia's Volcanoes</h2>
<ins><p>A new volcano erupted in 2003 along the northern coast...</p></ins>
```

*See also **`<del>`**.*

<kbd>

Indicate keyboard input.

Context

Placement	Inline
Content	Inline and text

Attributes

Optional

Core
Internationalization
Standard events

Usage Example

```
<li>At the username prompt, type <kbd>einstein</kbd>.</li>
```

<label>

Associate explanatory text with a form input control.

Context

Placement	Inline
Content	Inline and text

Attributes

Optional

```
accesskey="<character>"
for="<IDREF>"
onblur="<script>"
onfocus="<script>"
```
Core
Internationalization
Standard events

Usage Example

See <form>.

This element can significantly add to the user-friendliness of a form, especially for accessibility purposes. A browser should treat the label as an extension of the control — for example, clicking on a label next to a checkbox will toggle the checkbox.

\<legend>

Provide a caption for a set of form input controls.

Context

Parent	\<fieldset>
Content	Inline and text

Attributes

Optional

```
accesskey="<character>"
```
Core
Internationalization
Standard events

Usage Example

See \<form>.

If used, this must be the first child of a **\<fieldset>** *element, with nothing but whitespace preceding it.*

\<li>

Wrap a list item for an ordered or unordered list.

Context

Parent	\<ol>
	\<ul>
Content	Block, inline, and text

Attributes

Optional

Core
Internationalization
Standard events

Usage Example

See <ol>.

*Vertical whitespace between list items will expand when including nested **<p>** elements. If **<p>** elements are necessary to separate paragraphs within a single list item, CSS can be used to shrink the vertical whitespace if desired.*

<link>

Semantically associate related documents.

Context

Parent	<head>

Attributes

Optional

```
charset="<character encoding>"
href="<URL>"
hreflang="<language code>"
media="<media descriptor, ...>"
rel="<linktype ...>"
rev="<linktype ...>"
type="<MIME type>"
```
Core
Internationalization
Standard events

Usage Example

```
<head>
  <link rel="start" href="introduction.html"/>
  <link rel="prev" href="chapter-21.html"/>
  <link rel="next" href="chapter-23.html"/>
  <title>Freedonia History: Chapter 22</title>
</head>
```

See http://www.w3.org/TR/html401/struct/links.html for a good overview of the use of this element. The DTD does not constrain the link types that can be used.

<map>

Define an image map for navigation.

Context

Placement	Block

Content	`<area>`
	`<script>`
	`<noscript>`
	Block

Attributes

Required	Optional

`id="<ID>"`	`class="<text>"`
	`name="<map name>"`
	`style="<CSS>"`
	`title="<text>"`
	Internationalization
	Standard events

Usage Example

```
<h3>Freedonia Regions</h3>
<div>
  <img src="/images/image-map.gif" usemap="map-links"/>
  <map id="map-links" name="map-links">
    <area alt="Northern provinces" shape="rectangle" coords="0,0,100,50"
          href="/regions/north.html"/>
    <area alt="Eastern provinces" shape="rectangle" coords="50,50,100,100"
          href="/regions/east.html"/>
  </map>
</div>
```

*To maximize compatibility across browsers, specify both the **id** and **name** attributes with the same value.*

`<meta>`

Describe metadata for the document.

Context

Parent	`<head>`

Attributes

Required	Optional

`content="<TEXT>"`	`http-equiv="<HTTP header>"`
	`id="<ID>"`
	`name="<metadata key>"`
	`scheme="<metadata scheme identifier>"`
	Internationalization

Usage Example

See <head>.

*The XHTML DTD does not constrain the values for the **name** attribute, and there are many possible uses, including supplementary HTTP information and search engine hints regarding the content of the document.*

<noscript>

Offer alternative content for browsers that do not understand (or do not have enabled) the scripting language in use for the document.

Context

Placement	Block
Content	Block, inline, and text

Attributes

Optional
Core
Internationalization
Standard events

Usage Example

See <script>.

*Contrary to the example provided under **<script>**, **<noscript>** elements should not be used to nag the user about script support. They should be used only to convey information when the missing functionality is important.*

<object>

Embed external content into the document.

Context

Placement	Inline
Content	First children (if used): <param>
	Block, inline, and text

Attributes

Optional

```
archive="<URL,...>"
classid="<URL>"
codebase="<URL>"
codetype="<MIME type>"
data="<URL>"
declare="declare"
height="<length (pixels or percentage)>"
name="<object name>"
standby="<text>"
tabindex="<number>"
type="<MIME type>"
usemap="<URL>"
width="<length (pixels or percentage)>"
```
Core
Internationalization
Standard events

Usage Example

```
<object classid="cls d:8AD9C840-044E-11D1-B3E9-00805F499D93"
        height="400" width="600">
  <param name="code" value="Lifter"/>
  <param name="archive" value="Lifter.jar"/>
</object>
```

This element can be used to incorporate applications, images, and even other (X)HTML documents into the presentation of the current document.

<ol>

Define an ordered list (that is, one that uses numbers or characters as sequence indicators).

Context

Placement	Block
Content	<li>

Attributes

Optional

Core
Internationalization
Standard events

Usage Example

```
<ol style="list-style-type: lower-roman">
  <li>Register to vote</li>
  <li>Research candidates</li>
  <li>Vote on election day</li>
  <li>Complain about election results</li>
  <li>Rinse, repeat</li>
</ol>
```

*There is no equivalent to the **<caption>** tag in a table available for lists, but you can associate a header directly with the list by placing both inside a dedicated **<div>**.*

*See also: **<ul>**.*

<optgroup>

Group form selection options into a hierarchical structure.

Context

Parent	<select>
Content	<option>

Attributes

Required	Optional
label="<text>"	disabled="disabled" *Core* *Internationalization* *Standard events*

Usage Example

See <select>.

<option>

Define a form value to be selected from a list.

Context

Parents	<select> <optgroup>
Content	Text

Attributes

Optional

```
disabled="disabled"
label="<text>"
selected="selected"
value="<text sent to application>"
```
Core
Internationalization
Standard events

Usage Example

See <select>.

<p>

Demarcate the enclosed contents as a semantic paragraph.

Context

Placement	Block
Content	Inline and text

Attributes

Optional

Core
Internationalization
Standard events

Usage Example

```
<p>It was a dark and stormy night.</p>
<p><i>No, that's a lousy way to start a book</i>, she thought to herself,
forcefully erasing the first sentence.</p>
```

If a block is desired but the contents are not a paragraph, consider **<div>** *instead, or* **<pre>** *for preformatted text.*

<param>

Define values to be passed to a software object loaded into the document.

Context

Parent	<object>

Attributes

Optional

```
id="<ID>"
name="<parameter name>"
type="<MIME type>"
value="<parameter value>"
valuetype="data|ref|object"
Core
Internationalization
Standard events
```

Usage Example

See <object>.

<pre>

Specify that the contents of this block should preserve the whitespace as written, instead of compressing multiple spaces into one and breaking lines as dictated by the width of the container.

Context

Placement	Block
Content	Inline and text Disallowed: <img>, <object>, <big>, <small>

Attributes

Optional

```
Core
Internationalization
Standard events
```

Usage Example

```
<pre style="font-family: serif">
Down by the salley gardens my love and I did meet;
She passed the salley gardens with little snow-white feet.
She bid me take love easy, as the leaves grow on the tree;
But I, being young and foolish, with her would not agree.</pre>
```

If preformatted text is desired but a monospaced font is not, CSS can be used to correct the presentation, as in the preceding example.

<q>

Demarcate text that should be quoted appropriately for the language encoding.

Context

Placement	Inline
Content	Inline and text

Attributes

Optional

```
cite="<URL>"
```
Core
Internationalization
Standard events

Usage Example

```
<p>She said <q>Bite me,</q>, and Vlad took her literally.</p>
```

Internet Explorer is the only major browser that does not place quotes around the text as required by HTML 4 and XHTML 1.0.

<samp>

Indicate that the contents reflects sample output, as from software.

Context

Placement	Inline
Content	Inline and text

Attributes

Optional

Core
Internationalization
Standard events

Usage Example

```
<p>While working in the MacOS X Terminal, if you see <samp>command not
found</samp>, that means that you mistyped the command name.</p>
```

*See also **<kbd>** and **<tt>**.*

\<script>

Define a script to be used within the document.

Context

Placement	Inline or inside \<head>
Content	Text

Attributes

Required	Optional

`type="<MIME type>"`	`charset="<character encoding>"`
	`defer="defer"`
	`id="<ID>"`
	`src="<URL>"`

Usage Example

```
<body onload="place_cursor(document.getElementById('searchbar'))">
  <script type="text/javascript">
    function place_cursor(o) {
      o.focus();
    }
  </script>
  <noscript>
    <p>This page best viewed with JavaScript enabled.</p>
  </noscript>
  <div>
    <form action="/actions/do-search">
      <input type="text" id="searchbar"/>
    </form>
  </div>
```

The script can be written int the document or defined outside the document and linked in via the **src** *attribute.*

\<select>

Wrap a list of options in a form.

Context

Placement	Inline
Content	\<optgroup> \<option>

Attributes

Optional

```
disabled="disabled"
multiple="multiple"
name="<select name>"
onblur="<script>"
onchange="<script>"
onfocus="<script>"
size="<number>"
tabindex="<number>"
```
Core
Internationalization
Standard events

Usage Example

```
<select name="operating systems">
  <optgroup label="UNIX">
    <option label="HP-UX" value="HPUX">HP-UX</option>
    <option label="Solaris" value="Solaris">Solaris</option>
    <option label="MacOS X" value="Darwin" selected='selected'>
      MacOS X
    </option>
    <option label="I nux" value="Linux">Linux</option>
  </optgroup>
  <optgroup label="Macintosh">
    <option label="MacOS Classic (through v9)" value="MacOS">
      MacOS Classic (through v9)
    </option>
    <option label="MacOS X" value="Darwin">MacOS X</option>
  </optgroup>
  <optgroup label="Other">
    <option label="Windows" value="Windows">Windows</option>
    <option label="Amiga" value="Amiga">Amiga</option>
    <option label="Mainframe" value="mainframe">Mainframe</option>
  </optgroup>
</select>
```

*In the absence of a **value** attribute, the contents of the **<option>** tag will be passed to the Web application. It is better to use **value** so that the appearance of the option can be changed without breaking the application.*

<small>

Request that the enclosed contents be rendered with a smaller font.

Context

Placement	Inline
Content	Inline and text

Attributes

Optional

Core
Internationalization
Standard events

Usage Example

```
<p>The oxonium ion is represented as
[H<small><sub>3</sub></small>O<small>]<sup>+</sup></small>.</p>
```

See also **<big>** *for the converse.*

<span>

Demarcate inline text and elements for assigning attributes.

Context

Placement	Inline
Content	Inline and text

Attributes

Optional

Core
Internationalization
Standard events

Usage Example

```
<p>You can use CSS <span style="font-variant: small-caps">to achieve all sorts
of interesting effects</span>.</p>
```

See also **<div>** *for assigning attributes to a block.*

<strong>

Demarcate text that should be rendered with strong emphasis.

Context

Placement	Inline
Content	Inline and text

Attributes

Optional
Core
Internationalization
Standard events

Usage Example

```
<p>"There is <strong>no one</strong> better qualified to be dog catcher than
me," he reiterated.</p>
```

See also **<em>** *and* **<b>**.

<style>

Define style rules for the document.

Context

Parent	<head>
Content	Text

Attributes

Required	Optional
type="<MIME type>"	id="<ID>"
	media="<media descriptor, ...>"
	title="<text>"
	Internationalization

Usage Example

```
<head>
  <style type="text/css">
    .booktitle { font-style: italic }
  </style>
</head>
<body>
  <p>The first book I read in college was <span class="booktitle">Pride and
Prejudice</span>.</p>
```

Linking an external stylesheet into the document is often preferable to achieve greater consistency across a site and limit the amount of spurious bandwidth usage. To do so, use **<link>**.

<sub>

Indicate text that should be rendered as a subscript.

Context

Placement	Inline
Content	Inline and text

Attributes

Optional
Core Internationalization Standard events

Usage Example

See `<small>`.

`<sup>`

Indicate text that should be rendered as a superscript.

Context

Placement	Inline
Content	Inline and text

Attributes

Optional
Core Internationalization Standard events

Usage Example

See `<small>`.

`<table>`

Define content to be presented in a tabular format.

Context

Placement	Block	
Content	`<caption>`	`<thead>`
	`<col>`	`<tfoot>`
	`<colgroup>`	`<tbody>`
		`<tr>`

Attributes

```
border="<pixel length>"
cellpadding="<length (pixels or percentage)>"
cellspacing="<length (pixels or percentage)>"
frame="void|above|below|hsides|lhs|rhs|vsides|box|border"
rules="none|groups|rows|cols|all"
summary="<text>"
width="<length (pixels or percentage)>"
```
Core
Internationalization
Standard events

Usage Example

```
<table>
  <caption>Freedonia National Debt: 1400-1800</caption>
  <col width="30%">
  <colgroup style="text-align: right">
    <col width="30%">
    <col width="30%">
  </colgroup>
  <thead>
    <tr><th>Decade</th><th>Debt (in Freds)</th><th>Percentage of GDP</th></tr>
  </thead>
  <tfoot>
    <tr><th>Decade</th><th>Debt (in Freds)</th><th>Percentage of GDP</th></tr>
  </tfoot>
  <tbody>
    <tr><th>1400-1410</th><td>3000</td><td>7%</td></tr>
    <tr><th>1410-1420</th><td>5000</td><td>8%</td></tr>
...
    <tr><th>1780-1790</th><td>425,000,000</td><td>10%</td></tr>
    <tr><th>1790-1800</th><td>500,000,000</td><td>10%</td></tr>
  </tbody>
</table>
```

CSS provides for very granular control over the presence and rendering of table borders, both internal and external.

<tbody>

Define the main body of a table.

Context

Parent	<table>
Content	<tr>

Attributes

Optional

```
align="left|center|right|justify|char"
char="<character>"
charoff="<length (pixels or percentage)>"
valign="top|middle|bottom|baseline"
```
Core
Internationalization
Standard events

Usage Example

See <table>.

<td>

Demarcate a data cell in a table.

Context

Parent	<tr>
Content	Block, inline, and text

Attributes

Optional

```
abbr="<text>"
align="left|center|right|justify|char"
axis="<category,...>"
char="<character>"
charoff="<length (pixels or percentage)>"
colspan="<number>"
headers="<IDREFS>"
rowspan="<number>"
scope="row|col|rowgroup|colgroup"
valign="top|middle|bottom|baseline"
```
Core
Internationalization
Standard events

Usage Example

See <table>.

<textarea>

Define a block for text input in a form.

Context

Placement	Inline
Content	Text

Attributes

Required	Optional

`cols="<number>"`
`rows="<number>"`
	`accesskey="<character>"`
	`disabled="disabled"`
	`name="<textarea name>"`
	`onblur="<script>"`
	`onchange="<script>"`
	`onfocus="<script>"`
	`onselect="<script>"`
	`readonly="readonly"`
	`tabindex="<number>"`
	Core
	Internationalization
	Standard events

Usage Example

```
<textarea name="address" cols='50' rows='5'>Please replace this text with your
billing address.</textarea>
```

For a single line of text input, use **`<input type="text">`** *instead.*

<tfoot>

Define the footer for a table.

Context

Parent	`<table>`
Content	`<tr>`

Attributes

Optional

```
align="left|center|right|justify|char"
char="<character>"
charoff="<length (pixels or percentage)>"
valign="top|middle|bottom|baseline"
```
Core
Internationalization
Standard events

Usage Example

See <table>.

Defining footers and headers separately from the body for a table allows the browser to render them repeatedly, as appropriate, when the table spans multiple pages (for example, in printed output).

<th>

Demarcate a data cell in a table that serves as a heading.

Context

Parent	<tr>
Content	Block, inline, and text

Attributes

Optional

```
abbr="<text>"
align="left|center|right|justify|char"
axis="<category,...>"
char="<character>"
charoff="<length (pixels or percentage)>"
colspan="<number>"
headers="<IDREFS>"
rowspan="<number>"
scope="row|col|rowgroup|colgroup"
valign="top|middle|bottom|baseline"
```
Core
Internationalization
Standard events

Usage Example

See <table>.

\<thead\>

Define the header for a table.

Context

Parent	\<table\>
Content	\<tr\>

Attributes

Optional

```
align="left|center|right|justify|char"
char="<character>"
charoff="<length (pixels or percentage)>"
valign="top|middle|bottom|baseline"
Core
Internationalization
Standard events
```

Usage Example

See \<table\>.

\<title\>

Define the title for a document.

Context

Parent	\<head\>
Content	Text

Attributes

Optional

```
id="<ID>"
Internationalization
```

Usage Example

```
<head>
  <title>Flora and Fauna of Freedonia</title>
</head>
```

A meaningful title is very useful when browsing search engine results.

\<tr>

Define a row of data in a table.

Context

Parents	`<table>`
	`<thead>`
	`<tfoot>`
Content	`<th>`
	`<td>`

Attributes

Optional

```
align="left|center|right|justify|char"
char="<character>"
charoff="<length (pixels or percentage)>"
valign="top|middle|bottom|baseline"
```
Core
Internationalization
Standard events

Usage Example

See `<table>`.

\<tt>

Demarcate text that should be rendered in a monospace typeface.

Context

Placement	Inline
Content	Inline and text

Attributes

Optional

Core
Internationalization
Standard events

Usage Example

```
<p>If you want to IM me, my username is <tt>frd42</tt>.</p>
```

Consider instead a semantic element such as **<samp>**, **<var>**, *or* **<kbd>** *when appropriate.*

<ul>

Define an unordered list.

Context

Placement	Block
Content	<li>

Attributes

Optional

Core
Internationalization
Standard events

Usage Example

```
<div>
  <h3>Grocery list</h3>
  <ul style="list-style-type: square">
    <li>Milk</li>
    <li>Paper towels</li>
    <li>Salt</li>
  </ul>
</div>
```

<var>

Demarcate text as a variable name.

Context

Placement	Inline
Content	Inline and text

Attributes

Optional

Core
Internationalization
Standard events

Usage Example

```
<p>Changing the environment variable <var>HOME</var> can have unexpected
consequences.</p>
```

*See also **<kbd>**, **<samp>**, and **<tt>**.*

Event Attributes

The following section lists those attributes relevant to providing script hooks for responding to events such as page loading and mouse movement.

Standard Events

The standard event attributes that are supported by most elements:

Attribute	Triggered By
onclick	Pointer button was clicked.
ondblclick	Pointer button was double clicked.
onmousedown	Pointer button was pressed down.
onmouseup	Pointer button was released.
onmouseover	Pointer was moved into.
onmousemove	Pointer was moved within.
onmouseout	Pointer was moved away.
onkeypress	Key was pressed and released.
onkeydown	Key was pressed.
onkeyup	Key was released.

Other Events

Less-common event attributes:

Attribute	Triggered By
onload	Document has been loaded.
onunload	Document has been removed.
onblur	Element lost focus.
onfocus	Element gained focus.

Attribute	Triggered By
onreset	Form was reset.
onsubmit	Form was submitted.
onchange	Form element value changed.
onselect	Text in a form field has been selected.

Other Common Attributes

This section lists the other attributes that are supported by most elements.

Core Attributes

Attribute	Description
id	ID value unique to this document
class	Space-separated list of classes useful for selecting this element for style and other purposes
style	Local style information
title	Advisory title, typically rendered by a graphical browser when the pointer is over the element

Internationalization Attributes

Attribute	Description
lang	Language code for this element's contents
dir	Direction (ltr or rtl) for the text

Common Color Codes

This table lists the available color codes in both text and their name format.

The palette and color depth used on the user agent's platform may affect how colors are rendered on individual platforms.

Color Name	Color Code
Aliceblue	F0F8FF
Antiquewhite	FAEBD7
Aqua	00FFFF
Aquamarine	7FFFD4
Azure	F0FFF
Beige	F5F5DC
Bisque	FFE4C4
Black	000000
Blanchedalmond	FFEBCD
Blue	0000FF
Blueviolet	8A2BE2
Brown	A52A2A
Burlywood	DEB887
Cadetblue	5F9EA0
Chartreuse	7FFF00
Chocolate	D2691E
Coral	FF7F50
Cornflowerblue	6495ED
Cornsilk	FFF8DC
Crimson	DC143C
Cyan	00FFFF
Darkblue	00008B
Darkcyan	008B8B
Darkgoldenrod	B8860B
Darkgray	A9A9A9
Darkgreen	006400
Darkkhaki	BDB76B
Darkmagenta	8B008B
Darkolivegreen	556B2F
Darkorange	FF8C00
Darkorchid	9932CC

Color Name	Color Code
Darkred	8B0000
Darksalmon	E9967A
Darkseagreen	8FBC8F
Darkslateblue	483D8B
Darkslategray	2F4F4F
Darkturquoise	00CED1
Darkviolet	9400D3
Deeppink	FF1493
Deepskyblue	00BFFF
Dimgray	696969
Dodgerblue	1E90FF
Firebrick	B22222
Floralwhite	FFFAF0
Forestgreen	228B22
Fuchsia	FF00FF
Gainsboro	DCDCDC
Ghostwhite	F8F8FF
Gold	FFD700
Goldenrod	DAA520
Gray	808080
Green	008000
Greenyellow	ADFF2F
Honeydew	F0FFF0
Hotpink	FF69B4
Indianred	CD5C5C
Indigo	4B0082
Ivory	FFFFF0
Khaki	F0E68C
Lavender	E6E6FA
Lavenderblush	FFF0F5

Table continued on following page

Color Name	Color Code
Lawngreen	7CFC00
Lemonchiffon	FFFACD
Lightblue	ADD8E6
Lightcoral	F08080
Lightcyan	E0FFFF
Lightgoldenrodyellow	FAFAD2
Lightgreen	90EE90
Lightgrey	D3D3D3
Lightpink	FFB6C1
Lightsalmon	FFA07A
Lightseagreen	20B2AA
Lightskyblue	87CEFA
Lightslategray	778899
Lightsteelblue	B0C4DE
Lightyellow	FFFFE0
Lime	00FF00
Limegreen	32CD32
Linen	FAF0E6
Magenta	FF00FF
Maroon	800000
Mediumauqamarine	66CDAA
Mediumblue	0000CD
Mediumorchid	BA55D3
Mediumpurple	9370D8
Mediumseagreen	3CB371
Mediumslateblue	7B68EE
Mediumspringgreen	00FA9A
Mediumturquoise	48D1CC
Mediumvioletred	C71585
Midnightblue	191970
Mintcream	F5FFFA

Color Name	Color Code
Mistyrose	FFE4E1
Moccasin	FFE4B5
Navajowhite	FFDEAD
Navy	000080
Oldlace	FDF5E6
Olive	808000
Olivedrab	688E23
Orange	FFA500
Orangered	FF4500
Orchid	DA70D6
Palegoldenrod	EEE8AA
Palegreen	98FB98
Paleturquoise	AFEEEE
Palevioletred	D87093
Papayawhip	FFEFD5
Peachpuff	FFDAB9
Peru	CD853F
Pink	FFC0CB
Plum	DDA0DD
Powderblue	B0E0E6
Purple	800080
Red	FF0000
Rosybrown	BC8F8F
Royalblue	4169E1
Saddlebrown	8B4513
Salmon	FA8072
Sandybrown	F4A460
Seagreen	2E8B57
Seashell	FFF5EE
Sienna	A0522D
Silver	C0C0C0

Table continued on following page

Color Name	Color Code
Skyblue	87CEEB
Slateblue	6A5ACD
Slategray	708090
Snow	FFFAFA
Springgreen	00FF7F
Steelblue	4682B4
Tan	D2B48C
Teal	008080
Thistle	D8BFD8
Tomato	FF6347
Turquoise	40E0D0
Violet	EE82EE
Wheat	F5DEB3
White	FFFFFF
Whitesmoke	F5F5F5
Yellow	FFFF00
YellowGreen	9ACD32

CSS Properties

This appendix follows CSS 2.1, which is a specification intended to represent the most commonly supported properties in modern browsers.

> *Aural stylesheet properties are not covered in this appendix because adequate coverage of their use and capabilities goes well beyond a quick reference. For information on aural properties and their use, visit The Alliance for Technology Access Web site:* http://www.ataccess.org/.

Selector Examples

The following table should be used as a quick reference of CSS selector syntax. For more on selectors, see Chapter 13 and the end of this appendix.

Type of Selector	Example	Sample Match (matched tag in bold for reference)
By name	h1, h2, h3	**\<h2\>**
By class	.booktitle	**\<span class="booktitle"\>**
By id	div#logo	**\<div id="logo"\>**
By any attribute	acronym[title]	**\<acronym title="Ta Ta For Now"\>**
As child	div > p	\<div\>**\<p\>**
As grandchild or deeper	div * p	\<div\>\<form\>**\<p\>**
As child, grandchild, or deeper	div p	\<div\>**\<p\>**
As sibling	th + td	\<tr\>\<th scope="row"\>. . . \</th\>**\<td\>**
Pseudo-class	:visited	**\<a\>** (after being visited)

Property Listings

In each table that follows, words under Supported Values that are capitalized are placeholders for either a set of possible values or values drawn from a related property. Examples of placeholders include the following:

Length	Number followed by a unit of measurement, such as "px" for pixel
Percentage	Number followed by a percent sign
Integer	Whole number

Inherited refers to whether a given property will be drawn from the element's parents if it is not explicitly provided.

The set of elements to which a property applies may well be smaller than the set under which it may be defined. For example, the list styles apply to `<li>` elements, but are commonly defined at the list level when the XHTML `style` attribute is used.

> *Support for many of these properties is spotty. Testing on a wide variety of Web browsers is recommended, and there are Web sites that provide extensive information on CSS support across the popular browsers. Among the most comprehensive sites is http://www.blooberry.com.*

Background

The properties listed in this section control the color or image displayed behind an element.

background-image

Place an image behind an element (typically the body of a document).

```
table { background-image: url("/images/draft.gif"); }
```

Supported values:	`url()`, `none`, `inherit`
Default value:	`none`
Inherited:	No
Applies to:	All

background-repeat

Define the background image behavior if it fails to fill its element.

```
table { background-repeat: none; }
```

Supported values:	repeat, repeat-x, repeat-y, no-repeat, inherit
Default value:	repeat
Inherited:	No
Applies to:	All

background-attachment

Specify whether the background image scrolls with its enclosing element.

```
table { background-attachment: fixed; }
```

Supported values:	scroll, fixed, inherit
Default value:	scroll
Inherited:	No
Applies to:	All
Note(s):	Browsers not required to support "fixed"

background-position

Declare the initial position of a background image.

```
table { background-position: 25% 25%; }
```

Supported values:	Percentage, Length, top, center, bottom, left, right, inherit
Default value:	0 0
Inherited:	No
Applies to:	All
Note(s):	If two values are supplied, the first is a horizontal position and the second vertical. If one numeric value is supplied, it is treated as a horizontal position, and vertical will be 50%.

background-color

Define the background color for an element.

```
body { background-color: black; }
```

Supported values:	Color, transparent, inherit
Default value:	transparent
Inherited:	No
Applies to:	All

background

Consolidate background properties.

```
table { background: url("/images/draft.gif") none fixed 25% 25%; }
```

Supported values:	Color Image Repeat Attachment Position, inherit
Default value:	transparent none repeat scroll 0 0
Inherited:	No
Applies to:	All

List

These properties apply to the rendering of lists.

See also `counter-increment` and `counter-reset` under the "Generated Content" section later in this appendix.

list-style-type

Bullet markers for a list.

```
ul.nobullet { list-style-type: none; }
```

Supported values:	disc, circle, square, decimal, decimal-leading-zero, lower-roman, upper-roman, lower-greek, lower-latin, upper-latin, armenian, georgian, none, inherit
Default value:	disc
Inherited:	Yes
Applies to:	`<li>`

list-style-position

Indicate whether the list markers should be treated as internal to the box enclosing each list item.

```
ol.paragraphs { list-style-position: inside; }
```

Supported values:	inside, outside, inherit
Default value:	outside
Inherited:	Yes
Applies to:	`<li>`

list-style-image

Refer to an image to be used for bullet markers.

```
ul { list-style-image: url("/images/daggers.gif"); }
```

Supported values:	url(), none, inherit
Default value:	none
Inherited:	Yes
Applies to:	<li>
Note(s):	

list-style

Consolidate list style properties.

```
ul { list-style: circle outside url("/images/daggers.gif"); }
```

Supported values:	Type Position Image, inherit
Default value:	disc outside none
Inherited:	Yes
Applies to:	<li>
Note(s):	If both a type and image are supplied, the list style type will be used if the image cannot be retrieved.

Generated Content

CSS provides for the insertion of new text in certain locations via the content property.

The other properties in this section affect the text inserted by content by modifying the open/close quotes or by impacting a named counter value. Counters are not widely supported.

content

Text to be displayed before or after an element.

```
.quote:before { content: open-quote; }
.quote:after { content: close-quote; }
```

Supported values:	normal, String, url(), counter(), counters(), attr(), open-quote, close-quote, no-open-quote, no-close-quote, inherit
Default value:	normal
Inherited:	No
Applies to:	:before, :after pseudo-elements

quotes

Define quotation marks for use with <q> and content properties.

```
body { quotes: "\00AB" "\00BB"; }
```

Supported values:	String String, none, inherit
Default value:	Browser-defined
Inherited:	Yes
Applies to:	All

counter-increment

Indicate that the named counter should be incremented by one or the numeric value provided. The value stored in that counter may be retrieved via a counter() or counters() invocation from a content property.

```
div.section { counter-increment: sectionheading; }
div.section h2:before { "Section " counter(sectionheading); }
```

Supported values:	Identifier Integer, none, inherit
Default value:	none
Inherited:	No
Applies to:	All

counter-reset

Indicate that the named counter should be set back to zero or the numeric value provided.

```
div.section { counter-reset: sectionsubheading; }
```

Supported values:	Identifier Integer, none, inherit
Default value:	none
Inherited:	No
Applies to:	All

Font and Text

These properties are used to specify the way text is rendered.

text-align

Specify the text alignment within the block.

```
pre.poem { text-align: center; }
```

Supported values:	center, left, right, justify, inherit
Default value:	left (but see Note line of this table)
Inherited:	Yes
Applies to:	Block elements, <td>, <th>, and form input fields
Note(s):	The default value is 'right' if 'direction: rtl' is set.

text-decoration

Augment the text with underlining or similar properties.

```
p.annoying { text-decoration: line-through blink; }
```

Supported values:	none, underline, overline, line-through, blink, inherit
Default value:	none
Inherited:	No
Applies to:	All
Note(s):	Several decorations may be listed with whitespace separation.

text-indent

Specify the indentation for the first line in a block.

```
p { text-indent: 1em; }
```

Supported values:	Length, Percentage, inherit
Default value:	0
Inherited:	Yes
Applies to:	Block elements, <td>, <th>, and form input fields.

text-transform

Convert text to uppercase or lowercase.

```
span.customername { text-transform: uppercase; }
```

Supported values:	capitalize, uppercase, lowercase, none, inherit
Default value:	none
Inherited:	Yes
Applies to:	All

color

Define text color.

```
div.hardtoread { color: yellow; }
```

Supported values:	Color, inherit
Default value:	Browser-defined
Inherited:	Yes
Applies to:	All
Note(s):	Any borders in this scope will default to this color.

font-family

Define the desired typeface.

```
body { font-family: Garamond, serif; }
```

Supported values:	Family (1 or more comma-separated values), inherit
Default value:	Browser-defined
Inherited:	Yes
Applies to:	All
Note(s):	Use quotes around font family names that include spaces. Be sure to provide generic families as alternatives should the browser not be able to locate the font you prefer.

font-size

Specify the type size.

```
caption { font-size: x-large; }
```

Supported values:	Length, Percentage, xx-large, x-large, large, medium, small, x-small, xx-small, larger, smaller, inherit
Default value:	medium
Inherited:	Yes
Applies to:	All

font-style

Render the enclosed text as italic, oblique, or normal.

```
.booktitle { font-style: italic; }
```

Supported values:	`normal, italic, oblique, inherit`
Default value:	`normal`
Inherited:	Yes
Applies to:	All

font-variant

Render the enclosed text as small capitals or normal.

```
span.manufacturername { font-variant: small-caps; }
```

Supported values:	`normal, small-caps, inherit`
Default value:	`normal`
Inherited:	Yes
Applies to:	All

font-weight

Specify the "boldness" of text.

```
caption { font-weight: 900; }
```

Supported values:	`normal, bolder, bold, lighter, 100, 200, 300, 400, 500, 600, 700, 800, 900`
Default value:	`normal`
Inherited:	Yes
Applies to:	All
Note(s):	`'normal'` is equivalent to `400`; `'bold'` to `700`

font

Consolidate font properties or specify system fonts.

```
h6 { font: menu; }
```

Supported values:	`caption`, `icon`, `menu`, `message-box`, `small-caption`, `status-bar`, `inherit` (and see Note(s) section in this table)
Default value:	See `font-style`, `font-variant`, `font-weight`, `font-size`
Inherited:	Yes
Applies to:	All
Note(s):	The value can be one of the preceding or a combination of the other font properties with line-height thrown in to confuse things.

letter-spacing

Add to the spacing between letters.

```
blockquote { letter-spacing: 0.1em; }
```

Supported values:	Length, `normal`, `inherit`
Default value:	`normal`
Inherited:	Yes
Applies to:	All
Note(s):	The value may be negative.

word-spacing

Add to the spacing between words.

```
h2 { word-spacing: 1em; }
```

Supported values:	Length, `normal`, `inherit`
Default value:	`normal`
Inherited:	Yes
Applies to:	All

white-space

Specify the handling of whitespace, including line wrapping. The `normal` value is reasonably self-explanatory; `pre` is effectively the same as the `<pre>` XHTML element; `nowrap` allows text to exceed the width of the page; `pre-wrap` preserves whitepace like `pre`, but will wrap as necessary; `pre-line` is as `normal`, but it will honor line breaks in the XHTML.

```
blockquote.poem { white-space: pre; }
```

Supported values:	`normal`, `pre`, `nowrap`, `pre-wrap`, `pre-line`, `inherit`
Default value:	`normal`
Inherited:	Yes
Applies to:	All

Text Direction

These properties are required to deal with the problems arising from the fact that some languages read right to left, and others left to right.

unicode-bidi

This, combined with the `direction` property, handles the directionality of text for a document. This property is useful only when two languages of different directionality are present.

```
span.arabic { unicode-bidi: embed; direction: rtl; }
span.english { unicode-bidi: embed; direction: ltr; }
```

Supported values:	`normal`, `embed`, `bidi-override`, `inherit`
Default value:	`normal`
Inherited:	No
Applies to:	All

direction

Define the direction for the enclosed text.

```
p.english { direction: ltr; }
```

Supported values:	`ltr`, `rtl`, `inherit`
Default value:	`ltr`
Inherited:	Yes
Applies to:	All except for inline elements with `unicode-bidi: normal`

Block

Graphical browsers lay out a page as a sequence of boxes. These properties specify the way the box sizes and other internal properties should be handled.

The key differentiator between padding and margin: the padding is inside any border around a block, and the margin is outside that border.

margin-left, margin-right, margin-top, margin-bottom

Define the size of the margin on a given side of a block.

```
blockquote { margin-left: 10%; }
```

Supported values:	Length, Percentage, auto
Default value:	0
Inherited:	No
Applies to:	All except for table components (e.g. `<td>`, `<tfoot>`, `<tr>`)

margin

Consolidate margin widths.

```
p { margin: 1em 0 1em 0; }
```

Supported values:	Length, Percentage, auto (up to 4 values)
Default value:	0 0 0 0
Inherited:	No
Applies to:	All except for table components (e.g. `<td>`, `<tfoot>`, `<tr>`)
Note(s):	Order of values: top, right, bottom, left

padding-left, padding-right, padding-top, padding-bottom

Define the size of the padding on a given side of a block.

```
div.withborder { padding-top: 2%; }
```

Supported values:	Length, Percentage, inherit
Default value:	0
Inherited:	No
Applies to:	All excluding table components (but including `<td>`, `<th>`)

padding

Consolidate padding widths.

```
div.withborder { padding: 2% 0 0 0; }
```

Supported values:	Length, Percentage, inherit (up to 4 values)
Default value:	0 0 0 0
Inherited:	No
Applies to:	All excluding table components (but including <td>, <th>)
Note(s):	Order of values: top, right, bottom, left

clip

Define a boundary for an element outside of which any presentation (text, border) should be clipped.

```
blockquote { clip: rect(5px, 20px, 20px, 5px); overflow: scroll; }
```

Supported values:	Shape, auto, inherit
Default value:	auto
Inherited:	No
Applies to:	Absolutely positioned elements
Note(s):	If overflow is visible, this has no effect. The only recognized shape is rect(). The arguments to rect() are offsets from the border edge of the containing box: top (offset from top), right (offset from left), bottom (offset from top), left (offset from left). If the text direction is right to left, the right and left arguments are offsets from the right border.

overflow

Specify what happens when a block's content is larger than the clipping area.

```
blockquote { clip: rect(5px, 20px, 20px, 5px); overflow: scroll; }
```

Supported values:	visible, hidden, scroll, auto, inherit
Default value:	visible
Inherited:	No
Applies to:	Block elements, <img>, <object>, <td>, <th>

height, width

Specify the height or width of an element.

```
img.logo { height: 5cm; width: 5cm; }
```

Supported values:	Length, Percentage, auto, inherit
Default value:	auto
Inherited:	No
Applies to:	Block elements, `<img>`, `<object>`, and form input fields

max-height, max-width

Constrain element size.

```
table { max-width: 50%; }
```

Supported values:	Length, Percentage, none, inherit
Default value:	none
Inherited:	No
Applies to:	Block elements, `<img>`, `<object>`, and form input fields

min-height, min-width

Define a minimum element size.

```
textarea { min-width: 25%; }
```

Supported values:	Length, Percentage, inherit
Default value:	0
Inherited:	No
Applies to:	Block elements, `<img>`, `<object>`, and form input fields

line-height

Define line height. For block elements, this is the minimal line height; for inline, it is the specific height.

```
p { line-height: 150%; }
```

Supported values:	Number, Length, Percentage, normal, inherit
Default value:	normal
Inherited:	Yes
Applies to:	All
Note(s):	Unless an absolute measurement such as cm is used, this will be relative to the font size.

vertical-align

Define the vertical alignment characteristics of this element relative to its line box (when 'top' or 'bottom' are specified) or its parent.

```
span.superscript { vertical-align: super; }
```

Supported values:	Length, Percentage, baseline, sub, super, top, text-top, middle, bottom, text-bottom, inherit
Default value:	baseline
Inherited:	No
Applies to:	Inline, <td>, <th>

Positioning

The preceding Block properties specify the internal characteristics of the boxes that are used to lay out a page; the properties in this section can be used to describe the desired positions of those boxes.

visibility

Specify whether an element should be visible.

```
li.answer { visibility: hidden; }
```

Supported values:	visible, hidden, collapse, inherit
Default value:	visible
Inherited:	Yes
Applies to:	All
Note(s):	Unless display: none is set, the element will still occupy space, even if hidden.

display

Specify how an element should be presented.

```
.invisible { display: none; }
```

Supported values:	none, inline, block, list-item, run-in, inline-block, table, inline-table, table-row-group, table-header-group, table-footer-group, table-row, table-column-group, table-column, table-cell, table-caption, inherit
Default value:	inline
Inherited:	No
Applies to:	All
Note(s):	Other than removing objects from the document flow by setting display to "none", this property is most valuable for defining the presentation of XML documents with no inherent style.

position

Specify the algorithm to be used for placing this element's containing box on the page.

```
div#menu { position: absolute; top: 3.8cm; left: 0;}
```

Supported values:	static, relative, absolute, fixed, inherit
Default value:	static
Inherited:	No
Applies to:	All

float

For elements that are not absolutely positioned, define their relationship with elements surrounding them.

```
div#logo { float: left; }
```

Supported values:	left, right, none, inherit
Default value:	none
Inherited:	No
Applies to:	All elements without display: none

top, bottom, left, right

For absolutely positioned elements, define the distance to the enclosing box's edges.

```
div#menu { position: absolute; top: 3.8cm; left: 0;}
```

Supported values:	Length, Percentage, auto, inherit
Default value:	auto
Inherited:	No
Applies to:	Positioned elements

z-index

Define stacking order for overlapping elements.

```
div#logo { z-index: 99; }
```

Supported values:	Integer, auto, inherit
Default value:	auto
Inherited:	No
Applies to:	Positioned elements
Note(s):	The higher the number, the higher on the stack.

clear

Specify which sides of an element's box may not be adjacent to a floating element.

```
h1 { clear: both; }
```

Supported values:	none, left, right, both, inherit
Default value:	none
Inherited:	No
Applies to:	Block elements
Note(s):	This element will be shifted to be below any floater.

Borders

Specify borders and outlines for the boxes used to lay out the page. Outlines are not widely supported.

border-color, border-top-color, border-bottom-color, border-left-color, border-right-color

Specify border colors.

```
div#logo { border-color: green; }
```

Supported values:	Color, transparent, inherit
Default value:	color property value
Inherited:	No
Applies to:	All

border-style, border-top-style, border-bottom-style, border-left-style, border-right-style

Specify the border design.

```
div#logo { border-style: groove; }
```

Supported values:	none, hidden, dotted, dashed, solid, double, groove, ridge, inset, outset, inherit
Default value:	none
Inherited:	No
Applies to:	All

border-width, border-top-width, border-bottom-width, border-left-width, border-right-width

Specify the border size.

```
div#logo { border-width: thin; }
```

Supported values:	Length, thin, medium, thick, inherit
Default value:	medium
Inherited:	No
Applies to:	All

border

Consolidate border properties.

```
div#logo { border: green groove thin; }
```

Supported values:	Color Style Width, inherit
Default value:	color none medium
Inherited:	No
Applies to:	All

outline-color

Specify outline color.

```
span.acronym { outline-color: blue; }
```

Supported values:	Color, inherit, invert
Default value:	invert
Inherited:	No
Applies to:	All

outline-style

Specify outline style.

```
span.acronym { outline-style: dotted; }
```

Supported values:	none, dotted, dashed, solid, double, groove, ridge, inset, outset, inherit
Default value:	none
Inherited:	No
Applies to:	All

outline-width

Specify outline width.

```
span.acronym { outline-width: thin; }
```

Supported values:	Length, thin, medium, thick, inherit
Default value:	medium
Inherited:	No
Applies to:	All

outline

Consolidate outline properties.

```
span.acronym { outline: blue dotted thin; }
```

Supported values:	Color Style Width, inherit
Default value:	invert none medium
Inherited:	No
Applies to:	All

Table

Specify how tables are rendered, primarily pertaining to table cell borders.

table-layout

Specify a table layout algorithm. If "auto", the table's contents will be scanned before generation to calculate the proper width of each column; otherwise the table will be rendered as it is read, which may result in a suboptimal rendering if the cell width (or quantity) varies significantly across different rows.

```
table.huge { table-layout: fixed; }
```

Supported values:	auto, fixed, inherit
Default value:	auto
Inherited:	No
Applies to:	<table>

border-collapse

Specify whether adjacent table cell borders should be consolidated.

```
table { border-collapse: collapse; }
```

Supported values:	collapse, separate, inherit
Default value:	separate
Inherited:	Yes
Applies to:	<table>

border-spacing

Define the space between internal table borders.

```
table { border-spacing: 2pt 4pt; }
```

Supported values:	Length (1 or 2 values), inherit
Default value:	0
Inherited:	Yes
Applies to:	<table>
Note(s):	If two values, the first is horizontal, and the second vertical; otherwise, the value is applied to both dimensions.

empty-cells

Specify whether empty cells should be rendered with background and border.

```
table { empty-cells: hide; }
```

Supported values:	show, hide, inherit
Default value:	show
Inherited:	Yes
Applies to:	<td>, <th>

caption-side

Specify whether a caption goes above or below its table.

```
table.figure { caption-side: bottom; }
```

Supported values:	top, bottom, inherit
Default value:	top
Inherited:	Yes
Applies to:	<caption>

Printing

Provide instructions to the browser on how the page should be handled when printed. These can be used to help prevent page breaks in the middle of important content (although there are inherent limitations to how strictly the browser can follow these guidelines: page breaks must occur *somewhere*).

page-break-after, page-break-before

Specify whether a printed page break should occur before or after this block element.

```
h1 { page-break-after: avoid; }
```

Supported values:	auto, always, avoid, left, right, inherit
Default value:	auto
Inherited:	No
Applies to:	Block elements

page-break-inside

Specify a preference regarding page breaks internal to a block element.

```
table { page-break-inside: avoid; }
```

Supported values:	avoid, auto, inherit
Default value:	auto
Inherited:	Yes
Applies to:	Block elements

orphans

Define the number of lines in a paragraph that must be left at the bottom of a page. Any fewer and the entire paragraph will wrap to the following page.

```
body { orphans: 3; }
```

Supported values:	Integer, inherit
Default value:	2
Inherited:	Yes
Applies to:	Block elements

widows

Define the number of lines in a paragraph that must be available for the top of a page. Any fewer and the entire paragraph will wrap to that page.

```
body { widows: 4; }
```

Supported values:	Integer, inherit
Default value:	2
Inherited:	Yes
Applies to:	Block elements

Miscellaneous

The cursor property is a bit unusual, and it is rarely desirable. The Web browser will generally provide a mouse cursor that the user has been trained through experience to recognize and understand.

cursor

Define the type of cursor to be used when the mouse is over this element.

```
body.annoyuser { cursor: wait; }
```

Supported values:	auto, crosshair, default, pointer, move, nw-resize, n-resize, ne-resize, e-resize, se-resize, s-resize, sw-resize, w-resize, text, wait, help, progress, inherit, url()
Default value:	auto
Inherited:	Yes (but see Note)
Applies to:	All
Note(s):	The specification states that this is inherited, but browsers do not consistently do so. Use the inherit value if you wish for the parent's cursor to carry over to elements such as hyperlinks that would ordinarily have their own cursor type.

Selector Review

Preceding any block of CSS property assignments is a description of the HTML elements to which the properties apply. There are four basic mechanisms for matching properties to tags:

- ❑ By tag name
- ❑ By attribute presence or value
- ❑ By position within the document
- ❑ By pseudo-class

There is also a mechanism for assigning properties to portions of the document that are not elements as such: by pseudo-element.

These methods are frequently combined to minimize collateral damage. Conversely, selectors may be grouped with commas to allow the same property assignments to apply in different contexts.

Selectors are covered in-depth in Chapter 13.

Name Matching

This is fairly straightforward, and many selectors include at least one element name. There are two issues involving name matches that may surprise the unwary:

- ❑ With XHTML (or any XML grammar), the element names are case sensitive.
- ❑ The asterisk (*) serves as a wildcard that matches any tag, although it cannot be used to match a substring. For example, t* may *not* be used to represent table-related element names.

Attribute Matching

The most general syntax, which can be used to match any attribute, involves square brackets: [colspan] will match any element (presumably td or th) with the colspan attribute set, and [colspan="3"] will match any element with colspan defined with a value of 3.

There exist variations on the preceding syntax for matching a part of an attribute value; see Chapter 13 for more details.

Two attributes have a shorthand notation for use when matching values: class (.) and id (#).

Thus, .suspicious matches any element with a class value of "suspicious;" #logo matches any element with an id value of "logo."

Position Matching

Elements may be selected by matching another element that is an ancestor or immediately preceding sibling. Unlike attribute matching, position matching requires the use of element names (or, less often, the name wildcard).

❑ Whitespace between names indicates that the second name must be a descendent of an element with the preceding name for the match to occur.

❑ A greater-than sign (>) indicates that the second name must be a direct child of the first.

❑ A plus sign (+) indicates that the second name must immediately follow the first name as its sibling.

See also the information on pseudo-classes for the `:first-child` selector.

Pseudo-classes

These are specific strings prefaced with a colon (:) that refer to elements in certain states.

❑ `:first-child`—Matches elements that have no preceding siblings.

❑ `:link`—Matches elements that refer to a hypertext link that has not (recently) been visited.

❑ `:visited`—Matches elements that refer to a hypertext link that *has* recently been visited.

❑ `:hover`—Matches elements over which the mouse is hovering (or are otherwise designated by the user without being activated).

❑ `:active`—Matches clicked-on elements during the duration of the mouse button press.

❑ `:focus`—Matches input elements in which the cursor is active.

❑ `:lang`—Matches elements that are designated as containing text in the specified (natural) language.

Pseudo-elements

These syntactically look like pseudo-classes, but are used to designate a portion of the document inside of, preceding, or following an element.

❑ `:first-line`—Selects the text that the browser displays as the first line of a block of text.

❑ `:first-letter`—Selects the first character within an element.

❑ `:before`—Allows content to be inserted before an element.

❑ `:after`—Allows content to be inserted after an element.

JavaScript Language Reference

This section provides a comprehensive reference to the JavaScript language. Within this appendix, you will find listings for JavaScript's many language conventions, including its objects, methods, and properties. For more information on using the language, see Part III of this book.

To appropriately cover standard JavaScript, browser-specific objects, properties, and methods have been omitted from this reference. This appendix covers the ECMA-262 standard (`http://www.ecma-international.org/publications/standards/ Ecma-262.htm`).

Constants

Constant	Description
Infinity	Represents positive infinity. This constant is used in place of a number that exceeds the upper limit of the floating-point type.
NaN	Not a number. This constant is used in place of a number when a legal number cannot be returned when expected. You can use the function isNaN() to test for NaN.
Undefined	This constant is used to indicate a value that has not been defined — whether a variable that has not been declared or a variable that has been declared but not assigned a value. Not all platforms support undefined the same way in the same instances.

Operators

JavaScript Arithmetic Operators

Operator	Use
+	Addition
–	Subtraction
*	Multiplication
/	Division
%	Modulus
++	Increment
– –	Decrement

JavaScript Assignment Operators

Operator	Use
=	Assignment
+=	Increment assignment
–=	Decrement assignment
*=	Multiplication assignment
/=	Division assignment
%=	Modulus assignment

JavaScript Comparison Operators

Operator	Use
==	Is equal to
===	Exactly equal to, in value and type
!=	Is not equal to
!==	Is not exactly equal to
>	Is greater than
<	Is less than
>=	Is greater than or equal to
<=	Is less than or equal to

JavaScript Logical Operators

Operator	Use
&&	And
||	Or
!	Not

JavaScript Bitwise Operators

Operator	Use
&	And
|	Or
^	Xor
~	Not
<<	Left shift
>>	Right shift
>>>	Zero fill right shift

JavaScript Miscellaneous Operators

Operator	Use
.	Object/property/method separator
?	Condition operator
,	Specify multiple expressions in place of one expression. For example, you can use this operator to specify two variables to initialize at the beginning of a `for` loop: ```for (x=0, y=0; x<=20; x++) {` ` // loop code` `}```
delete	Delete specified object
new	Create new object
this	Reference current object
typeof	Type of object (number, string, and so on)
void	Evaluate expression without return value

String Operators

Operator	Use
+	Concatenation

Escape Characters

Characters	Description
\'	Single quote
\"	Double quote
\\	Backslash
\b	Backspace
\f	Form feed
\n	Newline
\r	Carriage return
\t	Tab

The backslash can also be used to escape any character simply by prefixing the character with a backslash.

Statements

Statement	Description
break [*label*]	Breaks out of the current loop, or the loop designated by the optional *label*. Program execution continues on the first line outside the corresponding loop.

comment (// and /* */)	Use either construct (double-slash or slash-asterisk) to create a comment in the code. The double-slash method can be used for a one-line or end-of-line comment:
	
	`// this is a comment`
	`i++; // increment I`
	
	The slash-asterisk method can be used for multiline comments:
	
	`/* function circle_area`
	`    arguments: radius`
	`    returns: area of circle */`

Statement	Description
continue [*label*]	Causes the current loop, or the loop designated by the optional *label*, to end the current iteration and begin the next. Program execution resumes at the beginning of the appropriate loop, performing any increment or other action as appropriate at the start of another iteration.

do {
  // loop code
} while (*expr*);
	Perform the loop code while *expr* evaluates to `true`. Note that since the conditional statement is at the end of the loop, the loop code will execute at least once.

export *mixed1* [, *mixed2*..., *mixedN*]	Exports the functions, objects, properties, or methods specified (*mixed*), making them available for other scripts to import.

for (*init_expr*;
cond_expr; *loop_expr*) {
  // loop code
}
	The `for` loop is a complex loop structure typically used to iterate over a sequence of numbers (for example, 1–10). At the start of the loop the *init_expr* is evaluated and the *cond_expr* is also evaluated. The loop executes as long as *cond_expr* remains true, evaluating the *loop_expr* on the second and subsequent iterations. For example, the following loop executes 10 times, assigning the variable x values of 1 through 10:
	
	```for (x = 1; x <= 10; x++) { // loop code }```

for (*var_name* in *mixed*) {
  // loop code
}
	Performs the loop code once for every property in *mixed*, assigning the variable *var_name* to each property in turn. For example, the following code will output every available property name and value of the `window` object:
	
	```for (p in window) { document.write("Property: "+p+" / "); document.writeln("Value: "+window[p]); }```

function *func_name* (
[*arg1, arg2...,argN*])
{
  // function code
  [return (*expr*);]
}
	Declares and defines a user-defined function. The optional arguments become variables local to the function, and the optional `return` statement provides the function's return value. If the `return` statement is omitted, the value of the last statement executed is returned. For example, the following function returns the area of a circle, given the circle's radius:
	
	```function circle_area (radius) { // area = pi * radius-squared with (Math) { var area = PI * pow(radius,2); } return area; }```

Table continued on following page

Statement	Description
```if (expr) {` ` // code to do if` `expr = true` `} [else {` ` // code to do if` `expr = false` `}]```	Performs code based on the evaluation of the expression, *expr*. If *expr* evaluates to true, the block of code in the if section is executed. If *expr* evaluates to false, the code in the if section is not executed, but the code in the optional else section is.
`import mixed1[,` `mixed2..., mixedN]`	Imports the functions, objects, properties, or methods specified (*mixed*), available via another script's export.
`label:`	Declares a label in the code that can be referenced via a break or continue statement. The label text (*label*) can be any valid nonreserved name and must end in a colon. For example, the following code utilizes a label named loop1: ```loop1:` `for (i = 1; i <= 20; i++) {` ` for (j = i+1; j <= 20; j++) {` ` // loop code` ` // if k ever exceeds 20, break out of loops` ` if (k > 20) { break loop1; }` ` }` `}```
`return [expr]`	Causes current execution of a function to end and returns the optional value of the expression expr.
```switch (expr) {` ` case value1:` ` // code to do if` `expr = value1` ` break;` ` case value2:` ` // code to do if` `expr = value2` ` break;` ` . . .` ` case valueN:` ` // code to do if` `expr = valueN` ` break;` ` [default:` ` // code to do if` `expr != any values]` `}```	Performs segments of code based on the value of expression *expr*. At the beginning of the switch construct, *expr* is evaluated and matched against each case *value*. If a match is found, the matching code (in the appropriate case section) is executed. If a match is not found, the code in the optional default section is executed. For example, the following switch construct outputs appropriate text based on the value of the variable *x*: ```switch (x) {` ` case 1:` ` document.write("x = 1");` ` break;` ` case 2:` ` document.write("x = 2");` ` break;` ` default:` ` document.write("x != 1 or 2");` `}```

Statement	Description
throw *string*	Creates an exception that breaks out of the current `try` construct and can be caught by a corresponding `catch` construct. (See the next entry for information about `try` and `catch`.)

try {
  // code to try
  [throw *value*; //
throw an error]
}
catch (*value*) {
  // code to diagnose/
report error
}
	Creates a testing structure for code. Using `throw` statements in the `try` section can create specific exceptions (errors) that can then be caught by the `catch` construct.
	For example, the following code throws an exception if k = 12 or 24, informing the catch construct of the value of k:
	
	```\ntry: {\n // code to try\n if (k = 12 || k = 24) { throw k; }\n}\ncatch (err) {\n // now err = value of k when exception\n // was thrown, handle and/or report\n // appropriately\n}\n```

var *var_name* [= *value*] | [= new *object_type*]	Declares a variable and optionally assigns it an initial value, type, or type with initial values. For example, the following `var` statements are all valid: ```\nvar x;\nvar x = 3;\nvar myImage = new Image();\nvar myArray = new Array("dog","cat","ferret");\n```

while (*expr*) {
  // loop code while
expr = true
}
	Perform the loop code while *expr* evaluates to true. Note that since the conditional statement is at the beginning of the loop, the loop code may not execute (if *expr* is initially false).

with (*object*) {
  // code using object
}
	Perform multiple actions using a particular object. If code within the `with` construct calls for an object, an attempt is made to match the *object* specified in the `with` statement. For example, the following code eliminates the need for having to repeatedly specify the `Math` object for each method and property (`PI` and `pow()`):
	
	```\nwith (Math) {\n var area = PI * pow(radius,2);\n}\n```

Standard Elements

This section details the methods, properties, and events that are common to many objects. The listings within this section only explain the meaning of the items; see the listing for specific objects to determine whether a specific object supports the item listed here.

Standard Methods

Methods	Description
blur	Removes focus from an object
select	Highlights all or a portion of text in a textarea element
click	Triggers the object's onclick handler
focus	Applies focus to an object
handleEvent(event)	Calls the handler for a specified event

Standard Properties

Properties	Description
constructor	A reference to the function that created the object
prototype	A reference to the object's prototype, which can be used to assign additional properties to an object

Standard Event Handlers

Event Handlers	Description
onAbort	Is triggered whenever an abort event occurs, such as a user navigating away from a page before it completes loading or clicking the Stop button
onBlur	Is triggered when an object loses focus
onClick	Is triggered when an object is clicked
onDblClick	Is triggered when an object is double-clicked
onError	Is triggered when a JavaScript syntax or runtime error occurs
onFocus	Is triggered when an object obtains focus
onKeyDown	Is triggered when a key is pressed
onKeyPress	Is triggered when a key is pressed and held down
onKeyUp	Is triggered when a key is released

Event Handlers	Description
onMouseDown	Is triggered when a mouse button is depressed
onMouseOut	Is triggered when the mouse pointer is moved away from an object (after being over the object)
onMouseOver	Is triggered when the mouse pointer is placed over an object
onMouseUp	Is triggered when a mouse button is released
onReset	Is triggered when the user clicks the Reset button on the corresponding form
onSelect	Is triggered when text is selected
onSubmit	Is triggered when the user clicks the Submit button on the corresponding form

Top-Level Functions

Function	Returns	Description
escape(*string*)	string	This function encodes the supplied *string* to make it portable — that is, able to be used in conditions where extended characters are not allowed. To make a string portable, characters other than the following must be encoded: ABCDEFGHIJKLMNOPQRSTUVWXYZ abcdefghijklmnopqrstuvwxyz 1234567890 @*-_+./ All other characters are converted to their two- or four-digit hexadecimal equivalent (%xx or %uxxxx). For example, a space is converted to hexadecimal %20. Escaped strings are commonly used to embed plain text in URLs and other restricted constructs. Use the unescape() function to translate an encoded string back to its ASCII equivalent.
eval(*string*)	Value of last statement	This function evaluates the given *string* and parses it for valid JavaScript code. If valid code is found in the *string*, the function executes the code and returns the value of the last statement encountered. This function is useful for dynamic scripting — where code is built on the fly by the script.

Function	Returns	Description
isFinite(*object*)	Boolean	This function evaluates the given *object* and returns `true` if the *object* is finite (non-infinity) or `false` if the *object* is infinite.
isNaN(*object*)	Boolean	This function evaluates the given *object* and returns `true` if the *object* cannot be evaluated as a number or `false` if the object can be evaluated as a number.
number(*object*)	number or NaN	This function evaluates the given *object* and parses it to obtain a number. If the object can be evaluated as a number, the evaluated number is returned. If the *object* cannot be evaluated as a number, the function returns NaN. (Note that the `number()` function can be used to translate Boolean objects into their numeric equivalents — 0 or 1.)
parseFloat(*object*)	float or NaN	This function evaluates the given *object* and parses it to obtain a floating-point number. If the object can be evaluated as a floating-point number, the evaluated number is returned. If the object cannot be evaluated as a number, the function returns NaN.
parseInt(*object*)	integer or NaN	This function evaluates the given *object* and parses it to obtain an integer number. If the object can be evaluated as an integer, the evaluated number is returned. If the object cannot be evaluated as an integer, the function returns NaN.
string(*object*)	string	This function translates the given *object* into a valid string object.
unescape(*string*)	string	This function decodes the given *string* into its ASCII equivalent. It detects two- and four-digit hexadecimal sequences (%xx and %uxxxx) and translates them back into their appropriate characters. This function is the opposite of the `escape()` function.

Objects

This section provides details on the multitude of objects available in JavaScript.

Anchor Object

The `Anchor` object corresponds to the XHTML anchor tag (`<a>`). You can use this object to create an anchor with the `document.write()` method in addition to writing specific code for the anchor. The following examples are identical:

```
var myheader = "Chapter 1";
document.write(myheader.anchor("Chapter_1"));

document.write('<a name="Chapter_1">Chapter 1</a>');
```

Properties

There are no properties specific to the Anchor object.

Methods

There are no methods specific to the Anchor object.

Area Object

An Area object is a type of Link object and has the same attributes. This object corresponds to the XHTML <area> tag. For more information on the Area object, see the Link object.

Properties

There are no properties specific to the Area object.

Methods

There are no methods specific to the Area object.

Array Object

The JavaScript Array object is similar to other languages' array objects, holding an ordered set of values. The following example creates an array of four string elements:

```
fruits = new Array("banana", "pear", "apple", "strawberry");
```

Elements of an array can be accessed by their numeric index, corresponding to their position in the array, starting with 0. For example, you could access the second element in the preceding array ("pear") as fruit[1].

Properties

Properties	Description
index	The index property created by a regular expression match, containing the zero-based index of that match. Read-only.
input	The input property created by a regular expression match, containing the original string against which the match was made. Read-only.
length	The length of the array (number of assigned elements).

Methods

Methods	Description
concat(array1, array2, ... arrayN)	Joins multiple Array objects to create a new array.
join(separator)	Joins the elements of an array into a single string separated by the given separator (the default is a comma).
reverse	Reverses the order of the elements in an array.
sort(function)	Sorts the elements of an array via the function specified. If no function is specified, the sort method sorts the array lexicographically. To sort an array numerically, you can define and specify one of the following functions in your code: function numAcending(a, b) { return (a-b); } function numDecending(a, b) { return (b-a); }
toString	Inherited from the Object object. For more details see the Object.toString method.
valueOf	Inherited from the Object object. For more details see the Object.valueOf method.

Boolean Object

The Boolean object is an object wrapper for a Boolean value. The following constructors will all create a Boolean object with a value of false:

```
new Boolean()
new Boolean(0)
new Boolean(-0)
new Boolean(null)
new Boolean(false)
new Boolean("")
```

A constructor with any other value will create a Boolean object with a value of true, even if the argument is the string false.

A Boolean object, unlike a Boolean primitive, will always evaluate to true when used in a conditional statement:

```
b = new Boolean(false);
if (b) {
  // Always true
}

b = false;
if (b) {
  // Not always true
}
```

Properties

Standard object properties.

Methods

Methods	Description
toString	Converts the Boolean object to a string (for example, true or false). This method is called automatically whenever a Boolean object is used in a situation requiring a string.
valueOf	Returns a primitive value (true or false) of the Boolean object.

Button Object

A Button object is created with every instance of an XHTML <input type="button"> tag within the document. The objects are stored in the array of the parent form and accessed using the name defined within the XHTML tag or an integer representing the order in which the element appears in the form (with 0 being the first element).

Properties

Properties	Description
form	Returns a reference to the object's parent form.
name	Sets or returns the value of the object's name attribute.
type	The value of this property is always button.
value	Sets or returns the object's value attribute.

Methods

Methods	Description
blur	Removes the focus from the object.
click	Simulates a mouse-click on the object.
focus	Gives focus to the object.
handleEvent(event)	Calls the handler for the given event.

Event Handlers

Even Handlers
onBlur
onClick
onFocus
onMouseDown
onMouseUp

Checkbox Object

A Checkbox object is created with every instance of an XHTML `<input type="checkbox">` tag within the document. The objects are stored in the array of the parent form and accessed using the name defined within the XHTML tag or an integer representing the order in which the element appears in the form (with 0 being the first element).

Properties

Properties	Description
checked	A Boolean value that sets or returns the current state of the object — true if the box is checked and false if it is not checked.
defaultChecked	Sets or returns the default value of the checked property — that is, what the attribute was originally set to in the XHTML code.
form	Returns a reference to the object's parent form.
name	Sets or returns the value of the object's name attribute.
type	The value of this property is always checkbox.
value	Sets or returns the value of the object's value attribute.

Methods

Methods
blur
click
focus
handleEvent (event)

Event Handlers

Event Handlers
onBlur
onClick
onFocus

Date Object

The Date object allows you to work with dates and times. You create a Date object using the Date constructor:

```
today = new Date(parameters);
```

The available parameters are shown in the following table.

Parameter	
milliseconds	An integer specifying the number of milliseconds since 01/01/1970 00:00:00
dateString	A string representing the date in a format that can be recognized by the Date.parse method
year_num, month_num, day_num	Integers representing the year, month, and day
hour_num, min_num, sec_num, ms_num	Integers representing the hours, minutes, seconds, and milliseconds

If you don't supply any parameters, JavaScript creates an object using the current time on the local machine.

Properties

Properties
constructor
prototype

Methods

Methods	Description
getDate()	Returns an integer (between 1 and 31) representing the day of the month for the specified Date object.
getDay()	Returns an integer (between 0 and 6) representing the day of the week for the specified Date object.
getFullYear()	Returns an integer representing the 4-digit year for the specified Date object.
getHours()	Returns an integer (between 0 and 23) that represents the hour for the specified Date object.
getMilliseconds()	Returns an integer (between 0 and 999) that represents the milliseconds for the specified Date object.
getMinutes()	Returns an integer (between 0 and 59) that represents the minutes for the specified Date object.
getMonth()	Returns an integer (between 0 and 11) that represents the month for the specified Date object.
getSeconds()	Returns an integer (between 0 and 59) that represents the seconds for the specified Date object.
getTime()	Returns an integer representing the number of milliseconds since midnight 01/01/1970 for the specified Date object.
getTimezoneOffset()	Returns an integer representing the difference in minutes between local time and Greenwich Mean Time.
getUTCDate()	Returns an integer (between 1 and 31) that represents the day of the month, according to universal time, for the specified Date object.
getUTCDay()	Returns an integer (between 0 and 6) that represents the day of the week, according to universal time, for the specified Date object.
getUTCFullYear()	Returns an integer representing the 4-digit year, according to universal time, for the specified Date object.
getUTCHours()	Returns an integer (between 0 and 23) representing the hours, according to universal time, for the specified Date object.
getUTCMilliseconds()	Returns an integer (between 0 and 999) representing the milliseconds, according to universal time, for the specified Date object.
getUTCMinutes()	Returns an integer (between 0 and 59) representing the minutes, in universal time, for the specified Date object.
getUTCMonth()	Returns an integer (between 0 and 11) representing the month, according to universal time, for the specified Date object.

Methods	Description
getUTCSeconds()	Returns an integer (between 0 and 59) representing the seconds, according to universal time, for the specified Date object.
parse(date_string)	Parses a string representing a date and returns the number of milliseconds since January 1, 1970 00:00:00.
setDate(integer)	Sets the day of the month for the specified Date object.
setFullYear(integer)	Sets the full year for the specified Date object.
setHours(integer)	Sets the hour for the specified Date object.
setMilliseconds(integer)	Sets the milliseconds for the specified Date object.
setMinutes(integer)	Sets the minutes for the specified Date object.
setMonth(integer)	Sets the month for the specified Date object.
setSeconds(integer)	Sets the seconds for the specified Date object.
setTime(integer)	Sets the time for the specified Date object as the number of milliseconds since January 1, 1970 00:00:00.
setUTCDate(integer)	Sets the day of the month for the specified Date object according to universal time.
setUTCFullYear(integer)	Sets the full year for the specified Date object according to universal time.
setUTCHours(integer)	Sets the hours for the specified Date object according to universal time.
setUTCMilliseconds(integer)	Sets the milliseconds for the specified Date object, according to universal time.
setUTCMinutes(integer)	Sets the minutes for the specified Date object, according to universal time.
setUTCMonth(integer)	Sets the month for the specified Date object, according to universal time.
setUTCSeconds(integer)	Sets the seconds for the specified Date object, according to universal time.
toGMTString()	Converts a local date to Greenwich Mean Time.
toLocaleString()	Converts the specified Date object to a string using the relevant locale's date conventions.
toSource()	Returns the source code that created the specified Date object.
toString()	Converts the specified Date object to a string. This method is automatically called whenever a Date object is needed as text.

Table continued on following page

Methods	Description
toUTCString()	Converts the specified Date object to a string using the universal time convention.
UTC()	Returns the number of milliseconds since January 1, 1970 00:00:00, according to universal time.
valueOf()	Returns a primitive value representing the number of milliseconds since January 1, 1970 00:00:00, of the specified Date object.

*The non-UTC **Date** functions use local date and time conventions when converting or constructing date values.*

Document Object

The Document object provides access to the XHTML elements in a document. This includes properties of forms, links, and anchors, as well as general Document properties.

Properties

Properties	Description
alinkColor [= "color"]	Returns or sets the color of active links within the specified document. The color value is either the hexadecimal definition of the color (for example, #FF0000) or its textual description (for example, red).
anchors[ ]	An array containing all the named Anchor objects in the specified document.
bgColor [= "color"]	Returns or sets the background color of the specified document. The color value is either the hexadecimal definition of the color (for example, #FF0000) or its textual description (for example, red).
cookie [= "expression"]	Returns or sets cookies that are associated with the specified document. Note that this property only returns visible and unexpired cookies.
domain [= "domain"]	Returns or sets the domain name from which the specified document originated.
embeds[ ]	An array containing all the embedded objects in the specified document.
fgColor [= "color"]	Returns or sets the specified document's foreground color. The color value is either the hexadecimal definition of the color (for example, #FF0000) or its textual description (for example, red).
formname."formname"	Returns a reference to the form that has formname as the value of its name attribute.

Properties	Description
forms[ ]	An array containing all the Form objects in the specified document.
images[ ]	An array containing all the Image objects in the specified document.
lastModified	Returns the date that the specified document was last modified.
layers[ ]	An array containing all the Layer objects in the specified document.
linkColor [= "color"]	Returns or sets the specified document's hyperlink color. The color value is either the hexadecimal definition of the color (for example, #FF0000) or its textual description (for example, red).
links[ ]	An array containing all the Area and Link objects in the specified document.
referrer	Returns the referring URL of the specified document.
title	Returns the specified document's title — that is, the text between the <title> tags.
URL	Returns the specified document's full URL.
vlinkColor	Returns or sets the specified document's visited links color. The color value is either the hexadecimal definition of the color (for example, #FF0000) or its textual description (for example, red).

Methods

Methods	Description
captureEvents(event_type)	Causes the specified document to capture and handle all events of a particular type. See the Event object for a list of valid event types.
close()	Closes the output stream previously opened with the document.open method and forces data from any document.write or document.writeln methods to be displayed.
handleEvent(event)	Calls the handler for the specified event.
open([mimetype[, replace]])	Used to open an output stream in the specified document for write or writeln methods.
releaseEvents(event_type)	Releases any events of the specified type to be passed along to objects further down the event hierarchy.
routeEvent(event)	Used to send the specified event through the normal event hierarchy.
write("expression(s)")	Used to write text (which may or may not include XHTML or other code) to the specified document.
writeln("expression(s)")	Identical to the write method, except that writeln ends the write with a newline.

Event Handlers

Event Handlers
onClick
onDblClick
onKeyDown
onKeyPress
onKeyUp
onMouseDown
onMouseUp

Event Object

JavaScript creates an Event object automatically on the occurrence of an event. The object's various properties can provide information about the event, such as event type, the position of the cursor at the time the event occurred, and so on.

Properties

Properties	Description
screenX / screenY	Returns the position of the cursor relative to the screen, in pixels, when the event occurred
type	Returns a string that represents the type of the event (click, key down, and so on)

The Event object supports the following types:

- ❑ ABORT
- ❑ BLUR
- ❑ CHANGE
- ❑ CLICK
- ❑ DBLCLICK
- ❑ DRAGDROP
- ❑ ERROR
- ❑ FOCUS
- ❑ KEYDOWN

- ❑ KEYPRESS
- ❑ KEYUP
- ❑ LOAD
- ❑ MOUSEDOWN
- ❑ MOUSEOUT
- ❑ MOUSEOVER
- ❑ MOUSEUP
- ❑ MOVE
- ❑ RESET
- ❑ RESIZE
- ❑ SELECT
- ❑ SUBMIT
- ❑ UNLOAD

For example, to capture all click events, you could use code similar to the following:

```
window.captureEvents(Event.CLICK)
```

Methods

There are no methods specific to the Event object.

FileUpload Object

The FileUpload object is created with every instance of an XHTML <input type="file"> tag within the document. The objects are stored in the array of the parent form and accessed using the name defined within the XHTML tag or an integer representing the order in which the element appears in the form (with 0 being the first element).

Properties

Properties	Description
form	Returns a reference to the object's parent form
name	Sets or returns the value of the object's name attribute
type	The value of this property is always file
value	Sets or returns the value of the object's value attribute

Methods

Methods
blur
click
focus
handleEvent(event)

Event Handlers

Event Handlers
onBlur
onChange
onFocus

Form Object

A Form object is created with every instance of an XHTML <form> tag within the document. The objects are stored in the Document object and can be accessed using the name defined within the XHTML tag or an integer representing the order in which the element appears in the document (with 0 being the first element).

Properties

Properties	Description
action [= "string"]	Returns or sets the action attribute for the specified form
elements[ ]	An array containing objects corresponding to elements within the specified form
encoding [= "string"]	Returns or sets the enctype attribute of the specified form
Length	Returns the number of elements in the specified form
method [= "GET|POST"]	Returns or sets the method attribute for the specified form
name [= "string"]	Returns or sets the name attribute for the specified form
target [= "string"]	Returns or sets the target attribute for the specified form

Methods

Methods	Description
`handleEvent(event)`	Invokes the event handler for the specified event
`Reset`	Emulates the clicking of a Reset button
`Submit`	Emulates the clicking of a Submit button

Event Handlers

Event Handlers
`onReset`
`onSubmit`

Function Object

The `Function` object corresponds to functions defined in your JavaScript code. Function definitions using the standard `function` statement have the following, basic syntax:

```
function function_name (function_argument(s)) {
  // function code
  return return_value;
}
```

For example, to define a function to add two values, you could use the following code:

```
function add_values (value1, value2) {
  var total = value1 + value2;
  return total;
}

alert("The sum of 2 and 4 is: "+add_values(2,4));
```

The function can also be defined using the function constructor in standard object form:

```
var function_name = new Function("argument1", "argument2"...,
  "argumentN", "expression(s)");
```

Converting our example function to this format yields the following:

```
var add_values = new Function("value1","value2",
  "var total=value1+value2; return total;");

alert("The sum of 2 and 4 is: "+add_values(2,4));
```

Properties

Properties	Description
arguments[ ]	An array containing all the arguments passed to the specified function.
arguments.callee	Used within the body of a function this property returns a string specifying the function.
arguments.length	Returns the number of arguments passed to the specified function.
arity	Returns the number of arguments expected by the specified function.
constructor	Returns a direct reference to the function that created the specified object. See the constructor property of the Object object for more details.
length	Similar to the arity property in this table.
prototype	Allows the addition of other properties and methods to an object. See also the prototype property of the Object object for more details.

Methods

Methods	Description
toString	Returns a string containing the source code of a function.
valueOf	Like toString, this returns a string containing the source code of a function.

Hidden Object

A Hidden object is created with every instance of an XHTML <input type="hidden"> tag within the document. The objects are stored in the array of the parent form and accessed using the name defined within the XHTML tag or an integer representing the order in which the element appears in the form (with 0 being the first element).

Properties

Properties	Description
form	Returns a reference to the object's parent form.
name	Sets or returns the value of the object's name attribute.
type	The value of this property is always hidden.
value	Sets or returns the button's value attribute.

Methods

There are no methods specific to the Hidden object.

History Object

The History object is a predefined JavaScript object accessible through the history property of a window object. The window.history property returns an array of URLs as strings, reflecting entries in the History object; these entries correspond to the URLs accessible through the browser's history function.

Properties

Properties	Description
length	Returns the number of entries in the history list

Methods

Methods	Description
back	Causes the browser to move one entry backward in the history list (similar to pressing the browser's Back button).
forward	Causes the browser to move one entry forward in the history list (similar to pressing the browser's Forward button).
go(delta|location)	Causes the browser to load a specific entry in the history list. The entry can be specified using a positive or negative delta (negative numbers move back the specified number of entries, positive numbers move forward) or a string containing text to match to the closest URL in the history list (for example, specifying "example.com" will move to the closest entry containing example.com).

Image Object

An Image object is created with every instance of an XHTML <img> tag. The objects are stored in the array of the document.images property and accessed using the name defined within the XHTML tag or an integer representing the order in which the element appears in the document (with 0 being the first element).

You can also use the Image constructor and the new operator to create an Image object, which can then be displayed within an existing displayed element. For example, the following code creates a new Image object called myImage containing the image cat.gif:

```
var myImage = new Image()
myImage.src = "cat.gif"
```

You could then have this image replace an existing image when a button is pressed, creating an event linked to code that swaps the source.

Properties

Properties	Description
border	Returns a string containing the border width of the specified image (in pixels). Read-only.
complete	Returns a Boolean value indicating whether the browser has finished loading the specified image. Read-only.
height	Returns a string containing the height attribute of the specified image (in pixels). Read-only.
hspace	Returns a string containing the hspace attribute of the specified image (in pixels). Read-only.
lowsrc	Sets or returns the value of the object's lowsrc attribute.
name	Sets or returns the value of the object's name attribute.
src	Sets or returns the value of the object's src attribute.
vspace	Returns a string containing the vspace attribute of the specified image (in pixels). Read-only.
width	Returns a string containing the width attribute of the specified image (in pixels). Read-only.

Methods

Methods
handleEvent(event)

Event Handlers

*All of the **Image** object's event handlers have an equivalent property (in lowercase) that can be used with the **Image** constructor.*

Event Handlers
onAbort
onError
onKeyDown
onKeyPress
onKeyUp
onload

Link Object

A Link object is created with every instance of an XHTML <a> or <area> tag within the document. The objects are stored in the array of the document.links property and accessed using the name defined within the XHTML tag or an integer representing the order in which the element appears in the document (with 0 being the first element).

*A **Link** object is also a **Location** object and therefore shares the same properties.*

Properties

Properties	Description
hash	Returns the anchor portion (#anchor) of the specified object.
host	Returns the host and port portions (for example, www.example.com:80) of the specified object.
hostname	Returns the server name and domain name (for example, www.example.com) or IP address of the specified object.
href	Returns the entire URL (protocol, hostname, port, and so on) of the specified object.
pathname	Returns the path and name (for example, /samples/index.html) of the specified object.
port	Returns the port number (for example, 80) of the specified object.
protocol	Returns the protocol (for example, http:) of the specified object.
search	Returns any query information (also known as GET information, for example, ?name=Steve&id=245) of the specified object.
target	Sets or returns the value of the object's target attribute.
text	Returns the text embedded in the specified object (text that comprises the visible hyperlink).

Methods

Methods
handleEvent(event)

Event Handlers

Event Handlers
onClick
onDblClick
onKeyDown
onKeyPress
onKeyUp
onMouseDown
onMouseOut
onMouseUp
onMouseOver

Location Object

The Location object is part of a Window object, accessed through the window.location property. This object contains the complete URL of a specified Window object.

Properties

Properties	Description
hash	Returns the anchor portion (#anchor) of the specified object.
host	Returns the host and port portions (for example, www.example.com:80) of the specified object.
hostname	Returns the server name and domain name (for example, www.example.com) or IP address of the specified object.
href	Returns the entire URL (protocol, hostname, port, and so on) of the specified object.
pathname	Returns the path and name (for example, /samples/index.html) of the specified object.
port	Returns the port number (for example, 80) of the specified object.
protocol	Returns the protocol (for example, http:) of the specified object.
search	Returns any query information (also known as GET information, for example, ?name=Steve&id=245) of the specified object.

Methods

Methods	Description
reload	Causes the browser to reload the window's current document
replace(URL)	Replaces the object's history entry with the specified URL

Math Object

The Math object is a top-level, built-in JavaScript object used to perform advanced calculations.

Properties

Properties	Description
E	Provides Euler's constant and the base of natural logarithms (approximately 2.7183)
LN10	Provides the natural logarithm of 10 (approximately 2.3026)
LN2	Provides the natural logarithm of 2 (approximately 0.6931)
LOG10E	Provides the base 10 logarithm of E (approximately 0.4343)
LOG2E	Provides the base 2 logarithm of E (approximately 1.4427)
PI	Provides the value of pi, (approximately 3.1416)
SQRT1_2	Provides the value of 1 divided by the square root of 2 (approximately 0.7071)
SQRT2	Provides the square root of 2 (approximately 1.4142)

Methods

Methods	Description
abs(*number*)	Returns the absolute value of *number*
acos(*number*)	Returns the arccosine of *number*
asin(*number*)	Returns the arcsine of *number*
atan(*number*)	Returns the arctangent of *number*
atan2(*number1*, *number2*)	Returns the arctangent of the quotient of its arguments
ceil(*number*)	Returns an integer equal to or the next integer greater than *number*
cos(*number*)	Returns the cosine of *number*
exp(*number*)	Returns the value of E^{number} where E is Euler's constant
floor(*number*)	Returns an integer equal to or the next integer less than *number*

Table continued on following page

Methods	Description
log(*number*)	Returns the natural logarithm (base E) of *number*
max(*number1*, *number2*)	Returns the greater of the two supplied numbers
min(*number1*, *number2*)	Returns the lesser of the two supplied numbers
pow(*number1*, *number2*)	Returns the value of number1 to the power of number2 (number1number2), where number1 is the base and number2 is the exponent
random()	Returns a pseudo-random number between 0 and 1
round(*number*)	Returns *number* rounded to the nearest integer
sin(*number*)	Returns the sine of *number*
sqrt(*number*)	Returns the square root of *number*
tan(*number*)	Returns the tangent of *number*

Navigator Object

The *Navigator* object contains information about the user agent. Designed originally for Netscape Navigator, it can also be used with Internet Explorer.

Properties

Properties	Description
appCodeName	Contains the code name of the browser
appName	Contains the name of the browser
appVersion	Contains information about the browser version
platform	Contains a string containing the machine type for which the browser was compiled
userAgent	Contains a string containing the value of the User-agent header sent by the client to the server

Methods

Methods	Description
javaEnabled	Tests whether Java is enabled, returning true if it is and false if not.
taintEnabled	Determines whether data tainting is enabled, returning true if it is and false if not. Note that tainting has been deprecated in the latest versions of JavaScript.

Number Object

The Number object is an object wrapper for primitive numeric values.

Properties

Properties	Description
constructor	Specifies the function that created the object. See also the Object.constructor property.
MAX_VALUE	Contains the largest number possible in JavaScript (approximately 1.79769e+308).
MIN_VALUE	Contains the number closest to 0 in JavaScript (approximately 5e-324).
NaN	Represents the special value Not a Number (NaN).
POSITIVE_INFINITY	Contains a special value representing infinity, which is returned on overflow.
prototype	Represents the prototype for this object, allowing you to add methods and properties to the object.

Methods

Methods	Description
valueOf	Returns the primitive value of a Number object as a number data type.

Object Object

Object is the primitive JavaScript object from which all other objects are derived.

Properties

Properties
constructor
prototype

Methods

Methods	Description
toString	Returns a string representing a specified object
valueOf	Returns a primitive value for a specified object

Option Object

An Option object is created with every instance of an XHTML <option> tag within the document. The objects are stored in the array of the parent form and accessed using the name defined within the XHTML tag or an integer representing the order in which the element appears in the form (with 0 being the first element).

Properties

Properties	Description
defaultSelected	Sets or returns the value of the object's selected attribute
selected	Sets or returns the current state of the object (selected returns true, not selected returns false)
text	Sets or returns the value of the text of the object (text that composes the visible portion of the option)
value	Sets or returns the value of the object's value attribute

Methods

There are no methods specific to the Option object.

Password Object

A Password object is created with every instance of an XHTML <input type="password"> tag within the document. The objects are stored in the array of the parent form and accessed using the name defined within the XHTML tag or an integer representing the order in which the element appears in the form (with 0 being the first element).

Properties

Properties	Description
defaultValue	Sets or returns the value of the object's value attribute.
form	Returns a reference to the object's parent form.
name	Sets or returns the value of the object's name attribute.
type	The value of this property is always password.
value	Returns the value entered by the user.

Methods

Methods
blur
focus
handleEvent(event)
select

Event Handlers

Event Handlers
onBlur
onFocus

Radio Object

A Radio object is created with every instance of an XHTML `<input type="radio">` tag within the document. The objects are stored in the array of the parent form and accessed using the name defined within the XHTML tag or an integer representing the order in which the element appears in the form (with 0 being the first element). Because radio buttons share the same name, they are stored in an array using the name of the group of buttons.

Properties

Properties	Description
checked	Contains a Boolean value corresponding to whether the item is selected.
defaultChecked	Contains a Boolean value corresponding to the original value of the checked attribute of the object (the value specified in the XHTML code).
form	Returns a reference to the object's parent form.
name	Sets or returns the value of the object's name attribute.
type	The value of this property is always radio.
value	Sets or returns the object's value attribute.

Methods

Methods
blur
click
focus
handleEvent(event)

Event Handlers

Event Handlers
onBlur
onClick
onFocus

RegExp Object

The RegExp object contains a regular expression and is used to match strings using its methods and properties.

Properties

Properties	Description
$1, ..., $9	Properties containing substrings (if any) from a regular expression
constructor	Specifies the function that creates an object
prototype	Represents the prototype for this class, allowing you to add your own properties and methods

Methods

Methods	Description
compile(pattern[, flags])	Compiles the specified regular expression
exec([string])	Executes a search using the specified regular expression within the string and returns a result array
toString	Returns a string representing the RegExp object
valueOf	Returns a primitive value for the RegExp object as a string data type

Reset Object

A Reset object is created with every instance of an XHTML <input type="reset"> tag within the document. The objects are stored in the array of the parent form and accessed using the name defined within the XHTML tag or an integer representing the order in which the element appears in the form (with 0 being the first element).

Properties

Properties	Description
form	Returns a reference to the object's parent form.
name	Sets or returns the value of the object's name attribute.
type	The value of this property is always reset.
value	Sets or returns the object's value attribute.

Methods

Methods
blur
click
focus
handleEvent(event)

Event Handlers

Event Handlers
onBlur
onClick
onFocus

Screen Object

The Screen object contains and returns information about the user agent's display screen.

Properties

Properties	Description
availHeight()	Returns the usable height of the screen (in pixels), minus OS interface features (such as the Windows taskbar)
availWidth()	Returns the usable width of the screen (in pixels), minus OS interface features (such as the Windows taskbar)
colorDepth()	Returns the color bit depth of the palette in use or the bit depth of the screen if no palette is in use
height()	Returns the full height of the screen (in pixels)
pixelDepth()	Returns the color bit depth of the screen
width()	Returns the full width of the screen (in pixels)

Methods

There are no methods specific to the Screen object.

Select Object

A Select object is created with every instance of an XHTML <select> tag within the document. The objects are stored in the array of the parent form and accessed using the name defined within the XHTML tag or an integer representing the order in which the element appears in the form (with 0 being the first element).

Properties

Properties	Description
form	Returns a reference to the object's parent form.
length	Contains the number of items (options) in the select list.
name	Sets or returns the value of the object's name attribute.
options[ ]	An array containing all of the options in the specified object.
selectedIndex	Returns the index of the currently selected item (option). If the list allows for multiple selections, this property will only return the index of the first item selected.
type	Returns the value of the select object's type — returns select-one if the list only allows a single selection or select-multiple if the list allows multiple selections.

Methods

Methods
blur
focus
handleEvent(event)

Event Handlers

Event Handlers
onBlur
onChange
onFocus

String Object

A String object represents a series of characters in a string.

Properties

Properties	Description
constructor	Returns a reference to the function that created the object
length	Returns the length of the string
prototype	Can be used to assign additional properties to an object

Methods

Methods	Description
anchor("name")	Embeds the string in anchor tags (<a>) using name for the name of the anchor (for example, <a name="name">string</a>).
big	Embeds the string in big tags (<big>).
blink	Embeds the string in blink tags (<blink>).
bold	Embeds the string in bold tags (<b>).
charAt(integer)	Returns the character at position integer in the string. (Note that the first character in a string has an index of 0.)
charCodeAt(integer)	Returns the Unicode value of the character at position integer in the string.
concat(string1, string2..., stringN)	Concatenates the given strings with the specified object and returns the resulting string.
fixed	Embeds the string in teletype tags (<tt>).
fontcolor("colorvalue")	Embeds the string in font tags using colorvalue as the value for the color attribute (for example, <font color="colorvalue">string</font>).
fontsize("sizevalue")	Embeds the string in font tags using sizevalue as the value for the size attribute (for example, <font size="sizevalue">string</font>).
fromCharCode(code1, code2...,codeN)	Returns a string comprised of the supplied Unicode values. (Static method does not return an object.)
indexOf(searchstring, [index])	Returns the index of the first occurrence of searchstring in the specified string, starting at the optional index position in the string.
italics	Embeds the string in italic tags (<i>).
lastIndexOf(search string, [index])	Returns the index of the last occurrence of searchstring in the specified string, starting backwards at the optional index position in the string.
link(url)	Embeds the string in anchor tags (<a>) using url as the URL in the href attribute (for example, <a href="url">string</a>).
match(regexp)	Matches the regular expression regexp against the specified string. Returns the matched portion of the string or null if no match can be made.
replace(regexp, newstring)	Matches the regular expression regexp against the specified string, replacing any matches with the specified newstring. Returns the string with the replacements.
search(regexp)	Searches the specified string for text matching the regular expression regexp. Returns 1 if a match was found or 0 if a match was not found.

Methods	Description
slice(start,end)	Returns a slice of the specified string from index start to index end, inclusive.
small	Embeds the specified string in small tags (<small>).
split(separator)	Splits the specified string at each occurrence of separator, creating an array containing the resulting substrings. (Note: The separator is discarded and does not appear in the resulting substrings.)
strike	Embeds the specified string in strikeout tags (<strike>).
sub	Embeds the specified string in subscript tags (<sub>).
substr(start[,length]);	Returns a substring from the specified string starting at the start index for a total of length characters. If length is not specified, the substring contains the characters from the start index through the end of the string.
substring(start,end)	Returns a substring of the specified string between the start and end indexes, inclusive.
sup	Embeds the specified string in superscript tags (<sup>).
toLowerCase	Returns the specified string converted to lowercase.
toSource	Returns a string representing the source code of the object.
toString	Returns the string representation of the specified object.
toUpperCase	Returns the specified string converted to uppercase.
valueOf	Returns the primitive value of a String object as a string datatype.

Submit Object

A Submit object is created with every instance of an XHTML <input type="submit"> tag within the document. The objects are stored in the array of the parent form and accessed using the name defined within the XHTML tag or an integer representing the order in which the element appears in the form (with 0 being the first element).

Properties

Properties	Description
form	Returns a reference to the object's parent form.
name	Sets or returns the value of the object's name attribute.
type	The value of this property is always submit.
value	Sets or returns the object's value attribute.

Methods

Methods
blur
click
focus
handleEvent(event)

Event Handlers

Event Handlers
onBlur
onClick
onFocus

Text Object

A Text object is created with every instance of an XHTML `<input type="text">` tag within the document. The objects are stored in the array of the parent form and accessed using the name defined within
the XHTML tag or an integer representing the order in which the element appears in the form (with 0
being the first element).

Properties

Properties	Description
defaultValue	Sets or returns the object's initial value attribute.
form	Returns a reference to the object's parent form.
name	Sets or returns the value of the object's name attribute.
type	The value of this property is always text.
value	Sets or returns the object's value attribute.

Methods

Methods
blur
focus
handleEvent(event)
select

Event Handlers

Event Handlers
onBlur
onChange
onFocus
onSelect

Textarea Object

A Textarea object is created with every instance of an XHTML <textarea> tag within the document. The objects are stored in the array of the parent form and accessed using the name defined within the XHTML tag or an integer representing the order in which the element appears in the form (with 0 being the first element).

Properties

Properties	Description
defaultValue	Sets or returns the object's initial value attribute.
form	Returns a reference to the object's parent form.
name	Sets or returns the value of the object's name attribute.
type	The value of this property is always textarea.
value	Sets or returns the object's value attribute.

Methods

Methods
blur
focus
handleEvent(event)
select

Event Handlers

Event Handlers
onBlur
onChange

Table continued on following page

Event Handlers
onFocus
onKeyDown
onKeyPress
onKeyUp
onSelect

Window Object

As the top-level object in the JavaScript client hierarchy, a `Window` object is created for every user agent window and frame (every instance of an XHTML `<body>` or `<frameset>` tag).

Properties

Properties	Description
closed	Returns a Boolean value corresponding to whether a window has been closed. If the window has been closed, this property is `true`.
defaultStatus [= "message"]	Returns or sets the message displayed in a window's status bar.
document	Returns a reference to the document currently displayed in the window. See `Document` object.
frames[]	An array containing all the child frames in the current window.
history	A reference to the window's `History` object. See the `History` object.
length	Returns the number of child frames contained within a window.
location	A reference to the window's `Location` object. See the `Location` object.
name[="name"]	Returns or sets a window's name.
opener	Returns a reference to the object (usually window) that opened the specified window.
outerheight / outerwidth	Determines the dimensions (in pixels) of the outside boundary of a window (including all interface elements).
pageXOffset / pageYOffset	Returns the X and Y positions (in pixels) of the current document's upper left corner in relation to the upper left corner of a window's display area.
parent	Returns a reference to the window or frame that contains the calling frame.
personalbar[.visible = true|false]	Sets the visibility of the window's personal bar (or directories bar).

Properties	Description
scrollbars[.visible = true|false]	Sets the visibility of the window's scroll bars.
self	Returns a reference to the current active window or frame.
status[= "message"]	Returns or sets the message displayed in a window's status bar.
statusbar[.visible = true|false]	Sets the visibility of the window's status bar.
toolbar[.visible = true|false]	Sets the visibility of the window's toolbar. Note that this property can be set only prior to the window being opened and requires the UniversalBrowserWrite privilege.
top	Returns a reference to the topmost browser window.
window	Returns a reference to the current window or frame.

Methods

Methods	Description
alert("message")	Displays an alert box containing message and an OK button (to clear the box).
blur	Removes the focus from the specified window.
captureEvents (event_types)	Instructs the window to capture all events of a particular type. See the Event object for a list of event types.
clearInterval (intervalID)	Used to cancel a timeout previously set with the setInterval method.
clearTimeout (timeoutID)	Used to cancel a timeout previously set with the setTimeout method.
close	Causes the specified window to close.
confirm("message")	Displays a dialog box containing message along with OK and Cancel buttons. If the user clicks the OK button, this method returns true; if the user clicks the Cancel button (or otherwise closes the dialog box), the method returns false.
disableExternal Capture	Disables the capturing of events previously enabled using the enableExternalCapture method.
enableExternalCapture	Allows a window that contains frames to capture events in documents that are loaded from other servers.
focus	Assigns focus to the specified window.
forward	Causes the window to move one entry forward in the history list (similar to pressing the browser's Forward button).

Table continued on following page

Methods	Description
`handleEvent(event)`	Used to call the handler for the specified event.
`home`	Mimics the user pressing the Home button, causing the window to display the document designated as the user's home page.
`moveBy(horizPixels, vertPixels)`	Moves the window horizontally by `horizPixels` and vertically by `vertPixels` in relation to its current position.
`moveTo(Xposition, Yposition)`	Moves the window upper left corner to the position `Xposition` (horizontal) and `Yposition` (vertically).
`open(URL, windowname [, features])`	Opens a new window named `windowname`, displaying the document referred to by URL, with the optional specified `features`. The specified `features` are contained in a string, with the features separated by commas. Features can include the following: `toolbar=yes|no`—Controls the visibility of the window's toolbar `location=yes|no`—Controls the visibility of the window's location bar `directories=yes|no`—Controls the visibility of the window's directory buttons `status=yes|no`—Controls the visibility of the window's status bar `menubar=yes|no`—Controls the visibility of the window's menu bar `resizable=yes|no`—Controls whether the window can be resized `scrollbars=yes|no`—Controls the visibility of the window's scroll bars `width=pixels`—Sets the width of the new window `height=pixels`—Sets the height of the new window For example, to create a new window that is 400 pixels square, is not resizable, and has no scroll bars, you could use the following string for `features`: `"height=400,width=400,resizeable=no,scrollbars=no"`
`print`	Calls the `print` routine for the user agent to print the current document.
`prompt(message[, input])`	Displays a dialog box containing `message` and a text box with the default `input` (if specified). The content of the text box is returned if the user clicks OK. If the user clicks Cancel or otherwise closes the dialog box, the method returns `null`.
`releaseEvents(event_type)`	Used to release any captured events of the specified type and to send them on to objects further down the event hierarchy.
`resizeBy(horizPixels, vertPixels)`	Resizes the specified window by the specified horizontal and vertical pixels. The window retains its upper left position; the resize moves the lower right corner appropriately.

Methods	Description
resizeTo(horizPixels, vertPixels)	Resizes the specified window to the specified dimensions.
routeEvent(event_type)	Used to send an event further down the normal event hierarchy.
scrollBy(horizPixels, vertPixels)	Scrolls the specified window by the amount (horizontal and vertically) specified. The visible property of the window's scrollbar must be set to true for this method to work. Note that this method has been largely deprecated in favor of scrollTo.
scrollTo(Xposition, Yposition)	Scrolls the specified window to the specified coordinates, with the specified coordinate becoming the top left corner of the viewable area.
setInterval (expression/function, milliseconds)	Causes the expression to be evaluated or the function called every milliseconds. Returns the ID of the interval. Use the clearInterval method to stop the iterations.
setTimeout (expression/function, milliseconds)	Causes the expression to be evaluated or the function called after the specified milliseconds elapse. Returns the ID of the interval. Use the clearTimeout method to stop the iteration.
stop	Mimics the user clicking the Stop button on their user agent.

Event Handlers

Event Handlers
onBlur
onDragDrop
onError
onFocus
onLoad
onMove
onResize
onUnload

Perl Language Reference

This appendix provides a comprehensive reference to the Perl language. Within this appendix you will find listings for Perl's many language conventions, including its variables, statements, and functions. For more information on using the language, see Chapters 25 and 28 of this book.

Command Line Arguments

The following table lists the various command line arguments that you can use with Perl. Note that you can also specify arguments on the #! line within individual scripts similar to the following code:

```
#!/usr/bin/perl -U
```

Argument	Use
-a	Turns on autosplit mode. Used with the -n or -p options. (Splits to @F.)
-c	Checks syntax. (Does not execute program.)
-d	Starts the Perl symbolic debugger.
-D *number*	Sets debugging flags.
-e *command*	Enters a single line of script. Multiple -e arguments can be used to create a multiline script.
-F *regexp*	Specifies a regular expression to split on if -a is used.
-i[*extension*]	Edits < > files in place.
-I[*directory*]	Used with -P, specifies where to look for include files. The *directory* is prepended to @INC.
-l [*octnum*]	Enables line-end processing on *octnum*.

Table continued on following page

Argument	Use
-n	Assumes a while (<>) loop around the script. Does not print lines.
-p	Similar to -n, but lines are printed.
-P	Executes the C preprocessor on the script before Perl.
-s	Enables switch parsing after program name.
-S	Enables PATH environment variable searching for program.
-T	Forces taint checking.
-u	Compiles program and dumps core.
-U	Enables Perl to perform unsafe operations.
-v	Outputs the version of the Perl executable.
-w	Enables checks and warning output for spelling errors and other error-prone constructs in the script.
-x [directory]	Extracts a Perl program from input stream. Specifying directory changes to that directory before running the program.
-X	Disables all warnings.
-0[octal]	Designates an initial value for the record separator, $/. See also -l.

Perl Symbolic Debugger Commands

Start the debugger with the Perl -d command line argument. Specifying a script on the command line will start the debugger with that script. The debugger supports the commands in the following table.

Command	Use
h	Prints out a help message.
T	Prints a stack trace.
s	Single-steps forward.
n	Single-steps forward around a subroutine call.
RETURN (key)	Repeats the last s or n debugger command.
r	Returns from the current subroutine.
c [line]	Continues until line, breakpoint, or exit.
p expr	Prints expr.

Command	Use
l [*range*]	Lists a range of lines. *range* may be a number, a subroutine name, or one of the following formats: `start-end`, `start+amount`. (Omitting *range* lists the next window.)
w	Lists window around current line.
–	Lists previous window.
f *file*	Switches to *file*.
l *sub*	Lists the subroutine *sub*.
S	List the names of all subroutines.
/*pattern*/	Searches forward for *pattern*.
?*pattern*?	Searches backward for *pattern*.
b [*line* [*condition*]]	Sets breakpoint at *line* for the specified *condition*. If *line* is omitted, the current line is used.
b *sub* [*condition*]	Sets breakpoint at the subroutine *sub* for the specified *condition*.
d [*line*]	Deletes breakpoint at *line*.
D	Deletes all breakpoints.
L	Lists lines that currently have breakpoints or actions.
a *line command*	Sets an action for line.
A	Deletes all line actions.
< *command*	Sets *command* to be executed before every debugger prompt.
> *command*	Sets *command* to be executed before every s, c, or n command.
V [*package* [*vars*]]	Lists all variables or specified *vars* in *package*. If *package* is omitted, lists main.
X [*vars*]	Similar to V, but lists the current package.
! [[-]*number*]	Re-executes a command. If *number* is not specified, the previous command is used.
H [-*number*]	Displays the last -*number* commands of more than one letter.
t	Toggles trace mode.
= [*alias value*]	Sets *alias* to *value*, or lists current aliases.
q	Quits the debugger.
command	Executes *command* as a Perl statement.

Operators

The following tables detail the various operators present in the Perl language.

Perl Arithmetic Operators

Operator	Use
+	Addition
−	Subtraction
*	Multiplication
/	Division
%	Modulus
**	Exponent
++	Increment
−−	Decrement

Perl Assignment Operators

Operator	Use
=	Assignment
+=	Increment assignment
−=	Decrement assignment
*=	Multiplication assignment
/=	Division assignment
%=	Modulus assignment
**=	Exponential assignment
.=	String concatenation assignment

Perl Comparison Operators

Operator	Use
==	Numeric is equal to
!=	Numeric is not equal to
>	Numeric is greater than

Operator	Use
<	Numeric is less than
>=	Numeric is greater than or equal to
<=	Numeric is less than or equal to
eq	String equality
ne	String nonequality
gt	String greater than
lt	String less than
ge	String greater than or equal to
le	String less than or equal to

Perl Logical Operators

Operator	Use
&&	And
||	Or
!	Not

Perl Bitwise Operators

Operator	Use
&	And
|	Or
^	Xor
~	Not
<<	Left shift
>>	Right shift

Perl Miscellaneous Operators

Operator	Use
.	Object/property/method separator
?	Condition operator
delete	Delete specified object
new	Create new object
this	Reference current object
ref	Type of object (number, string, and so on)
void	Evaluate expression without return value

String Operators

Operator	Use
.	Concatenation
x	Repetition

String Tokens

Token	Character
\b	Backspace
\e	Escape
\t	Horizontal tab
\n	Line feed
\v	Vertical tab
\f	Form feed
\r	Carriage return
\"	Double quote
\'	Single quote
\$	Dollar sign
\@	At sign
\\	Backslash

Standard Variables

The following tables detail the various standard variables in the Perl language.

Global Variables

Variable	Use
$_	The default input and pattern-searching space.
$.	The current input line number of the last filehandle read.
$/	The input record separator (newline is the default).
$,	The output field separator for the print operator.
$"	The separator joining elements of arrays interpolated in strings.
$\	The output record separator for the print operator.
$?	The status returned by the last ` ... ` command, pipe close, or system operator.
$]	The Perl version number.
$;	The subscript separator for multidimensional array emulation (default is \034).
$!	In a numeric context, is the current value of errno. In a string context, is the corresponding error string.
$@	The Perl error message from the last eval or do command.
$:	The set of characters after which a string may be broken to fill continuation fields in a format.
$0	The name of the file containing the Perl script being executed.
$$	The process ID of the currently executing Perl program.
$<	The real user ID of the current process.
$>	The effective user ID of the current process.
$(	The real group ID of the current process.
$)	The effective group ID of the current process.
$^A	The accumulator for formline and write operations.
$^D	The debug flags; passed to Perl using the -D command line argument.
$^F	The highest system file descriptor.
$^I	In-place edit extension, passed to Perl using the -i command line argument.
$^L	Formfeed character used in formats.
$^P	Internal debugging flag.

Table continued on following page

Variable	Use
$^T	The time (as delivered by time) when the program started. Value is used by the file test operators -M, -A, and -C.
$^W	The value of the -w command line argument.
$^X	The name used to invoke the current program.

Context-Dependent Variables

Variable	Use
$%	The current page number of the current output channel.
$=	The page length of the current output channel. (Default is 60.)
$-	The number of lines remaining on the page.
$~	The name of the current report format.
$^	The name of the current top-of-page format.
$|	Used to force a flush after every write or flush on the current output channel. Set to nonzero to force flush.
$ARGV	The name of the file when reading from < >.

Localized Variables

Variable	Use
$&	The string matched by the last successful pattern match.
$`	The string preceding what was matched by the last successful pattern match.
$'	The string following what was matched by the last successful pattern match.
$+	The last bracket matched by the last search pattern.
$1...$9	Contains the subpatterns from the corresponding parentheses in the last successful pattern match. (Subpatterns greater than $9 are available if the match contained more than 9 matched subpatterns.)

Special Arrays

Array	Use
@ARGV	Contains the command-line arguments for the program. Does not include the command name.
@EXPORT	Names of methods a package exports by default.

Array	Use
@EXPORT_OK	Names of methods a package can export upon explicit request.
@INC	Contains a list of places to look for Perl scripts for require or do.
@ISA	Contains a list of the base classes of a package.
@_	Contains the parameter array for subroutines. Also used by split (not in array context).
%ENV	Contains the current environment.
%INC	Contains a list of files that have been included with require or do. The key to each entry is the filename of the inclusion, and the value is the location of the actual file used. (The require command uses this array to determine if a particular file has already been included or not.)
%OVERLOAD	Overload operators in a package.
%SIG	Sets signal handlers for various signals.

Statements

The following tables detail the various statements present in the Perl language.

Subroutines, Packages, and Modules

Function/Statement	Use
&subroutine list	Executes *subroutine*. Note: The & may be omitted if the subroutine has been declared before being used.
bless ref [, package]	Turns the object *ref* into an object in *package*. Returns *ref*.
caller [expr]	Returns an array containing the context for a specific subroutine call ($package,$file,$line). Using *expr* specifies how many call frames to go back from the current frame. When *expr* is used, the routine returns extra information in the array ($package, $filename, $line, $subroutine, $hasargs, $wantarray, $evaltext, $is_require, $hints, $bitmask). Returns false if there is no caller. (If *expr* is used, this function returns additional debugging info.)
goto &subroutine	Substitutes a call to *subroutine* for the currently running subroutine.
import module [[version] list]	Imports the named subroutines from *module* into the current program.
no module [list]	Cancels imported semantics.

Table continued on following page

Function/Statement	Use
`package name`	Designates the remainder of the current block as a package.
`require expr`	Can be used in multiple contexts: If *expr* is numeric, statement requires Perl to be at least the version in *expr*. If *expr* is nonnumeric, it indicates a name of a file to be included from the Perl library. (The `.pm` extension is assumed if none is given.)
`return expr`	Returns from a subroutine with the value specified.
`sub name { expr ; ... }`	Designates *name* as a subroutine. Parameters are passed by reference as array `@_`. Returns the value of the last expression evaluated in the subroutine or the value indicated with the `return` statement.
`[ sub ] BEGIN { expr ; ... }`	Defines a setup block to be called before execution of the rest of the script.
`[ sub ] END { expr ; ... }`	Defines a cleanup block to be called upon termination of the script.
`tie var, package, [ list ]`	Ties a variable to a package that will handle it.
`untie var`	Breaks the binding between *var* and its package.
`use module [ [ version ] list ]`	Imports semantics from module into the current package.

Loops and Conditions

Statement	Use
`do {` `} while|until expr`	Perform the loop code while *expr* evaluates to `true` (while) or until *expr* evaluates to `true` (until). Note that because the conditional statement is at the end of the loop, the loop code will execute at least once.

`elsif (expr) {`
 `  # code to do if expr = true`
 `} [ else {`
 ` # code to do if expr = false`
 `} ]`
	An optional construct that can be used instead of `else` in an `if` construct. The `elsif` (else if) construct evaluates *expr* and performs actions accordingly. An example of an extended `if` construct with an `elsif` block follows:
	
	 `if (expr1) {`
	 ` # code to do if expr1 = true`
	 `} elsif (expr2) {`
	 ` # code to do if expr1 = false and expr2 = true`
	 `}`
	
	 Note: The `elsif` construct can also employ an `else` block.

Statement	Use

``for (init_expr; cond_expr;
loop_expr) {
 // loop code
}```
	The `for` loop is a complex loop structure typically used to iterate over a sequence of numbers (for example, 1–10). At the start of the loop the *init_expr* is evaluated and the *cond_expr* is also evaluated. The loop executes as long as *cond_expr* remains true, evaluating the *loop_expr* on the second and subsequent iterations. For example, the following loop executes 10 times, assigning the variable x values of 1 through 10:
	
	``for (x = 1; x <= 10; x++) {
	 // loop code
	}```

``foreach [var] (mixed) {
 // loop code
}```
	Performs the loop code once for every item in *mixed*, assigning the variable *var* to each item in turn. For example, the following code will output all the values in array @arr:
	
	``foreach $value (@arr) {
	 print $value;
	}```
	
	If *var* is omitted, the iteration variable ($_) is used instead.

``if (expr) {
 # code to do if expr = true
} [else {
 # code to do if expr = false
}]```
	Performs code based on the evaluation of the expression, *expr*. If *expr* evaluates to `true`, the block of code in the `if` section is executed. If *expr* evaluates to `false`, the code in the `if` section is not executed, but the code in the optional `else` section is. See also `elsif`.

label:	Declares a `label` in the code that can be referenced via statements such as `next`, `last`, or `redo`. The label text (*label*) can be any valid nonreserved name and must end in a colon.
last [*label*]	Causes the loop to advance to the end condition (condition statement = `true`) ending the loop. This statement skips the `continue` section of the loop if it exists. If *label* is specified, it performs the action on the appropriately labeled loop instead of the current one.
next [*label*]	Causes the loop to end the current iteration and start the next iteration (evaluating the conditional statement in the process). If *label* is specified, it performs the action on the appropriately labeled loop instead of the current one.

Table continued on following page

Statement	Use
redo [*label*]	Causes the loop to redo the current iteration of the loop (*not* evaluating the conditional statement in the process). If *label* is specified, it performs the action on the appropriately labeled loop instead of the current one.

until (*expr*) {
  # statement(s) to execute
  # while expression is true
} [continue {
  # statements to do at end
  # of loop or explicit continue
}]
	Perform the loop code until *expr* evaluates to true. Note that because the conditional statement is at the beginning of the loop, the loop code may not execute (if *expr* is initially true).

while (*expr*) {
  # statement(s) to execute
} [continue {
  # statements to do at end
  # of loop or explicit continue
}]
	Perform the loop code while *expr* evaluates to true. Note that because the conditional statement is at the beginning of the loop, the loop code may not execute (if *expr* is initially false).

Functions

The following tables detail the various default functions available in the Perl language.

Arithmetic Functions

Function	Use
abs *expr*	Returns the absolute value of *expr*.
atan2 *x*, *y*	Returns the arctangent of x/y.
cos *expr*	Returns the cosine of *expr*.
exp *expr*	Returns e (the natural logarithm base) to the power of *expr*.
int *expr*	Returns the integer portion of *expr*.
log *expr*†	Returns the natural logarithm of *expr*.
rand [*expr*]	Returns a random number between 0 and the value of *expr*. If *expr* is omitted, returns a value between 0 and 1.
sin *expr*	Returns the sine of *expr*.
sqrt *expr*	Returns the square root of *expr*.
srand [*expr*]	Sets the random number seed for the rand operator.
time	Returns the number of seconds since January 1, 1970.

Conversion Functions

Function	Use
chr *expr*	Returns the character represented by the decimal value *expr*.
gmtime *expr*	Returns a 9-element array (0 = $sec, 1 = $min, 2 = $hour, 3 = $mday, 4 = $mon, 5 = $year, 6 = $wday, 7 = $yday, 8 = $isdst) with the time formatted for the Greenwich time zone. Note that *expr* should be in a form returned from a time function.
hex *expr*	Returns the decimal value of *expr*, with *expr* interpreted as a hex string.
localtime *expr*	Returns a 9-element array (0 = $sec, 1 = $min, 2 = $hour, 3 = $mday, 4 = $mon, 5 = $year, 6 = $wday, 7 = $yday, 8 = $isdst) with the time formatted for the local time zone. Note that *expr* should be in a form returned from a time function.
oct *expr*	Returns the decimal value of *expr*, with *expr* interpreted as an octal string. If *expr* begins with 0x, *expr* is interpreted as a hex string instead of an octal string.
ord *expr*	Returns the ASCII value of the first character of *expr*.
vec *expr*, *offset*, *bits*	Using *expr* as a vector of unsigned integers, returns the bit at *offset*. Note that *bits* must be between 1 and 32.

Structure Conversion

Function	Use
pack *template*, *list*	Returns a binary structure, packing the list of values using template. See the template listing in the next table.
unpack *template*, *expr*	Returns an array unpacking the structure *expr*, using template. See the template listing in the next table.

*For the **pack** and **unpack** functions, template is a sequence of characters containing the characters in the following table.*

Pack and Unpack Template Characters

Character	Use
a	A string with binary data (null padded).
A	A text (ASCII) string (space padded).
z	A null-terminated (ASCIZ) string (null padded).
b	A bit string (ascending bit order inside each byte).

Table continued on following page

Character	Use
B	A bit string (descending bit order inside each byte).
h	A hex string (low nybble first).
H	A hex string (high nybble first).
c	A signed char value.
C	An unsigned char value. (See U for Unicode chars.)
s	A signed short value.
S	An unsigned short value.
i	A signed integer value.
I	An unsigned integer value.
l	A signed long value.
L	An unsigned long value.
n	An unsigned short in "network" (big-endian) order.
N	An unsigned long in "network" (big-endian) order.
v	An unsigned short in "VAX" (little-endian) order.
V	An unsigned long in "VAX" (little-endian) order.
q	A signed quad (64-bit) value.
Q	An unsigned quad value.
j	A signed integer value.
J	An unsigned integer value.
f	A single-precision float (native format).
d	A double-precision float (native format).
F	A floating-point value (native format).
D	A long double-precision float (native format).
p	A pointer to a null-terminated string.
P	A pointer to a structure (fixed-length string).
u	A uuencoded string.
U	A Unicode character number.
w	A BER compressed integer.
x	A null byte.
X	Back up a byte.

Character	Use
@	Null fill to absolute position, counted from the start of the innermost group.
(	Start of a group.
)	End of a group.

Each character can be followed by a decimal number that is used as a repeat count. An asterisk specifies all remaining arguments. If the format begins with %N, the unpack function will return an N-bit checksum. Spaces can be included in the *template* for legibility — they are ignored when the *template* is processed.

String Functions

Function	Use
chomp *string* | *list*	Removes the trailing record separator (as set in $/) from *string* or all elements of *list*. Returns the total number of characters removed.
chop *list*	Removes the last character from all elements of *list*. Returns the last character removed.
crypt *string*, *salt*	Encrypts *string*.
eval *expr*	Parses *expr* and executes it as if it contained Perl code. Returns the value of the last expression evaluated.
index *string*, *substr* [, *offset*]	Returns the position of *substr* in *string* at or after *offset*. If *substr* is not found, index returns -1.
length *expr*	Returns the length of *expr* in characters.
lc *expr*	Returns a lowercase version of *expr*.
lcfirst *expr*	Returns *expr* with the first character in lowercase.
quotemeta *expr*	Returns *expr* with all regular expression metacharacters quoted.
rindex *string*, *substr* [, *offset*]	Returns the position of the last *substr* in *string* at or before *offset*.
substr *expr*, *offset* [, *len*]	Extracts a substring of length *len* out of *expr* and returns it. If *offset* is negative, substr counts from the end of the string.
uc *expr*	Returns an uppercase version of *expr*.
ucfirst *expr*	Returns *expr* with the first character in uppercase.

Array and List Functions

Function	Use
delete $hash{key}	Deletes the specified value from *hash*. Returns the deleted value.
each %hash	Returns an array consisting of the key and value for the next pair in *hash*. Entries are returned in a random order. After all values have been returned, each returns a null array. Subsequent calls will iterate through *hash* again.
exists *expr*	Checks if the specified *expr* key exists in its hash.
grep *expr|block*, *list*	Evaluates *expr* or *block* for each element of *list*, setting $_ to refer to the element. (Note that modifying $_ will also modify the corresponding element from *list*.) Returns an array of *list* elements for which *expr* returned true.
join *expr*, *list*	Joins the strings in *list* into a single string with each field separated by the value of *expr*. Returns the new, combined string.
keys %hash	Returns an array containing the keys of *hash*.
map *expr|block*, *list*	Evaluates *expr* or *block* for each element of *list*, setting $_ to refer to the element. (Note that modifying $_ will also modify the corresponding element from *list*.) Returns the list of results.
pop @array	Pops off (removes) and returns the last value *array*.
push @array, *list*	Pushes (adds) the values in *list* onto the end of *array*.
reverse *list*	In array context, reverse returns the *list* in reverse order. In scalar context, reverse returns the first element of *list* with its bytes reversed.
scalar @array	Returns the number of elements in *array*.
scalar %hash	Returns a true value if *hash* has elements defined.
shift [@array]	Shifts the first value of *array* off and returns it. If @array is omitted, shift will operate on @argv in main and @_ in subroutines.
sort [*subroutine*] *list*	Sorts *list* and returns the sorted array value. If *subroutine* is specified, determines how the list is sorted. The *subroutine* must return less than zero, zero, or greater than zero — the elements of the array are available *subroutine* as $a and $b are to be ordered. (Note that *subroutine* may refer to the name of a user-defined routine, or a *block*.)

Function	Use
splice @array, offset [, length [, list]]	Removes the elements of @array designated by offset and length and replaces them with list (if specified). Returns the elements removed from @array.
split [pattern [, expr [, limit]]]	Splits a string into an array and returns the array. If limit is specified, split creates at most the number of fields specified. If pattern is omitted, the string is split at white space. If split is not in array context, it returns number of fields and splits to @_.
unshift @array, list	Prepends list to the front of @array, and returns the number of elements in the new array.
values %hash	Returns an array containing all the values of hash.

Search and Replace Functions

Function	Use
[expr =~] [m] /pattern/ [g] [i] [m] [o] [s] [x]	Searches expr (or the default $_) for pattern. If used in array context, an array is returned consisting of the expressions matched by the parentheses in pattern, that is, ($1,$2,$3,...). (Note: If pattern is empty, the last pattern from a previous search or replace function is used.) See the next table for descriptions of options.
[$var =~] s/pattern/ replacement/ [e] [g] [i] [m] [o] [s] [x]	Searches a string for a pattern, and if pattern is found, it is replaced by the replacement text. Returns the number of substitutions made, or returns false if no substitutions were made. See the next table for descriptions of options.
[$var =~] tr/searchlist/ replacelist/ [c] [d] [s]	Translates all occurrences of the characters found in searchlist with the corresponding character in the replacelist. It returns the number of characters replaced. See the next table for descriptions of options.
pos scalar	Returns the position where the last m//g search left off for scalar.
study [$var]	Study $var in anticipation of performing many pattern matches on it.

The following table explains the options mentioned in the preceding "Search and Replace Functions" table.

Search and Replace Options

Option	Use
c	Complements *searchlist*.
d	Deletes all characters in *searchlist* that do not appear in *replacelist*.
e	Evaluates *replacement* string as a Perl expression.
g	Matches as many times as possible (global).
i	Case-insensitive search manner.
m (prepend option)	(Prepend) Uses alternate delimiters instead of slashes.
m (suffixed option)	Treats the string as multiple lines.
o	Interpolates variables only once.
s	Treats the string as a single line.
x	Allows regular expression extensions.

File and File Handle Test Functions

Test	Use
-r	File is readable by effective uid/gid.
-w	File is writable by effective uid/gid.
-x	File is executable by effective uid/gid.
-o	File is owned by effective uid.
-R	File is readable by real uid/gid.
-W	File is writable by real uid/gid.
-X	File is executable by real uid/gid.
-O	File is owned by real uid.
-e	File exists.
-z	File has zero size (empty).
-s	File has nonzero size (returns file size, in bytes).
-f	File is a plain file.
-d	File is a directory.
-l	File is a symbolic link.

Test	Use
-p	File is a named pipe (FIFO), or filehandle is a pipe.
-S	File is a socket.
-b	File is a block special file.
-c	File is a character special file.
-t	Filehandle is opened to a tty.
-u	File has a setuid bit set.
-g	File has a setgid bit set.
-k	File has a sticky bit set.
-T	File is an ASCII text file.
-B	File is a binary file (opposite of -T).
-M	Script start time minus file modification time (in days).
-A	Script start time minus access time (in days).
-C	Script start time minus inode change time (in days).

File Operations

Function	Use
chmod *list*	Changes the permissions of the files in *list*. The first element of *list* is the mode to use.
chown *list*	Changes the owner and group of the files in *list*. The first two elements of the *list* are the numerical userid and groupid to set.
truncate *file*, *size*	Truncates *file* to *size*. The *file* can be a filename or a filehandle.
link *oldfile*, *newfile*	Creates *newfile* as a link to *oldfile*.
lstat *file*	Identical to the stat function, but lstat does not traverse symbolic links.
mkdir *directory*, *mode*	Creates *directory* with permissions in *mode*. Sets $! if operation fails.
readlink *expr*	Returns the value of a symbolic link. Sets $! on system error, uses $_ if *expr* is omitted.
rename *oldname*, *newname*	Changes the name *oldname* to *newname*.
rmdir *directory*	Deletes *directory* if it is empty. Sets $! if operation fails.

Table continued on following page

Function	Use
stat *file*	Returns a 13-element array where 0 = $dev, 1 = $ino, 2 = $mode, 3 = $nlink, 4 = $uid, 5 = $gid, 6 = $rdev, 7 = $size, 8 = $atime, 9 = $mtime, 10 = $ctime, 11 = $blksize, 12 = $blocks. Note that *file* can be a filehandle, an expression evaluating to a filename, or _ (underline filehandle), which will use the file referred to in the last file test operation or stat call. Returns a null list on failure.
symlink *oldfile*, *newfile*	Creates *newfile* symbolically linked *oldfile*.
unlink *list*	Deletes the *list* of files.
utime *list*	Changes the access and modification times of files in *list*. The first two elements of *list* are the access and modification times to use.

Input and Output Functions

Function	Use
<*filehandle*>	Reads a line from *filehandle* (in scalar context) or reads the whole file (in array context).
< >	Reads from the input stream formed by entries in @argv, or reads from STDIN if no arguments are supplied.
binmode *filehandle*	Prepares *filehandle* to be read or written in binary mode (as opposed to text mode). Not valid under UNIX.
close *filehandle*	Closes the file or pipe associated with *filehandle*.
eof *filehandle*	Returns true if the end of file (EOF) on *filehandle* has been reached.
fcntl *filehandle*, *function*, $var	Implements a fcntl(2) function, using the parameters specified, with nonstandard return values.
fileno *filehandle*	Returns the file descriptor for *filehandle*.
flock *filehandle*, *operation*	Calls flock(2) on *filehandle*. Note that *operation* is formed by adding the following values for the following operations: 1 = shared, 2 = exclusive, 4 = nonblocking, or 8 = unlock. Note that such a lock is only advisory and that systems or programs not supporting flock will be able to write through the lock. Returns true on success or false on failure.
getc [*filehandle*]	Returns the next character from *filehandle*, or an empty string if EOF. Reads from STDIN if *filehandle* is not specified.

Function	Use
`ioctl filehandle, function, $var`	Performs `ioctl(2)` on *filehandle*, using the supplied parameters, with nonstandard return values.
`open filehandle [ , filename ]`	Opens a file and associates it with *filehandle*. If *filename* is not , specified the scalar variable *filehandle* must contain the filename. Returns `true` on success or `undef` on failure.
	The following conventions apply to the filename specification when opening a file:
	file or <*file* : open *file* for reading >*file* : open *file* for writing, creating *file* first if necessary. >>*file* : open *file* for writing in append mode. +<*file* : open *file* with read/write access (*file* must exist). +>*file* : open *file* with read/write access (*file* is truncated). |*cmd* : open a pipe to command *cmd*; creates a fork if *cmd* is -. *cmd*| : open a pipe from command *cmd*; creates a fork if *cmd* is -.
	Note that *file* may be specified as &*filehandle*, in which case the new filehandle is connected to the previously used filehandle.
`pipe readhandle, writehandle`	Returns a pair of connected pipes.
`print [ filehandle ] [ list ]`	Equivalent to print *filehandle* sprintf *list*.
`printf[([filehandle] list)]`	Equivalent to print *filehandle* sprintf(*list*).
`read filehandle, $var, length [ , offset ]`	Reads *length* binary bytes from *filehandle* into $*var* at *offset*. Returns the number of bytes read.
`seek filehandle, position, whence`	Arbitrarily positions the file pointer. Returns `true` if the operation was successful.
`select [ filehandle ]`	Returns the current default *filehandle*. If *filehandle* is specified, it becomes the current default filehandle.
`select rbits, wbits, nbits, timeout`	Performs a `select(2)` system call with the parameters specified.
`sprintf format, list`	Returns a string formatted by `printf(3)` conventions.
`sysread filehandle, $var, length [ , offset ]`	Reads *length* bytes from *filehandle* into $*var* at *offset*.
`syswrite filehandle, scalar, length [ , offset ]`	Writes *length* bytes from *scalar* at *offset* to *filehandle*.

Table continued on following page

Function	Use
tell [*filehandle*]	Returns the current file pointer position for *filehandle*. Assumes the last file accessed if *filehandle* is omitted.
write [*filehandle*]	Writes a formatted record to *filehandle*, using the data format associated with that filehandle.

Directory Functions

Function	Use
closedir *dirhandle*	Closes a directory opened by opendir.
opendir *dirhandle*, *dirname*	Opens *dirname* on the *dirhandle* specified.
readdir *dirhandle*	Returns the next entry or an array of entries from *dirhandle*.
rewinddir *dirhandle*	Positions the directory pointer at the beginning of the *dirhandle* list.
seekdir *dirhandle*, *pos*	Sets the directory pointer on *dirhandle* to *pos*.
telldir *dirhandle*	Returns the directory pointer position in the *dirhandle* list.

System Functions

Function	Use
alarm *expr*	Schedules a SIGALRM after *expr* seconds.
chdir [*expr*]	Changes the working directory to *expr*. If *expr* is omitted, alarm uses $ENV{"HOME"} or $ENV{"LOGNAME"}.
chroot *dirname*	Changes the root directory to *dirname* for the process and its children.
die [*list*]	Prints *list* to STDERR and exits with the current value of $!.
exec *list*	Executes the system command(s) *list*. Does not return.
exit [*expr*]	Exits the program immediately with the value of *expr*. Calls appropriate end routines and object destructors before exiting.
fork	Performs a fork(2) system call. Returns the process ID of the child to the parent process and 0 to the child process.
getlogin	Returns the effective login name.
getpgrp [*pid*]	Returns the process group for process *pid*. If pid is 0 or omitted, getgrp returns the current process.
getppid	Returns the process ID of the parent process.

Function	Use
getpriority *which*, *who*	Returns the current priority for a process, a process group, or a user.
glob *pattern*	Returns a list of filenames that match the pattern *pattern*.
kill *list*	Sends a signal to the processes in *list*. The first element of the list is the signal to send in numeric or name form.
setpgrp *pid*, *pgrp*	Sets the process group to *pgrp* for the process specified by *pid*. If *pid* is omitted or 0, setpgrp uses the current process.
setpriority *which*, *who*, *priority*	Sets the current priority for a process, a process group, or a user.
sleep [*expr*]	Causes the program to sleep for *expr* seconds. If *expr* is omitted, the program sleeps forever. Returns the number of seconds slept.
syscall *list*	Calls a system call. The first element in *list* is the system call; the rest of *list* is used as arguments.
system *list*	Similar to exec except that a fork is performed first, and the parent process waits for the child process to complete.
times	Returns a four-element array giving the user and system times, in seconds, for this process and the children of this process (0= $user, 1= $system, 2= $cuser, 3= $csystem).
umask [*expr*]	Sets the umask for the process. Returns the old umask. Omitting *expr* causes the current umask to be returned.
wait	Behaves like a wait(2) system process — waits for a child process to terminate. Returns the process ID of the terminated process (-1 if none). The status is returned in $?.
waitpid *pid*, *flags*	Performs the same function as the waitpid(2) system call.
warn [*list*]	Similar to *die*, warn prints list on STDERR but doesn't exit.

Networking Functions

Function	Use
accept *newsocket*, *genericsocket*	Accepts a new socket similar to the accept(2) system call.
bind *socket*, *name*	Binds *name* to *socket*. The *name* should be a packed address of an appropriate type for *socket*.
connect *socket*, *name*	Attempts to connect *name* to *socket*, similar to the system call.
getpeername *socket*	Returns the socket address of the other end of *socket*.

Table continued on following page

Function	Use
getsockname *socket*	Returns the name of *socket*.
getsockopt *socket*, *level*, *optionname*	Returns the *socket* option identified by *optionname*, queried at *level*.
listen *socket*, *queuesize*	Similar to the listen system call, starts listening on *socket*. Returns true or false depending on success.
recv *socket*, *scalar*, *length*, *flags*	Attempts to receive *length* characters of data into *scalar* from the specified *socket*. Specified *flags* are the same as the recv system call.
send *socket*, *msg*, *flags* [, *to*]	Attempts to send *msg* to socket. Takes the same *flags* as the send system call. Use *to* when necessary to specify an unconnected socket.
setsockopt *socket*, *level*, *optionname*, *optionvalue*	Sets the *socket* option *optionname* to *optionvalue* using the *level* specified.
shutdown *socket*, *method*	Shuts down a *socket* using the specified *method*. The *method* can be any valid method for the shutdown system call.
socket *socket*, *domain*, *type*, *protocol*	Similar to the socket system call, creates a *socket* in *domain* with the *type* and *protocol* specified.
socketpair *socket1*, *socket2*, *domain*, *type*, *protocol*	Similar to socket but creates a pair of bidirectional sockets.

Miscellaneous Functions

Function	Use
defined *expr*	Tests whether *expr* has an actual value.
do *filename*	Executes *filename* as a Perl script.
dump [*label*]	Performs an immediate core dump to a new binary executable. When new binary runs, execution starts at optional *label* or at the beginning of the executable if *label* is not specified.
eval { *expr1* ; *expr2*; ... *exprN*}	Evaluates and executes any code between the braces ({ and }).
local *variable* local (*list*) my *variable* my (*list*)	Creates locally scoped *variable* or *list*.
ref *expr*	Tests *expr* and returns true if *expr* is a reference. Returns a package name if *expr* has been blessed into a package. (See the "Subroutines, Packages, and Modules" table in the "Statements" section.)

Function	Use
reset [*list*]	Resets all variables and arrays that begin with a letter in *list*.
scalar *expr*	Evaluates *expr* in scalar context.
undef [*value*]	Undefines *value*. Returns undefined.
wantarray	Tests the current context to see if an array is expected. Returns true if array is expected or false if array is not expected.

Regular Expressions

The following tables provide information used with Perl's regular expressions and regex handling functions.

Matching Expressions and Characters

Expression/Character	Use
.	Matches an arbitrary character but not a newline.
(...)	Groups a series of elements into a single element; that single element can be used as subexpressions (later referenced with $1 to $9 or \1 to \9, if matched).
^	Matches the beginning of a line or the beginning of the pattern.
$	Matches the end of a line.
[...]	Matches a class of characters. Use ^ to negate the class ([^ ...]).
(... | ... | ...)	Matches one of the alternatives.
character	Escape *character*.
(?# *text*)	Use *text* as a comment.
(?: *regexp*)	Similar to (*regexp*) but does not make back-references.
(?= *regexp*)	Zero width, positive look-ahead assertion.
(?! *regexp*)	Zero width, negative look-ahead assertion.
(? *modifier*)	Embedded pattern-match modifier. The *modifier* can be one or more of the following: i, m, s, or x.

Match Count Modifiers

Modifier	Use
+	Matches the preceding character or pattern element one or more times.
?	Matches the preceding character or pattern element zero or one times.
*	Matches the preceding character or pattern element zero or more times.
{N,M}	Matches the preceding character or pattern element a minimum of N and maximum of M match count. Use {N} for exactly N matches; use {N, } for at least N matches.

Escape Characters

Escaped Character	Use
\w	Matches alphanumeric (including underscore).
\W	Matches nonalphanumeric.
\s	Matches white space.
\S	Matches non–white space.
\d	Matches numeric.
\D	Matches nonnumeric.
\A	Matches the beginning of the string.
\Z	Matches the end of the string.
\b	Matches word boundaries.
\B	Matches nonword boundaries.
\G	Matches where a previous m//g search left off.
\1 ... \9	Are used to refer to previously matched subexpressions (grouped with parenthesis inside the match pattern). Note: \10 and up can be used if the pattern matches more than nine subexpressions.

E

Python Language Reference

This appendix lists various functions and variables available for CGI programming in Python. Their syntax and general use are shown, and short examples are included, where necessary, for clarity. Although care has been taken to include those functions most likely to be used in CGI programming, Python is evolving, so older code might include deprecated functions that aren't listed here. Because Python is highly modularized, the functions and variables are grouped by the module to which they belong. In most cases, the module must be imported before the functions listed become available.

Built-in Functions

The following sections cover the functions built into Python. These functions are always available and do not require that a specific module be imported for their use.

Syntax	Description

__import__(*mod*)	Imports the module represented by the string mod, especially useful for dynamically importing a list of modules:
	
	`myModules = ['sys','os','cgi','cgitb']`
	`modules = map(__import__,myModules)`

abs(*n*)	Returns the absolute value of *n*.
basestring()	Constructor for the built-in type that can be used to test whether an object is an instance of `str` or `Unicode`. This function can't be called or instantiated but is used like this: `if isinstance(obj, basestring):`

Table continued on following page

Syntax	Description
bool([x])	Returns True or False depending on the value of x. If x is a false statement or empty, returns False; otherwise, returns True.
callable(obj)	Returns 1 if obj can be called; otherwise, returns 0.
chr(i)	Returns a string of one character whose ASCII code is the integer i.

classmethod(func)	Returns a class method for func in the following format:
	
	    class C:
	      @classmethod
	      def func(cls, arg1, arg2...):

cmp(a,b)	Compares values a and b, returning a negative value if a < b, 0 if a == b, and a positive value if a > b.
compile(string, filename, kind [, flags [, don't inherit]])	Compiles string into a code object. Filename is the file containing the code. Kind denotes what kind of code to compile.
complex([real[, imag]])	Returns a complex number with value real+imag*j.
delattr(obj, string)	Removes the attribute of obj whose name is string.
dict([mapping or sequence])	Returns a dictionary whose initial value is set to mapping or sequence. Returns empty dictionary if no mapping or sequence is provided.
dir(obj)	Returns attributes and methods of obj. Works on nearly any data type.
divmod(a,b)	Returns quotient and remainder of two noncomplex numbers, a and b.
enumerate(iterable)	Returns an enumerate object based on the specified iterable object.
eval(expression [, globals [, locals]])	Returns evaluation of expression by Python rules using globals (which must be a dictionary) as global namespace and locals (which can be any mapping object) as local namespace.
execfile(filename [, globals [, locals]])	Parses filename, evaluating as series of Python expressions, using globals and locals as global and local namespaces. globals and locals are dictionaries. If no locals are given, locals are set to provided globals.
file(filename [, mode [, bufsize]])	Returns new file object of specified mode. Modes are r for reading, w for writing, and a for appending: + appended to mode indicates that file is changeable, and b appended to mode indicates that file is to be binary. bufsize may be 0 for unbuffered, 1 for line buffered, or any other positive value for a specific buffer size.

Syntax	Description
filter(*function*, *list*)	Returns a list of items from *list* where *function* is True.
float([*x*])	Returns string or number *x* as converted to a floating-point value. If no argument *x* is given, returns 0.0.
frozenset([*iterable*])	Returns set (with elements taken from *iterable*) that has no update methods but can be hashed and used as the member of other sets or as dictionary keys (called a frozen set).
getattr(*obj*, *name*[, *default*])	Returns the value of the named attribute of *obj* or default if it does not exist.
globals()	Returns a dictionary containing the current global symbol table.
hasattr(*obj*, *name*)	Returns True if *name* is the name of one of *obj*'s attributes; otherwise, returns False.
hash(*obj*)	Returns the hash value of *obj*.
help([*obj*])	Invokes the built-in help system.
hex(*x*)	Converts *x* to a hexadecimal value.
id(*obj*)	Returns the unique integer representing *obj*.
input([*prompt*])	Returns the equivalent of eval(*raw_input(prompt)*).
int[*x*[, *radix*]]	Returns the integer version of *x* to the base specified by *radix*.
isinstance(*obj*, *classinfo*)	Returns True if *obj* is an instance of *classinfo*; otherwise, False. For example, if issubclass(*A*,*B*), then isinstance(*x*,*A*) => isinstance(*x*,*B*).
iter(*o*[, *sentinel*])	Returns an iterator object. If *sentinel* is not specified, *o* must be a collection object that supports the iteration protocol or must support the sequence protocol. If it does not support either of those protocols, TypeError is raised. If *sentinel* is given, then *o* must be a callable object. The iterator created in this case will call *o* with no arguments for each call to its next() method; if the value returned is equal to *sentinel*, StopIteration will be raised; otherwise, the value will be returned.
len(*obj*)	Returns the length of *obj*. Works with string, tuple, list, or dictionary.
list([*sequence*])	Returns a list whose items are the same and in the same order as the objects in *sequence*. If no *sequence* is specified, returns an empty list.
locals()	Returns a dictionary representing the local symbol table.

Table continued on following page

Syntax	Description
long([x[,radix]])	Returns a long integer converted from x to base radix. x may be a string or a regular or long integer or a floating-point number. A floating-point number is truncated toward zero.
map(func, list)	Returns list of results from applying func to every member of list.
max(s[, args])	Returns the largest member of sequence s. If additional args are specified, returns the largest of args.
min(s[, args])	Returns the smallest member of sequence s. If additional args are specified, returns the smallest of args.
object()	Returns a new featureless object.
oct(x)	Returns octal form of integer x.
open(filename[mode[,bufsize]])	Alias for the file function.
ord(c)	Returns the ASCII character represented by the one-character string or Unicode character c. ord('c') returns the integer 99.
pow(x,y[,z])	Returns x to the power y; if z is present, returns x to the power y, modulo z.

property[fget[,fset[,fdel][,doc]]])	Returns a property attribute for a new-style class with functions to get, set, and delete an attribute.
	
	 class C(object):
	     def getx(self): return self.__x
	     def setx(self, val): return self.__x = val
	     def delx(self): del self.__x
	     x=property(getx,setx,delx,"doc of the 'x' property.")

range([start,]stop[,step]])	Creates a progression list of plain integers often used for loops. If all arguments are specified, the list looks like [start,start+step,start+step+step,...].
raw_input(prompt)	Prints prompt to standard output with no newline. Then reads the next line from standard input and returns it (without a newline). s=raw_input('prompt>') prompt> Phrase I typed in. >>>s "Phrase I typed in."

Syntax	Description
reduce(*function*, *sequence*[,*initializer*])	Applies function of two arguments cumulatively to items of *sequence*, from left to right, for the purpose of reducing *sequence* to a single value. Example: reduce(*lambda x,y:x+y*, [*1,2,3,4,5*]) means ((((1+2)+3)+4)+5). Argument *x* is the accumulated value created by adding each of the values in the array as argument *y*. If the initializer value is present, it is placed before the items of the sequence in the calculation and serves as a default when the sequence is empty.
reload(*module*)	Returns the module object of a previously loaded module. The reload function causes the module code to be recompiled and executed (with the exception of the init function), updating the name and dataspace with any changed values and reclaiming any old objects with a reference count of zero. The dictionary is retained from the first loading but redefined names override old definitions. Example: If a module is syntactically correct but its initialization fails, the first import statement for it does not bind its name locally but does store a (partially initialized) module object in sys.modules. To reload the module, you must first import it again (this will bind the name to the partially initialized module object) before you can reload() it.
repr(*obj*)	Returns a printable representation of *obj*.
reversed(*seq*)	Returns the reverse of any object that supports the sequence protocol.
round(*x*[,*n*])	Returns floating point *x* rounded to *n* digits after the decimal point.
set([*iterable*])	Returns a set whose immutable elements are taken from *iterable*.
setattr(*obj*,*string*,*val*)	Assigns the value *val* to *string*, which is an element of *obj*, provided *obj* allows it.
slice([*start*,]*stop*[,*step*])	Returns a slice object representing the set of indices specified by range(*start*, *stop*, *step*).
sorted(*iterable*[,*cmp*[,*key*[,*reverse*]]])	Returns a new sorted list of the elements in *iterable*. Mostly replaced by the list.sort() function, which acts the same way.
staticmethod(*func*)	Returns a static method for function. Static methods in Python are similar to those in Java and C++.

Table continued on following page

Syntax	Description
str(*x*)	Converts *x* into string form. Works on any available data type.
sum(*sequence*[, *start*])	Returns the sum of *start* and the items of sequence that are not allowed to be strings.
super(*type*[,*obj* or *type*])	Returns the superobject of type. If the second argument is an object, isinstance(*obj*, *type*) must be true. If the second argument is a type, issubclass(*type2*,*type*) must be true.
tuple([*sequence*])	Returns a tuple whose items are the same and in the same order as those in sequence.
type(*obj*)	Returns datatype of obj. Works on any available data type.
unichr(*i*)	Return the Unicode string of one character whose Unicode code is the integer *i*. For example, unichr(99) returns the string u'c'.
Unicode([*obj*[,*encoding*[,*errors*]]])	Returns the Unicode version of *obj*. If no optional parameters are specified, this function will behave like the str() function except that it returns Unicode strings instead of eight-bit strings. If encoding and/or errors are given, Unicode() will decode the object, which can either be an eight-bit string or a character buffer using the codec for encoding.
vars([*obj*])	Without arguments, this function returns dictionary corresponding to the current local symbol table. If a module is specified, this function returns a dictionary corresponding to the specified object's symbol table.
xrange([*start*,]*stop*[,*step*])	This function is very similar to range(), but returns an "xrange object'' instead of a list.

array Module

These functions define functionality in support of the array object type, which can represent an array of characters, integers, and floating-point numbers. Arrays are sequence types, behave very much like lists, and are supported by the following functions:

Syntax	Description
array(*typecode*[,*initializer*])	Returns a new array whose items are restricted by *typecode* and initialized from the optional *initializer* value, which must be a list or string in versions prior to 2.4 but may also contain an iterable over elements of the appropriate type. The *typecode* is a character that defines the item type.
append(*x*)	Appends a new item of value *x* to the end of the array.

Syntax	Description
buffer_info()	Return a tuple (address, length) giving the current memory address and the length in elements of the buffer used to hold the array's contents.
byteswap()	Switches byte order of arguments that are 1, 2, 4, or 8 bytes in size (endianness).
count(*x*)	Returns the number of times *x* occurs in the array.
extend(*iterable*)	Appends items from iterable (which prior to version 2.4 had to be another array but has been changed to include any iterable containing elements of the same type as those in array) to end of array.
fromfile(*file*, *num*)	Appends *num* items from *file* to array or returns EOFError if less than *num* are available.
fromlist(*list*)	Appends items from list to array; equivalent to "for x in list: array.append(x)".
fromstring(*string*)	Appends items from string to array, interpreting *string* as an array of machine values.
fromUnicode(*string*)	Extends any type 'u' array with data from the given Unicode string.
index(*x*)	Returns the index of the first occurrence of *x* in the array.
insert(*a*, *x*)	Inserts a new item with value *x* in the array before position *a*.
pop([*i*])	Pops the item with index *i* off the array and returns it.
remove(*x*)	Removes the first occurrence of item *x* from the array.
reverse()	Returns the items in the array in reverse order.
tofile(*file*)	Writes all items (machine values) to *file*.
tolist()	Converts the array to a normal list.
tostring()	Converts the array to an array of machine values and returns the string representation.
toUnicode()	Converts a type 'u' array to a Unicode string.

asyncore Module

This module provides the basic functionality in support of writing asynchronous socket service clients and servers.

Syntax	Description
loop([timeout[,use_poll[,map[,count]]]])	Enters a polling loop that terminates after *count* passes or after all open channels have been closed. The *use_poll* parameter, which defaults to False, can be set to True to indicate that the poll() should be used in preference to select(). *timeout* specifies the number of seconds before the select() or poll() function should timeout. *map* is a dictionary of channels to watch. If the map parameter is omitted, a global map is used. This map is updated by the default class __init__() — make sure you extend, rather than override, __init__() if you want to retain this behavior.
CLASS dispatcher()	Class is a wrapper around a low-level socket object with some methods for event handling called from the asynchronous loop.
handle_read()	Called when the asynchronous loop detects that a read() call on the socket will succeed.
handle_write()	Called when the asynchronous loop detects that a writable socket can be written. Performance may be enhanced if this method implements buffering.
handle_expt()	Called when there is out-of-band data for a socket connection.
handle_connect()	Performs some function such as sending a welcome banner or initiating protocol negotiation when the active opener's socket makes a connection.
handle_close()	Called when the socket is closed.
handle_error()	Called when an exception is raised and not otherwise handled.
handle_accept()	Called on listening channels when a connection can be established to a new remote system that has issued a connect() for the local system.
readable()	Called when the asynchronous loop determines that the socket should be added to the list on which read events can occur.
writable()	Called when the asynchronous loop determines that the socket should be added to the list on which write events can occur.
create_socket(*family*, *type*)	Creates a socket just like the normal socket object.
connect(*address*)	Connects to the socket object indicated by *address*, which is a tuple of the host and the port number.
send(*data*)	Sends data to the remote end-point of the socket.

Syntax	Description
recv(*buffer_size*)	Reads at most *buffer_size* bytes from the socket's remote end-point. If *buffer_size* is an empty string, the connection has been closed from the remote end.
listen(*backlog*)	Listens for *backlog* connections made to the socket. *backlog* should be at least one and not more than the number allowed by the operating system.
bind(*address*)	Binds the socket to *address* as long as it is not already bound.
accept()	Accepts a connection for a socket that is bound to an address and is listening for connection.
close()	Closes the socket.

asynchat Module

This module builds on the basic functionality of the asyncore module for the purpose of simplifying asynchronous communication between clients and servers. It especially helps with protocols whose elements are terminated by arbitrary strings or are of variable length.

Syntax	Description
CLASS ASYNC_CHAT()	Abstract class of asyncore.dispatcher. To make practical use of it, you should subclass async_chat, providing meaningful methods of collect_incoming_data() and found_terminator().
close_when_done()	Pushes a None on the producer fifo, which, when popped off, causes the channel to be closed.
collect_incoming_data(*data*)	Called with data holding some amount of received *data*. The default method, which must be overridden, raises a NotImplementedError exception.
discard_buffers()	Discards any data held in the input or output buffers and the producer fifo.
found_terminator()	Called when the incoming data stream matches the termination condition set by the set_terminator() method.
get_terminator()	Returns the current terminator for the channel.
handle_close()	Called when the channel is closed.
handle_read()	Called when a read event fires on the channel's socket in the asynchronous loop. By default, it checks the termination condition set by set_terminator(), which can be the appearance of a particular string as input or the receipt of a particular number of characters, and upon finding it, calls found_terminator().

Table continued on following page

Syntax	Description
handle_write()	Called when the application may write to the channel. handle_write() calls the initiate_send() method.
push(*data*)	Creates a simple producer object containing *data* and pushes it onto the channel's producer_fifo.
push_with_producer(*producer*)	Takes a *producer* object as input and adds it to the producer_fifo associated with the channel.
readable()	Should return True for the channel to be included in the set of channels to be tested by the select() loop for readability.
refill_buffer()	Refills the output buffer by calling the more() method of the producer object at the head of the fifo.
set_terminator(*term*)	Sets the terminating condition to be recognized on the channel to string (looks for a certain string in the input stream), integer (counts a number of characters received), and None (no terminating condition is set).
writable()	Should return True if the item remains on the producer_fifo or if the channel is connected and the channel's output buffer is not empty.
CLASS simple_producer (*data* [, *buffer_size*=512])	A simple_producer instance takes a chunk of *data* and an optional buffer size. Calls to the more() method may only receive chunks of data no larger than *buffer_size*.
more()	Retrieves the next chunk of data from the producer and returns it. Returns empty string if no data is available.
CLASS fifo([*list*=None])	Each channel maintains a fifo, which holds data pushed on by an application but not yet popped for writing to a channel.
is_empty()	Returns True if the fifo is empty.
first()	Returns the oldest item from the fifo.
push(*data*)	Adds the given *data* to the producer fifo. *data* should be a string or a producer object.
pop()	Deletes the item returned by first() from the fifo and returns True. If the fifo is empty, returns False.

binascii Module

The following section covers the functions in Python's binascii module. The binascii module provides functionality for conversion between binary and various ASCII-encoded representations.

Syntax	Description
ab2_uu (*string*)	Returns the binary data converted from the single line of uuencoded data *string*.
b2a_uu (*data*)	Returns a line of ASCII characters ending in a newline, as converted from binary *data*.
a2b_base64 (*string*)	Returns binary data as converted from the block of base64 data specified by *string*.
b2a_base64 (*string*)	Returns a line of ASCII characters in base64 coding ending in a newline, as converted from a 57-character or shorter binary *string*.
a2b_qp (*string* [, *header*])	Returns binary data as converted from a block of quoted-printable data. If the optional argument header is present and true, underscores will be decoded as spaces.
b2a_qp (*data* [, *quotetabs*, *istext*, *header*])	Returns a line or lines of ASCII characters in quoted-printable format as converted from a line or lines of binary data. If the optional argument header is present and true, spaces will be encoded as underscores.
a2b_hqx (*string*)	Converts binhex4-formatted ASCII data *string* to binary, without doing RLE-decompression.
rledecode_hqx (*data*)	Performs RLE-decompression on the data and returns the decompressed data. The decompression algorithm uses 0x90 after a byte as a repeat indicator, followed by a count. A count of 0 specifies a byte value of 0x90. The routine returns the decompressed data, unless data input data ends in an orphaned repeat indicator, in which case the Incomplete exception is raised.

cgi Module

The following section covers the functions in Python's Common Gateway Interface module. This module defines a number of utilities for use by CGI scripts written in Python.

Syntax	Description
parse (*file* [, *keep_blanks* [, *strict_parsing*]])	Parses a query from the specified file or from sys.stdin if none is specified. For details on the *keep_blanks* and *strict_parsing* parameters, see the parse_qs function.
parse_qs (*querystr* [, *keep_blanks* [, *strict_parsing*]])	Returns a dictionary containing data from the parsed query string *querystr*. The *keep_blanks* parameter is a flag indicating whether blank values in URL encoded queries should be treated as blank strings. The *strict_parsing* parameter indicates whether or not to raise an exception when parsing errors are found.

Table continued on following page

Syntax	Description
parse_qsl (*querystr* [, *keep_blanks* [, *strict_parsing*]])	Returns a list of name,value pairs from the parsed query string *querystr*. The *keep_blanks* parameter is a flag indicating whether blank values in URL encoded queries should be treated as blank strings. The *strict_parsing* parameter indicates whether or not to raise an exception when parsing errors are found.
parse_multipart (*file*, *pdict*)	Parses multipart/form-data for file uploads. Arguments include file *file* and a dictionary containing other parameters in the Content-Type Header. Returns a dictionary just like the parse_qs() function: keys are the field names, each value is a list of values for that field.
parse_header (*string*)	Parses MIME Header *string* into a main value and a dictionary of parameters.
test()	Writes minimal HTTP headers and formats all information provided to the script in HTML form for use in testing.
print_environ()	Formats the shell environment in HTML format.
print_form()	Formats a form in HTML.
print_directory()	Formats the current directory in HTML.
print_environ_usage()	Prints a list of cgi environment variables in HTML.
escape(*s* [, *quote*])	Convert the characters &, <, and > in string *s* to HTML-safe sequences. If quote is True, double-quotes are translated as well.

cgitb Module

The following section covers the functions in Python's CGI Traceback module. Although this module was originally developed to provide extensive traceback information in HTML for troubleshooting Python CGI scripts, it has more recently been generalized to also provide information in plain text. Output includes a traceback showing excerpts of the source code for each level, as well as the values of the arguments and local variables to currently running functions to assist in debugging. To use this module, add the following to the top of the script to be debugged:

```
import cgitb; cgitb.enable()
```

Syntax	Description
enable([display[, logdir [, context[, format]]]])	This function causes the cgitb module to take over the interpreter's default handling for exceptions by setting the value of sys.excepthook. The *display* argument may be 1, which enables sending the traceback to the browser, or 0 to disable it. The *logdir* argument specifies to write tracebacks to files in the directory named by *logdir*. The *context* value is the number of lines of context to display around the current line of source code in the traceback. The *format* option may be either "html" to format the output to HTML or any other value that formats it as plain text.
handler([info])	This function handles an exception using the default settings (show a report in the browser, but don't log to a file). The optional *info* argument should be a 3-tuple containing an exception type, exception value, and traceback object.

Cookie Module

The Cookie Module provides a mechanism for state management in HTML primarily on the server side. It supports both simple string-only cookies, and provides an abstraction for having any serializable data-type as cookie value. The Cookie Module originally strictly applied the parsing rules described in RFC 2109 and RFC 2068 specifications, but modifications have made its parsing less strict. Due to security concerns, two classes have been deprecated from this module: CLASS SerialCookier([input]) and CLASS SmartCookier([input]). For backwards compatibility, the Cookie Module exports a class named Cookie, which is just an alias for SmartCookie. This is probably a mistake and will likely be removed in a future version. You should not use the Cookie class in your applications, for the same reason you should not use the SerialCookie class.

Syntax	Description
exception CookieError	Exception raised when the cookie in question is invalid according to RFC 2109.
CLASS BaseCookie ([input])	This class is a dictionary-like object with keys that are strings and values that are Morse1 instances. Upon setting a key to a value, the value is converted to a Morse1 containing the key and the value. If input is given, this class passes it to the load() method.
CLASS SimpleCookie ([input])	This class derives from BaseCookie and overrides value_decode() and value_encode() to be the identity and str(), respectively.

cookielib Module

The cookielib module defines classes in support of the automatic handling of HTTP cookies, for accessing Web sites that require cookies to be set on the client machine by an HTTP response from a Web server and then to be returned to the server in later HTTP requests.

Syntax	Description
exception LoadError	Error returned if the cookies fail to load from the specified file.
CLASS CookieJar(*policy*=None)	The CookieJar class stores HTTP cookies, extracts HTTP requests, and returns them in HTTP responses. Instances of the CookieJar class automatically expire contained cookies when necessary.
CLASS FileCookieJar(*filename*, *delayload*=None, *policy*=None)	A CookieJar that can load cookies from and save cookies to a file. Cookies are NOT loaded from the named file until either the load() or revert() method is called.
CLASS CookiePolicy()	This class is responsible for deciding whether each cookie should be accepted from or returned to the server.
CLASS DefaultCookiePolicy (*blocked_domains*=None, *allowed_domains*=None, *netscape*=True, *rfc2965*=False, *hide_cookie2*=False, *strict_domain*=False, *strict_rfc2965_unverifiable*=True, *strict_ns_unverifiable*=False, *strict_ns_domain*= DefaultCookiePolicy. DomainLiberal, *strict_ns_set_initial_dollar*=False, *strict_ns_set_path*=False)	Constructor class should be passed as keyword arguments only. *blocked_domains* is a sequence of domain names that we never accept cookies from or return cookies to. *allowed_domains* is a sequence of the only domains for which we accept and return cookies or None.
CLASS Cookie()	This class represents Netscape, RFC 2109, and RFC 2965 cookies.

email Module

The following functions are available from the email module for use in setting and querying header fields and for accessing message bodies. This module replaces the functionality of the mimetools module from before Python version 2.3.

Syntax	Description
CLASS Message()	The basic message constructor. Message objects provide a mapping style interface for accessing the message headers and an explicit interface for accessing both the headers and the payload, which can be either a string or a list of Message objects for MIME container documents (for example, multipart/* and message/rfc822).
as_string([*unixfrom*])	Return the entire message flattened as a string. When optional *unixfrom* is True, the envelope header is included in the returned string. *unixfrom* defaults to False.

Syntax	Description
__str__()	Equivalent to as_string with *unixfrom* set to True.
is_multipart()	Returns True if the message's payload is a list of sub-Message objects; otherwise (if it is a string) returns False.
set_unixfrom(*unixfrom*)	Sets the message's envelope header to *unixfrom*, which should be a string.
get_unixfrom()	Returns the message's envelope header.
attach(*payload*)	Adds *payload* to the current payload, which must be None or a list of Message objects prior to the call of attach(). After the call, the payload will always be a list of Message objects.
get_payload([*i*[,*decode*]])	Returns a reference to the current payload, which can be either a string or a list of Message objects. With optional argument *i*, get_payload() will return the *i*-th element of the payload, counting from zero, if payload is a list of Message objects. Optional *decode* is a flag indicating whether or not the payload should be decoded, according to the Content-Transfer-Encoding: header.
set_payload(*payload*[,*charset*])	Set the entire message object's payload to *payload*. If *charset* is specified, it sets the message's default character set.
set_charset(*charset*)	Sets the character set to *charset*.
get_charset(*charset*)	Retrieves the character set being used in the message's payload.
__len__()	Returns the total number of headers including duplicates.
__contains__(*name*)	Returns true if the message object has a field named *name*.
__getitem__(*name*)	Returns the value of the named header field, *name*.
__setitem__(*name*,*val*)	Appends a header to the end of the message's existing fields with field name *name* and value *val*.
__delitem__(*name*)	Removes all occurrences of the field with name *name* in the message's headers.
has_key(*name*)	Returns True if the message contains a header field named *name*; otherwise, returns False.
keys()	Returns a list of all the message's header field names.
values()	Returns a list of all the message's field values.
items()	Returns a list of 2-tuples containing all the message's field headers and values.
get_all(*name*[,*failobj*])	Returns a list of all the values for the field named *name*. If there is no such named header in the message, *failobj* is returned.

Table continued on following page

Syntax	Description

add_header (_name,_value, **_params)	The add_header() method is similar to __setitem__() except that additional header parameters can be provided as keyword arguments. _name is the header field to add and _value is the primary value for the header.
	
	```\nmsg.add_header('Content-Disposition',\n 'attachment',filename='example.gif')\n```
	adds a header which looks like:
	```\nContent-Disposition: attachment;\nfilename="example.gif"\n```

replace_header (_name,_value)	Replaces the first header found in the message that matches _name, retaining header order and field name case.
get_content_type()	Returns the message's content type in lowercase of the form maintype/subtype or the default content type if there is no Content-Type Header in the message.
get_content_maintype()	Returns the message's main content type. This is the maintype part of the string returned by get_content_type().
get_content_subtype()	Returns the message's sub-content type. This is the subtype part of the string returned by get_content_type().
get_default_type()	Returns the default content type. Most messages have a default content type of text/plain, except those that are subparts of multipart/digest containers and have a default content type of message/rfc822.
set_default_type(ctype)	Sets the default content type. ctype should either be text/plain or message/rfc822, although this is not enforced.
get_params ([failobj [, header [, unquote]]])	Returns the message's Content-Type: parameters, as a list of 2-tuples of key/value pairs, as split on the = sign. The left-hand side of the = is the key, and the right-hand side is the value.
get_param(param [, failobj [, header [, unqote]]])	Returns the value of the Content-Type: header's parameter param as a string. If the message has no Content-Type: header or if there is no such parameter, then failobj is returned (defaults to None). The header parameter specifies an alternative header to Content-Type:. If optional unquote is True, all parameters will be quoted as necessary. unquote defaults to False.
set_param(param, value [, header [, requote [, charset [, language]]]])	Replaces the value of param in the header if it exists or sets the Context-Type to text/plain. If optional requote is provided and set to True, all parameters will be quoted as necessary. requote defaults to False.
del_param(param [, header [, requote]])	Removes the given parameter completely from the Content-Type: header. header specifies an alternative to Content-Type:. All values will be quoted as necessary unless requote is False (the default is True).

Syntax	Description
set_type(*type*[,*header*[,*requote*]])	Set the main type and subtype for the Content-Type: header where *type* is a string in the form maintype/subtype. If *requote* is False, this leaves the existing header's quoting as is; otherwise, the parameters will be quoted.
get_filename([*failobj*])	Returns the value of the filename parameter of the Content-Disposition: header of the message, or *failobj* if either the header is missing or has no filename parameter.
get_boundary([*failobj*])	Returns the value of the boundary parameter of the Content-Type: header of the message, or *failobj* if the header is missing or has no boundary parameter.
set_boundary(*boundary*)	Sets the *boundary* parameter of the Content-Type: header to boundary. set_boundary().
get_content_charset([*failobj*])	Returns the charset parameter of the Content-Type: header in lowercase if it exists; otherwise returns *failobj*.
get_charsets([*failobj*])	Returns a list containing the character set names in the message, one element for each subpart of the payload or *failobj* if no content header exists.
walk()	This method is an all-purpose generator used to iterate over all parts and subparts of the message object tree.
preamble	MIME document format allows some text between the blank line following the headers and the first multipart boundary string. The preamble attribute contains this leading extra-armor text.
epilogue	Text that appears between the last boundary and the end of the message is stored in the epilogue attribute.
defects	The defects attribute contains a list of all problems occurring during message parsing.

file Object

The following section covers the functions available when the built-in function file() is called. The file object returned has the inherent functionality described in the following table. These functions are called like this:

```
filename.function()
```

Syntax	Description
close()	Closes the file.
flush()	Flushes the internal file buffer.

Table continued on following page

Syntax	Description
`fileno()`	Returns the integer "file descriptor" that is used by the underlying implementation to request I/O operations from the operating system.
`isatty()`	Returns `True` if the filename describes a TTY device; otherwise, returns `False`.
`read([size])`	Returns, in the form of a string object, *size* bytes from the file or fewer if the read hits EOF before obtaining that many bytes. If the size argument is negative or omitted, returns all data until EOF is reached.
`readline([size])`	Reads and returns a line from the file, including the trailing newline character.
`readlines([size])`	Reads and returns all lines from file as a list, including the trailing newline characters.
`seek(offset[, pos])`	Sets the file's current position, for example, stdio's `fseek()`. The *pos* argument defaults to 0, which turns on absolute file positioning. Other values are 1, seek relative to the current position and 2, seek relative to the end of the file.
`tell()`	Returns the file's current position.
`truncate([size])`	Truncates the file to length *size* bytes or 0 if *size* is not specified.
`write(string)`	Writes *string* to the file.
`writelines(sequence)`	Writes a sequence of strings to the file. The sequence can be any iterable object producing strings, typically a list of strings.

gc Module Functions and Variables (Garbage Collection)

This module provides an interface to the optional garbage collector, which is available only if the interpreter was built with the optional cyclic garbage detector (enabled by default).

Syntax	Description
`enable()`	Enables the garbage collector.
`disable()`	Disables the garbage collector.
`isenabled()`	Returns `True` if the garbage collector is enabled.
`collect()`	Runs a full garbage collection, examining all generations and returning the number of unreachable objects found.

Syntax	Description
set_debug()	Sets debugging flags for garbage collection and writing the resulting debugging information out to stderr. The flags may be any of the following: DEBUG_STATS (print statistics during collection), DEBUG_COLLECTABLE (print information on collectable objects), DEBUG_UNCOLLECTABLE (print information on uncollectible objects), DEBUG_INSTANCES (print information about instance objects found when DEBUG_COLLECTABLE or DEBUG_UNCOLLECTABLE is set), DEBUG_OBJECTS (print information about objects other than instances found when DEBUG_COLLECTABLE or DEBUG_UNCOLLECTABLE is set), DEBUG_SAVEALL (append all unreachable objects found to garbage instead of freeing), and DEBUG_LEAK (DEBUG_COLLECTABLE | DEBUG_UNCOLLECTABLE | DEBUG_INSTANCES | DEBUG_OBJECTS | DEBUG_SAVEALL)
get_debug()	Returns the debugging flags currently set.
get_objects()	Returns a list of all objects tracked by the collector.
set_threshold (*threshold0* [, *threshold1* [, *threshold2*]])	Sets the garbage collection frequency. Setting *threshold0* to zero disables collection. The GC classifies objects into three generations (*threshold0*, *threshold1*, *threshold2*) depending on how many collection sweeps they have survived.
get_threshold()	Returns the current collection thresholds as a tuple of (*threshold0*, *threshold1*, *threshold2*).
get_referrers(**objs*)	Returns the list of objects that directly refer to any of *objs* for the purpose of debugging.
get_referents(**objs*)	Returns a list of objects directly referred to by any of the arguments specified as *objs*.
garbage	Variable that contains a list of objects that the collector found to be unreachable but could not be freed (uncollectible objects).

httplib Module Functions and Variables

This module defines classes that implement the client side of the HTTP and HTTPS protocols. It is normally not used directly — the module urllib uses it to handle URLs that use HTTP and HTTPS.

Syntax	Description
CLASS HTTPConnection(*host*[,*port*])	An instance of this class represents one transaction to the HTTP server. If *port* is not provided and *host* is of the form *host::port*, the port to connect to is taken from this string. If host does not contain this port section and the port parameter is not provided, the connection is made to the default HTTP port, usually 80.
request(*method*,*url*[,*body*[,*headers*]])	This will send a request to the server using the HTTP request method *method* and the selector *url*. If the body argument is present, it should be a string of data to send after the headers are finished. The *headers* argument should be a mapping of extra HTTP headers to send with the request.
get_response()	Should be called after a request is sent to get the response from the server. Returns an HTTPResponse instance.
set_debuglevel(*level*)	Sets the default debugging level; defaults to no debugging data printing out.
connect()	Connects to the server specified when the object was created.
close()	Closes the connection to the server.
send(*data*)	Sends specified *data* to the server. This method should be called directly only after the endheaders() method and before the getreply() method.
putrequest(*request*,*selector*[,*skip_host* [,*skip_accept_encoding*]])	First call made to server after a connection has been made. It sends a line to the server consisting of the request string, the selector string, and the HTTP version. *skip_host* and *skip_accept_encoding* are Boolean variables.
putheader(*header*,*arguments*)	Sends an RFC 822-style header to the server. It sends a line to the server consisting of the header, a colon and a space, and the first argument. If more arguments are given, continuation lines are sent, each consisting of a tab and an argument.
endheaders()	Sends a blank line to the server, signaling the end of the headers.

Syntax	Description
CLASS HTTPSConnection(*host* [, *port* , key_file , cert_file])	An instance of this class represents one transaction to the secure HTTP server. If *port* is not provided and *host* is of the form *host::port*, the port to connect to is taken from this string. If host does not contain this port section and the port parameter is not provided, the connection is made to the default HTTPS port, usually 443. *key_file* is the name of a Privacy Enhanced Mail (PEM) Security Certificate formatted file that contains your private key. *cert_file* is a PEM formatted certificate chain file.
CLASS HTTPResponse(*sock* [, *debuglevel*=0] [, *strict*=0]	Class whose instance is returned upon successful connection. Not instantiated directly.
read([*byte*])	Reads the *byte* bytes of the response body.
getheader(*name* [, *default*])	Gets the content of the header *name* or default if no header name is specified.
getheaders()	Returns a list of (header, value) tuples.
msg	Instance of mimetools.message (deprecated) or email.message, which contains the response headers.
version	HTTP protocol version used by server. 10 for HTTP/1.0, 11 for HTTP/1.1.
status	Status code returned by the server.
reason	Reason code returned by the server.
exception HTTPException	Base class for the other exceptions in this module.
exception NotConnected	Subclass of HTTPException raised when no connection can be established.
exception InvalidURL	Subclass of HTTPException raised when a port is given and is either nonnumeric or empty.
exception UnknownProtocol	Subclass of HTTPException raised when the specified protocol isn't recognized.
exception UnknownTransferEncoding	Subclass of HTTPException raised when the transfer encoding mechanism is not recognized.
exception UnimplementedFileMode	Subclass of HTTPException raised when the expected file mode is not supported.
exception IncompleteRead	Subclass of HTTPException.
exception ImproperConnectionState	Subclass of HTTPException.
exception CannotSendRequest	Subclass of ImproperConnectionState.

Table continued on following page

Syntax	Description
exception `CannotSendHeader`	Subclass of `ImproperConnectionState`.
exception `ResponseNotReady`	Subclass of `ImproperConnectionState`.
exception `BadStatusLine`	Subclass of `HTTPException` raised when the server responds with an unknown HTTP status code.
HTTP_PORT	Variable holding default value for HTTP Port, 80.
HTTPS_PORT	Variable holding default value for HTTPS Port, 443.

imaplib Module

The `imaplib` module defines three classes, `IMAP4`, `IMAP4_SSL`, and `IMAP4_stream`, which encapsulate a connection to an `IMAP4` server and implement a large subset of the `IMAP4rev1` client protocol, as defined in RFC 2060.

Syntax	Description
CLASS `IMAP4([host[,port]])`	Initializes the instance thereby creating the connection and determining the protocol (`IMAP4` or `IMAP4rev1`). If *host* is not specified, localhost is used. If *port* is omitted, the standard `IMAP4` port (143) is used.
exception `IMAP4.error`	Exception raised on any error.
exception `IMAP4.abort`	Subclass of `IMAP4.error`, which is raised upon `IMAP4` server errors.
exception `IMAP4.readonly`	Subclass of `IMAP4.error`, which is raised when a writable mailbox has its status changed by the server.
CLASS `IMAP4_SSL([host [,port[,keyfile[,certfile]]]])`	This is a subclass derived from `IMAP4` that connects over an SSL-encrypted socket (to use this class, you need a socket module that was compiled with SSL support).
CLASS `IMAP4_stream` (*command*)	This is a subclass derived from `IMAP4` that connects to the `stdin/stdout` file descriptors created by passing command to `os.popen2()`.
`Internaldate2tuple` (*datestr*)	Converts an `IMAP4` `INERNALDATE` string to Coordinated Universal Time and returns that time in a time module tuple.
`Int2AP`(*num*)	Converts an integer into a string representation using characters from the set `[A...P]`.
`ParseFlags`(*flagstr*)	Converts an `IMAP4` `"FLAGS"` response to a tuple of individual flags.
`Time2Internaldate` (*date_time*)	Converts a time module tuple to an `IMAP4` `"INTERNALDATE"` representation. Returns a string in the form `"DD-Mmm-YYYY HH:MM:SS +HHMM"`.

mimetools Module

Deprecated. Use the `email` module now.

os Module

The following table covers the functions in Python's `os` module. This module provides more portable access to the underlying operating system functionality than the `posix` module. Extensions to particular operating systems exist but make the use of the `os` module much less portable. These functions perform such functions as file processing, directory traversing, and access/permissions assignment.

Syntax	Description
`remove()`	Deletes the file.
`unlink()`	Same as `remove()`.
`rename()`	Renames the file.
`stat()`	Returns file statistics for the file.
`lstat()`	Returns file statistics for a symbolic link.
`symlink()`	Creates a symbolic link.
`utime()`	Updates the timestamp for the file.
`chdir()`	Changes the working directory.
`listdir()`	Lists files in the current directory.
`getcwd()`	Returns the current working directory.
`mkdir(dir)`	Creates directory as specified by *dir*.
`makedirs()`	Same as `mkdir()` except with multiple directories being created.
`rmdir(dir)`	Removes directory as specified by *dir*.
`removedirs()`	Same as `rmdir()` except with multiple directories being removed.
`access()`	Verifies permission modes for the file.
`chmod()`	Changes permission modes for the file.
`umask()`	Sets default permission modes for the file.
`basename()`	Removes the directory path and returns the leaf name.
`dirname()`	Removes leaf name and returns directory path.
`join()`	Joins separate components into a single pathname.
`split()`	Returns a tuple containing a `dirname()` and a `basename()`.
`splitdrive()`	Returns tuple containing drivename and pathname.
`splitext()`	Returns tuple containing filename and extension.

Table continued on following page

Syntax	Description
getatime()	Returns last access time for file. This varies a bit with different operating systems.
getmtime()	Returns last file modification time for file.
getsize()	Returns file size in bytes.
exists()	Returns True if pathname, file, or directory exists.
isdir()	Returns True if pathname exists and is a directory.
isfile()	Returns True if pathname exists and is a file.
islink()	Returns True if pathname exists and is a symbolic link.
samefile()	Returns True if both pathnames refer to the same file.

os.path Module

The following table covers the functions in Python's os.path module. This module provides support for manipulation of command paths.

Syntax	Description
abspath(*path*)	Returns a normalized absolute version of the pathname *path*.
basename(*path*)	Returns the base name of pathname *path*, the second half of the pair returned by split(*path*).
commonprefix(*list*)	Returns the longest *path* prefix that is a prefix of all paths in list. If there is none, an empty string is returned.
dirname(*path*)	Return the directory name of pathname *path*, the first half of the pair returned by split(*path*).
exists(*path*)	Returns True if *path* exists and False if *path* is a broken symbolic link.
lexists(*path*)	Same as exists() for use on platforms lacking os.lstat().
expanduser(*path*)	Returns *path* with an initial component of "~" or "~user" replaced by that user's home directory.
expandvars(*path*)	Returns *path* with environment variables expanded.
getatime(*path*)	Returns the time since the last time *path* was accessed in seconds since the last epoch.
getmtime(*path*)	Returns the time since the last time *path* was modified in seconds since the last epoch.
getctime(*path*)	Returns the system's ctime, which, on some systems (such as Unix), is the time of the last change, and on others (such as Windows) is the creation time for *path* in seconds since the last epoch.

Syntax	Description
getsize(*path*)	Returns the size in bytes of *path*.
isabs(*path*)	Returns True if *path* is an absolute path (starting with /).
isfile(*path*)	Return True if *path* is an existing regular file. This function follows symbolic links, so both islink() and isfile() can be True for the same path.
isdir(*path*)	Returns True if *path* is an existing directory. This function follows symbolic links, so both islink() and isdir() can be true for the same path.
islink(*path*)	Returns True if *path* refers to a directory entry that is a symbolic link. Always False if symbolic links are not supported.
ismount(*path*)	Returns True if pathname *path* is a mount point.
join(*path*[,*path2*[,...]])	Joins *path* and *path2* and subsequent *path* components intelligently. If any component is an absolute path, all previous components are thrown away and joining continues. The return value is the concatenation of *path* and any other provided path components with exactly one directory separator inserted.
normcase(*path*)	Returns the normalized case of a pathname. On UNIX, this returns the path unchanged; on case-insensitive filesystems, it converts the path to lowercase. On Windows, it also converts forward slashes to backward slashes.
normpath(*path*)	Returns a normalized pathname. This function collapses redundant separators and up-level references, for example, a//b, a/./b, and a/foo/../b all become a/b. It does not normalize the case (use normcase() for that). On Windows, it converts forward slashes to backward slashes.
realpath(*path*)	Returns the canonical path of the specified filename, eliminating any symbolic links encountered in the *path*.
samefile(*path1*,*path2*)	Returns True if both pathname arguments refer to the same file or directory.
sameopenfile(*fileptr1*, *fileptr2*)	Returns True if *fileptr1* and *fileptr2* refer to the same file.
samestat(*stat1*,*stat2*)	Returns True if the stat tuples *stat1* and *stat2* refer to the same file. Stat tuples are returned from stat, lstat, and fstat functions.
split(*path*)	Splits the pathname path into a pair, where tail is the last pathname component and head is everything leading up to that. The tail part will never contain a slash; if path ends in a slash, tail will be empty.

Table continued on following page

Syntax	Description
splitdrive(*path*)	Splits the pathname path into a pair (drive, tail), where drive is either a drive specification or an empty string. On systems that do not use drive specifications, drive will always be an empty string.
splittext(*path*)	Strips the rightmost file extension, which can include only one period and returns the remainder. path("etc/myfile.txt").stripext() == path("etc/myfile")
walk(*path*, *visit*, *arg*)	Calls the function *visit* with arguments (*arg, dirname, names*) for each directory in the directory tree rooted at path (including path itself, if it is a directory). The argument *dirname* specifies the visited directory; the argument *names* lists the files in the directory. The *visit* function may modify names to influence the set of directories visited below *dirname*.

poplib Module

The following table covers the functions in Python's poplib module, which defines a class, POP3, that supports connecting to a POP3 server and implements the protocol as defined in RFC 1725, and a class POP3_SSL, which supports connecting to a POP3 server that uses SSL as an underlying protocol layer as defined in RFC 2595. Instances of the POP3 class include all of the methods listed. Instances of POP3_SSL have no additional methods. The interface of this subclass is identical to its parent.

Syntax	Description
CLASS POP3 (*host* [, *port*])	This class is for implementing a connection to the mail server host using the POP3 protocol. The connection is created when an instance of the class is initialized. If port is omitted, the standard POP3 port (110) is used.
CLASS POP3_SSL (*host* [, *port* [, *keyfile* [, *certfile*]]])	This class is for implementing a connection to the mail server host using the POP3 protocol over an SSL-encrypted port. The connection is created when an instance of the class is initialized. If port is omitted, the standard POP3 over SSL port (995) is used. A PEM formatted private key and certificate chain file for the SSL connection may be provided.
set_debuglevel(*level*)	Sets the instances debugging level to 0, which produces no debugging output, 1, which produces a moderate amount of debugging output, or 2, which produces the maximum amount of debugging output. Any number higher than 2 produces the same amount as specifying 2.
getwelcome()	Returns the welcome screen for the POP3 server to which the connection is made.

Syntax	Description
user(*username*)	Sends the user command for the specified *username* to the POP3 server.
pass_(*password*)	Sends the password command with the specified *password* to the POP3 server. The mailbox will be locked until quit is sent.
apop(*user*, *secret*)	Uses the more secure APOP authentication to log into the POP3 server.
rpop(*user*)	Uses RPOP commands to log into POP3 server.
stat()	Returns tuple representing mailbox status (message count, mailbox size)
list([*msg*])	Requests message list of message *msg*. If no parameters are sent, response is in the form (response, ['mesg_num octets']).
retr(*msg*)	Retrieves the whole message *msg* and marks it as seen. Response is in format (response, ['line',...], octets).
dele(*msg*)	Flags message number *msg* for deletion, which, on most servers, occurs when the quit command is issued.
rset()	Resets the deletion marks on any messages in the mailbox.
noop()	Does nothing. Is sometimes used to keep the connection alive.
quit()	Commits changes, unlocks mailbox, and drops the connection.
top(*msg*, *amount*)	Retrieves the message header plus amount lines of the message after the header of message number *msg*.
uidl([*msg*])	Returns message digest list for message identified by *msg* or for all if *msg* is not specified.

smtpd Module

These functions define functionality in support of the creation and usage of sockets in Python.

Syntax	Description
CLASS SMTPServer (*localaddr*, *remoteaddr*)	Creates a new SMTPServer object that binds to *localaddr*, treating *remoteaddr* as an upstream SMTP relayer. SMTPServer inherits form asyncore.dispatcher and is thus inserted into asyncore's event loop when instantiated.
process_message (*peer*, *mailfrom*, *rcpttos*, *data*)	Raises NotImplementedError exception but may be overridden in subclasses to do something useful with this message. The value of the class's remoteaddr parameter is available as the _remoteaddr attribute. *peer* is the remote host address, *mailfrom* is the envelope originator, *rcpttos* are the envelope recipients, and *data* is the string that contains the e-mail's contents.

smtplib Module

These functions supply Simple Mail Transport Protocol (SMTP) functionality for use in Python scripts.

Syntax	Description
CLASS SMTP ([host [, port [, local_hostname]]])	Encapsulates an SMTP connection. Has methods that support SMTP and ESMTP operations. If the optional host and port parameters are included, they are passed to the connect() method when it is called.
set_debuglevel (level)	Sets the level of debug output. If level is set to True, debug logging is enabled for the connection and all messages sent to and received from the server.
connect ([host [, port]])	Connects to host on port port. If host contains a colon followed by a number, the number will be interpreted as the port number.
docmd (cmd [, argstring])	Sends the command cmd and optional arguments argstring to the server and returns a 2-tuple containing the numeric response code and the actual response line.
helo ([hostname])	Identifies user to SMTP server using "HELO". This is usually called by sendmail and not directly.
ehlo ([hostname])	Identifies user to ESMTP server using "EHLO". This is usually called by sendmail and not directly.
has_extn (name)	Returns True if name is in the set of SMTP service extensions returned by the server; otherwise, returns False.
verify (address)	Verifies address on the server using SMTP "VRFY", which returns a tuple of code 250 and a full address if the user address is valid.
login (user, password)	Logs onto an SMTP server, which requires authentication using user and password. Automatically tries either "EHLO" or "HELO" if this login attempt was not preceded by it.
SMTPHeloError	Error returned if the server doesn't reply correctly to the "HELO" greeting.
SMTPAuthenticationError	Error most likely returned if the server doesn't accept the username/password combination.
SMTPError	Error returned if no suitable authentication method was found.
starttls ([keyfile [, certfile]])	Puts the SMTP connections into Transport Layer Security mode. Requires that ehlo() be called again afterwards. If keyfile and certfile are provided, they are passed to the socket module's ssl() function.
sendmail (from_addr, to_addr, msg [, mail_opts , rcpt_opts])	Sends mail to to_addr from from_addr consisting of msg. Automatically tries either "EHLO" or "HELO" if this sendmail attempt was not preceded by it.
SMTPRecipientsRefused	Error returned if all recipient addresses are refused.

Syntax	Description
SMTPHeloError	Error returned if the server doesn't reply correctly to the "HELO" greeting.
SMTPSenderRefused	Error returned if the server doesn't accept from_addr.
SMTPDataError	Error returned if the server replies with an unexpected error code.
quit()	Terminates the SMTP session and closes the connection.

socket Module

These functions define functionality in support of the creation and usage of sockets in Python.

Syntax	Description
socket(*socket_family*, *socket_type*, *protocol*)	Creates a socket of socket_family AF_UNIX or AF_INET, as specified. The socket_type is either SOCK_STREAM or SOCK_DGRAM. The protocol is usually left to default to 0.
bind()	Binds specified hostname, port number pair to socket.
listen()	Sets up and starts a TCP listener on the socket.
accept()	Passively accepts TCP client connections.
connect()	Actively initiates TCP server connection.
recv()	Receives TCP message.
send()	Transmits TCP message.
recvfrom()	Receives UDP message.
sendto()	Transmits UDP message.
close()	Closes socket.
fromfd()	Creates a socket object from an open file descriptor.
gethostname()	Returns the current hostname.
gethostbyname()	Maps a hostname to a numeric IP.
gethostbyaddr()	Maps a numeric IP or a hostname to DNS information.
getservbyname()	Maps a service name and a protocol name to a port number.
getprotobyname()	Maps a protocol name to a number.
ssl()	Invokes Secure Socket Layer support.

Appendix E

string Module

The following table covers the functions in Python's `string` module. The term *string* is used to represent the string variable to be acted upon by the function. For example, the function to capitalize a string variable named `myString` would be called as follows:

```
myString.capitalize()
```

Syntax	Description
string.capitalize()	Returns a copy of *string* with only its first character capitalized.
string.center(*width*)	Returns a copy of string centered in a *string* of length *width*.
string.count(*sub*[,*start* [,*end*]])	Returns number of occurrences of substring *sub* in *string*.
string.encode([*encoding* [,*errors*]])	Returns an encoded version of *string*. Default encoding is the current default string encoding.
string.endswith(*suffix* [,*start*[,*end*]])	Returns True if *string* ends with the specified suffix; otherwise, returns False. If *start* is supplied, search for string begins at that position. If *end* is supplied, search ends at that position.
string.expandtabs ([*tabsize*])	Returns *string* with tabs replaced by spaces.
string.find(*sub* [,*start*[,*end*]])	Returns the lowest index in *string* where substring sub is found. Return -1 if sub is not found.
string.index(*sub* [,*start*[,*end*]])	Behaves like *string*.find() but raises ValueError if sub is not found within *string*.
string.isalnum()	Returns True if all characters in *string* are alphanumeric, otherwise, returns False.
string.isalpha()	Returns True if all characters in *string* are alphabetic; otherwise, returns False.
string.isdigit()	Returns True if all characters in *string* are digits; otherwise, returns False.
string.islower()	Returns True if all characters in *string* are lowercase; otherwise, returns False.
string.isspace()	Returns True if all characters in *string* are space characters; otherwise, returns False.
string.istitle()	Returns True if all characters in *string* are title case; otherwise, returns False.
string.isupper()	Returns True if all characters in *string* are uppercase; otherwise, returns False.
separator.join(*seq*)	Returns a concatenation of strings in *seq*, separated by separator (for example, "+".join(['H', 'I', '!']) -> "H+I+!")

Syntax	Description
string.ljust(*width*)	Returns *string* left justified in a string of length *width*.
string.lower()	Returns string with each character converted to lowercase.
string.lstrip([*chars*])	Returns a copy of *string* with leading *chars* removed. Default chars is set to `whitespace`.
string.replace(*old*, *new* [, *maxsplit*])	Returns a copy of *string* with all occurrences of substring *old* replaced by *new*.
string.rfind(*sub* [, *start*[, *end*]])	Returns the highest index in *string* where substring *sub* is found. Returns -1 if *sub* is not found.
string.rindex(*sub* [, *start*[, *end*]])	Behaves like `rfind()`, but raises `ValueError` when the substring *sub* is not found.
string.rjust(*width*)	Returns *string* right justified in a string of length *width*.

sys Module

This module provides access to some variables used or maintained by the interpreter and to functions that interact strongly with the interpreter. It is always available.

Syntax	Description
argv	This variable represents the list of command line arguments passed to a Python script. argv[0] is the script name or has zero length if none was passed. If other arguments were passed, they are assigned argv[*i*] where *i* is 1 — the number of arguments.
byteorder	This variable is set to big or little depending on the endian-ness of the system.
builtin_module_name	This variable is a tuple of strings giving the names of all modules that are compiled into this Python interpreter.
copyright	This variable is a string containing the copyright information for the Python interpreter.
dllhandler	This variable is an integer representing the handle of the Python DLL (only in Windows).
displayhook(*value*)	This function writes the value of displayhook to stdout and saves it in __builtin__._.
excepthook(*type,value, traceback*)	When an exception is raised and uncaught, the interpreter calls sys.excepthook with three arguments, the exception class, exception instance, and a traceback object. In a Python program, this happens just before the program exits.
__displayhook__	The original value of displayhook is stored in this variable.

Table continued on following page

Syntax	Description
__excepthook__	The original value of excepthook is stored in this variable.
exc_info()	This function returns a tuple of three values that give information about the exception that is currently being handled. The information returned is specific both to the current thread and to the current stack frame. If the current stack frame is not handling an exception, the information is taken from the calling stack frame, or its caller, and so on until a stack frame is found that is handling an exception.
exc_clear()	This function clears all information relating to the current or last exception that occurred in the current thread.
exec_prefix	A variable giving the site-specific directory prefix where the platform-dependent Python files are installed; by default, this is '/usr/local'.
executable	A variable containing the path to the Python binary.
exit([*arg*])	Exits from Python.
getcheckinterval()	Returns the interpreter's "check interval"; see setcheckinterval().
getdefaultencoding()	Returns the name of the current default string encoding used by the Unicode implementation.
getdlopenflags()	Returns the current value of the flags that are used for dlopen() calls.
getfilesystemencoding()	Returns the name of the encoding used to convert Unicode filenames into system filenames. Returns None if the system default encoding is used. The return value is dependent on the filesystem.
getrefcount(*obj*)	Returns the reference count of the object *obj*.
getrecursionlimit()	Returns the current value of the recursion limit, the maximum depth of the Python interpreter stack. This limit serves to prevent the crashing of Python inherent to infinite recursion.
getwindowsversion()	Returns one of the following strings, which represent the various Windows versions: VER_PLATFORM_WIN32s — Win32s on Win3.1 VER_PLATFORM_WIN32_WINDOWS — Win95/98/ME VER_PLATFORM_WIN32_NT — WinNT/2000/XP VER_PLATFORM_WIN32_CE — WinCE
hexversion	This variable contains the version number converted to hexadecimal.
maxint	This variable represents the maximum size of an integer in the current environment. This is at least 2**31-1.

Syntax	Description
maxUnicode	This variable is an integer giving the largest supported code point for a Unicode character.
modules	This variable is a dictionary of all the loaded modules.
path	This variable is a list of strings that specifies the search path for modules as initialized from the environment variable PYTHON-PATH plus an installation-dependent default.
platform	This variable contains a string containing a platform identifier.
prefix	This variable is a string containing the directory prefix for location of the Python files.
ps1	This variable contains a string representing the primary prompt for the Python interpreter.
setcheckinterval(*interval*)	Sets the *interval* for how often the interpreter checks for periodic things, such as thread switches and signal handlers.
setdefaultencoding(*name*)	Sets the current default string encoding used by the Unicode implementation to *name*.
setdlopenflags(*name*)	Sets the flags used by the interpreter for dlopen() calls, such as when the interpreter loads extension modules.
setprofile(*profilefunc*)	Sets the system's profile function, which allows you to implement a Python source code profiler in Python.
setrecursionlimit(*limit*)	Sets the maximum depth of the Python interpreter's stack to *limit*.
settrace(*function*)	Sets the system's trace function, allowing the implementation of a Python source code debugger in Python.
stdin, stdout, stderr	File objects corresponding to the interpreter's standard input, output, and error streams.
__stdin__, __stdout__, __stderr__	Variables that store the original values of the interpreter's standard input, output, and error streams.
tracebacklimit()	A variable that determines the maximum number of levels of traceback information printed when an unhandled exception occurs. The default is 1000. When set to 0 or less, all traceback information is suppressed and only the exception type and value are printed.
version	A string variable containing the version number of the Python interpreter as well as the build number and compiler used.
api_version	A variable containing the C API version for this interpreter.
version_info	A tuple containing the five components of the Python interpreter version number: major, minor, micro, releaselevel, and serial.

Table continued on following page

Syntax	Description
warnoptions	An implementation detail of the warnings framework; this value is not to be modified.
winver	A variable containing the version number used to form registry keys on Windows platforms, stored as string resource 1000 in the Python DLL. winver is normally the first three characters of version. It is provided in the sys module for informational purposes only and has no effect on Windows registry keys.

random Module

This module provides functionality in support of obtaining pseudo-random numbers. Different operating systems handle this differently — some using randomness sources as hash sources and others instead using system time.

Syntax	Description
seed(x)	Initializes the basic random number generator using hash object x if it is provided.
getstate()	Returns the current internal state of the random number generator.
setstate(state)	Resets the internal state of the random number generator to the supplied state.
jumpahead(n)	Changes the internal state to one different from the current state. n is a nonnegative integer that is used to scramble the current state vector. This is commonly used in multithreaded programs, in conjunction with multiple instances of the Random class: setstate() or seed() can be used to force all instances into the same internal state, and then jumpahead() can be used to force the instances' states far apart.
getrandbits(x)	Returns a python long int with x random bits.
randrange([start,]stop[,step])	Returns a randomly selected element from range(start, stop, step).
randint(a,b)	Returns a random integer int such that $a <= int <= b$.
choice(seq)	Returns a random element from seq.
shuffle(x[,random])	Shuffles the sequence x, using the random function random if specified.
sample(sequence,length)	Returns a list of num unique elements from sequence.
random()	Returns a random floating-point number between 0.0 and 1.0.
uniform(a,b)	Returns a random real number N where $a <= N > b$.

urllib Module

This module provides high-level functionality for fetching data across the World Wide Web. The functionality is similar to the built-in function open() except that it accepts Universal Resource Locators (URLs) instead of filenames.

Syntax	Description
CLASS URLopener([proxies [, **509]])	Base class for opening and reading URLs. In most cases, you will want to use the CLASS FancyURLopener instead. An empty *proxies* variable turns off proxies completely.

CLASS FancyURLopener ([proxies[, **509]])	Class for opening and reading URLs providing default handling for the following HTTP response codes: 301, 302, 303, 307, and 401. An empty *proxies* variable turns off proxies completely.
	
	 ```>>>import urllib```
	 ```>>>proxies =```
	 ```{'http':'http://proxy.server.com:8080/'}```
	 ```>>>opener = urllib.FancyURLopener(proxies)```

urlopen(*url*[, *data*[, *proxies*]])	Opens a connection to the specified *url* and returns a file-like object. If no protocol or download scheme is specified or if the scheme is file, *url* is assumed to be a local file. The object returned by the urlopen function may then be acted upon by file object methods.
urlretrieve(*url*[, *filename* [, *reporthook*[, *data*]]])	Copies a network object denoted by the provided *url* to a local file, returning a tuple containing the filename of the local file and headers information as returned from the info() method of the object.
urlcleanup()	Clears the cache that may have been populated by previous calls to urlretrieve().
pathname2url(*path*)	Converts the pathname *path* from the syntax for a local path to a URL. Returned URL requires further processing before being a complete URL.
url2pathname(*path*)	Converts the path component URL to a pathname. Returned path requires further decoding to be a true path.

urllib2 Module

This module defines functions and classes needed to facilitate opening URLs—basic and digest authentication, redirections, cookies, and such. If a class is listed, functions belonging to that class are grouped with it.

Syntax	Description
urlopen(*url*[,*data*])	Opens the specified *url*, which can be a string or a REQUEST object. The data parameter is for use in passing extra information as needed for http and should be a buffer in the format of application/x-www-form-urlencoded. The urlopen function returns a file-like object with a geturl() method to retrieve the URL of the resource received and an info() method to return the meta-information of the page.
install_opener(*opener*)	Installs an OpenerDirector instance as the default global opener.
build_opener(*handlers*)	Returns an OpenerDirector instance, which chains the handlers in the order given. These handlers can be instances of BaseHandler or subclasses of it. The following exceptions may be raised: URLError (on handler errors), HTTPError (a subclass of URLError that handles exotic HTTP errors), and GopherError (another subclass of URLError that handles errors from the Gopher handler).
CLASS Request(*url*[,*data*[,*headers* [,*origin_req_host*[,*unverifiable*]]]])	This class is an abstraction of a URL Request. *url* should be a valid URL in string format. For a description of *data*, see the add_data() description. *headers* should be in dictionary format. *origin_req_host* should be the request-host of the origin transaction. *unverifiable* should indicate whether or not the request is verifiable, as specified in RFC 2965.
add_data(*data*)	Sets the Request data to *data*.
get_method()	Posts a string indicating the HTTP request method, which may be either GET or POST.
has_data()	Returns True when the instance has data and False when instance is None.
get_data()	Returns the instance's data.
add_header(*key*, *val*)	Adds another header to the request. Later calls will overwrite earlier ones with the same key value.
add_undirected_header (*key*,*header*)	Adds a header that will not be added in the case of a redirected request.
has_header(*header*)	Returns whether the instance (either regular or redirected) has a header.
get_full_url()	Returns the URL given in the constructor.
get_type()	Returns the type (or scheme) of the URL.
get_host()	Returns the host to which the connection will be made.
get_selector()	Returns the selector, the part of the URL that is sent to the server.

Syntax	Description
set_proxy(*host*, *type*)	Prepares the request by connecting to a proxy server. *host* and *type* will replace the ones for the instance.
get_origin_req_host()	Returns the request-host of the origin transaction.
is_unverifiable()	Returns whether the request is unverifiable as defined in RFC 2965.
CLASS OpenerDirector()	The OpenerDirector class opens URLs via BaseHandlers chained together and is responsible for managing their resources and error recovery.
add_handler(*handler*)	Searches and adds to the possible chains any of the following handlers: protocol_open() —Signals that the handler knows how to handle open protocol URLs http_error_type() —Signals that the handler knows how to handle HTTP errors protocol_error() —Signals that the handler knows how to handle non-HTTP errors. protocol_request() —Signals that the handler knows how to preprocess protocol requests. protocol_response() —Signals that the handler knows how to post-process protocol requests.
open(*url*[, *data*])	Opens the given URL and passes *data* if provided.
error(*proto*[, *args*])	Handles an error of the given protocol by calling the given protocol with the specified *args*.
CLASS BaseHandler()	This is the base class for all registered handlers and handles the basics of registration.
add_parent(*director*)	Adds a director as a parent.

Table continued on following page

Syntax	Description
close()	Removes any parents.
parent	A valid `OpenerDirector` to be used to open a URL using a different protocol.
default_open(*req*)	This method is not defined in `BaseHandler`, but should be defined to catch all URLs.
protocol_open(*req*)	This method is not defined in `BaseHandler`, but should be defined to handle URLs of the given protocol.
unknown_open(*req*)	This method is not defined in `BaseHandler`, but should be defined to handle catching URLs with no specific registered handler to open them.
http_error_default(*req,fp,code,msg,hdrs*)	This method is not defined in `BaseHandler` but should be overridden by the subclass to provide a catchall for otherwise unhandled HTTP errors. *req* is a `Request` object, *fp* is a file-like object with the HTTP error body, *code* is the three-digit error code, *msg* is a user-visible explanation of the error code, and *hdrs* is the mapping object with the header of the error.
http_error_nnn(*req,fp,code,msg,hdrs*)	This method is not defined in `BaseHandler` but is called on an instance of subclass when an HTTP error with code nnn is encountered.
protocol_request(*req*)	This method is not defined in `BaseHandler` but should be called by the subclass to pre-process requests of the specified protocol.
protocol_response(*req,response*)	This method is not defined in `BaseHandler` but should be called by the subclass to post-process requests of the specified protocol.
CLASS HTTPDefaultErrorHandler()	A class that defines a default handler for HTTP error responses; all responses are turned into `HTTPError` exceptions.
CLASS HTTPRedirectHandler()	A class to handle redirection.
redirect_request(*req,fp,code,msg,hdrs*)	Returns a request or none in response to a redirect request.

Syntax	Description
http_error_301(*req*, *fp*, *code*, *msg*, *hdrs*)	Redirects to the URL.
http_error_302(*req*, *fp*, *code*, *msg*, *hdrs*)	Redirects for a "found" response.
http_error_303(*req*, *fp*, *code*, *msg*, *hdrs*)	Redirects for "see other" response.
http_error_307(*req*, *fp*, *code*, *msg*, *hdrs*)	Redirects for "temporary redirect" response.
CLASS HTTPCookieProcessor(*cookies*)	A class to handle HTTP cookies.
cookiejar	The cookielib.CookieJar in which cookies are stored.
CLASS ProxyHandler(*proxies*)	A class to handle routing requests through a proxy. If *proxies* is specified, it must be in the form of a dictionary that maps protocol names to URLs of proxies.
protocol_open(*req*)	ProxyHandler will assign a method protocol_open() for every protocol that has a proxy in the proxies dictionary given in the constructor.
CLASS HTTPPasswordMgr()	A class that supports a database of (realm, url) -> (user, password) mappings.
add_password(*realm*, *uri*, *user*, *password*)	Sets user authentication token for given *user*, *realm*, and *uri*.
find_user_password(*realm*, *authuri*)	Gets username and password for the given realm.
CLASS HTTPPasswordMgrWithDefaultRealm()	A class that performs the same function as HTTPPasswordMgr() except that a realm of None is considered a catchall and is searched if no other real fits.
CLASS AbstractBasicAuthHandler([*password_mgr*])	A class that supports HTTP authentication to the remote host and to the proxy server. The *password_mgr* variable must be compatible with HTTPPasswordMgr.
handle_authentication_request(*authreq*, *host*, *req*, *headers*)	Reattempts authentication using the given user information. *authreq* is a header in which information about the realm exists. *host* is the host to which to authenticate, *req* is the failed request object, and *headers* are the error headers.

Table continued on following page

Syntax	Description
CLASS HTTPBasicAuthHandler([password_mgr])	A class that supports HTTP authentication with the remote host. The *password_mgr* variable must be compatible with HTTP-PasswordMgr.
http_error_401(*req,fp,code,msg,headers*)	Retries the HTTP request with user-provided authentication information, if included.
CLASS ProxyBasicAuthHandler([password_mgr]	A class that supports plaintext password HTTP authentication with the proxy. The *password_mgr* variable must be compatible with HTTPPasswordMgr.
http_error_407(*req,fp,code,msg,headers*)	Retries the proxy request with user-provided authentication information, if included.
CLASS AbstractDigestAuthHandler ([*password_mgr*])	A class that helps with hashed password HTTP authentication to the remote host and to a proxy. The *password_mgr* variable must be compatible with HTTPPasswordMgr.
handle_authentication_request (authreq host req headers)	Performs the same function as in AbstractBasicAuthHandler class except with hashed passwords.
CLASS HTTPDigestAuthHandler([*password_mgr*])	A class that handles authentication with the remote host. The *password_mgr* variable must be compatible with HTTPPasswordMgr.
http_error_401(*req,fp,code,msg,headers*)	Performs the same function as in AbstractBasicAuthHandler class.
CLASS ProxyDigestAuthHandler([*password_mgr*])	A class that handles authentication with the proxy. *password_mgr* variable must be compatible with HTTPPasswordMgr.
http_error_407(*req,fp,code,msg,headers*)	Performs the same function as in ProxyBasicAuthHandler class.
CLASS HTTPHandler()	A class that handles HTTP URLs.
http_open(*req*)	Sends an HTTP request, either GET or POST, depending on the value of req.has_data().
CLASS HTTPSHandler()	A class that handles secure HTTP URLs.
https_open(*req*)	Sends an HTTPS request, either GET or POST, depending on the value of req.has_data().

Syntax	Description
CLASS `FileHandler()`	A class that handles opening local files.
`file_open(`*req*`)`	Opens the local file if localhost or no host is specified, and otherwise initiates an ftp connection and reattempts opening the file.
CLASS `FTPHandler()`	A class that handles FTP URLs.
`ftp_open(`*req*`)`	Opens the file indicated by *req* using an empty username and password.
CLASS `CacheFTPHandler()`	A class that handles FTP URLs and caches FTP connections to minimize delay.
`setTimeout(`*t*`)`	Sets timeout of connections to *t* seconds.
`setMaxConns(`*n*`)`	Sets the maximum number of cached connections to *n*.
CLASS `GopherFTPHandler()`	A class that handles gopher URLs.
`gopher_open(`*req*`)`	Opens the gopher resource denoted by *req*.
CLASS `UnknownHandler()`	A catchall class to handle unknown URLs.
`unknown_open()`	Raises a `URLError` exception on URLs with no specific register handler.

PHP Language Reference

This appendix cannot provide an exhaustive list of all of the PHP functions (or it would be hundreds of pages long), but it presents a subset of functions that the authors think you will encounter in your everyday use of PHP along with brief descriptions of what those functions do. The core language functions are included, as well as the functions for PHP extensions that are in popular use.

This appendix is meant as a quick reference for you to check the input and return types of parameters — more of a reminder of how the function works than a verbose description of how to use the function in your scripts. If you need to see how a particular function should be used, or to read up on a function that isn't covered here, check out the PHP documentation online at www.php.net/docs.php.

This appendix originally appeared in Beginning PHP 5 written by Dave W. Mercer, Allan Kent, Steven D. Nowicki, David Mercer, Dan Squier, and Wankyu Choi and published by Wrox, ISBN: 0-7645-5783-1, copyright 2004, Wiley Publishing, Inc. The author is grateful to those authors and the publisher for allowing it to be reused here.

Apache

Function	Returns	Description
apache_child_terminate(void)	bool	Terminates apache process after this request.
apache_note(string note _name [, string note_value])	string	Gets and sets Apache request notes.
virtual(string filename)	bool	Performs an Apache subrequest.
getallheaders(void)	array	Alias for apache_request_headers().
apache_request_headers(void)	array	Fetches all HTTP request headers.
apache_response_headers(void)	array	Fetches all HTTP response headers.

Table continued on following page

Function	Returns	Description
`apache_setenv(string variable, string value [, bool walk_to_top])`	bool	Sets an Apache `subprocess_env` variable.
`apache_lookup_uri(string URI)`	object	Performs a partial request of the given URI to obtain information about it.
`apache_get_version(void)`	string	Fetches Apache version.
`apache_get_modules(void)`	array	Gets a list of loaded Apache modules.

Arrays

Function	Returns	Description
`krsort(array array_arg [, int sort_flags])`	bool	Sorts an array by key value in reverse order.
`ksort(array array_arg [, int sort_flags])`	bool	Sorts an array by key.
`count(mixed var [, int mode])`	int	Counts the number of elements in a variable (usually an array).
`natsort(array array_arg)`	void	Sorts an array using natural sort.
`natcasesort(array array_arg)`	void	Sorts an array using case-insensitive natural sort.
`asort(array array_arg [, int sort_flags])`	bool	Sorts an array and maintains index association.
`arsort(array array_arg [, int sort_flags])`	bool	Sorts an array in reverse order and maintains index association.
`sort(array array_arg [, int sort_flags])`	bool	Sorts an array.
`rsort(array array_arg [, int sort_flags])`	bool	Sorts an array in reverse order.
`usort(array array_arg, string cmp_function)`	bool	Sorts an array by values using a user-defined comparison function.
`uasort(array array_arg, string cmp_function)`	bool	Sorts an array with a user-defined comparison function and maintains index association.
`uksort(array array_arg, string cmp_function)`	bool	Sorts an array by keys using a user-defined comparison function.

Function	Returns	Description
end(array array_arg)	mixed	Advances array argument's internal pointer to the last element and returns it.
prev(array array_arg)	mixed	Moves array argument's internal pointer to the previous element and returns it.
next(array array_arg)	mixed	Moves array argument's internal pointer to the next element and returns it.
reset(array array_arg)	mixed	Sets array argument's internal pointer to the first element and returns it.
current(array array_arg)	mixed	Returns the element currently pointed to by the internal array pointer.
key(array array_arg)	mixed	Returns the key of the element currently pointed to by the internal array pointer.
min(mixed arg1 [, mixed arg2 [, mixed ...]])	mixed	Returns the lowest value in an array or a series of arguments.
max(mixed arg1 [, mixed arg2 [, mixed ...]])	mixed	Returns the highest value in an array or a series of arguments.
array_walk(array input, string funcname [, mixed userdata])	bool	Applies a user function to every member of an array.
array_walk_recursive(array input, string funcname [, mixed userdata])	bool	Applies a user function recursively to every member of an array.
in_array(mixed needle, array haystack [, bool strict])	bool	Checks if the given value exists in the array.
array_search(mixed needle, array haystack [, bool strict])	mixed	Searches the array for a given value and returns the corresponding key if successful.
extract(array var_array [, int extract_type [, string prefix]])	int	Imports variables into symbol table from an array.
compact(mixed var_names [, mixed ...])	array	Creates a hash containing variables and their values.
array_fill(int start_key, int num, mixed val)	array	Creates an array containing num elements starting with index start_key each initialized to val.
range(mixed low, mixed high [, int step])	array	Creates an array containing the range of integers or characters from low to high (inclusive).
shuffle(array array_arg)	bool	Randomly shuffles the contents of an array.

Table continued on following page

Function	Returns	Description
`array_push(array stack, mixed var [, mixed ...])`	int	Pushes elements onto the end of the array.
`array_pop(array stack)`	mixed	Pops an element off the end of the array.
`array_shift(array stack)`	mixed	Pops an element off the beginning of the array.
`array_unshift(array stack, mixed var [, mixed ...])`	int	Pushes elements onto the beginning of the array.
`array_splice(array input, int offset [, int length [, array replacement]])`	array	Removes the elements designated by off set and length and replaces them with a supplied array.
`array_slice(array input, int offset [, int length])`	array	Returns elements specified by offset and length.
`array_merge(array arr1, array arr2 [, array ...])`	array	Merges elements from passed arrays into one array.
`array_merge_recursive(array arr1, array arr2 [, array ...])`	array	Recursively merges elements from passed arrays into one array.
`array_keys(array input [, mixed search_value])`	array	Returns just the keys from the input array, optionally only for the specified `search_value`.
`array_values(array input)`	array	Returns just the values from the input array.
`array_count_values(array input)`	array	Returns the value as key and the frequency of that value in input as value.
`array_reverse(array input [, bool preserve keys])`	array	Returns input as a new array with the order of the entries reversed.
`array_pad(array input, int pad_size, mixed pad_value)`	array	Returns a copy of input array padded with `pad_value` to size `pad_size`.
`array_flip(array input)`	array	Returns array with key <-> value flipped.
`array_change_key_case(array input [, int case=CASE_LOWER])`	array	Returns an array with all string keys lower-cased (or uppercased).
`array_unique(array input)`	array	Removes duplicate values from array.
`array_intersect(array arr1, array arr2 [, array ...])`	array	Returns the entries of arr1 that have values that are present in all the other arguments.
`array_uintersect(array arr1, array arr2 [, array ...], callback data_compare_func)`	array	Returns the entries of arr1 that have values that are present in all the other arguments. Data is compared by using a user-supplied callback.

Function	Returns	Description
`array_intersect_assoc(array arr1, array arr2 [, array ...])`	array	Returns the entries of `arr1` that have values that are present in all the other arguments. Keys are used to do more restrictive check.
`array_uintersect_assoc(array arr1, array arr2 [, array ...], callback data_compare_func)`	array	Returns the entries of `arr1` that have values that are present in all the other arguments. Keys are used to do more restrictive check. Data is compared by using a user-supplied callback.
`array_intersect_uassoc(array arr1, array arr2 [, array ...], callback key_compare_func)`	array	Returns the entries of arr1 that have values that are present in all the other arguments. Keys are used to do more restrictive check and they are compared by using a user-supplied callback.
`array_uintersect_uassoc (array arr1, array arr2 [, array ...], callback data_ compare_func, callback key_ compare_func)`	array	Returns the entries of `arr1` that have values that are present in all the other arguments. Keys are used to do more restrictive check. Both data and keys are compared by using user-supplied callbacks.
`array_diff(array arr1, array arr2 [, array ...])`	array	Returns the entries of `arr1` that have values that are not present in any of the others arguments.
`array_udiff(array arr1, array arr2 [, array ...], callback data_comp_func)`	array	Returns the entries of `arr1` that have values that are not present in any of the other arguments. Elements are compared by a user-supplied function.
`array_diff_assoc(array arr1, array arr2 [, array ...])`	array	Returns the entries of `arr1` that have key value pairs that are not present in any of the other arguments.
`array_diff_uassoc(array arr1, array arr2 [, array ...], callback data_comp_func)`	array	Returns the entries of `arr1` that have key value pairs that are not present in any of the other arguments. Elements are compared by a user-supplied function.
`array_udiff_assoc(array arr1, array arr2 [, array ...], callback key_comp_func)`	array	Returns the entries of `arr1` that have key value pairs that are not present in any of the other arguments. Keys are compared by a user-supplied function.
`array_udiff_uassoc(array arr1, array arr2 [, array ...], callback data_comp_func, callback key_comp_func)`	array	Returns the entries of `arr1` that have key value pairs that are not present in any of the others arguments. Keys and elements are compared by user-supplied functions.

Table continued on following page

Function	Returns	Description
array_multisort(array ar1 [, SORT_ASC|SORT_DESC [, SORT_REGULAR|SORT_NUMERIC|SORT_STRING]] [, array ar2 [, SORT_ASC|SORT_DESC [, SORT_REGULAR|SORT_NUMERIC|SORT_STRING]] , ...])	bool	Sorts multiple arrays at once (similar to how ORDER BY clause works in SQL).
array_rand(array input [, int num_req])	mixed	Returns key/keys for random entry/entries in the array.
array_sum(array input)	mixed	Returns the sum of the array entries.
array_reduce(array input, mixed callback [, int initial])	mixed	Iteratively reduces the array to a single value via the callback.
array_filter(array input [, mixed callback])	array	Filters elements from the array via the callback.
array_map(mixed callback, array input1 [, array input2 , ...])	array	Applies the callback to the elements in given arrays.
array_key_exists(mixed key, array search)	bool	Checks if the given key or index exists in the array.
array_chunk(array input, int size [, bool preserve_keys])	array	Splits array into chunks.
array_combine(array keys, array values)	array	Creates an array by using the elements of the first parameter as keys and the elements of the second as corresponding keys.
each(array arr)	array	Returns the currently pointed key value pair in the passed array, and advances the pointer to the next element.
error_reporting(int new_error_level=null)	int	Returns the current error_reporting level and, if an argument was passed, changes to the new level.

BCMath

Function	Returns	Description
bcadd(string left_operand, string right_operand [, int scale])	string	Returns the sum of two arbitrary precision numbers.

Function	Returns	Description
bcsub(string left_operand, string right_operand [, int scale])	string	Returns the difference between two arbitrary precision numbers.
bcmul(string left_operand, string right_operand [, int scale])	string	Returns the multiplication of two arbitrary precision numbers.
bcdiv(string left_operand, string right_operand [, int scale])	string	Returns the quotient of two arbitrary precision numbers (division).
bcmod(string left_operand, string right_operand)	string	Returns the modulus of the two arbitrary precision operands (remainder).
bcpowmod(string x, string y, string mod [, int scale])	string	Returns the value of an arbitrary precision number raised to the power of another reduced by a modulus.
bcpow(string x, string y [, int scale])	string	Returns the value of an arbitrary precision number raised to the power of another.
bcsqrt(string operand [, int scale])	string	Returns the square root of an arbitrary precision number.
bccomp(string left_operand, string right_operand [, int scale])	int	Compares two arbitrary precision numbers.
bcscale(int scale)	bool	Sets default scale parameter for all bc math functions.

BZip2

Function	Returns	Description
bzopen(string|int file| fp, string mode)	resource	Opens a new BZip2 stream.
bzread(int bz [, int length])	string	Reads up to length bytes from a BZip2 stream, or 1024 bytes if length is not specified.
bzwrite(int bz, string data [, int length])	int	Writes the contents of the string data to the BZip2 stream.
bzerrno(resource bz)	int	Returns the error number.
bzerrstr(resource bz)	string	Returns the error string.

Table continued on following page

Function	Returns	Description
bzerror(resource bz)	array	Returns the error number and error string in an associative array.
bzcompress(string source [, int blocksize100k [, int workfactor]])	string	Compresses a string into BZip2 encoded data.
bzdecompress(string source [, int small])	string	Decompresses BZip2 compressed data.
bzclose((resource bz)	int	Closes a BZip2 file pointer.
bzflush(resource bz)	int	Forces a write of all buffered BZip2 data.

Calendar

Function	Returns	Description
unixtojd([int timestamp])	int	Converts UNIX timestamp to Julian Day.
jdtounix(int jday)	int	Converts Julian Day to UNIX timestamp.
cal_info(int calendar)	array	Returns information about a particular calendar.
cal_days_in_month (int calendar, int month, int year)	int	Returns the number of days in a month for a given year and calendar.
cal_to_jd(int calendar, int month, int day, int year)	int	Converts from a supported calendar to Julian Day Count.
cal_from_jd(int jd, int calendar)	array	Converts from Julian Day Count to a supported calendar and returns extended information.
jdtogregorian (int juliandaycount)	string	Converts a Julian Day Count to a Gregorian calendar date.
gregoriantojd(int month, int day, int year)	int	Converts a Gregorian calendar date to Julian Day Count.
jdtojulian (int juliandaycount)	string	Converts a Julian Day Count to a Julian calendar date.
juliantojd (int month, int day, int year)	int	Converts a Julian calendar date to Julian Day Count.

Function	Returns	Description
jdtojewish(int juliandaycount [, bool hebrew [, int fl]])	string	Converts a Julian Day Count to a Jewish calendar date.
jewishtojd(int month, int day, int year)	int	Converts a Jewish calendar date to a Julian Day Count.
jdtofrench(int juliandaycount)	string	Converts a Julian Day Count to a French Republic calendar date.
frenchtojd(int month, int day, int year)	int	Converts a French Republic calendar date to Julian Day Count.
jddayofweek(int juliandaycount [, int mode])	mixed	Returns name or number of day of week from Julian Day Count.
jdmonthname(int juliandaycount, int mode)	string	Returns name of month for Julian Day Count.
easter_date([int year])	int	Returns the timestamp of midnight on Easter of a given year (defaults to current year).
easter_days([int year, [int method]])	int	Returns the number of days after March 21 that Easter falls on for a given year (defaults to current year).

Class/Object

Function	Returns	Description
class_exists (string classname)	bool	Checks if the class exists.
get_class(object object)	string	Retrieves the class name.
get_parent_class (mixed object)	string	Retrieves the parent class name for object or class.
is_subclass_of (object object, string class_name)	bool	Returns true if the object has this class as one of its parents.
is_a(object object, string class_name)	bool	Returns true if the object is of this class or has this class as one of its parents.
get_class_vars (string class_name)	array	Returns an array of default properties of the class.
get_object_vars(object obj)	array	Returns an array of object properties.

Table continued on following page

Function	Returns	Description
get_class_methods (mixed class)	array	Returns an array of method names for class or class instance.
method_exists (object object, string method)	bool	Checks if the class method exists.
Get_class_vars (string class_name)	array	Returns an array of default properties of the class.
get_declared_classes (string class_name)	array	Returns an array with the names of the declared classes in the current script.

Character Type

Function	Returns	Description
ctype_alnum(string text)	bool	Checks for alphanumeric character(s).
ctype_alpha(string text)	bool	Checks for alphabetic character(s).
ctype_cntrl(string text)	bool	Checks for control character(s).
ctype_digit(string text)	bool	Checks for numeric character(s).
ctype_graph(string text)	bool	Checks for any printable character(s) except space.
ctype_lower(string text)	bool	Checks for lowercase character(s).
ctype_print(string text)	bool	Checks for printable character(s).
ctype_punct(string text)	bool	Checks for any printable character that is not whitespace or an alphanumeric character.
ctype_space(string text)	bool	Checks for whitespace character(s).
ctype_upper(string text)	bool	Checks for uppercase character(s).
ctype_xdigit(string text)	bool	Checks for character(s) representing a hexadecimal digit.

Curl

Function	Returns	Description
curl_version([int version])	array	Returns CURL version information.
curl_init([string url])	resource	Initializes a CURL session.

Function	Returns	Description
curl_setopt(resource ch, string option, mixed value)	bool	Sets an option for a CURL transfer.
curl_exec(resource ch)	bool	Performs a CURL session.
curl_getinfo (resource ch, int opt)	mixed	Gets information regarding a specific transfer.
curl_error(resource ch)	string	Returns a string containing the last error for the current session.
curl_errno(resource ch)	int	Returns an integer containing the last error number.
curl_close(resource ch)	void	Closes a CURL session.
curl_multi_init(void)	resource	Returns a new CURL multi handle.
curl_multi_add_handle (resource multi, resource ch)	int	Adds a normal CURL handle to a CURL multi handle.
curl_multi_remove_handle (resource mh, resource ch)	int	Removes a multi handle from a set of CURL handles.
curl_multi_select (resource mh[, double timeout])	int	Gets all the sockets associated with the CURL extension, which can then be selected.
curl_multi_exec(resource mh)	int	Runs the subconnections of the current CURL handle.
curl_multi_getcontent (resource ch)	string	Returns the content of a CURL handle if CURLOPT_RETURNTRANSFER is set.
curl_multi_info_read (resource mh)	array	Gets information about the current transfers.
curl_multi_close(resource mh)	void	Closes a set of CURL handles.

Date and Time

Function	Returns	Description
time(void)	int	Returns current UNIX timestamp.
mktime(int hour, int min, int sec, int mon, int day, int year)	int	Gets UNIX timestamp for a date.

Table continued on following page

Function	Returns	Description
`gmmktime(int hour, int min, int sec, int mon, int day, int year)`	int	Gets UNIX timestamp for a GMT date.
`date(string format [, int timestamp])`	string	Formats a local time/date.
`gmdate(string format [, int timestamp])`	string	Formats a GMT/UTC date/time.
`idate(string format [, int timestamp])`	int	Formats a local time/date as integer.
`localtime([int timestamp [, bool associative_array]])`	array	Returns the results of the C system call local time as an associative array if the `associative_array` argument is set to 1 (otherwise it's a regular array).
`getdate([int timestamp])`	array	Gets date/time information.
`checkdate(int month, int day, int year)`	bool	Returns `true(1)` if it is a valid date in Gregorian calendar.
`strftime(string format [, int timestamp])`	string	Formats a local time/date according to locale settings.
`gmstrftime(string format [, int timestamp])`	string	Formats a GMT/UTC time/date according to locale settings.
`strtotime (string time, int now)`	int	Converts string representation of date and time to a timestamp.
`microtime(void)`	string	Returns a string containing the current time in seconds and microseconds.
`gettimeofday(void)`	array	Returns the current time as array.
`getrusage([int who])`	array	Returns an array of usage statistics.
`date_sunrise(mixed time [, int format [, float latitude [, float longitude [, float zenith [, float gmt_offset]]]]])`	mixed	Returns time of sunrise for a given day and location.
`date_sunset(mixed time [, int format [, float latitude [, float longitude [, float zenith [, float gmt_offset]]]]])`	mixed	Returns time of sunset for a given day and location.

Directory

Function	Returns	Description
opendir(string path)	mixed	Opens a directory and returns a dir_handle.
dir(string directory)	object	Directory class with properties handle and path, and methods read, rewind, and close.
closedir([resource dir_handle])	void	Closes directory connection identified by the dir_handle.
chroot(string directory)	bool	Changes root directory.
chdir(string directory)	bool	Changes the current directory.
getcwd(void)	mixed	Gets the current directory.
rewinddir([resource dir_handle])	void	Rewinds dir_handle back to the start.
readdir([resource dir_handle])	string	Reads directory entry from dir_handle.
glob(string pattern [, int flags])	array	Finds pathnames matching a pattern.
scandir(string dir [, int sorting_order])	array	Lists files and directories inside the specified path.
dl(string extension_filename)	int	Loads a PHP extension at runtime.

Error Handling

Function	Returns	Description
error_log(string message [, int message_type [, string destination [, string extra_headers]]])	bool	Sends an error message somewhere.
debug_print_backtrace(void) */	void	Prints a backtrace.
debug_backtrace(void)	array	Returns backtrace as array.
restore_error_handler(void)	void	Restores the previously defined error handler function.

Table continued on following page

Function	Returns	Description
set_exception_handler (string exception_handler)	string	Sets a user-defined exception handler function. Returns the previously defined exception handler, or `false` on error.
restore_exception_ handler(void)	void	Restores the previously defined exception handler function.
trigger_error(string messsage [, int error_type])	void	Generates a user-level error/warning/ notice message.
set_error_handler (string error_handler)	string	Sets a user-defined error handler function. Returns the previously defined error handler, or `false` on error.
leak(int num_bytes=3)	void	Causes an intentional memory leak, for testing/debugging purposes.

Filesystem

Function	Returns	Description
flock(resource fp, int operation [, int &wouldblock])	bool	Portable file locking.
file_get_contents (string filename [, bool use_include_path [, resource context]])	string	Reads the entire file into a string.
file_put_contents (string file, mixed data [, int flags [, resource context]])	int	Writes/creates a file with contents data and returns the number of bytes written.
file(string filename [, int flags [, resource context]])	array	Reads entire file into an array
tempnam(string dir, string prefix)	string	Creates a unique filename in a directory.
tmpfile(void)	resource	Creates a temporary file that will be deleted automatically after use.
fopen(string filename, string mode [, bool use_ include_path [, resource context]])	resource	Opens a file or a URL and returns a file pointer.

Function	Returns	Description
`fclose(resource fp)`	bool	Closes an open file pointer.
`popen(string command, string mode)`	resource	Executes a command and opens either a read or a write pipe to it.
`pclose(resource fp)`	int	Closes a file pointer opened by `popen()`.
`feof(resource fp)`	bool	Tests for end-of-file on a file pointer.
`fgets(resource fp [, int length])`	string	Gets a line from file pointer.
`fgetc(resource fp)`	string	Gets a character from file pointer.
`fgetss(resource fp [, int length, string allowable_tags])`	string	Gets a line from file pointer and strips HTML tags.
`fscanf(resource stream, string format [, string ...])`	mixed	Implements a mostly ANSI-compatible `fscanf()`.
`fwrite(resource fp, string str [, int length])`	int	Binary-safe file write.
`fflush(resource fp)`	bool	Flushes output.
`rewind(resource fp)`	bool	Rewinds the position of a file pointer.
`ftell(resource fp)`	int	Gets file pointer's read/write position.
`fseek(resource fp, int offset [, int whence])`	int	Seeks on a file pointer.
`mkdir(string pathname [, int mode [, bool recursive [, resource context]]])`	bool	Creates a directory.
`rmdir(string dirname [, resource context])`	bool	Removes a directory.
`readfile(string filename [, bool use_include_path [, resource context]])`	int	Outputs a file or a URL.
`umask([int mask])`	int	Returns or changes the umask.
`fpassthru(resource fp)`	int	Outputs all remaining data from a file pointer.
`rename(string old_name, string new_name [, resource context])`	bool	Renames a file.
`unlink(string filename [, context context])`	bool	Deletes a file.

Table continued on following page

Function	Returns	Description
`ftruncate (resource fp, int size)`	bool	Truncates file to size length.
`fstat (resource fp)`	int	Performs `stat()` on a file handle.
`copy (string source_file, string destination_file)`	bool	Copies a file.
`fread (resource fp, int length)`	string	Binary-safe file read.
`fgetcsv (resource fp [, int length [, string delimiter [, string enclosure]]])`	array	Gets line from file pointer and parses for CSV fields.
`realpath (string path)`	string	Returns the resolved path.
`fnmatch (string pattern, string filename [, int flags])`	bool	Matches filename against pattern.
`disk_total_space (string path)`	float	Gets total disk space for filesystem that path is on.
`disk_free_space (string path)`	float	Gets free disk space for filesystem that path is on.
`chgrp (string filename, mixed group)`	bool	Changes file group.
`chown (string filename, mixed user)`	bool	Changes file owner.
`chmod (string filename, int mode)`	bool	Changes file mode.
`touch (string filename [, int time [, int atime]])`	bool	Sets modification time of file.
`clearstatcache (void)`	void	Clears file stat cache.
`fileperms (string filename)`	int	Gets file permissions.
`fileinode (string filename)`	int	Gets file inode.
`filesize (string filename)`	int	Gets file size.
`fileowner (string filename)`	int	Gets file owner.
`filegroup (string filename)`	int	Gets file group.
`fileatime (string filename)`	int	Gets last access time of file.
`filemtime (string filename)`	int	Gets last modification time of file.
`filectime (string filename)`	int	Gets inode modification time of file.

Function	Returns	Description
filetype(string filename)	string	Gets file type.
is_writable(string filename)	bool	Returns true if file can be written.
is_readable(string filename)	bool	Returns true if file can be read.
is_executable(string filename)	bool	Returns true if file is executable.
is_file(string filename)	bool	Returns true if file is a regular file.
is_dir(string filename)	bool	Returns true if file is a directory.
is_link(string filename)	bool	Returns true if file is a symbolic link.
file_exists(string filename)	bool	Returns true if filename exists.
lstat(string filename)	array	Gives information about a file or symbolic link.
stat(string filename)	array	Gives information about a file.
readlink(string filename)	string	Returns the target of a symbolic link.
linkinfo(string filename)	int	Returns the st_dev field of the UNIX C stat structure describing the link.
symlink(string target, string link)	int	Creates a symbolic link.
link(string target, string link)	int	Creates a hard link.
is_uploaded_file(string path)	bool	Checks if file was created by RFC1867 upload.
move_uploaded_file(string path, string new_path)	bool	Moves a file if and only if it was created by an upload.
parse_ini_file(string filename [, bool process_sections])	array	Parses configuration file.

FTP

Function	Returns	Description
ftp_connect(string host [, int port [, int timeout]])	resource	Opens an FTP stream.
ftp_ssl_connect(string host [, int port [, int timeout]])	resource	Opens an FTP-SSL stream.

Table continued on following page

Function	Returns	Description
`ftp_login(resource stream, string username, string password)`	bool	Logs into the FTP server.
`ftp_pwd(resource stream)`	string	Returns the present working directory.
`ftp_cdup(resource stream)`	bool	Changes to the parent directory.
`ftp_chdir(resource stream, string directory)`	bool	Changes directories.
`ftp_exec(resource stream, string command)`	bool	Requests execution of a program on the FTP server.
`ftp_raw(resource stream, string command)`	array	Sends a literal command to the FTP server.
`ftp_mkdir(resource stream, string directory)`	string	Creates a directory and returns the absolute path for the new directory or `false` on error.
`ftp_rmdir(resource stream, string directory)`	bool	Removes a directory.
`ftp_chmod(resource stream, int mode, string filename)`	int	Sets permissions on a file.
`ftp_alloc(resource stream, int size[, &response])`	bool	Attempts to allocate space on the remote FTP server.
`ftp_nlist(resource stream, string directory)`	array	Returns an array of filenames in the given directory.
`ftp_rawlist(resource stream, string directory [, bool recursive])`	array	Returns a detailed listing of a directory as an array of output lines.
`ftp_systype(resource stream)`	string	Returns the system type identifier.
`ftp_fget(resource stream, resource fp, string remote_ file, int mode [, int resumepos])`	bool	Retrieves a file from the FTP server and writes it to an open file.
`ftp_nb_fget(resource stream, resource fp, string remote_ file, int mode[, int resumepos])`	int	Retrieves a file from the FTP server asynchronly and writes it to an open file.
`ftp_pasv(resource stream, bool pasv)`	bool	Turns passive mode on or off.
`ftp_get(resource stream, string local_file, string remote_file, int mode [, int resume_pos])`	bool	Retrieves a file from the FTP server and writes it to a local file.

Function	Returns	Description
`ftp_nb_get(resource stream, string local_file, string remote_file, int mode[, int resume_pos])`	int	Retrieves a file from the FTP server nbhronly and writes it to a local file.
`ftp_nb_continue (resource stream)`	int	Continues retrieving/sending a file nbronously.
`ftp_fput(resource stream, string remote_file, resource fp, int mode [, int startpos])`	bool	Stores a file from an open file to the FTP server.
`ftp_nb_fput(resource stream, string remote_file, resource fp, int mode[, int startpos])`	int	Stores a file from an open file to the FTP server nbronly.
`ftp_put(resource stream, string remote_file, string local_file, int mode [, int startpos])`	bool	Stores a file on the FTP server.
`ftp_nb_put(resource stream, string remote_file, string local_file, int mode [, int startpos])`	int	Stores a file on the FTP server.
`ftp_size(resource stream, string filename)`	int	Returns the size of the file, or -1 on error.
`ftp_mdtm(resource stream, string filename)`	int	Returns the last modification time of the file, or -1 on error.
`ftp_rename(resource stream, string src, string dest)`	bool	Renames the given file to a new path.
`ftp_delete(resource stream, string file)`	bool	Deletes a file.
`ftp_site(resource stream, string cmd)`	bool	Sends a SITE command to the server.
`ftp_close(resource stream)`	bool	Closes the FTP stream.
`ftp_set_option (resource stream, int option, mixed value)`	bool	Sets an FTP option.
`ftp_get_option(resource stream, int option)`	mixed	Gets an FTP option.

Function Handling

Function	Returns	Description
call_user_func (string function_name [, mixed parmeter] [, mixed ...])	mixed	Calls a user function that is the first parameter.
call_user_func_array (string function_name, array parameters)	mixed	Calls a user function that is the first parameter with the arguments contained in array.
call_user_method (string method_name, mixed object [, mixed parameter] [, mixed ...])	mixed	Calls a user method on a specific object or class.
call_user_method_array (string method_name, mixed object, array params)	mixed	Calls a user method on a specific object or class using a parameter array.
register_shutdown_ function (string function_name)	void	Registers a user-level function to be called on request termination.
register_tick_function (string function_name [, mixed arg [, mixed ...]])	bool	Registers a tick callback function.
unregister_tick_function (string function_name)	void	Unregisters a tick callback function.
create_function(string args, string code)	string	Creates an anonymous function, and returns its name.
function_exists (string function_name)	bool	Checks if the function exists.
func_num_args(void)	int	Gets the number of arguments that were passed to the function.
func_get_arg(int arg_num)	mixed	Gets the $arg_num'th argument that was passed to the function.
func_get_args()	array	Gets an array of the arguments that were passed to the function.

HTTP

Function	Returns	Description
header(string header [, bool replace, [int http_response_code]])	void	Sends a raw HTTP header.
setcookie(string name [, string value [, int expires [, string path [, string domain [, bool secure]]]]])	bool	Sends a cookie.
setrawcookie(string name [, string value [, int expires [, string path [, string domain [, bool secure]]]]])	bool	Sends a cookie with no URL encoding of the value.
headers_sent([string &$file [, int &$line]])	bool	Returns true if headers have already been sent, false otherwise.
headers_list(void)	string	Returns a list of headers to be sent/already sent.

Iconv Library

Function	Returns	Description
iconv(tring in_charset, string out_charset, string str)	string	Returns str converted to the out_charset character set.
ob_iconv_handler (string contents, int status)		Returns str in output buffer converted to the iconv.output_encoding character set.
iconv_get_encoding ([string type])	mixed	Gets internal encoding and output encoding for ob_iconv_handler().
iconv_set_encoding (string type, string charset)	bool	Sets internal encoding and output encoding for ob_iconv_handler().

Image

Function	Returns	Description
exif_tagname(index)	string	Gets headername for index or false if not defined.
exif_read_data(string filename [, sections_needed [, sub_arrays [, read_thumbnail]]])	array	Reads header data from the JPEG/TIFF image filename and optionally reads the internal thumbnails.
exif_thumbnail (string filename [, &width, &height [, &imagetype]])	string	Reads the embedded thumbnail.
exif_imagetype (string imagefile)	int	Gets the type of an image.
gd_info()	array	Retrieves information about the currently installed GD library.
imageloadfont(string filename)	int	Loads a new font.
imagesetstyle (resource im, array styles)	bool	Sets the line drawing styles for use with imageline and IMG_COLOR_STYLED.
imagecreatetruecolor (int x_size, int y_size)	resource	Creates a new true color image.
imageistruecolor(resource im)	bool	Returns true if the image uses true color.
imagetruecolortopalette (resource im, bool ditherFlag, int colorsWanted)	void	Converts a true color image to a palette-based image with a number of colors, optionally using dithering.
imagecolormatch (resource im1, resource im2)	bool	Makes the colors of the palette version of an image more closely match the true color version.
imagesetthickness (resource im, int thickness)	bool	Sets line thickness for drawing lines, ellipses, rectangles, polygons, and so on.
imagefilledellipse (resource im, int cx, int cy, int w, int h, int color)	bool	Draws an ellipse.
imagefilledarc(resource im, int cx, int cy, int w, int h, int s, int e, int col, int style)	bool	Draws a filled partial ellipse.
imagealphablending (resource im, bool on)	bool	Turns alpha blending mode on or off for the given image.

Function	Returns	Description
imagesavealpha (resource im, bool on)	bool	Includes alpha channel to a saved image.
imagelayereffect (resource im, int effect)	bool	Sets the alpha blending flag to use the bundled libgd layering effects.
imagecolorallocatealpha (resource im, int red, int green, int blue, int alpha)	int	Allocates a color with an alpha level. Works for true color and palette-based images.
imagecolorresolvealpha (resource im, int red, int green, int blue, int alpha)	int	Resolves/allocates a color with an alpha level. Works for true color and palette-based images.
imagecolorclosestalpha (resource im, int red, int green, int blue, int alpha)	int	Finds the closest matching color with alpha transparency.
imagecolorexactalpha (resource im, int red, int green, int blue, int alpha)	int	Finds exact match for color with transparency.
imagecopyresampled (resource dst_im, resource src_im, int dst_x, int dst_y, int src_x, int src_y, int dst_w, int dst_h, int src_w, int src_h)	bool	Copies and resizes part of an image using resampling to help ensure clarity.
imagerotate (resource src_im, float angle, int bgdcolor)	resource	Rotates an image using a custom angle.
imagesettile (resource image, resource tile)	bool	Sets the tile image to $tile when filling $image with the IMG_COLOR_TILED color.
imagesetbrush (resource image, resource brush)	bool	Sets the brush image to $brush when filling $image with the IMG_COLOR_BRUSHED color.
imagecreate (int x_size, int y_size)	resource	Creates a new image.
imagetypes(void)	int	Returns the types of images supported in a bitfield — 1=GIF, 2=JPEG, 4=PNG, 8=WBMP, 16=XPM.
imagecreatefromstring (string image)	resource	Creates a new image from the image stream in the string.

Table continued on following page

Function	Returns	Description
`imagecreatefromgif (string filename)`	resource	Creates a new image from GIF file or URL.
`imagecreatefromjpeg (string filename)`	resource	Creates a new image from JPEG file or URL.
`imagecreatefrompng (string filename)`	resource	Creates a new image from PNG file or URL.
`imagecreatefromxbm (string filename)`	resource	Creates a new image from XBM file or URL.
`imagecreatefromxpm (string filename)`	resource	Creates a new image from XPM file or URL.
`imagecreatefromwbmp (string filename)`	resource	Creates a new image from WBMP file or URL.
`imagecreatefromgd (string filename)`	resource	Creates a new image from GD file or URL.
`imagecreatefromgd2 (string filename)`	resource	Creates a new image from GD2 file or URL.
`imagecreatefromgd2part (string filename, int srcX, int srcY, int width, int height)`	resource	Creates a new image from a given part of GD2 file or URL.
`imagexbm(int im, string filename [, int foreground])`	int	Outputs XBM image to browser or file.
`imagegif(resource im [, string filename])`	bool	Outputs GIF image to browser or file.
`imagepng(resource im [, string filename])`	bool	Outputs PNG image to browser or file.
`imagejpeg(resource im [, string filename [, int quality]])`	bool	Outputs JPEG image to browser or file.
`imagewbmp(resource im [, string filename, [, int foreground]])`	bool	Outputs WBMP image to browser or file.
`imagegd(resource im [, string filename])`	bool	Outputs GD image to browser or file.
`imagegd2(resource im [, string filename, [, int chunk_size, [, int type]]])`	bool	Outputs GD2 image to browser or file.

Function	Returns	Description
imagedestroy(resource im)	bool	Destroys an image.
imagecolorallocate (resource im, int red, int green, int blue)	int	Allocates a color for an image.
imagepalettecopy (resource dst, resource src)	void	Copies the palette from the src image onto the dst image.
imagecolorat(resource im, int x, int y)	int	Gets the index of the color of a pixel.
imagecolorclosest (resource im, int red, int green, int blue)	int	Gets the index of the closest color to the specified color.
imagecolorclosesthwb (resource im, int red, int green, int blue)	int	Gets the index of the color that has the hue, white, and blackness nearest to the given color.
imagecolordeallocate (resource im, int index)	bool	De-allocates a color for an image.
imagecolorresolve (resource im, int red, int green, int blue)	int	Gets the index of the specified color or its closest possible alternative.
imagecolorexact (resource im, int red, int green, int blue)	int	Gets the index of the specified color.
imagecolorset (resource im, int col, int red, int green, int blue)	void	Sets the color for the specified palette index.
imagecolorsforindex (resource im, int col)	array	Gets the colors for an index.
imagegammacorrect (resource im, float inputgamma, float outputgamma)	bool	Apply a gamma correction to a GD image.
imagesetpixel (resource im, int x, int y, int col)	bool	Sets a single pixel.
imageline (resource im, int x1, int y1, int x2, int y2, int col)	bool	Draws a line.

Table continued on following page

Function	Returns	Description
imagedashedline (resource im, int x1, int y1, int x2, int y2, int col)	bool	Draws a dashed line.
imagerectangle (resource im, int x1, int y1, int x2, int y2, int col)	bool	Draws a rectangle.
imagefilledrectangle (resource im, int x1, int y1, int x2, int y2, int col)	bool	Draws a filled rectangle.
imagearc (resource im, int cx, int cy, int w, int h, int s, int e, int col)	bool	Draws a partial ellipse.
imageellipse (resource im, int cx, int cy, int w, int h, int color)	bool	Draws an ellipse.
imagefilltoborder (resource im, int x, int y, int border, int col)	bool	Flood fills to specific color.
imagefill (resource im, int x, int y, int col)	bool	Flood fills with given color col.
imagecolorstotal (resource im)	int	Finds out the number of colors in an image's palette.
imagecolortransparent (resource im [, int col])	int	Defines a color as transparent.
imageinterlace (resource im [, int interlace])	int	Enables or disables interlace.
imagepolygon (resource im, array point, int num_points, int col)	bool	Draws a polygon.
imagefilledpolygon (resource im, array point, int num_points, int col)	bool	Draws a filled polygon.
imagefontwidth (int font)	int	Gets font width.
imagefontheight (int font)	int	Gets font height.

Function	Returns	Description
imagechar(resource im, int font, int x, int y, string c, int col)	bool	Draws a character.
imagecharup(resource im, int font, int x, int y, string c, int col)	bool	Draws a character rotated 90 degrees counterclockwise.
imagestring(resource im, int font, int x, int y, string str, int col)	bool	Draws a string horizontally.
imagestringup (resource im, int font, int x, int y, string str, int col)	bool	Draws a string vertically rotated 90 degrees counterclockwise.
imagecopy (resource dst_im, resource src_im, int dst_x, int dst_y, int src_x, int src_y, int src_w, int src_h)	bool	Copies part of an image.
imagecopymerge (resource src_im, resource dst_im, int dst_x, int dst_y, int src_x, int src_y, int src_w, int src_h, int pct)	bool	Merges one part of an image with another.
imagecopymergegray (resource src_im, resource dst_im, int dst_x, int dst_y, int src_x, int src_y, int src_w, int src_h, int pct)	bool	Merges one part of an image with another while preserving hue of source.
imagecopyresized (resource dst_im, resource src_im, int dst_x, int dst_y, int src_x, int src_y, int dst_w, int dst_h, int src_w, int src_h)	bool	Copies and resizes part of an image.
imagesx(resource im)	int	Gets image width.
imagesy(resource im)	int	Gets image height.

Table continued on following page

Function	Returns	Description
imageftbbox(int size, int angle, string font_file, string text[, array extrainfo])	array	Gives the bounding box of a text block using fonts via freetype2.
imagefttext(resource im, int size, int angle, int x, int y, int col, string font_file, string text, [array extrainfo])	array	Writes text to the image using fonts via freetype2.
imagettfbbox (int size, int angle, string font_file, string text)	array	Gives the bounding box of a text block using TrueType fonts.
imagettftext (resource im, int size, int angle, int x, int y, int col, string font_file, string text)	array	Writes text to the image using a TrueType font.
imagepsloadfont (string pathname)	resource	Loads a new font from specified file.
imagepscopyfont (int font_index)	int	Makes a copy of a font for purposes such as extending or re-encoding.
imagepsfreefont (resource font_index)	bool	Frees memory used by a font.
imagepsencodefont (resource font_index, string filename)	bool	Changes the character-encoding vector of a font.
imagepsextendfont (resource font_index, float extend)	bool	Extends or condenses (if extend < 1) a font.
imagepsslantfont (resource font_index, float slant)	bool	Slants a font.
imagepstext (resource image, string text, resource font, int size, int xcoord, int ycoord [, int space, int tightness, float angle, int antialias])	array	Rasterizes a string over an image.
imagepsbbox(string text, resource font, int size [, int space, int tightness, int angle])	array	Returns the bounding box needed by a string if rasterized.

Function	Returns	Description
image2wbmp(resource im [, string filename [, int threshold]])	bool	Outputs WBMP image to browser or file.
jpeg2wbmp (string f_org, string f_dest, int d_height, int d_width, int threshold)	bool	Converts JPEG image to WBMP image.
png2wbmp (string f_org, string f_dest, int d_height, int d_width, int threshold)	bool	Converts PNG image to WBMP image.
imagefilter (resource src_im, int filtertype, [args])	bool	Applies Filter an image using a custom angle.
imageantialias (resource im, bool on)	bool	Determines if antialiased functions should be used or not.
image_type_to_mime_type (int imagetype)	string	Gets Mime-Type for image-type returned by getimagesize, exif_read_data, exif_thumbnail, exif_imagetype.
image_type_to_extension (int imagetype [, bool include_dot])	string	Gets file extension for image-type returned by getimagesize, exif_read_data, exif_thumbnail, exif_imagetype.
getimagesize (string imagefile [, array info])	array	Gets the size of an image as four-element array.
iptcembed (string iptcdata, string jpeg_file_name [, int spool])	array	Embeds binary IPTC data into a JPEG image.
iptcparse(string iptcdata)	array	Parses binary IPTC-data into associative array.

IMAP

Function	Returns	Description
imap_open(string mailbox, string user, string password [, int options])	resource	Opens an IMAP stream to a mailbox.

Table continued on following page

Function	Returns	Description
`imap_reopen(resource stream_id, string mailbox [, int options])`	bool	Reopens an IMAP stream to a new mailbox.
`imap_append (resource stream_id, string folder, string message [, string options])`	bool	Appends a new message to a specified mailbox.
`imap_num_msg (resource stream_id)`	int	Gives the number of messages in the current mailbox.
`imap_ping (resource stream_id)`	bool	Checks if the IMAP stream is still active.
`imap_num_recent (resource stream_id)`	int	Gives the number of recent messages in current mailbox.
`imap_get_quota (resource stream_id, string qroot)`	array	Returns the quota set to the mailbox account qroot.
`imap_get_quotaroot (resource stream_id, string mbox)`	array	Returns the quota set to the mailbox account mbox.
`imap_set_quota (resource stream_id, string qroot, int mailbox_size)`	bool	Sets the quota for qroot mailbox.
`imap_setacl (resource stream_id, string mailbox, string id, string rights)`	bool	Sets the ACL for a given mailbox.
`imap_getacl (resource stream_id, string mailbox)`	array	Gets the ACL for a given mailbox.
`imap_expunge (resource stream_id)`	bool	Permanently deletes all messages marked for deletion.
`imap_close (resource stream_id [, int options])`	bool	Closes an IMAP stream.
`imap_headers (resource stream_id)`	array	Returns headers for all messages in a mailbox.
`imap_body(resource stream_id, int msg_no [, int options])`	string	Reads the message body.

Function	Returns	Description
imap_mail_copy (resource stream_id, int msg_no, string mailbox [, int options])	bool	Copies the specified message to a mailbox.
imap_mail_move (resource stream_id, int msg_no, string mailbox [, int options])	bool	Moves the specified message to a mailbox.
imap_createmailbox (resource stream_id, string mailbox)	bool	Creates a new mailbox.
imap_renamemailbox (resource stream_id, string old_name, string new_name)	bool	Renames a mailbox.
imap_deletemailbox (resource stream_id, string mailbox)	bool	Deletes a mailbox.
imap_list (resource stream_id, string ref, string pattern)	array	Reads the list of mailboxes.
imap_getmailboxes (resource stream_id, string ref, string pattern)	array	Reads the list of mailboxes and returns a full array of objects containing name, attributes, and delimiter.
imap_scan (resource stream_id, string ref, string pattern, string content)	array	Reads a list of mailboxes containing a certain string.
imap_check (resource stream_id)	object	Gets mailbox properties.
imap_delete (resource stream_id, int msg_no [, int options])	bool	Marks a message for deletion.
imap_undelete (resource stream_id, int msg_no)	bool	Removes the delete flag from a message.
imap_headerinfo (resource stream_id, int msg_no [, int from_length [, int subject_length [, string default_host]]])	object	Reads the headers of the message.

Table continued on following page

Function	Returns	Description
`imap_rfc822_parse_headers` `(string headers` `[, string default_host])`	object	Parses a set of mail headers contained in a string, and returns an object similar to `imap_headerinfo()`.
`imap_lsub` `(resource stream_id,` `string ref, string pattern)`	array	Returns a list of subscribed mailboxes.
`imap_getsubscribed` `(resource stream_id,` `string ref, string pattern)`	array	Returns a list of subscribed mailboxes, in the same format as `imap_getmailboxes()`.
`imap_subscribe` `(resource stream_id,` `string mailbox)`	bool	Subscribes to a mailbox.
`imap_unsubscribe` `(resource stream_id,` `string mailbox)`	bool	Unsubscribes from a mailbox.
`imap_fetchstructure` `(resource stream_id,` `int msg_no [, int options])`	object	Reads the full structure of a message.
`imap_fetchbody` `(resource stream_id,` `int msg_no, int section` `[, int options])`	string	Gets a specific body section.
`imap_base64(string text)`	string	Decodes BASE64 encoded text.
`imap_qprint(string text)`	string	Converts a quoted-printable string to an 8-bit string.
`imap_8bit(string text)`	string	Converts an 8-bit string to a quoted-printable string.
`imap_binary(string text)`	string	Converts an 8-bit string to a base64 string.
`imap_mailboxmsginfo` `(resource stream_id)`	object	Returns info about the current mailbox.
`imap_rfc822_write_address` `(string mailbox, string host,` `string personal)`	string	Returns a properly formatted e-mail address given the mailbox, host, and personal info.
`imap_rfc822_parse_adrlist` `(string address_string,` `string default_host)`	array	Parses an address string.
`imap_utf8` `(string mime_encoded_text)`	string	Converts mime-encoded text to UTF-8.

Function	Returns	Description
imap_utf7_decode(string buf)	string	Decodes a modified UTF-7 string.
imap_utf7_encode(string buf)	string	Encodes a string in modified UTF-7.
imap_setflag_full (resource stream_id, string sequence, string flag [, int options])	bool	Sets flags on messages.
imap_clearflag_full (resource stream_id, string sequence, string flag [, int options])	bool	Clears flags on messages.
imap_sort (resource stream_id, int criteria, int reverse [, int options [, string search_criteria [, string charset]]])	array	Sorts an array of message headers, optionally including only messages that meet specified criteria.
imap_fetchheader (resource stream_id, int msg_no [, int options])	string	Gets the full unfiltered header for a message.
imap_uid(resource stream_id, int msg_no)	int	Gets the unique message id associated with a standard sequential message number.
imap_msgno (resource stream_id, int unique_msg_id)	int	Gets the sequence number associated with a UID.
imap_status (resource stream_id, string mailbox, int options)	object	Gets status info from a mailbox.
imap_bodystruct (resource stream_id, int msg_no, int section)	object	Reads the structure of a specified body section of a specific message.
imap_fetch_overview (resource stream_id, int msg_no [, int options])	array	Reads an overview of the information in the headers of the given message sequence.
imap_mail_compose (array envelope, array body)	string	Creates a MIME message based on given envelope and body sections.
imap_mail(string to, string subject, string message [, string additional_headers [, string cc [, string bcc [, string rpath]]]])	bool	Sends an e-mail message.

Table continued on following page

Function	Returns	Description
imap_search (resource stream_id, string criteria [, int options [, string charset]])	array	Returns a list of messages matching the given criteria.
imap_alerts(void)	array	Returns an array of all IMAP alerts that have been generated since the last page load or since the last imap_alerts() call, whichever came last. The alert stack is cleared after imap_alerts() is called.
imap_errors(void)	array	Returns an array of all IMAP errors generated since the last page load, or since the last imap_errors() call, whichever came last. The error stack is cleared after imap_errors() is called.
imap_last_error(void)	string	Returns the last error that was generated by an IMAP function. The error stack is not cleared after this call.
imap_mime_header_ decode(string str)	array	Decodes mime header element in accordance with RFC 2047and returns an array of objects containing charset encoding and decoded text.
imap_thread (resource stream_id [, int options])	array	Returns are threaded by REFERENCES tree.
imap_timeout (int timeout_type [, int timeout])	mixed	Sets or fetches IMAP timeout.

Mail

Function	Returns	Description
ezmlm_hash(string addr)	int	Calculates EZMLM list hash value.
mail(string to, string subject, string message [, string additional_headers [, string additional_ parameters]])	int	Sends an e-mail message.

Math

Function	Returns	Description
`abs(int number)`	int	Returns the absolute value of the number.
`ceil(float number)`	float	Returns the next highest integer value of the number.
`floor(float number)`	float	Returns the next lowest integer value from the number.
`round(float number [, int precision])`	float	Returns the number rounded to specified precision.
`sin(float number)`	float	Returns the sine of the number in radians.
`cos(float number)`	float	Returns the cosine of the number in radians.
`tan(float number)`	float	Returns the tangent of the number in radians.
`asin(float number)`	float	Returns the arc sine of the number in radians.
`acos(float number)`	float	Returns the arc cosine of the number in radians.
`atan(float number)`	float	Returns the arc tangent of the number in radians.
`atan2(float y, float x)`	float	Returns the arc tangent of y/x, with the resulting quadrant determined by the signs of y and x.
`sinh(float number)`	float	Returns the hyperbolic sine of the number, defined as `(exp(number) - exp(-number))/2`.
`cosh(float number)`	float	Returns the hyperbolic cosine of the number, defined as `(exp(number) + exp(-number))/2`.
`tanh(float number)`	float	Returns the hyperbolic tangent of the number, defined as `sinh(number)/cosh(number)`.
`asinh(float number)`	float	Returns the inverse hyperbolic sine of the number, that is, the value whose hyperbolic sine is number.
`acosh(float number)`	float	Returns the inverse hyperbolic cosine of the number, that is, the value whose hyperbolic cosine is number.

Table continued on following page

Function	Returns	Description
`atanh(float number)`	float	Returns the inverse hyperbolic tangent of the number, that is, the value whose hyperbolic tangent is number.
`pi(void)`	float	Returns an approximation of pi.
`is_finite(float val)`	bool	Returns whether argument is finite.
`is_infinite(float val)`	bool	Returns whether argument is infinite.
`is_nan(float val)`	bool	Returns whether argument is not a number.
`pow(number base, number exponent)`	number	Returns base raised to the power of exponent. Returns integer result when possible.
`exp(float number)`	float	Returns e raised to the power of the number.
`expm1(float number)`	float	Returns `exp(number) - 1`, computed in a way that's accurate even when the value of number is close to zero.
`log1p(float number)`	float	Returns `log(1 + number)`, computed in a way that's accurate even when the value of number is close to zero.
`log(float number, [float base])`	float	Returns the natural logarithm of the number, or the base log if the base is specified.
`log10(float number)`	float	Returns the base-10 logarithm of the number.
`sqrt(float number)`	float	Returns the square root of the number.
`hypot(float num1, float num2)`	float	Returns `sqrt(num1*num1 + num2*num2)`.
`deg2rad(float number)`	float	Converts the number in degrees to the radian equivalent.
`rad2deg(float number)`	float	Converts the radian number to the equivalent number in degrees.
`bindec(string binary_number)`	int	Returns the decimal equivalent of the binary number.
`hexdec(string hexadecimal_number)`	int	Returns the decimal equivalent of the hexadecimal number.
`octdec(string octal_number)`	int	Returns the decimal equivalent of an octal string.

Function	Returns	Description
decbin(int decimal_number)	string	Returns a string containing a binary representation of the number.
decoct(int decimal_number)	string	Returns a string containing an octal representation of the given number.
dechex(int decimal_number)	string	Returns a string containing a hexadecimal representation of the given number.
base_convert(string number, int frombase, int tobase)	string	Converts a number in a string from any base <= 36 to any base <= 36.
number_format(float number [, int num_decimal_places [, string dec_seperator, string thousands_seperator]])	string	Formats a number with grouped thousands.
fmod(float x, float y)	float	Returns the remainder of dividing x by y as a float.
srand([int seed])	void	Seeds random number generator.
mt_srand([int seed])	void	Seeds Mersenne Twister random number generator.
rand([int min, int max])	int	Returns a random number.
mt_rand([int min, int max])	int	Returns a random number from Mersenne Twister.
getrandmax(void)	int	Returns the maximum value a random number can have.
mt_getrandmax(void)	int	Returns the maximum value a random number from Mersenne Twister can have.

MIME

Function	Returns	Description
mime_content_type (string filename |resource stream)	string	Returns content-type for file.

Miscellaneous

Function	Returns	Description
get_browser([string browser_name [, bool return_array]])	mixed	Gets information about the capabilities of a browser.
constant(string const_name)	mixed	Given the name of a constant this function returns the constant's associated value.
getenv(string varname)	string	Gets the value of an environment variable.
putenv(string setting)	bool	Sets the value of an environment variable.
getopt(string options [, array longopts])	array	Gets options from the command line argument list.
flush(void)	void	Flushes the output buffer.
sleep(int seconds)	void	Delays for a given number of seconds.
usleep(int micro_seconds)	void	Delays for a given number of micro seconds.
time_nanosleep (long seconds, long nanoseconds)	mixed	Delays for a number of seconds and nanoseconds.
highlight_file(string file_name [, bool return])	bool	Syntax highlights a source file.
php_strip_whitespace (string file_name)	string	Returns source with stripped comments and whitespace.
php_check_syntax (string file_name [, &$error_message])	bool	Checks the syntax of the specified file.
highlight_string (string string [, bool return])	bool	Syntax highlights a string or optionally returns it.
uniqid([string prefix , bool more_entropy])	string	Generates a unique ID.
version_compare(string ver1, string ver2 [, string oper])	int	Compares two PHP-standardized version number strings.
connection_aborted(void)	int	Returns true if client disconnected.
connection_status(void)	int	Returns the connection status bitfield.
ignore_user_abort(bool value)	int	Sets whether you want to ignore a user abort event or not.

Function	Returns	Description

`define(string constant_`
`name, mixed value, case_`
`sensitive=true)`
	bool	Defines a new constant.

`defined(string constant_name)`	bool	Checks whether a constant exists.

MS SQL

Function	Returns	Description

`mssql_connect`
`([string servername`
`[, string username`
`[, string password]]])`
	int	Establishes a connection to an MS-SQL server.

`mssql_pconnect`
`([string servername`
`[, string username`
`[, string password]]])`
	int	Establishes a persistent connection to an MS-SQL server.

`mssql_close` `([resource conn_id])`	bool	Closes a connection to an MS-SQL server.

`mssql_select_db`
`(string database_name`
`[, resource conn_id])`
	bool	Select an MS-SQL database.

`mssql_fetch_batch` `(resource result_index)`	int	Returns the next batch of records.

`mssql_query(string query`
`[, resource conn_id`
`[, int batch_size]])`
	resource	Performs an SQL query on an MS-SQL server database.

`mssql_rows_affected` `(resource conn_id)`	int	Returns the number of records affected by the query.
`mssql_free_result` `(resource result_index)`	bool	Frees an MS-SQL result index.
`mssql_get_last_message(void)`	string	Gets the last message from the MS-SQL server.
`mssql_num_rows` `(resource mssql_result_index)`	int	Returns the number of rows fetched in from the `result_id` specified.
`mssql_num_fields` `(resource mssql_result_index)`	int	Returns the number of fields fetched in from the `result_id` specified.

Table continued on following page

Function	Returns	Description
mssql_fetch_row (resource result_id)	array	Returns an array of the current row in the result set specified by result_id.
mssql_fetch_object (resource result_id [, int result_type])	object	Returns a psuedo-object of the current row in the result set specified by result_id.
mssql_fetch_array (resource result_id [, int result_type])	array	Returns an associative array of the current row in the result set specified by result_id.
mssql_fetch_assoc (resource result_id)	array	Returns an associative array of the current row in the result set specified by result_id.
mssql_data_seek (resource result_id, int offset)	bool	Moves the internal row pointer of the MS-SQL result associated with the specified result identifier to point to the specified row number.
mssql_fetch_field (resource result_id [, int offset])	object	Gets information about certain fields in a query result.
mssql_field_length (resource result_id [, int offset])	int	Gets the length of an MS-SQL field.
mssql_field_name (resource result_id [, int offset])	string	Returns the name of the field given by offset in the result set given by result_id.
mssql_field_type (resource result_id [, int offset])	string	Returns the type of a field.
mssql_field_seek (int result_id, int offset)	bool	Seeks to the specified field offset.
mssql_result (resource result_id, int row, mixed field)	string	Returns the contents of one cell from an MS-SQL result set.
mssql_next_result (resource result_id)	bool	Moves the internal result pointer to the next result.
mssql_min_error_severity (int severity)	void	Sets the lower error severity.
mssql_min_message_severity (int severity)	void	Sets the lower message severity.

Function	Returns	Description
mssql_init(string sp_name [, resource conn_id])	int	Initializes a stored procedure or a remote stored procedure.
mssql_bind(resource stmt, string param_name, mixed var, int type [, int is_output [, int is_null[, int maxlen]]])	bool	Adds a parameter to a stored procedure or a remote stored procedure.
mssql_execute(resource stmt [, bool skip_results = false])	mixed	Executes a stored procedure on an MS-SQL server database.
mssql_free_statement (resource result_index)	bool	Frees an MS-SQL statement index.
mssql_guid_string (string binary [,int short_format])	string	Converts a 16-byte binary GUID to a string.

MySQL

Function	Returns	Description
mysql_connect ([string hostname[:port] [:/path/to/socket] [, string username [, string password [, bool new [, int flags]]]]])	resource	Opens a connection to a MySQL Server.
mysql_pconnect ([string hostname[:port] [:/path/to/socket] [, string username [, string password [, int flags]]]])	resource	Opens a persistent connection to a MySQL Server.
mysql_close ([int link_identifier])	bool	Closes a MySQL connection.
mysql_select_db (string database_name [, int link_identifier])	bool	Selects a MySQL database.
mysql_get_client_info(void)	string	Returns a string that represents the client library version.
mysql_get_host_info ([int link_identifier])	string	Returns a string describing the type of connection in use, including the server host name.

Table continued on following page

Function	Returns	Description
mysql_get_proto_info ([int link_identifier])	int	Returns the protocol version used by current connection.
mysql_get_server_info ([int link_identifier])	string	Returns a string that represents the server version number.
mysql_info ([int link_identifier])	string	Returns a string containing information about the most recent query.
mysql_thread_id ([int link_identifier])	int	Returns the thread id of current connection.
mysql_stat ([int link_identifier])	string	Returns a string containing status information.
mysql_client_encoding ([int link_identifier])	string	Returns the default character set for the current connection.
mysql_create_db (string database_name [, int link_identifier])	bool	Creates a MySQL database.
mysql_drop_db (string database_name [, int link_identifier])	bool	Drops (deletes) a MySQL database.
mysql_query(string query [, int link_identifier])	resource	Sends an SQL query to MySQL.
mysql_unbuffered_query (string query [, int link_identifier])	resource	Sends an SQL query to MySQL, without fetching and buffering the result rows.
mysql_db_query (string database_name, string query [, int link_identifier])	resource	Sends an SQL query to MySQL.
mysql_list_dbs ([int link_identifier])	resource	Lists databases available on a MySQL server.
mysql_list_tables (string database_name [, int link_identifier])	resource	Lists tables in a MySQL database.
mysql_list_fields(string database_name, string table_name [, int link_identifier])	resource	Lists MySQL result fields.
mysql_list_processes ([int link_identifier])	resource	Returns a result set describing the current server threads.
mysql_error ([int link_identifier])	string	Returns the text of the error message from the previous MySQL operation.

Function	Returns	Description
mysql_errno ([int link_identifier])	int	Returns the number of the error message from the previous MySQL operation.
mysql_affected_rows ([int link_identifier])	int	Gets number of affected rows in the previous MySQL operation.
mysql_escape_string (string to_be_escaped)	string	Escapes string for mysql query.
mysql_real_escape_string (string to_be_escaped [, int link_identifier])	string	Escapes special characters in a string for use in a SQL statement, taking into account the current charset of the connection.
mysql_insert_id ([int link_identifier])	int	Gets the ID generated from the previous INSERT operation.
mysql_result (resource result, int row [, mixed field])	mixed	Gets result data.
mysql_num_rows (resource result)	int	Gets number of rows in a result.
mysql_num_fields (resource result)	int	Gets number of fields in a result.
mysql_fetch_row (resource result)	array	Gets a result row as an enumerated array.
mysql_fetch_object (resource result [, int result_type])	object	Fetches a result row as an object.
mysql_fetch_array (resource result [, int result_type])	array	Fetches a result row as an array (associative, numeric or both).
mysql_fetch_assoc (resource result)	array	Fetches a result row as an associative array.
mysql_data_seek (resource result, int row_number)	bool	Moves internal result pointer.
mysql_fetch_lengths (resource result)	array	Gets max data size of each column in a result.
mysql_fetch_field (resource result [, int field_offset])	object	Gets column information from a result and returns as an object.

Table continued on following page

Function	Returns	Description
mysql_field_seek (resource result, int field_offset)	bool	Sets result pointer to a specific field offset.
mysql_field_name (resource result, int field_index)	string	Gets the name of the specified field in a result.
mysql_field_table (resource result, int field_offset)	string	Gets name of the table the specified field is in.
mysql_field_len (resource result, int field_offset)	int	Returns the length of the specified field.
mysql_field_type (resource result, int field_offset)	string	Gets the type of the specified field in a result.
mysql_field_flags (resource result, int field_offset)	string	Gets the flags associated with the specified field in a result.
mysql_free_result (resource result)	bool	Frees result memory.
mysql_ping ([int link_identifier])	bool	Pings a server connection. If no connection exists, it reconnects.

Network Functions

Function	Returns	Description
define_syslog_variables(void)	void	Initializes all syslog-related variables.
openlog(string ident, int option, int facility)	bool	Opens connection to system logger.
closelog(void)	bool	Closes connection to system logger.
syslog(int priority, string message)	bool	Generates a system log message.
ip2long(string ip_address)	int	Converts a string containing an (IPv4) Internet Protocol dotted address into a proper address.
long2ip(int proper_address)	string	Converts an (IPv4) Internet network address into a string in Internet standard dotted format.

Function	Returns	Description
getservbyname (string service, string protocol)	int	Returns port number associated with service. Protocol must be tcp or udp.
getservbyport (int port, string protocol)	string	Returns service name associated with port. Protocol must be tcp or udp.
getprotobyname(string name)	int	Returns protocol number associated with name as per /etc/protocols.
getprotobynumber(int proto)	string	Returns protocol name associated with protocol number.

ODBC

Function	Returns	Description
odbc_close_all(void)	void	Closes all ODBC connections.
odbc_binmode (int result_id, int mode)	bool	Handles binary column data.
odbc_longreadlen (int result_id, int length)	bool	Handles LONG columns.
odbc_prepare (resource connection_id, string query)	resource	Prepares a statement for execution.
odbc_execute (resource result_id [, array parameters_array])	bool	Executes a prepared statement.
odbc_cursor (resource result_id)	string	Gets cursor name.
odbc_data_source (resource connection_id, int fetch_type)	array	Returns information about the currently connected data source.
odbc_exec (resource connection_id, string query [, int flags])	resource	Prepares and executes an SQL statement.
odbc_fetch_object (int result [, int rownumber])	object	Fetches a result row as an object.
odbc_fetch_array (int result [, int rownumber])	array	Fetches a result row as an associative array.

Table continued on following page

Function	Returns	Description
odbc_fetch_into (resource result_id, array result_array, [, int rownumber])	int	Fetches one result row into an array.
odbc_fetch_row (resource result_id [, int row_number])	bool	Fetches a row.
odbc_result (resource result_id, mixed field)	mixed	Gets result data.
odbc_result_all (resource result_id [, string format])	int	Prints result as HTML table.
odbc_free_result (resource result_id)	bool	Frees resources associated with a result.
odbc_connect (string DSN, string user, string password [, int cursor_option])	resource	Connects to a datasource.
odbc_pconnect (string DSN, string user, string password [, int cursor_option])	resource	Establishes a persistent connection to a datasource.
odbc_close (resource connection_id)	void	Closes an ODBC connection.
odbc_num_rows (resource result_id)	int	Gets number of rows in a result.
odbc_next_result (resource result_id)	bool	Checks if multiple results are available.
odbc_num_fields (resource result_id)	int	Gets number of columns in a result.
odbc_field_name (resource result_id, int field_number)	string	Gets a column name.
odbc_field_type (resource result_id, int field_number)	string	Gets the datatype of a column.
odbc_field_len (resource result_id, int field_number)	int	Gets the length (precision) of a column.

Function	Returns	Description
odbc_field_scale (resource result_id, int field_number)	int	Gets the scale of a column.
odbc_field_num (resource result_id, string field_name)	int	Returns column number.
odbc_autocommit (resource connection_id [, int OnOff])	mixed	Toggles autocommit mode or gets autocommit status.
odbc_commit (resource connection_id)	bool	Commits an ODBC transaction.
odbc_rollback (resource connection_id)	bool	Rolls back a transaction.
odbc_error ([resource connection_id])	string	Gets the last error code.
odbc_errormsg ([resource connection_id])	string	Gets the last error message.
odbc_setoption (resource conn_id| result_id, int which, int option, int value)	bool	Sets connection or statement options.
odbc_tables (resource connection_id [, string qualifier, string owner, string name, string table_types])	resource	Calls the SQLTables function.
odbc_columns (resource connection_id, string qualifier, string owner, string table_name, string column_name)	resource	Returns a result identifier that can be used to fetch a list of column names in specified tables.
odbc_columnprivileges (resource connection_id, string catalog, string schema, string table, string column)	resource	Returns a result identifier that can be used to fetch a list of columns and associated privileges for the specified table.

Table continued on following page

Function	Returns	Description
odbc_foreignkeys (resource connection_id, string pk_qualifier, string pk_owner, string pk_table, string fk_qualifier, string fk_owner, string fk_table)	resource	Returns a result identifier to either a list of foreign keys in the specified table or a list of foreign keys in other tables that refer to the primary key in the specified table.
odbc_gettypeinfo (resource connection_id [, int data_type])	resource	Returns a result identifier containing information about data types supported by the data source.
odbc_primarykeys (resource connection_id, string qualifier, string owner, string table)	resource	Returns a result identifier listing the column names that comprise the primary key for a table.
odbc_procedurecolumns (resource connection_id [, string qualifier, string owner, string proc, string column])	resource	Returns a result identifier containing the list of input and output parameters, as well as the columns that make up the result set for the specified procedures.
odbc_procedures (resource connection_id [, string qualifier, string owner, string name])	resource	Returns a result identifier containing the list of procedure names in a datasource.
odbc_specialcolumns (resource connection_id, int type, string qualifier, string owner, string table, int scope, int nullable)	resource	Returns a result identifier containing either the optimal set of columns that uniquely identifies a row in the table or columns that are automatically updated when any value in the row is updated by a transaction.
odbc_statistics (resource connection_id, string qualifier, string owner, string name, int unique, int accuracy)	resource	Returns a result identifier that contains statistics about a single table and the indexes associated with the table.
odbc_tableprivileges (resource connection_id, string qualifier, string owner, string name)	resource	Returns a result identifier containing a list of tables and the privileges associated with each table.

Output Buffering

Function	Returns	Description
ob_list_handlers()	false|array	Lists all output_buffers in an array.
ob_start([string|array user_function [, int chunk_size [, bool erase]]])	bool	Turns on Output Buffering (specifying an optional output handler).
ob_flush(void)	bool	Flushes (sends) contents of the output buffer. The last buffer content is sent to next buffer.
ob_clean(void)	bool	Cleans (deletes) the current output buffer.
ob_end_flush(void)	bool	Flushes (sends) the output buffer, and deletes current output buffer.
ob_end_clean(void)	bool	Cleans the output buffer, and deletes current output buffer.
ob_get_flush(void)	bool	Gets current buffer contents, flushes (sends) the output buffer, and deletes current output buffer.
ob_get_clean(void)	bool	Gets current buffer contents and deletes current output buffer.
ob_get_contents(void)	string	Returns the contents of the output buffer.
ob_get_level(void)	int	Returns the nesting level of the output buffer.
ob_get_length(void)	int	Returns the length of the output buffer.
ob_get_status([bool full_status])	false|array	Returns the status of the active or all output buffers.
ob_implicit_flush([int flag])	void	Turns implicit flush on/off and is equivalent to calling flush() after every output call.
output_reset_rewrite_vars(void)	bool	Resets (clears) URL rewriter values.
output_add_rewrite_var(string name, string value)	bool	Adds URL rewriter values.

PCRE

Function	Returns	Description
`preg_match(string pattern, string subject [, array subpatterns [, int flags [, int offset]]])`	int	Performs a Perl-style regular expression match.
`preg_match_all(string pattern, string subject, array subpatterns [, int flags [, int offset]])`	int	Performs a Perl-style global regular expression match.
`preg_replace(mixed regex, mixed replace, mixed subject [, int limit])`	string	Performs Perl-style regular expression replacement.
`preg_replace_callback (mixed regex, mixed callback, mixed subject [, int limit])`	string	Performs Perl-style regular expression replacement using replacement callback.
`preg_split(string pattern, string subject [, int limit [, int flags]])`	array	Splits string into an array using a Perl-style regular expression as a delimiter.
`preg_quote(string str, string delim_char)`	string	Quotes regular expression characters plus an optional character.
`preg_grep(string regex, array input)`	array	Searches an array and returns entries that match regex.

PHP Options and Info

Function	Returns	Description
`assert(string|bool assertion)`	int	Checks if assertion is false.
`assert_options(int what [, mixed value])`	mixed	Sets/gets the various assert flags.
`phpinfo([int what])`	void	Outputs a page of useful information about PHP and the current request.
`phpversion([string extension])`	string	Returns the current PHP version.
`phpcredits([int flag])`	void	Prints the list of people who've contributed to the PHP project.

Function	Returns	Description
php_logo_guid(void)	string	Returns the special ID used to request the PHP logo in phpinfo screens.
php_real_logo_guid(void)	string	Returns the special ID used to request the PHP logo in phpinfo screens.
php_egg_logo_guid(void)	string	Returns the special ID used to request the PHP logo in phpinfo screens.
zend_logo_guid(void)	string	Returns the special ID used to request the Zend logo in phpinfo screens.
php_sapi_name(void)	string	Returns the current SAPI module name.
php_uname(void)	string	Returns information about the system PHP was built on.
php_ini_scanned_files(void)	string	Returns comma-separated string of .ini files parsed from the additional ini dir.
getmyuid(void)	int	Gets PHP script owners UID.
getmygid(void)	int	Gets PHP script owners GID.
getmypid(void)	int	Gets current process ID.
getmyinode(void)	int	Gets the inode of the current script being parsed.
getlastmod(void)	int	Gets time of last page modification.
set_time_limit(int seconds)	bool	Sets the maximum time a script can run.
ini_get(string varname)	string	Gets a configuration option.
ini_get_all([string extension])	array	Gets all configuration options.
ini_set(string varname, string newvalue)	string	Sets a configuration option; returns false on error and the old value of the configuration option on success.
ini_restore(string varname)	void	Restores the value of a configuration option specified by varname.
set_include_path(string varname, string newvalue)	string	Sets the include_path configuration option.
get_include_path()	string	Gets the current include_path configuration option.
restore_include_path()	void	Restores the value of the include_path configuration option.

Table continued on following page

Function	Returns	Description
`get_current_user(void)`	string	Gets the name of the owner of the current PHP script.
`get_cfg_var(string option_name)`	string	Gets the value of a PHP configuration option.
`set_magic_quotes_runtime(int new_setting)`	bool	Sets the current active configuration setting of `magic_quotes_runtime` and returns previous setting.
`get_magic_quotes_runtime(void)`	int	Gets the current active configuration setting of `magic_quotes_runtime`.
`get_magic_quotes_gpc(void)`	int	Gets the current active configuration setting of `magic_quotes_gpc`.
`get_declared_classes()`	array	Returns an array of all declared classes.
`get_declared_interfaces()`	array	Returns an array of all declared interfaces.
`get_defined_functions(void)`	array	Returns an array of all defined functions.
`get_defined_vars(void)`	array	Returns an associative array of names and values of all currently defined variable names (variables in the current scope).
`get_resource_type(resource res)`	string	Gets the resource type name for a given resource.
`get_loaded_extensions(void)`	array	Returns an array containing names of loaded extensions.
`get_defined_constants(void)`	array	Returns an array containing the names and values of all defined constants.
`extension_loaded(string extension_name)`	bool	Returns `true` if the named extension is loaded.
`get_extension_funcs(string extension_name)`	array	Returns an array with the names of functions belonging to the named extension.
`get_included_files(void)`	array	Returns an array with the names of included or required files.
`zend_version(void)`	string	Gets the version of the Zend Engine.

Program Execution

Function	Returns	Description
exec(string command [, array &output [, int &return_value]])	string	Executes an external program.
system(string command [, int &return_value])	int	Executes an external program and displays output.
passthru(string command [, int &return_value])	void	Executes an external program and displays raw output.
escapeshellcmd(string command)	string	Escapes shell metacharacters.
escapeshellarg(string arg)	string	Quotes and escapes an argument for use in a shell command.
shell_exec(string cmd)	string	Executes command via shell and returns complete output as string.
proc_nice(int priority)	bool	Changes the priority of the current process.
proc_terminate(resource process [, long signal])	int	Kills a process opened by proc_open.
proc_close(resource process)	int	Closes a process opened by proc_open.
proc_get_status(resource process)	array	Gets information about a process opened by proc_open.
proc_open(string command, array descriptorspec, array &pipes [, string cwd [, array env [, array other_options]]])	resource	Runs a process with more control over its file descriptors.

Regular Expressions

Function	Returns	Description
ereg(string pattern, string string [, array registers])	int	Matches a regular expression.
eregi(string pattern, string string [, array registers])	int	Matches a case-insensitive regular expression.
ereg_replace(string pattern, string replacement, string string)	string	Replaces a regular expression.

Table continued on following page

Function	Returns	Description
eregi_replace(string pattern, string replacement, string string)	string	Replaces a case-insensitive regular expression.
split(string pattern, string string [, int limit])	array	Splits a string into an array by regular expression.
spliti(string pattern, string string [, int limit])	array	Splits a string into an array by regular case-insensitive expression.
sql_regcase(string string)	string	Creates a regular expression for a case-insensitive match on a string.

Sessions

Function	Returns	Description
session_set_cookie_params(int lifetime [, string path [, string domain [, bool secure]]])	void	Sets session cookie parameters.
session_get_cookie_params(void)	array	Returns the session cookie parameters.
session_name([string newname])	string	Returns the current session name. If newname is given, the session name is replaced with newname.
session_module_name([string newname])	string	Returns the current module name used for accessing session data. If newname is given, the module name is replaced with newname.
session_set_save_handler(string open, string close, string read, string write, string destroy, string gc)	void	Sets user-level functions.
session_save_path([string newname])	string	Returns the current save path passed to module_name. If newname is given, the save path is replaced with newname.
session_id([string newid])	string	Returns the current session_id. If newid is given, the session_id is replaced with newid.
session_regenerate_id()	bool	Updates the current session_id with a newly generated one.

Function	Returns	Description
session_cache_limiter([string new_cache_limiter])	string	Returns the current cache limiter. If new_cache_limiter is given, the current cache_limiter is replaced with new_cache_limiter.
session_cache_expire([int new_cache_expire])	int	Returns the current cache expire. If new_cache_expire is given, the current cache_expire is replaced with new_cache_expire.
session_register(mixed var_names [, mixed ...])	bool	Adds varname(s) to the list of variables that are frozen at the session end.
session_unregister(string varname)	bool	Removes varname from the list of variables that are frozen at the session end.
session_is_registered(string varname)	bool	Checks if a variable is registered in session.
session_encode(void)	string	Serializes the current setup and returns the serialized representation.
session_decode(string data)	bool	Deserializes data and reinitializes the variables.
session_start(void)	bool	Begins session — reinitializes frozen variables, registers browsers, and so on.
session_destroy(void)	bool	Destroys the current session and all data associated with it.
session_unset(void)	void	Unsets all registered variables.
session_write_close(void)	void	Writes session data and ends session.

Simple XML

Function	Returns	Description
simplexml_load_file (string filename)	simplemxml_element	Loads a filename and returns a simplexml_element object to allow for processing.
simplexml_load_string (string data)	simplemxml_element	Loads a string and returns a simplexml_element object to allow for processing.
simplexml_import_dom (domNode node)	simplemxml_element	Gets a simplexml_element object from dom to allow for processing.

Sockets

Function	Returns	Description
`socket_select(array &read_fds, array &write_fds, &array except_fds, int tv_sec[, int tv_usec])`	int	Runs the `select()` system call on the sets mentioned with a timeout specified by `tv_sec` and `tv_usec`.
`socket_create_listen(int port[, int backlog])`	resource	Opens a socket on port to accept connections.
`socket_accept(resource socket)`	resource	Accepts a connection on the listening socket fd.
`socket_set_nonblock (resource socket)`	bool	Sets nonblocking mode on a socket resource.
`socket_set_block(resource socket)`	bool	Sets blocking mode on a socket resource.
`socket_listen(resource socket[, int backlog])`	bool	Sets the maximum number of connections allowed to be waited for on the socket specified by fd.
`socket_close(resource socket)`	void	Closes a file descriptor.
`socket_write(resource socket, string buf[, int length])`	int	Writes the buffer to the socket resource; length is optional.
`socket_read(resource socket, int length [, int type])`	string	Reads a maximum of length bytes from socket.
`socket_getsockname(resource socket, string &addr[, int &port])`	bool	Queries the remote side of the given socket, which may either result in host/port or in a UNIX filesystem path, dependent on its type.
`socket_getpeername(resource socket, string &addr[, int &port])`	bool	Queries the remote side of the given socket, which may either result in host/port or in a UNIX filesystem path, dependent on its type.
`socket_create(int domain, int type, int protocol)`	resource	Creates an endpoint for communication in the domain specified by domain, of type specified by type.
`socket_connect(resource socket, string addr [, int port])`	bool	Opens a connection to addr:port on the socket specified by socket.

Function	Returns	Description
`socket_strerror(int errno)`	string	Returns a string describing an error.
`socket_bind(resource socket, string addr [, int port])`	bool	Binds an open socket to a listening port. Port is only specified in AF_INET family.
`socket_recv(resource socket, string &buf, int len, int flags)`	int	Receives data from a connected socket.
`socket_send(resource socket, string buf, int len, int flags)`	int	Sends data to a connected socket.
`socket_recvfrom(resource socket, string &buf, int len, int flags, string &name [, int &port])`	int	Receives data from a socket, connected or not.
`socket_sendto(resource socket, string buf, int len, int flags, string addr [, int port])`	int	Sends a message to a socket, whether it is connected or not.
`socket_get_option(resource socket, int level, int optname)`	mixed	Gets socket options for the socket.
`socket_set_option(resource socket, int level, int optname, int|array optval)`	bool	Sets socket options for the socket.
`socket_create_pair(int domain, int type, int protocol, array &fd)`	bool	Creates a pair of indistinguishable sockets and stores them in an array.
`socket_shutdown(resource socket [, int how])`	bool	Shuts down a socket for receiving, sending, or both.
`socket_last_error([resource socket])`	int	Returns the last socket error (either the last used or the provided socket resource).
`socket_clear_error([resource socket])`	void	Clears the error on the socket or the last error code.
`fsockopen(string hostname, int port [, int errno [, string errstr [, float timeout]]])`	int	Opens Internet or UNIX domain socket connection.
`pfsockopen(string hostname, int port [, int errno [, string errstr [, float timeout]]])`	int	Opens persistent Internet or UNIX domain socket connection.

SQLite

Function	Returns	Description
sqlite_popen(string filename [, int mode [, string &error_message]])	resource	Opens a persistent handle to a SQLite database. Will create the database if it does not exist.
sqlite_open(string filename [, int mode [, string &error_message]])	resource	Opens a SQLite database. Will create the database if it does not exist.
sqlite_factory(string filename [, int mode [, string &error_message]])	object	Opens a SQLite database and creates an object for it. Will create the database if it does not exist.
sqlite_busy_timeout(resource db, int ms)	void	Sets busy timeout duration. If ms <= 0, all busy handlers are disabled.
sqlite_close(resource db)	void	Closes an open sqlite database.
sqlite_unbuffered_query(string query, resource db [, int result_type])	resource	Executes a query that does not prefetch and buffer all data.
sqlite_query(string query, resource db [, int result_type])	resource	Executes a query against a given database and returns a result handle.
sqlite_fetch_all(resource result [, int result_type [, bool decode_binary]])	array	Fetches all rows from a result set as an array of arrays.
sqlite_fetch_array(resource result [, int result_type [, bool decode_binary]])	array	Fetches the next row from a result set as an array.
sqlite_fetch_object(resource result [, string class_name [, NULL|array ctor_params [, bool decode_binary]]])	object	Fetches the next row from a result set as an object.
sqlite_array_query(resource db, string query [, int result_type [, bool decode_binary]])	array	Executes a query against a given database and returns an array of arrays.
sqlite_single_query(resource db, string query [, bool first_row_only [, bool decode_binary]])	array	Executes a query and returns either an array for one single column or the value of the first row.
sqlite_fetch_single(resource result [, bool decode_binary])	string	Fetches the first column of a result set as a string.
sqlite_current(resource result [, int result_type [, bool decode_binary]])	array	Fetches the current row from a result set as an array.

Function	Returns	Description
`sqlite_column(resource result, mixed index_or_name [, bool decode_binary])`	mixed	Fetches a column from the current row of a result set.
`sqlite_libversion()`	string	Returns the version of the linked SQLite library.
`sqlite_libencoding()`	string	Returns the encoding (iso8859 or UTF-8) of the linked SQLite library.
`sqlite_changes(resource db)`	int	Returns the number of rows that were changed by the most recent SQL statement.
`sqlite_last_insert_rowid (resource db)`	int	Returns the rowid of the most recently inserted row.
`sqlite_num_rows(resource result)`	int	Returns the number of rows in a buffered result set.
`sqlite_has_more(resource result)`	bool	Returns whether more rows are available.
`sqlite_has_prev(resource result)`	bool	Returns whether a previous row is available.
`sqlite_num_fields(resource result)`	int	Returns the number of fields in a result set.
`sqlite_field_name(resource result, int field_index)`	string	Returns the name of a particular field of a result set.
`sqlite_seek(resource result, int row)`	bool	Seeks to a particular row number of a buffered result set.
`sqlite_rewind(resource result)`	bool	Seeks to the first row number of a buffered result set.
`sqlite_next(resource result)`	bool	Seeks to the next row number of a result set.
`sqlite_prev(resource result)`	bool	Seeks to the previous row number of a result set.
`sqlite_escape_string(string item)`	string	Escapes a string for use as a query parameter.
`sqlite_last_error(resource db)`	int	Returns the error code of the last error for a database.
`sqlite_error_string(int error_ code)`	string	Returns the textual description of an error code.

Table continued on following page

Function	Returns	Description
sqlite_create_aggregate (resource db, string funcname, mixed step_func, mixed finalize_ func[, long num_args])	bool	Registers an aggregate function for queries.
sqlite_create_function (resource db, string funcname, mixed callback[, long num_args])	bool	Registers a regular function for queries.
sqlite_udf_encode_binary (string data)	string	Applies binary encoding (if required) to a string to return from a UDF.
sqlite_udf_decode_binary (string data)	string	Decodes binary encoding on a string parameter passed to a UDF.

Streams

Function	Returns	Description
stream_socket_client(string remoteaddress [, long &errcode, string &errstring, double timeout, long flags, resource context])	resource	Opens a client connection to a remote address.
stream_socket_server(string localaddress [, long &errcode, string &errstring, long flags, resource context])	resource	Creates a server socket bound to localaddress.
stream_socket_accept(resource serverstream, [double timeout, string &peername])	resource	Accepts a client connection from a server socket.
stream_socket_get_name(resource stream, bool want_peer)	string	Returns either the locally bound or remote name for a socket stream.
stream_socket_sendto(resouce stream, string data [, long flags [, string target_addr]])	long	Sends data to a socket stream. If target_addr is specified, it must be in dotted quad (or [ipv6]) format.
stream_socket_recvfrom(resource stream, long amount [, long flags [, string &remote_addr]])	string	Receives data from a socket stream.
stream_get_contents(resource source [, long maxlen])	long	Reads all remaining bytes (up to maxlen bytes) from a stream and returns them as a string.

Function	Returns	Description
stream_copy_to_stream(resource source, resource dest [, long maxlen])	long	Reads up to maxlen bytes from source stream and writes them to destination stream.
stream_get_meta_data(resource fp)	resource	Retrieves header/meta data from streams/file pointers.
stream_get_transports()	array	Retrieves list of registered socket transports.
stream_get_wrappers()	array	Retrieves list of registered stream wrappers.
stream_select(array &read_streams, array &write_streams, array &except_streams, int tv_sec[, int tv_usec])	int	Runs the select() system call on the sets of streams with a timeout specified by tv_sec and tv_usec.
stream_context_get_options (resource context|resource stream)	array	Retrieves options for a stream/wrapper/context.
stream_context_set_option(resource context|resource stream, string wrappername, string optionname, mixed value)	bool	Sets an option for a wrapper.
stream_context_set_params(resource context|resource stream, array options)	bool	Sets parameters for a file context.
stream_context_create([array options])	resource	Creates a file context and optionally sets parameters.
stream_filter_prepend(resource stream, string filtername[, int read_write[, string filterparams]])	bool	Prepends a filter to a stream.
stream_filter_append(resource stream, string filtername[, int read_write[, string filterparams]])	bool	Appends a filter to a stream.
stream_get_line(resource stream, int maxlen, string ending)	string	Reads up to maxlen bytes from a stream or until the ending string is found.
stream_set_blocking(resource socket, int mode)	bool	Sets blocking/nonblocking mode on a socket or stream.
set_socket_blocking(resource socket, int mode)	bool	Sets blocking/nonblocking mode on a socket.
stream_set_timeout(resource stream, int seconds, int microseconds)	bool	Sets timeout on stream read to seconds + microseconds.

Table continued on following page

Function	Returns	Description
stream_set_write_buffer(resource fp, int buffer)	int	Sets file write buffer.
stream_wrapper_register(string protocol, string classname)	bool	Registers a custom URL protocol handler class.
stream_bucket_make_writeable (resource brigade)	object	Returns a bucket object from the brigade for operating on.
stream_bucket_prepend(resource brigade, resource bucket)	void	Prepends bucket to brigade.
stream_bucket_append(resource brigade, resource bucket)	void	Appends bucket to brigade.
stream_bucket_new(resource stream, string buffer)	resource	Creates a new bucket for use on the current stream.
stream_get_filters(void)	array	Returns a list of registered filters.
stream_filter_register(string filtername, string classname)	bool	Registers a custom filter handler class.

Strings

Function	Returns	Description
crc32(string str)	string	Calculates the crc32 polynomial of a string.
crypt(string str [, string salt])	string	Encrypts a string.
convert_cyr_string(string str, string from, string to)	string	Converts from one Cyrillic character set to another.
lcg_value()	float	Returns a value from the combined linear congruential generator.
levenshtein(string str1, string str2)	int	Calculates Levenshtein distance between two strings.
md5(string str, [bool raw_output])	string	Calculates the md5 hash of a string.
md5_file(string filename [, bool raw_output])	string	Calculates the md5 hash of given filename.
metaphone(string text, int phones)	string	Breaks English phrases down into their phonemes.

Function	Returns	Description
pack(string format, mixed arg1 [, mixed arg2 [, mixed ...]])	string	Takes one or more arguments and packs them into a binary string according to the format argument.
unpack(string format, string input)	array	Unpacks binary string into named array elements according to format argument.
sha1(string str [, bool raw_output])	string	Calculates the sha1 hash of a string.
sha1_file(string filename [, bool raw_output])	string	Calculates the sha1 hash of given filename.
soundex(string str)	string	Calculates the soundex key of a string.
bin2hex(string data)	string	Converts the binary representation of data to hex.
strspn(string str, string mask [, start [, len]])	int	Finds length of initial segment consisting entirely of characters found in mask. If start and/or length is provided, works like strspn(substr($s,$start, $len),$good_chars).
strcspn(string str, string mask [, start [, len]])	int	Finds length of initial segment consisting entirely of characters not found in mask. If start and/ or length is provided, works like strcspn(substr($s,$start, $len),$bad_chars).
nl_langinfo(int item)	string	Queries language and locale information.
strcoll(string str1, string str2)	int	Compares two strings using the current locale.
trim(string str [, string character_mask])	string	Strips whitespace from the beginning and end of a string.
rtrim(string str [, string character_mask])	string	Removes trailing whitespace.
ltrim(string str [, string character_mask])	string	Strips whitespace from the beginning of a string.
wordwrap(string str [, int width [, string break [, boolean cut]]])	string	Wraps buffer to selected number of characters using string break char.

Table continued on following page

Function	Returns	Description
explode(string separator, string str [, int limit])	array	Splits a string on string separator and returns array of components.
join(array src, string glue)	string	An alias for implode function.
implode([string glue,] array pieces)	string	Joins array elements placing glue string between items and returns one string.
strtok([string str,] string token)	string	Tokenizes a string.
strtoupper(string str)	string	Makes a string uppercase.
strtolower(string str)	string	Makes a string lowercase.
basename(string path [, string suffix])	string	Returns the filename component of the path.
dirname(string path)	string	Returns the directory name component of the path.
pathinfo(string path)	array	Returns information about a certain string.
stristr(string haystack, string needle)	string	Finds first occurrence of a string within another, case insensitive.
strstr(string haystack, string needle)	string	Finds first occurrence of a string within another.
strchr(string haystack, string needle)	string	An alias for strstr.
strpos(string haystack, string needle [, int offset])	int	Finds position of first occurrence of a string within another.
stripos(string haystack, string needle [, int offset])	int	Finds position of first occurrence of a string within another, case insensitive.
strrpos(string haystack, string needle [, int offset])	int	Finds position of last occurrence of a string within another string.
strripos(string haystack, string needle [, int offset])	int	Finds position of last occurrence of a string within another string.
strrchr(string haystack, string needle)	string	Finds the last occurrence of a character in a string within another.
chunk_split(string str [, int chunklen [, string ending]])	string	Returns split line.
substr(string str, int start [, int length])	string	Returns part of a string.
substr_replace(mixed str, mixed repl, mixed start [, mixed length])	mixed	Replaces part of a string with another string.

Function	Returns	Description
quoted_printable_decode(string str)	string	Converts a quoted-printable string to an 8-bit string.
quotemeta(string str)	string	Quotes (escapes with \) meta characters.
ord(string character)	int	Returns ASCII value of character.
chr(int ascii)	string	Converts ASCII code to a character.
ucfirst(string str)	string	Makes a string's first character uppercase.
ucwords(string str)	string	Uppercases the first character of every word in a string.
strtr(string str, string from, string to)	string	Translates characters in str using given translation tables.
strrev(string str)	string	Reverses a string.
similar_text(string str1, string str2 [, float percent])	int	Calculates the similarity between two strings.
addcslashes(string str, string charlist)	string	Escapes all chars mentioned in charlist with backslash. It creates octal representations if asked to backslash characters with 8-bit set or with ASCII<32 (except '\n', '\r', '\t', and so on).
addslashes(string str)	string	Escapes single quote, double quotes, and backslash characters in a string with backslashes.
stripcslashes(string str)	string	Strips backslashes from a string. Uses C-style conventions.
stripslashes(string str)	string	Strips backslashes from a string.
str_replace(mixed search, mixed replace, mixed subject [, int &replace_count])	mixed	Replaces all occurrences of search in haystack with replace.
str_ireplace(mixed search, mixed replace, mixed subject [, int &replace_count])	mixed	Replaces all (case-insensitive) occurrences of search in haystack with replace.
hebrev(string str [, int max_chars_per_line])	string	Converts logical Hebrew text to visual text.
hebrevc(string str [, int max_chars_per_line])	string	Converts logical Hebrew text to visual text with newline conversion.

Table continued on following page

Function	Returns	Description
`nl2br(string str)`	string	Converts newlines to HTML line breaks.
`strip_tags(string str [, string allowable_tags])`	string	Strips HTML and PHP tags from a string.
`setlocale(mixed category, string locale [, string ...])`	string	Sets locale information.
`parse_str(string encoded_string [, array result])`	void	Parses GET/POST/COOKIE data and sets global variables.
`str_repeat(string input, int mult)`	string	Returns the input string repeat mult times.
`count_chars(string input [, int mode])`	mixed	Returns info about what characters are used in input.
`strnatcmp(string s1, string s2)`	int	Returns the result of string comparison using "natural" algorithm.
`localeconv(void)`	array	Returns numeric formatting information based on the current locale.
`strnatcasecmp(string s1, string s2)`	int	Returns the result of case-insensitive string comparison using "natural" algorithm.
`substr_count(string haystack, string needle)`	int	Returns the number of times a substring occurs in the string.
`str_pad(string input, int pad_length [, string pad_string [, int pad_type]])`	string	Returns input string padded on the left or right to specified length with `pad_string`.
`sscanf(string str, string format [, string ...])`	mixed	Implements an ANSI C-compatible `sscanf`.
`str_rot13(string str)`	string	Performs the `rot13` transform on a string.
`str_shuffle(string str)`	void	Shuffles string. One permutation of all possible is created.
`str_word_count(string str, [int format])`	mixed	Counts the number of words inside a string. If format of 1 is specified, it returns an array containing all the words found. A format of 2 returns an associative array where the key is the numeric position of the word.

Function	Returns	Description
money_format(string format , float value)	string	Converts monetary value(s) to string.
str_split(string str [, int split_length])	array	Converts a string to an array. If split_length is specified, breaks the string down into chunks each split_length characters long.
strpbrk(string haystack, string char_list)	array	Searches a string for any of a set of characters.
substr_compare(string main_str, string str, int offset [, int length [, bool case_sensitivity]])	int	Binary safe optionally case-insensitive comparison of two strings from an offset, up to length characters.
uuencode(string data)	string	Unencode a string.
uudecode(string data)	string	Decode a uuencoded string.
sprintf(string format [, mixed arg1 [, mixed ...]])	string	Returns a formatted string.
vsprintf(string format, array args)	string	Returns a formatted string.
printf(string format [, mixed arg1 [, mixed ...]])	int	Outputs a formatted string.
vprintf(string format, array args)	int	Outputs a formatted string.
fprintf(resource stream, string format [, mixed arg1 [, mixed ...]])	int	Outputs a formatted string into a stream.
vfprintf(resource stream, string format, array args)	int	Outputs a formatted string into a stream.
htmlspecialchars(string string [, int quote_style] [, string charset])	string	Converts special characters to HTML entities.
html_entity_decode(string string [, int quote_style] [, string charset])	string	Converts all HTML entities to their applicable characters.
htmlentities(string string [, int quote_style] [, string charset])	string	Converts all applicable characters to HTML entities.
get_html_translation_table([int table [, int quote_style]])	array	Returns the internal translation table used by htmlspecialchars and htmlentities.
strlen(string str)	int	Gets string length.
strcmp(string str1, string str2)	int	Binary safe string comparison.

Table continued on following page

Function	Returns	Description
`strncmp(string str1, string str2, int len)`	int	Binary safe string comparison.
`strcasecmp(string str1, string str2)`	int	Binary safe case-insensitive string comparison.
`strncasecmp(string str1, string str2, int len)`	int	Binary safe string comparison.

URL

Function	Returns	Description
`http_build_query(mixed formdata [, string prefix])`	string	Generates a form-encoded query string from an associative array or object.
`parse_url(string url)`	array	Parses a URLand returns its components.
`get_headers(string url)`	array	Fetches all the headers sent by the server in response to an HTTP request.
`urlencode(string str)`	string	URL-encodes all non alphanumeric characters except -_.
`urldecode(string str)`	string	Decodes URL-encoded string.
`rawurlencode(string str)`	string	URL-encodes all non alphanumeric characters.
`rawurldecode(string str)`	string	Decodes URL-encoded string.
`base64_encode(string str)`	string	Encodes string using MIME base64 algorithm.
`base64_decode(string str)`	string	Decodes string using MIME base64 algorithm.
`get_meta_tags(string filename [, bool use_include_path])`	array	Extracts all meta tag content attributes from a file and returns an array.

Variable Functions

Function	Returns	Description
`gettype(mixed var)`	string	Returns the type of the variable.
`settype(mixed var, string type)`	bool	Sets the type of the variable.

Function	Returns	Description
`intval(mixed var [, int base])`	int	Gets the integer value of a variable using the optional base for the conversion.
`floatval(mixed var)`	float	Gets the float value of a variable.
`strval(mixed var)`	string	Gets the string value of a variable.
`is_null(mixed var)`	bool	Returns `true` if variable is null.
`is_resource(mixed var)`	bool	Returns `true` if variable is a resource.
`is_bool(mixed var)`	bool	Returns `true` if variable is a Boolean.
`is_long(mixed var)`	bool	Returns `true` if variable is a long (integer).
`is_float(mixed var)`	bool	Returns `true` if variable is a float point.
`is_string(mixed var)`	bool	Returns `true` if variable is a string.
`is_array(mixed var)`	bool	Returns `true` if variable is an array.
`is_object(mixed var)`	bool	Returns `true` if variable is an object.
`is_numeric(mixed value)`	bool	Returns `true` if value is a number or a numeric string.
`is_scalar(mixed value)`	bool	Returns `true` if value is a scalar.
`is_callable(mixed var [, bool syntax_only [, string callable_name]])`	bool	Returns `true` if var is callable.
`var_dump(mixed var)`	void	Dumps a string representation of variable to output.
`debug_zval_dump(mixed var)`	void	Dumps a string representation of an internal `zend` value to output.
`var_export(mixed var [, bool return])`	mixed	Outputs or returns a string representation of a variable.
`serialize(mixed variable)`	string	Returns a string representation of variable (which can later be unserialized).
`unserialize(string variable_representation)`	mixed	Takes a string representation of variable and recreates it.
`memory_get_usage()`	int	Returns the allocated by PHP memory.
`print_r(mixed var [, bool return])`	mixed	Prints out or returns information about the specified variable.
`import_request_variables (string types [, string prefix])`	bool	Imports GET/POST/Cookie variables into the global scope.

XML

Function	Returns	Description
xml_parser_create([string encoding])	resource	Creates an XML parser.
xml_parser_create_ns([string encoding [, string sep]]).	resource	Creates an XML parser.
xml_set_object(resource parser, object &obj)	int	Sets up object which should be used for callbacks.
xml_set_element_handler(resource parser, string shdl, string ehdl)	int	Sets up start and end element handlers.
xml_set_character_data_handler (resource parser, string hdl)	int	Sets up character data handler.
xml_set_processing_instruction_ handler(resource parser, string hdl)	int	Sets up processing instruction (PI) handler.
xml_set_default_handler(resource parser, string hdl)	int	Sets up default handler.
xml_set_unparsed_entity_decl_ handler(resource parser, string hdl)	int	Sets up unparsed entity declaration handler.
xml_set_notation_decl_handler (resource parser, string hdl)	int	Sets up notation declaration handler.
xml_set_external_entity_ref_ handler(resource parser, string hdl)	int	Sets up external entity reference handler.
xml_set_start_namespace_decl_ handler(resource parser, string hdl)	int	Sets up character data handler.
xml_set_end_namespace_decl_handler (resource parser, string hdl)	int	Sets up character data handler.
xml_parse(resource parser, string data [, int isFinal])	int	Starts parsing an XML document.
xml_parse_into_struct(resource parser, string data, array &struct, array &index)	int	Parses an XML document.
xml_get_error_code(resource parser)	int	Gets XML parser error code.
xml_error_string(int code)	string	Gets XML parser error string.
xml_get_current_line_number (resource parser)	int	Gets current line number for an XML parser.
xml_get_current_column_number (resource parser)	int	Gets current column number for an XML parser.

Function	Returns	Description
`xml_get_current_byte_index` `(resource parser)`	int	Gets current byte index for an XML parser.
`xml_parser_free(resource parser)`	int	Frees an XML parser.
`xml_parser_set_option(resource parser, int option, mixed value)`	int	Sets options in an XML parser.
`xml_parser_get_option(resource parser, int option)`	int	Gets options from an XML parser.
`utf8_encode(string data)`	string	Encodes an ISO-8859-1 string to UTF-8.
`utf8_decode(string data)`	string	Converts a UTF-8 encoded string to ISO-8859-1.

ZLib

Function	Returns	Description
`gzfile(string filename [, int use_include_path])`	array	Reads and uncompresses entire `.gz-file` into an array.
`gzopen(string filename, string mode [, int use_include_path])`	resource	Opens a `.gz-file` and returns a `.gz-file` pointer.
`readgzfile(string filename [, int use_include_path])`	int	Outputs a `.gz-file`.
`gzcompress(string data [, int level])`	string	Gzip-compresses a string.
`gzuncompress(string data [, int length])`	string	Unzips a gzip-compressed string.
`gzdeflate(string data [, int level])`	string	Gzip-compresses a string.
`gzinflate(string data [, int length])`	string	Unzips a gzip-compressed string.
`zlib_get_coding_type(void)`	string	Returns the coding type used for output compression.
`gzencode(string data [, int level [, int encoding_mode]])`	string	GZ-encodes a string.
`ob_gzhandler(string str, int mode)`	string	Encodes `str` based on accept-encoding setting; designed to be called from `ob_start()` as a callback function.

Index